SHURLEY ENGLISH

HOMESCHOOL MADE EASY

LEVEL 4

Teacher's Edition

By

Brenda Shurley

Shurley Instructional Materials, Inc., Cabot, Arkansas

In Loving Memory of
Gilbert Edwin Strackbein
(Gil)

Dedication

This book is gratefully dedicated to my husband, Billy Shurley, for his love, support, and encouragement during this momentous undertaking.

Acknowledgements

We gratefully thank the following people for their help and support in the preparation of this book:

Rachel Andrews	Janice Graham	Shurley Method Staff
Ardean Coffman	Stacey See	Arlene Strackbein
Keith Covington	Billy Ray Shurley, Jr.	Andrea Turkia
Jamie Geneva	Kim Shurley	Jani-Petri Rainer Turkia
		Bob Wilson, Ph.D.

11-05
Homeschool Edition
ISBN 1-58561-036-4 (Level 4 Teacher's Manual)

TABLE OF CONTENTS

TABLE OF CONTENTS

Level 4 Homeschool Teacher's Manual

TABLE OF CONTENTS

TABLE OF CONTENTS

Level 4 Homeschool Teacher's Manual

TABLE OF CONTENTS

SHURLEY ENGLISH ABBREVIATIONS FOR LEVEL 4

Abbreviation	Description
N	Noun
SN	Subject Noun
CSN	Compound Subject Noun
Pro	Pronoun
SP	Subject Pronoun
CSP	Compound Subject Pronoun
V	Verb
HV	Helping Verb
CV	Compound Verb
V-t	Verb-transitive
CV-t	Compound Verb-transitive
LV	Linking Verb
CLV	Compound Linking Verb
A	Article Adjective
Adj	Adjective
CAdj	Compound Adjective
Adv	Adverb
CAdv	Compound Adverb
P	Preposition
OP	Object of the Preposition
COP	Compound Object of the Preposition

	Description
PPA	Possessive Pronoun Adjective
PNA	Possessive Noun Adjective
C	Conjunction
I	Interjection
DO	Direct Object
CDO	Compound Direct Object
IO	Indirect Object
CIO	Compound Indirect Object
PrN	Predicate Noun
CPrN	Compound Predicate Noun
PA	Predicate Adjective
CPA	Compound Predicate Adjective

Sentences	
D	Declarative Sentence
E	Exclamatory Sentence
Int	Interrogative Sentence
Imp	Imperative Sentence

Level 4 Patterns	
SN V P1	Subject Noun Verb Pattern 1
SN V-t DO P2	Subject Noun Verb-transitive Direct Object Pattern 2
SN V-t IO DO P3	Subject Noun Verb-transitive Indirect Object Direct Object Pattern 3

CHAPTER 1   LESSON 1

Objectives: Long-term goals and short-term goals.

STUDY SKILLS TIME

TEACHING SCRIPT FOR SETTING GOALS

Good organizational skills are the foundation for good study skills. You must learn to manage your time, your materials, and your work environment. Good study skills do not just happen. It takes time, determination, and the practice of certain guidelines to get organized. The study skills chapter will concentrate on the guidelines you need for success in developing good study habits. Follow them carefully until they become habits that will help you for a lifetime.

Everyone has the same 24 hours, but everyone does not use his/her 24 hours in the same way. In order to get the most for your time, it is important to set goals. Goals will keep you pointed in the direction you want to go, will focus your time, and will keep you on track. With a list of goals, you can check your progress. Long-term goals are what you want to accomplish in life, usually concentrating on your education and your career. Short-term goals will help you plan things to do this school year, and guidelines will give you specific things to do each day to help you achieve your goals. Listen to examples of long-term and short-term goals as I read them. (*Read the examples below or write them on the board.*)

Examples of goals for a person interested in computers:

Long-term Goals	Short-term Goals
1. Get a technology scholarship for college.	1. Make a schedule to plan each day.
2. Earn a degree in Computer Science.	2. Earn good grades this school year.
3. Own a computer software company.	3. Set aside at least 30 minutes per night for study time.
	4. Earn spending money by having a paper route.
	5. Spend 30 minutes per day learning about different kinds of computer software.

Examples of goals for a person interested in teaching:

Long-term Goals	Short-term Goals
1. Get an academic scholarship for college.	1. Make a schedule to plan each day.
2. Earn a degree in elementary education.	2. Earn good grades this school year.
3. Become an elementary school teacher.	3. Set aside at least 30 minutes per night for study time.
	4. Earn spending money by pet sitting.
	5. Spend 15 minutes per day reading to younger sisters, brothers, or cousins.

Notice that getting organized and setting aside study time are always important short-term goals because they help you achieve your long-term goals. You will now write down your own long-term and short-term goals. Write two or three long-term goals and four or five short-term goals. You can add more as you think of them. (*Give students time to write down their long-term and short-term goals. You may want to discuss what kind of goals were written. Have students make English folders and put their goals in the folders.*)

(End of lesson.)

CHAPTER 1   LESSON 2
Objectives: Beginning setup plan for homeschool.

STUDY SKILLS TIME

TEACHING SCRIPT FOR STUDY PLANS

We have learned that goals are important because they are a constant reminder of what you want to happen in your future. To make the most of your goals, you should take time to evaluate your goals at the end of every month to see if there are any adjustments you wish to make. Goals change as your needs change and as your abilities increase.

Remember, goals are your destination. A schedule is your road map. You may take a few detours, but you still know the direction you are headed in and how to get there. (*Have discussion time with your students at the beginning of each month to evaluate goals and schedules. Help students make any necessary adjustments. This is a worthwhile learning activity that is done nine times for the whole school year. It should be a meaningful experience for your students.*)

I will introduce the first step in good organization: learning how to make and follow a daily schedule, or routine. Turn to page 10 and look at Reference 1. Follow along as I read the guidelines that will help you establish a daily schedule to follow during study time and school time. These guidelines will help you get organized with the least amount of wasted effort. (*Read and discuss the plan reproduced below with your students.*)

Reference 1: Beginning Setup Plan for Homeschool

You should use this plan to keep things in order!

1. Have separate color-coded pocket folders for each subject.
2. Put unfinished work in the right-hand side and finished work in the left-hand side of each subject folder.
3. Put notes to study, graded tests, and study guides in the brads so you will have them to study for scheduled tests.
4. Have a paper folder to store clean sheets of paper. Keep it full at all times.
5. Have an assignment folder to be reviewed every day.

Things to keep in your assignment folder:

A. Keep a monthly calendar of assignments, test dates, report-due dates, project-due dates, extra activities, dates and times, review dates, etc.

B. Keep a grade sheet to record the grades received in each subject. (*You might also consider keeping your grades on the inside cover of each subject folder. However you keep your grades, just remember to record them accurately. Your grades are your business, so keep up with them! Grades help you know which areas need attention.*)

C. Make a list every day of the things you want to do so you can keep track of what you finish and what you have not finished. Move the unfinished items to your new list the next day. (*Making this list takes time, but it's your road map to success. You will always know at a glance what you set out to accomplish and what still needs to be done.*)

6. Keep all necessary school supplies in a handy, heavy-duty Ziploc bag or a pencil bag.

(End of Lesson.)

CHAPTER 1   LESSON 3
Objectives: Skills (Synonyms, Antonyms, Five-Step Vocabulary Plan), and Vocabulary #1.

SKILL TIME

TEACHING SCRIPT FOR SYNONYMS AND ANTONYMS

Words are your tools for the future. Having a strong command of different vocabulary words can help you express exactly what is on your mind, and it will also help others to fully understand your thoughts and ideas. The ability to communicate is more effective when you do not use the same words over and over again. That is why it is necessary to learn a wide variety of vocabulary words. Think of it as having a large bank account from which you can draw the right words to best express your thoughts.

Today, we will learn about synonyms and antonyms and how to mark them. Turn to page 10 in the Reference Section of your book and look at Reference 2. (*The first part of Reference 2 is reproduced below.*) This format will be used for identifying vocabulary words as synonyms or antonyms.

Reference 2: Synonyms, Antonyms, and Five-Step Vocabulary Plan		
Part 1: Synonyms and Antonyms		
Definitions: Synonyms are words that have similar, or almost the same, meanings. Antonyms are words that have opposite meanings.		
Directions: Identify each pair of words as synonyms or antonyms by putting parentheses ( ) around *syn* or *ant*.		
1. bashful, shy **(syn)** ant	2. reply, answer **(syn)** ant	3. absent, present syn **(ant)**

Listen carefully as I read the definition for synonyms and antonyms. **Synonyms** are words that have similar, or almost the same, meanings. **Antonyms** are words that have opposite meanings. Look at the words ***bashful*** and ***shy*** beside number 1. What are the meanings of the words **bashful** and **shy?** (*Discuss the meanings of the words **bashful** and **shy**.*) Do the words ***bashful*** and ***shy*** have almost the same meanings, or do they have opposite meanings? (*almost the same meanings*) Since they have almost the same meanings, are they synonyms or antonyms? (*synonyms*) How do we indicate that they are synonyms? (*By putting parentheses around the **syn***) (*For number 1, have students note the parentheses around the **syn** in their practice box.*)

Look at number 2. Let's discuss the meanings of the words **reply** and **answer**. (*Discuss the meanings of the words **reply** and **answer**.*) Do these words have almost the same meanings, or do they have opposite meanings? (*almost the same meanings*) Since they have almost the same meanings, are they synonyms or antonyms? (*synonyms*) How do we indicate that they are synonyms? (*By putting parentheses around the **syn***) (*For number 2, have students note the parentheses around the **syn** in their practice box.*) Remember, synonyms may not have the same meanings, but their meanings will be similar. That is why they are called synonyms.

Look at number 3. Let's discuss the meanings of the words **absent** and **present**. (*Discuss the meanings of the words **absent** and **present**.*) Do these words have almost the same meanings, or do they have opposite meanings? (*opposite meanings*) Since they have opposite meanings, are they synonyms or antonyms? (*antonyms*) How do we indicate that they are antonyms? (*By putting parentheses around the **ant***) (*For number 3, have students note the parentheses around the **ant** in their practice box.*) Remember, antonyms have different meanings because they are opposite words. They do not mean the same thing. That is why they are called antonyms.

CHAPTER 1 LESSON 3 CONTINUED

If the thought of learning new words is overwhelming, think about what you have available. You have two valuable tools to help you in this task: the dictionary and the thesaurus. The nice thing about these tools is that you alone, at any time, can use the dictionary or thesaurus (*for free*) to learn more words with which to express yourself.

Today, you will begin building your "bank account" of words. You will advance your vocabulary by learning synonyms and antonyms. Remember that synonyms are words that have almost the same meanings, and antonyms are words that have opposite meanings. Now that we have discussed several synonym and antonym words, I want you to name two pairs of words and identify one pair as synonyms and one pair as antonyms. (*Allow students to use a dictionary or a thesaurus to look up each pair of words if needed. Check students' identification of the words for accuracy.*)

Since we will be learning or reviewing synonyms and antonyms in almost every chapter, we will call this time **Vocabulary Time**. The purpose of Vocabulary Time is to learn new words; so, you will keep a Vocabulary notebook. During Vocabulary Time, you will always follow the Five-Step Vocabulary Plan. You will find this plan in the second part of Reference 2 on page 10 in your book. You will use this plan every time you enter vocabulary words in your notebook. (*Have students follow along as you read and discuss the vocabulary plan with them.*)

Reference 2: Synonyms, Antonyms, and Five-Step Vocabulary Plan (continued)
Part 2: Five-Step Vocabulary Plan
(1) Write a title for the vocabulary words in each chapter. Example: **Chapter 1, Vocabulary Words**
(2) Write each vocabulary word in your vocabulary notebook.
(3) Look up each vocabulary word in a dictionary or thesaurus.
(4) Write the meaning beside each vocabulary word.
(5) Write a sentence that helps you remember how each vocabulary word is used.

You will have a list of synonyms and antonyms to define in each chapter. These words are listed on pages 8 and 9 in the Reference Section of your workbook. (*Have students turn to page 8 and look at the eight words listed for Chapter 1.*)

I will tell you the words you will define during Vocabulary Time. Today, you will define and write sentences for four words. Any of the words you learn during Vocabulary Time could be used in the Vocabulary section of your test. You may also use your vocabulary notebook to record any vocabulary word you wish to define for future reference.

 VOCABULARY TIME

Assign Chapter 1, Vocabulary Words **#1** on page 8 in the Reference Section for students to define in their Vocabulary notebooks. Tell students they are to use a dictionary or thesaurus to look up the meanings of the vocabulary words. After they write each word and its meaning, students are to write a sentence using the vocabulary word.

Chapter 1, Vocabulary Words #1
(bold, timid, slumber, sleep)

(End of lesson.)

CHAPTER 1 LESSON 4

Objectives: Skills (A/An choices), Practice Exercise, Writing (Journal), and Vocabulary #2.

SKILL TIME

TEACHING SCRIPT FOR A / AN CHOICES

I am going to introduce how to use the words ***a*** and ***an*** correctly. Even though this skill should already be familiar to you, we will go step by step through an easy review method that will make it even easier for you to remember how to use the words ***a*** and ***an*** correctly. Look at Reference 3 on page 11 in your Reference Section. These are the rules for choosing *a* or *an*. (*Read the information in the reference box below.*)

Reference 3: A and An Choices
Rule 1: Use the word ***a*** when the next word begins with a consonant sound.   (*Example: a red apple.*) Rule 2: Use the word ***an*** when the next word begins with a vowel sound.   (*Example: an apple.*)
Example Sentences: Write ***a*** or ***an*** in the blanks.
1. Would you like __**an**__ angel necklace?   3. We saw __**a**__ statue in the courtyard. 2. Would you like __**a**__ gold angel necklace?   4. I saw __**an**__ old statue in the courtyard.

We will discuss the sample sentences in the reference box. Always read the directions very carefully before you start the exercise. The directions say to write *a* or *an* in the blanks.

Look at number 1. Before we can choose *a* or *an* to put in the blank, we have to look at the word that comes next. Does ***angel*** start with a consonant or vowel sound? (*vowel sound*) The rule says to use the word *an* before words that begin with a vowel sound. We will write the word *an* in the blank before the word ***angel***.

Look at number 2. Does the word ***gold*** start with a consonant or vowel sound? (*consonant sound*) The rule says to use the word *a* before words that begin with a consonant sound. We will write the word *a* in the blank before the word ***gold***.

Look at number 3. Does the word ***statue*** start with a consonant or a vowel sound? (*consonant sound*) The rule says to use the word *a* before words that begin with a consonant sound. We will write the word *a* in the blank before the word ***statue***.

Look at number 4. Does the word ***old*** start with a consonant or a vowel sound? (*vowel sound*) The rule says to use the word *an* before words that begin with a vowel sound. We will write the word *an* in the blank before the word ***old***.

CHAPTER 1 LESSON 4 CONTINUED

PRACTICE TIME

Have students turn to page 66 in the Practice Section of their book and find Chapter 1, Lesson 4, Practice. Go over the directions to make sure they understand what to do. Check and discuss the Practice after students have finished. (*Chapter 1, Lesson 4, Practice key is given below.*)

Chapter 1, Lesson 4, Practice: Write *a* or *an* in the blanks.

1. Did you find **an** answer yet?
2. We saw **an** icicle.
3. He ate **a** large steak.

4. We found **a** lost puppy.
5. Mom ate **an** apple.
6. I baked **a** pie.

7. **an** octopus
8. **a** friend
9. **an** elevator

10. **a** light
11. **an** ax
12. **a** box

WRITING TIME

TEACHING SCRIPT FOR JOURNAL WRITING

Now, turn to your Reference Section and look at Reference 4 on page 11. You will begin journal writing today, but, before you begin, I want to share some important information about this type of writing. (*Read the information in the reference box below and on the next page.*)

Reference 4: What is Journal Writing?

Journal Writing is a written record of your personal thoughts and feelings about things or people that are important to you. Recording your thoughts in a journal is a good way to remember how you felt about what was happening in your life at a particular time. You can record your dreams, memories, feelings, and experiences. You can ask questions and answer some of them. It is fun to go back later and read what you have written because it shows how you have changed in different areas of your life. A journal can also be an excellent place to look for future writing topics, creative stories, poems, etc. Writing in a journal is an easy and enjoyable way to practice your writing skills without worrying about a writing grade.

What do I write about?

Journals are personal, but sometimes it helps to have ideas to get you started. Remember, in a journal, you do not have to stick to one topic. Write about someone or something you like. Write about what you did last weekend or on vacation. Write about what you hope to do this week or on your next vacation. Write about home, school, friends, hobbies, special talents (yours or someone else's), or present and future hopes and fears. Write about what is wrong in your world and what you would do to "fix" it. Write about the good things and the bad things in your world. If you think about a past event and want to write an opinion about it now, put it in your journal. If you want to give your opinion about a present or future event that could have an impact on your life or the way that you see things, put it in your journal. If something bothers you, record it in your journal. If something interests you, record it. If you just want to record something that doesn't seem important at all, write it in your journal. After all, it is your journal!

CHAPTER 1 LESSON 4 CONTINUED

Reference 4: What is Journal Writing? (continued)

How do I get started writing in my personal journal?

You need to put the day's date on the title line of your paper: **Month, Day, Year.** Skip the next line and begin your entry. You might write one or two sentences, a paragraph, a whole page, or several pages. Except for the journal date, no particular organizational style is required for journal writing. You decide how best to organize and express your thoughts. Feel free to include sketches, diagrams, lists, etc., if they will help you remember your thoughts about a topic or an event. You will also need a spiral notebook, a pen, a quiet place, and at least 5-10 minutes of uninterrupted writing time.

Note: Use a pen if possible. Pencils have lead points that break, and erasers, both of which slow down your thoughts. Any drawings you might include do not have to be masterpieces—stick figures will do nicely.

TEACHER INSTRUCTIONS

Have students write the title *My Personal Journal for the Year* ____, indicating the current year on the front covers of their journal notebooks or folders. Students should use their journal notebooks for their journal writing assignments.

Have students make the first entry in their journals at this time.

Teacher's Notes about Journal Writing: Journal writing helps students express themselves in written form, helps students feel comfortable with writing, and gives students an opportunity to practice what they are learning. Check to make sure students are making their entries. Make it a writing routine to have a five-to-ten minute journal-writing time whenever it is assigned. If students finish early, have them go back and read earlier entries. Keeping a journal should develop into a life-long habit.

 VOCABULARY TIME

Assign Chapter 1, Vocabulary Words **#2** on page 8 in the Reference Section for students to define in their Vocabulary notebooks. Tell students they are to use a dictionary or thesaurus to look up the meanings of the vocabulary words. After they write each word and its meaning, students are to write a sentence using the vocabulary word.

Chapter 1, Vocabulary Words #2
(modest, forward, depart, leave)

(End of lesson.)

CHAPTER 1   LESSON 5

Objectives: Study, Test, Check, Writing (revising, editing), and Writing (journal).

STUDY TIME

Have students study the vocabulary words in their vocabulary notebooks. Remind students that any vocabulary word in their notebook could be on their test.

TEST TIME

Have students turn to page 98 in the Test Section of their book and find the Chapter 1 Test *(Exercises 1–2)*. Tell them that grammar is not tested yet. Go over the directions to make sure they understand what to do. *(Chapter 1 Test keys are given below.)*

Exercise 1: Identify each pair of words as synonyms or antonyms by putting parentheses ( ) around *syn* or *ant*. Write numbers 5 and 6 on notebook paper. For number 5, write two synonym words and identify them with *syn*. For number 6, write two antonym words and identify them with *ant*.

| 1. timid, bold | syn **(ant)** | 3. modest, forward | syn **(ant)** | 5. **(Answers will vary.)** |
| 2. slumber, sleep | **(syn)** ant | 4. depart, leave | **(syn)** ant | 6. **(Answers will vary.)** |

Exercise 2: Write *a* or *an* in the blanks.

1. We found __a__ bird's nest.
2. They saw __an__ odd bird.
3. I have __an__ awful cold.
4. We are __a__ good team.
5. It was __an__ empty box.
6. He has __a__ new friend.
7. __an__ eagle
8. __a__ test
9. __an__ accident
10. __a__ fur
11. __an__ orange
12. __a__ nose

CHECK TIME

After students have finished, check and discuss their test papers. Make sure they understand why their answers are right or wrong. *(For total points, count each required answer as a point.)*

Teacher's Notes: Grading Ideas
1. **One Grade:** You can take one grade on the whole test.
2. **Two Grades:** You can take one grade on the grammar sentences and another grade on the skill exercises.
3. **Possible Points:** For total points, count each required answer as a point.

CHAPTER 1 LESSON 5 CONTINUED

 **WRITING TIME**

TEACHING SCRIPT FOR REVISING AND EDITING

Before you start your writing assignments in another chapter, there are a few basic things I want you to know. First, writing is a process. You usually do not have a finished product the first time you write. When you write, you start out by writing a rough draft. A rough draft is a rough copy of your writing. It is not a finished piece of writing. In fact, you do not have to worry about errors as you write your rough draft. You will usually make changes in the rough draft to improve it. Today, we will learn the different terminology used as you go through the process of changing your writing to make it better.

Listen to the words, **revise** and **edit**. Both revising and editing make your writing better. It's usually called revising when you find ways to make the content better. Look at Reference 5 on page 12 in your book. Let's read some of the things you need to know about revision. (*Read and discuss only the Revision Checklist on the next page.*)

After you have made revisions in your writing content, your next step is to check your paper for mistakes in spelling, grammar, usage, and punctuation. This is called editing. It begins with careful proofreading. Look at the second part of Reference 5. It is called a Beginning Editing Checklist because it contains only some of the first skills necessary for you to know as you edit.

The editing list will continue to grow as more skills are introduced. We will go through the skills listed under "More Editing Skills" in later chapters. (*Teaching scripts for these additional skills will also be given to the teacher in later chapters.*) Eventually, you will have a regular editing checklist that will have most of the skills added. We will discuss only the beginning editing skills to make sure you understand each of them at this point. (*Read and discuss the Beginning Editing Checklist on the next page.*)

We will now study four paragraphs. Look at the four paragraphs in Reference 6. (*Your copy of Reference 6 is located on page 11 of this chapter.*) Nothing has been done to the first paragraph. It is a rough draft. Notice that the second paragraph has been revised, and the third paragraph has been edited. (*Read and discuss the differences in the first three paragraphs.*) Once you have revised and edited your rough draft, you will make a final copy of your work. Look at the third checklist. It is called "Final Paper Checklist." This will tell you what to expect as you write your final paper. (*Read and discuss the Final Paper Checklist on the next page.*) The last paragraph has gone through the "Final Paper Checklist" and is ready for publishing.

Let's review the procedure you should use for each writing assignment. This procedure is called the "Writing Process Checklist." Look at the last section of Reference 5. You will refer to this section to help you remember the writing procedures used in your writing assignments. (*Read and discuss the Writing Process Checklist on the next page.*)

Listen carefully as I repeat the writing process again. It is too important to forget. First, you gather information. Next, you write a rough draft. Then, you revise and edit the rough draft. Finally, you rewrite the rough draft and turn in a final paper. If your writing assignment takes more than one session, you will finish it in your free time. Make sure you refer to Reference 5 anytime you forget what to do.

CHAPTER 1 LESSON 5 CONTINUED

Reference 5: Checklists

Revision Checklist

1. Eliminate unnecessary or needlessly repeated words or ideas.
2. Combine or reorder sentences.
3. Change word choices for clarity and expression.
4. Know the purpose: to explain, to describe, to entertain, or to persuade.
5. Know the audience: the reader(s) of the writing.

Beginning Editing Checklist

1. Did you indent the paragraph?
2. Did you capitalize the first word and put an end mark at the end of every sentence?
3. Did you spell words correctly?

More Editing Skills

4. Did you follow the writing guidelines? (*located in Reference 13 on student page 17*)
5. Did you list the topic and three points on separate lines at the top of the paper?
6. Did you follow the three-point paragraph pattern?
7. Did you write in the point of view assigned? (*first or third person*)
8. Did you use the correct homonyms?
9. Did you follow all other capitalization and punctuation rules?
10. Did you follow the three-paragraph essay pattern?

Final Paper Checklist

1. Have you written the correct heading on your paper?
2. Have you written your final paper in ink?
3. Have you single-spaced your final paper?
4. Have you written your final paper neatly?
5. Have you stapled the final paper to the rough draft and handed them in to your teacher?

Writing Process Checklist

1. Gather information.
2. Write a rough draft.
3. Revise the rough draft.
4. Edit the rough draft.
5. Write a final paper.

CHAPTER 1 LESSON 5 CONTINUED

Reference 6: Rough Drafts and Final Paragraph
Rough Draft
When Melissa arrived, at the airport last weak, the terminial were so conjested that she could hardly move. Melissa quickly moved through the airports crowded hallways, because she was already late. She arrived at the right terminial just in time to bored her flight. Melissa was out of breath and her hart was beating hard too. When she reached her seat on the plain, she was tired. Before she fell asleep she promised to allow extra time on the next trip for the large crowds.
Revision of Draft
When Melissa arrived, at the airport last weak, the terminial were so conjested she could **barely** move. **Because she was already late, Melissa rushed through the airports crowded corridors.** She arrived at the **correct** terminial just in time to bored her flight. Melissa was out of breath and **her hart was pounding rapidly from her mad dash through the airport**. When she **finally** reached her seat on the plain, she was **exhausted**. Before she fell asleep she promised **herself that on the next trip, she would allow extra time for the enormous crowds at the airport.**
Edit Draft
When Melissa arrived [**delete comma**] at the airport last week, [**week, not weak**] the terminal [**terminal, not terminial**] was [**was, not were**] so congested [**congested, not conjested**] she could barely move. Because she was already late, Melissa rushed through the airport's [**apostrophe added**] crowded corridors. She arrived at the correct terminal [**terminal, not terminial**] just in time to board [**board, not bored**] her flight. Melissa was out of breath, [**comma inserted**] and her heart [**heart, not hart**] was pounding rapidly from her mad dash through the airport. When she finally reached her seat on the plane [**plane, not plain**], she was exhausted. Before she fell asleep, [**comma inserted**] she promised herself that on the next trip, she would allow extra time for the enormous crowds at the airport.
Final Paragraph
When Melissa arrived at the airport last week, the terminal was so congested she could barely move. Because she was already late, Melissa rushed through the airport's crowded corridors. She arrived at the correct terminal just in time to board her flight. Melissa was out of breath, and her heart was pounding rapidly from her mad dash through the airport. When she finally reached her seat on the plane, she was exhausted. Before she fell asleep, she promised herself that on the next trip, she would allow extra time for the enormous crowds at the airport.

 WRITING TIME

Have students make an entry in their journals.

(End of lesson.)

CHAPTER 2   LESSON 1

Objectives: How to Get Started, Jingles (noun, verb, sentence), Grammar (noun, verb), Activity, Vocabulary #1 and #2, and Writing (journal).

HOW TO GET STARTED

1. The word *students* will be used throughout the text in reference to the child/children you are teaching. The adult teaching this program will be referred to as *teacher*.

2. Stay one lesson ahead of your students. Study the entire lesson thoroughly before you present it. Then, read each lesson like you read a storybook: word-for-word. Your teacher's manual will give you teaching scripts to read out loud to your students. It will give you teacher's notes, and it will tell you when your students are to participate with you. Do not skip anything, and do not jump ahead. In just a few days, you will be in a comfortable routine that will help your students develop a love of learning.

3. All jingles and references are found in the **Jingle and Reference Section** in the front of the student book. A **Practice Section** is located after the Jingle and Reference Sections to give students practice on the skills they are learning. A **Test Section** is located after the Practice Section to test students on the skills taught.

4. The lessons in this book are divided into chapters. Each lesson takes approximately twenty to fifty minutes to complete. For best results, you should do one lesson everyday.

5. Your Shurley kit contains a teacher's manual, a student workbook, and an audio CD which demonstrates the Jingles and the Question and Answer Flows for the Introductory Sentences.

Read the six *Jingle Guidelines* below before you teach jingles to your students. These guidelines will give you ideas and help you establish procedures for the oral recitation of jingles.

Jingle Guidelines

1. **Jingles are used** to learn English definitions. Jingle Time should be fun as well as educational.

2. **Knowing English definitions** makes learning English concepts easier because children can use the definitions to remember how to classify words used in sentences.

3. **Approach Jingle Time** as a learning time. Most of the jingles are presented as choral chants with enough rhythm to make them easy to remember, but you can also sing, rap, or just read them. Learning definitions in jingle form makes this necessary practice more fun. Listen to the CD for examples of one way the jingles can be done.

4. **Jingles are more fun** if you make up motions for each jingle. Motions use the kinesthetic learning style of students and help them learn faster. Motions should be incorporated for several of the jingles. Relax and have fun. Have your children help make up motions they enjoy.

5. **You only need** to spend a short time on jingles (five to ten minutes) because you will be working with the jingles every day.

6. **Demonstrate each new jingle** for your students and then lead them in reciting the jingles. Let your students lead the jingles as soon as they are ready.

CHAPTER 2 LESSON 1 CONTINUED

JINGLE TIME

Have students turn to page 2 in the Jingle Section of their books. The teacher will lead the students in reciting the new jingles (*Noun, Verb, and Sentence*) below. Practice the jingles several times until students can recite the jingles smoothly. Emphasize reciting with a rhythm. Students and teacher should be together! (*Do not try to explain the jingles at this time. Just have fun reciting them. Add motions for more fun and laughter.*)

Teacher's Notes: Do not spend a large amount of time practicing the new jingles. Students learn the jingles best by spending a small amount of time consistently, **every** day. (*Lead your students as they jiggle, wiggle, and jingle! Everyone should enjoy Jingle Time.*)

Jingle 1: Noun Jingle
This little noun Floating around Names a person, place, or thing. With a knick knack, paddy wack, These are English rules. Isn't language fun and cool?

Jingle 2: Verb Jingle		
A verb, a verb. What is a verb? Haven't you heard? There are two kinds of verbs: The action verb and the linking verb.	The action verb shows a state of action, Like **stand** and **sit** and **smile**. The action verb is always doing Because it tells what the subject does. We **stand**! We **sit**! We **smile**!	The linking verb is a state of being, Like **am, is, are, was**, and **were**, **Looks, becomes, grows**, and **feels**. A linking verb shows no action Because it tells what the subject is. *He* **is** *a* *clown*. *He* **looks** *funny*.

Jingle 3: Sentence Jingle	
A sentence, sentence, sentence Is complete, complete, complete When 5 simple rules It meets, meets, meets.	Add a capital letter, letter And an end mark, mark. Now, we're finished, and aren't we smart! Now, our sentence has all its parts!
It has a subject, subject, subject And a verb, verb, verb. It makes sense, sense, sense With every word, word, word.	REMEMBER Subject, Verb, Com-plete sense, Capital letter, and an end mark, too. That's what a sentence is all about!

GRAMMAR TIME

TEACHING SCRIPT FOR THE NOUN AND VERB

The purpose of studying English is to learn the vocabulary and skills that will help you become effective in speaking and writing. We will begin our study of English with nouns and verbs.

CHAPTER 2 LESSON 1 CONTINUED

The Noun Jingle that you learned today says a **noun** names a person, place, or thing. The noun is also known as a naming word. Words like **baby** and **Bill** name people. Can you tell me two more nouns that name people? (*Give students time to respond.*) Words like **horses** and **cows** name animals. Can you tell me two more nouns that name animals? (*Give students time to respond.*)

Words like **restaurant** and **school** name places, and words like **pots** and **pans** name things. Can you tell me two more nouns that name places and things? (*Give students time to respond.*) (*Then, give students time to identify several nouns in the room.*) We use the abbreviation **N** for the word **noun** when we do not spell it out.

You have already learned several things about the verb from the Verb Jingle. A word that shows action is a verb. The **verb** tells what a person or thing does. Words like **swim** and **hop** tell what children do. Can you tell me two more verbs that tell what children do? (*Give students time to respond.*) We use the abbreviation **V** for the word **verb** when we do not spell it out.

 ## ACTIVITY / ASSIGNMENT TIME

For independent practice, have students write this title on notebook paper: Family Car. Have them make two columns and write a number 1 at the top of the first column and a number 2 at the top of the second column. Have students list as many nouns related to the car as possible and record the nouns under the first column. Next, have students actually examine the family car and list all the additional nouns under the second column. (*Compare and discuss the two noun lists after students have finished.*)

 ## VOCABULARY TIME

Assign Chapter 2, Vocabulary Words **#1** and **#2** on page 8 in the Reference Section for students to define in their Vocabulary notebooks. Tell students they are to use a dictionary or thesaurus to look up the meanings of the vocabulary words. After they write each word and its meaning, students are to write a sentence using the vocabulary word.

Chapter 2, Vocabulary Words #1
(calamity, disaster, admire, detest)

Chapter 2, Vocabulary Words #2
(easy, complicated, precise, exact)

 ## WRITING TIME

Have students make an entry in their journals.

(End of lesson.)

CHAPTER 2   LESSON 2

Objectives: Jingles, Grammar (Introductory Sentences, Question & Answer Flow, classifying, labeling, subject noun, verb), Skills (five parts of a complete sentence).

JINGLE TIME

Have students turn to the Jingle Section in their books. The teacher will lead the students in reciting the previously-taught jingles.

GRAMMAR TIME

Put the introductory sentences from the box below on the board. Use these sentences as you go through the new concepts covered in your teaching scripts. For the greatest benefit, students must participate orally with the teacher. (*You might put the introductory sentences on notebook paper if you are doing one-on-one instruction with your students.*)

Chapter 2, Introductory Sentences for Lesson 2
1. Ice melted.
2. Clown juggled.
3. Pioneers traveled.

TEACHING SCRIPT FOR THE QUESTION & ANSWER FLOW

Understanding how all the parts of a sentence work together makes writing sentences easier and more interesting. Learning how to ask the right questions to get answers will help you identify the parts of a sentence. The questions you ask and the answers you get are called a **Question and Answer Flow**.

You will use a Question and Answer Flow to find what each word in a sentence is called. This method is called **classifying** because you classify, or tell, what each word in a sentence is called. After you classify a word, you will write the abbreviation above it. This is called **labeling** because you identify the words by writing abbreviations above them.

CHAPTER 2 LESSON 2 CONTINUED

TEACHING SCRIPT FOR SUBJECT NOUN AND VERB IN A SENTENCE

I am going to show you how to use the noun and verb definitions and the Question and Answer Flow to find the subject noun and verb in a sentence. The subject of a sentence tells who or what a sentence is about. Since a noun names a person, place, or thing, a subject noun tells who or what a sentence is about. **The abbreviation *SN* is used for the words *subject noun* when we do not spell them out.** We ask a subject question to find the noun that works as the subject of the sentence. The subject questions are **who**, or **what**. We ask **who** if the sentence is **about people**. We ask **what** if the sentence is **not about people,** but about an animal, a place, or a thing.

Look at Sentence 1: Ice melted.
What melted? ice - subject noun (*Write SN above ice.*)
Since the word *ice* is a thing, we ask the subject question *what*.
The subject noun *ice* tells *what* the sentence is about.

Now, let's learn the Question and Answer Flow to find the verb. The verb definition says the verb shows action. The verb tells what the subject is doing. To find the verb, ask **what is being said about** the subject. Let's say **what is being said about** five times. Go. (*Have your students recite "what is being said about" with you at least five times. This will help them remember this important verb question.*)

What is being said about ice? ice melted - verb (*Write V above melted.*)

Remember, the questions you ask and the answers you get are called a Question and Answer Flow. I will classify Sentence 1 again, but this time you will classify the sentence with me. After we finish Sentence 1, you will classify Sentences 2 and 3 with me.

Teacher's Note: Make sure students say the Question and Answer Flows correctly.

Question and Answer Flow for Sentence 1: Ice melted.

1. What melted? ice - subject noun (Trace over the SN above *ice*.)
2. What is being said about ice? ice melted - verb (Trace over the V above *melted*.)

Classified Sentence: SN   V
     Ice melted.

Question and Answer Flow for Sentence 2: Clown juggled.

1. Who juggled? clown - subject noun (Write SN above *clown*.)
 (Since *clown* is a person, we begin the subject question with *who*. The subject noun *clown* tells *who* the sentence is about.)
2. What is being said about clown? clown juggled - verb (Write V above *juggled*.)

Classified Sentence: SN   V
     Clown juggled.

Question and Answer Flow for Sentence 3: Pioneers traveled.

1. Who traveled? pioneers - subject noun (Write SN above *pioneers*.)
 (Since *pioneers* are people, we begin the subject question with *who*. The subject noun *pioneers* tells *who* the sentence is about.)
2. What is being said about pioneers? pioneers traveled - verb (Write V above *traveled*.)

Classified Sentence: SN   V
     Pioneers traveled.

CHAPTER 2 LESSON 2 CONTINUED

TEACHER INSTRUCTIONS

Have students recite the Question and Answer Flows for the first two sentences with you again, but this time they are to trace the labels on their desks with the first three fingers of their writing hand as they classify. This is excellent practice to develop dexterity and to learn at a faster pace.

Have students write the third sentence on notebook paper. Then, students should go through the Question and Answer Flow with you again, but this time they are to write the labels above the words they classify. This will give them practice writing the labels before they are tested on them.

The key to success is to keep students constantly saying the Question and Answer Flows until they know them automatically. Follow the suggestions below for your students to get the greatest benefits from the grammar lessons.

1. Be sure to have the students read each sentence with you, in unison, before classifying it.
2. Make sure students are saying the **questions** and the **answers** with you as each Question and Answer Flow is recited.

 SKILL TIME

TEACHING SCRIPT FOR THE 5 PARTS OF THE COMPLETE SENTENCE

Let's recite just the Sentence Jingle again. As you recite the Sentence Jingle, listen for the five parts that make a complete sentence. (*Recite the Sentence Jingle.*) Did you hear the five parts that make a complete sentence when we recited the Sentence Jingle? Of course, you did. Listen carefully as I go over the definition and the crucial parts of a complete sentence.

A **complete sentence** is a group of words that has a subject, a verb, and expresses a complete thought. A complete sentence should also begin with a capital letter and end with an end mark. Since you will be required to know the five parts of a sentence on a definition test later, you will learn the five parts of a sentence the easy way: by reciting the Sentence Jingle during Jingle Time. Now, listen for the five parts of a sentence as you recite the Sentence Jingle one more time. (*Recite the Sentence Jingle again.*) I want you to recite only the five parts of a sentence. (*Have students recite the section under REMEMBER several times.*)

> **REMEMBER**
> Subject, Verb, Com-plete sense,
> Capital letter, and an end mark, too.
> That's what a sentence is all about!

(End of lesson.)

CHAPTER 2   LESSON 3

Objectives: Jingles (adverb, adjective, article adjective), Skills (four kinds of sentences), and Activity.

 JINGLE TIME

Have students turn to the Jingle Section in their books and recite the previously-taught jingles. Then, lead students in reciting the new jingles (*Adverb, Adjective, Article Adjective*) below. Practice the new jingles several times until students can recite them smoothly. Emphasize reciting with a rhythm. Students and teacher should be together! (*Do not try to explain the jingles at this time. The jingles are taught now so they can be used as a reference in future lessons. Just have fun reciting them. Add motions for more fun and laughter.*)

Teacher's Notes: Again, do not spend a large amount of time practicing the new jingles. Students learn the jingles best by spending a small amount of time consistently, **every** day.

Jingle 4: Adverb Jingle
An adverb modifies a verb, adjective, or another adverb.
An adverb asks *How? When? Where?*
To find an adverb: **Go, Ask, Get**.
Where do I **go**? To a verb, adjective, or another adverb.
What do I **ask**? How? When? Where?
What do I **get**? An ADVERB! (Clap) (Clap) That's what!

Jingle 5: Adjective Jingle
An adjective modifies a noun or pronoun.
An adjective asks *What kind? Which one? How many?*
To find an adjective: **Go, Ask, Get**.
Where do I **go**? To a noun or pronoun.
What do I **ask**? What kind? Which one? How many?
What do I **get**? An ADJECTIVE! (Clap) (Clap)That's what!

Jingle 6: Article Adjective
We are the article adjectives, Teeny, tiny adjectives: **A, AN, THE - A, AN, THE.** We are called article adjectives and noun markers; We are memorized and used every day. So, if you spot us, you can mark us With the label A. We are the article adjectives, Teeny, tiny adjectives: **A, AN, THE - A, AN, THE.**

 SKILL TIME

TEACHING SCRIPT FOR THE FOUR KINDS OF SENTENCES

There are four kinds of sentences. They are declarative, interrogative, imperative, and exclamatory. Let's recite the four kinds of sentences together five times. Go. (*Have your students recite "declarative, interrogative, imperative, and exclamatory" with you at least five times. This will help them remember the vocabulary necessary when discussing the kinds of sentences.*)

CHAPTER 2 LESSON 3 CONTINUED

These sentences have four purposes: to tell, to ask, to request/command, or to show strong feeling. Now, you will learn more about the four kinds of sentences. Look at Reference 7 on page 14 in the Reference Section of your book. (*Read and discuss the information in the reference box below with your students.*)

Reference 7: The Four Kinds of Sentences and the End Mark Flow

1. A **declarative** sentence makes a statement.
   It is labeled with a *D*.
   Example: Lisa bought a video.
   (*Period, statement, declarative sentence*)

2. An **imperative** sentence gives a command.
   It is labeled with an *Imp*.
   Example: Take the mail to the post office.
   (*Period, command, imperative sentence*)

3. An **interrogative** sentence asks a question.
   It is labeled with an *Int*.
   Example: What is in your lunch box?
   (*Question mark, question, interrogative sentence*)

4. An **exclamatory** sentence expresses strong feeling.
   It is labeled with an *E*.
   Example: The roller coaster is awesome!
   (*Exclamation point, strong feeling, exclamatory sentence*)

Examples: Read each sentence, recite the end-mark flow in parentheses, and put the end mark and the abbreviation for the sentence type in the blank at the end of each sentence.

1. Monday is a holiday **. D**
   (*Period, statement, declarative sentence*)

2. The car rolled down the street **! E**
   (*Exclamation point, strong feeling, exclamatory sentence*)

3. Peel the apples in the kitchen **. Imp**
   (*Period, command, imperative sentence*)

4. Will your mother be home tonight **? Int**
   (*Question mark, question, interrogative sentence*)

Go to the examples listed at the bottom of your reference box and follow along as I identify each sentence by reciting the end-mark flow. Remember, the end-mark flow identifies the punctuation mark, the kind of sentence, and the name of that type of sentence. (*Read the examples with your students and recite the end-mark flow that is provided in parentheses.*)

ACTIVITY / ASSIGNMENT TIME

Sentence Hopscotch
Suggestions: (1) Use an old window shade for the hopscotch board—tape it down; (2) Use tape on the floor; (3) Use an old shower curtain—tape it down; (4) draw a hopscotch design outside on the sidewalk.

Draw a hopscotch design with three single front squares, a double square, two more single squares, and a circle. Make the squares large enough for the student to jump easily from square to square. Mark each square with a sentence abbreviation (*D, E, Int, Imp*). Some of the abbreviations will be used more than once.

Using four index cards, write a sentence abbreviation on each card. Arrange the cards so the student cannot see the abbreviations. Have the student select a card and recite a sentence that matches the abbreviation on the card. If the sentence is correct, the student may start the hopscotch activity. The student cannot jump in a square marked with the sentence abbreviation they selected. After the student has jumped the hopscotch correctly, he/she chooses another index card and repeats the activity until all cards have been selected. **Variation:** If the student recites the sentence named on the index card incorrectly, he/she must write three correct sentences. After the teacher has checked the sentences, the student may begin the hopscotch activity again.

(End of lesson.)

CHAPTER 2   LESSON 4

Objectives: Jingles, and Grammar (Introductory Sentences, adverb, modify).

JINGLE TIME

Have students turn to the Jingle Section in their books. The teacher will lead the students in reciting the previously-taught jingles.

GRAMMAR TIME

Put the introductory sentences from the box below on the board. Use these sentences as you go through the new concepts covered in your teaching scripts. For the greatest benefit, students must participate orally with the teacher. (*You might put the introductory sentences on notebook paper if you are doing one-on-one instruction with your students.*)

Chapter 2, Introductory Sentences for Lesson 4

1. Ice melted rapidly away.
2. Clowns juggled happily today.
3. Pioneers traveled onward.

TEACHING SCRIPT FOR THE ADVERB

You are learning that jingles give you a lot of information quickly and easily. I will review several things that the Adverb Jingle tells us about the adverb. Listen carefully. **The Adverb Definition:** An adverb modifies a verb, adjective, or another adverb. **The Adverb Questions:** How? When? Where?

The adverb definition uses the word *modifies*. The word **modify** means to describe. When the adverb definition says that an adverb modifies a verb, it means that an adverb describes a verb. The abbreviation you will use for an adverb is **Adv**.

You will now learn how to use the adverb definition and the Question and Answer Flow to find the adverbs in sentences. But first, we will classify the main parts of a sentence, the subject and verb, before we find the adverbs.

Classify Sentence 1: Ice melted rapidly away.
What melted rapidly away? ice - subject noun (*Write SN above ice.*)
What is being said about ice? ice melted - verb (*Write V above melted.*)

The Adverb Jingle tells you the adverb definition and the adverb questions. Look at the Adverb Jingle in the Jingle Section on page 3 and repeat the Adverb Jingle with me. (*Repeat the Adverb Jingle with your students again.*) I am going to ask you some questions that will show you how to use the Adverb Jingle to find adverbs. You may look at the Adverb Jingle in your book so you can answer my questions about adverbs.

CHAPTER 2 LESSON 4 CONTINUED

1. Where do you go to find an adverb? (*to the verb, adjective, or another adverb*)
2. Where do you go **first** to find an adverb? (*to the verb*)
3. What is the verb in Sentence 1? (*melted*)
4. What do you ask after you go to the verb *melted*?
   (*one of the adverb questions: how? when? where?*)
5. How do you know which adverb question to ask?
   Look at the words around the verb: (rapidly, away). (Let these words guide you.)
6. Which adverb question would you use to find the first adverb in this sentence? (*how?*)

This is how you would ask an adverb question and give an adverb answer in the Question and Answer Flow: **Melted how? rapidly - adverb** (*Write Adv above the word **rapidly**.*)

Look at the sentence again. As you can see, there is another word that needs to be classified. In order to classify this word, you must again ask the questions that you have learned. You will continue this question and answer procedure until all words in the sentence have been identified. That is why we call it the Question and Answer Flow.

Let's go back to the verb and do the Question and Answer Flow for another adverb:
Melted where? away - adverb (*Write Adv above the word **away**.*)

I will classify Sentence 1 again, but this time you will classify it with me. I will lead you as we follow the series of questions and answers that I have just demonstrated. Then, we will classify Sentences 2-3 together.

Question and Answer Flow for Sentence 1: Ice melted rapidly away.

1. What melted rapidly away? ice - subject noun (Trace over the SN above *ice*.)
2. What is being said about ice? ice melted - verb (Trace over the V above *melted*.)
3. Melted how? rapidly - adverb (Trace over the Adv above *rapidly*.)
4. Melted where? away - adverb (Trace over the Adv above *away*.)

Classified Sentence: SN   V   Adv   Adv
                               Ice melted rapidly away.

Question and Answer Flow for Sentence 2: Clowns juggled happily today.

1. Who juggled happily today? clowns - subject noun (Write SN above *clowns*.)
2. What is being said about clowns? clowns juggled - verb (Write V above *juggled*.)
3. Juggled how? happily - adverb (Write Adv above *happily*.)
4. Juggled when? today - adverb (Write Adv above *today*.)

Classified Sentence: SN   V   Adv   Adv
                               Clowns juggled happily today.

Question and Answer Flow for Sentence 3: Pioneers traveled onward.

1. Who traveled onward? pioneers - subject noun (*SN*)
2. What is being said about pioneers? pioneers traveled - verb (*V*)
3. Traveled where? onward - adverb (*Adv*)

Classified Sentence: SN   V   Adv
                               Pioneers traveled onward.

(End of lesson.)

CHAPTER 2   LESSON 5

Objectives: Jingles, Grammar (Introductory Sentences, adjective, article adjective, modify) Skills (indefinite articles, definite article), Activity, Practice Exercise, and Test.

 **JINGLE TIME**

Have students turn to the Jingle Section in their books. The teacher will lead the students in reciting the previously-taught jingles.

 GRAMMAR TIME

Put the introductory sentences from the box below on the board. Use these sentences as you go through the new concepts covered in your teaching scripts. For the greatest benefit, students must participate orally with the teacher. (*You might put the introductory sentences on notebook paper if you are doing one-on-one instruction with your students.*)

Chapter 2, Introductory Sentences for Lesson 5

1. The frozen ice melted rapidly away.
2. The hilarious clowns juggled happily today.
3. The five exhausted pioneers traveled onward.

TEACHING SCRIPT FOR THE ADJECTIVE

Remember, jingles give you a lot of information quickly and easily. I will review several things that the Adjective Jingle tells us about the adjective. **The Adjective Definition:** An adjective modifies a noun or pronoun. **The Adjective Questions:** What kind? Which one? How many?

The adjective definition also uses the word *modifies*. The word **modify** means to describe. When the adjective definition says that an adjective modifies a noun, it means that an adjective describes a noun. The abbreviation you will use for an adjective is **Adj**.

You will now learn how to use the adjective definition and the Question and Answer Flow to find the adjectives in sentences. But first, we will classify the subject, verb, and adverb before we find the adjectives.

Classify Sentence 1: The frozen ice melted rapidly away.
What melted rapidly away? ice - subject noun (*Write SN above ice.*)
What is being said about ice? ice melted - verb (*Write V above melted.*)
Melted how? rapidly - adverb (*Write Adv above the word **rapidly**.*)
Melted where? away - adverb (*Write Adv above the word **away**.*)

Level 4 Homeschool Teacher's Manual

CHAPTER 2 LESSON 5 CONTINUED

We will use the same procedure to find the adjectives. The Adjective Jingle tells you the adjective definition and the adjective questions. Look at the Adjective Jingle in the Jingle Section on page 3 and repeat the Adjective Jingle with me. (*Repeat the Adjective Jingle with your students again.*)

I am going to ask you some questions that will show you how to use the Adjective Jingle to find adjectives. You may look at the Adjective Jingle in your book so you can answer my questions about adjectives.

1. Where do you go to find an adjective? (*to the noun or pronoun*)
2. Where do you go **first** to find an adjective? (*to the subject noun*)
3. What is the subject noun in Sentence 1? (*ice*)
4. What do you ask after you go to the subject noun *ice*?
   (*one of the adjective questions: what kind? which one? how many?*)
5. How do you know which adjective question to ask?
   (*Look at the word or words around the noun: (frozen)   (That word will guide you.)*)
6. Which adjective question would you use to find an adjective in this sentence? (*what kind?*)

This is how you would ask an adjective question and give the adjective answer in the Adjective Question and Answer Flow: **What kind of ice? frozen - adjective** (*Write Adj above the word **frozen**.*)

TEACHING SCRIPT FOR THE ARTICLE ADJECTIVE

We have another adjective to identify. This new adjective is known as the article adjective. There are only three article adjectives. Let's recite the Article Adjective Jingle to learn more about the article adjectives. (*Recite the Article Adjective Jingle with your students.*)

Article Adjectives are the three most commonly-used adjectives. The three article adjectives are *a, an,* and *the.* Everyone recite the words *article adjective* three times. (*article adjective, article adjective, article adjective*) Article adjectives are sometimes called noun markers because they tell that a noun is close by. The article adjectives must be <u>memorized</u> because there are no questions in the Question and Answer Flow to find the article adjectives. Article adjectives are labeled with an **A**.

This is how you would identify an article adjective in the Question and Answer Flow: **The - article adjective** (*Write **A** above the word **The**.*)

I will classify Sentence 1 again, but this time you will classify it with me. I will lead you as we follow the series of questions and answers that I have just demonstrated. Then, we will classify Sentences 2-3 together.

Question and Answer Flow for Sentence 1: The frozen ice melted rapidly away.

1. What melted rapidly away? ice - subject noun (Trace over the SN above *ice.*)
2. What is being said about ice? ice melted - verb (Trace over the V above *melted.*)
3. Melted how? rapidly - adverb (Trace over the Adv above *rapidly.*)
4. Melted where? away - adverb (Trace over the Adv above *away.*)
5. What kind of ice? frozen - adjective (Trace over the Adj above *frozen.*)
6. The - article adjective (Trace over the A above *The.*)

Classified Sentence: A   Adj SN   V   Adv   Adv
                          The frozen ice melted rapidly away.

CHAPTER 2 LESSON 5 CONTINUED

Question and Answer Flow for Sentence 2: The hilarious clowns juggled happily today.

1. Who juggled happily today? clowns - subject noun (Write SN above *clowns.*)
2. What is being said about clowns? clowns juggled - verb (Write V above *juggled.*)
3. Juggled how? happily - adverb (Write Adv above *happily.*)
4. Juggled when? today - adverb (Write Adv above *today.*)
5. What kind of clowns? hilarious - adjective (Write Adj above *hilarious.*)
6. The - article adjective (Write A above *The.*)

Classified Sentence:

      A   Adj   SN   V   Adv Adv
      The hilarious clowns juggled happily today.

Question and Answer Flow for Sentence 3: The five exhausted pioneers traveled onward.

1. Who traveled onward? pioneers - subject noun (*SN*)
2. What is being said about pioneers? pioneers traveled - verb (*V*)
3. Traveled where? onward - adverb (*Adv*)
4. What kind of pioneers? exhausted - adjective (*Adj*)
5. How many pioneers ? five - adjective (*Adj*)
6. The - article adjective (A)

Classified Sentence:

      A   Adj   Adj   SN   V   Adv
      The five exhausted pioneers traveled onward.

SKILL TIME

TEACHING SCRIPT FOR ARTICLE ADJECTIVE SKILLS

You have seen how the article adjective is used in the Question and Answer Flows to classify sentences. Now, I will give you more information about article adjectives. Turn to Reference 8 on page 14 in the Reference Section of your book. (*Have students follow along as you read the information in the reference box below.*)

Reference 8: Additional Article Adjective Information

1. **A/An** are called <u>indefinite</u> articles, meaning one of several.
   (Examples: **a** brown cow—**an** arrow.)

2. **The** is called a <u>definite</u> article, meaning there is only one.
   (Examples: **the** brown cow—**the** arrow.)

3. The article **The** has two pronunciations:

   a. As a long **e** (*where the article precedes a word that begins with a vowel sound: the elbow, the infant*)

   b. As a short **u** (*where the article precedes a word that begins with a consonant sound: the book, the tree*)

CHAPTER 2 LESSON 5 CONTINUED

ACTIVITY / ASSIGNMENT TIME

On notebook paper, write five nouns that begin with a vowel sound. Write the letter **(e)** in *parentheses* after each word to indicate that the article would be pronounced with the long e sound. Next, write ten nouns that begin with a consonant sound. Write the letter **(u)** in parentheses after each word to indicate that the article would be pronounced with the short **u** sound. After you have finished, we will say the words aloud with the proper pronunciation of the article **t-h-e** in front of each word. (*After students have finished, listen to them as they pronounce the article correctly for each word they have written on their paper.*)

PRACTICE TIME

Have students turn to page 66 in the Practice Section of their book and find the skills under Chapter 2, Lesson 5, Practice *(1-2)*. Go over the directions to make sure they understand what to do. Check and discuss the Practices after students have finished. (*Chapter 2, Lesson 5, Practice keys are given below.*)

Chapter 2, Lesson 5, Practice 1: Put the end mark and the abbreviation for each kind of sentence in the blanks.

1. Close your eyes and try to sleep   **. Imp**
2. Did you get new glasses   **? Int**
3. I see the tornado   **! E**
4. I'm leaving on my trip tomorrow   **. D**

Chapter 2, Lesson 5, Practice 2: On notebook paper, write a sentence to demonstrate each of these four kinds of sentences: (1) Declarative (2) Interrogative (3) Exclamatory (4) Imperative. Write the correct punctuation and the abbreviation that identifies it at the end. Use these abbreviations: **D, Int, E, Imp.**

TEST TIME

Have students turn to page 98 in the Test Section of their book and find the Chapter 2 Test *(Exercise 1)*. Go over the directions to make sure they understand what to do. Check and discuss the test after students have finished. (*Chapter 2 Test key is given below.*)

Exercise 1: Match the definitions by writing the correct letter beside each numbered concept.

G	1. exclamatory sentence	A.	verb, adjective, or adverb
H	2. a/an are also called	B.	who
I	3. adjective modifies	C.	what is being said about
C	4. verb question	D.	person, place, or thing
J	5. a definite article	E.	what
E	6. subject-noun question (thing)	F.	period
K	7. article adjective can be called	G.	shows strong feeling
L	8. makes a request or gives a command	H.	indefinite articles
D	9. noun	I.	noun or pronoun
B	10. subject-noun question (person)	J.	the
F	11. punctuation for declarative	K.	noun marker
A	12. adverb modifies	L.	imperative sentence

(End of Lesson.)

CHAPTER 3   LESSON 1

Objectives: Jingles, Grammar (Introductory Sentences, identifying adverbs that modify adjectives and adverbs), Skills (Skill Builder Checks, Noun Checks).

 JINGLE TIME

Have students turn to the Jingle Section in their books. The teacher will lead the students in reciting the previously-taught jingles.

 GRAMMAR TIME

Put the introductory sentences from the box below on the board. Use these sentences as you go through the new concepts covered in your teaching scripts. For the greatest benefit, students must participate orally with the teacher. (*You might put the introductory sentences on notebook paper if you are doing one-on-one instruction with your students.*)

Chapter 3, Introductory Sentences for Lesson 1

1. The incredibly talented musician played extremely well.
2. Several hungry wolves ran quickly away.
3. Two express trains collided suddenly!

TEACHING SCRIPT FOR IDENTIFYING ADVERBS THAT MODIFY ADJECTIVES AND ADVERBS

How do you find and classify adjectives? (*Go to the noun, ask an adjective question, and label the answer as an adjective.*) How do you find and classify adverbs? (*Go to the verb, ask an adverb question, and label the answer as an adverb.*)

The adverb definition tells you that an adverb modifies a verb, adjective, or another adverb. Today, I will show you how to find adverbs that do not modify a verb. You will go to an adjective or an adverb instead of the verb to ask an adverb question. Notice how these new concepts are demonstrated in the Question and Answer Flow. Begin.

Teacher's Notes: At this time, your manual will no longer have the entire name written out for each part of speech used in the Question and Answer Flow. Instead of *adverb*, you will see **Adv**. You will continue to say *adverb* even though you see only the abbreviation **Adv**. You will say *subject noun* whenever you see the abbreviation **SN**. Always say *verb* whenever you see the abbreviation **V**, etc.

Question and Answer Flow for Sentence 1: The incredibly talented musician played extremely well.

1. Who played extremely well? musician - SN
2. What is being said about musician? musician played - V
3. Played how? well - Adv
4. How well? extremely - Adv

5. What kind of musician? talented - Adj
6. How talented? incredibly - Adv
7. The - A

Note: "incredibly" is an adverb that modifies an adjective in the complete subject. It is part of the complete subject.

Classified Sentence: A   Adv   Adj   SN   V   Adv   Adv

The incredibly talented musician played extremely well.

CHAPTER 3 LESSON 1 CONTINUED

Question and Answer Flow for Sentence 2: Several hungry wolves ran quickly away.

1. What ran quickly away? wolves - SN
2. What is being said about wolves? wolves ran - V
3. Ran how? quickly - Adv
4. Ran where? away - Adv
5. What kind of wolves? hungry - Adj
6. How many wolves? several - Adj

Classified Sentence: Adj   Adj   SN   V   Adv   Adv
Several hungry wolves ran quickly away.

Question and Answer Flow for Sentence 3: Two express trains collided suddenly!

1. What collided suddenly? trains - SN
2. What is being said about trains? trains collided - V
3. Collided when? suddenly - Adv
4. What kind of trains? express - Adj
5. How many trains? two - Adj

Classified Sentence: Adj   Adj   SN   V   Adv
Two express trains collided suddenly!

Teacher's Notes: Adverbs are classified in the order they appear after the verb because it is easier for the students. Only when an adverb modifies another adverb does the order change. The second adverb is classified first.

Example: *Tom ran very well.* Ran how? well - Adv; How well? very - Adv.

SKILL TIME

TEACHING SCRIPT FOR INTRODUCING SKILL BUILDER CHECKS AND NOUN CHECKS

Now that we have classified all three sentences, I am going to use them to do a Skill Builder Check. **A Skill Builder Check** is an oral review of certain skills. Skill Builder Checks are designed to make sure you keep basic skills sharp and automatic. The first skill that will be covered by the Skill Builder Check is the **Noun Check.** Even though a noun is only one part of speech, a noun can do many jobs or perform many functions in a sentence. The first noun job you have learned is that a noun can function as the subject of a sentence. The first noun job will be the subject noun.

Look at Sentences 1-3. In a Noun Check, we will identify the nouns in all three sentences by drawing circles around them. It will be easy today because we have only one noun job at this point. I will use Sentence 1 to demonstrate the four things that you say: **Number 1** (*You say the sentence number.*) **Subject Noun:** *musician* (*You say the noun job and the noun used for the noun job.*) **Yes** (*You say the word* **yes** *to verify that the word* **musician** *is a noun, not a pronoun.*) So it will not be confusing, I will repeat number 1 again. We will say, "Number 1: subject noun *musician*, yes." I will circle *musician* because we have identified it as a noun.

Let's start with number 1 again and do a Noun Check. Begin. (*Circle the nouns for all three sentences as your students recite the Noun Check with you: Number 1: subject noun* **musician***, yes. Number 2: subject noun* **wolves***, yes. Number 3: subject noun* **trains***, yes.*)

(End of lesson.)

CHAPTER 3 LESSON 2
Objectives: Jingles, Grammar (Introductory Sentences, Pattern 1 Sentences, complete subject, complete predicate, end punctuation), Skills (Review Skill Builder Checks, Noun Checks) and Vocabulary #1.

JINGLE TIME

Have students turn to the Jingle Section in their books. The teacher will lead the students in reciting the previously-taught jingles.

GRAMMAR TIME

Put the introductory sentences from the box below on the board. Use these sentences as you go through the new concepts covered in your teaching scripts. For the greatest benefit, students must participate orally with the teacher. (*You might put the introductory sentences on notebook paper if you are doing one-on-one instruction with your students.*)

Chapter 3, Introductory Sentences for Lesson 2
1. _____ The two fishing boats sailed swiftly away.
2. _____ The four spotted cheetahs attacked very abruptly!
3. _____ The extremely late flight landed safely.

TEACHING SCRIPT FOR PATTERN 1, COMPLETE SUBJECT/COMPLETE PREDICATE, AND END PUNCTUATION

We will now classify Sentence 1. This time, there will be more information added to the Question and Answer Flow. You will classify the sentence with me until we get to the new part. The new part will be at the end of the Question and Answer Flow. Begin.

Sentence 1: The two fishing boats sailed swiftly away.
What sailed swiftly away? boats - SN
What is being said about boats? boats sailed - V
Sailed how? swiftly - Adv
Sailed where? away - Adv
What kind of boats? fishing - Adj
How many boats? two - Adj
The - A

I will now explain the new parts and show you how to add them to the Question and Answer Flow. First, I will say the new parts in the Question and Answer Flow, and then I will explain each new part to you. Listen carefully as I repeat the three new parts.

1. Subject Noun Verb Pattern 1 Check. (*Write SN V P1 in the blank in front of the sentence. Be sure to say* **check**. *You will use the check to identify any new skill that is added to the Question and Answer Flow.*)
2. Period, statement, declarative sentence. (*Write a D at the end of the sentence.*)
3. Go back to the verb - divide the complete subject from the complete predicate.
   (*As you say* **divide**, *put a slash mark before your verb.*)

CHAPTER 3 LESSON 2 CONTINUED

Note: Your sentence should look like this:

```
                  A  Adj  Adj   SN    V   Adv   Adv
      SN  V       The two fishing boats / sailed swiftly away.  D
      P1
```

I will explain each new part, one at a time. Listen to the definition for a Pattern 1 sentence. The pattern of a sentence is the **order of the main parts** in that sentence. **Pattern 1** has only two main parts: the subject and the verb. (*The subject can be a noun or pronoun.*) Adjectives and adverbs add information to sentences, but they are not part of a sentence pattern. A **Pattern 1** sentence is labeled **SN V P1**. (*Put the SN V P1 on the board for your students to see.*) When you see or write the **SN V P1** labels, you will say, "Subject Noun, Verb, Pattern 1."

You will add a <u>check</u> to the sentence pattern to check for any additional skills to be identified. You will say, **"Subject Noun, Verb, Pattern 1, Check."** Remember these things:

1. The pattern of a sentence is <u>the order of its main parts</u>. <u>The subject and the verb are the main parts of a Pattern 1 sentence</u>.
2. Adjectives and adverbs are extra words that are not considered essential parts of a sentence pattern because they are used freely with all sentence patterns.
3. To identify the Pattern 1 sentences, you will write *SN V P1* on the line in front of any Pattern 1 sentence.

The second new part is to identify the sentence as a declarative, imperative, interrogative, or exclamatory sentence. As soon as you say the pattern, you will immediately go to the end of the sentence, identify the end mark, the kind of sentence, and the name of that sentence. Look at Sentence 1. You will say, **"Period, statement, declarative sentence."** After you have identified the sentence as a declarative sentence, you will write a *D* after the period, but you will always say, "Period, statement, declarative sentence."

Now, I will explain the third new part. Listen carefully as I repeat the new part again. **"Go back to the verb - divide the complete subject from the complete predicate."** First, I will give you information about the complete subject and the complete predicate. Listen carefully. The **complete subject** is the subject and all the words that modify the subject. The complete subject usually starts at the beginning of the sentence and includes every word up to the verb of the sentence. The vertical line in front of the verb shows where the subject parts end and the predicate parts begin.

The **complete predicate** is the verb and all the words that modify the verb. The complete predicate usually starts with the verb and includes every word after the verb. The vertical line in front of the verb shows where the predicate parts start. The vertical line is a dividing line that divides or separates all the subject parts from the predicate parts in the sentence.

Remember, the words you say in the Question and Answer Flow are these: **Go back to the verb - divide the complete subject from the complete predicate.** Then, you will draw a line in front of the verb to indicate that the verb and everything after the verb is the complete predicate, and everything in front of the verb is the complete subject. (*Exceptions to this general rule are addressed later in Level 4.*) This is an easy way to identify all the subject parts and all the predicate parts.

I will classify Sentence 1 again, and you will classify it with me this time. Then, we will classify Sentences 2-3 together.

CHAPTER 3 LESSON 2 CONTINUED

Question and Answer Flow for Sentence 1: The two fishing boats sailed swiftly away.

1. What sailed swiftly away? boats - SN
2. What is being said about boats? boats sailed - V
3. Sailed how? swiftly - Adv
4. Sailed where? away - Adv
5. What kind of boats? fishing - Adj
6. How many boats? two - Adj
7. The - A

8. SN V P1 Check (Say: Subject Noun, Verb, Pattern 1, Check)
   (Write *SN V P1* in the blank beside the sentence.)
9. Period, statement, declarative sentence
   (Write *D* at the end of the sentence.)
10. Go back to the verb - divide the complete subject from the complete predicate.
    (As you say <u>divide</u>, put a slash mark before the verb.)

Classified Sentence:

          A   Adj   Adj   SN   V   Adv   Adv
SN V   The two fishing boats **/** sailed swiftly away. **D**
P1

Question and Answer Flow for Sentence 2: The four spotted cheetahs attacked very abruptly!

1. What attacked very abruptly? cheetahs - SN
2. What is being said about cheetahs?
   cheetahs attacked - V
3. Attacked how? abruptly - Adv
4. How abruptly? very - Adv
5. What kind of cheetahs? spotted – Adj
6. How many cheetahs? four - Adj
7. The - A

8. SN V P1 Check (Say: Subject Noun, Verb, Pattern 1, Check)
   (Write *SN V P1* in the blank beside the sentence.)
9. Exclamation point, strong feeling, exclamatory sentence
   (Write E at the end of the sentence.)
10. Go back to the verb - divide the complete subject from the complete predicate.
    (As you say <u>divide</u>, put a slash mark before the verb.)

Classified Sentence:

          A   Adj   Adj   SN   V   Adv   Adv
SN V   The four spotted cheetahs **/** attacked very abruptly! **E**
P1

Question and Answer Flow for Sentence 3: The extremely late flight landed safely.

1. What landed safely? flight - SN
2. What is being said about flight? flight landed - V
3. Landed how? safely - Adv
4. What kind of flight? late - Adj
5. How late? extremely - Adv

Note: "extremely" is an adverb that modifies an adjective in the complete subject. It is part of the complete subject.

6. The - A
7. SN V P1 Check
   (Say: Subject Noun, Verb, Pattern 1, Check)
8. Period, statement, declarative sentence
   (Write D at the end of the sentence.)
9. Go back to the verb - divide the complete subject from the complete predicate.
   (As you say <u>divide</u>, put a slash mark before the verb.)

Classified Sentence:

          A   Adv   Adj SN   V   Adv
SN V   The extremely late flight **/** landed safely. **D**
P1

I want you to look at Reference 9 on page 14 in the Reference Section of your book. You are given a Question and Answer Flow as an example so it will be easy for you to study. Let's read it together. Remember, we always begin by reading the sentence. (*Read and discuss the Question and Answer Flow in the reference box on the next page with your students.*)

CHAPTER 3 LESSON 2 CONTINUED

Reference 9: Question and Answer Flow Sentence	
Question and Answer Flow for Sentence 1: The excited little girl cheered very loudly.	
1. Who cheered very loudly? girl - SN	7. The - A
2. What is being said about girl? girl cheered - V	8. SN V P1 Check
3. Cheered how? loudly - Adv	9. Period, statement, declarative sentence
4. How loudly? very - Adv	10. Go back to the verb - divide the complete subject from the complete predicate.
5. What kind of girl? little - Adj	
6. What kind of girl? excited - Adj	

Classified Sentence:

```
                        A    Adj  Adj SN    V     Adv  Adv
         SN  V     The excited little girl / cheered very loudly.  D
         P1
```

SKILL TIME

TEACHING SCRIPT FOR REVIEWING SKILL BUILDER CHECKS AND NOUN CHECKS

Now that we have classified all three sentences, I am going to use them to do a Skill Builder Check. We will begin with a **Noun Check**. You have already learned the first noun job: a noun can function as the subject of a sentence.

Look at Sentences 1-3. In a Noun Check, we will identify the nouns in all three sentences by drawing circles around them. It will be easy today because we have only one noun job at this point. Let's start with number 1 and do a Noun Check. Begin. (*Circle the nouns for all three sentences as your students recite the Noun Check with you. Number 1: subject noun **boats**, yes. Number 2: subject noun **cheetahs**, yes. Number 3: subject noun **flight**, yes.*)

VOCABULARY TIME

Assign Chapter 3, Vocabulary Words **#1** on page 8 in the Reference Section for students to define in their Vocabulary notebooks. Tell students they are to use a dictionary or thesaurus to look up the meanings of the vocabulary words. After they write each word and its meaning, students are to write a sentence using the vocabulary word.

Chapter 3, Vocabulary Words #1
(idle, busy, hinted, implied)

(End of lesson.)

CHAPTER 3   LESSON 3

Objectives: Jingles, Grammar (Practice Sentences), Skills (reviewing a noun check, singular nouns, plural nouns, common nouns, proper nouns, simple subject, simple predicate), Practice Exercise, and Vocabulary #2.

 JINGLE TIME

Have students turn to the Jingle Section in their books. The teacher will lead the students in reciting the previously-taught jingles.

 GRAMMAR TIME

Put the Practice Sentences from the box below on the board. Use these sentences as you practice the concepts that have been taught. For the greatest benefit, students must participate orally with the teacher. (*You might put the Practice Sentences on notebook paper if you are doing one-on-one instruction with your students.*)

Chapter 3, Practice Sentences for Lesson 3
1. _____ The beautiful woman sang incredibly high.
2. _____ The three strong lumberjacks worked vigorously yesterday.
3. _____ The very excited fans cheered wildly!

TEACHING SCRIPT FOR PRACTICING PATTERN 1 SENTENCES

We will classify three different sentences to practice grammar as we recite the Question and Answer Flows. We will classify the sentences together. Begin. (*Have students write the labels above the sentences at this time.*)

Question and Answer Flow for Sentence 1: The beautiful woman sang incredibly high.

1. Who sang incredibly high? woman - SN
2. What is being said about woman? woman sang - V
3. Sang how? high - Adv
4. How high? incredibly - Adv
5. What kind of woman? beautiful - Adj

6. The - A
7. SN V P1 Check
8. Period, statement, declarative sentence
9. Go back to the verb - divide the complete subject from the complete predicate.

Classified Sentence:

```
                  A   Adj    SN      V    Adv    Adv
          SN V    The beautiful woman / sang incredibly high.  D
          ‾‾‾‾
          P1
```

CHAPTER 3 LESSON 3 CONTINUED

Question and Answer Flow for Sentence 2: The three strong lumberjacks worked vigorously yesterday.

1. Who worked vigorously yesterday? lumberjacks - SN
2. What is being said about lumberjacks? lumberjacks worked - V
3. Worked how? vigorously - Adv
4. Worked when? yesterday - Adv
5. What kind of lumberjacks? strong - Adj
6. How many lumberjacks? three - Adj

7. The - A
8. SN V P1 Check
9. Period, statement, declarative sentence
10. Go back to the verb - divide the complete subject from the complete predicate.

Classified Sentence:

		A	Adj	Adj	SN	V	Adv	Adv

<u>SN V</u>   The three strong lumberjacks / worked vigorously yesterday. **D**
P1

Question and Answer Flow for Sentence 3: The very excited fans cheered wildly!

1. Who cheered wildly? fans - SN
2. What is being said about fans? fans cheered - V
3. Cheered how? wildly - Adv
4. What kind of fans? excited - Adj
5. How excited? very - Adv
6. The - A

7. SN V P1 Check
8. Exclamation point, strong feeling, exclamatory sentence
9. Go back to the verb - divide the complete subject from the complete predicate.

Classified Sentence:

	A	Adv	Adj	SN	V	Adv

<u>SN V</u>   The very excited fans / cheered wildly! **E**
P1

Teacher's Notes: <u>Options Available for Classifying Sentences:</u>

- **Option 1:** If this is your student's first year in Shurley English, the program should stay teacher-student oriented. Students should classify all Introductory and Practice Sentences with the teacher to reinforce the new concepts.

- **Option 2:** If your student is experiencing no difficulty with the Practice Sentences, allow him/her to classify them independently on notebook paper. Use the Practice Sentence keys in the teacher's manual to check student's practice work.

- **Note:** Practice Booklets and Practice CDs are available as an alternative to putting the Introductory and Practice Sentences on the board or notebook paper. These booklets and CDs are supplemental and can be purchased separately.

SKILL TIME

TEACHING SCRIPT FOR REVIEWING A NOUN CHECK

Now that we have classified all three sentences, I am going to use them to do a **Noun Check** during Skill Builder Time. Look at Sentences 1-3. We will identify the nouns in all three sentences by drawing circles around them. Let's start with number 1 and do a Noun Check. Begin. (*Circle the nouns for all three sentences as your students recite the Noun Check with you. Number 1: subject noun **woman**, yes. Number 2: subject noun **lumberjacks**, yes. Number 3: subject noun **fans**, yes.*)

CHAPTER 3 LESSON 3 CONTINUED

We will now discuss several definitions that we will use as we learn more skills during Skill Builder Checks. Look at Reference 10 on page 15 in the Reference Section of your book. (*Reference 10 is located below. Read the definitions with your students. You will discuss each one in the teaching scripts throughout this lesson.*)

Reference 10: Definitions for a Skill Builder Check
1. A **noun** names a person, place, or thing.
2. A **singular noun** usually does not end in *s* or *es* and means only one. (*book, flower, shoe*)   <u>Exception:</u> Some nouns that end in s are singular and mean only one. (*recess, dress*)
3. A **plural noun** usually ends in *s* or *es* and means more than one. (*books, flowers, shoes*)   <u>Exception:</u> Some nouns are made plural by changing their spelling. (*woman-women, child-children*)
4. A **common noun** names ANY person, place, or thing. A common noun is not capitalized because it does not name a specific person, place, or thing. (*watch, purse*)
5. A **proper noun** is a noun that names a specific, or particular, person, place, or thing. Proper nouns are always capitalized no matter where they are located in the sentence. (*David, Texas*)
6. A **simple subject** is another name for the subject noun or subject pronoun.
7. A **simple predicate** is another name for the verb.

TEACHING SCRIPT FOR IDENTIFYING NOUNS AS SINGULAR OR PLURAL

The next skill we will learn in our Skill Builder Check is identifying nouns as singular or plural. This is an easy skill, but you would be surprised at the number of people who have trouble with it. We must first learn the general definitions for singular and plural.

A **singular noun** usually does not end in *s* or *es* and means only one. (*book, flower, shoe*) There are a few exceptions: Some nouns end in s and are singular and mean only one. (*recess, dress*)

A **plural noun** usually ends in *s* or *es* and means more than one. (*books, flowers, shoes*) There are a few exceptions: Some nouns are made plural by changing their spelling. (*woman-women, child-children*)

We will identify each circled noun in Sentences 1-3 as singular or plural. I will write **S** for singular or **P** for plural above each noun as we identify it. We will say "woman - singular," and I will write a **S** above *woman*. Begin. (*woman – singular, lumberjacks – plural, fans – plural. Mark the nouns with the letter "S" or "P" in all three sentences. Discuss why the nouns are singular or plural.*)

TEACHING SCRIPT FOR IDENTIFYING NOUNS AS COMMON OR PROPER

Next, you will learn about common and proper nouns. A **common noun** is a noun that names ANY person, place, or thing. A common noun is not capitalized because it does not name a specific person, place, or thing. (*watch, purse*) A **proper noun** is a noun that names a specific, or particular, person, place, or thing. Proper nouns are always capitalized no matter where they are located in the sentence. (*David, Texas*)

CHAPTER 3 LESSON 3 CONTINUED

We will look at the nouns that are circled in the three sentences and tell whether they are common or proper. How do we recognize a proper noun? (*It begins with a capital letter no matter where it is located in the sentence.*) Do we have any proper nouns in our sentences? (*No.*) How do you know? (*None of the nouns that are circled begin with a capital letter.*) Since we do not have a proper noun in the three sentences that we have just classified, I want you to think of a proper noun. (*Get several responses and discuss why the nouns named are proper nouns.*) Do we have any common nouns in our sentences? (*Yes.*) Are all the nouns common? (*Yes.*) How do you know? (*All the nouns that are circled begin with a lowercase letter.*)

TEACHING SCRIPT FOR IDENTIFYING THE SIMPLE SUBJECT AND THE SIMPLE PREDICATE

We have already discussed the **complete subject** and the **complete predicate**, but I will review them again. The **complete subject** is the subject and all the words that modify the subject. The **complete predicate** is the verb and all the words that modify the verb.

We will now learn about the simple subject and the simple predicate. The **simple subject** is another name for the subject noun or subject pronoun. The simple subject is just the subject; it does not include the other words in the complete subject. The **simple predicate** is another name for the verb. The simple predicate is just the verb; it does not include the other words in the complete predicate.

Look at Sentence 1 again. I will draw one line under the simple subject and two lines under the simple predicate as you identify them in the sentence. To identify the simple subject, make sure you respond with the words "the subject noun" before you name the simple subject. **What is the simple subject?** (*the subject noun, woman*) I will draw one line under the simple subject woman.

To identify the simple predicate, make sure you say "the verb" before you name the simple predicate. **What is the simple predicate?** (*the verb, sang*) I will draw two lines under the simple predicate *sang*. (*Mark the answers for Sentences 2-3 in the same way. The three strong lumberjacks worked vigorously yesterday. The very excited fans cheered wildly.*)

Look at Reference 11 on page 15 in your book to see how to use the skills you have just learned in a classified sentence. This example is set up in the same format, as it will appear on your test. (*Read the directions to your students and then go through the sentence, showing them how to find the answers for the noun job chart. Reference 11 is located below.*)

Reference 11: Noun Job Chart					
Directions: Classify the sentence below. Underline the complete subject once and the complete predicate twice. Then, complete the table.					
SN V A Adj SN V Adv Adv The happy children / played quietly today. D P1					
List the Noun Used	List the Noun Job	Singular or Plural	Common or Proper	Simple Subject	Simple Predicate
children	**SN**	**P**	**C**	**children**	**played**

CHAPTER 3 LESSON 3 CONTINUED

 PRACTICE TIME

Have students turn to pages 66 and 67 in the Practice Section of their book and find Chapter 3, Lesson 3, Practice (*1-3*). Go over the directions to make sure they understand what to do. Check and discuss the Practices after students have finished. (*Chapter 3, Lesson 3, Practice keys are given below.*)

Chapter 3, Lesson 3, Practice 1: Classify the sentence below. Underline the complete subject once and the complete predicate twice. Then, complete the table.

```
              A   Adj  SN    V    Adv   Adv
SN  V         The pirate ship / sailed hastily away.  D
P1
```

List the Noun Used	List the Noun Job	Singular or Plural	Common or Proper	Simple Subject	Simple Predicate
ship	SN	S	C	ship	sailed

Chapter 3, Lesson 3, Practice 2: Write *a* or *an* in the blanks.

1. She wore **a** blue dress.
2. I rode **a** motorcycle.
3. They saw **an** elephant.
4. He is **an** excellent cook.
5. She is **an** active child.
6. It was **a** new book.
7. **an** ear
8. **a** desk
9. **an** article
10. **a** dream
11. **an** oven
12. **a** swing

Chapter 3, Lesson 3, Practice 3: On notebook paper, write a sentence to demonstrate each of these four kinds of sentences: (1) Declarative (2) Interrogative (3) Exclamatory (4) Imperative. Write the correct punctuation and the abbreviation that identifies it at the end. Use these abbreviations: **D, Int, E, Imp.**

 VOCABULARY TIME

Assign Chapter 3, Vocabulary Words **#2** on page 8 in the Reference section for students to define in their Vocabulary notebooks. Tell students they are to use a dictionary or thesaurus to look up the meanings of the vocabulary words. After they write each word and its meaning, students are to write a sentence using the vocabulary word.

Chapter 3, Vocabulary Words #2
(quiver, shake, aggression, retreat)

(End of lesson.)

CHAPTER 3   LESSON 4

Objectives: Jingles, Study, Test, Check, Activity and Writing (journal).

 JINGLE TIME

Have students turn to the Jingle Section in their books. The teacher will lead the students in reciting the previously-taught jingles.

 STUDY TIME

Have students study the vocabulary words in their vocabulary notebooks. Remind students that any vocabulary word in their notebooks could be on their test. Also, have students study any of the skills in the Practice Section that they need to review.

 TEST TIME

Have students turn to page 99 in the Test Section of their books and find the Chapter 3 Test. Go over the directions to make sure they understand what to do. (*Chapter 3 Test key is on the next page.*)

 CHECK TIME

After students have finished, check and discuss their test papers. Make sure they understand why their answers are right or wrong. (*For total points, count each required answer as a point.*)

 ACTIVITY / ASSIGNMENT TIME

Make a list of five fruits and five vegetables. Write the name of each fruit or vegetable on an index card. On the back of each index card, write descriptive sentences about the fruit or vegetable listed on the front. Be sure to include as many adjectives and adverbs as possible.

Finally, play a guessing game with different members of your family. Read aloud or hold up the side of the card with the description and let family members guess the name of the fruit or vegetable that is written on the other side. Discuss the fruits and vegetables that were the hardest and easiest to guess. Also, discuss the fruits and vegetables that were the hardest and easiest to describe.

(End of lesson.)

Chapter 3 Test
(Student Page 99)

Exercise 1: Classify each sentence.

```
              A    Adj   Adj    Adj      SN     V      Adv
1.  SN  V     The four little cheerful toddlers / laughed loudly.  D
    P1
```

```
              A    Adj   Adj   SN     V      Adv    Adv
2.  SN  V     The huge scary ape / walked suddenly away.  D
    P1
```

```
              A    Adj    Adj    SN      V      Adv     Adv
3.  SN  V     The young baseball team / played extremely well.  D
    P1
```

Exercise 2: Use Sentence 1 to underline the complete subject once and the complete predicate twice and to complete the table below.

List the Noun Used	List the Noun Job	Singular or Plural	Common or Proper	Simple Subject	Simple Predicate
1. toddlers	2. SN	3. P	4. C	5. toddlers	6. laughed

Exercise 3: Identify each pair of words as synonyms or antonyms by putting parentheses ( ) around *syn* or *ant*.

1. implied, hinted	(syn) ant	3. precise, exact	(syn) ant	5. detest, admire	syn (ant)
2. idle, busy	syn (ant)	4. calamity, disaster	(syn) ant	6. aggression, retreat	syn (ant)

Exercise 4: Write *a* or *an* in the blanks.

1. We found __an__ egg.
2. He wore __a__ fancy costume.
3. We ate __a__ jelly donut.
4. Did you see __an__ eagle?
5. I have __a__ bad cold.
6. I need __an__ aspirin.
7. __a__ pie
8. __a__ churn
9. __an__ echo
10. __an__ airport
11. __an__ anchovy
12. __a__ game

Exercise 5: Match the definitions by writing the correct letter beside each numbered concept.

__K__	1. tells what the subject does	A.	verb, adjective, or adverb
__E__	2. a/an are also called	B.	what
__I__	3. adjective modifies	C.	what is being said about?
__C__	4. verb question	D.	person, place, or thing
__J__	5. a definite article	E.	indefinite articles
__B__	6. subject-noun question (thing)	F.	period
__G__	7. article adjective can be called	G.	noun marker
__L__	8. makes a request or gives a command	H.	who
__D__	9. noun	I.	noun or pronoun
__H__	10. subject-noun question (person)	J.	the
__F__	11. punctuation for declarative	K.	verb
__A__	12. adverb modifies	L.	imperative sentence

Exercise 6: On notebook paper, write one of each kind of the following sentences: Declarative, Interrogative, Exclamatory, Imperative. Write the punctuation and the abbreviation that identifies it at the end. Use these abbreviations: **D, Int, E, Imp**.

Exercise 7: In your journal, write a paragraph summarizing what you have learned this week.

CHAPTER 3 LESSON 4 CONTINUED

TEACHER INSTRUCTIONS

Use the Question and Answer Flows below for the sentences on the Chapter 3 Test.

Question and Answer Flow for Sentence 1: The four little cheerful toddlers laughed loudly.

1. Who laughed loudly? toddlers - SN
2. What is being said about toddlers? toddlers laughed - V
3. Laughed how? loudly - Adv
4. What kind of toddlers? cheerful - Adj
5. What kind of toddlers? little - Adj
6. How many toddlers? four - Adj

7. The - A
8. SN V P1 Check
9. Period, statement, declarative sentence
10. Go back to the verb - divide the complete subject from the complete predicate.

Classified Sentence:

                                A   Adj   Adj   Adj   SN   V   Adv

           SN   V   The four little cheerful toddlers / laughed loudly. **D**

             P1

Question and Answer Flow for Sentence 2: The huge scary ape walked suddenly away.

1. What walked suddenly away? ape - SN
2. What is being said about ape? ape walked - V
3. Walked how? suddenly - Adv
4. Walked where? away - Adv
5. What kind of ape? scary - Adj
6. What kind of ape? huge - Adj

7. The - A
8. SN V P1 Check
9. Period, statement, declarative sentence
10. Go back to the verb - divide the complete subject from the complete predicate.

Classified Sentence:

                                A   Adj   Adj   SN   V   Adv   Adv

           SN   V   The huge scary ape / walked suddenly away. **D**

             P1

Question and Answer Flow for Sentence 3: The young baseball team played extremely well.

1. Who played extremely well? team - SN
2. What is being said about team? team played - V
3. Played how? well - Adv
4. How well? extremely - Adv
5. What kind of team? baseball - Adj
6. What kind of team? young - Adj

7. The - A
8. SN V P1 Check
9. Period, statement, declarative sentence
10. Go back to the verb - divide the complete subject from the complete predicate.

Classified Sentence:

                                A   Adj   Adj   SN   V   Adv   Adv

           SN   V   The young baseball team / played extremely well. **D**

             P1

CHAPTER 3   LESSON 5

Objectives: Writing (expository, writing definitions) and Writing Assignment #1.

WRITING TIME

Teacher's Notes:
As students write their three-point paragraphs, it is very important that they follow the exact writing pattern that this lesson teaches. If this is done consistently, the students will learn to organize their writing by learning how to do these things: write a topic sentence for any given topic, write sentences that support the topic, and write a concluding sentence that summarizes their paragraph.

Teaching students how to write a three-point paragraph gives students several advantages:

1. It gives students a definite, concrete pattern to follow when asked to write a paragraph.
2. It gives students the practice they need in organizing their writing.
3. It gives students a chance to greatly improve their self-confidence because, as they advance in the program, they become stronger and more independent in all areas of their grammar and writing skills.

TEACHER INSTRUCTIONS

Put the following writing definitions on the board:

1. **Paragraph** - a group of sentences that is written about one particular subject or topic.
2. **Topic** - the subject of the paragraph; the topic tells what the paragraph is about.
3. **Expository writing** - the discussion or telling of ideas by giving facts, directions, explanations, definitions, and examples.

TEACHING SCRIPT FOR INTRODUCING EXPOSITORY WRITING AND WRITING DEFINITIONS

As a fourth grade student, you want to be prepared to be a good writer. As a part of that preparation, today, we are going to learn about expository writing and how to organize your writing by writing a three-point paragraph. First, let's look at some key definitions to be sure that we know what we are talking about.

Look at the first two definitions. A **paragraph** is a group of sentences that is written about one particular subject or topic. A **topic** is the subject of the paragraph; the topic tells what the paragraph is about.

Now, let's look at the last definition: **expository writing**. I want you to say "expository writing" with me so we can feel this type of writing on our tongues: **Expository writing!** Expository writing is the discussion or telling of ideas by giving facts, directions, explanations, definitions, and examples.

CHAPTER 3 LESSON 5 CONTINUED

In other words, expository writing is informational. Its purpose is to inform, to give facts, to give directions, to explain, or to define something. Remember that expository writing is informational because it gives some type of information.

Since expository writing deals with information of some kind, it is very important to focus on making the meaning clear and understandable. The reader must be able to understand exactly what the writer means.

Now that we know what expository writing is, we must learn more about it because the first type of paragraph that we learn to write is an EXPOSITORY paragraph. What makes any type of writing easy is knowing exactly what to do when you are given a writing assignment. And the first thing you learn to do is organize your writing.

Expository writing may be organized in different ways. One of the most common ways to write an expository paragraph is by using a **three-point paragraph** format. The three-point paragraph format is a way of organizing the sentences in your expository paragraph that will help make your meaning clear and understandable.

Now, you will learn how to write a three-point expository paragraph. I am going to give you a topic about which you are to write your paragraph. Remember that a topic tells what the paragraph is about; it is the subject of the paragraph. In order to make sure you understand, we are going to write a three-point expository paragraph together, following specific steps.

TEACHING SCRIPT FOR SELECTING THE THREE POINTS OF THE PARAGRAPH

The first thing we learn is how to select and list the points that we are going to write about. Let's begin with our topic. Remember that a topic is a subject. The topic about which we are going to write our paragraph is "My Favorite Subjects." I will write this on the board under "Topic" (*Demonstrate by writing on the board.*)

Topic: My Favorite Subjects

Do you have some favorite subjects that you could write about? (*Discuss some of the students' favorite courses.*) Now, let's see how we are going to write this paragraph. Remember that I told you this paragraph is called a three-point paragraph. First, we are going to look at our topic, "My Favorite subjects," and see if we can list three favorite subjects about which we can write.

Teacher's Note:
Even though students have named their favorite subjects, the teaching sample will use geography, English, and science.

CHAPTER 3 LESSON 5 CONTINUED

Geography, English, and science: These are three good favorite subjects. I will list these three subjects on the board under "Three points about the topic." They will be the three points for our three-point expository paragraph. (*Demonstrate by writing on the board.*)

Three points about the topic:

1. _____geography_____   2. _____English_____   3. _____science_____

Now, let's set them aside for a minute and begin our paragraph. We are going to use these three items shortly.

Teacher's Notes: The simplified outline below will give you a quick view of what you will be covering with your students in your discussion of the three-point expository paragraph. Write each part on the board only as it is being discussed so that your students will not be overwhelmed by the amount of written work that they see on the board.

The Three-Point Expository Paragraph Outline

Topic

3 points about the topic

Sentence #1: Topic sentence

Sentence #2: A three-point sentence

Sentence #3: A **first**-point sentence

Sentence #4: A **supporting** sentence for the first point

Sentence #5: A **second**-point sentence

Sentence #6: A **supporting** sentence for the second point

Sentence #7: A **third**-point sentence

Sentence #8: A **supporting** sentence for the third point

Sentence #9: A concluding sentence

Teacher's Note: As you work through the steps, be sure to show students how the sentences are divided into three categories: the introduction (*topic and three-point sentence*), the body (*the three main points and their supporting sentences*), and the conclusion (*the concluding sentence*).

TEACHING SCRIPT FOR WRITING THE TOPIC SENTENCE

First, we must write what is called a topic sentence. A topic sentence is very important because it tells the main idea of our paragraph. We are going to let the topic sentence be the first sentence in our paragraph because it tells everyone what our paragraph is going to be about. In many paragraphs, it is not the first sentence. Later, we can learn to put the topic sentence in other places in the paragraph, but, for now, it is important that we make it the first sentence in our three-point paragraph.

CHAPTER 3 LESSON 5 CONTINUED

The topic sentence for a three-point paragraph needs three things:

1. It needs to tell the main idea of the paragraph.
2. It needs to be general because the other sentences in the paragraph must tell about the topic sentence.
3. It needs to tell the number of points that will be discussed in the paragraph.

When you write a topic sentence for a three-point paragraph, follow these two easy steps:

1. You will use all or some of the words in the topic.
2. You will tell the number of points, or ideas, you will discuss in your paragraph.

Now, we are going to write a topic sentence by following the two easy steps we have just discussed. Look at our topic, "My Favorite Subjects." Without actually listing the three specific points – geography, English, and science – let's write a sentence that makes a general statement about the main idea of our topic and tells the number of points we will list later.

How about using "I have three favorite subjects" as the topic sentence? I will write this on the board under "Sentence #1: Topic sentence." (*Demonstrate by writing on the board. Read the sentence to the students.*)

Sentence #1. Topic sentence: I have three favorite subjects.

Look at the topic sentence on the board. Notice that in this sentence, we have mentioned our topic, "My Favorite Subjects," and we have stated that there are three of these subjects; we will tell what the three are in the three-point sentence that follows.

Also, notice that we did not say, "I am going to tell you about my three favorite subjects." We do not need to tell the reader we are going to tell him/her something; we simply do it. To say "I am going to tell you" is called "writing about your writing," and it is not effective writing. Do not "write about your writing."

TEACHING SCRIPT FOR WRITING THE THREE-POINT SENTENCE

Now that we have our topic sentence, our next sentence will list the three specific points our paragraph will discuss. Our next sentence could be, "These subjects are geography, English, and science." I will write this on the board under "Sentence #2: A three-point sentence." (*Demonstrate by writing the information below on the board. Read the sentence to the students.*)

Sentence #2. A three-point sentence: These subjects are geography, English, and science.

Look at the order in which I have listed the three subjects. You must always be aware of the order in which you put your points because that will be the order in which you discuss these points in your paragraph.

I have chosen to place these in this order: geography, English, and science. I chose to put "science" last because it is usually thought of as a laboratory class. I did not have any particular reason for placing geography before English. Depending upon your three points as well as your purpose in writing, you will select the order of your three points.

CHAPTER 3 LESSON 5 CONTINUED

Notice three things we have done here:

1. We have put our three items in the order we have chosen, remembering that we will be discussing these points in this order later in our paragraph. (*geography, English, and science*)

2. We have written our first sentence, and our first sentence tells us the number of points that will be discussed in the rest of the paragraph. (*I have three favorite subjects.*)

3. We have started our listing sentence with words that helped us connect it to our first sentence. (*These subjects are* **geography, English, and science**.)

Notice how we have used repetition to link our two sentences. Our first sentence mentions **"favorite subjects"** by stating **"I have three favorite subjects."** Sentence number two, **"These subjects are geography, English, and science,"** refers to sentence number one by stating **"These subjects,"** meaning the favorite subjects just mentioned in sentence number one. Although you will not want to use repetition in every sentence to link sentences, repetition is a good device for making your paragraph flow smoothly.

TEACHING SCRIPT FOR DEVELOPING AND SUPPORTING THE POINTS OF THE PARAGRAPH

After you have stated the general topic sentence and then followed it by the more specific three-point sentence, you will begin to discuss each of the three points, one at a time. DO NOT FORGET: You are going to discuss them in the order in which you listed them in sentence number two. You will begin your third sentence by stating, "My first favorite subject is geography." This is your first listed point. I will write this on the board under "Sentence #3: A first-point sentence." (*Demonstrate by writing the information below on the board. Read the sentence to the students.*)

Sentence #3. A first-point sentence: My first favorite subject is geography.

Next, you will write one sentence about geography. It can be a descriptive sentence about geography. It can be a reason why you like geography, but it must be about geography's being your favorite subject. This is called a supporting sentence. I will now write a supporting sentence on the board under "Sentence #4: A supporting sentence for the first point." You can use this sentence or make up your own: "I like geography because it lets me travel to different countries all over the world." (*Demonstrate by writing the information below on the board. Read the sentence to the students.*)

Sentence #4. A supporting sentence for the first point: I like geography because it lets me travel to countries all over the world.

When you keep your writing targeted to the topic you are assigned, your paragraph will have what we call "unity," or will be a "unified" paragraph. In a unified paragraph, all sentences work together to form one idea about the subject, or topic.

As you get more skilled at three-point writing, you may write two or more sentences about each of your listed points, but, for now, stay with one sentence for each point. Each of the sentences that you write following your points should support what you have stated in that point. Use only ideas that support. Discard non-supporting ideas.

CHAPTER 3 LESSON 5 CONTINUED

So far, we have introduced our topic and listed our three specific points. We have begun to discuss our three points and have completed the first point along with a sentence that supports the first point. So far, we have four sentences.

Your fifth sentence will introduce the second point of the three-point paragraph. Your second point is "English." Since "English" is the second item you listed, your fifth sentence should state, "My second favorite subject is English." I will write this on the board under "Sentence #5: A second-point sentence." (*Demonstrate by writing the information below on the board. Read the sentence to the students.*)

Sentence #5. A second-point sentence: My second favorite subject is English.

Just as you wrote the sentence supporting the statement of your first point, so now you must write a sentence supporting your statement about English's being your second favorite subject. I will write the next supporting sentence on the board under "Sentence #6: A supporting sentence for the second point." (*Demonstrate by writing the information below on the board. Read the sentence to the students.*)

Sentence #6. A supporting sentence for the second point: I especially enjoy the opportunity to write stories and be creative.

By now, you can begin to see a pattern to your paragraph. However, you still have another point about which to write. So far, you have written six sentences in your paragraph. Your seventh sentence will list your third favorite subject, science. I will write this sentence on the board under "Sentence #7: A third-point sentence." (*Demonstrate by writing the information below on the board. Read the sentence to the students.*)

Sentence #7. A third-point sentence: My third favorite subject is science.

Following this sentence, your eighth sentence should make a supporting statement about science's being your third favorite subject. I will write this supporting sentence on the board under "Sentence #8: A supporting sentence for the third point." (*Demonstrate by writing the information below on the board. Read the sentence to the students.*)

Sentence #8. A supporting sentence for the third point: I love science because I get to study creatures of all kinds.

TEACHING SCRIPT FOR WRITING THE CONCLUSION OF THE PARAGRAPH

We have now introduced our topic, or subject, listed each of our three points, and made one supporting statement about each point. Now, we need to complete our paragraph, leaving the reader with the impression that he/she has read a finished product. In order to complete our paragraph, we need a conclusion, or final sentence.

There are different ways to write a concluding sentence, but one of the best and simplest is the summary statement. This means that the main points of the paragraph are stated again, briefly, in one sentence.

When you write a concluding sentence, follow these two easy steps:
1. You will use some of the words in your topic sentence.
2. You will add an extra, or concluding, thought about your paragraph.

CHAPTER 3 LESSON 5 CONTINUED

You might try a good compound sentence, such as, "I enjoy studying all kinds of subjects, but my favorites will probably always be geography, English, and science." I will write this on the board under "Sentence #9: A concluding sentence." (*Demonstrate by writing the information below on the board. Read the sentence again to the students.*)

Sentence #9. A concluding sentence: I enjoy studying all kinds of subjects, but my favorites will probably always be geography, English, and science.

TEACHING SCRIPT FOR CHECKING THE FINISHED PARAGRAPH

It is good to get in the habit of checking over your writing after you have finished. Just reading your finished paragraph several times slowly will help you see and hear things that you may want to correct. It also helps to have a checklist that tells specific areas to check to make sure you do not lose points for careless mistakes.

Turn to page 16 and look at Reference 12 as I read what it tells you to do as you write each sentence of your three-point paragraph. (*Read and discuss each section of the three-point paragraph example in Reference 12. Tell students to use this reference page if they need it when they write a three-point paragraph. It will help them organize their writing, and it will help them see the pattern of a three-point expository paragraph.*) (*Reference 12 is reproduced for you on the next page.*)

Teacher's Notes: There was neither discussion nor guidelines provided for writing a title for the paragraph. Single paragraphs are often written without titles; the decision is left to the teacher or writer. Remind students that this is an expository paragraph, which means that its purpose is to inform or explain. The three-point format is a way of underlining organizing an expository paragraph.

TEACHER INSTRUCTIONS FOR WRITING ASSIGNMENT #1

Give Writing Assignment #1 from the box below. Remind students to use the three-point paragraph example in Reference 12 on page 16 in the Reference Section if they need it. **If this is their first year in the program, tell students that this writing assignment will be done on a writing page in their books.** The writing page is already set up in a three-point format that will help them follow the form of the three-point paragraph. Direct students to page 67 in the Practice Section of their books. (*The practice page is reproduced for you at the end of this lesson on page 49.*)

Writing Assignment Box

Writing Assignment #1: Three-Point Expository Paragraph

Writing topic choices: My Favorite Subjects   or   My Favorite Sports/Hobbies

---

After students have filled out the three-point practice page, have them transfer their sentences to a sheet of notebook paper or type them on a computer. Before students begin, go over the Writing Guidelines on page 48 so they will know how to arrange their writing assignment on notebook paper or on the computer.

CHAPTER 3 LESSON 5 CONTINUED

Reference 12: Three-Point Paragraph Example

Topic: **My Favorite Subjects**

Three main points: 1. **geography**   2. **English**   3. **science**

Sentence #1 – <u>Topic Sentence</u> (*Use words in the topic and tell how many points will be used.*)
I have three favorite subjects.

Sentence #2 – <u>3-Point Sentence</u> (*List the 3 points in the order you will present them.*)
These subjects are geography, English, and science.

Sentence #3 – <u>First Point</u>
My first favorite subject is geography.

Sentence #4 – <u>Supporting Sentence</u> for the first point.
I like geography because it lets me travel to countries all over the world.

Sentence #5 – <u>Second Point</u>
My second favorite subject is English.

Sentence #6 – <u>Supporting Sentence</u> for the second point.
I especially enjoy the opportunity to write stories and be creative.

Sentence #7 – <u>Third Point</u>
My third favorite subject is science.

Sentence #8 – <u>Supporting Sentence</u> for the third point.
I love science because I get to study creatures of all kinds.

Sentence #9 – <u>Concluding (final) Sentence</u> (*Restate the topic sentence and add an extra thought.*)
I enjoy studying all kinds of subjects, but my favorites will probably always be geography, English, and science.

SAMPLE PARAGRAPH

My Favorite Subjects

    I have three favorite subjects. These subjects are geography, English, and science. My first favorite subject is geography. I like geography because it lets me travel to countries all over the world. My second favorite subject is English. I especially enjoy the opportunity to write stories and be creative. My third favorite subject is science. I love science because I get to study creatures of all kinds. I enjoy studying all kinds of subjects, but my favorites will probably always be geography, English, and science.

CHAPTER 3 LESSON 5 CONTINUED

TEACHING SCRIPT FOR WRITING GUIDELINES

Today, we will go through some guidelines for your writing. Turn to page 17 in your book and look at Reference 13. You will use these guidelines every time you are given a writing assignment. (*Read and discuss the Writing Guidelines with your students.*)

Reference 13: Writing Guidelines

1. Label your writing assignment in the top right-hand corner of your page with the following information:
    A. Your Name
    B. The Writing Assignment Number. *(Example: WA#1, WA#2, etc.)*
    C. Type of Writing (*Examples: Expository Paragraph, Persuasive Essay, Descriptive Paragraph, etc.*)
    D. The title of the writing on the top of the first line.
2. Think about the topic that you are assigned.
3. Think about the type of writing assigned, which is the purpose for the writing.
    (Is your writing intended to explain, persuade, describe, or narrate?)
4. Think about the writing format, which is the organizational plan you are expected to use.
    (Is your assignment a paragraph, a 3-paragraph essay, a 5-paragraph essay, or a letter?)
5. Use your writing time wisely.
    (Begin work quickly and concentrate on your assignment until it is finished.)

TEACHING SCRIPT FOR USING THE WRITING PROCESS FOR WRITING ASSIGNMENT #1

As you begin this writing assignment, you will use the writing process discussed in Reference 13. I will give you a quick review of that writing process. First, you will think about your topic and gather any information you might need in order to do the writing. Second, you will write a rough draft. Remember that it is called a rough draft because it will be revised and edited. You do not have to worry about mistakes as you write your rough draft. After you write the first draft, you will make revisions, using the Revision Checklist in Reference 5. After you revise your writing, you will edit it, using the Beginning Editing Checklist in Reference 5. Finally, after you are satisfied with your revising and editing, you will write a final paper, using the Final Paper Checklist in Reference 5. You will then give the finished writing assignment to me.

TEACHER INSTRUCTIONS FOR CHECKING WRITING ASSIGNMENT #1

Read, check, and discuss Writing Assignment #1 after students have finished their final paper. Use the editing checklist (*Reference 5 on teacher's page 10*) as you check and discuss students' papers. Make sure students are using the editing checklist correctly. In the beginning, you must also check students' papers carefully for <u>form</u> mistakes. This will ensure that students are learning the three-point format correctly.

Teacher's Notes: It's okay for students to pattern their sentences after the examples. As they get stronger in this system and change topics, you will see more independent sentences. In fact, you will see a lot of variety in these paragraphs because students will probably choose at least two different subjects and write different supporting sentences. Remind students that they now know how to add adjectives and adverbs to make their sentences more interesting and more expressive.

CHAPTER 3 LESSON 5 CONTINUED

Chapter 3, Lesson 5, Practice Writing Page: Use the three-point outline form below to guide you as you write a three-point expository paragraph.

Write a topic: _____

List 3 points about the topic:

1. _____ 2. _____ 3. _____

Sentence #1   Topic sentence (*Use words in the topic and tell how many points will be used.*)

_____

Sentence #2   3-point sentence (*List your 3 points in the order that you will present them.*)

_____

Sentence #3   State your first point in a complete sentence.

_____

Sentence #4   Write a supporting sentence for the first point.

_____

Sentence #5   State your second point in a complete sentence.

_____

Sentence #6   Write a supporting sentence for the second point.

_____

Sentence #7   State your third point in a complete sentence.

_____

Sentence #8   Write a supporting sentence for the third point.

_____

Sentence #9   Concluding sentence (*Restate the topic sentence and add an extra thought.*)

_____

Student Note: Rewrite your nine-sentence paragraph on notebook paper. Be sure to indent and use the checklists to help you edit your paragraph. Make sure you re-read your paragraph several times, slowly.

(End of lesson.)

CHAPTER 4   LESSON 1

Objectives: Jingles, Grammar (Practice Sentences, Oral Skill Builder Check), Skills (parts of speech), Practice Exercise, and Vocabulary #1.

 **JINGLE TIME**

Have students turn to the Jingle Section in their books. The teacher will lead the students in reciting the previously-taught jingles.

 GRAMMAR TIME

First-Year Option: Put the Practice Sentences from the box below on the board or on notebook paper. Use these sentences as you practice the concepts that have been taught. For the greatest benefit, students must participate orally with the teacher. **Second-Year Option:** Have students classify the Practice Sentences independently on notebook paper. Check students' sentences with the answers provided below. (*If you have the CDs for Practice Sentences, have students check their sentences with the CDs.*)

Chapter 4, Practice Sentences for Lesson 1
1. _____ The inexperienced telephone operator spoke too fast.
2. _____ The large snowflakes fell steadily outside.
3. _____ The clever red fox raced away quickly.

TEACHING SCRIPT FOR PRACTICING PATTERN 1 SENTENCES

We will classify three different sentences to practice grammar as we recite the Question and Answer Flows. We will classify the sentences together. Begin. (*You might have students write the labels above the sentences at this time.*)

Teacher's Notes: Make sure students say the Question and Answer Flow orally for each sentence. Be sure to lead them so they will say the Question and Answer Flows correctly.

Question and Answer Flow for Sentence 1: The inexperienced telephone operator spoke too fast.

1. Who spoke too fast? operator - SN
2. What is being said about operator? operator spoke - V
3. Spoke how? fast - Adv
4. How fast? too - Adv
5. What kind of operator? telephone - Adj
6. Which operator? inexperienced - Adj
7. The - A
8. SN V P1 Check
9. Period, statement, declarative sentence
10. Go back to the verb - divide the complete subject from the complete predicate.

Classified Sentence:

```
                        A      Adj     Adj    SN      V   Adv Adv
          SN  V     The inexperienced telephone operator / spoke too fast.  D
          P1
```

CHAPTER 4 LESSON 1 CONTINUED

Question and Answer Flow for Sentence 2: The large snowflakes fell steadily outside.

1. What fell steadily outside? snowflakes - SN
2. What is being said about snowflakes? snowflakes fell - V
3. Fell how? steadily - Adv
4. Fell where? outside - Adv
5. What kind of snowflakes? large - Adj

6. The - A
7. SN V P1 Check
8. Period, statement, declarative sentence
9. Go back to the verb - divide the complete subject from the complete predicate.

Classified Sentence:

<pre>
                          A   Adj   SN   V   Adv   Adv
           SN V   The large snowflakes / fell steadily outside. D
           P1
</pre>

Question and Answer Flow for Sentence 3: The clever red fox raced away quickly.

1. What raced away quickly? fox - SN
2. What is being said about fox? fox raced - V
3. Raced where? away - Adv
4. Raced how? quickly - Adv
5. What kind of fox? red - Adj
6. What kind of fox? clever - Adj

7. The - A
8. SN V P1 Check
9. Period, statement, declarative sentence
10. Go back to the verb - divide the complete subject from the complete predicate.

Classified Sentence:

<pre>
                          A   Adj   Adj SN   V   Adv   Adv
           SN V   The clever red fox / raced away quickly. D
           P1
</pre>

TEACHER INSTRUCTIONS

Use Sentences 1-3 that you just classified with your students to do an Oral Skill Builder Check. From this time forward, the skills for an Oral Skill Builder Check and a short explanation will be listed in a Skill Builder box. As more skills are covered, they will be added to the skill box. These guidelines will help you know the skills you have covered.

Oral Skill Builder Check

1. **Noun check.**
   (Say the job and then say the noun. Circle each noun.)
2. **Identify the nouns as singular or plural.**
   (Write **S** or **P** above each noun.)
3. **Identify the nouns as common or proper.**
   (Follow established procedure for oral identification.)

4. **Identify the complete subject and the complete predicate.** (Underline the complete subject once and the complete predicate twice.)
5. **Identify the simple subject and simple predicate.**
   (Underline the simple subject once and the simple predicate twice. Bold, or highlight, the lines to distinguish them from the complete subject and complete predicate.)

CHAPTER 4 LESSON 1 CONTINUED

SKILL TIME

TEACHING SCRIPT FOR THE PARTS OF SPEECH

To have a keen understanding of different subject areas, you must understand the vocabulary used to communicate in any given area. English is no different. In fact, there are several areas in English where vocabulary is important. Knowing the vocabulary for grammar, mechanics, and usage will make it easier to communicate in writing and editing.

First, we must know why it is so important to have an excellent command of grammar. It is important to learn grammar well because it is the vocabulary for the sentences used in writing. We can talk to each other about writing and editing when we know how to talk about the sentences we write and how we put them together in paragraphs.

Second, we must gain mastery in the areas of grammar, mechanics, and usage to have a command of editing. Your study of English this year will help you in all these areas.

We will now discuss the eight parts of speech. Do you know that all words in the English language have been put into eight groups called the **Parts of Speech**? How a word is used in a sentence determines its part of speech. The sentences you have been classifying are made from four parts of speech. Do you know the names of these four parts of speech? _(noun, verb, adjective, and adverb)_

These first four parts of speech are easy to remember because you are using them every day. Make sure you remember them because you will also have them on your test. You will learn the other parts of speech later. _(Have students repeat the four parts of speech four or five times together, orally, and in a rhythmic fashion. Students will learn an Eight-Parts-of-Speech Jingle after the eight parts have been introduced.)_

CHAPTER 4 LESSON 1 CONTINUED

TEACHING SCRIPT FOR ONLY ONE PART OF SPEECH IN A SENTENCE

(Note: Have the example below on the board or on a sheet of paper.)

Adjective(s): 1. The tiny silver hummingbird flew gently away.

I am going to show you the steps to use whenever you need to identify only one part of speech in a sentence. No matter what part of speech you are looking for, always identify the subject and verb, first. This will give you the foundation from which to work. In the example on the board, we are looking for only one part of speech: the adjective.

1. Is Sentence 1 about a person, animal, place, or thing? animal
2. What is the sentence about? hummingbird _(Write **SN** above hummingbird.)_
3. What is being said about hummingbird? hummingbird flew _(Write **V** above flew.)_
4. What part of speech is listed to be identified? adjective
5. Where do we go to find adjectives? to nouns or pronouns
6. What is the noun in the sentence? hummingbird
7. Are there any adjectives modifying the noun _hummingbird_? yes
8. What are they? the, tiny, and silver
9. We will do an adjective check to verify the adjectives:

> What kind of hummingbird? silver - adjective (Underline the adjective _silver._)
> What kind of hummingbird? tiny - adjective (Underline the adjective _tiny._)
> The - article adjective (Underline the adjective _the._)

Your finished sentence should look like this:

SN   V

Adjective(s): 1. The tiny silver hummingbird flew gently away.

If you follow this procedure, you should have no trouble finding a specific part of speech without having to classify the whole sentence. But if you are ever in doubt, classify the whole sentence to be sure of your answers.

You will now practice not only this skill, but you will also practice classifying a sentence and completing a noun job table.

CHAPTER 4 LESSON 1 CONTINUED

 PRACTICE TIME

Have students turn to page 68 in the Practice Section of their books and find the skill under Chapter 4, Lesson 1, Practice. Go over the directions to make sure they understand what to do. Check and discuss the Lesson 1, Practice after students have finished. (*Chapter 4, Lesson 1, Practice key is given below.*)

Chapter 4, Lesson 1, Practice: Classify the sentence below. Underline the complete subject once and the complete predicate twice. Then, complete the table.

```
          A   Adj   SN      V      Adv   Adv
SN V      The feisty poodle / strolled proudly away.  D
P1
```

List the Noun Used	List the Noun Job	Singular or Plural	Common or Proper	Simple Subject	Simple Predicate
poodle	SN	S	C	poodle	strolled

Finding One Part of Speech: For each sentence, write **SN** above the simple subject and **V** above the simple predicate. Underline the word(s) for the part of speech listed to the left of each sentence.

Adjective(s):
                         SN   V
1. The crisp, crunchy candies disappeared quickly today.

Adverb(s):
                         SN   V
2. The nervous young driver drove very safely away.

Noun(s):
                        SN   V
3. The talented artist painted extremely well.

Adjective(s):
                      SN   V
4. The canoe floated away.

Verb(s):
                         SN   V
5. The academic team performed splendidly.

 VOCABULARY TIME

Assign Chapter 4, Vocabulary Words **#1** on page 8 in the Reference Section for students to define in their Vocabulary notebooks. Tell students they are to use a dictionary or thesaurus to look up the meanings of the vocabulary words. After they write each word and its meaning, students are to write a sentence using the vocabulary word.

Chapter 4, Vocabulary Words #1
(reply, answer, vivid, dingy)

(End of lesson.)

CHAPTER 4   LESSON 2

Objectives: Jingles, Grammar (Introductory Sentences, predicate words located in the complete subject, Practice and Improved Sentences), and Vocabulary #2.

JINGLE TIME

Have students turn to the Jingle Section in their books. The teacher will lead the students in reciting the previously-taught jingles.

GRAMMAR TIME

Put the introductory sentences from the box below on the board. Use these sentences as you go through each new concept covered in your teaching script. For the greatest benefit, students must participate orally with the teacher. (*You might put the introductory sentences on notebook paper if you are doing one-on-one instruction with your students.*)

Chapter 4, Introductory Sentences for Lesson 2
1. _____ Yesterday, the adorable little puppies whimpered very softly.
2. _____ The scared, wounded soldier lay perfectly still.
3. _____ Suddenly, a beautiful rainbow appeared overhead.

TEACHING SCRIPT FOR PREDICATE WORDS LOCATED IN THE COMPLETE SUBJECT

We will classify Sentence 1 together, but this time there will be more information added to the Question and Answer Flow. You will classify the sentence with me until we get to the new part. I will explain the new skill and show you how to add it to the Question and Answer Flow. Remember, it is very important that you say the questions with me as well as the answers. Just follow me. Begin. (*Classify Sentence 1 with your students.*)

Question and Answer Flow for Sentence 1: Yesterday, the adorable little puppies whimpered very softly.

1. What whimpered very softly? puppies - SN
2. What is being said about puppies? puppies whimpered - V
3. Whimpered how? softly - Adv
4. How softly? very - Adv
5. What kind of puppies? little - Adj
6. What kind of puppies? adorable - Adj
7. The - A
8. Whimpered when? yesterday - Adv
9. SN V P1 Check

10. Period, statement, declarative sentence
11. Go back to the verb - divide the complete subject from the complete predicate.

   STOP! (Go to the teaching script on the next page.)

12. This sentence has predicate words in the complete subject. Underline the adverb at the beginning of the sentence twice.

Classified Sentence:

		Adv	A	Adj	Adj	SN	V	Adv	Adv
SN V		Yesterday,	the	adorable	little	puppies /	whimpered	very	softly. **D**
P1									

CHAPTER 4 LESSON 2 CONTINUED

Now, we are going to add another part to the Question and Answer Flow. This new part will show us how to handle **predicate words located in the complete subject**. Sometimes, predicate words come at the beginning of the sentence. These words modify the verb even though they are located at the beginning of the complete subject.

These predicate words are really easy to identify because they are always located at the beginning of the sentence. The predicate words that may be located at the beginning of the complete subject are **adverbs, helping verbs, and prepositional phrases**. Say these words with me five times: *adverbs, helping verbs, and prepositional phrases*.

Look at Reference 14 on page 17 in the Reference Section of your book while I read the information about predicate words located in the complete subject to make sure you understand it before we classify the rest of the sentence. (*Read the information below to your students.*)

Reference 14: Predicate Words Located in the Complete Subject

1. An adverb at the beginning of the sentence will modify the verb.

   (Example: <u>Yesterday</u>, <u>we</u> / <u>went to the park</u>.) (<u>We</u> / <u>went to the park yesterday</u>.)

2. A helping verb at the beginning of a sentence will always be part of the verb.

   (Example: <u>Are</u> <u>we</u> / <u>going to the park</u>?) (<u>We</u> / <u>are going to the park</u>.)

3. A prepositional phrase at the beginning of a sentence will modify the verb.

   (Example: <u>At the park</u>, <u>we</u> / <u>played with the children</u>.) (<u>We</u> / <u>played with the children at the park</u>.)

To add *predicate words in the complete subject* to the Question and Answer Flow, say, *"This sentence has predicate words in the complete subject. Underline the (adverb), (helping verb), or (prepositional phrase) twice."* If there are no predicate words in the complete subject, then you will not do this step.

Now, I will complete the Question and Answer Flow for Sentence 1 and show you how to mark it. (*Read: This sentence has predicate words in the complete subject. Underline the adverb at the beginning of the sentence twice.*)

We will now classify Sentence 1 again. I will lead you as we say the questions and answers together. Remember, it is very important that you say the questions with me as well as the answers. (*Classify Sentence 1 again with your students. Use the Question and Answer Flow on the previous page, but this time do not stop for the teaching script.*)

Remember, we will only add the "predicate words in the complete subject" to the Q & A Flow when we have an adverb, a helping verb, or a prepositional phrase at the beginning of a sentence. We will identify only adverbs in this chapter. We will add helping verbs and prepositional phrases in later chapters as they are introduced.

We will now classify the rest of the sentences. You must say the **questions** and **answers** with me. By asking and answering the questions together orally, you will learn everything faster because you see it, hear it, say it, and then do it. Begin.

CHAPTER 4 LESSON 2 CONTINUED

Question and Answer Flow for Sentence 2: The scared, wounded soldier lay perfectly still.

1. Who lay perfectly still? soldier - SN
2. What is being said about soldier? soldier lay - V
3. Lay how? still - Adv
4. How still? perfectly - Adv
5. What kind of soldier? wounded - Adj
6. What kind of soldier? scared - Adj
7. The - A
8. SN V P1 Check
9. Period, statement, declarative sentence
10. Go back to the verb - divide the complete subject from the complete predicate.

Classified Sentence:

	A	Adj	Adj	SN	V	Adv	Adv

SN V / P1   The scared, wounded soldier / lay perfectly still. **D**

Question and Answer Flow for Sentence 3: Suddenly, a beautiful rainbow appeared overhead.

1. What appeared overhead? rainbow - SN
2. What is being said about rainbow? rainbow appeared - V
3. Appeared where? overhead - Adv
4. What kind of rainbow? beautiful - Adj
5. A - A
6. Appeared when? suddenly - Adv
7. SN V P1 Check
8. Period, statement, declarative sentence
9. Go back to the verb - divide the complete subject from the complete predicate.
10. This sentence has predicate words in the complete subject. Underline the adverb at the beginning of the sentence twice.

Classified Sentence:

	Adv	A	Adj	SN	V	Adv

SN V / P1   <u>Suddenly</u>, a beautiful rainbow / appeared overhead. **D**

TEACHING SCRIPT FOR THE PRACTICE SENTENCE

Sentences are the foundation of writing; so, you must first learn how sentences are put together. Next, you will learn how to improve and expand sentences, and then you will learn to combine sentences into paragraphs.

The first two areas we will address are how sentences are put together and how to improve them. In order to talk about sentences, we must know the vocabulary that is used to build sentences. If you are building a house, you need to know about hammers and nails. You need to know the names of the tools and materials that you will be using.

In the same way, when you are building or writing sentences, you need to know the names of the parts you will be using and what to do with them. Your writing vocabulary will develop as you learn all the parts of a sentence. We will start by learning how to write a sentence from a given set of English labels. This is called a **Practice Sentence**.

A **Practice Sentence** is a sentence that is written following certain sentence labels (**A**, **Adj**, **SN**, **V**, **Adv**, etc.). The difficulty level of the sentence labels will increase as your ability increases. To write a Practice Sentence, you will follow the labels given to you in your assignment. You must think of words that fit the labels and that make sense.

Look at the Practice Sentence in Reference 15 on page 17 in your Reference Section. Since we have learned only four parts of a sentence so far, the Practice Sentence will demonstrate only these four parts. Notice that by using these sentence parts (*article adjective/adjective, subject noun, verb,* and *adverb*), we can make a seven-word sentence: **The harmless little insect crawled quietly away.**

CHAPTER 4 LESSON 2 CONTINUED

Reference 15: Practice Sentence							
Labels:	A	Adj	Adj	SN	V	Adv	Adv
Practice:	**The**	**harmless**	**little**	**insect**	**crawled**	**quietly**	**away.**

There are three adjectives used in this sentence: *the, harmless,* and *little.* There are two adverbs: *quietly* and *away.* And, of course, there is the subject noun *insect,* and there is the verb *crawled.* We could just as easily have written a sentence with the bare essentials: *The insect crawled.* That is a correct sentence, but, by adding more parts, we are able to make the picture of the insect even clearer.

As you learn how to use more sentence parts to expand your sentences, you will use them automatically because they make your writing better.

Put these labels on the board: **A Adj SN V Adv**

Look at the sentence labels on the board: **A Adj SN V Adv**. Now, I am going to guide you through the process of writing a sentence using all the parts that you have learned thus far. Most of these steps will become automatic in a very short time.

Get out a sheet of notebook paper. On the top line of your notebook paper, write the title *Practice Sentence.* Copy the sentence labels from the board onto your notebook paper. Be sure to leave plenty of writing space between each label. Now, I will guide you through the process you will use whenever you write a Practice Sentence.

1. Go to the **SN** label for the subject noun. Think of a noun that you want to use as your subject. Write the noun you have chosen on the line *under* the **SN** label.

2. Go to the **V** label for the verb. Think of a verb that tells what your subject does. Make sure that your verb makes sense with the subject noun. Write the verb you have chosen on the line *under* the **V** label.

3. Go to the **Adv** label for the adverb. Go to the verb in your sentence and ask an adverb question. What are the adverb questions? (*How, When, Where*) Choose one adverb question to ask and write your adverb answer *under* the **Adv** label.

4. Go to the **Adj** label for the adjective. Go to the subject noun of your sentence and ask an adjective question. What are the adjective questions? (*What kind, Which one, How many*) Choose one adjective question to ask and write your adjective answer *under* the **Adj** label next to the subject noun. Always check to make sure your answers are making sense in the sentence.

5. Go to the **A** label for article adjective. What are the three article adjectives? (*a, an,* and *the*) You will choose the article adjective that makes the best sense in your sentence. Write the article adjective you have chosen *under* the **A** label.

CHAPTER 4 LESSON 2 CONTINUED

6. Finally, check the Practice Sentence to make sure it has the necessary parts to be a complete sentence. What are the five parts of a complete sentence? (*subject, verb, complete sense, capital letter, and an end mark*) Does this Practice Sentence have all the parts necessary to make a complete sentence? (*Allow time for students' responses and for any corrections to be made on the board or on students' papers.*)

TEACHING SCRIPT FOR AN IMPROVED SENTENCE

Now that we have written a correct sentence using all the parts that we have studied, we must now concentrate on improving what we have written. The result is called an **Improved Sentence**. An **Improved Sentence** is a sentence made from the Practice Sentence that is improved through the use of synonyms, antonyms, or complete word changes. Writing Improved Sentences will help you make better word choices as you write because your writing vocabulary increases.

Look at the Improved Sentence in Reference 16 on page 17 in your Reference Section. The original English labels are on the first line. The sample Practice Sentence is on the second line. On the last line, you see an Improved Sentence made from synonyms, antonyms, and complete word changes. Knowing how to make improvements in what you have written means that you are beginning to revise and edit. (*Read the Practice and Improved Sentences in the box as your students follow along. Make sure students see the difference that improving sentences can make.*)

Reference 16: Improved Sentence							
Labels:	A	Adj	Adj	SN	V	Adv	Adv
Practice:	The	harmless	little	insect	crawled	quietly	away.
Improved:	**An**	**innocent**	**red**	**ladybug**	**scurried**	**frantically**	**around.**
	(word change)	(synonym)	(word change)	(synonym)	(synonym)	(antonym)	(word change)

Put these directions on the board or on notebook paper:

Make at <u>least</u> one synonym change, one antonym change, and one complete word change.

The directions on the board tell you to make these changes in your Practice Sentence: **Make at <u>least</u> one synonym change, one antonym change, and a complete word change.** I am going to show you how to improve your Practice Sentence by making synonym, antonym, and complete word changes with some of the words.

The changed sentence will be called an **Improved Sentence** because you will make several improvements. Most of these steps will become automatic in a very short time. Now, on another line, under your Practice Sentence, write the title *Improved Sentence.*

1. Look at our Practice Sentence on the board. Let's find a word that can be improved with an antonym. (*Identify the word to be changed.*) Give me an antonym suggestion, and I will write your suggested antonym to improve, or change, the word.

CHAPTER 4 LESSON 2 CONTINUED

Remember, antonyms are powerful because they completely change the direction or meaning of your sentence. (*Discuss several antonym suggestions from students.*) Let's write the antonym we have chosen *under* the word we want to change in the Practice Sentence. (*Write the antonym choice on the board and have students write it on their papers.*)

2. Let's find a word in the Practice Sentence that can be improved with a synonym. (*Identify the word to be changed.*) Give me a synonym suggestion, and I will write your suggested synonym to improve the word. Remember, synonyms improve your writing vocabulary faster because they give you more word choices. (*Discuss several synonym suggestions from students.*) Let's write the synonym we have chosen *under* the word we want to improve in the Practice Sentence. (*Write the synonym choice on the board and have students write it on their papers.*)

3. Sometimes, you will think of a better word to use to improve your sentence that is not a synonym or antonym. We call this type of improvement a complete word change. It will give you more flexibility as you work to improve your sentences. Look at the Practice Sentence again. Is there another word that we want to change by simply making a complete word change? (*Discuss several complete word change suggestions from students.*) Let's write the complete word change we have chosen *under* the word we want to change in the Practice Sentence. (*Write the complete word change on the board and have students write it on their papers.*) If you cannot think of a complete word change, you can always use a synonym or antonym change.

4. Let's look at our Improved Sentence. Do you want to make any more improvements or changes? (*Discuss and then make extra improvements or changes as indicated by student participation.*)

5. Finally, let's check the Improved Sentence to make sure it has the necessary parts to be a complete sentence. Does our Improved Sentence have all the parts necessary to make a complete sentence? (*Allow time for students' responses and for corrections to be made on the board and on students' papers.*)

I want you to write your own Practice and Improved Sentences. You may use the same English labels that I listed on the board: **A Adj SN V Adv**. Make sure you follow the procedures we have just gone through. Remember, any time you write an Improved Sentence, you are actually editing your writing, and that's why it is so important that you learn to write Improved Sentences. (*Check and discuss students' Practice and Improved Sentences after they have finished. They will add more adjectives and adverbs to their Practice Sentence in the next lesson, but if they want to add them now, allow them to do so.*)

 VOCABULARY TIME

Assign Chapter 4, Vocabulary Words **#2** on page 8 in the Reference Section for students to define in their Vocabulary notebooks. Tell students they are to use a dictionary or thesaurus to look up the meanings of the vocabulary words. After they write each word and its meaning, students are to write a sentence using the vocabulary word.

Chapter 4, Vocabulary Words #2
(muscle, brawn, delight, displease)

(End of lesson.)

Level 4 Homeschool Teacher's Manual

CHAPTER 4   LESSON 3

Objectives: Jingles, Grammar (Practice Sentences), Skills (Oral Skill Builder Check, add a vocabulary check to Skill Builder, Expanded Practice Sentence), Practice Exercise.

JINGLE TIME

Have students turn to the Jingle Section in their books. The teacher will lead the students in reciting the previously-taught jingles.

GRAMMAR TIME

First-Year Option: Put the Practice Sentences from the box below on the board or notebook paper. Use these sentences as you practice the concepts that have been taught. For the greatest benefit, students must participate orally with the teacher. **Second-Year Option:** Have students classify the Practice Sentences independently on notebook paper. Check students' sentences with the answers provided below. (*If you have the CDs for Practice Sentences, have students check their sentences with the CDs.*)

Chapter 4, Practice Sentences for Lesson 3
1. _____ The ancient clanking car chugged noisily away.
2. _____ Finally, the very tired little baby rested quietly.
3. _____ The weary, thirsty riders dismounted slowly today.

TEACHING SCRIPT FOR PRACTICING PATTERN 1 SENTENCES

We will classify three different sentences to practice grammar as we recite the Question and Answer Flows. We will classify the sentences together. Begin. (*You might have students write the labels above the sentences at this time.*)

Teacher's Notes: Make sure students say the **questions** and **answers** orally for each sentence. Be sure to lead them so they will say the Question and Answer Flows correctly.

Question and Answer Flow for Sentence 1: The ancient clanking car chugged noisily away.

1. What chugged noisily away? car - SN
2. What is being said about car? car chugged - V
3. Chugged how? noisily - Adv
4. Chugged where? away - Adv
5. What kind of car? clanking - Adj
6. What kind of car? ancient - Adj
7. The - A
8. SN V P1 Check
9. Period, statement, declarative sentence
10. Go back to the verb - divide the complete subject
     from the complete predicate.

Classified Sentence:

```
                          A    Adj    Adj    SN    V     Adv  Adv
         SN  V           The  ancient clanking car / chugged noisily away.  D
         P1
```

CHAPTER 4 LESSON 3 CONTINUED

Question and Answer Flow for Sentence 2: Finally, the very tired little baby rested quietly.

1. Who rested quietly? baby - SN
2. What is being said about baby? baby rested - V
3. Rested how? quietly - Adv
4. What kind of baby? little - Adj
5. What kind of baby? tired - Adj
6. How tired? very - Adv
7. The - A
8. Rested when? finally - Adv

9. SN V P1 Check
10. Period, statement, declarative sentence
11. Go back to the verb - divide the complete subject from the complete predicate.
12. This sentence has predicate words in the complete subject. Underline the adverb at the beginning of the sentence twice.

Classified Sentence:

```
              Adv   A   Adv  Adj  Adj SN     V     Adv
   SN V   Finally, the very tired little baby / rested quietly.  D
    P1
```

Question and Answer Flow for Sentence 3: The weary, thirsty riders dismounted slowly today.

1. Who dismounted slowly today? riders - SN
2. What is being said about riders? riders dismounted - V
3. Dismounted how? slowly - Adv
4. Dismounted when? today - Adv
5. What kind of riders? thirsty - Adj

6. What kind of riders? weary - Adj
7. The - A
8. SN V P1 Check
9. Period, statement, declarative sentence
10. Go back to the verb - divide the complete subject from the complete predicate.

Classified Sentence:

```
            A   Adj   Adj   SN      V      Adv  Adv
   SN V   The weary, thirsty riders / dismounted slowly today.  D
    P1
```

SKILL TIME

TEACHING SCRIPT FOR ADDING A VOCABULARY CHECK TO SKILL BUILDER TIME

We will use the three sentences that we just classified to learn a new Skill Builder. We will add a Vocabulary Check to the Oral Skill Builder Check time. The Vocabulary Check will give me an opportunity to expand your vocabulary. I will select different words from the three sentences that we classify together for a Vocabulary Check. We will define the words, use them in new sentences, and name synonyms and antonyms for them.

CHAPTER 4 LESSON 3 CONTINUED

TEACHER INSTRUCTIONS

Look over the words in the classified sentences. Select any words you think your students may not understand or words for which you want students to develop a broader understanding. Use the guidelines below for a Vocabulary Check. (*For some words, you might use all the guidelines presented for a Vocabulary Check. For the reinforcement of other words, you might ask only for synonyms and antonyms. Talk about how synonym and antonym changes can affect the meaning of the original sentence. Tell your students that synonyms and antonyms are powerful writing tools, and they must learn to use them well. It is very important that each student has a thesaurus of his/her own.*)

Guidelines for a Vocabulary Check

1. Give a definition for the word.
2. Use the word correctly in a sentence.
3. Think of a synonym for the word.
4. Think of an antonym for the word.

TEACHER INSTRUCTIONS

Use Sentences 1-3 that you just classified with your students to do an Oral Skill Builder Check. Use the guidelines below.

Oral Skill Builder Check

1. Noun check. (Say the job and then say the noun. Circle each noun.) **2. Identify the nouns as singular or plural.** (Write **S** or **P** above each noun.) **3. Identify the nouns as common or proper.** (Follow established procedure for oral identification.) **4. Do a vocabulary check.** (Follow established procedure for oral identification.)	**5. Identify the complete subject and the complete predicate.** (Underline the complete subject once and the complete predicate twice.) **6. Identify the simple subject and simple predicate.** (Underline the simple subject once and the simple predicate twice. Bold, or highlight, the lines to distinguish them from the complete subject and complete predicate.)

Teacher's Notes: A Vocabulary Check is an excellent way to enrich your students' writing vocabulary. There will be times when you may just ask for a synonym and an antonym for different words. This will give students a better command of the options they have when making word choices as they write sentences. Remind students of the power of words and give them plenty of practice as you utilize the three sentences they have classified. Again, it is very important that each student has a thesaurus of his/her own.

CHAPTER 4 LESSON 3 CONTINUED

TEACHING SCRIPT FOR AN EXPANDED PRACTICE SENTENCE

Put these labels on the board: **A Adj Adj SN V Adv Adv**

In the previous lesson, I guided you through the process of writing a Practice Sentence and an Improved Sentence for the first time. Today, I am going to guide you through the same process again, but this time you will write an expanded sentence by adding a few more sentence labels. Look at the new sentence labels on the board: **A Adj Adj SN V Adv Adv**.

Get out a sheet of notebook paper and write the title *Practice Sentence* on the top line. Copy the labels on the board across the page: **A Adj Adj SN V Adv Adv**. Make sure you leave plenty of room for the words that you will write under the labels.

I will guide you through the process of writing a sentence using a given set of labels again. I will lead you each time we cover a new concept in Pattern 1. Writing a sentence using English labels is total sentence control. It is very easy if you know how, but it is also something very few people can do without training.

1. Go to the **SN** label for the subject noun. Think of a noun that you want to use as your subject. Write the noun you have chosen on the line *under* the **SN** label.

2. Go to the **V** label for the verb. Think of a verb that tells what your subject does. Make sure that your verb makes sense with the subject noun. Write the verb you have chosen on the line *under* the **V** label.

3. Go to the **Adv** label for the adverb. Go to the verb in your sentence and ask an adverb question. What are the adverb questions? (*How, When, Where*) Choose one adverb question to ask and write your adverb answer *under* the first **Adv** label.

4. Go to the **Adv** label for another adverb. Go to the verb again and ask another adverb question. You can use the same adverb question, or you can use a different adverb question. Write another adverb *under* the second **Adv** label.

5. Go to the **Adj** label for the adjective. Go to the subject noun of your sentence and ask an adjective question. What are the adjective questions? (*What kind, Which one, How many*) Choose one adjective question to ask and write your adjective answer *under* the **Adj** label next to the subject noun. Always check to make sure your answers are making sense in the sentence.

6. Go to the next **Adj** label for another adjective. Go to the subject noun again and ask another adjective question. You can use the same adjective question, or you can use a different adjective question. Write another adjective *under* the second **Adj** label.

7. Go to the **A** label for the article adjective. What are the three article adjectives? (*a, an*, and *the*) Choose the article adjective that makes the best sense in your sentence. Write the article adjective you have chosen *under* the **A** label.

CHAPTER 4 LESSON 3 CONTINUED

8. Finally, check your Practice Sentence to make sure it has the necessary parts to be a complete sentence. What are the five parts of a complete sentence? *(subject, verb, complete sense, capital letter, and an end mark)* Does your Practice Sentence have the five parts of a complete sentence? *(Allow time for students to read over their sentences and to make the necessary corrections.)*

9. Under your Practice Sentence, write the title *Improved Sentence* on another line. To improve your Practice Sentence, you will make two synonym changes, one antonym change, and your choice of a complete word change or another synonym or antonym change.

Since it is harder to find words that can be changed to an antonym, it is usually wise to go through your sentence to find an antonym change first. Then, look through your sentence again to find words that can be improved with synonyms. Finally, make a decision about whether your last change will be a complete word change, a synonym change, or an antonym change.

I will give you time to write your Improved Sentence. *(Always encourage students to use a thesaurus, synonym-antonym book, or a dictionary to help them develop an interesting and improved writing vocabulary. After students have finished, check and discuss students' Practice and Improved Sentences.)*

 PRACTICE TIME

Have students turn to page 68 in the Practice Section of their book and find Chapter 4, Lesson 3, Practice. Go over the directions to make sure they understand what to do. Check and discuss the Practice after students have finished. *(Chapter 4, Lesson 3, Practice key is given below.)*

Chapter 4, Lesson 3, Practice: Put this 3-part assignment on notebook paper: (1) Write the four parts of speech that you have studied so far (in any order). (2) Write out the Question and Answer Flow in exact order for the sentence listed below. (3) Classify the sentence.			
1. noun	**2. verb**	**3. adjective**	**4. adverb**

Practice Sentence: Yesterday, the new youth minister preached fervently.

Question and Answer Flow Key for Practice Sentence: Yesterday, the new youth minister preached fervently.

1. Who preached fervently? minister - SN
2. What is being said about minister? minister preached - V
3. Preached how? fervently - Adv
4. What kind of minister? youth - Adj
5. What kind of minister? new - Adj
6. The - A
7. Preached when? yesterday - Adv

8. SN V P1 Check
9. Period, statement, declarative sentence
10. Go back to the verb - divide the complete subject from the complete predicate.
11. This sentence has predicate words in the complete subject. Underline the adverb at the beginning of the sentence twice.

Classified Sentence:

<pre>
                        Adv   A   Adj Adj   SN   V   Adv
        SN V   Yesterday, the new youth minister / preached fervently. D
        P1
</pre>

(End of lesson.)

CHAPTER 4   LESSON 4

Objectives: Jingles, Study, Test, Check, Activity, and Writing (journal).

 **JINGLE TIME**

Have students turn to the Jingle Section in their books. The teacher will lead the students in reciting the previously-taught jingles.

 STUDY TIME

Have students study the vocabulary words in their vocabulary notebooks. Remind students that any vocabulary word in their notebooks could be on their test. Also, have students study any of the skills in the Practice Section they need to review.

 TEST TIME

Have students turn to page 100 in the Test Section of their books and find the Chapter 4 Test. Go over the directions to make sure they understand what to do. (*Chapter 4 Test key is on the next page.*)

 **CHECK TIME**

After students have finished, check and discuss their test papers. Make sure they understand why their answers are right or wrong. (*For total points, count each required answer as a point.*)

 ACTIVITY / ASSIGNMENT TIME

Make a list of seven different animals. Write the name of each animal on an index card. On the back of each index card, write descriptive sentences about the animal listed on the front. Be sure to include as many adjectives and adverbs as possible. Finally, play a guessing game with different members of your family. Read aloud or hold up the side of the card with the description and let family members guess which animal's name is written on the other side. Discuss which animals were the hardest and easiest to guess. Also, discuss which animals were the hardest and easiest to describe.

(End of lesson.)

Chapter 4 Test
(Student Page 100)

Exercise 1: Classify each sentence.

                 Adv   A Adj Adj   SN   V   Adv   Adv

1. **SN V**   Today, the two hungry children **/** ate rather quickly. **D**
    P1

                 A   Adv   Adj SN   V   Adv   Adv

2. **SN V**   The incredibly tall man **/** stood up suddenly. **D**
    P1

                 A Adj Adj SN   V   Adv   Adv

3. **SN V**   The wise old owl **/** looked piercingly everywhere. **D**
    P1

Exercise 2: Use Sentence 2 to underline the complete subject once and the complete predicate twice and to complete the table below.

List the Noun Used	List the Noun Job	Singular or Plural	Common or Proper	Simple Subject	Simple Predicate
1. man	2. SN	3. S	4. C	5. man	6. stood

Exercise 3: Name the four parts of speech that you have studied so far. **(The order of answers may vary.)**

1. **noun**   2. **verb**   3. **adjective**   4. **adverb**

Exercise 4: Identify each pair of words as synonyms or antonyms by putting parentheses ( ) around *syn* or *ant*.

1. quiver, shake	**(syn)** ant	5. precise, exact	**(syn)** ant	9. implied, hinted	**(syn)** ant
2. vivid, dingy	syn **(ant)**	6. complicated, easy	syn **(ant)**	10. calamity, disaster	**(syn)** ant
3. admire, detest	syn **(ant)**	7. brawn, muscle	**(syn)** ant	11. delight, displease	syn **(ant)**
4. reply, answer	**(syn)** ant	8. idle, busy	syn **(ant)**	12. aggression, retreat	syn **(ant)**

Exercise 5: Write *a* or *an* in the blanks.

1. My friend lives in **an** igloo.   3. Do you want **an** egg?   5. **a** boot 7. **an** apology

2. He drove **a** new car.   4. We need **a** vacation.   6. **a** tree 8. **an** entertainer

Exercise 6: Match the definitions by writing the correct letter beside each numbered concept.

F	1. asks a question	A.	verb, adjective, or adverb
E	2. a/an are also called	B.	a definite article
I	3. adjective modifies	C.	person, place, or thing
B	4. the	D.	imperative sentence
H	5. subject question	E.	indefinite articles
G	6. article adjective can be called	F.	interrogative sentence
D	7. makes a request or gives a command	G.	noun marker
C	8. noun	H.	who or what
J	9. tells what the subject does	I.	noun or pronoun
A	10. adverb modifies	J.	verb

Exercise 7: On notebook paper, write one of each kind of the following sentences: Declarative, Interrogative, Exclamatory, Imperative. Write the punctuation and the abbreviation that identifies it at the end. Use these abbreviations: **D, Int, E, Imp.**

Exercise 8: In your journal, write a paragraph summarizing what you have learned this week.

CHAPTER 4 LESSON 4 CONTINUED

TEACHER INSTRUCTIONS

Use the Question and Answer Flows below for the sentences on the Chapter 4 Test.

Question and Answer Flow for Sentence 1: Today, the two hungry children ate rather quickly.

1. Who ate rather quickly? children - SN
2. What is being said about children? children ate - V
3. Ate how? quickly - Adv
4. How quickly? rather - Adv
5. What kind of children? hungry - Adj
6. How many children? two - Adj
7. The - A
8. Ate when? today - Adv
9. SN V P1 Check
10. Period, statement, declarative sentence
11. Go back to the verb - divide the complete subject from the complete predicate.
12. This sentence has predicate words in the complete subject. Underline the adverb at the beginning of the sentence twice.

Classified Sentence:

<pre>
                       Adv   A Adj   Adj   SN   V Adv   Adv
  SN V   Today, the two hungry children / ate rather quickly. D
  P1
</pre>

Question and Answer Flow for Sentence 2: The incredibly tall man stood up suddenly.

1. Who stood up suddenly? man - SN
2. What is being said about man? man stood - V
3. Stood where? up - Adv
4. Stood how? suddenly - Adv
5. What kind of man? tall - Adj
6. How tall? incredibly - Adv
7. The - A
8. SN V P1 Check
9. Period, statement, declarative sentence
10. Go back to the verb - divide the complete subject from the complete predicate.

Classified Sentence:

<pre>
                    A   Adv   Adj SN   V Adv Adv
  SN V   The incredibly tall man / stood up suddenly. D
  P1
</pre>

Question and Answer Flow for Sentence 3: The wise old owl looked piercingly everywhere.

1. What looked piercingly everywhere? owl - SN
2. What is being said about owl? owl looked - V
3. Looked how? piercingly - Adv
4. Looked where? everywhere - Adv
5. What kind of owl? old - Adj
6. What kind of owl? wise - Adj
7. The - A
8. SN V P1 Check
9. Period, statement, declarative sentence
10. Go back to the verb - divide the complete subject from the complete predicate.

Classified Sentence:

<pre>
                  A   Adj Adj SN   V   Adv   Adv
  SN V   The wise old owl / looked piercingly everywhere. D
  P1
</pre>

Level 4 Homeschool Teacher's Manual

CHAPTER 4   LESSON 5

Objectives: Writing assignment #2, Bonus Option.

 WRITING TIME

TEACHER INSTRUCTIONS FOR WRITING ASSIGNMENT

Give Writing Assignment #2 from the box below. Remind students to follow the Writing Guidelines as they prepare their writings.

Writing Assignment Box

Writing Assignment #2: Three-Point Expository Paragraph
Writing topic choices: **Why I Like to Camp**   or   **My Favorite Adults**   or   **My Favorite Movies/Games**

Bonus Option: Write the following questions in your Journal along with today's date. Leave space in your Journal to record the answers.

(1) **What is the name of the character in the Bible who was sold into slavery by his own brothers?** *(Joseph)*
(2) **Where does this story begin in the Bible?** *(Genesis 37)*
(3) **How many pieces of silver did his brothers get for him?** *(20 pieces of silver—or 8 ounces of silver)*
(4) **Write the story in your own words.**
(5) **Draw the special piece of clothing described in the story.** *(coat of many colors)*

TEACHING SCRIPT FOR USING THE WRITING PROCESS FOR THIS WRITING ASSIGNMENT

As you begin this writing assignment, you will use the writing process again. First, you will think about your topic and gather any information you might need in order to do the writing. Second, you will write a rough draft. Remember, it is called a rough draft because it will be revised and edited. You do not have to worry about mistakes as you write your rough draft. After you write the first draft, you will make revisions, using the Revision Checklist in Reference 5. After you revise your writing, you will edit, using the Beginning Editing Checklist in Reference 5. Finally, after you are satisfied with your revising and editing, you will write a final paper, using the Final Paper Checklist in Reference 5. You will then give the finished writing assignment to me. (*Students should finish their writing during their free time if they do not finish during this lesson.*)

TEACHER INSTRUCTIONS FOR CHECKING WRITING ASSIGNMENT #2

Read, check, and discuss Writing Assignment #2 after students have finished their final papers. Use the editing checklist (*Reference 5 on teacher's page 10*) as you check and discuss students' papers. Make sure students are using the editing checklist correctly. In the beginning, you must also check students' papers carefully for <u>form</u> mistakes. This will ensure that students are learning the three-point format correctly.

(End of lesson.)

CHAPTER 5   LESSON 1

Objectives: Jingles (preposition, object of the prep, preposition flow), Grammar (Introductory Sentences, preposition, object of the preposition, prepositional phrase, add object of the preposition to the Noun Check, add the preposition to the parts of speech, Oral Skill Builder Check), Vocabulary #1.

 **JINGLE TIME**

Have students turn to the Jingle Section in their books and recite the previously-taught jingles. Then, lead students in reciting the new jingles (*Preposition, Object of the Preposition, and Preposition Flow*) below. Practice the new jingles several times until students can recite them smoothly. Emphasize reciting with rhythm. Students and teacher should be together! (*Do not try to explain the jingles at this time. Just have fun reciting them. Remember, add motions for more fun and laughter.*)

Teacher's Notes: Again, do not spend a large amount of time practicing the new jingles. Students learn the jingles best by spending a small amount of time consistently, **every** day.

Jingle 7: Preposition Jingle

A PREP PREP PREPOSITION
Is a special group of words
That connects a
NOUN, NOUN, NOUN
Or a PRO, PRO, PRONOUN
To the rest of the sentence.

Jingle 8:   Object of the Prep Jingle

Dum De Dum Dum!
An O-P is a N-O-U-N or a P-R-O
After the P-R-E-P
In a S-E-N-T-E-N-C-E.
Dum De Dum Dum - DONE!

Jingle 9:   Preposition Flow Jingle

1. **Preposition, Preposition
Starting with an A.**

   (Fast)
   aboard, about, above,
   across, after, against,
   (Slow)
   along, among, around, at.

2. **Preposition, Preposition
Starting with a B.**

   (Fast)
   before, behind, below,
   beneath, beside, between,
   (Slow)
   beyond, but, by.

3. **Preposition, Preposition
Starting with a D.**

   down (slow & long),
   during (snappy).

4. **Preposition, Preposition
Don't go away.
Go to the middle
And see what we say.
E-F-I and L-N-O**

   except, for, from,
   in, inside, into,
   like,
   near, of, off,
   on, out, outside, over.

5. **Preposition, Preposition
Almost through.
Start with P and end with W.**

   past, since, through,
   throughout, to, toward,
   under, underneath,
   until, up, upon,
   with, within, without.

6. **Preposition, Preposition
Easy as can be.
We're all finished,
And aren't you pleased?
We've just recited
All 49 of these.**

CHAPTER 5 LESSON 1 CONTINUED

 GRAMMAR TIME

Put the introductory sentences from the box below on the board. Use these sentences as you go through each new concept covered in your teaching script. For the greatest benefit, students must participate orally with the teacher. (*You might put the introductory sentences on notebook paper if you are doing one-on-one instruction with your students.*)

Chapter 5, Introductory Sentences for Lesson 1
1. _____ The young performers walked happily across the stage after the concert.
2. _____ The small digital camera worked well on the new computer with the specialized software.
3. _____ The two mysterious strangers walked silently around the empty house.

TEACHING SCRIPT FOR PREPOSITION, OBJECT OF THE PREPOSITION, AND PREPOSITIONAL PHRASE

We will now begin the really "fun stuff" in English. We are going to start with prepositions! The Preposition Jingles have already told you a lot about prepositions, but now we are going to learn even more. A **preposition** is a joining word. It joins a noun or a pronoun to the rest of the sentence. To know whether a word is a preposition, say the preposition word and ask *What* or *Whom*. If the answer is a noun or pronoun, then the word is a preposition. Prepositions are labeled with a *P*.

An **object of the preposition** is a noun or pronoun after the preposition in a sentence. An object of the preposition is labeled with an *OP*.

It is important for you to know the difference between prepositions and adverbs. Look at Reference 17 on page 18 as I explain how you can tell the difference between prepositions and adverbs.

A word can be a preposition or an adverb, depending on how it is used in a sentence. For example, the word *down* can be an adverb or a preposition. How do you decide if the word *down* is an adverb or a preposition? If *down* is used alone, with no noun after it, it is an adverb. If *down* has a noun after it that answers the question *what* or *whom*, then *down* is a preposition, and the noun after *down* is an object of the preposition. (*Have students follow along as you read and discuss the information in the reference box below.*)

Reference 17: Knowing the Difference Between Prepositions and Adverbs

Adv
In the sample sentence, *Susan fell* **down**, the word **down** is an adverb because it does not have a noun after it.
         P   noun (OP)
In the sample sentence, *Susan fell* **down the stairs**, the word **down** is a preposition because it has the noun **stairs**
(the object of the preposition) after it. To find the preposition and object of the preposition in the Question and Answer
Flow, say: **down – P**   (Say: *down – preposition*)
           down what? stairs – OP   (Say: *down what? stairs – object of the preposition*)

CHAPTER 5 LESSON 1 CONTINUED

Now, we will learn about prepositional phrases. A **prepositional phrase** starts with the preposition and ends with an object of the preposition. It includes any modifiers between the preposition and the object of the preposition.

A prepositional phrase adds meaning to a sentence and can be located anywhere in the sentence. Prepositional phrases can modify like adjectives or adverbs. For example, the prepositional phrase (*down the stairs*) tells where Susan fell.

A single word that modifies a verb is called an adverb. A prepositional phrase that modifies a verb is called an adverb phrase, or adverbial phrase. Prepositional phrases can also modify like adjectives. (*Students are not required to identify adjectival and adverbial phrases in sentences until seventh grade.*)

Prepositional phrases are identified in the Question and Answer Flow after you say the word *Check*. Now, when you say *Check*, you are also looking for prepositional phrases in the sentence. If you find a prepositional phrase, you will read the whole prepositional phrase and put parentheses around it.

If there is more than one prepositional phrase in a sentence, read all prepositional phrases during this check time. For example, after you classify the sentence, *Janice walked around the pool*, you say, **Subject Noun Verb Pattern 1 Check: (Around the pool) - Prepositional phrase.**

You will learn prepositional phrases very quickly simply by identifying and using them everyday. I will show you how quick and easy it is to identify prepositional phrases by using the Question and Answer Flow. Remember, the Question and Answer Flow will make learning prepositional phrases easy and fun. (*Classify Sentence 1 to demonstrate prepositional phrases in the Question and Answer Flow. You could also use the audio CD to introduce the Introductory Sentences.*)

Question and Answer Flow for Sentence 1: The young performers walked happily across the stage after the concert.

1. Who walked happily across the stage after the concert? performers - SN
2. What is being said about performers? performers walked - V
3. Walked how? happily - Adv
4. Across - P (Preposition)
5. Across what? stage - OP (Object of the Preposition)

Note: To test whether a word is a preposition, say your preposition and ask "what" or "whom." If your answer is a noun or pronoun, you will have a preposition. All prepositions will have a noun or pronoun object. (When the object of the preposition is a person, use "whom" instead of "what.")

6. The - A
7. After - P
8. After what? concert - OP

9. The - A
10. What kind of performers? young - Adj
11. The - A
12. SN V P1 Check
13. (Across the stage) - Prepositional phrase

Note: Say "across the stage - Prepositional phrase" as you put parentheses around the words. This also teaches your students how to read in complete phrases, so keep it smooth.

14. (After the concert) - Prepositional phrase
15. Period, statement, declarative sentence
16. Go back to the verb - divide the complete subject from the complete predicate.

Classified Sentence:

			A	Adj	SN	V	Adv	P	A	OP	P	A	OP
	SN V		The	young	performers /	walked	happily	(across	the	stage)	(after	the	concert). D
	P1												

CHAPTER 5 LESSON 1 CONTINUED

I will now classify Sentence 1 again, but this time you classify it with me. I will lead you as we say the questions and answers together. Remember, it is very important that you say the **questions** with me as well as the **answers**. *(Classify Sentence 1 again with your students.)*

We will classify Sentences 2 and 3 together to practice the new grammar concepts in the Question and Answer Flows. You must say the **questions and answers** with me. By asking and answering the questions orally, you will learn everything faster because you see it, hear it, say it, and then do it. Begin.

Question and Answer Flow for Sentence 2: The small digital camera worked well on the new computer with the specialized software.

1. What worked well on the new computer with the specialized software? camera - SN
2. What is being said about camera? camera worked - V
3. Worked how? well - Adv
4. On - P
5. On what? computer - OP
6. Which computer? new - Adj
7. The - A
8. With - P
9. With what? software - OP
10. What kind of software? specialized - Adj
11. The - A
12. What kind of camera? digital - Adj
13. What kind of camera? small - Adj
14. The - A
15. SN V P1 Check
16. (On the new computer) - Prepositional phrase
17. (With the specialized software) - Prepositional phrase
18. Period, statement, declarative sentence
19. Go back to the verb - divide the complete subject from the complete predicate.

Classified Sentence:

```
              A  Adj  Adj   SN      V   Adv  P A  Adj  OP       P   A
   SN V    The small digital camera / worked well (on the new computer) ( with the
  ─────                       Adj        OP
   P1      specialized software). D
```

Question and Answer Flow for Sentence 3: The two mysterious strangers walked silently around the empty house.

1. Who walked silently around the empty house? strangers - SN
2. What is being said about strangers? strangers walked - V
3. Walked how? silently - Adv
4. Around - P
5. Around what? house - OP
6. What kind of house? empty - Adj
7. The - A
8. What kind of strangers? mysterious - Adj
9. How many strangers? two - Adj
10. The - A
11. SN V P1 Check
12. (Around the empty house) - Prepositional phrase
13. Period, statement, declarative sentence
14. Go back to the verb - divide the complete subject from the complete predicate.

Classified Sentence:

```
              A  Adj      Adj      SN       V    Adv    P   A   Adj   OP
   SN V    The two mysterious strangers / walked silently (around the empty house). D
  ─────
   P1
```

CHAPTER 5 LESSON 1 CONTINUED

TEACHING SCRIPT FOR ADDING THE OBJECT OF THE PREPOSITION TO THE NOUN CHECK

We are going to use the sentences we have just classified to do an Oral Skill Builder Check. You have already learned how to do a Noun Check with the subject of the sentence. Today, we are going to add a new noun job, the object of the preposition, to the Noun Check. We will learn to identify nouns in the object of the preposition job. Therefore, to find nouns, you will go to the words marked **SN** and **OP** in the classified sentences.

Look at Sentences 1-3 that we have just classified on the board. Remember, we will go to the subject nouns **and** the objects of the prepositions to find nouns. We will circle each noun as we find it.

Look at Sentence 1. You will say, "Number 1: subject noun *performers, yes;* object of the preposition *stage, yes;* object of the preposition *concert, yes.*" I will circle each noun as you identify it. *(Have students repeat number 1 with you as you circle each noun identified.)* We will find and circle the nouns in Sentences 2 and 3 the same way. *(Work through the rest of the sentences, identifying and circling the subject nouns and object-of-the-preposition nouns.)* *(Number 1:* subject noun *performers, yes;* object of the preposition *stage, yes;* object of the preposition *concert, yes. Number 2:* subject noun *camera, yes;* object of the preposition *computer, yes;* object of the preposition *software, yes. Number 3:* subject noun *strangers, yes;* object of the preposition *house, yes.)*

Use the same Skill Builder procedures that were taught in previous chapters to have students identify each noun as singular or plural. Ask students to tell which nouns are common and which are proper. Check the vocabulary words used for each sentence. Select the ones your students may not know and do a Vocabulary Check. For each word selected, make sure it is defined, used in a new sentence, and given a synonym and/or an antonym. You might also ask for synonyms and antonyms of several words just to check students' understanding of different words.

Now that you have finished the Noun Check, the Singular/Plural Check, the Common/Proper Check, and the Vocabulary Check, continue using Sentences 1-3 to do the rest of the Skill Builders from the checklist below. This checklist will always be given to you every time you do an Oral Skill Builder Check.

Teacher's Notes: You will be given directions for a Skill Builder Check only with the first set of sentences in a chapter. You could do Skill Builder Checks with every set of sentences, but it is usually not necessary. Your time allotment and the needs of your students will influence your decision.

Oral Skill Builder Check	
1. Noun check. (Say the job and then say the noun. Circle each noun.)	**5. Identify the complete subject and the complete predicate.** (Underline the complete subject once and the complete predicate twice.)
2. Identify the nouns as singular or plural. (Write **S** or **P** above each noun.)	
3. Identify the nouns as common or proper. (Follow established procedure for oral identification.)	**6. Identify the simple subject and simple predicate.** (Underline the simple subject once and the simple predicate twice. Bold, or highlight, the lines to distinguish them from the complete subject and complete predicate.)
4. Do a vocabulary check. (Follow established procedure for oral identification.)	

CHAPTER 5 LESSON 1 CONTINUED

TEACHING SCRIPT FOR ADDING THE PREPOSITION TO THE PARTS OF SPEECH

Until now, we have had only four parts of speech. Do you remember the names of the four parts of speech we have already learned? _(noun, verb, adjective,_ and _adverb)_ Today, we have learned about prepositions. A preposition is also a part of speech; so, we will add it to our list. We do not add the object of the preposition because it is a noun, and nouns are already on our list. Now, you know five of the eight parts of speech. What are the five parts of speech we have studied? _(noun, verb, adjective, adverb,_ and _preposition)_ _(Recite the five parts of speech several times. Students will learn an Eight-Parts-of-Speech Jingle after the eight parts have been introduced.)_

 VOCABULARY TIME

Assign Chapter 5, Vocabulary Words **#1** on page 8 in the Reference Section for students to define in their Vocabulary notebooks. Tell students they are to use a dictionary or thesaurus to look up the meanings of the vocabulary words. After they write each word and its meaning, students are to write a sentence using the vocabulary word.

Chapter 5, Vocabulary Words #1
(accept, reject, tales, stories)

(End of lesson.)

CHAPTER 5   LESSON 2

Objectives: Jingles, Grammar (Introductory Sentences, prepositional phrase at the beginning of a sentence), Practice and Improved sentence with a prepositional phrase, and Vocabulary #2.

JINGLE TIME

Have students turn to the Jingle Section in their books and recite the previously-taught jingles.

GRAMMAR TIME

Put the introductory sentences from the box below on the board. Use these sentences as you go through each new concept covered in your teaching script. For the greatest benefit, students must participate orally with the teacher. (*You might put the introductory sentences on notebook paper if you are doing one-on-one instruction with your students.*)

Chapter 5, Introductory Sentences for Lesson 2

1. _____ During the reception, the wedding guests danced until the wee hours of the morning!
2. _____ Today, the library club meets for thirty minutes in the cafeteria after school.
3. _____ The unexpected company arrived in the middle of the afternoon yesterday.

TEACHING SCRIPT FOR A PREPOSITIONAL PHRASE AT THE BEGINNING OF A SENTENCE

I want to do a quick review of predicate words in the complete subject. Look at Reference 14 on page 17 in your book. *(Page 56 in TM.)* A sentence with predicate words in the complete subject has one of these predicate words at the beginning of the complete subject: **an adverb, a helping verb, or a prepositional phrase**. We have had the adverb at the beginning of the sentence.

Today, we will identify a prepositional phrase at the beginning of the sentence. If a prepositional phrase is located at the beginning of a sentence, it usually modifies the verb and is identified as predicate words in the complete subject. We will identify a prepositional phrase at the beginning of the sentence the same way that we identified an adverb at the beginning of the sentence, and we will underline it twice. Starting a sentence with an adverb or prepositional phrase is a quick, easy way to add variety to your writing.

Identifying predicate words at the beginning of the sentence will come at the end of the Question and Answer Flow. Just follow me as we recite the Question and Answer Flows for the three new sentences, and I will show you how to add this new information. We will classify the sentences together. Begin. (*You might have students write the labels above the sentences.*)

CHAPTER 5 LESSON 2 CONTINUED

Question and Answer Flow for Sentence 1: During the reception, the wedding guests danced until the wee hours of the morning!

1. Who danced until the wee hours of the morning? guests - SN
2. What is being said about guests? guests danced - V
3. Until - P
4. Until what? hours - OP
5. What kind of hours? wee - Adj
6. The - A
7. Of - P
8. Of what? morning - OP
9. The - A
10. What kind of guests? wedding - Adj
11. The - A
12. During - P

13. During what? reception - OP
14. The - A
15. SN V P1 Check
16. (During the reception) - Prepositional phrase
17. (Until the wee hours) - Prepositional phrase
18. (Of the morning) - Prepositional phrase
19. Exclamation point, strong feeling, exclamatory sentence
20. Go back to the verb - divide the complete subject from the complete predicate.
21. This sentence has predicate words in the complete subject. Underline the prepositional phrase at the beginning of the sentence twice.

Classified Sentence:

		P	A	OP	A	Adj	SN	V	P	A	Adj	OP	P	A	OP	

SN V / P1   (During the reception), the wedding guests / danced (until the wee hours) (of the morning)! E

Question and Answer Flow for Sentence 2: Today, the library club meets for thirty minutes in the cafeteria after school.

1. Who meets for thirty minutes in the cafeteria after school? club - SN
2. What is being said about club? club meets - V
3. For - P
4. For what? minutes - OP
5. How many minutes? thirty - Adj
6. In - P
7. In what? cafeteria - OP
8. The - A
9. After - P
10. After what? school - OP
11. What kind of club? library - Adj

12. The - A
13. Meets when? today - Adv
14. SN V P1 Check
15. (For thirty minutes) - Prepositional phrase
16. (In the cafeteria) - Prepositional phrase
17. (After school) - Prepositional phrase
18. Period, statement, declarative sentence
19. Go back to the verb - divide the complete subject from the complete predicate.
20. This sentence has predicate words in the complete subject. Underline the adverb at the beginning of the sentence twice.

Classified Sentence:

Adv	A	Adj	SN	V	P	Adj	OP	P	A	OP	P	OP

SN V / P1   Today, the library club / meets (for thirty minutes) (in the cafeteria) (after school). D

Question and Answer Flow for Sentence 3: The unexpected company arrived in the middle of the afternoon yesterday.

1. Who arrived in the middle of the afternoon yesterday? company - SN
2. What is being said about company? company arrived - V
3. In - P
4. In what? middle - OP
5. The - A
6. Of - P
7. Of what? afternoon - OP
8. The - A

9. Arrived when? yesterday - Adv
10. What kind of company? unexpected - Adj
11. The - A
12. SN V P1 Check
13. (In the middle) - Prepositional phrase
14. (Of the afternoon) - Prepositional phrase
15. Period, statement, declarative sentence
16. Go back to the verb - divide the complete subject from the complete predicate.

Classified Sentence:

A	Adj	SN	V	P	A	OP	P	A	OP	Adv

SN V / P1   The unexpected company / arrived (in the middle) (of the afternoon) yesterday. D

CHAPTER 5 LESSON 2 CONTINUED

TEACHING SCRIPT FOR A PRACTICE SENTENCE WITH A PREPOSITIONAL PHRASE

Put these labels on the board: **A Adj Adj SN V Adv P A Adj OP**

Look at the new sentence labels on the board: **A Adj Adj SN V Adv P A Adj OP**. I will guide you again through the process of writing a sentence to practice all the parts that you have learned.

Get out a sheet of notebook paper. On the top line of your notebook paper, write the title *Practice Sentence*. Copy the sentence labels from the board onto your notebook paper. Be sure to leave plenty of writing space between each label. Now, I will guide you through the process you will use whenever you write a Practice Sentence with a prepositional phrase.

1. Go to the **SN** label for the subject noun. Think of a noun that you want to use as your subject. Write the noun you have chosen on the line *under* the **SN** label.

2. Go to the **V** label for the verb. Think of a verb that tells what your subject does. Make sure that your verb makes sense with the subject noun. Write the verb you have chosen on the line *under* the **V** label.

3. Go to the **Adv** label for the adverb. Immediately go to the verb in your sentence and ask an adverb question. What are the adverb questions? (*How, When, Where*) Choose one adverb question to ask and write your adverb answer *under* the **Adv** label.

4. Go to the **P** label for the preposition. Think of a preposition word that tells something about your verb. You must be careful to choose a preposition word that makes sense with the noun you will choose for the object of the preposition in your next step. Write the word you have chosen for a preposition *under* the **P** label.

5. Go to the **OP** label for the object of the preposition. If you like the noun you thought of while thinking of a preposition, write it down under the **OP** label. If you prefer, think of another noun by asking **what** or **whom** after your preposition. Check to make sure the preposition and object of the preposition make sense together and also make sense with the rest of the sentence. Remember, the object of the preposition will always answer the question **what** or **whom** after the preposition. Write the word you have chosen for the object of the preposition *under* the **OP** label.

6. Go to the **Adj** label for an adjective. Go to the object of the preposition that you just wrote and ask an adjective question to describe the object of the preposition noun. What are the adjective questions? (*What kind, Which one, How many*) Choose one adjective question to ask and write your adjective answer *under* the **Adj** label next to the object of the preposition. Always check to make sure your answers are making sense in the sentence.

7. Go to the **A** label for the article adjective that is part of your prepositional phrase. What are the three article adjectives? (*a, an,* and *the*) Choose the article adjective that makes the best sense in your sentence. Write the article adjective you have chosen *under* the **A** label.

CHAPTER 5 LESSON 2 CONTINUED

8. Go to the **Adj** label for another adjective. Go to the subject noun of your sentence and ask an adjective question. What are the adjective questions again? (*What kind, Which one, How many*) Choose one adjective question to ask and write your adjective answer *under* the **Adj** label next to the subject noun.

9. Go to the **Adj** label for a third adjective. Go to the subject noun again and ask another adjective question. You can use the same adjective question, or you can use a different adjective question. Write another adjective *under* the third **Adj** label.

10. Go to the **A** label for the article adjective in the subject area. What are the three article adjectives again? (*a, an,* and *the*) Choose the article adjective that makes the best sense in your sentence. Write the article adjective you have chosen *under* the **A** label.

11. Finally, check your Practice Sentence to make sure it has the necessary parts to be a complete sentence. What are the five parts of a complete sentence? (*subject, verb, complete sense, capital letter, and an end mark*) Does your Practice Sentence have the five parts of a complete sentence? (*Allow time for students to read over their sentences and to make any corrections they need to make.*)

TEACHING SCRIPT FOR THE IMPROVED SENTENCE

Under your Practice Sentence, write the title *Improved Sentence* on another line. To improve your Practice Sentence, you will make two synonym changes, one antonym change, and your choice of a complete word change or another synonym or antonym change.

Since it is harder to find words that can be changed to an antonym, it is usually wise to go through your sentence to find an antonym change first. Then, look through your sentence again to find words that can be improved with synonyms. Finally, make a decision about whether your last change will be a complete word change, another synonym change, or another antonym change.

I will give you time to write your Improved Sentence. (*Always encourage students to use a thesaurus, synonym-antonym book, or a dictionary to help them develop an interesting and improved writing vocabulary. After students have finished, check and discuss students' Practice and Improved Sentences.*)

VOCABULARY TIME

Assign Chapter 5, Vocabulary Words **#2** on page 8 in the Reference Section for students to define in their Vocabulary notebooks. Tell students they are to use a dictionary or thesaurus to look up the meanings of the vocabulary words. After they write each word and its meaning, students are to write a sentence using the vocabulary word.

Chapter 5, Vocabulary Words #2
(pursue, follow, proceed, cease)

(End of lesson.)

> ## CHAPTER 5   LESSON 3
> Objectives: Jingles, Grammar (Practice Sentences), and an Activity.

 **JINGLE TIME**

Have students turn to the Jingle Section in their books and recite the previously-taught jingles.

 GRAMMAR TIME

First-Year Option: Put the Practice Sentences from the box below on the board or notebook paper. Use these sentences as you practice the concepts that have been taught. For the greatest benefit, students must participate orally with the teacher. **Second-Year Option:** Have students classify the Practice Sentences independently on notebook paper. Check students' sentences with the answers provided below. (*If you have the CDs for Practice Sentences, have students check their sentences with the CDs.*)

> ### Chapter 5, Practice Sentences for Lesson 3
>
> 1. _____ Tonight, the determined football players plowed forward against an exceptionally strong line.
> 2. _____ During the pool party, the bumblebee flew menacingly around the pool.
> 3. _____ The young bomber pilot flew over the beautiful green valley on a brilliant, cloudless day.

TEACHING SCRIPT FOR PRACTICING PREPOSITIONAL PHRASES

We will classify three different sentences to practice using prepositional phrases in the Question and Answer Flows. We will classify the sentences together. Begin.

> **Question and Answer Flow for Sentence 1: Tonight, the determined football players plowed forward against an exceptionally strong line.**
>
> 1. Who plowed forward against an exceptionally strong line? players - SN
> 2. What is being said about players? players plowed - V
> 3. Plowed where? forward - Adv
> 4. Against - P
> 5. Against what? line - OP
> 6. What kind of line? strong - Adj
> 7. How strong? exceptionally - Adv
> 8. An - A
> 9. What kind of players? football - Adj
> 10. What kind of players? determined - Adj
> 11. The - A
> 12. Plowed when? tonight - Adv
> 13. SN V P1 Check
> 14. (Against an exceptionally strong line) - Prepositional phrase
> 15. Period, statement, declarative sentence
> 16. Go back to the verb - divide the complete subject from the complete predicate.
> 17. This sentence has predicate words in the complete subject. Underline the adverb at the beginning of the sentence twice.
>
> **Classified**   Adv   A   Adj   Adj   SN   V   Adv   P   A   Adv   Adj   OP
> **Sentence:**   SN V   <u>Tonight</u>, the determined football players / plowed forward (against an exceptionally strong line). **D**
>   P1

CHAPTER 5 LESSON 3 CONTINUED

Question and Answer Flow for Sentence 2: During the pool party, the bumblebee flew menacingly around the pool.

1. What flew menacingly around the pool? bumblebee - SN
2. What is being said about bumblebee? bumblebee flew - V
3. Flew how? menacingly - Adv
4. Around - P
5. Around what? pool - OP
6. The - A
7. The - A
8. During - P
9. During what? party - OP

10. What kind of party? pool - Adj
11. The - A
12. SN V P1 Check
13. (During the pool party) - Prepositional phrase
14. (Around the pool) - Prepositional phrase
15. Period, statement, declarative sentence
16. Go back to the verb - divide the complete subject from the complete predicate.
17. This sentence has predicate words in the complete subject. Underline the prepositional phrase at the beginning of the sentence twice.

		P	A	Adj	OP	A	SN	V	Adv	P	A	OP
Classified Sentence: SN V / P1 (During the pool party), the bumblebee / flew menacingly (around the pool). D

Question and Answer Flow for Sentence 3: The young bomber pilot flew over the beautiful green valley on a brilliant, cloudless day.

1. Who flew over the beautiful green valley on a brilliant, cloudless day? pilot - SN
2. What is being said about pilot? pilot flew - V
3. Over - P
4. Over what? valley - OP
5. What kind of valley? green - Adj
6. What kind of valley? beautiful - Adj
7. The - A
8. On - P
9. On what? day - OP
10. What kind of day? cloudless - Adj

11. What kind of day? brilliant - Adj
12. A - A
13. What kind of pilot? bomber - Adj
14. What kind of pilot? young - Adj
15. The - A
16. SN V P1 Check
17. (Over the beautiful green valley) - Prepositional phrase
18. (On a brilliant, cloudless day) - Prepositional phrase
19. Period, statement, declarative sentence
20. Go back to the verb - divide the complete subject from the complete predicate.

	A	Adj	Adj	SN	V	P	A	Adj	Adj	OP	P	A	Adj	Adj	OP
Classified Sentence: SN V / P1 The young bomber pilot / flew (over the beautiful green valley) (on a brilliant, cloudless day). D

ACTIVITY / ASSIGNMENT TIME

Divide a white poster board into four parts. (*Draw one vertical line and one horizontal line through the center of the board. They do not have to be equal parts.*) Put one of the sentences below in each of the four sections. Each sentence will be the title of that section. Using the title sentence as the core, write as many prepositional phrases as possible that will fit that sentence. Use the Preposition Flow to help you think of prepositions. Illustrate and color each section. Discuss what you liked best about your project. Show your finished project to family members, friends, and relatives.

The boy ran...
1. Under the bridge.
2. Around the house.

The soldiers fought...
1. For their country.
2. In the jungle.

The cougar hunted...
1. After dark.
2. During the day.

Make up your own sentence...

(End of lesson.)

CHAPTER 5   LESSON 4

Objectives: Jingles, Study, Test, Check, and Writing (journal).

 JINGLE TIME

Have students turn to the Jingle Section in their books and recite the previously-taught jingles.

 STUDY TIME

Have students study the vocabulary words in their vocabulary notebooks. Remind students that any vocabulary word in their notebooks could be on their test. Also, have students study any of the skills in the Practice Section that they need to review.

 TEST TIME

Have students turn to page 101 in the Test Section of their book and find the Chapter 5 Test section. Go over the directions to make sure they understand what to do. (*Chapter 5 Test key is on the next page.*)

 **CHECK TIME**

After students have finished, check and discuss their test papers. Make sure they understand why their answers are right or wrong. (*For total points, count each required answer as a point.*)

(End of lesson.)

Level 4 Homeschool Teacher's Manual

Chapter 5 Test
(Student Page 101)

Exercise 1: Classify each sentence.

           A   Adj   Adj   SN   P   A   OP   V   Adv   P   A   OP

1. <u>SN V</u>   The explosive, fiery volcano (on the mountainside) / erupted violently (during the night)! **E**
   <u>P1</u>

           A   Adj   Adj   Adj   SN   V   Adv P A   Adj   OP   P   Adj   OP

2. <u>SN V</u>   A keen, old mule deer / stood still (in the heavy thicket) (during hunting season). **D**
   <u>P1</u>

           A   Adj   Adj   SN   V   Adv   P   A   OP   P A Adj   OP

3. <u>SN V</u>   <u>An expensive diamond necklace</u> / <u>sparkled brightly (through the window) (of the jewelry store)</u>. **D**
   <u>P1</u>

Exercise 2: Use Sentence 3 to underline the complete subject once and the complete predicate twice and to complete the table below.

List the Noun Used	List the Noun Job	Singular or Plural	Common or Proper	Simple Subject	Simple Predicate
1. **necklace**	2. **SN**	3. **S**	4. **C**	5. **necklace**	6. **sparkled**
7. **window**	8. **OP**	9. **S**	10. **C**		
11. **store**	12. **OP**	13. **S**	14. **C**		

Exercise 3: Name the five parts of speech that you have studied. (*You may use abbreviations.*) **(The order may vary.)**

1. <u>**Noun**</u>   2. <u>**Verb**</u>   3. <u>**Adjective**</u>   4. <u>**Adverb**</u>   5. <u>**Preposition**</u>

Exercise 4: Identify each pair of words as synonyms or antonyms by putting parentheses ( ) around *syn* or *ant*.

1. pursue, follow	**(syn)** ant	5. precise, exact	**(syn)** ant	9. implied, hinted	**(syn)** ant
2. proceed, cease	syn **(ant)**	6. accept, reject	syn **(ant)**	10. quiver, shake	**(syn)** ant
3. brawn, muscle	**(syn)** ant	7. tales, stories	**(syn)** ant	11. delight, displease	syn **(ant)**
4. reply, answer	**(syn)** ant	8. vivid, dingy	syn **(ant)**	12. aggression, retreat	syn **(ant)**

Exercise 5: Write *a* or *an* in the blanks.

1. He whistled <u>**a**</u> happy tune.   3. It was <u>**an**</u> isolated event.   5. <u>**a**</u> quilt   7. <u>**an**</u> octopus

2. We saw <u>**an**</u> antelope.   4. They bought <u>**a**</u> big boat.   6. <u>**a**</u> fish   8. <u>**an**</u> instructor

Exercise 6: Match the definitions by writing the correct letter beside each numbered concept.

<u>F</u>   1. joins a noun or a pronoun to the rest of the sentence   A.   verb, adjective, or adverb

<u>E</u>   2. a/an are also called   B.   object of the preposition

<u>I</u>   3. adjective modifies   C.   person, place, or thing

<u>B</u>   4. noun or pronoun after a preposition   D.   imperative sentence

<u>H</u>   5. subject question   E.   indefinite articles

<u>G</u>   6. article adjective can be called   F.   preposition

<u>D</u>   7. makes a request or gives a command   G.   noun marker

<u>C</u>   8. noun   H.   who or what

<u>J</u>   9. tells what the subject does   I.   noun or pronoun

<u>A</u>   10. adverb modifies   J.   verb

Exercise 7: On notebook paper, write as many prepositions as you can. **(Check prepositions with the Preposition Flow Jingle.)**

Exercise 8: In your journal, write a paragraph summarizing what you have learned this week.

CHAPTER 5 LESSON 4 CONTINUED

TEACHER INSTRUCTIONS

Use the Question and Answer Flows below for the sentences on the Chapter 5 Test.

Question and Answer Flow for Sentence 1: The explosive, fiery volcano on the mountainside erupted violently during the night!

1. What erupted violently during the night? volcano - SN
2. What is being said about volcano? volcano erupted - V
3. Erupted how? violently - Adv
4. During - P
5. During what? night - OP
6. The - A
7. On - P
8. On what? mountainside - OP
9. The - A
10. What kind of volcano? fiery - Adj
11. What kind of volcano? explosive - Adj
12. The - A
13. SN V P1 Check
14. (On the mountainside) - Prepositional phrase
15. (During the night) - Prepositional phrase
16. Exclamation point, strong feeling, exclamatory sentence
17. Go back to the verb - divide the complete subject from the complete predicate.

			A	Adj	Adj	SN	P	A	OP	V	Adv	P	A	OP
Classified Sentence:	SN V		The explosive, fiery volcano (on the mountainside) / erupted violently (during the night)!											E
	P1													

Question and Answer Flow for Sentence 2: A keen, old mule deer stood still in the heavy thicket during hunting season.

1. What stood still in the heavy thicket during hunting season? deer - SN
2. What is being said about deer? deer stood - V
3. Stood how? still - Adv
4. In - P
5. In what? thicket - OP
6. What kind of thicket? heavy - Adj
7. The - A
8. During - P
9. During what? season - OP
10. What kind of season? hunting - Adj
11. What kind of deer? mule - Adj
12. What kind of deer? old - Adj
13. What kind of deer? keen - Adj
14. A - A
15. SN V P1 Check
16. (In the heavy thicket) - Prepositional phrase
17. (During hunting season) - Prepositional phrase
18. Period, statement, declarative sentence
19. Go back to the verb - divide the complete subject from the complete predicate.

		A	Adj	Adj	Adj	SN		V	Adv	P	A	Adj	OP	P	Adj	OP
Classified Sentence:	SN V	A keen, old mule deer / stood still (in the heavy thicket) (during hunting season).														D
	P1															

Question and Answer Flow for Sentence 3: An expensive diamond necklace sparkled brightly through the window of the jewelry store.

1. What sparkled brightly through the window of the jewelry store? necklace - SN
2. What is being said about necklace? necklace sparkled - V
3. Sparkled how? brightly - Adv
4. Through - P
5. Through what? window - OP
6. The - A
7. Of - P
8. Of what? store - OP
9. What kind of store? jewelry - Adj
10. The - A
11. What kind of necklace? diamond - Adj
12. What kind of necklace? expensive - Adj
13. An - A
14. SN V P1 Check
15. (Through the window) - Prepositional phrase
16. (Of the jewelry store) - Prepositional phrase
17. Period, statement, declarative sentence
18. Go back to the verb - divide the complete subject from the complete predicate.

		A	Adj	Adj	SN		V	Adv	P	A	OP	P	A	Adj	OP
Classified Sentence:	SN V	An expensive diamond necklace / sparkled brightly (through the window) (of the jewelry store).													D
	P1														

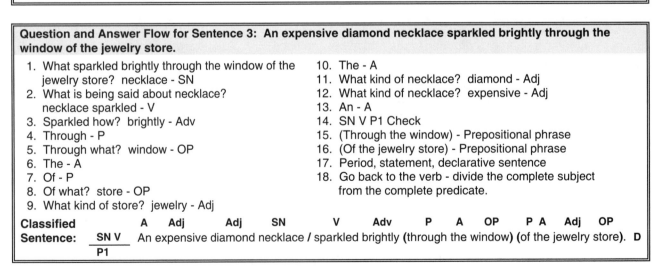

CHAPTER 5 LESSON 5

Objectives: Writing (point of view, writing in first and third person), Writing Assignments #3 and #4, Bonus Option.

 **WRITING TIME**

TEACHING SCRIPT FOR INTRODUCING POINT OF VIEW AND WRITING IN FIRST AND THIRD PERSON

When you write, you usually write from a certain point of view. Point of view refers to the writer's use of personal pronouns to determine who is telling a story. There are commonly two points of view used in literature and writing: first person point of view and third person point of view.

Second person point of view is not used very often in writing except when you are telling someone how to do something. Second person point of view will use the second person pronouns *you, your,* and *yours* to name the person or thing spoken to. Very few stories, paragraphs, or essays are written in second person. Mostly, second person point of view is used in giving directions, and it uses the pronoun **you** almost exclusively.

Since you will not be using second person point of view in your writing at this time, we will concentrate on learning how to write in first and third person. Look at Reference 18 on page 18 in the Reference Section of your book while I read the information.

Reference 18: Writing in First Person or Third Person

Events and stories can be told from different viewpoints.

First Person Point of View uses the first person pronouns *I, we, us, me, my, mine, our,* and *ours* to name the speaker. If any of the first person pronouns are used in a writing, the writing is usually considered a first person writing, even though second and third person pronouns may also be used. First person shows that you (*the writer*) are speaking, and that you (*the writer*) are personally involved in what is happening.

(Examples: **I** am going to the store in **my** new car. She likes **my** car.)

Third Person Point of View uses the third person pronouns *he, his, him, she, her, hers, it, its, they, their, theirs,* and *them* to name the person or thing spoken about. You should <u>not</u> use the first person pronouns *I, we, us, me, my, mine, our* and *ours* for third person writing because using the first person pronouns usually puts a writing in a first person point of view. Third person means that you (*the writer*) must write as if you are watching the events take place. Third person shows that you are writing about another person, thing, or event.

(Examples: **He** is going to the store in **his** new car. **She** likes **his** car.)

CHAPTER 5 LESSON 5 CONTINUED

It is simple to see the difference in first and third person by listening to the following paragraphs. Listen as I read a paragraph written in first person.

First Person Point of View

Last year, <u>my</u> sister and <u>I</u> entered a local talent contest. <u>Our</u> act was a violin and piano duet. <u>We</u> practiced for weeks beforehand until <u>we</u> had <u>our</u> music memorized. When <u>we</u> stood on stage to perform, <u>I</u> felt butterflies in <u>my</u> stomach. After <u>our</u> performance the crowd cheered. <u>Our</u> mom and dad were so proud of <u>us</u> and treated <u>us</u> to ice cream after <u>our</u> debut.

Listen as I read a second paragraph, this time in third person point of view. As I read, notice that the first person pronouns have been changed to third person or to a person's name. Remember that when you write in third person, you should not use any of the first person pronouns (*I, we, us, me, my, mine,* our and *ours*) because using any first person pronoun usually puts a writing in a first person point of view. *(There are exceptions when you use quotations, but this is a good rule of thumb to follow.)*

Third Person Point of View

Last year, <u>Jennifer</u> and <u>her</u> sister entered a local talent contest. <u>Their</u> act was a violin and piano duet. <u>They</u> practiced for weeks beforehand until <u>they</u> had <u>their</u> music memorized . When <u>they</u> stood on stage to perform, <u>Jennifer</u> felt butterflies in <u>her</u> stomach. After <u>their</u> performance, the crowd cheered. <u>Their</u> mom and dad were so proud of <u>them</u> and treated <u>them</u> to ice cream after <u>their</u> debut.

Remember, it is good to get in the habit of checking over your writing after you have finished. Just reading your finished paragraph several times slowly will help you see and hear things that you may want to correct.

TEACHER INSTRUCTIONS FOR WRITING ASSIGNMENTS

Give Writing Assignment #3 and Writing Assignment #4 from the box on the next page. Remind students to follow the Writing Guidelines as they prepare their writings. For Writing Assignment #3, have students underline all first person pronouns in their paragraph. For Writing Assignment #4, have students underline all third person pronouns in their paragraph.

CHAPTER 5 LESSON 5 CONTINUED

Writing Assignment Box

Writing Assignment #3: Three-Point Expository Paragraph (First Person)
(Remind students that first person pronouns are *I, we, me, us, my, mine, our,* and *ours.*)

Writing topic choices: **My Favorite Snack** or **My Favorite Place** or **My Favorite Holidays**

Writing Assignment #4: Three-Point Expository Paragraph (Third Person)
(Remind students that third person pronouns are *he, his, him, she, her, hers, it, its, they, their, theirs, and them.*)

Writing topic choices: **My Mom's (Dad's) Favorite Snack** or **My Mom's (Dad's) Favorite Place** or
My Mom's (Dad's) Favorite Holidays

<u>Bonus Option:</u> **To solve the puzzle for Matthew 7:7, cross out every third letter to read the message. (King
James Version)**

ASAKASNDFITQSHWALELBREGGIVHENJYOKU
SEPEKOANIDYUESYHATLLRFIEND
KNMOCNKABNDVITCSHXALZLBLEOKPEJNEHDUGNTFOYDOU

Answer: (Ask, and it shall be given you; seek, and ye shall find; knock, and it shall be opened unto you.)

Have students design their own puzzles and share them with other family members and friends.

TEACHING SCRIPT FOR USING THE WRITING PROCESS FOR THIS WRITING ASSIGNMENT

As you begin this writing assignment, you will again go through the writing process. First, you will think
about your topic and gather any information you might need in order to do the writing. Second, you will
write a rough draft. Remember, it is called a rough draft because it will be revised and edited. You do not
have to worry about mistakes as you write your rough draft. After you write the first draft, you will make
revisions, using the Revision Checklist in Reference 5. After you revise your writing, you will edit, using
the Beginning Editing Checklist in Reference 5. Finally, after you are satisfied with your revising and
editing, you will write a final paper, using the Final Paper Checklist in Reference 5. You will then give
the finished writing assignment to me. (*Students should finish their writing during their free time if they do not
finish during this lesson.*)

TEACHER INSTRUCTIONS FOR CHECKING WRITING ASSIGNMENTS

Read, check, and discuss Writing Assignments #3 and #4 after students have finished their final papers.
Use the editing checklist (*Reference 5 on teacher's page 10*) as you check and discuss students' papers. Make
sure students are using the editing checklists correctly. In the beginning, you must also check students'
papers carefully for <u>form</u> mistakes. This will ensure that students are learning the three-point format
correctly.

(End of lesson.)

CHAPTER 6 LESSON 1

Objectives: Jingles (Pronoun, Subject Pronoun), Grammar (Introductory Sentences, pronoun, subject pronoun, understood subject pronoun, Noun Checks with pronouns, adding the pronoun to the parts of speech, Oral Skill Builder Check), and Vocabulary #1.

JINGLE TIME

Have students turn to the Jingle Section in their books and recite the previously-taught jingles. Then, lead students in reciting the new jingles (*Pronoun, Subject Pronoun*) below. Practice the new jingles several times until students can recite them smoothly. Emphasize reciting with a rhythm. Students and teacher should be together! (*Do not try to explain the jingles at this time. Just have fun reciting them. Remember, add motions for more fun and laughter.*)

Teacher's Notes: Again, do not spend a large amount of time practicing the new jingles. Students learn the jingles best by spending a small amount of time consistently, **every** day.

Jingle 10: Pronoun Jingle
This little pronoun, Floating around, Takes the place of a little old noun. With a knick knack, paddy wack, These are English rules. Isn't language fun and cool?

Jingle 11: Subject Pronoun Jingle
There are seven subject pronouns That are easy as can be: I and we,   (clap 2 times) He and she,   (clap 2 times) It and they and you.   (clap 3 times)

GRAMMAR TIME

Put the introductory sentences from the box below on the board. Use these sentences as you go through each new concept covered in your teaching script. For the greatest benefit, students must participate orally with the teacher. (*You might put the introductory sentences on notebook paper if you are doing one-on-one instruction with your students.*)

Chapter 6, Introductory Sentences for Lesson 1
1. _____ They live in the small white house on the corner of Maple Street.
2. _____ Play quietly with the toys in the kitchen until lunchtime.
3. _____ We went to the baseball tournament on Saturday with Tyler.

CHAPTER 6 LESSON 1 CONTINUED

TEACHING SCRIPT FOR THE PRONOUN AND THE SUBJECT PRONOUN

Today, we will learn about pronouns and the different kinds of pronouns. Let's look at the Pronoun Jingle again. It tells us that a **pronoun** takes the place of a noun. A pronoun may take the place of a person, place, or thing in a sentence. Without pronouns, everyone would be forced to repeat the same nouns again and again. Frequently-used pronouns are usually memorized.

The first kind of pronoun we will study is the subject pronoun. Look at Reference 19 on page 18 as I explain the five things you should know about the subject pronoun.

Reference 19: Subject Pronoun
1. A **subject pronoun** takes the place of a noun that is used as the subject of a sentence.
2. These are the most common subject pronouns: *I, we, he, she, it, they*, and *you*. Use the Subject Pronoun Jingle to remember the common subject pronouns.
3. To find a subject pronoun, ask the subject question *who* or *what*.
4. Label a subject pronoun with *SP*.
5. Call the *SP* abbreviation a subject pronoun.

If you are ever in doubt about whether the subject is a noun or pronoun, just recite the Subject Pronoun Jingle. If the subject is one of the pronouns in the Subject Pronoun Jingle; it is a Subject Pronoun. (*Have students recite the Subject Pronoun Jingle.*)

We will use that information as you classify Sentence 1 with me to find the subject pronoun. Remember, you use the same subject question, starting with *who* or *what*, to find the subject pronoun. Begin.

Question and Answer Flow for Sentence 1: They live in the small white house on the corner of Maple Street.	
1. Who live in the small white house on the corner of Maple Street? they - SP (subject pronoun)	12. Of what? Maple Street - OP
2. What is being said about they? they live - V	13. SN V P1 Check
3. In - P	**Note:** When writing the sentence pattern, write SN even though the subject may be a subject pronoun. See teacher's notes below.
4. In what? house - OP	
5. What kind of house? white - Adj	14. (In the small white house) - Prepositional phrase
6. What kind of house? small - Adj	15. (On the corner) - Prepositional phrase
7. The - A	16. (Of Maple Street) - Prepositional phrase
8. On - P	17. Period, statement, declarative sentence
9. On what? corner - OP	18. Go back to the verb - divide the complete subject from the complete predicate.
10. The - A	
11. Of - P	

Classified Sentence:

```
                      SP    V   P A  Adj Adj  OP     P A  OP   P   OP
           SN  V      They / live (in the small white house) (on the corner) (of Maple Street).  D
           P1
```

Teacher's Notes: Each sentence pattern is still identified with *SN* even though the actual subject is identified and labeled as *SP* in the sentence. The *SN* is part of the pattern identification, not the actual identification of the subject in the sentence.

CHAPTER 6 LESSON 1 CONTINUED

TEACHING SCRIPT FOR UNDERSTOOD SUBJECT PRONOUN

The second kind of pronoun we will study is the <u>understood subject pronoun</u>. Look at Reference 20 on page 19 as I explain the four things you should know about the understood subject pronoun.

Reference 20: Understood Subject Pronoun
1. A sentence has an **understood subject** when someone gives a command or makes a request and leaves the subject unwritten or unspoken. It is understood that the unspoken subject will always be the pronoun *you*.
2. An imperative sentence gives a command or makes a request. It ends with a period or an exclamation point and always has the word *you* understood, but not expressed, as the subject.
3. The understood subject pronoun *you* is always written in parentheses at the beginning of the sentence with the label *SP* beside or above it: **(You) SP**.
4. Call the abbreviation **(You) SP** an understood subject pronoun.

As you can see, an understood subject is not spoken or written down. Whenever a sentence gives a command or makes a request and leaves the subject unwritten and unspoken, the subject is always called an UNDERSTOOD SUBJECT. This understood subject will always be the pronoun YOU.

In this example, *Turn quickly,* who is being commanded to turn quickly? It is understood that someone is being commanded to turn quickly even though the name is not mentioned. The person receiving the command is always the understood subject pronoun YOU.

Let's classify Sentence 2 for identification of the understood subject pronoun *you.*

Question and Answer Flow for Sentence 2: Play quietly with the toys in the kitchen until lunchtime.

1. Who play quietly with the toys in the kitchen until lunchtime? (You) - SP (Understood subject pronoun)

Note: Say, "you - understood subject pronoun." Demonstrate how to write (You) - SP above the pattern to the left of the sentence.

2. What is being said about you? you play - V
3. Play how? quietly - Adv
4. With - P
5. With what? toys - OP
6. The - A
7. In - P
8. In what? kitchen - OP
9. The - A

10. Until - P
11. Until what? lunchtime - OP
12. SN V P1 Check
13. (With the toys) - Prepositional phrase
14. (In the kitchen) - Prepositional phrase
15. (Until lunchtime) - Prepositional phrase
16. Period, command, imperative sentence

Note: Emphasize that when they have an understood subject pronoun, they will usually have an imperative sentence.

17. Go back to the verb - divide the complete subject from the complete predicate.

Classified Sentence:

```
                  (You) SP      V    Adv    P    A   OP    P  A    OP      P     OP
                  SN V       / Play quietly (with the toys) (in the kitchen) (until lunchtime).  Imp
                  P1
```

CHAPTER 6 LESSON 1 CONTINUED

Teacher's Notes: Question and Answer Flow Disclaimer.

For consistency, the Question and Answer Flow will use the verb form that is written in each sentence to complete the subject question, regardless of whether the verb is singular or plural.
Example: They <u>are</u> dancing. Q & A: Who <u>are</u> dancing?
If you prefer using the singular verb form, just make the necessary change whenever it occurs.

At this point, it is wise to note an exception because you will have to make decisions based on this knowledge. When a sentence has an understood subject pronoun, it will <u>usually</u> be an imperative sentence. The only time an imperative sentence is not classified as imperative is when it is a command that shows very strong feeling or excitement and has (or should have) an exclamation point. Then, it is classified as an exclamatory sentence. (*Examples: Yell for help! Call immediately for the ambulance!*)

Question and Answer Flow for Sentence 3: We went to the baseball tournament on Saturday with Tyler.

1. Who went to the baseball tournament on Saturday with Tyler? we - SP (subject pronoun)
2. What is being said about we? we went - V
3. To - P
4. To what? tournament - OP
5. What kind of tournament? baseball - Adj
6. The - A
7. On - P
8. On what? Saturday - OP
9. With - P
10. With whom? Tyler - OP
11. SN V P1 Check
12. (To the baseball tournament) - Prepositional phrase
13. (On Saturday) - Prepositional phrase
14. (With Tyler) - Prepositional phrase
15. Period, statement, declarative sentence
16. Go back to the verb - divide the complete subject from the complete predicate.

Classified Sentence:

	SP	V	P	A	Adj	OP	P	OP	P	OP
<u>SN V</u> P1	We /	went	(to	the	baseball	tournament)	(on	Saturday)	(with	Tyler). **D**

TEACHING SCRIPT FOR A NOUN CHECK WHEN PRONOUNS ARE IN THE SENTENCES

A Noun Check is a check for nouns. Since nouns are located in noun jobs, it is essential to know the noun jobs so that you know where to go to find nouns. You have had two noun jobs so far: the subject noun job and the object of the preposition noun job.

Since we are looking for nouns, we will say the noun job, say the noun or pronoun, and then say *yes* if it is a noun or *no* if it is a pronoun. Let's start with number one and go through the Noun Check for Sentences 1-3, identifying nouns by using the procedure below.

Sentence 1: Subject pronoun *they*, no. Object of the preposition *house*, yes. (Circle **house** because it is a noun.) Object of the preposition *corner, yes. (Circle **corner** because it is a noun.) Object of the preposition *Maple Street*, yes. (Circle **Maple Street** because it is a noun.)

Sentence 2: Understood subject pronoun *you*, no. Object of the preposition *toys*, yes. (Circle **toys** because it is a noun.) Object of the preposition *kitchen*, yes. (Circle **kitchen** because it is a noun.) Object of the preposition *lunchtime*, yes. (Circle **lunchtime** because it is a noun.)

Sentence 3: Subject pronoun *we*, no. Object of the preposition *tournament*, yes. (Circle **tournament** because it is a noun.) Object of the preposition *Saturday*, yes. (Circle **Saturday** because it is a noun.) Object of the preposition *Tyler*, yes. (Circle **Tyler** because it is a noun.)

CHAPTER 6 LESSON 1 CONTINUED

Use Sentences 1-3 that you just classified with your students to do an Oral Skill Builder Check. Use the guidelines below.

Oral Skill Builder Check	
1. Noun check. (Say the job and then say the noun. Circle each noun.) **2. Identify the nouns as singular or plural.** (Write **S** or **P** above each noun.) **3. Identify the nouns as common or proper.** (Follow established procedure for oral identification.) **4. Do a vocabulary check.** (Follow established procedure for oral identification.)	**5. Identify the complete subject and the complete predicate.** (Underline the complete subject once and the complete predicate twice.) **6. Identify the simple subject and simple predicate.** (Underline the simple subject once and the simple predicate twice. Bold, or highlight, the lines to distinguish them from the complete subject and complete predicate.)

TEACHING SCRIPT FOR ADDING THE PRONOUN TO THE PARTS OF SPEECH

Do you remember that all words in the English language have been put into one of eight groups called the **Parts of Speech**? We learned that how a word is used in a sentence determines its part of speech. Do you remember the names of the five parts of speech we have already studied? *(noun, verb, adjective, adverb,* and *preposition)*

Today, we have learned about pronouns. A pronoun is also a part of speech; so, we will add it to our list. Now, we know six of the eight parts of speech. What are the six parts of speech? *(noun, verb, adjective, adverb, preposition,* and *pronoun)* *(Chant the six parts of speech that the students have learned several times for immediate reinforcement. Students will learn an Eight-Parts-of-Speech Jingle after the eight parts have been introduced.)*

 VOCABULARY TIME

Assign Chapter 6, Vocabulary Words **#1** on page 8 in the Reference Section for students to define in their Vocabulary notebooks. Tell students they are to use a dictionary or thesaurus to look up the meanings of the vocabulary words. After they write each word and its meaning, students are to write a sentence using the vocabulary word.

Chapter 6, Vocabulary Words #1
(soiled, dirty, calm, turmoil)

(End of lesson.)

CHAPTER 6   LESSON 2

Objectives: Jingles (possessive pronoun), Grammar (Introductory Sentences, possessive pronouns, Practice and Improved Sentences with pronouns), and Vocabulary #2.

JINGLE TIME

Have students turn to the Jingle Section in their books and recite the previously-taught jingles. Then, lead students in reciting the new jingle (*Possessive Pronoun*) below. Practice the new jingle several times until students can recite it smoothly. Emphasize reciting with a rhythm. Students and teacher should be together! (*Do not try to explain the jingles at this time. Just have fun reciting them. Remember, add motions for more fun and laughter.*)

Jingle 12: Possessive Pronoun Jingle	
There are seven possessive pronouns	
That are easy as can be:	
My and our,	(clap 2 times)
His and her,	(clap 2 times)
Its and their and your.	(clap 3 times)

GRAMMAR TIME

Put the introductory sentences from the box below on the board. Use these sentences as you go through each new concept covered in your teaching script. For the greatest benefit, students must participate orally with the teacher. (*You might put the introductory sentences on notebook paper if you are doing one-on-one instruction with your students.*)

Chapter 6, Introductory Sentences for Lesson 2
1. _____   Yesterday, a pretty brown bird sang in our apple tree.
2. _____   Go to our new art museum for a tour before closing time.
3. _____   My cute little brother bounced around the room with a mischievous smile on his face!

TEACHING SCRIPT FOR POSSESSIVE PRONOUNS

The third kind of pronoun we will study is the possessive pronoun. Look at Reference 21 on page 19 in the Reference Section of your book. Follow along as I explain the six things you should know about the possessive pronoun. (*Read and discuss the information about possessive pronouns in the reference box on the next page.*)

CHAPTER 6 LESSON 2 CONTINUED

Reference 21: Possessive Pronouns
1. A possessive pronoun takes the place of a possessive noun.
2. A possessive pronoun's spelling form makes it possessive. These are the most common possessive pronouns: *my, our, his, her, its, their,* and *your.* Use the Possessive Pronoun Jingle to remember the most common possessive pronouns.
3. A possessive pronoun has two jobs: to show ownership or possession and to modify like an adjective.
4. When classifying a possessive pronoun, both jobs will be recognized by labeling it as a possessive pronoun adjective. Use the abbreviation **PPA** (possessive pronoun adjective).
5. Include possessive pronouns when you are asked to identify pronouns, possessives, or adjectives.
6. To find a possessive pronoun, begin with the question *whose.* (*Whose book? His - PPA*)

You will use this information as you classify Sentence 1 with me to find the possessive pronoun. Remember, you use the question *whose* to find the possessive pronoun. Begin.

Question and Answer Flow for Sentence 1: Yesterday, a pretty brown bird sang in our apple tree.

1. What sang in our apple tree? bird - SN
2. What is being said about bird? bird sang - V
3. In - P
4. In what? tree - OP
5. What kind of tree? apple - Adj
6. Whose tree? our - PPA (Possessive Pronoun Adjective)
7. What kind of bird? brown - Adj
8. What kind of bird? pretty - Adj
9. A - A
10. Sang when? yesterday - Adv

11. SN V P1 Check
12. (In our apple tree) - Prepositional phrase
13. Period, statement, declarative sentence
14. Go back to the verb - divide the complete subject from the complete predicate.
15. This sentence has predicate words in the complete subject. Underline the adverb at the beginning of the sentence twice.

Classified Sentence:

```
              Adv    A  Adj   Adj   SN    V    P PPA  Adj   OP
     SN V    Yesterday, a pretty brown bird / sang (in our apple tree). D
     P1
```

Question and Answer Flow for Sentence 2: Go to our new art museum for a tour before closing time.

1. Who go to our new art museum for a tour before closing time? (You) - SP (Understood subject pronoun)
2. What is being said about you? you go - V
3. To - P
4. To what? museum - OP
5. What kind of museum? art - Adj
6. What kind of museum? new - Adj
7. Whose museum? our - PPA
8. For - P
9. For what? tour - OP

10. A - A
11. Before - P
12. Before what? time - OP
13. What kind of time? closing - Adj
14. SN V P1 Check
15. (To our new art museum) - Prepositional phrase
16. (For a tour) - Prepositional phrase
17. (Before closing time) - Prepositional phrase
18. Period, command, imperative sentence
19. Go back to the verb - divide the complete subject from the complete predicate.

Classified Sentence:

```
         (You) SP   V   P PPA Adj  Adj   OP     P  A  OP    P     Adj    OP
          SN V     / Go (to our new art museum) (for a tour) (before closing time). Imp
          P1
```

CHAPTER 6 LESSON 2 CONTINUED

Question and Answer Flow for Sentence 3: My cute little brother bounced around the room with a mischievous smile on his face!

1. Who bounced around the room with a mischievous smile on his face? brother - SN
2. What is being said about brother? brother bounced - V
3. Around - P
4. Around what? room - OP
5. The - A
6. With - P
7. With what? smile - OP
8. What kind of smile? mischievous - Adj
9. A - A
10. On - P
11. On what? face - OP
12. Whose face? his - PPA
13. What kind of brother? little - Adj
14. What kind of brother? cute - Adj
15. Whose brother? my - PPA
16. SN V P1 Check
17. (Around the room) - Prepositional phrase
18. (With a mischievous smile) - Prepositional phrase
19. (On his face) - Prepositional phrase
20. Exclamation point, strong feeling, exclamatory sentence
21. Go back to the verb - divide the complete subject from the complete predicate.

		PPA	Adj	Adj	SN		V		P	A	OP	P	A	Adj		OP	P	PPA	OP
Classified		My	cute	little	brother	**/**	bounced	(around	the	room)	(with	a	mischievous	smile)	(on	his	face)!	**E**
Sentence:	SN V																		
	P1																		

TEACHING SCRIPT FOR A PRACTICE SENTENCE WITH PRONOUNS

Put these labels on the board: **SP V Adv P PPA Adj OP**

Look at the new sentence labels on the board: **SP V Adv P PPA Adj OP**. I will guide you through the process of writing a sentence to practice the new parts that you have learned.

Get out a sheet of notebook paper. On the top line of your notebook paper, write the title *Practice Sentence*. Copy the sentence labels from the board onto your notebook paper. Be sure to leave plenty of writing space between each label. I will guide you through the process you will use whenever you write a Practice Sentence with pronouns.

1. Go to the **SP** label for the subject pronoun. Repeat the Subject Pronoun Jingle to help you think of a pronoun that you want to use as your subject. Write the pronoun you have chosen on the line *under* the **SP** label.

2. Go to the **V** label for the verb. Think of a verb that tells what your subject does. Make sure that your verb makes sense with the subject pronoun. Write the verb you have chosen on the line *under* the **V** label.

3. Go to the **Adv** label for the adverb. Immediately go to the verb in your sentence and ask an adverb question. What are the adverb questions? (*How, When, Where*) Choose one adverb question to ask and write your adverb answer *under* the **Adv** label.

4. Go to the **P** label for the preposition. Think of a preposition word that tells something about your verb. You must be careful to choose a preposition word that makes sense with the noun you will choose for the object of the preposition in your next step. Write the word you have chosen for a preposition *under* the **P** label.

5. Now, go to the **OP** label for the object of the preposition. If you like the noun you thought of while thinking of a preposition, write it down under the **OP** label. If you prefer, think of another noun by asking **what** or **whom** after your preposition. Check to make sure the preposition and object of the preposition make sense together and also make sense with the rest of the sentence. Remember, the object of the preposition will always answer the question **what** or **whom** after the preposition. Write the word you have chosen for the object of the preposition *under* the **OP** label.

6. Go to the **Adj** label for the adjective. Go to the object of the preposition that you just wrote and ask an adjective question to describe the object of the preposition noun. What are the adjective questions? (*What kind, Which one, How many*) Choose one adjective question to ask and write your adjective answer *under* the **Adj** label next to the object of the preposition. Always check to make sure your answers are making sense in the sentence.

7. Go to the **PPA** label for the possessive pronoun adjective that is part of your prepositional phrase. Repeat the Possessive Pronoun Jingle to help you think of a pronoun that you want to use as your possessive pronoun adjective. You will choose one of the possessive pronouns that makes the best sense in your sentence. Write the possessive pronoun you have chosen *under* the **PPA** label.

8. Finally, check your Practice Sentence to make sure it has the necessary parts to be a complete sentence. What are the five parts of a complete sentence? (*subject, verb, complete sense, capital letter, and an end mark*) Does your Practice Sentence have the five parts of a complete sentence? (*Allow time for students to read over their sentences and to make any corrections they need to make.*)

TEACHING SCRIPT FOR AN IMPROVED SENTENCE

Under your Practice Sentence, write the title *Improved Sentence* on another line. To improve your Practice Sentence, you will make two synonym changes, one antonym change, and your choice of a complete word change or another synonym or antonym change.

Since it is harder to find words that can be changed to an antonym, it is usually wise to go through your sentence to find an antonym change first. Look through your sentence again to find words that can be improved with synonyms. Finally, make a decision about whether your last change will be a complete word change, another synonym change, or another antonym change.

I will give you time to write your Improved Sentence. (*Always encourage students to use a thesaurus, synonym-antonym book, or a dictionary to help them develop an interesting and improved writing vocabulary. After students have finished, check and discuss students' Practice and Improved Sentences.*)

  VOCABULARY TIME

Assign Chapter 6, Vocabulary Words **#2** on page 8 in the Reference Section for students to define in their Vocabulary notebooks. Students may use a dictionary or thesaurus to look up the meanings of the vocabulary words and to help them write a sentence using the vocabulary words.

Chapter 6, Vocabulary Words #2
(arrange, prepare, encourage, belittle)

(End of lesson.)

CHAPTER 6   LESSON 3

Objectives: Jingles, Grammar (Practice Sentences), Skill (subject/verb agreement), Practice Exercise, and Activity.

JINGLE TIME

Have students turn to the Jingle Section in their books and recite the previously-taught jingles.

GRAMMAR TIME

First-Year Option: Put the Practice Sentences from the box below on the board or notebook paper. Use these sentences as you practice the concepts that have been taught. For the greatest benefit, students must participate orally with the teacher. **Second-Year Option:** Have students classify the Practice Sentences independently on paper. Check students' sentences with the answers provided below. (*If you have the CDs for Practice Sentences, have students check their sentences with the CDs.*)

Chapter 6, Practice Sentences for Lesson 3
1. _____ Yesterday, sixteen business executives climbed aboard the corporate jet for Chicago.
2. _____ During the afternoon party, she played with her friends in the swimming pool.
3. _____ The young teacher laughed at her excited kids on the playground during a fun game of tag.

TEACHING SCRIPT FOR PRACTICING PATTERN 1 SENTENCES

We will classify three different sentences to practice the grammar concepts in the Question and Answer Flows. We will classify the sentences together. Begin.

Question and Answer Flow for Sentence 1: Yesterday, sixteen business executives climbed aboard the corporate jet for Chicago.
1. Who climbed aboard the corporate jet for Chicago? executives - SN   10. How many executives? sixteen - Adj
2. What is being said about executives? executives climbed - V   11. Climbed when? yesterday - Adv
3. Aboard - P   12. SN V P1 Check
4. Aboard what? jet - OP   13. (Aboard the corporate jet) - Prepositional phrase
5. What kind of jet? corporate - Adj   14. (For Chicago) - Prepositional phrase
6. The - A   15. Period, statement, declarative sentence
7. For - P   16. Go back to the verb - divide the complete subject from the complete predicate.
8. For what? Chicago - OP   17. This sentence has predicate words in the complete subject. Underline the adverb at the beginning of the sentence twice.
9. What kind of executives? business - Adj

Classified Sentence:

	Adv	Adj	Adj	SN	V	P	A	Adj	OP	P	OP
SN V P1	Yesterday,	sixteen	business	executives /	climbed	(aboard	the	corporate	jet)	(for	Chicago). D

© SHURLEY INSTRUCTIONAL MATERIALS, INC.

CHAPTER 6 LESSON 3 CONTINUED

Question and Answer Flow for Sentence 2: During the afternoon party, she played with her friends in the swimming pool.

1. Who played with her friends in the swimming pool? she - SP
2. What is being said about she? she played - V
3. With - P
4. With whom? friends - OP
5. Whose friends? her - PPA
6. In - P
7. In what? pool - OP
8. What kind of pool? swimming - Adj
9. The - A
10. During - P
11. During what? party - OP

12. What kind of party? afternoon - Adj
13. The - A
14. SN V P1 Check
15. (During the afternoon party) - Prepositional phrase
16. (With her friends) - Prepositional phrase
17. (In the swimming pool) - Prepositional phrase
18. Period, statement, declarative sentence
19. Go back to the verb - divide the complete subject from the complete predicate.
20. This sentence has predicate words in the complete subject. Underline the prepositional phrase at the beginning of the sentence twice.

Classified
Sentence:
$\quad$ P $\quad$ A $\quad$ Adj $\quad$ OP $\quad$ SP $\quad$ V $\quad$ P $\quad$ PPA $\quad$ OP $\quad$ P $\quad$ A $\quad$ Adj $\quad$ OP

$\underline{\text{SN V}}$ (During the afternoon party), she / played (with her friends) (in the swimming pool). **D**
P1

Question and Answer Flow for Sentence 3: The young teacher laughed at her excited kids on the playground during a fun game of tag.

1. Who laughed at her excited kids on the playground during a fun game of tag? teacher - SN
2. What is being said about teacher? teacher laughed - V
3. At - P
4. At whom? kids - OP
5. What kind of kids? excited - Adj
6. Whose kids? her - PPA
7. On - P
8. On what? playground - OP
9. The - A
10. During - P
11. During what? game - OP
12. What kind of game? fun - Adj

13. A - A
14. Of - P
15. Of what? tag - OP
16. What kind of teacher? young - Adj
17. The - A
18. SN V P1 Check
19. (At her excited kids) - Prepositional phrase
20. (On the playground) - Prepositional phrase
21. (During a fun game) - Prepositional phrase
22. (Of tag) - Prepositional phrase
23. Period, statement, declarative sentence
24. Go back to the verb - divide the complete subject from the complete predicate.

Classified Sentence:
$\quad$ A $\quad$ Adj $\quad$ SN $\quad$ V $\quad$ P $\quad$ PPA $\quad$ Adj $\quad$ OP $\quad$ P $\quad$ A $\quad$ OP

$\underline{\text{SN V}}$ The young teacher / laughed (at her excited kids) (on the playground)
P1 $\quad$ P $\quad$ A Adj OP $\quad$ P OP
(during a fun game) (of tag). **D**

CHAPTER 6 LESSON 3 CONTINUED

SKILL TIME

TEACHING SCRIPT FOR SUBJECT/VERB AGREEMENT

A sentence must have correct subject-verb agreement. The word **agreement** means to work together; therefore, subject-verb agreement means the special way in which the subject and verb work together to make the sentence correct.

We will use the following sentence to demonstrate the subject-verb agreement concept: **The young robin splashed in the birdbath.** (_Put the demonstration sentence on the board._) Whenever you work with subject-verb agreement, you must remember to work only with the subject and verb. Therefore, you must isolate the subject and verb before you begin. What are the subject and verb in the demonstration sentence? (_robin splashed_)

I will write the subject and verb _robin splashed_ on a different section of the board so we can concentrate on what we need to do for subject-verb agreement. (_Write "robin splashed" on a clean area of the board so you will have room to work without other sentences distracting students._)

You only worry about subject-verb agreement with present tense verbs. When a verb is past tense or ends with -ed, it doesn't matter if the subject is singular or plural; the verb remains the same: past tense.

Example: Robin splashed. Robins splashed.

The example clearly demonstrates that we must change a past tense verb to present tense in order to work with singular and plural forms. How do we change _splashed_ to present tense? (_Take off the **-ed**._) Now that _splash_ is in present tense, we must check whether it agrees with its subject. If the subject is singular, we must use a singular verb form. If the subject is plural, we must use a plural verb form.

Is the subject _robin_ singular or plural? (_Singular_) Since the subject _robin_ is singular, we must choose the singular form of the verb _splash_. How do we make a verb singular? (_Add an **s** or **es** to the plain form to make the word **splashes**._)

Since we have checked to make sure the subject and verb are both singular, we know the subject agrees with the verb. Let's say both singular forms together so we can hear the singular combination as we say them. (_Have students say "robin splashes" several times to hear the subject-verb agreement forms._)

Now, we will form the plural forms of the subject and verb. Since the subject _robin_ is singular, how do we make it plural? (_Add an **s** to make the word **robins**._) We must also change the verb to a plural form. The plural form of a present tense verb is called the <u>plain form</u> because it does not end in _s_ or _es_.

How would we write the plural form of the verb _splashes_? (_splash_) The verb _splash_ is plural because it does not end in _s_ or _es_. Since we have changed both the subject and verb to plural forms, we know the subject agrees with the verb. Let's say both plural forms together so we can hear the plural combinations as we say them. (_Have students say "robins splash" several times to hear the subject-verb agreement forms._)

CHAPTER 6 LESSON 3 CONTINUED

Sometimes, a word does not follow the regular rules because of spelling form. These are called exceptions. One such exception is the word *child*. In the sentence, *Child laughed*, what are the subject and verb? *(child laughed)* What is the present tense of the verb *laughed*? *(laugh)* Is the subject *child* singular or plural? *(singular)* Since the subject is singular, we must use the singular verb form. How do we make the verb *laugh* singular? *(Add an **s** or **es** to the plain form to make the word **laughs**.)*

Since our subject and verb are both singular, we know the subject agrees with the verb. Let's say both singular forms together so we can hear the singular combination as we say them. *(Have students say "child laughs" several times to hear the subject-verb agreement forms.)*

Now, we will form the plural forms of the subject and verb. Since the subject *child* is singular, how do we make it plural? This is one of the exceptions. Some words are made plural by changing the spelling form, not by adding an "s" or "es". To make *child* plural, we must make a spelling change to make the plural word *children*. We must also change the verb to a plural form.

Remember, the plural form of a present tense verb is called the plain form because it does not end in *s* or *es*. What is the plural form of the verb *laughs*? *(laugh)* The verb *laugh* is plural because it does not end in *s* or *es*. Since we have changed both the subject and verb to plural forms, we know the subject agrees with the verb. Let's say both plural forms together so we can hear the plural combination as we say them. *(Have students say "children laugh" several times to hear the subject-verb agreement forms.)*

We will now discuss a set of rules that will also help you make the right subject-verb agreement choice with different kinds of verbs. Look at Reference 22 on page 19 in the Reference Section of your book. Rule 1 says that if you have a singular subject, you must use a singular verb form that ends in *s*: **is, was, has, does, or verbs ending with** *es*. Notice that singular verb forms end in *s*. The "s" stands for singular verb forms. Remember, a singular subject agrees with a singular verb form that ends in *s*.

Reference 22: Subject-Verb Agreement Rules			
Rule 1: A singular subject must use a singular verb form that ends in **s**: *is, was, has, does, or verbs ending with* **es**.			
Rule 2: A plural subject, a compound subject, or the subject **YOU** must use a plural verb form that has **no s** ending: *are, were, do, have, or verbs without* **s** *or* **es** *endings.* (A plural verb form is also called the *plain form*.)			
Examples: For each sentence, do these four things: (1) Write the subject. (2) Write **S** if the subject is singular or **P** if the subject is plural. (3) Write the rule number. (4) Underline the correct verb in the sentence.			
Subject	**S or P**	**Rule**	
book	S	1	1. The **book** (<u>was</u>, were) on the kitchen table.
cake and pie	P	2	2. **Cake** and **pie** (is, <u>are</u>) popular desserts.
You	P	2	3. **You** (cooks, <u>cook</u>) supper tonight.

Rule 2 says that if you have a plural subject, a compound subject, or the subject *YOU*, you must use these verbs: **are, were, have, do, or verbs without** *s* **or** *es* **endings** because these verbs are plural verb forms. Any time the pronoun YOU is the subject of a sentence, you do not have to decide whether it is singular or plural. The subject pronoun YOU always uses a plural verb, and you MUST choose a plural verb form. Remember, a plural subject agrees with a plural verb form that does not end in *s*.

CHAPTER 6 LESSON 3 CONTINUED

Look at the examples under the rules. The directions say you must write the subject, then write **S** if the subject is singular or write **P** if the subject is plural. You must also write the rule number (Rule 1 or 2) from the rule box and then underline the correct verb in the sentence. What is the subject in Sentence 1? (*book*) Is the subject *book* singular or plural? (*singular*)

Since the subject is singular, you will go to the rule box and find the rule that tells you which verb to choose if you have a singular subject. Which rule do we put in the blank? (*Rule 1*) Notice that a number 1 has been written in the blank for Rule 1. Using the list of singular verbs in Rule 1, which verb would we choose to agree with the singular subject *book*? (*was*, the verb with the s or es ending) The verb *was* has been underlined as the correct verb choice.

What is the subject in Sentence 2? (*cake and pie*) Is the subject *cake* and *pie* singular or plural? (*Plural - because it is compound*) Since the subject is plural, you will go to the rule box and find the rule that tells you which verb to choose if you have a plural subject. Which rule do we put in the blank? (*Rule 2*) A number 2 has been written in the blank for Rule 2. Using the list of plural verbs in Rule 2, which verb would we choose to agree with the plural subject *cake* and *pie*? (*are*) The verb *are* has been underlined as the correct verb choice.

What is the subject in Sentence 3? (*You*) Is the subject *you* singular or plural? (*Plural*) Since the subject is plural, you will go to the rule box and find the rule that tells you which verb to choose if you have a plural subject. Which rule do we put in the blank? (*Rule 2*) A number 2 has been written in the blank for Rule 2. Using the list of plural verbs in Rule 2, which verb would we choose to agree with the plural subject *you*? (*cook*) The verb *cook* has been underlined as the correct verb choice.

Choosing verbs to agree with the subjects in the sentences on your test will be easy if you follow the rules you have just learned. Remember, first you must decide if the subject of the sentence is singular or plural. Next, you must look at the verb choices in parentheses in the sentence. Last, you must choose the verb that is listed under the singular or plural rule in the box. (*Discuss the subject **I** as an exception. The subject **I** takes a plural verb form. Examples: I have, I want, I walk, I talk, etc.*)

Teacher's Notes: The singular subject **I** and the verb **be** present a special case of subject-verb agreement. Use the following examples to demonstrate the verb forms used with the pronoun **I**.
Examples: I am. I was. I have. I walk. I talk.

 PRACTICE TIME

Have students turn to page 69 in the Practice Section of their book and find the skills under Chapter 6, Lesson 3, Practice. Go over the directions to make sure they understand what to do. Check and discuss the Practice after students have finished. (*Chapter 6, Lesson 3, Practice key is given on the next page.*)

CHAPTER 6 LESSON 3 CONTINUED

Chapter 6, Lesson 3, Practice: For each sentence, do these four things: (1) Write the subject. (2) Write **S** if the subject is singular or **P** if the subject is plural. (3) Write the rule number. (4) Underline the correct verb in the sentence.

Rule 1: A singular subject must use a singular verb form that ends in **s**: *is, was, has, does, or verbs ending with* **es**.

Rule 2: A plural subject, a compound subject, or the subject **YOU** must use a plural verb form that has **no s** ending: *are, were, do, have, or verbs without* **s** *or* **es** *endings*. (A plural verb form is also called the *plain form*.)

Subject	S or P	Rule	
parents	P	2	1. The **parents** (was, <u>were</u>) talking in the kitchen.
Tim and John	P	2	2. **Tim** and **John** (is, <u>are</u>) good baseball players.
friend	S	1	3. My **friend** (<u>was</u>, were) drawing on the sidewalk with chalk.
driver	S	1	4. The **driver** (stop, <u>stops</u>) for the school bus.
You	P	2	5. **You** (is, <u>are</u>) my best friend.
They	P	2	6. **They** (was, <u>were</u>) swimming in the creek.
He	S	1	7. **He** (<u>rides</u>, ride) without a saddle.
hunters	P	2	8. The **hunters** (was, <u>were</u>) taken by surprise.
John and Carol	P	2	9. **John** and **Carol** (is, <u>are</u>) working in the garden today.

ACTIVITY / ASSIGNMENT TIME

Students will make and then play a Subject-Verb Agreement game. Have students follow the directions below to make the pieces necessary for this game.

1. Make 5 sentence cards. Use 5 index cards and write one sentence on each card. For the first game, use the sample sentences below.

    1. The lions _____ in the jungle.
    2. The children _____ into the house.
    3. We _____ down the street.
    4. They _____ in the parade.
    5. Kim and Billy _____ at the funny clowns.

2. Cut 5 index cards in half. With a black magic marker, write the word "singular" on 5 of the cards and the word "plural" on the other 5 cards.

3. Cut 5 more index cards in half. With a black magic marker, write the word "Rule 1" on 5 of the cards and the word "Rule 2" on the other 5 cards.

4. Make 10 verb cards. With a black magic marker, write each of these verbs on an index card: **walk, walks, run, runs, was, were, laugh, laughs, hunt, hunts.**

<u>To play the game:</u> First, arrange the five sentence cards on a flat surface. Next, place a singular or plural card beside the sentence to indicate a singular or plural subject. Then, place a Rule 1 or Rule 2 card beside the singular/plural card to indicate the rule to follow when choosing a verb. Finally, select the correct verb from the verb cards and place it beside the rule card. Make sure the verb makes sense in the sentence.

Add more verb cards as more sentences are added. For added fun, have other family members, relatives, or friends play the game. Develop extra rules as needed. This game should be timed. Keep a record of everyone's time. Discuss what you like best about this game. What did you learn?

(End of lesson.)

CHAPTER 6   LESSON 4

Objectives: Jingles, Study, Test, Check, and Writing (journal).

 **JINGLE TIME**

Have students turn to the Jingle Section in their books and recite the previously-taught jingles.

 STUDY TIME

Have students study the vocabulary words in their vocabulary notebooks. Remind students that any vocabulary word in their notebooks could be on their test. Also, have students study any of the skills in the Practice Section that they need to review.

 TEST TIME

Have students turn to page 102 in the Test Section of their book and find the Chapter 6 Test section. Go over the directions to make sure they understand what to do. (*Chapter 6 Test key is on the next page.*)

 **CHECK TIME**

After students have finished, check and discuss their test papers. Make sure they understand why their answers are right or wrong. (*For total points, count each required answer as a point.*)

Chapter 6 Test
(Student Page 102)

Exercise 1: Classify each sentence.

```
      (You) SP    V    Adv   P  PPA  Adj  OP     P   PPA  Adj  OP    P    OP
1.  SN V      / Sit quietly (at our kitchen table) (during your snack time) (after school).  Imp
    P1
```

```
                P    A    OP  PPA Adj SN   V   P  A   Adj    Adj  OP   P  PPA  Adj   OP
2.  SN V      (During the day), my pet frog / sits (on a large black rock) (in our little pond).  D
    P1
```

```
              SP    V    P    A   OP   P   A   Adj    OP    P  PPA  Adj   OP
3.  SN V      We / slept (through the end) (of the midnight movie) (at her slumber party).  D
    P1
```

Exercise 2: Use Sentence 3 to underline the complete subject once and the complete predicate twice and to complete the table below.

List the Noun Used	List the Noun Job	Singular or Plural	Common or Proper	Simple Subject	Simple Predicate
1. **end**	2. **OP**	3. **S**	4. **C**	5. **We**	6. **slept**
7. **movie**	8. **OP**	9. **S**	10. **C**		
11. **party**	12. **OP**	13. **S**	14. **C**		

Exercise 3: Name the six parts of speech that you have studied. (*You may use abbreviations.*) **(The order may vary.)**

1. **noun**　　2. **verb**　　3. **adjective**　　4. **adverb**　　5. **preposition**　　6. **pronoun**

Exercise 4: Identify each pair of words as synonyms or antonyms by putting parentheses ( ) around *syn* or *ant*.

1. vivid, dingy	syn **(ant)**	5. arrange, prepare	**(syn)** ant	9. pursue, follow	**(syn)** ant
2. calm, turmoil	syn **(ant)**	6. reply, answer	**(syn)** ant	10. proceed, cease	syn **(ant)**
3. idle, busy	syn **(ant)**	7. tales, stories	**(syn)** ant	11. accept, reject	syn **(ant)**
4. soiled, dirty	**(syn)** ant	8. belittle, encourage	syn **(ant)**	12. delight, displease	syn **(ant)**

Exercise 5: For each sentence, write the subject, then write **S** if the subject is singular or **P** if the subject is plural, write the rule number, and underline the correct verb in the sentence.

Rule 1: A singular subject must use a singular verb form that ends in **s**: *is, was, has, does, or verbs ending with **s** or **es**.*
Rule 2: A plural subject, a compound subject, or the subject **YOU** must use a plural verb form that has **no s** ending:
*are, were, do, have, or verbs without **s** or **es** endings.* (A plural verb form is also called the *plain form*.)

Subject	S or P	Rule
sister	S	1
Jerry and Jeff	P	2
roads	P	2
bush	S	1
teachers	P	2
wrist	S	1
horses	P	2
houses	P	2
garden	S	1
pilot	S	1

1. My **sister** (<u>was</u>, were) singing in the school choir.
2. **Jerry** and **Jeff** (is, <u>are</u>) building a house.
3. The **roads** (has, <u>have</u>) many twists and turns.
4. That **bush** (need, <u>needs</u>) pruning today.
5. Some **teachers** (is, <u>are</u>) very strict.
6. My **wrist** (<u>was</u>, were) broken in the fall.
7. **Horses** (is, <u>are</u>) my favorite animals.
8. (<u>Do</u>, Does) those **houses** have numbers on them?
9. The **garden** (appear, <u>appears</u>) to be very plentiful.
10. The **pilot** (<u>was</u>, were) eager to land the plane.

Exercise 6: On notebook paper, write as many prepositions as you can.

Exercise 7: In your journal, write a paragraph summarizing what you have learned this week.

CHAPTER 6 LESSON 4 CONTINUED

TEACHER INSTRUCTIONS

Use the Question and Answer Flows below for the sentences on the Chapter 6 Test.

Question and Answer Flow for Sentence 1: Sit quietly at our kitchen table during your snack time after school.

1. Who sit quietly at our kitchen table during your snack time after school? (You) - SP (Understood subject pronoun)
2. What is being said about you? you sit - V
3. Sit how? quietly - Adv
4. At - P
5. At what? table - OP
6. What kind of table? kitchen - Adj
7. Whose table? our - PPA
8. During - P
9. During what? time - OP
10. What kind of time? snack - Adj
11. Whose time? your - PPA
12. After - P
13. After what? school - OP
14. SN V P1 Check
15. (At our kitchen table) - Prepositional phrase
16. (During your snack time) - Prepositional phrase
17. (After school) - Prepositional phrase
18. Period, command, imperative sentence
19. Go back to the verb - divide the complete subject from the complete predicate.

Classified Sentence:	(You) SP	V	Adv	P	PPA	Adj	OP	P	PPA	Adj	OP	P	OP
	SN V ___ P1	/ Sit	quietly	(at	our	kitchen	table)	(during	your	snack	time)	(after	school). Imp

---

Question and Answer Flow for Sentence 2: During the day, my pet frog sits on a large black rock in our little pond.

1. What sits on a large black rock in our little pond? frog - SN
2. What is being said about frog? frog sits - V
3. On - P
4. On what? rock - OP
5. What kind of rock? black - Adj
6. What kind of rock? large - Adj
7. A - A
8. In - P
9. In what? pond - OP
10. What kind of pond? little - Adj
11. Whose pond? our - PPA
12. What kind of frog? pet - Adj
13. Whose frog? my - PPA
14. During - P
15. During what? day - OP
16. The - A
17. SN V P1 Check
18. (During the day) - Prepositional phrase
19. (On a large black rock) - Prepositional phrase
20. (In our little pond) - Prepositional phrase
21. Period, statement, declarative sentence
22. Go back to the verb - divide the complete subject from the complete predicate.
23. This sentence has predicate words in the complete subject. Underline the prepositional phrase at the beginning of the sentence twice.

Classified Sentence:		P	A	OP	PPA	Adj	SN	V	P	A	Adj	Adj	OP	P	PPA	Adj	OP
	SN V ___ P1	(During	the	day),	my	pet	frog	/ sits	(on	a	large	black	rock)	(in	our	little	pond). D

Question and Answer Flow for Sentence 3: We slept through the end of the midnight movie at her slumber party.

1. Who slept through the end of the midnight movie at her slumber party? we - SP
2. What is being said about we? we slept - V
3. Through - P
4. Through what? end - OP
5. The - A
6. Of - P
7. Of what? movie - OP
8. What kind of movie? midnight - Adj
9. The - A
10. At - P
11. At what? party - OP
12. What kind of party? slumber - Adj
13. Whose party? her - PPA
14. SN V P1 Check
15. (Through the end) - Prepositional phrase
16. (Of the midnight movie) - Prepositional phrase
17. (At her slumber party) - Prepositional phrase
18. Period, statement, declarative sentence
19. Go back to the verb - divide the complete subject from the complete predicate.

Classified Sentence:	SP	V	P	A	OP	P	A	Adj	OP	P	PPA	Adj	OP
	SN V ___ P1	We	/ slept	(through	the	end)	(of	the	midnight	movie)	(at	her	slumber	party). D

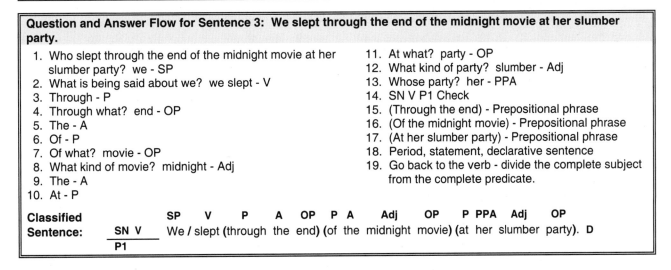

CHAPTER 6   LESSON 5

Objectives: Writing (changing plural categories to singular points) and Writing Assignments #5 and #6.

 WRITING TIME

TEACHING SCRIPT FOR CHANGING PLURAL CATEGORIES TO SINGULAR POINTS

When you have a topic such as *My favorite books*, you will usually name your favorite books by categories, or groups, like mysteries, spy novels, and autobiographies. When this happens, you need to know how to change plural points to singular points. I will demonstrate how this is done in a paragraph. Look at Reference 23 on page 20 as I read the paragraph to you. Then, I will show you how to change each of the three points in the paragraph. *(Read the paragraph to your students from beginning to end. Then, go through the teaching script given for each sentence in the paragraph.)*

Reference 23: Singular and Plural Points
Three-Point Expository Paragraph in First Person **Topic:** My favorite books **3-points:** 1. mysteries   2. spy novels   3. autobiographies   I have three favorite books. These books are mysteries, spy novels, and autobiographies. My first favorite book is a mystery. I love mysteries because they are suspenseful and fun to read. My second favorite book is a spy novel. I like spy novels because they are exciting and adventurous. My third favorite book is an autobiography. I enjoy reading autobiographies because I like reading about famous people. My three favorite books are entertaining, and I enjoy reading them as much as I can.

Notice that the topic is written first because it is the subject of the paragraph. Having the topic written first will help us focus on what the paragraph is about. Next, the three points that we will discuss are listed. Again, having the three points written down before we start will help us focus on what we will say in the paragraph.

We are now ready to begin our paragraph because we are clear about our topic and about the points we will cover as we write. We start with a topic sentence because it tells the reader what the paragraph is about: *I have three favorite books.* Knowing what the paragraph is about helps the reader focus on the main points as the reader progresses through the paragraph.

Our next sentence is the three-point sentence: *These books are mysteries, spy novels, and autobiographies.* The three-point sentence lists the three main points that will be discussed in the paragraph, so in this paragraph we know the three main points are *mysteries, spy novels*, and *autobiographies*. Now, I want you to notice that each of the three points listed is plural (*mysteries, spy novels*, and *autobiographies*). These main points are actually categories, or groups, of books, and that is why they are listed in plural form.

Level 4 Homeschool Teacher's Manual

CHAPTER 6 LESSON 5 CONTINUED

Let's look at the sentence written for the first point. The sentence for the first point starts out like this: *My first favorite book is*. Since this phrase is singular, we could change the plural listing to a singular listing to agree with the type of sentence that is written. To do this, we will change *mysteries* from plural to singular: *My first favorite book is a mystery*. Usually, an article adjective is needed to make the sentence sound better.

Just remember: If your three points are plural, you usually make them singular as you name them for your first point, second point, and third point. Use an article adjective with your singular form to make it sound better. Notice that the second and third main points follow this same format. Look at the forms as I read them to you. (**2nd point:** *My second favorite book is a spy novel.* **3rd point:** *My third favorite book is an autobiography.*)

After each main point, there is a supporting sentence. Supporting sentences make each point clearer by telling extra information about each main point. Remember, we have stated in the main points that mysteries, spy novels and autobiographies are three of our favorite books. Each supporting sentence should state some kind of information that proves each of the main points. (**1st Supporting sentence:** *I love **mysteries** because they are suspenseful and fun to read.* **2nd Supporting sentence:** *I like spy novels because they are exciting and adventurous.* **3rd Supporting sentence:** *I enjoy reading about **autobiographies** because I like reading about famous people.*) Notice that we also used the plural forms in the supporting sentences.

Our last sentence is a concluding sentence. It summarizes our three points by restating some of the words in the topic sentence and by adding an extra thought that finalizes the paragraph. (**Concluding sentence:** *My three favorite books are entertaining, and I enjoy reading them as much as I can.*)

Now, I will read the same paragraph to you in third person. Notice the change in pronouns. Listen carefully. (*Read the second part of Reference 23. Then, discuss the differences in the first person and third person paragraphs.*) (*Remind students that third person is the point of view in writing that uses the personal pronouns **he, his, she, it, its, they, them, their, theirs, him, hers, and her**. Usually, in third person writing, students <u>would not use any</u> of the first person pronouns: **I, me, my, mine, or we, us, our, and ours**).*

Reference 23: Singular and Plural Points (continued)
Three-Point Expository Paragraph in Third Person
Topic: Emily's favorite books **3-points:** 1. mysteries 2. spy novels 3. autobiographies   Emily has three favorite books. These books are mysteries, spy novels, and autobiographies. Emily's first favorite book is a mystery. She loves mysteries because they are suspenseful and fun to read. Emily's second favorite book is a spy novel. She likes spy novels because they are exciting and adventurous. Emily's third favorite book is an autobiography. She enjoys reading autobiographies because she likes reading about famous people. Emily's three favorite books are entertaining, and she enjoys reading them as much as she can.

As we study the two paragraphs, make sure you know that third person pronouns may be used in first person writing without changing the first person point of view. (Example: <u>I</u> like <u>her</u> work.) Remember, if even **one first person pronoun** is used in a sentence or paragraph, it is identified as first person even though third person pronouns are also used. On the other hand, only third person pronouns should be used in third person writing. No first person pronoun (including **my**) should be used in most third person writing. First person pronouns are very powerful and will change any writing to a first person point of view.

CHAPTER 6 LESSON 5 CONTINUED

TEACHER INSTRUCTIONS FOR WRITING ASSIGNMENTS #5 AND #6

Give Writing Assignment #5 and Writing Assignment #6 from the box below. Remind students to follow the Writing Guidelines from Chapter 3 as they prepare their writings.

For Writing Assignment #5, students are to write a three-point paragraph in first person. Have students underline all first person pronouns in their paragraph. Remind students that they can use third person pronouns in first person writing.

For Writing Assignment #6, students are to write a three-point paragraph in third person. Have students underline all third person pronouns in their second paragraph. Remind students that they normally would not use any first person pronouns (including *my*) in third person writing.

Writing Assignment Box

Writing Assignment #5: Three-Point Expository Paragraph (First Person)
(Remind students that first person pronouns are *I, we, me, us, my, our, mine, and ours.*)

Writing topics: My Favorite Books or **My Favorite Animals** or **People I Would Like to Meet**

Writing Assignment #6: Three-Point Expository Paragraph (Third Person)
(Remind students that third person pronouns are *he, his, him, she, her, hers, it, its, they, their, theirs, and them.*)

Writing topics: (Person's Name) Favorite Books or **(Person's Name) Favorite Animals** or
People That (Person's Name) Would Like to Meet

TEACHING SCRIPT FOR USING THE WRITING PROCESS FOR THIS WRITING ASSIGNMENT

As you begin this writing assignment, you will again go through the writing process. First, you will think about your topic and gather any information you might need in order to do the writing. Second, you will write a rough draft. Remember, it is called a rough draft because it will be revised and edited. You do not have to worry about mistakes as you write your rough draft. After you write the first draft, you will make revisions, using the Revision Checklist in Reference 5. After you revise your writing, you will edit, using the Beginning Editing Checklist in Reference 5. Finally, after you are satisfied with your revising and editing, you will write a final paper, using the Final Paper Checklist in Reference 5. You will then give the finished writing assignment to me.

TEACHER INSTRUCTIONS FOR CHECKING WRITING ASSIGNMENTS #5 AND #6

Read, check, and discuss Writing Assignments #5 and #6 after students have finished their final papers. Use the editing checklist (*Reference 5 on teacher's page 10*) as you check and discuss students' papers. Make sure students are using the editing checklist correctly. In the beginning, you must also check students' papers carefully for <u>form</u> mistakes. This will ensure that students are learning the three-point format correctly.

(End of lesson.)

CHAPTER 7   LESSON 1

Objectives: Jingles, Grammar (Introductory Sentences, possessive noun, Noun Check with possessive nouns, Oral Skill Builder Check), Practice Exercise, and Vocabulary #1.

JINGLE TIME

Have students turn to the Jingle Section in their books and recite the previously-taught jingles.

GRAMMAR TIME

Put the introductory sentences from the box below on the board. Use these sentences as you go through each new concept covered in your teaching script. For the greatest benefit, students must participate orally with the teacher. (*You might put the introductory sentences on notebook paper if you are doing one-on-one instruction with your students.*)

Chapter 7, Introductory Sentences for Lesson 1
1. _____ During our grandmother's visit, we sang happily with Mother's radio on the porch. 2. _____ His father drove to the doctor's office immediately after the phone call on Wednesday! 3. _____ Sleep well tonight with the new night-light in your bedroom.

TEACHING SCRIPT FOR POSSESSIVE NOUN

Today, we will learn about a very special noun: the possessive noun. Since there is not a jingle for a possessive noun, information about the possessive noun is listed in the Reference Section on page 20. Look at Reference 24. Follow along as I explain the six things you should know about the possessive noun. (*Read and discuss the information about possessive nouns in the reference box below.*)

Reference 24: Possessive Nouns
1. A possessive noun is the name of a person, place, or thing that owns something.
2. A possessive noun will always have an apostrophe after it. It will be either an *apostrophe <u>s</u> ('s)* or an *<u>s</u> apostrophe (s')*. The apostrophe makes a noun show ownership. (*Mitchell's scooter*)
3. A possessive noun has two jobs: to show ownership or possession and to modify like an adjective.
4. When classifying a possessive noun, both jobs will be recognized by labeling it as a possessive noun adjective. Use the abbreviation **PNA** (possessive noun adjective).
5. Include possessive nouns when you are asked to identify possessive nouns or adjectives. Do not include possessive nouns when you are asked to identify regular nouns.
6. To find a possessive noun, begin with the question *whose*. (*Whose scooter? Mitchell's - PNA*)

CHAPTER 7 LESSON 1 CONTINUED

Since you use the *whose* question to find a possessive noun and a possessive pronoun, you must remember one important fact about each one in order to tell them apart. Remember, all possessive nouns have an apostrophe, and the seven possessive pronouns are in the Possessive Pronoun Jingle you have learned. *(You may want your students to recite the Possessive Pronoun Jingle again to reinforce what you have just said.)* You will use this information as you classify Sentences 1-3 with me. Begin.

Question and Answer Flow for Sentence 1: During our grandmother's visit, we sang happily with Mother's radio on the porch.

1. Who sang happily with Mother's radio on the porch?
   we - SP
2. What is being said about we? we sang - V
3. Sang how? happily - Adv
4. With - P
5. With what? radio - OP
6. Whose radio? Mother's - PNA (Possessive Noun Adjective)
7. On - P
8. On what? porch - OP
9. The - A
10. During - P
11. During what? visit - OP
12. Whose visit? grandmother's - PNA

13. Whose grandmother?
    our - PPA (Possessive pronoun adjective)
14. SN V P1 Check
15. (During our grandmother's visit) - Prepositional phrase
16. (With Mother's radio) - Prepositional phrase
17. (On the porch) - Prepositional phrase
18. Period, statement, declarative sentence
19. Go back to the verb - divide the complete subject from the complete predicate.
20. This sentence has predicate words in the complete subject. Underline the prepositional phrase at the beginning of the sentence twice.

Classified
Sentence:
SN V
P1

P PPA PNA OP SP V Adv P PNA OP P A OP
(During our grandmother's visit), we / sang happily (with Mother's radio) (on the porch). **D**

Question and Answer Flow for Sentence 2: His father drove to the doctor's office immediately after the phone call on Wednesday!

1. Who drove to the doctor's office immediately after the phone call on Wednesday? father - SN
2. What is being said about father? father drove - V
3. To - P
4. To what? office - OP
5. Whose office? doctor's - PNA
6. The - A
7. Drove when? immediately - Adv
8. After - P
9. After what? call - OP
10. What kind of call? phone - Adj

11. The - A
12. On - P
13. On what? Wednesday - OP
14. Whose father? his - PPA
15. SN V P1 Check
16. (To the doctor's office) - Prepositional phrase
17. (After the phone call) - Prepositional phrase
18. (On Wednesday) - Prepositional phrase
19. Exclamation point, strong feeling, exclamatory sentence
20. Go back to the verb - divide the complete subject from the complete predicate.

Classified
Sentence:
SN V
P1

PPA SN V P A PNA OP Adv P A Adj OP P OP
His father / drove (to the doctor's office) immediately (after the phone call) (on Wednesday)! **E**

CHAPTER 7 LESSON 1 CONTINUED

Question and Answer Flow for Sentence 3: Sleep well tonight with the new night-light in your bedroom.

1. Who sleep well tonight with the new night-light in your bedroom? (You) - SP (Understood subject pronoun)
2. What is being said about you? you sleep - V
3. Sleep how? well - Adv
4. Sleep when? tonight - Adv
5. With - P
6. With what? night-light - OP
7. What kind of night-light? new - Adj
8. The - A
9. In - P

10. In what? bedroom - OP
11. Whose bedroom? your - PPA
12. SN V P1 Check
13. (With the new night-light) - Prepositional phrase
14. (In your bedroom) - Prepositional phrase
15. Period, command, imperative sentence
16. Go back to the verb - divide the complete subject from the complete predicate.

Classified Sentence:

(You) SP	V	Adv	Adv	P	A	Adj	OP	P	PPA	OP	
SN V	/ Sleep well tonight (with the new night-light) (in your bedroom). **Imp**										
P1											

TEACHING SCRIPT FOR A NOUN CHECK WHEN POSSESSIVE NOUNS ARE IN THE SENTENCES

We will only do a Noun Check today to show you how to deal with possessive nouns when you are identifying nouns. A possessive noun's part of speech is an adjective. Remember, a Noun Check is a check for nouns. If there is a possessive noun, we will not classify it as a noun because we are looking only for noun jobs that give us regular nouns, not special nouns that function as possessives and adjectives. Let's start with number one and go through the Noun Check for Sentences 1-3, looking for nouns. (*Recite the information below with your students.*)

Sentence 1: Subject pronoun *we*, no. Object of the preposition *visit, yes.* (*Circle **visit** because it is a noun.*) Object of the preposition *radio, yes.* (*Circle **radio** because it is a noun.*) Object of the preposition *porch, yes.* (*Circle **porch** because it is a noun.*)

Sentence 2: Subject noun, *father, yes.* (*Circle **father** because it is a noun.*) Object of the preposition *office, yes.* (*Circle **office** because it is a noun.*) Object of the preposition *call, yes.* (*Circle **call** because it is a noun.*) Object of the preposition *Wednesday, yes.* (*Circle **Wednesday** because it is a noun.*)

Sentence 3: Understood subject pronoun *you*, no. Object of the preposition *night-light, yes.* (*Circle **night-light** because it is a noun.*) Object of the preposition *bedroom, yes.* (*Circle **bedroom** because it is a noun.*)

Use Sentences 1-3 that you just classified with your students to do an Oral Skill Builder Check. Use the guidelines below.

Oral Skill Builder Check

1. **Noun check.**
   (Say the job and then say the noun. Circle each noun.)
2. **Identify the nouns as singular or plural.**
   (Write **S** or **P** above each noun.)
3. **Identify the nouns as common or proper.**
   (Follow established procedure for oral identification.)
4. **Do a vocabulary check.**
   (Follow established procedure for oral identification.)

5. **Identify the complete subject and the complete predicate.** (Underline the complete subject once and the complete predicate twice.)
6. **Identify the simple subject and simple predicate.**
   (Underline the simple subject once and the simple predicate twice. Bold, or highlight, the lines to distinguish them from the complete subject and complete predicate.)

CHAPTER 7 LESSON 1 CONTINUED

PRACTICE TIME

Have students turn to page 70 in the Practice Section of their book and find the skills under Chapter 7, Lesson 1, Practice. Go over the directions to make sure they understand what to do. Check and discuss the Practice after students have finished. (*Chapter 7, Lesson 1, Practice key is given below.*)

Chapter 7, Lesson 1, Practice: For each sentence, do these four things: (1) Write the subject. (2) Write **S** if the subject is singular or **P** if the subject is plural. (3) Write the rule number. (4) Underline the correct verb in the sentence.

Rule 1: A singular subject must use a singular verb form that ends in **s**: *is, was, has, does, or verbs ending with* **es**.

Rule 2: A plural subject, a compound subject, or the subject **YOU** must use a plural verb form that has **no s** ending: *are, were, do, have, or verbs without* **s** *or* **es** *endings.* (A plural verb form is also called the *plain form*.)

Subject	S or P	Rule		
ducks	P	2	1.	The **ducks** (has, <u>have</u>) webbed feet.
Buffey	S	1	2.	**Buffey** (<u>barks</u>, bark) all night.
cars	P	2	3.	The **cars** in the parking lot (is, <u>are</u>) locked.
flowers	P	2	4.	The **flowers** (grows, <u>grow</u>) fast during the summer.
You	P	2	5.	**You** (is, <u>are</u>) doing a good job.
They	P	2	6.	**They** (was, <u>were</u>) looking for a new pet.
She	S	1	7.	**She** (<u>goes</u>, go) home every weekend.
girls	P	2	8.	The **girls** (was, <u>were</u>) working on a science project.
Bill and Joe	P	2	9.	**Bill** and **Joe** (is, <u>are</u>) good friends.
keys	P	2	10.	(Was, <u>Were</u>) your **keys** in your pocket?
sled	S	1	11.	Our **sled** (<u>was</u>, were) sliding down the snowy hill.
players	P	2	12.	(<u>Do</u>, Does) the football **players** run every day?

VOCABULARY TIME

Assign Chapter 7, Vocabulary Words **#1** on page 8 in the Reference Section for students to define in their Vocabulary notebooks. Tell students they are to use a dictionary or thesaurus to look up the meanings of the vocabulary words. After they write each word and its meaning, students are to write a sentence using the vocabulary word.

Chapter 7, Vocabulary Words #1
(rival, competitor, fatigued, fresh)

(End of lesson.)

Level 4 Homeschool Teacher's Manual

CHAPTER 7 LESSON 2

Objectives: Jingles, Grammar (Practice Sentences, Practice and Improved Sentences), Practice Exercise, and Vocabulary #2.

JINGLE TIME

Have students turn to the Jingle Section in their books and recite the previously-taught jingles.

GRAMMAR TIME

First-Year Option: Put the Practice Sentences from the box below on the board or on notebook paper. Use these sentences as you practice the concepts that have been taught. For the greatest benefit, students must participate orally with the teacher. **Second-Year Option:** Have students classify the Practice Sentences independently on notebook paper. Check students' sentences with the answers provided below. *(If you have the CDs for Practice Sentences, have students check their sentences with the CDs.)*

Chapter 7, Practice Sentences for Lesson 2
1. _____ The young boy's quarter rolled under the parked car.
2. _____ My bottle of cold water disappeared from the bleachers during the third race.
3. _____ Molly's three little puppies ran excitedly toward their mother.

TEACHING SCRIPT FOR PRACTICING PRONOUNS AND POSSESSIVE NOUNS

We will classify three different sentences to practice the new skills in the Question and Answer Flows. We will classify the sentences together. Begin. *(You might have your students write the labels above the sentences at this time.)*

Question and Answer Flow for Sentence 1: The young boy's quarter rolled under the parked car.

1. What rolled under the parked car? quarter - SN
2. What is being said about quarter? quarter rolled - V
3. Under - P
4. Under what? car - OP
5. What kind of car? parked - Adj
6. The - A
7. Whose quarter? boy's - PNA
8. What kind of boy? young - Adj
9. The - A
10. SN V P1 Check
11. (Under the parked car) - Prepositional phrase
12. Period, statement, declarative sentence
13. Go back to the verb - divide the complete subject from the complete predicate.

Classified Sentence:

$$\frac{\text{SN V}}{\text{P1}}$$ A Adj PNA SN V P A Adj OP
The young boy's quarter / rolled (under the parked car). **D**

CHAPTER 7 LESSON 2 CONTINUED

Question and Answer Flow for Sentence 2: My bottle of cold water disappeared from the bleachers during the third race.

1. What disappeared from the bleachers during the third race? bottle - SN
2. What is being said about bottle? bottle disappeared - V
3. From - P
4. From what? bleachers - OP
5. The - A
6. During - P
7. During what? race - OP
8. Which race? third - Adj
9. The - A
10. Of - P
11. Of what? water - OP
12. What kind of water? cold - Adj
13. Whose bottle? my - PPA
14. SN V P1 Check
15. (Of cold water) - Prepositional phrase
16. (From the bleachers) - Prepositional phrase
17. (During the third race) - Prepositional phrase
18. Period, statement, declarative sentence
19. Go back to the verb - divide the complete subject from the complete predicate.

Classified Sentence:		PPA SN P Adj OP V P A OP P A Adj OP
	SN V P1	My bottle (of cold water) / disappeared (from the bleachers) (during the third race). D

Question and Answer Flow for Sentence 3: Molly's three little puppies ran excitedly toward their mother.

1. What ran excitedly toward their mother? puppies - SN
2. What is being said about puppies? puppies ran - V
3. Ran how? excitedly - Adv
4. Toward - P
5. Toward whom? mother - OP
6. Whose mother? their - PPA
7. What kind of puppies? little - Adj
8. How many puppies? three - Adj
9. Whose puppies? Molly's - PNA
10. SN V P1 Check
11. (Toward their mother) - Prepositional phrase
12. Period, statement, declarative sentence
13. Go back to the verb - divide the complete subject from the complete predicate.

Classified Sentence:	PNA Adj Adj SN V Adv P PPA OP
SN V P1	Molly's three little puppies / ran excitedly (toward their mother). D

TEACHING SCRIPT FOR THE PRACTICE SENTENCE

Put these labels on the board: **SP V Adv P PPA PNA Adj OP**

Look at the new sentence labels on the board: **SP V Adv P PPA PNA Adj OP**. I will guide you again through the process of writing a sentence to practice the different parts that you have learned.

Get out a sheet of notebook paper. On the top line of your notebook paper, write the title *Practice Sentence*. Copy the sentence labels from the board onto your notebook paper. Be sure to leave plenty of writing space between each label. I will guide you through the process you will use whenever you write a Practice Sentence with possessive pronouns and possessive nouns.

CHAPTER 7 LESSON 2 CONTINUED

1. Go to the **SP** label for the subject pronoun. Repeat the Subject Pronoun Jingle to help you think of a pronoun that you want to use as your subject. Write the pronoun you have chosen on the line *under* the **SP** label.

2. Go to the **V** label for the verb. Think of a verb that tells what your subject does. Make sure that your verb makes sense with the subject pronoun. Write the verb you have chosen on the line *under* the **V** label.

3. Go to the **Adv** label for the adverb. Immediately go to the verb in your sentence and ask an adverb question. What are the adverb questions? (*How, When, Where*) Choose one adverb question to ask and write your adverb answer *under* the **Adv** label.

4. Go to the **P** label for the preposition. Think of a preposition word that tells something about your verb. You must be careful to choose a preposition word that makes sense with the noun you will choose for the object of the preposition in your next step. Write the word you have chosen for a preposition *under* the **P** label.

5. Go to the **OP** label for the object of the preposition. If you like the noun you thought of while thinking of a preposition, write it down under the **OP** label. If you prefer, think of another noun by asking **what** or **whom** after your preposition. Check to make sure the preposition and object of the preposition make sense together and also make sense with the rest of the sentence. Remember, the object of the preposition will always answer the question **what** or **whom** after the preposition. Write the word you have chosen for the object of the preposition *under* the **OP** label.

6. Go to the **Adj** label for the adjective. Go to the object of the preposition that you just wrote and ask an adjective question to describe the object of the preposition noun. What are the adjective questions? (*What kind, Which one, How many*) Choose one adjective question to ask and write your adjective answer *under* the **Adj** label next to the object of the preposition. Always check to make sure your answers are making sense in the sentence.

7. Go to the **PNA** label for the possessive noun adjective that is part of your prepositional phrase. Think of a possessive noun that answers "whose" when you refer to the object of the preposition noun. Make sure the possessive noun makes sense in your sentence. Also, make sure you write the apostrophe correctly as you write the possessive noun you have chosen *under* the **PPA** label.

8. Go to the **PPA** label for the possessive pronoun adjective that is part of your prepositional phrase. Repeat the Possessive Pronoun Jingle to help you think of a pronoun that you want to use as your possessive pronoun adjective. Now, you will choose one of the possessive pronouns that makes the best sense in your sentence. Write the possessive pronoun you have chosen *under* the **PPA** label.

9. Finally, check your Practice Sentence to make sure it has the necessary parts to be a complete sentence. What are the five parts of a complete sentence? (*subject, verb, complete sense, capital letter, and an end mark*) Does your Practice Sentence have the five parts of a complete sentence? (*Allow time for students to read over their sentences and to make any corrections they need to make.*)

CHAPTER 7 LESSON 2 CONTINUED

TEACHING SCRIPT FOR THE IMPROVED SENTENCE

Under your Practice Sentence, write the title *Improved Sentence* on another line. To improve your Practice Sentence, you will make two synonym changes, one antonym change, and your choice of a complete word change or another synonym or antonym change.

Since it is harder to find words that can be changed to an antonym, it is usually wise to go through your sentence to find an antonym change first. Then, look through your sentence again to find words that can be improved with synonyms. Finally, make a decision about whether your last change will be a complete word change, another synonym change, or another antonym change.

I will give you time to write your Improved Sentence. *(Always encourage students to use a thesaurus, synonym-antonym book, or a dictionary to help them develop an interesting and improved writing vocabulary. After students have finished, check and discuss students' Practice and Improved Sentences.)*

 PRACTICE TIME

Have students write the three sentences that they classified at the beginning of the lesson on a sheet of paper. (See page 113) Have them tape-record the Question and Answer Flows for all three sentences. Students should write labels above the sentences as they classify them. They especially need the second practice if this is their first year in the program. *(After the students have finished, check the tape and sentence labels. Make sure students understand any mistakes they have made.)*

 VOCABULARY TIME

Assign Chapter 7, Vocabulary Words **#2** on page 8 in the Reference Section for students to define in their Vocabulary notebooks. Tell students they are to use a dictionary or thesaurus to look up the meanings of the vocabulary words. After they write each word and its meaning, students are to write a sentence using the vocabulary word.

Chapter 7, Vocabulary Words #2
(uplift, depress, pail, bucket)

(End of lesson.)

CHAPTER 7   LESSON 3
Objectives: Jingle (Object Pronoun), Grammar (Practice Sentences, object pronoun), Test, Activity, and Writing (journal).

 **JINGLE TIME**

Have students turn to the Jingle Section in their books and recite the previously-taught jingles. Then, lead students in reciting the new jingle (*Object Pronoun*) below. Practice the new jingle several times until students can recite it smoothly. Emphasize reciting with a rhythm. Students and teacher should be together! (*Do not try to explain the jingles at this time. Just have fun reciting them. Remember, add motions for more fun and laughter.*)

Teacher's Notes: Again, do not spend a large amount of time practicing the new jingle. Students learn the jingles best by spending a small amount of time consistently, **every** day.

Jingle 13: Object Pronoun Jingle	
There are seven object pronouns	
That are easy as can be:	
Me and us,	(clap 2 times)
Him and her,	(clap 2 times)
It and them and you.	(clap 3 times)

 GRAMMAR TIME

First-Year Option: Put the Practice Sentences from the box below on the board or on notebook paper. Use these sentences as you practice the concepts that have been taught. For the greatest benefit, students must participate orally with the teacher. **Second-Year Option:** Have students classify the Practice Sentences independently on notebook paper. Check students' sentences with the answers provided below. (*If you have the CDs for Practice Sentences, have students check their sentences with the CDs.*)

Chapter 7, Practice Sentences for Lesson 3
1. _____ The beautiful fish in the aquarium swam gracefully toward us.
2. _____ He talked to me on the telephone for an hour after school.
3. _____ Listen closely to the visiting professor's lecture on nuclear science.

TEACHING SCRIPT FOR PRACTICING PATTERN 1 SENTENCES

We will classify three different sentences to practice the new concepts in the Question and Answer Flows. We will classify the sentences together. Begin. (*You might have your students write the labels above the sentences at this time.*)

CHAPTER 7 LESSON 3 CONTINUED

Teacher's Notes: Make sure students say the Question and Answer Flow orally for each sentence. Be sure to lead them so they will say the Question and Answer Flows correctly.

Question and Answer Flow for Sentence 1: The beautiful fish in the aquarium swam gracefully toward us.

1. What swam gracefully toward us? fish - SN
2. What is being said about fish? fish swam - V
3. Swam how? gracefully - Adv
4. Toward - P
5. Toward whom? us - OP
6. In - P
7. In what? aquarium - OP
8. The - A
9. What kind of fish? beautiful - Adj
10. The - A
11. SN V P1 Check
12. (In the aquarium) - Prepositional phrase
13. (Toward us) - Prepositional phrase
14. Period, statement, declarative sentence
15. Go back to the verb - divide the complete subject from the complete predicate.

Classified Sentence:

	A	Adj	SN	P	A	OP		V	Adv		P	OP	
SN V	The	beautiful	fish	(in	the	aquarium)	/	swam	gracefully		(toward	us).	D
P1													

Question and Answer Flow for Sentence 2: He talked to me on the telephone for an hour after school.

1. Who talked to me on the telephone for an hour after school? he - SP
2. What is being said about he? he talked - V
3. To - P
4. To whom? me - OP
5. On - P
6. On what? telephone - OP
7. The - A
8. For - P
9. For what? hour - OP
10. An - A
11. After - P
12. After what? school - OP
13. SN V P1 Check
14. (To me) - Prepositional phrase
15. (On the telephone) - Prepositional phrase
16. (For an hour) - Prepositional phrase
17. (After school) - Prepositional phrase
18. Period, statement, declarative sentence
19. Go back to the verb - divide the complete subject from the complete predicate.

Classified Sentence:

	SP	V	P	OP	P	A	OP		P	A	OP	P	OP	
SN V	He	/ talked	(to	me)	(on	the	telephone)		(for	an	hour)	(after	school).	D
P1														

Question and Answer Flow for Sentence 3: Listen closely to the visiting professor's lecture on nuclear science.

1. Who listen closely to the visiting professor's lecture on nuclear science? (You) - SP (Understood subject pronoun)
2. What is being said about you? you listen - V
3. Listen how? closely - Adv
4. To - P
5. To what? lecture - OP
6. Whose lecture? professor's - PNA
7. Which professor? visiting - Adj
8. The - A
9. On - P
10. On what? science - OP
11. What kind of science? nuclear - Adj
12. SN V P1 Check
13. (To the visiting professor's lecture) - Prepositional phrase
14. (On nuclear science) - Prepositional phrase
15. Period, command, imperative sentence
16. Go back to the verb - divide the complete subject from the complete predicate.

Classified Sentence:

	(You) SP	V	Adv	P	A	Adj	PNA	OP	P	Adj	OP	
SN V		/ Listen	closely	(to	the	visiting	professor's	lecture)	(on	nuclear	science).	Imp
P1												

CHAPTER 7 LESSON 3 CONTINUED

TEACHING SCRIPT FOR OBJECT PRONOUN

We are now ready to learn another type of pronoun. But, first, let's review the two jingles that tell us about two other types of pronouns: the Subject Pronoun Jingle and the Possessive Pronoun Jingle. (*Recite the two jingles.*) Now, we are going to recite the Object Pronoun Jingle that you learned at the beginning of this lesson. (*Have students turn to page 5 in the Jingle section of their books and recite the Object Pronoun Jingle with you.*)

Look at Reference 25 on page 21 in your Reference Section. Follow along as I explain three things you need to know about object pronouns. (*You may want to write the example on the board as a visual aid for your students.*)

Reference 25: Object Pronoun

1. If a pronoun does any job that has the word *object* in it, that pronoun is an object pronoun. Object pronouns can be used as objects of the prepositions, direct objects, or indirect objects.

2. The object pronouns are listed in your Object Pronoun Jingle: *me, us, him, her, it, them,* and *you.*

3. An object pronoun does not have a special label. An object pronoun keeps the **OP**, **DO**, or **IO** label that tells its job.

	OP	DO	IO
Examples:	Lisa left with *her.*	My mother called *me.*	Mail *him* the letter.

Did you notice that these jobs all have the word *object* in them? Listen to the list again. *Object* pronouns are used as *objects* of the prepositions, direct *objects*, and indirect *objects*.

As you can see, an object pronoun can perform many jobs. Remember, the object pronoun will not be labeled object pronoun. It will take the name of the pronoun job that you use when you classify the sentence. For example, the object pronoun is labeled *OP* for object of the preposition (*not object pronoun*). It may also be labeled *DO* for direct object or *IO* for indirect object. You will learn about the other object pronoun jobs in later sentence patterns. For now, we will concentrate on using the object pronoun as an object of the preposition.

Look at Sentence 1, which we have just classified. It has two prepositional phrases. In the first prepositional phrase, the object of the preposition is a noun. In the second prepositional phrase, the object of the preposition is a pronoun. Notice that we classify both objects of the prepositions as "OP."

(*Put this sample sentence on the board: The car was given* **to me** *for graduation. Read and discuss the sample sentence.*) Can we substitute other object pronouns for the object pronoun that is used here? (*yes*) What are some of the object pronouns that we could substitute? (*her, him, them, us*) How would you label the object pronouns that we could substitute? (*Keep the same OP label for the object of the preposition.*)

CHAPTER 7 LESSON 3 CONTINUED

 TEST TIME

To develop listening skills, give students a definition test orally. Have them get out one sheet of paper and number it 1-11. They should listen carefully to the questions and write the answers on their paper. Ask the questions listed below. After students have finished, check and discuss the answers together. Discuss strong areas as well as weak areas. (*You may or may not want to take a grade on this oral test. Bonus points usually work nicely in place of grades.*)

1. What are the three article adjectives? *a, an, the*

2. What are the five parts of a correct sentence?
   subject, verb, complete sense, capital letter, and end mark

3. What is an interrogative sentence? *a question*

4. What is the understood subject pronoun? *you*

5. What punctuation is used for possessive nouns? *an apostrophe or (')*

6. What are the three adverb questions? *how, when, where*

7. What are the three adjective questions? *what kind, which one, how many*

8. What is the definition of a pronoun? *A pronoun takes the place of a noun*.

9. What are the seven subject pronouns? *I, we, he, she, it, they, you*

10. What are the seven possessive pronouns? *my, our, his, her, its, their, your*

11. What are the seven object pronouns? *me, us, him, her, it, them, you*

 ACTIVITY / ASSIGNMENT TIME

For the rest of the day, try not to use any pronouns. Down the left side of a sheet of paper, make a list of all the pronouns that are used in the pronoun jingles. Keep the list with you at all times. Every time you say a pronoun, place a tally mark beside that pronoun. At the end of the day, total up the number of times you used pronouns. Discuss the pronouns you used the most. Try this experiment again with family members or friends. Have a contest. Set up the rules and time frame for the pronoun contest. See if anyone can go several hours without saying any pronouns. Discuss the importance of pronouns in our communications.

 WRITING TIME

Have students make an entry in their journals.

(End of lesson.)

Level 4 Homeschool Teacher's Manual

CHAPTER 7   LESSON 4

Objectives: Jingles, Study, Test, Check, and Writing (journal).

 **JINGLE TIME**

Have students turn to the Jingle Section in their books and recite the previously-taught jingles.

 STUDY TIME

Have students study the vocabulary words in their vocabulary notebooks. Remind students that any vocabulary word in their notebooks could be on their test. Also, have students study any of the skills in the Practice Section that they need to review.

 TEST TIME

Have students turn to page 103 in the Test Section of their book and find the Chapter 7 Test section. Go over the directions to make sure they understand what to do. (*Chapter 7 Test key is on the next page.*)

 **CHECK TIME**

After students have finished, check and discuss their test papers. Make sure they understand why their answers are right or wrong. (*For total points, count each required answer as a point.*)

(End of lesson.)

Chapter 7 Test
(Student Page 103)

Exercise 1: Classify each sentence.

　　　　　　　　PPA　SN　　　　V　　Adv　　　P　A　OP　　P　PNA　　OP

1. **SN V** ___ My children / stared breathlessly (at the cows) (in Dad's pasture). **D**
   P1

　　　　　Adv　　Adj　　Adj　SN　　　V　　　Adv　P　A　Adj　OP　　　P　　A　OP　　P　A　OP

2. **SN V** ___ Today, several duck eggs / hatched slowly (in the soft grass) (beside the edge) (of the pond). **D**
   P1

　(You) SP　　　V　P　PPA　Adj　　Adj　　OP　P　A　　OP　　P　PPA　OP　P　PPA　OP

3. **SN V** ___ / Stop (by my favorite candy store) (in the mall) (on your way) (to our house). **Imp**
   P1

Exercise 2: Use Sentence 1 to underline the complete subject once and the complete predicate twice and to complete the table below.

List the Noun Used	List the Noun Job	Singular or Plural	Common or Proper	Simple Subject	Simple Predicate
1. **children**	2. **SN**	3. **P**	4. **C**	5. **children**	6. **stared**
7. **cows**	8. **OP**	9. **P**	10. **C**		
11. **pasture**	12. **OP**	13. **S**	14. **C**		

Exercise 3: Name the six parts of speech that you have studied. (*You may use abbreviations.*) **(The order may vary.)**

1. __noun__　　　2. __verb__　　　3. __adjective__　　4. __adverb__　　　5. __preposition__　　6. __pronoun__

Exercise 4: Identify each pair of words as synonyms or antonyms by putting parentheses ( ) around *syn* or *ant*.

1. soiled, dirty	**(syn)** ant	4. belittle, encourage	syn **(ant)**	7. arrange, prepare	**(syn)** ant
2. depress, uplift	syn **(ant)**	5. calm, turmoil	syn **(ant)**	8. fatigued, fresh	syn **(ant)**
3. brawn, muscle	**(syn)** ant	6. bucket, pail	**(syn)** ant	9. rival, competitor	**(syn)** ant

Exercise 5: Finding One Part of Speech. For each sentence, write **SN/SP** above the simple subject and **V** above the simple predicate. Underline the word(s) for the part of speech listed to the left of each sentence.

　　　　　　　　　　　　　　　　　SN　　　V

Adjective(s): 　1. Our elementary teacher rode on my sister's brand-new motorcycle.

　　　　　　　　SP　　　　　　V

Preposition(s): 　2. We carefully worked on the science project for the contest.

　　　　　　　　SP　V

Pronoun(s): 　3. I stayed at my sister's house during our family reunion.

Exercise 6: For each sentence, write the subject, then write **S** if the subject is singular or **P** if the subject is plural, write the rule number (Rule 1 for singular or Rule 2 for plural), and underline the correct verb in the sentence.

Subject	S or P	Rule		
people	P	2	1.	These **people** (<u>know</u>, knows) how to survive.
Beth and Gayle	P	2	2.	**Beth** and **Gayle** (is, <u>are</u>) this year's finalists.
car	S	1	3.	The **car** (<u>was</u>, were) in need of gas.
you	P	2	4.	**You** (was, <u>were</u>) two minutes too late.
uncle	S	1	5.	(<u>Doesn't</u>, Don't) your **uncle** live in the red house?
residents	P	2	6.	(<u>Do</u>, Does) the **residents** still want city water?
biscuits	P	2	7.	My **biscuits** in the microwave (was, <u>were</u>) stale.
Joan and sisters	P	2	8.	(Has, <u>Have</u>) **Joan** and her **sisters** stayed at the cabin?

Exercise 7: On notebook paper, write seven subject pronouns, seven possessive pronouns, and seven object pronouns.

Exercise 8: In your journal, write a paragraph summarizing what you have learned this week.

CHAPTER 7 LESSON 4 CONTINUED

TEACHER INSTRUCTIONS

Use the Question and Answer Flows below for the sentences on the Chapter 7 Test.

Question and Answer Flow for Sentence 1: My children stared breathlessly at the cows in Dad's pasture.

1. Who stared breathlessly at the cows in Dad's pasture? children - SN
2. What is being said about children? children stared - V
3. Stared how? breathlessly - Adv
4. At - P
5. At what? cows - OP
6. The - A
7. In - P
8. In what? pasture - OP
9. Whose pasture? Dad's - PNA
10. Whose children? my - PPA
11. SN V P1 Check
12. (At the cows) - Prepositional phrase
13. (In Dad's pasture) - Prepositional phrase
14. Period, statement, declarative sentence
15. Go back to the verb - divide the complete subject from the complete predicate.

Classified Sentence:

```
              PPA   SN      V        Adv        P  A  OP    P  PNA   OP
    SN V      My children / stared breathlessly (at the cows) (in Dad's pasture).  D
    P1
```

Question and Answer Flow for Sentence 2: Today, several duck eggs hatched slowly in the soft grass beside the edge of the pond.

1. What hatched slowly in the soft grass beside the edge of the pond? eggs - SN
2. What is being said about eggs? eggs hatched - V
3. Hatched how? slowly - Adv
4. In - P
5. In what? grass - OP
6. What kind of grass? soft - Adj
7. The - A
8. Beside - P
9. Beside what? edge - OP
10. The - A
11. Of - P
12. Of what? pond - OP
13. The - A
14. What kind of eggs? duck - Adj
15. How many eggs? several - Adj
16. Hatched when? today - Adv
17. SN V P1 Check
18. (In the soft grass) - Prepositional phrase
19. (Beside the edge) - Prepositional phrase
20. (Of the pond) - Prepositional phrase
21. Period, statement, declarative sentence
22. Go back to the verb - divide the complete subject from the complete predicate.
23. This sentence has predicate words in the complete subject. Underline the adverb at the beginning of the sentence twice.

Classified Sentence:

```
              Adv    Adj  Adj  SN      V      Adv  P  A  Adj  OP     P    A   OP      P  A  OP
    SN V      Today, several duck eggs / hatched slowly (in the soft grass) (beside the edge) (of the pond).  D
    P1
```

Question and Answer Flow for Sentence 3: Stop by my favorite candy store in the mall on your way to our house.

1. Who stop by my favorite candy store in the mall on your way to our house? (You) - SP (Understood subject pronoun)
2. What is being said about you? you stop - V
3. By - P
4. By what? store - OP
5. What kind of store? candy - Adj
6. What kind of store? favorite - Adj
7. Whose store? my - PPA
8. In - P
9. In what? mall - OP
10. The - A
11. On - P
12. On what? way - OP
13. Whose way? your - PPA
14. To - P
15. To what? house - OP
16. Whose house? our - PPA
17. SN V P1 Check
18. (By my favorite candy store) - Prepositional phrase
19. (In the mall) - Prepositional phrase
20. (On your way) - Prepositional phrase
21. (To our house) - Prepositional phrase
22. Period, command, imperative sentence
23. Go back to the verb - divide the complete subject from the complete predicate.

Classified Sentence:

```
              (You) SP      V    P  PPA  Adj     Adj    OP     P  A  OP     P  PPA OP  P  PPA OP
    SN V          / Stop (by my  favorite candy  store) (in the mall) (on  your  way) (to our  house).  Imp
    P1
```

CHAPTER 7   LESSON 5
Objectives: Writing (standard and time-order forms), Writing Assignment #7, and Bonus Option.

 WRITING TIME

TEACHING SCRIPT FOR STANDARD AND TIME-ORDER FORMS

When you learned to write a three-point paragraph, you learned to state your points by beginning each sentence that stated a point with an article adjective or a possessive pronoun. (**My** first favorite, **My** second favorite, **My** third favorite, or **The** first thing, **The** second thing, **The** third thing.) We will call what you have been doing the **standard form** because it is used often and is a good, reliable three-point form. But now you are ready to learn another way to state each point in a three-point paragraph. This will give you some versatility in your writing. We will call the new way to state each point the **time-order form**.

In the time-order form, you should begin each sentence that states a point with words that suggest a definite time or number order, such as *first, second, third*, etc. or *first, next, last,* or *finally*, etc. <u>When you begin your sentence with time order words, you leave out the article adjectives and possessive pronouns.</u> For example, instead of saying "**My first** favorite" you would say "**First**, I like." You must remember this word of caution. Whichever form you choose, you must use that same form throughout your paragraph to introduce each of your points. You cannot mix forms in the same paragraph.

I will demonstrate how to use the time-order form to write a paragraph. Turn to page 21 and look at Reference 26A as I read the paragraph to you. Then, I will go through each of the three points in the paragraph and show you how it was written in time-order form. *(Read the paragraph to your students from beginning to end. Then, go through the teaching script given for each sentence in the paragraph.)*

Reference 26A: Paragraphs Using Different Writing Forms
Topic: My favorite snacks **3-points:** 1. ice cream   2. popcorn   3. peanut butter crackers
Sample 1: <u>Three-point paragraph using a standard topic sentence with time-order points</u>
I have three favorite snacks. They are ice cream, popcorn, and peanut butter crackers. **First**, I like ice cream. I like all the different flavors of ice cream, and I laugh when the cold tickles my tongue. **Second**, I like popcorn. To me, popcorn is best when it is hot and covered with lots of melted butter. **Third**, I like peanut butter crackers. (*or* **Finally**, *I like peanut butter crackers.*) I like peanut butter crackers because they are so fun to make. I enjoy many different snacks, but my favorites will always be ice cream, popcorn, and peanut butter crackers.

Notice that the topic is written first because it is the subject of the paragraph. Having the topic written first will help us focus on what the paragraph is about. Next, the three points that we will discuss are listed. Again, having the three points written down before we start will help us focus on what we will say in the paragraph.

We are now ready to begin our paragraph because we are clear about our topic and about the points we will cover as we write. We start with a topic sentence because it tells the reader what the paragraph is about. Our topic sentence is, *"I have three favorite snacks."* Knowing what the paragraph is about helps the reader focus on the main points as the reader progresses through the paragraph.

Our next sentence is the three-point sentence: *They are ice cream, popcorn, and peanut butter crackers.* The three-point sentence lists the three main points that will be discussed in the paragraph, so in this paragraph, we know the three main points are *ice cream, popcorn* and *peanut butter crackers.*

Let's look at the sentence written for the first point. The sentence for the first point starts out like this: *First, I like ice cream.* As you can see, we do not use the possessive pronoun *my* or the article *the* in front of the word *first*, and a comma is placed after the order word because it is an introductory word.

Notice that the second and third main points have been written in the same format selected for the first point. Look at their form as I read them to you. (**2nd point:** *Second, I like popcorn.* **3rd point:** *Third, I like peanut butter crackers.*) Another interesting detail is that you could use *finally* instead of *third* to introduce your last point.

After each main point, there is a supporting sentence. The supporting sentences make each point clearer by telling extra information about each main point. Remember, we have stated in the main points that <u>ice cream</u>, <u>popcorn</u>, and <u>peanut butter crackers</u> are three of our favorite snacks. Each supporting sentence should state some kind of information that proves each of the main points. (**1st Supporting sentence:** *I like all the different flavors of **ice cream**, and I laugh when the cold tickles my tongue.* **2nd Supporting sentence:** *To me, **popcorn** is best when it is hot and covered with lots of melted butter.* **3rd Supporting sentence:** *I like **peanut butter crackers** because they are so much fun to make.*)

Our last sentence is a concluding sentence. It summarizes our three points by restating some of the words in the topic sentence and by adding an extra thought that finalizes the paragraph. (**Concluding sentence:** *I enjoy many different snacks, but my favorites will always be ice cream, popcorn, and peanut butter crackers.*)

I will read the same paragraph to you again, but this time I will use different order words to introduce each point. In the first example, the order words were *first, second*, and *third*. In the second example, the order words are *first, next*, and *last*. It is a minor change, but it definitely adds variety to the paragraph. (*As you read the following paragraph, emphasize the different words that introduce each point sentence.*)

Reference 26A: Paragraphs Using Different Writing Forms (continued)

Sample 2: <u>Three-point paragraph using a standard topic sentence with different time-order points</u>

   I have three favorite snacks. They are ice cream, popcorn, and peanut butter crackers. **<u>First</u>**, I like ice cream. I like all the different flavors of ice cream, and I laugh when the cold tickles my tongue. **<u>Next</u>**, I like popcorn. To me, popcorn is best when it is hot and covered with lots of melted butter. **<u>Last</u>**, I like peanut butter crackers. (*or* **<u>Finally</u>**, *I like peanut butter crackers.*) I like peanut butter crackers because they are so fun to make. I enjoy many different snacks, but my favorites will always be ice cream, popcorn, and peanut butter crackers.

As a review, I will go over the four things you need to know whenever you are using the time-order form to write a three-point paragraph. Listen carefully because I will ask you a few questions after I have finished the review. (*Go over the four items listed below. Then, discuss the questions on the next page.*)

Using the Time-Order Form

1. Use time-order words at the beginning of each of the main point sentences.
   (*first, second, third*, etc.) or (*first, next, last, finally*, etc.)
2. Do not use a possessive pronoun or article in front of the time-order word.
3. Put a comma after the introductory time-order word.
4. For consistency, use the same style to introduce each point in your paragraph.

CHAPTER 7 LESSON 5 CONTINUED

1. The words you use in the time-order form usually come in sets. We have discussed two sets. What are they? *(first, second, third, etc.)* or *(first, next, last, finally, etc.)*

2. What two kinds of words are generally not used in the time-order form? *(possessive pronouns and articles)*

3. When you use time-order words to introduce the point sentences, they are introductory words. What punctuation is required after the time-order words when they are used as introductory words? *(comma)*

4. If I am writing a three-point paragraph using the standard form, what form do I use for each of the points I introduce? *(the standard form)* In the standard form, am I allowed to use possessive pronouns and articles to help introduce my points? *(yes)*

5. If I am writing a three-point paragraph using the time-order form, what form do I use for each of the points I introduce? *(the time-order form)* In the time-order form, am I allowed to use possessive pronouns and articles to help introduce my points? *(no)*

TEACHER INSTRUCTIONS FOR WRITING ASSIGNMENT

For Writing Assignment #7, students are to write a three-point paragraph in first person, using the time-order form. They are to underline all time-order words used at the beginning of each sentence that states a point. Also, tell students to look up any words they cannot spell as they check over their writing. A spelling check is being added to the general editing list for the students. *(See "More Editing Skills" in Reference 5 on student page 12.)*

Writing Assignment Box

Writing Assignment #7: Three-Point Expository Paragraph (First Person, Time-Order Form)
(Remind students that first person pronouns are *I, we, me, us, my, mine, our,* and *ours.*)
Writing topics: Things That Make Me Laugh or **My Favorite Rides at the Fair** or **Problems Faced by Early Settlers**

<u>**Bonus Option:**</u> **Visit the nursing home or an elderly resident. Find out their favorite Bible verses and discuss them. Have them select a story from the Bible and read it to them. Write about your experiences in your Journal.**

TEACHING SCRIPT FOR USING THE WRITING PROCESS FOR THIS WRITING ASSIGNMENT

As you begin this writing assignment, you will start through the writing process. First, you will think about your topic and gather any information you might need in order to do the writing. Second, you will write a rough draft. Remember, it is called a rough draft because it will be revised and edited. You do not have to worry about mistakes as you write your rough draft. After you write the first draft, you will make revisions, using the Revision Checklist in Reference 5. After you revise your writing, you will edit, using the Beginning Editing Checklist in Reference 5. Finally, you will write a final paper, using the Final Paper Checklist in Reference 5. You will then give the finished writing assignment to me.

TEACHER INSTRUCTIONS FOR CHECKING WRITING ASSIGNMENT

Read, check, and discuss Writing Assignment #7 after students have finished their final paper. Use the editing checklist *(Reference 5 on teacher's page 10)* as you check and discuss students' papers. Make sure students are using the editing checklist correctly.

(End of lesson.)

CHAPTER 8 LESSON 1
Objectives: Jingles (The 23 Helping Verbs of the Mean, Lean Verb machine), Grammar (Introductory Sentences, helping verb, **not** adverb, question verb, Oral Skill Builder Check), Writing (journal), and Vocabulary #1.

 JINGLE TIME

Have students turn to the Jingle Section in their books and recite the previously-taught jingles. Then, lead students in reciting the new jingle (*The 23 Helping Verbs of the Mean, Lean Verb Machine*) below. Practice the new jingle several times until students can recite it smoothly. Emphasize reciting with a rhythm. Students and teacher should be together! (*Do not try to explain the jingle at this time. Just have fun reciting it. Remember, add motions for more fun and laughter.*)

Teacher's Notes: Again, do not spend a large amount of time practicing the new jingles. Students learn the jingles best by spending a small amount of time consistently, **every** day.

Jingle 14:   The 23 Helping Verbs of the Mean, Lean Verb Machine Jingle

These 23 helping verbs will be on my test.
I gotta remember them so I can do my best.
I'll start out with 8 and finish with 15;
Just call me the mean, lean verb machine.

There are 8 *be* verbs that are easy as can be:
   am, is, are – was and were,
   am, is, are – was and were,
   am, is, are – was and were,
   be, being, and been.

All together now, the 8 *be* verbs:
am, is, are – was and were – be, being, and been.
am, is, are – was and were – be, being, and been.

There're 23 helping verbs, and I've recited only 8.
That leaves fifteen more that I must relate:
   has, have, and had – do, does, and did,
   has, have, and had – do, does, and did,
   might, must, may – might, must, may.

Knowing these verbs will save my grade:
   can and could – would and should,
   can and could – would and should,
   shall and will,
   shall and will.

In record time, I did this drill.
I'm the mean, lean verb machine - STILL!

 GRAMMAR TIME

Put the introductory sentences from the box below on the board. Use these sentences as you go through each new concept covered in your teaching script. For the greatest benefit, students must participate orally with the teacher. (*You might put the introductory sentences on notebook paper if you are doing one-on-one instruction with your students.*)

Chapter 8, Introductory Sentences for Lesson 1
1. _____ Our choir has been singing softly for the children at the hospital.
2. _____ Sarah has not worked in her father's shop today.
3. _____ Was the medicine prepared carefully for his puppy?

CHAPTER 8 LESSON 1 CONTINUED

TEACHING SCRIPT FOR THE HELPING VERB

Today, we will learn about helping verbs. When there are two or more verbs used together in a sentence, the verbs in front are known as the **helping verbs**, and the last verb is the main verb. Helping verbs are also called **auxiliary verbs**. The main verb and helping verbs together are called a **verb phrase**.

When directions are given to underline the verb, the helping verb and the main verb will be underlined because they are both part of the verb phrase. (For example: The fox **is running** for his life!) Helping verbs are labeled with *HV*. *Is running* is the verb phrase and both verbs would be underlined. If you are labeling *is running*, you would label the helping verb *is* with the letters *HV* and the main verb *running* with the letter *V*.

You will use this information as you classify Sentence 1 with me to find the helping verb. Remember, you use the same subject question, *who* or *what*, to start classifying all sentences. Begin.

Question and Answer Flow for Sentence 1: Our choir has been singing softly for the children at the hospital.

1. Who has been singing softly for the children at the hospital? choir - SN
2. What is being said about choir? choir has been singing - V

Note: There are 3 verbs. *Singing* is the main verb and will be labeled with a <u>V</u>. *Has* and *been* are the helping verbs in front of *singing* and will be labeled with <u>HV</u>.

3. Has - HV (helping verb) (Write HV above *has*.)
4. Been - HV (helping verb) (Write HV above *been*.)
5. Has been singing how? softly - Adv
6. For - P
7. For whom? children - OP
8. The - A
9. At - P
10. At what? hospital - OP
11. The - A
12. Whose choir? our - PPA
13. SN V P1 Check
14. (For the children) - Prepositional phrase
15. (At the hospital) - Prepositional phrase
16. Period, statement, declarative sentence
17. Go back to the verb - divide the complete subject from the complete predicate.

Classified Sentence:

	PPA	SN	HV	HV	V	Adv	P	A	OP	P	A	OP
SN V	Our	choir /	has	been	singing	softly	(for	the	children)	(at	the	hospital). **D**
P1												

---

*TEACHING SCRIPT FOR THE **NOT** ADVERB*

Even though the word *NOT* is not a verb, we will study it now because it is so often confused as part of a verb phrase. The helping verb can be split from the main verb by the adverb *NOT*. The word *NOT* is usually an adverb telling *how*. Many negative words are adverbs telling *how* or *to what extent*. (*For example: Sandy is **not** singing in the play.*) We will now classify Sentence 2 to find the "*NOT*" adverb. Begin.

CHAPTER 8 LESSON 1 CONTINUED

Question and Answer Flow for Sentence 2: Sarah has not worked in her father's shop today.

1. Who has not worked in her father's shop today? Sarah - SN
2. What is being said about Sarah? Sarah has worked - V
3. Has - HV
4. Has worked how? not - Adv
5. In - P
6. In what? shop - OP
7. Whose shop? father's - PNA
8. Whose father? her - PPA
9. Has worked when? today - Adv
10. SN V P1 Check
11. (In her father's shop) - Prepositional phrase
12. Period, statement, declarative sentence
13. Go back to the verb - divide the complete subject from the complete predicate.

Classified Sentence:

           SN   HV Adv V   P PPA PNA   OP   Adv

    <u>SN V</u>   Sarah / has not worked (in her father's shop) today. **D**
       P1

TEACHING SCRIPT FOR THE QUESTION VERB

Earlier, we studied interrogative sentences. Now, we are going to review the interrogative sentence that starts with a helping verb. When the helping verb is placed before the subject, the sentence is usually a question. The subject will come between the helping verb and the main verb. You can check the parts of a question by making a statement: (For example: **Can** you **park** in the field? You **can park** in the field.)

Let's classify Sentence 3 for identification of the question verb. Begin.

Question and Answer Flow for Sentence 3: Was the medicine prepared carefully for his puppy?

1. What was prepared carefully for his puppy? medicine - SN
2. What is being said about medicine? medicine was prepared - V
3. Was - HV
4. Was prepared how? carefully - Adv
5. For - P
6. For what? puppy - OP
7. Whose puppy? his - PPA
8. The - A
9. SN V P1 Check
10. (For his puppy) - Prepositional phrase
11. Question mark, question, interrogative sentence
12. Go back to the verb - divide the complete subject from the complete predicate.
(With a question verb, divide in front of the main verb.)
13. This sentence has predicate words in the complete subject. Underline the helping verb at the beginning of the sentence twice.
(The question verb is located in the subject of the sentence, but it is part of the predicate.)

Classified Sentence:

           HV   A   SN   V   Adv   P PPA OP

    <u>SN V</u>   <u>Was</u> the medicine / prepared carefully (for his puppy)? **Int**
       P1

CHAPTER 8 LESSON 1 CONTINUED

TEACHER INSTRUCTIONS

Use Sentences 1-3 that you just classified with your students to do an Oral Skill Builder Check. Use the guidelines below.

Oral Skill Builder Check	
1. Noun check. (Say the job and then say the noun. Circle each noun.) **2. Identify the nouns as singular or plural.** (Write **S** or **P** above each noun.) **3. Identify the nouns as common or proper.** (Follow established procedure for oral identification.) **4. Do a vocabulary check.** (Follow established procedure for oral identification.)	**5. Identify the complete subject and the complete predicate.** (Underline the complete subject once and the complete predicate twice.) **6. Identify the simple subject and simple predicate.** (Underline the simple subject once and the simple predicate twice. Bold, or highlight, the lines to distinguish them from the complete subject and complete predicate.)

WRITING TIME

Have students make an entry in their journals.

VOCABULARY TIME

Assign Chapter 8, Vocabulary Words **#1** on page 8 in the Reference Section for students to define in their Vocabulary notebooks. Tell students they are to use a dictionary or thesaurus to look up the meanings of the vocabulary words. After they write each word and its meaning, students are to write a sentence using the vocabulary word.

Chapter 8, Vocabulary Words #1
(unique, common, promise, pledge)

(End of lesson.)

CHAPTER 8   LESSON 2

Objectives: Jingles, Grammar (Practice sentences, Practice and Improved Sentences), Practice Exercise, and Vocabulary #2.

 JINGLE TIME

Have students turn to the Jingle Section in their books and recite the previously-taught jingles.

 GRAMMAR TIME

First-Year Option: Put the Practice Sentences from the box below on the board or notebook paper. Use these sentences as you practice the concepts that have been taught. For the greatest benefit, students must participate orally with the teacher. **Second-Year Option:** Have students classify the Practice Sentences independently on notebook paper. Check students' sentences with the answers provided below. (*If you have the CDs for Practice Sentences, have students check their sentences with the CDs.*)

Chapter 8, Practice Sentences for Lesson 2
_____1. Has the chimney on the shabby old brick house fallen down?
_____2. The two squirmy baby puppies were yelping constantly for their mother's return.
_____3. The color of the picture in the main hallway has not faded through the years.

*TEACHING SCRIPT FOR PRACTICING WITH HELPING VERBS AND THE **NOT** ADVERB*

We will classify three different sentences to practice using our new skills in the Question and Answer Flows. We will classify the sentences together. Begin. (*You might have your child write the labels above the sentences at this time.*)

Question and Answer Flow for Sentence 1: Has the chimney on the shabby old brick house fallen down?
1. What has fallen down? chimney - SN   12. SN V P1 Check
2. What is being said about chimney? chimney has fallen - V   13. (On the shabby old brick house) - Prepositional phrase
3. Has - HV
4. Has fallen where? down - Adv   14. Question mark, question, interrogative sentence
5. On - P   15. Go back to the verb - divide the complete subject from the complete predicate.
6. On what? house - OP
7. What kind of house? brick - Adj   16. This sentence has predicate words in the complete subject. Underline the helping verb at the beginning of the sentence twice.
8. What kind of house? old - Adj
9. What kind of house? shabby - Adj
10. The - A
11. The - A

Classified Sentence:

                         HV   A   SN   P   A   Adj   Adj Adj   OP   V   Adv

       SN V   <u>Has</u> the chimney (on the shabby old brick house) / fallen down? **Int**

       P1

CHAPTER 8 LESSON 2 CONTINUED

Question and Answer Flow for Sentence 2: The two squirmy baby puppies were yelping constantly for their mother's return.

1. What were yelping constantly for their mother's return? puppies - SN
2. What is being said about puppies? puppies were yelping - V
3. Were - HV
4. Were yelping how? constantly - Adv
5. For - P
6. For what? return - OP
7. Whose return? mother's - PNA
8. Whose mother? their - PPA
9. What kind of puppies? baby - Adj
10. What kind of puppies? squirmy - Adj
11. How many puppies? two - Adj
12. The - A
13. SN V P1 Check
14. (For their mother's return) - Prepositional phrase
15. Period, statement, declarative sentence
16. Go back to the verb - divide the complete subject from the complete predicate. (You will divide in front of the helping verb.)

Classified Sentence:

SN V
P1

A   Adj   Adj   Adj   SN   HV   V   Adv   P PPA PNA   OP
The two squirmy baby puppies / were yelping constantly (for their mother's return). D

Question and Answer Flow for Sentence 3: The color of the picture in the main hallway has not faded through the years.

1. What has not faded through the years? color - SN
2. What is being said about color? color has faded - V
3. Has - HV
4. Has faded how? not - Adv
5. Through - P
6. Through what? years - OP
7. The - A
8. In - P
9. In what? hallway - OP
10. What kind of hallway? main - Adj
11. The - A
12. Of - P
13. Of what? picture - OP
14. The - A
15. The - A
16. SN V P1 Check
17. (Of the picture) - Prepositional phrase
18. (In the main hallway) - Prepositional phrase
19. (Through the years) - Prepositional phrase
20. Period, statement, declarative sentence
21. Go back to the verb - divide the complete subject from the complete predicate.

Classified Sentence:

SN V
P1

A   SN   P A   OP   P A Adj   OP   HV Adv V   P   A   OP
The color (of the picture) (in the main hallway) / has not faded (through the years). D

CHAPTER 8 LESSON 2 CONTINUED

TEACHING SCRIPT FOR THE PRACTICE SENTENCE

Put these labels on the board: **HV A Adj SN V P PPA OP**

Look at the new sentence labels on the board: **HV A Adj SN V P PPA OP**. I will guide you through the process of writing a sentence to practice the new parts that you have learned.

Get out a sheet of notebook paper. On the top line of your notebook paper, write the title *Practice Sentence*. Copy the sentence labels from the board onto your notebook paper. Be sure to leave plenty of writing space between each label. I will guide you through the process you will use whenever you write a Practice Sentence with helping verbs.

1. Go to the **SN** label for the subject noun. Think of a noun that you want to use as your subject. Write the noun you have chosen on the line *under* the **SN** label.

2. Go to the **V** label for verb. Think of a verb that tells what your subject does. Make sure that your verb makes sense with the subject noun. Write the verb you have chosen on the line *under* the **V** label.

3. Go to the **P** label for the preposition. Think of a preposition word that tells something about your verb. You must be careful to choose a preposition word that makes sense with the noun you will choose for the object of the preposition in your next step. Write the word you have chosen for a preposition *under* the **P** label.

4. Go to the **OP** label for object of the preposition. If you like the noun you thought of while thinking of a preposition, write it down under the **OP** label. If you prefer, think of another noun by asking **what** or **whom** after your preposition. Check to make sure the preposition and object of the preposition make sense together and also make sense with the rest of the sentence. Remember, the object of the preposition will always answer the question **what** or **whom** after the preposition. Write the word you have chosen for the object of the preposition *under* the **OP** label.

5. Go to the **PPA** label for the possessive pronoun adjective that is part of your prepositional phrase. Recite the Possessive Pronoun Jingle to help you think of a pronoun that you want to use as your possessive pronoun adjective. Choose the possessive pronoun that makes the best sense in your sentence. Write the possessive pronoun you have chosen *under* the **PPA** label.

6. Go to the **Adj** label for the adjective. Go to the subject noun of your sentence and ask an adjective question. What are the adjective questions again? (*What kind, Which one, How many*) Choose one adjective question to ask and write your adjective answer *under* the **Adj** label next to the subject noun.

7. Go to the **A** label for the article adjective in the subject area. What are the three article adjectives again? (*a, an, the*) Choose the article adjective that makes the best sense in your sentence. Write the article adjective you have chosen *under* the **A** label.

CHAPTER 8 LESSON 2 CONTINUED

8. Go to the **HV** label for the helping verb. Choose a helping verb that asks a question and that makes sense in your sentence. Write the helping verb you have chosen *under* the **HV** label.

9. Finally, check your Practice Sentence to make sure it has the necessary parts to be a complete sentence. What are the five parts of a complete sentence? (*subject, verb, complete sense, capital letter, and an end mark*) Does your Practice Sentence have the five parts of a complete sentence? (*Allow time for students to read over their sentences and to make any corrections they need to make.*)

TEACHING SCRIPT FOR THE IMPROVED SENTENCE

Under your Practice Sentence, write the title *Improved Sentence* on another line. To improve your Practice Sentence, you will make two synonym changes, one antonym change, and your choice of a complete word change or another synonym or antonym change.

Since it is harder to find words that can be changed to an antonym, it is usually wise to go through your sentence to find an antonym change first. Look through your sentence again to find words that can be improved with synonyms. Finally, make a decision about whether your last change will be a complete word change, another synonym change, or another antonym change.

I will give you time to write your Improved Sentence. (*Always encourage students to use a thesaurus, synonym-antonym book, or a dictionary to help them develop an interesting and improved writing vocabulary. After students have finished, check and discuss students' Practice and Improved Sentences.*)

PRACTICE TIME

Have students write the three sentences that they classified at the beginning of the lesson on notebook paper. (*See page 131.*) Have them tape-record the Question and Answer Flows for all three sentences. Students should write labels above the sentences as they classify them. They especially need the second practice if this is their first year in the program. (*After students have finished, check the tape and sentence labels. Make sure students understand any mistakes they have made.*)

VOCABULARY TIME

Assign Chapter 8, Vocabulary Words **#2** on page 8 in the Reference Section for students to define in their Vocabulary notebooks. Tell students they are to use a dictionary or thesaurus to look up the meanings of the vocabulary words. After they write each word and its meaning, students are to write a sentence using the vocabulary word.

Chapter 8, Vocabulary Words #2
(keen, sharp, impetuous, cautious)

(End of lesson.)

CHAPTER 8   LESSON 3
Objectives: Jingles, Grammar (Practice Sentences, add Irregular Verb Chart to the Skill Builder Check, Oral Skill Builder Check), Test, Activity, and Writing (journal).

 JINGLE TIME

Have students turn to the Jingle Section in their books and recite the previously-taught jingles.

 GRAMMAR TIME

First-Year Option: Put the Practice Sentences from the box below on the board or on notebook paper. Use these sentences as you practice the concepts that have been taught. For the greatest benefit, students must participate orally with the teacher. **Second-Year Option:** Have students classify the Practice Sentences independently on notebook paper. Check students' sentences with the answers provided below. (*If you have the CDs for Practice Sentences, have students check their sentences with the CDs.*)

Chapter 8, Practice Sentences for Lesson 3
____1. Those beautiful, thorny rosebushes were not damaged by the ice storm.
____2. The silly clown was driving in a very small car during the circus parade today.
____3. Was our class president campaigning for a longer lunch break?

*TEACHING SCRIPT FOR PRACTICING HELPING VERBS AND THE **NOT** ADVERB*

We will practice classifying the new concepts in the Question and Answer Flows. We will classify the sentences together. Begin. (*You might have your students write the labels above the sentences at this time.*)

Question and Answer Flow for Sentence 1: Those beautiful, thorny rosebushes were not damaged by the ice storm.
1. What were not damaged by the ice storm? rosebushes - SN
2. What is being said about rosebushes? rosebushes were damaged - V
3. Were - HV
4. Were damaged how? not - Adv
5. By - P
6. By what? storm - OP
7. What kind of storm? ice - Adj
8. The - A

9. What kind of rosebushes? thorny - Adj
10. What kind of rosebushes? beautiful - Adj
11. Which rosebushes? those - Adj
12. SN V P1 Check
13. (By the ice storm) - Prepositional phrase
14. Period, statement, declarative sentence
15. Go back to the verb - divide the complete subject from the complete predicate.

```
                       Adj   Adj    Adj    SN      HV  Adv   V     P  A Adj  OP
Classified
Sentence:    SN  V     Those beautiful, thorny rosebushes / were not damaged (by the ice storm). D
             P1
```

CHAPTER 8 LESSON 3 CONTINUED

Question and Answer Flow for Sentence 2: The silly clown was driving in a very small car during the circus parade today.

1. Who was driving in a very small car during the circus parade today? clown - SN
2. What is being said about clown? clown was driving - V
3. Was - HV
4. In - P
5. In what? car - OP
6. What kind of car? small - Adj
7. How small? very - Adv
8. A - A
9. During - P
10. During what? parade - OP
11. What kind of parade? circus - Adj

12. The - A
13. Was driving when? today - Adv
14. What kind of clown? silly - Adj
15. The - A
16. SN V P1 Check
17. (In a very small car) - Prepositional phrase
18. (During the circus parade) - Prepositional phrase
19. Period, statement, declarative sentence
20. Go back to the verb - divide the complete subject from the complete predicate.

		A	Adj	SN		HV	V	P	A	Adv	Adj	OP	P	A	Adj	OP	Adv	
Classified Sentence:	SN V P1	The	silly	clown	/	was	driving	(in	a	very	small	car)	(during	the	circus	parade)	today.	D

Question and Answer Flow for Sentence 3: Was our class president campaigning for a longer lunch break?

1. Who was campaigning for a longer lunch break? president - SN
2. What is being said about president? president was campaigning - V
3. Was - HV
4. For - P
5. For what? break - OP
6. What kind of break? lunch - Adj
7. What kind of break? longer - Adj
8. A - A

9. What kind of president? class - Adj
10. Whose president? our - PPA
11. SN V P1 Check
12. (For a longer lunch break) - Prepositional phrase
13. Question mark, question, interrogative sentence
14. Go back to the verb - divide the complete subject from the complete predicate.
15. This sentence has predicate words in the complete subject. Underline the helping verb at the beginning of the sentence twice.

		HV	PPA	Adj	SN		V	P	A	Adj	Adj	OP	
Classified Sentence:	SN V P1	Was	our	class	president	/	campaigning	(for	a	longer	lunch	break)?	Int

---

CHAPTER 8 LESSON 3 CONTINUED

TEACHER INSTRUCTIONS

Use Sentences 1-3 that you just classified with your students to do an Oral Skill Builder Check. Use the guidelines below.

Oral Skill Builder Check	
1. Noun check. (Say the job and then say the noun. Circle each noun.) **2. Identify the nouns as singular or plural.** (Write **S** or **P** above each noun.) **3. Identify the nouns as common or proper.** (Follow established procedure for oral identification.) **4. Do a vocabulary check.** (Follow established procedure for oral identification.)	**5. Identify the complete subject and the complete predicate.** (Underline the complete subject once and the complete predicate twice.) **6. Identify the simple subject and simple predicate.** (Underline the simple subject once and the simple predicate twice. Bold, or highlight, the lines.) **7. Recite the irregular verb chart.** (This new skill is explained below.)

TEACHING SCRIPT FOR ADDING AN IRREGULAR VERB CHART TO THE SKILL BUILDER CHECK

We will now add an Irregular Verb Chart to the Skill Builder Check. Look at the Irregular Verb Chart that is located in Reference 27 on page 23 in your book. (*The irregular verb chart is reproduced for you on the next page.*) We will recite the Irregular Verb Chart during the Skill Builder Checks to help you learn the different principal parts of some irregular verbs.

Even though this is only a partial listing of irregular verbs, it will expose you to the correct forms on a consistent basis. We can add more irregular verbs as we think of them. (*You do not need to chant all of the verb chart for every Skill Builder Check. Pick only a few verbs to chant if your child does not have a problem with irregular verb usage.*)

If you use an irregular verb incorrectly, either spoken or written, I will say, "I need a correction for the verb ___," and you will be expected to recite the verb correctly two ways. You will recite the two corrections several times in short sentences. If you cannot remember how to use the two corrections in short sentences, you should use the chart to help you. (*Explain the example below.*)

Example: He **driven** before.   Verb used incorrectly: **driven**

1. Correction with the past tense form: He **drove** before; He **drove** before; He **drove** before; He **drove** before.

2. Correction with a helping verb: He **had driven** before; He **had driven** before; He **had driven** before; He **had driven** before.

CHAPTER 8 LESSON 3 CONTINUED

Reference 27: Irregular Verb Chart			
PRESENT	**PAST**	**PAST PARTICIPLE**	**PRESENT PARTICIPLE**
become	became	(has) become	(is) becoming
blow	blew	(has) blown	(is) blowing
break	broke	(has) broken	(is) breaking
bring	brought	(has) brought	(is) bringing
burst	burst	(has) burst	(is) bursting
buy	bought	(has) bought	(is) buying
choose	chose	(has) chosen	(is) choosing
come	came	(has) come	(is) coming
drink	drank	(has) drunk	(is) drinking
drive	drove	(has) driven	(is) driving
eat	ate	(has) eaten	(is) eating
fall	fell	(has) fallen	(is) falling
fly	flew	(has) flown	(is) flying
freeze	froze	(has) frozen	(is) freezing
get	got	(has) gotten	(is) getting
give	gave	(has) given	(is) giving
grow	grew	(has) grown	(is) growing
know	knew	(has) known	(is) knowing
lie	lay	(has) lain	(is) lying
lay	laid	(has) laid	(is) laying
make	made	(has) made	(is) making
ride	rode	(has) ridden	(is) riding
ring	rang	(has) rung	(is) ringing
rise	rose	(has) risen	(is) rising
sell	sold	(has) sold	(is) selling
sing	sang	(has) sung	(is) singing
sink	sank	(has) sunk	(is) sinking
set	set	(has) set	(is) setting
sit	sat	(has) sat	(is) sitting
shoot	shot	(has) shot	(is) shooting
swim	swam	(has) swum	(is) swimming
take	took	(has) taken	(is) taking
tell	told	(has) told	(is) telling
throw	threw	(has) thrown	(is) throwing
wear	wore	(has) worn	(is) wearing
write	wrote	(has) written	(is) writing

Level 4 Homeschool Teacher's Manual

CHAPTER 8 LESSON 3 CONTINUED

 TEST TIME

To develop listening skills, give students a knowledge test orally. Have them get out one sheet of paper and number it 1-11. They should listen carefully to the questions and write the answers on their paper. Ask the questions listed below. After students have finished, check and discuss the answers together. Discuss strong areas as well as weak areas.

1. What part of speech is the word NOT? **adverb**
2. Name the understood subject pronoun. **you**
3. What is an imperative sentence? **a command**
4. What is a declarative sentence? **a statement**
5. What is an interrogative sentence? **a question**
6. What punctuation mark does a possessive noun always have? **an apostrophe**
7. What part of speech is a possessive noun classified as, and what is the abbreviation used? **adjective, PNA**

8. List the 8 *be* verbs.
    am, is, are, was, were, be, being, been
9. What are the parts of a verb phrase?
    helping verb and main verb
10. Name the seven subject pronouns.
    I, we, he, she, it, you, they
11. Name the seven possessive pronouns.
    my, our, his, her, its, their, your

 ACTIVITY / ASSIGNMENT TIME

Write the letters of each of your family member's names vertically, including your own name. Beside each letter, write an adjective or short phrase that starts with that letter to describe each family member. Have students research the word **acrostic**. Discuss this type of poem. (*Write the example below on the board for your students.*)

Example:

S –sweet
A –artistic
R –reads a lot
A –athletic
H –honest

 WRITING TIME

Have students make an entry in their journals.

(End of lesson.)

CHAPTER 8   LESSON 4

Objectives: Jingles, Study, Test, Check, and Writing (journal).

JINGLE TIME

Have students turn to the Jingle Section in their books and recite the previously-taught jingles.

STUDY TIME

Have students study the vocabulary words in their vocabulary notebooks. Remind students that any vocabulary word in their notebooks could be on their test. Also, have students study any of the skills in the Practice Section that they need to review.

TEST TIME

Have students turn to page 104 in the Test Section of their book and find the Chapter 8 Test. Go over the directions to make sure they understand what to do. (*Chapter 8 Test key is on the next page.*)

CHECK TIME

After students have finished, check and discuss their test papers. Make sure they understand why their answers are right or wrong. (*For total points, count each required answer as a point.*)

(End of lesson.)

Chapter 8 Test
(Student Page 104)

Exercise 1: Classify each sentence.

             HV A   SN   V   Adv   P   A   OP

1. **SN V**   Did the giraffe / walk quietly (by the children)? **Int**
   P1

            Adj   SN   P PPA OP   HV HV V   P A   OP

2. **SN V**   Several pictures (of my school) / could be seen (in the paper). **D**
   P1

           A   Adj   Adj   SN   HV Adv   V   P PPA OP

3. **SN V**   The three black bears / have not returned (to their den). **D**
   P1

Exercise 2: Use Sentence 2 to underline the complete subject once and the complete predicate twice and to complete the table below.

List the Noun Used	List the Noun Job	Singular or Plural	Common or Proper	Simple Subject	Simple Predicate
1. **pictures**	2. **SN**	3. **P**	4. **C**	5. **pictures**	6. **could be seen**
7. **school**	8. **OP**	9. **S**	10. **C**		
11. **paper**	12. **OP**	13. **S**	14. **C**		

Exercise 3: Name the six parts of speech that you have studied. (*You may use abbreviations.*) **(The order may vary.)**

1.   **noun**   2.   **verb**   3.   **adjective**   4.   **adverb**   5.   **preposition**   6.   **pronoun**

Exercise 4: Identify each pair of words as synonyms or antonyms by putting parentheses ( ) around *syn* or *ant*.

1. implied, hinted	**(syn)** ant	5. arrange, prepare	**(syn)** ant	9. pursue, follow	**(syn)** ant
2. keen, sharp	**(syn)** ant	6. encourage, belittle	syn **(ant)**	10. rival, competitor	**(syn)** ant
3. admire, detest	syn **(ant)**	7. pledge, promise	**(syn)** ant	11. impetuous, cautious	syn **(ant)**
4. calm, turmoil	syn **(ant)**	8. unique, common	syn **(ant)**	12. proceed, cease	syn **(ant)**

Exercise 5: For each sentence, write the subject, then write **S** if the subject is singular or **P** if the subject is plural, write the rule number (Rule 1 for singular or Rule 2 for plural), and underline the correct verb in the sentence.

Subject	S or P	Rule
Chris	S	1
windows	P	2
you	P	2
Brandon and Danny	P	2
pup	S	1
celery	S	1
violets	P	2

1. **Chris** (<u>decides</u>, decide) not to go.
2. Two **windows** (was, <u>were</u>) broken last night.
3. **You** (wasn't, <u>weren't</u>) home last night.
4. **Brandon** and **Danny** (has, <u>have</u>) left home.
5. His **pup** (<u>is</u>, are) on a leash.
6. The **celery** (<u>is</u>, are) covered with mold.
7. Wild **violets** (was, <u>were</u>) in bloom on the ridge.

Exercise 6: Finding One Part of Speech. For each sentence, write **SN/SP** above the simple subject and **V** (or **HV** and **V**) above the simple predicate. Underline the word(s) for the part of speech listed to the left of each sentence.

                                 SP   V

Noun(s):   1. At the <u>beach</u>, we swam in the <u>water</u> with our <u>aunt</u>.

                                 SP HV   V

Pronoun(s):   2. <u>He</u> will not advertise in <u>her</u> school newspaper.

                                 SP   V

Preposition(s): 3. <u>After</u> dark, we waded <u>through</u> the creek <u>in</u> our bare feet.

Exercise 7: In your journal, write a paragraph summarizing what you have learned this week.

CHAPTER 8 LESSON 4 CONTINUED

TEACHER INSTRUCTIONS

Use the Question and Answer Flows below for the sentences on the Chapter 8 Test.

Question and Answer Flow for Sentence 1: Did the giraffe walk quietly by the children?

1. What did walk quietly by the children? giraffe - SN
2. What is being said about giraffe? giraffe did walk - V
3. Did - HV
4. Did walk how? quietly - Adv
5. By - P
6. By whom? children - OP
7. The - A
8. The - A

9. SN V P1 Check
10. (By the children) - Prepositional phrase
11. Question mark, question, interrogative sentence
12. Go back to the verb - divide the complete subject from the complete predicate.
13. This sentence has predicate words in the complete subject. Underline the helping verb at the beginning of the sentence twice.

Classified Sentence:

<pre>
                      HV A   SN   V   Adv   P   A   OP
        SN V   Did the giraffe / walk quietly (by the children)? Int
        P1
</pre>

Question and Answer Flow for Sentence 2: Several pictures of my school could be seen in the paper.

1. What could be seen in the paper? pictures - SN
2. What is being said about pictures?
   pictures could be seen - V
3. Could - HV
4. Be - HV
5. In - P
6. In what? paper - OP
7. The - A
8. Of - P

9. Of what? school - OP
10. Whose school? my - PPA
11. How many pictures? several - Adj
12. SN V P1 Check
13. (Of my school) - Prepositional phrase
14. (In the paper) - Prepositional phrase
15. Period, statement, declarative sentence
16. Go back to the verb - divide the complete subject from the complete predicate.

Classified Sentence:

<pre>
                    Adj   SN   P PPA OP   HV HV V   P   A   OP
        SN V   Several pictures (of my school) / could be seen (in the paper). D
        P1
</pre>

Question and Answer Flow for Sentence 3: The three black bears have not returned to their den.

1. What have not returned to their den? bears - SN
2. What is being said about bears?
   bears have returned - V
3. Have - HV
4. Have returned how? not - Adv
5. To - P
6. To what? den - OP
7. Whose den? their - PPA

8. What kind of bears? black - Adj
9. How many bears? three - Adj
10. The - A
11. SN V P1 Check
12. (To their den) - Prepositional phrase
13. Period, statement, declarative sentence
14. Go back to the verb - divide the complete subject from the complete predicate.

Classified Sentence:

<pre>
                  A Adj Adj SN   HV Adv   V   P PPA OP
        SN V   The three black bears / have not returned (to their den). D
        P1
</pre>

CHAPTER 8   LESSON 5

Objectives: Writing (topic sentences) and Writing Assignment #8.

 **WRITING TIME**

TEACHING SCRIPT FOR INTRODUCING ANOTHER WAY TO WRITE TOPIC SENTENCES
WITHOUT STATING THE NUMBER OF POINTS

When we learned how to write a topic sentence, we listed three things we needed to know about a topic sentence in order to recognize it and to write one correctly. I will go over those three things again.

1. A topic sentence should tell the main idea of a paragraph. The topic sentence will give you a general overview of what the paragraph is about. Notice that I said a **general** overview, not a detailed overview. A topic sentence does not give details because its job is to inform the reader very quickly what the reader can expect to find in the paragraph.

2. Most of the time, the topic sentence is the first sentence in the paragraph because most writers prefer to tell their readers at the very beginning what they can expect from the paragraph. Placing the topic sentence first also helps the writer stay focused on the topic of the paragraph. Occasionally, writers will place the topic sentence last or in the middle of a paragraph, but we will concentrate on what happens the majority of the time.

3. A topic sentence usually tells the number of points that will be discussed in the paragraph. This helps narrow the topic and keeps the writer on target.

We are going to look more closely at the third thing a topic sentence usually does. It usually tells the number of points that will be discussed in the paragraph. Let's look at the topic sentence and the three-point sentence from our earlier paragraph about snacks. (*Write the following sentences on the board.* ***Topic sentence****: I have three favorite snacks.* ***Three-point****: They are ice cream, popcorn, and peanut butter crackers.*)

Notice the topic sentence tells that there will be three points in the paragraph, and the points are then listed in the three-point sentence. Remember, this way of writing a topic sentence is used often and is a good reliable form in the three-point paragraph.

In today's lesson, we will learn that the topic sentence does not always have to state the exact number of points. I will show you how to write a topic sentence without actually stating the total number of points. Instead, you will tell the number of points in the three-point sentence. Look carefully at the new sentences I am writing on the board to demonstrate this change. (*Write these new sentences on the board or on notebook paper.* ***Topic sentence****: I enjoy the county fair for many reasons.* ***Three-point****: Three of these reasons are livestock judging, riding the Ferris wheel, and eating cotton candy.*)

CHAPTER 8 LESSON 5 CONTINUED

Topic sentence: I enjoy the county fair for many reasons.
Three-point sentence: Three of these reasons are livestock judging, riding the Ferris wheel, and eating cotton candy.

Notice that words such as **several, many, some, numerous, etc.**, can be used in the topic sentence instead of the exact number of points you will discuss. When you choose to make the topic sentence **more general** by not stating the exact number of points, you force the three-point sentence to supply more information. The three-point sentence must now state the number of points along with listing them.

After you have written a general topic sentence (*by not stating the exact number of points*) and the new three-point sentence, you may write the rest of your paragraph by using the original way of stating your point sentences (*the standard form*) or by using the form you learned in the last lesson (*the time-order form*).

Turn to page 22 and look at Reference 26B. I am going to read the third and fourth sample paragraphs to show you the different ways to combine the things you have learned about three-point paragraphs. (*Read and discuss the third and fourth paragraphs below.*)

Reference 26B: Paragraphs Using Different Writing Forms

Sample 3: Three-point paragraph using a general topic sentence with standard points

    I enjoy the county fair for many reasons. Three of these reasons are livestock judging, riding the Ferris wheel, and eating cotton candy. My first reason for enjoying the county fair is the livestock judging. I enjoy showing my prize bull in the judge's ring before dozens of my friends. **My second** reason for enjoying the county fair is riding the Ferris wheel. I especially like the thrill of coming down fast and getting that hollow feeling in my stomach. **My third** reason for enjoying the county fair is eating cotton candy. I love its sticky texture and getting it all over my fingers and hands. Given the fact that the fair comes but once a year, I make the most of enjoying it for these three reasons.

Sample 4: Three-point paragraph using a general topic sentence with time-order points

    I enjoy the county fair for many reasons. Three of these reasons are livestock judging, riding the Ferris wheel, and eating cotton candy. First, I enjoy the county fair for the livestock judging. I enjoy showing my prize bull in the judge's ring before dozens of my friends. **Next**, I enjoy the county fair for riding the Ferris wheel. I especially like the thrill of coming down fast and getting that hollow feeling in my stomach. **Last**, I enjoy the county fair because I love to eat cotton candy. (or **Finally**, *I enjoy the county fair because I love to eat cotton candy.*) I love its sticky texture and getting it all over my fingers and hands. Given the fact that the fair comes but once a year, I make the most of enjoying it for these three reasons.

TEACHER INSTRUCTIONS FOR WRITING ASSIGNMENT

Give Writing Assignment #8 from the box on the next page. For Writing Assignment #8, students are to write a three-point expository paragraph. They will choose the point of view (first or third person) and the writing form (standard or time order). They are to underline all time-order words used at the beginning of each point sentence. Remind students that they can use third person pronouns in first person writing. Have them follow the Writing Guidelines as they prepare their writing.

CHAPTER 8 LESSON 5 CONTINUED

Writing Assignment Box

Writing Assignment #8: Three-Point Expository Paragraph (You choose the point of view and the writing form.)
(Remind students that first person pronouns are *I, we, me, us, my, mine, our,* and *ours.*)

Writing topics: Things I Remember Most About Grandma or **Ways to Stop Hiccups** or **Ways to Conserve Energy**

TEACHING SCRIPT FOR USING THE WRITING PROCESS FOR THIS WRITING ASSIGNMENT

As you begin this writing assignment, you will start through the writing process. First, you will think about your topic and gather any information you might need in order to do the writing. Second, you will write a rough draft. Remember, it is called a rough draft because it will be revised and edited. You do not have to worry about mistakes as you write your rough draft. After you write the first draft, you will make revisions, using the Revision Checklist in Reference 5. After you revise your writing, you will edit, using the Beginning Editing Checklist in Reference 5.

Finally, after you are satisfied with your revising and editing, you will write a final paper, using the Final Paper Checklist in Reference 5. You will then give the finished writing assignment to me.

TEACHER INSTRUCTIONS FOR CHECKING WRITING ASSIGNMENT

Read, check, and discuss Writing Assignment #8 after students have finished their final paper. Use the editing checklist (*Reference 5 on teacher's page 12*) as you check and discuss students' papers. Make sure students are using the editing checklist correctly.

TEACHING SCRIPT FOR CHOOSING THE BEST WRITING FORM

We have studied two forms for a three-point paragraph, the standard form and the time-order form. Learning to use general number words in the topic sentence of either form gives you the ability to add a lot more variety to your writing. As you write three-point paragraphs, you may choose either the standard or the time-order form, and you may use general number words or exact points.

Since both forms produce effective paragraphs, I will leave it up to you which form you choose each time. Some of you may enjoy the variety of choosing a different form each time you write a paragraph. Others may be more comfortable using only one paragraph form for all your writing assignments.

Even though you are allowed to choose the form you use to write your paragraph, you must follow the directions given for writing in either first or third person. If a point of view is not assigned, you may choose to write in either first or third person. Be aware that the point of view you choose could make it necessary to change the wording of your title.

(End of lesson.)

CHAPTER 9   LESSON 1
Objectives: Jingle (eight parts of speech), Grammar (Introductory Sentences, conjunctions, compound parts, interjection, eight parts of speech, Oral Skill Builder Check), Activity, and Vocabulary #1.

 JINGLE TIME

Have students turn to the Jingle Section in their books and recite the previously-taught jingles. Then, lead students in reciting the new jingle (*The Eight Parts of Speech*) below. Practice the new jingle several times until students can recite it smoothly. Emphasize reciting with a rhythm. Students and teacher should be together! (*Do not try to explain the jingle at this time. Just have fun reciting it. Remember, add motions for more fun and laughter.*)

Teacher's Notes: Again, do not spend a large amount of time practicing the new jingles. Students learn the jingles best by spending a small amount of time consistently, **every** day.

Jingle 15:   Eight Parts of Speech Jingle
Want to know how to write?   Use the eight parts of speech - They're dynamite!   **N**ouns, **V**erbs, and **P**ronouns - They rule!   They're called the **NVP's**, and they're really cool!   The **Double A's** are on the move;   **A**djectives and **A**dverbs help you groove!   Next come the **PIC's**, and then we're done!   The **PIC's** are **P**reposition, **I**nterjection, and **C**onjunction!   All together now, the eight parts of speech, abbreviations please: NVP, AA, PIC   NVP, AA, PIC!

 GRAMMAR TIME

Put the introductory sentences from the box below on the board. Use these sentences as you go through each new concept covered in your teaching script. For the greatest benefit, students must participate orally with the teacher. (*You might put the introductory sentences on notebook paper if you are doing one-on-one instruction with your students.*)

Chapter 9, Introductory Sentences for Lesson 1
1. _____ Maggie and Leslie will be staying with us for a week during the summer.   2. _____ The ore was mined and sold by the mining company in Minnesota.   3. _____ Dear me! The rush-hour traffic is moving very slowly on the freeway!

CHAPTER 9 LESSON 1 CONTINUED

TEACHING SCRIPT FOR CONJUNCTIONS AND COMPOUND PARTS

Today, we will learn about conjunctions and compound parts. A **conjunction** is a word that joins words or groups of words together. The three most common conjunctions are *and, or,* and *but*. The conjunctions *and, or,* and *but* are used so often that they should be memorized. Since conjunctions are memorized, there are no questions to ask to find a conjunction. Conjunctions are labeled with a **C**. Let's chant the three most common conjunctions together several times. (*Have students chant the three most common conjunctions with you several times. Try "**and** (stand up), **or** (sit down), **but** (arms up in a V)" as you recite them. Other motions will also work well.*)

When words or groups of words in a sentence are joined by a conjunction, the parts that are joined are called **compound parts**. The label *C* is written in front of the regular labels for the compound parts. Example: **CSN** for each compound subject noun or **CV** for each compound verb.

You will use what you have just learned as you classify Sentences 1-2 with me to find the conjunction and compound parts. We will classify the sentences together, and I will show you how to say the new part as we say the Question and Answer Flow. Begin.

Question and Answer Flow for Sentence 1: Maggie and Leslie will be staying with us for a week during the summer.

1. Who will be staying with us for a week during the summer? Maggie and Leslie - CSN, CSN (compound subject noun, compound subject noun)
2. What is being said about Maggie and Leslie? Maggie and Leslie will be staying - V
3. Will - HV
4. Be - HV
5. With - P
6. With whom? us - OP
7. For - P
8. For what? week - OP
9. A - A

10. During - P
11. During what? summer - OP
12. The - A
13. And - C

Note: Say: and - conjunction. Label "and" with a "C."

14. SN V P1 Check
15. (With us) - Prepositional phrase
16. (For a week) - Prepositional phrase
17. (During the summer) - Prepositional phrase
18. Period, statement, declarative sentence
19. Go back to the verb - divide the complete subject from the complete predicate.

Classified Sentence:

```
                            CSN   C  CSN  HV HV   V    P  OP   P A OP    P    A   OP
         SN  V      Maggie  and  Leslie / will  be  staying (with  us) (for  a  week) (during  the  summer).  D
         P1
```

Question and Answer Flow for Sentence 2: The ore was mined and sold by the mining company in Minnesota.

1. What was mined and sold by the mining company in Minnesota? ore - SN
2. What is being said about ore? ore was mined and sold - CV, CV (compound verb, compound verb)
3. Was - HV
4. And - C
5. By - P
6. By what? company - OP
7. What kind of company? mining - Adj

8. The - A
9. In - P
10. In what? Minnesota - OP
11. The - A
12. SN V P1 Check
13. (By the mining company) - Prepositional phrase
14. (In Minnesota) - Prepositional phrase
15. Period, statement, declarative sentence
16. Go back to the verb - divide the complete subject from the complete predicate.

Classified Sentence:

```
                         A  SN   HV   CV   C  CV  P  A  Adj      OP      P    OP
         SN  V      The ore / was mined and sold (by the mining company) (in Minnesota).  D
         P1
```

CHAPTER 9 LESSON 1 CONTINUED

TEACHING SCRIPT FOR INTERJECTION

We will now learn about interjections. An **interjection** is one or more words used to express mild or strong emotion. Interjections are usually located at the beginning of a sentence and are separated from the rest of the sentence with a punctuation mark. Mild interjections are followed by a comma or period; strong interjections are followed by an exclamation point. Example: **Oh! Well, Wow! Yes, Hey!**

Interjections are not to be considered when you are deciding whether a sentence is declarative, interrogative, exclamatory, or imperative. There are no questions to find interjections. Interjections are named and then labeled with the abbreviation *I* above them.

You will use what you have just learned about interjections as you classify Sentence 3 with me. We will classify the sentence together, and I will show you how to say the new part as we say the Question and Answer Flow. Begin.

Question and Answer Flow for Sentence 3: Dear me! The rush-hour traffic is moving very slowly on the freeway!	
1. What is moving very slowly on the freeway? traffic - SN	9. What kind of traffic? rush-hour - Adj
2. What is being said about traffic? traffic is moving - V	10. The - A
3. Is - HV	11. Dear me - I
4. Is moving how? slowly - Adv	**Note:** Say, "Dear me - interjection." Label "Dear me" with an 'I'.
5. How slowly? very - Adv	12. SN V P1 Check
6. On - P	13. (On the freeway) - Prepositional phrase
7. On what? freeway - OP	14. Exclamation point, strong feeling, exclamatory sentence
8. The - A	15. Go back to the verb - divide the complete subject from the complete predicate.

Classified Sentence:

```
                            I     A    Adj      SN   HV  V    Adv  Adv    P   A    OP
        SN  V    Dear me! The rush-hour traffic / is moving very slowly (on the freeway)! E
        P1
```

TEACHER INSTRUCTIONS

Use Sentences 1-3 that you just classified with your students to do an Oral Skill Builder Check. Use the guidelines below.

Oral Skill Builder Check	
1. **Noun check.** (Say the job and then say the noun. Circle each noun.)	5. **Identify the complete subject and the complete predicate.** (Underline the complete subject once and the complete predicate twice.)
2. **Identify the nouns as singular or plural.** (Write **S** or **P** above each noun.)	
3. **Identify the nouns as common or proper.** (Follow established procedure for oral identification.)	6. **Identify the simple subject and simple predicate.** (Underline the simple subject once and the simple predicate twice. Bold, or highlight, the lines.)
4. **Do a vocabulary check.** (Follow established procedure for oral identification.)	7. **Recite the irregular verb chart.** (Located on student page 23 and teacher page 138.)

CHAPTER 9 LESSON 1 CONTINUED

TEACHING SCRIPT FOR ALL EIGHT PARTS OF SPEECH

We can add the final two parts of speech, conjunctions and interjections, to our eight parts of speech list. Remember, all words in the English language have been put into one of eight groups called the **Parts of Speech**. How a word is used in a sentence determines its part of speech.

It is very important to know the eight parts of speech because they are the vocabulary for writing. We will now celebrate learning the eight parts of speech by reciting the Eight Parts of Speech Jingle. This jingle will help you remember the eight parts of speech quickly and easily. Turn to page 5 in the Jingle Section of your books and recite Jingle 15, the Eight Parts of Speech Jingle.

ACTIVITY / ASSIGNMENT TIME

Create a word search puzzle and a crossword puzzle, using all the English terms and English definitions that you have studied so far. Make a "key" for each puzzle. Continue to upgrade your puzzles as you have time. Your work on this project may take several days. If you use the computer for this project, generate several puzzles for friends and for other members of your family.

VOCABULARY TIME

Assign Chapter 9, Vocabulary Words **#1** on page 8 in the Reference Section for students to define in their Vocabulary notebooks. Tell students they are to use a dictionary or thesaurus to look up the meanings of the vocabulary words. After they write each word and its meaning, students are to write a sentence using the vocabulary word.

Chapter 9, Vocabulary Words #1
(quill, feather, rip, mend)

(End of lesson.)

CHAPTER 9   LESSON 2

Objectives: Jingles, Grammar (Practice Sentences, Practice and Improved Sentences), Practice Exercise, and Vocabulary #2.

JINGLE TIME

Have students turn to the Jingle Section in their books and recite the previously-taught jingles.

GRAMMAR TIME

First-Year Option: Put the Practice Sentences from the box below on the board or on notebook paper. Use these sentences as you practice the concepts that have been taught. For the greatest benefit, students must participate orally with the teacher. **Second-Year Option:** Have students classify the Practice Sentences independently on notebook paper. Check students' sentences with the answers provided below. (*If you have the CDs for Practice Sentences, have students check their sentences with the CDs.*)

Chapter 9, Practice Sentences for Lesson 2
1. _____ Many varieties of roses were budding and blooming brilliantly in the garden.
2. _____ Dark clouds and a heavy mist hovered over the village throughout the afternoon.
3. _____ We did not camp during the cold winter months.

TEACHING SCRIPT FOR PRACTICING PATTERN 1 SENTENCES WITH THE 8 PARTS OF SPEECH

We will classify three different sentences to practice using the eight parts of speech in the Question and Answer Flows. We will classify the sentences together. Begin. (*You might have your students write the labels above the sentences at this time.*)

Question and Answer Flow for Sentence 1: Many varieties of roses were budding and blooming brilliantly in the garden.

1. What were budding and blooming brilliantly in the garden? varieties - SN
2. What is being said about varieties? varieties were budding and blooming - CV, CV (compound verb, compound verb)
3. Were - HV
4. And - C
5. Were budding and blooming how? brilliantly - Adv
6. In - P
7. In what? garden - OP
8. The - A
9. Of - P
10. Of what? roses - OP
11. How many varieties? many - Adj
12. SN V P1 Check
13. (Of roses) - Prepositional phrase
14. (In the garden) - Prepositional phrase
15. Period, statement, declarative sentence
16. Go back to the verb - divide the complete subject from the complete predicate.

Classified Sentence:

		Adj	SN	P	OP	HV	CV	C	CV	Adv	P	A	OP
SN V P1		Many	varieties	(of	roses)	/ were	budding	and	blooming	brilliantly	(in	the	garden). D

Level 4 Homeschool Teacher's Manual

CHAPTER 9 LESSON 2 CONTINUED

Question and Answer Flow for Sentence 2: Dark clouds and a heavy mist hovered over the village throughout the afternoon.

1. What hovered over the village throughout the afternoon?
   clouds and mist - CSN, CSN
2. What is being said about clouds and mist?
   clouds and mist hovered - V
3. Over - P
4. Over what? village - OP
5. The - A
6. Throughout - P
7. Throughout what? afternoon - OP
8. The - A
9. What kind of mist? heavy - Adj

10. A - A
11. And - C
12. What kind of clouds? dark - Adj
13. SN V P1 Check
14. (Over the village) - Prepositional phrase
15. (Throughout the afternoon) - Prepositional phrase
16. Period, statement, declarative sentence
17. Go back to the verb - divide the complete subject from the complete predicate.

Classified
Sentence:

      Adj   CSN C A Adj CSN   V   P A OP   P   A   OP
<u>SN V</u> Dark clouds and a heavy mist / hovered (over the village) (throughout the afternoon). D
P1

Question and Answer Flow for Sentence 3: We did not camp during the cold winter months.

1. Who did not camp during the cold winter months?
   we - SP
2. What is being said about we? we did camp - V
3. Did - HV
4. Did camp how? not - Adv
5. During - P
6. During what? months - OP
7. What kind of months? winter - Adj

8. What kind of months? cold - Adj
9. The - A
10. SN V P1 Check
11. (During the cold winter months) - Prepositional phrase
12. Period, statement, declarative sentence
13. Go back to the verb - divide the complete subject from the complete predicate.

Classified Sentence:

             SP HV Adv V   P   A   Adj Adj   OP
<u>SN V</u> We / did not camp (during the cold winter months). D
P1

© SHURLEY INSTRUCTIONAL MATERIALS, INC.

CHAPTER 9 LESSON 2 CONTINUED

TEACHING SCRIPT FOR THE PRACTICE SENTENCE

Put these labels on the board: **I CSN C CSN HV V P PPA OP**

Look at the new sentence labels on the board: **I CSN C CSN HV V P PPA OP**. I will guide you again through the process of writing a sentence to practice the different parts that you have learned.

Get out a sheet of notebook paper. On the top line of your notebook paper, write the title _Practice Sentence_. Copy the sentence labels from the board onto your notebook paper. Be sure to leave plenty of writing space between each label. I will guide you through the process you will use whenever you write a Practice Sentence with pronouns and possessive nouns.

1. Go to the two **CSN** labels for compound subject nouns. Think of two nouns that you want to use as your compound subject. Remember, these two nouns must make sense together and with the verb that you choose. Write the two nouns you have chosen on the line _under_ the two **CSN** labels.

2. Go to the **HV** and the **V** labels for the helping verb and the main verb. Think of a helping verb and a main verb that tell what your subjects do. Make sure that your verb makes sense with the two subject nouns. Also, check to make sure you have proper subject-verb agreement. Write the two verbs you have chosen on the line _under_ the **HV** and the **V** labels.

3. Go to the **P** label for the preposition. Think of a preposition word that tells something about your verb. You must be careful to choose a preposition word that makes sense with the noun you will choose for the object of the preposition in your next step. Write the word you have chosen for a preposition _under_ the **P** label.

4. Go to the **OP** label for object of the preposition. If you like the noun you thought of while thinking of a preposition, write it down under the **OP** label. If you prefer, think of another noun by asking **what** or **whom** after your preposition. Check to make sure the preposition and object of the preposition make sense together and also make sense with the rest of the sentence. Remember, the object of the preposition will always answer the question **what** or **whom** after the preposition. Write the word you have chosen for the object of the preposition _under_ the **OP** label.

5. Go to the **PPA** label for the possessive pronoun adjective that is part of your prepositional phrase. Repeat the Possessive Pronoun Jingle to help you think of a pronoun that you want to use as your possessive pronoun adjective. Choose the possessive pronoun that makes the best sense in your sentence. Write the possessive pronoun you have chosen _under_ the **PPA** label.

CHAPTER 9 LESSON 2 CONTINUED

6. Go to the **C** label for the conjunction in your sentence and choose a conjunction that makes sense. What are the three main conjunctions again? (*and, but, or*) Write the conjunction you have chosen *under* the **C** label.

7. Go to the **I** label for the interjection at the beginning of the sentence. Choose an interjection that makes the best sense in your sentence. Write the interjection you have chosen *under* the **I** label.

8. Finally, check your Practice Sentence to make sure it has the necessary parts to be a complete sentence. What are the five parts of a complete sentence? (*subject, verb, complete sense, capital letter, and an end mark*) Does your Practice Sentence have the five parts of a complete sentence? (*Allow time for students to read over their sentences and to make any corrections they need to make.*)

TEACHING SCRIPT FOR THE IMPROVED SENTENCE

Under your Practice Sentence, write the title *Improved Sentence* on another line. To improve your Practice Sentence, you will make two synonym changes, one antonym change, and your choice of a complete word change or another synonym or antonym change.

Since it is harder to find words that can be changed to an antonym, it is usually wise to go through your sentence to find an antonym change first. Look through your sentence again to find words that can be improved with synonyms. Finally, make a decision about whether your last change will be a complete word change, another synonym change, or another antonym change.

I will give you time to write your Improved Sentence. (*Always encourage students to use a thesaurus, synonym-antonym book, or a dictionary to help them develop an interesting and improved writing vocabulary.*) (*After students have finished, check and discuss students' Practice and Improved Sentences.*)

 PRACTICE TIME

Have students write the three sentences that they classified at the beginning of the lesson on notebook paper. Have them tape-record the Question and Answer Flows for all three sentences. Students should write labels above the sentences as they classify them. They especially need the second practice if this is their first year in the program. (*After the students have finished, check the tape and sentence labels. Make sure students understand any mistakes they have made.*)

 VOCABULARY TIME

Assign Chapter 9, Vocabulary Words **#2** on page 8 in the Reference Section for students to define in their Vocabulary notebooks. Tell students they are to use a dictionary or thesaurus to look up the meanings of the vocabulary words. After they write each word and its meaning, students are to write a sentence using the vocabulary word.

Chapter 9, Vocabulary Words #2
(hardy, robust, creeping, rushing)

(End of lesson.)

CHAPTER 9   LESSON 3

Objectives: Jingles, Grammar (Practice Sentences), Skill (homonyms), Writing (journal), and Activity (continued).

 JINGLE TIME

Have students turn to the Jingle Section in their books and recite the previously-taught jingles.

 **GRAMMAR TIME**

First-Year Option: Put the Practice Sentences from the box below on the board or on notebook paper. Use these sentences as you practice the concepts that have been taught. For the greatest benefit, students must participate orally with the teacher. **Second-Year Option:** Have students classify the Practice Sentences independently on notebook paper. Check students' sentences with the answers provided below. (*If you have the CDs for Practice Sentences, have students check their sentences with the CDs.*)

Chapter 9, Practice Sentences for Lesson 3

1. _____ Ouch! I stepped on a sharp rock in the yard and fell down!
2. _____ Horse carriages and classic automobiles cruised down the street during the parade.
3. _____ Oh, no! The skydiver's parachute has not opened yet!

TEACHING SCRIPT FOR PRACTICING PATTERN 1 SENTENCES WITH THE 8 PARTS OF SPEECH

We will classify three different sentences to practice using the eight parts of speech in the Question and Answer Flows. We will classify the sentences together. Begin. (*You might have your students write the labels above the sentences at this time.*)

Question and Answer Flow for Sentence 1: Ouch! I stepped on a sharp rock in the yard and fell down!

1. Who stepped on a sharp rock in the yard and fell down? I - SP
2. What is being said about I? I stepped and fell - CV, CV
3. Fell where? down - Adv
4. And - C
5. In - P
6. In what? yard - OP
7. The - A
8. On - P
9. On what? rock - OP
10. What kind of rock? sharp - Adj
11. A - A
12. Ouch - I
13. SN V P1 Check
14. (On a sharp rock) - Prepositional phrase
15. (In the yard) - Prepositional phrase
16. Exclamation point, strong feeling, exclamatory sentence
17. Go back to the verb - divide the complete subject from the complete predicate.

Classified Sentence:

		I	SP	CV		P	A	Adj	OP		P	A	OP	C	CV	Adv
SN	V	Ouch! I / stepped (on a sharp rock) (in the yard) and fell down! **E**														
	P1															

Level 4 Homeschool Teacher's Manual

CHAPTER 9 LESSON 3 CONTINUED

Question and Answer Flow for Sentence 2: Horse carriages and classic automobiles cruised down the street during the parade.

1. What cruised down the street during the parade?
   carriages and automobiles - CSN, CSN
2. What is being said about carriages and automobiles?
   carriages and automobiles cruised - V
3. Down - P
4. Down what? street - OP
5. The - A
6. During - P
7. During what? parade - OP
8. The - A
9. What kind of automobiles? classic - Adj
10. And - C
11. What kind of carriages? horse - Adj
12. SN V P1 Check
13. (Down the street) - Prepositional phrase
14. (During the parade) - Prepositional phrase
15. Period, statement, declarative sentence
16. Go back to the verb - divide the complete subject
    from the complete predicate.

Classified   Adj   CSN   C   Adj   CSN   V   P   A   OP   P   A   OP
Sentence: __SN V__   Horse carriages and classic automobiles / cruised (down the street) (during the parade). **D**
                    P1

Question and Answer Flow for Sentence 3: Oh, no! The skydiver's parachute has not opened yet!

1. What has not opened yet? parachute - SN
2. What is being said about parachute?
   parachute has opened - V
3. Has - HV
4. Has opened how? not - Adv
5. Has opened when? yet - Adv
6. Whose parachute? skydiver's - PNA
7. The - A
8. Oh, no - I
9. SN V P1 Check
10. No prepositional phrases.
11. Exclamation point, strong feeling, exclamatory sentence
12. Go back to the verb - divide the complete subject
    from the complete predicate.

Classified Sentence: I   A   PNA   SN   HV Adv   V   Adv
                        __SN V__   Oh, no! The skydiver's parachute / has not opened yet! **E**
                            P1

SKILL TIME

TEACHING SCRIPT FOR HOMONYMS

Today, we will learn about homonyms. Look at Reference 28 on page 24 in the Reference section of your book. The definition says that homonyms are words that sound the same but have different meanings and different spellings. You should study the Homonym Chart until you are familiar enough with each homonym that you can choose the correct form easily. Since this is only a partial listing, you must look up homonyms that you do not know and that are not listed on the chart. (*The homonym chart is located on the next page.*)

Look at the examples for choosing the right homonyms at the bottom of the reference box. The directions say to underline the correct homonym. Read number 1. Look at the homonyms *council* and *counsel*. Go to the Homonym Chart and read the definition for each spelling. How do we spell the homonym that means *assembly* ? (*c-o-u-n-c-i-l*) How do we spell the homonym that means *advice* ? (*c-o-u-n-s-e-l*)

Which homonym would you choose to complete the first sentence correctly? (*council*) How did you decide? It makes sense for Mr. Davis to be a member of an assembly. The word *council* means the same thing as *assembly*

CHAPTER 9 LESSON 3 CONTINUED

Now, look at number 2. Which homonym would you choose to complete the second sentence correctly? (*counsel*) How did you decide? It makes sense for Mr. and Mrs. Smith to give advice to troubled teenagers. The word *counsel* means the same thing as *advice*. Always check the Homonym Chart or use a dictionary if you have a question about which homonym to use.

Reference 28: Homonym Chart		
Homonyms are words that sound the same but have different meanings and different spellings.		
1. **capital** - upper part, main	15. **lead** - metal	29. **their** - belonging to them
2. **capitol** - statehouse	16. **led** - guided	30. **there** - in that place
3. **coarse** - rough	17. **no** - not so	31. **they're** - they are
4. **course** - route	18. **know** - to understand	32. **threw** - did throw
5. **council** - assembly	19. **right** - correct	33. **through** -from end to end
6. **counsel** - advice	20. **write** - to form letters	34. **to** - toward, preposition
7. **forth** - forward	21. **principle** - a truth/rule/law	35. **too** - denoting excess
8. **fourth** - ordinal number	22. **principal** - chief/head person	36. **two** - a couple
9. **its** - possessive pronoun	23. **stationary** - motionless	37. **your** - belonging to you
10. **it's** - it is	24. **stationery** - paper	38. **you're** - you are
11. **hear** - to listen	25. **peace** - quiet	39. **weak** - not strong
12. **here** - in this place	26. **piece** - a part	40. **week** - seven days
13. **knew** - understood	27. **sent** - caused to go	41. **days** - more than one day
14. **new** - not old	28. **scent** - odor	42. **daze** - a confused state
Directions: Underline the correct homonym.		

1. Mr. Davis is a member of the church (counsel, **council**).
2. Mr. and Mrs. Smith give (council, **counsel**) to troubled teenagers.

WRITING TIME

Have students make an entry in their journals.

ACTIVITY / ASSIGNMENT TIME

Continue working on your word search puzzle and crossword puzzle. Make sure you are using all the English terms and English definitions that you have studied so far. Make a "key" for each puzzle. Give your finished project to family members and friends and have them complete your puzzles. Check the puzzles they work with your puzzle key. Keep notes in your Journal about your puzzles for future reference. Continue to upgrade your puzzles as you have time. Remember, if you use the computer for this project, generate several puzzles for friends and for other members of your family.

STUDY TIME

Have students study the skills in the Practice Section that they need to review. They should study the homonym chart and the jingles. Chapter 9 Test will include homonyms and matching English definitions.

(End of lesson.)

Level 4 Homeschool Teacher's Manual

CHAPTER 9   LESSON 4

Objectives: Jingles, Study, Test, Check, Activity, and Writing (journal)

JINGLE TIME

Have students turn to the Jingle Section in their books and recite the previously-taught jingles.

STUDY TIME

Have students study the vocabulary words in their vocabulary notebooks. Remind students that any vocabulary word in their notebooks could be on their test. Also, have students study any of the skills in the Practice Section that they need to review.

TEST TIME

Have students turn to page 105 in the Test Section of their book and find the Chapter 9 Test. Go over the directions to make sure they understand what to do. (*Chapter 9 Test key is on the next page.*)

CHECK TIME

After students have finished, check and discuss their test papers. Make sure they understand why their answers are right or wrong. (*For total points, count each required answer as a point.*)

ACTIVITY / ASSIGNMENT TIME

Today, you will evaluate your "puzzle" project. Write the evaluation of this project in your Journal. Tell what you enjoyed most about this project. Tell what you would do differently next time. Share the most interesting and inspiring part of the project. Share the most frustrating part of the project. Did you finish your project on time? Did you share your project and get feedback from friends and family members? Did you create more puzzles? Compare your creative efforts with other projects that you have done. Are you happy with the finished product? What grade would you give this project? Explain why.

(End of lesson.)

Chapter 9 Test
(Student Page 105)

Exercise 1: Classify each sentence.

```
       (You) SP      V    P  Adj  A   Adj      OP    P   A    OP    P   A   Adj    OP
1.  SN V        / Look (at all the  broken branches) (on the  ground) (after the severe storm). Imp
    P1
```

```
                       I   SP   V     P   A  Adj   Adj    OP   P  Adj  OP
2.  SN V        Whew! I / studied (for the annual spelling contest) (for six weeks)! E
    P1
```

```
                    A   CSN   CSN   C  CSN  HV   V    P  OP
3.  SN V        The nickel, quarter, and dime / were minted (in 1975). D
    P1
```

Exercise 2: Use Sentence 2 to underline the complete subject once and the complete predicate twice and to complete the table below.

List the Noun Used	List the Noun Job	Singular or Plural	Common or Proper	Simple Subject	Simple Predicate
1. **contest**	2. **OP**	3. **S**	4. **C**	5. **I**	6. **studied**
7. **weeks**	8. **OP**	9. **P**	10. **C**		

Exercise 3: Name the eight parts of speech that you have studied. (*You may use abbreviations*.) **(The order may vary.)**

1. **noun**   2. **verb**   3. **adjective**   4. **adverb**   5. **preposition**   6. **pronoun**   7. **conjunction**   8. **interjection**

Exercise 4: Answer each question below.

1. List the 8 *be* verbs. **am, is, are, was, were, be, being, been**

2. What are the parts of a verb phrase? **helping verb and main verb**

3. Name the seven subject pronouns. **I, we, he, she, it, you, they**

4. Name the seven possessive pronouns. **my, our, his, her, its, their, your**

5. Name the seven object pronouns. **me, us, him, her, it, them, you**

6. What part of speech is the word NOT? **adverb**

Exercise 5: Identify each pair of words as synonyms or antonyms by putting parentheses ( ) around *syn* or *ant*.

1. bucket, pail	**(syn)** ant	5. hardy, robust	**(syn)** ant	9. pledge, promise	**(syn)** ant
2. rip, mend	syn **(ant)**	6. depress, uplift	syn **(ant)**	10. creeping, rushing	syn **(ant)**
3. fresh, fatigued	syn **(ant)**	7. unique, common	syn **(ant)**	11. sharp, keen	**(syn)** ant
4. soiled, dirty	**(syn)** ant	8. quill, feather	**(syn)** ant	12. impetuous, cautious	syn **(ant)**

Exercise 6: Underline the correct homonym in each sentence.

1. I really need some (<u>coarse</u>, course) sandpaper.
2. (Its, <u>It's</u>) a perfect day for a picnic.
3. I need (<u>to</u>, too, two) be absent tomorrow.
4. Look again at the (forth, <u>fourth</u>) question.
5. The (coarse, <u>course</u>) was too difficult for freshmen.
6. We traced the river to (<u>its</u>, it's) origin.
7. There are (to, too, <u>two</u>) rivers to cross in town.
8. She was (to, <u>too</u>, two) late for the appointment.

Exercise 7: In your journal, write a paragraph summarizing what you have learned this week.

CHAPTER 9 LESSON 4 CONTINUED

TEACHER INSTRUCTIONS

Use the Question and Answer Flows below for the sentences on the Chapter 9 Test.

Question and Answer Flow for Sentence 1: Look at all the broken branches on the ground after the severe storm.

1. Who look at all the broken branches on the ground after the severe storm?
   (You) - SP (Understood subject pronoun)
2. What is being said about you? you look - V
3. At - P
4. At what? branches - OP
5. What kind of branches? broken - Adj
6. The - A
7. How many branches? all - Adj
8. On - P
9. On what? ground - OP
10. The - A
11. After - P
12. After what? storm - OP
13. What kind of storm? severe - Adj
14. The - A
15. SN V P1 Check
16. (At all the broken branches) - Prepositional phrase
17. (On the ground) - Prepositional phrase
18. (After the severe storm) - Prepositional phrase
19. Period, command, imperative sentence
20. Go back to the verb - divide the complete subject from the complete predicate.

Classified Sentence:
```
          (You) SP      V     P Adj A   Adj      OP        P   A    OP     P   A   Adj    OP
          SN V         / Look (at all the broken branches) (on the ground) (after the severe storm). Imp
          P1
```

Question and Answer Flow for Sentence 2: Whew! I studied for the annual spelling contest for six weeks!

1. Who studied for the annual spelling contest for six weeks? I - SP
2. What is being said about I? I studied - V
3. For - P
4. For what? contest - OP
5. What kind of contest? spelling - Adj
6. What kind of contest? annual - Adj
7. The - A
8. For - P
9. For what? weeks - OP
10. How many weeks? six - Adj
11. Whew - I
12. SN V P1 Check
13. (For the annual spelling contest) - Prepositional phrase
14. (For six weeks) - Prepositional phrase
15. Exclamation point, strong feeling, exclamatory sentence
16. Go back to the verb - divide the complete subject from the complete predicate.

Classified Sentence:
```
                         I   SP  V      P A  Adj     Adj     OP       P Adj OP
          SN V          Whew! I / studied (for the annual spelling contest) (for six weeks)! E
          P1
```

Question and Answer Flow for Sentence 3: The nickel, quarter, and dime were minted in 1975.

1. What were minted in 1975? nickel, quarter, and dime - CSN, CSN, CSN
2. What is being said about nickel, quarter, and dime? nickel, quarter, and dime were minted - V
3. Were - HV
4. In - P
5. In what? 1975 - OP
6. And - C
7. The - A
8. SN V P1 Check
9. (In 1975) - Prepositional phrase
10. Period, statement, declarative sentence
11. Go back to the verb - divide the complete subject from the complete predicate.

Classified Sentence:
```
                        A    CSN     CSN   C   CSN   HV   V    P  OP
          SN V         The nickel, quarter, and dime / were minted (in 1975). D
          P1
```

CHAPTER 9   LESSON 5
Objectives: Writing (essay) and Writing Assignments #9 and #10.

 **WRITING TIME**

TEACHING SCRIPT FOR INTRODUCING AN ESSAY

You have been writing expository paragraphs in a three-point paragraph format. Remember, writing in a three-point paragraph format is a way to organize your paragraph by defining your topic, listing each of your points, supporting each of your points, and ending with a conclusion. Now, in this writing section, you will learn to expand your basic three-point format into several paragraphs. When you write several paragraphs about a certain topic, it is called an essay.

The essay is an easy and fun form of writing. The **essay** is a written discussion of one idea and is made up of several paragraphs. It might be interesting to know that the word *essay* comes from the French word *essai*, meaning "a trial" or "a try." Many students consider essay writing a real "trial." However, with the Shurley Method, you will find essay writing quite easy and even pleasant. In fact, anyone who reads your essays will be very impressed with your ability to organize and discuss any writing topic.

In this writing section, you will write expository essays. **Expository essays** give facts or directions, explain ideas, or define words, just like the expository paragraphs. Expository writing is often used for writing assignments in different subject areas. Any time you do an expository writing, whether it is an essay or a paragraph, you should focus on making your meaning clear and understandable. The three-point format you use will help your reader understand exactly what you mean. You will now learn to expand a three-point paragraph into an expository essay.

TEACHING SCRIPT FOR INTRODUCING HOW TO WRITE A 3-PARAGRAPH ESSAY

To make essay writing easier, you will first learn how to develop a three-paragraph essay using the three-point format. Remember, the three-point format is a way of organizing your essay that will help make your meaning clear and understandable.

A three-paragraph essay has three parts: **1. Introduction 2. Body 3. Conclusion**. All these parts will always be written in that order. Although a title will be the first item appearing at the top of your essay, you will not write the title until you have finished the essay. In effect, the title will become the fourth part of a three-paragraph essay. In a three-paragraph essay, there will be three paragraphs, no more and no fewer. The introduction forms the first paragraph, the body forms the second paragraph, and the conclusion forms the third paragraph of the essay.

As you are learning to write a three-paragraph essay, it will help to remember the outline for the three-point paragraph that you have already learned. Look at the two outlines in Reference 29 on page 24 in your book. Let's compare and discuss the differences in the paragraph and essay. Notice that there are more sentences in the introduction and conclusion for the essay. Of course, the second paragraph contains all the points and their supporting sentences. (*Reference 29 is on the next page.*)

CHAPTER 9 LESSON 5 CONTINUED

Reference 29: Three-Point Paragraph and Essay	
Outline of a Three-Point Paragraph	**Outline of a Three-Paragraph Essay**

I. Title
II. Paragraph (9 sentences)
  A. Topic sentence
  B. A three-point sentence
  C. A **first-point** sentence
  D. A **supporting** sentence for the first point
  E. A **second-point** sentence
  F. A **supporting** sentence for the second point
  G. A **third-point** sentence
  H. A **supporting** sentence for the third point
  I. A concluding sentence
	I. Title
	II. Paragraph 1 - Introduction (3 sentences)
	  A. Topic and general number sentence
	  B. Extra information about the topic sentence
	  C. Three-point sentence
	III. Paragraph 2 - Body (6-9 sentences)
	  A. **First-point** sentence
	  B. One or two **supporting** sentences for the first point
	  C. **Second-point** sentence
	  D. One or two **supporting** sentences for the second point
	  E. **Third-point** sentence
	  F. One or two **supporting** sentences for the third point
	IV. Paragraph 3 - Conclusion (2 sentences)
	  A. Concluding general statement
	  B. Concluding summary sentence

You will learn how to write each sentence and paragraph in the three-paragraph expository essay by following the steps in Reference 30 on pages 25 and 26 in your book. (*Read and discuss Reference 30 with your students.*)

Reference 30: Steps in Writing a Three-Paragraph Expository Essay

WRITING TOPIC: Playing a Musical Instrument

LIST THE POINTS FOR THE TOPIC

♦ Select three points to list about the topic.
  1. **Opens the door to a new world of art**
  2. **Teaches self-discipline**
  3. **Creates a lifelong enjoyment of music**

WRITING THE INTRODUCTION AND TITLE

1. Sentence #1 - Topic Sentence
   Write the topic sentence by using the words in your topic and adding a general number word, such as *several, many, some,* or *numerous,* instead of the exact number of points you will discuss.
   (I have discovered that playing a musical instrument can provide many opportunities for people who love music.)

2. Sentence #2 - Extra Information about the topic sentence
   This sentence can clarify, explain, define, or just be an extra interesting comment about the topic sentence. If you need another sentence to complete your information, write an extra sentence here. If you write an extra sentence, your introductory paragraph will have four sentences in it instead of three.
   (Although many people focus solely on developing sports-related abilities, I think musical talents are just as important to develop.)

3. Sentence #3 - Three-point sentence
   This sentence will list the three points to be discussed in the order that you will present them in the body of your paper. You can list the points with or without the specific number in front.
   (Playing a musical instrument opens the door to a new world of art, teaches self-discipline, and creates a lifelong enjoyment of music.) or **(The three reasons why I enjoy playing a musical instrument are that it opens the door to a new world of art, teaches self-discipline, and creates a lifelong enjoyment of music.)**

CHAPTER 9 LESSON 5 CONTINUED

Reference 30: Steps in Writing a Three-Paragraph Expository Essay (continued)

♦ The Title - Since there are many possibilities for titles, look at the topic and the three points listed about the topic. Use some of the words in the topic and write a phrase to tell what your paragraph is about. Your title can be short or long. Capitalize the first, last, and important words in your title. **(The Benefits of Playing a Musical Instrument)**

WRITING THE BODY

4. Sentence #4 - First Point - Write a sentence stating your first point.
   (One of the reasons I enjoy playing a musical instrument is that it opens the door to a new world of art.)

5. Sentence #5 - Supporting Sentence(s) - Write one or two sentences that give more information about your first point. **(In learning to play different pieces of music on an instrument, one explores a wide range of artistic styles.)**

6. Sentence #6 - Second Point - Write a sentence stating your second point.
   (Another reason I enjoy playing a musical instrument is that it teaches self-discipline.)

7. Sentence #7 - Supporting Sentence(s) - Write one or two sentences that give more information about your second point. **(Without a doubt, it requires devotion to the instrument.)**

8. Sentence #8 - Third Point - Write a sentence stating your third point.
   (I also enjoy playing a musical instrument because it creates a lifelong enjoyment of music.)

9. Sentence #9 - Supporting Sentence(s) - Write one or two sentences that give more information about your third point. **(Acquiring these special skills creates many opportunities for one to perform for business or pleasure throughout the rest of his or her life.)**

WRITING THE CONCLUSION

10. Sentence #10 - Concluding General Statement - Read the topic sentence again and then rewrite it, using some of the same words to say the same thing in a different way.
    (Clearly, there are many advantages of playing a musical instrument.)

11. Sentence #11 - Concluding Summary (Final) Sentence - Read the three-point sentence again and then rewrite it using some of the same words to say the same thing in a different way.
    (For those who play a musical instrument, the skill can be very valuable in many ways.)

SAMPLE THREE-PARAGRAPH ESSAY

The Benefits of Playing a Musical Instrument

I have discovered that playing a musical instrument can provide many opportunities for people who love music. Although many people focus solely on developing sports-related abilities, I think musical talents are just as important to develop. Playing a musical instrument opens the door to a new world of art, teaches self-discipline, and creates a lifelong enjoyment of music.

One of the reasons I enjoy playing a musical instrument is that it opens the door to a new world of art. In learning to play different pieces of music on an instrument, one explores a wide range of artistic styles. Another reason I enjoy playing a musical instrument is that it teaches self-discipline. Without a doubt, it requires devotion to the instrument. I also enjoy playing a musical instrument because it creates a lifelong enjoyment of music. Acquiring these special skills creates many opportunities for one to perform for business or pleasure throughout the rest of his or her life.

Clearly, there are many advantages of playing a musical instrument. For those who play a musical instrument, the skill can be very valuable in many ways.

CHAPTER 9 LESSON 5 CONTINUED

TEACHER INSTRUCTIONS FOR WRITING ASSIGNMENTS

Give Writing Assignment #9 and Writing Assignment #10 from the box below. Remind students to follow the Writing Guidelines as they prepare their writings. For Writing Assignment #9, students are to write a three-point **paragraph** in first person. Have students underline all first person pronouns in their paragraph. Remind students that they can use third person pronouns in first person writing.

For Writing Assignment #10, students are to write a **three-paragraph essay** in first person. Have students use the three-paragraph essay steps and the essay outline to do the writing assignment below. After students have finished writing their essay, have them circle the capital letter and end mark at the beginning and end of each sentence. (*Students can expand their three-point paragraph from writing assignment #9 into a three-paragraph essay, or they can choose a different topic for their three-point essay.*)

Writing Assignment Box

Writing Assignment #9: Three-Point Expository Paragraph (First Person)
(Remind students that first person pronouns are *I, we, me, us, my, our, mine,* and *ours.*)

Writing topics: What I Like/Dislike about Shopping or **Reasons for Having a Fire-Drill Plan at Home**

Writing Assignment #10: Three-Paragraph Expository Essay (First Person)
(Remind students that the 3-paragraph essay has four parts: 1. Title 2. Introduction 3. Body 4. Conclusion)

Writing topics: What I Like/Dislike about Shopping or **Reasons for Having a Fire-Drill Plan at Home** or
Important Inventions in America or **Things That Make Me Angry**

TEACHING SCRIPT FOR USING THE WRITING PROCESS FOR THIS WRITING ASSIGNMENT

As you begin this writing assignment, you will start through the writing process. First, you will think about your topic and gather any information you might need in order to do the assignment. Second, you will write a rough draft. Remember, it is called a rough draft because it will be revised and edited. You do not have to worry about mistakes as you write your rough draft. After you write the first draft, you will make revisions, using the Revision Checklist in Reference 5. After you revise your writing, you will edit, using the Beginning Editing Checklist in Reference 5. Finally, after you are satisfied with your revising and editing, you will write a final paper, using the Final Paper Checklist in Reference 5. You will then give the finished writing assignment to me.

TEACHER INSTRUCTIONS FOR CHECKING WRITING ASSIGNMENTS

Read, check, and discuss Writing Assignments #9 and #10 after students have finished their final papers. Use the editing checklist (*Reference 5 on teacher's page 12*) as you check and discuss students' papers. Make sure students are using the editing checklist correctly. In the beginning, you must also check students' papers carefully for <u>form</u> mistakes. This will ensure that students are learning the three-point essay format correctly.

(End of lesson.)

CHAPTER 10   LESSON 1
Objectives: Jingles, Grammar (Practice Sentences), Oral Skill Builder Check, Skill (capitalization), Activity, and Vocabulary #1.

 JINGLE TIME

Have students turn to the Jingle Section in their books and recite the previously-taught jingles.

 GRAMMAR TIME

First-Year Option: Put the Practice Sentences from the box below on the board or on notebook paper. Use these sentences as you practice the concepts that have been taught. For the greatest benefit, students must participate orally with the teacher. **Second-Year Option:** Have students classify the Practice Sentences independently on notebook paper. Check students' sentences with the answers provided below. *(If you have the CDs for Practice Sentences, have students check their sentences with the CDs.)*

Chapter 10, Practice Sentences for Lesson 1
1. _____ Did you sleep well at night during your vacation cruise?   2. _____ Listen carefully to the words of the beautiful song.

TEACHING SCRIPT FOR PRACTICING PATTERN 1 SENTENCES

We will practice classifying Pattern 1 Sentences. We will classify the sentences together. Begin. *(You might have your students write the labels above the sentences at this time.)*

Question and Answer Flow for Sentence 1: Did you sleep well at night during your vacation cruise?
1. Who did sleep well at night during your vacation cruise? 　you - SP   2. What is being said about you? you did sleep - V   3. Did - HV   4. Did sleep how? well - Adv   5. At - P   6. At what? night - OP   7. During - P   8. During what? cruise - OP   9. What kind of cruise? vacation - Adj   10. Whose cruise? your - PPA

11. SN V P1 Check
12. (At night) - Prepositional phrase
13. (During your vacation cruise) - Prepositional phrase
14. Question mark, question, interrogative sentence
15. Go back to the verb - divide the complete subject from the complete predicate.
16. This sentence has predicate words in the complete subject. Underline the helping verb at the beginning of the sentence twice.

Classified Sentence:

```
                          HV SP    V    Adv  P  OP      P   PPA  Adj    OP
              SN  V       Did you / sleep well (at night) (during your vacation cruise)?  Int
              P1
```

CHAPTER 10 LESSON 1 CONTINUED

Question and Answer Flow for Sentence 2: Listen carefully to the words of the beautiful song.	
1. Who listen carefully to the words of the beautiful song? (You) - SP (Understood subject pronoun)	9. What kind of song? beautiful - Adj
2. What is being said about you? you listen - V	10. The - A
3. Listen how? carefully - Adv	11. SN V P1 Check
4. To - P	12. (To the words) - Prepositional phrase
5. To what? words - OP	13. (Of the beautiful song) - Prepositional phrase
6. The - A	14. Period, command, imperative sentence
7. Of - P	15. Go back to the verb - divide the complete subject from the complete predicate.
8. Of what? song - OP	

Classified Sentence:
```
                    (You) SP      V    Adv    P  A   OP    P  A   Adj    OP
                    SN  V       / Listen carefully (to the words) (of the beautiful song).  Imp
                    _____
                    P1
```

Use Sentences 1-2 that you just classified with your students to do an Oral Skill Builder Check. Use the guidelines below.

Oral Skill Builder Check	
1. **Noun check.** (Say the job and then say the noun. Circle each noun.)	5. **Identify the complete subject and the complete predicate.** (Underline the complete subject once and the complete predicate twice.)
2. **Identify the nouns as singular or plural.** (Write **S** or **P** above each noun.)	6. **Identify the simple subject and simple predicate.** (Underline the simple subject once and the simple predicate twice. Bold, or highlight, the lines.)
3. **Identify the nouns as common or proper.** (Follow established procedure for oral identification.)	7. **Recite the irregular verb chart.** (Located on student page 23 and teacher page 138.)
4. **Do a vocabulary check.** (Follow established procedure for oral identification.)	

SKILL TIME

TEACHING SCRIPT FOR INTRODUCING THE CAPITALIZATION RULES

Turn to page 27 in the Reference Section and look at Reference 31 in your student book. These are the rules for capitalization. The capitalization rules are organized into sections of similar rules. (*Read and discuss each section and the rules contained in each section.*) Your knowledge of capitalization rules will help you as you write and edit your writing. You will find that readers appreciate writers who use capitalization rules well. (*The capitalization rules are reproduced for you on page 167.*)

CHAPTER 10 LESSON 1 CONTINUED

ACTIVITY / ASSIGNMENT TIME

Students will make and then play a Capitalization Memory game. Have students follow the directions below to play Capitalization Memory.

1. Gather 24 index cards. Write one capitalization rule on the back of each card. On the front of each card, write an example that demonstrates that rule.

2. Play with a partner if possible (family member, friend, etc.).

3. Shuffle the 24 cards and spread them out in your hand. Have a player point to a card. Hold the card so the player can read the example. See if the player can recite the capitalization rule that applies to the example.

4. Variation: Have a player point to a card. Hold the card so the player can read the capitalization rule. See if the player can recite 5 examples that apply to the capitalization rule.

5. Assign points to the different capitalization rules. Harder rules could be worth more points. Total up the points for each player.

6. Discuss the rules players do and do not know. Think of new capitalization games to play.

VOCABULARY TIME

Assign Chapter 10, Vocabulary Words **#1** on page 8 in the Reference Section for students to define in their Vocabulary notebooks. Tell students they are to use a dictionary or thesaurus to look up the meanings of the vocabulary words. After they write each word and its meaning, students are to write a sentence using the vocabulary word.

Chapter 10, Vocabulary Words #1
(complex, difficult, petite, large)

(End of lesson.)

CHAPTER 10 LESSON 1 CONTINUED

Reference 31: Capitalization Rules

SECTION 1: CAPITALIZE THE FIRST WORD

1. The first word of a sentence. (*He likes to take a nap.*)
2. The first word in the greeting and closing of letters. (*Dear, Yours truly*)
3. The first and last word and important words in titles of literary works.
    (*books, songs, short stories, poems, articles, movie titles, magazines*)
    (*Note: Conjunctions, articles, and prepositions with fewer than five letters are not capitalized unless they are the first or last word.*)
4. The first word of a direct quotation. (*Dad said, "We are going home."*)
5. The first word in each line of a topic outline.

SECTION 2: CAPITALIZE NAMES, INITIALS, AND TITLES OF PEOPLE

6. The pronoun I. (*May I go with you?*)
7. The names and nicknames of people. (*Sam, Joe, Jones, Slim, Shorty*)
8. Family names when used in place of or with the person's name.
    (*Grandmother, Auntie, Uncle Joe, Mother – Do NOT capitalize <u>my mother</u>.*)
9. Titles used with, or in place of, people's names.
    (*Mr., Ms., Miss, Dr. Smith, Doctor, Captain, President, Sir*)
10. People's initials. (*J. D., C. Smith*)

SECTION 3: CAPITALIZE WORDS OF TIME

11. The days of the week and months of the year. (*Monday, July*)
12. The names of holidays. (*Christmas, Thanksgiving, Easter*)
13. The names of historical events, periods, laws, documents, conflicts, and distinguished awards.   (*Civil War, Middle Ages, Medal of Honor*)

SECTION 4: CAPITALIZE NAMES OF PLACES

14. The names and abbreviations of cities, towns, counties, states, countries, and nations.
    (*Dallas, Texas, Fulton County, Africa, America, USA, AR, TX*)
15. The names of avenues, streets, roads, highways, routes, and post office boxes.
    (*Main Street, Jones Road, Highway 89, Rt. 1, Box 2, P.O. Box 45*)
16. The names of lakes, rivers, oceans, mountain ranges, deserts, parks, stars, planets, and constellations.
    (*Beaver Lake, Rocky Mountains, Venus*)
17. The names of schools and titles of school courses that are numbered or are languages.
    (*Walker Elementary School, Mathematics II*)
18. North, south, east, and west when they refer to sections of the country.
    (*up North, live in the East, out West*)

SECTION 5: CAPITALIZE NAMES OF OTHER NOUNS AND PROPER ADJECTIVES

19. The names of pets. (*Spot, Tweety Bird, etc.*)
20. The names of products. (*Campbell's soup, Kelly's chili, Ford cars, etc.*)
21. The names of companies, buildings, ships, planes, space ships.
    (*Empire State Building, Titanic, IBM, The Big Tire Co.*)
22. Proper adjectives. (*the English language, Italian restaurant, French test*)
23. The names of clubs, organizations, or groups. (*Lion's Club, Jaycees, Beatles*)
24. The names of political parties, religious preferences, nationalities, and races.
    (*Democratic party, Republican, Jewish synagogue, American*)

CHAPTER 10   LESSON 2

Objectives: Jingles, Grammar (Practice Sentences, Pattern 1 Practice and Improved Sentences), Skill (punctuation), Activity, and Vocabulary #2.

 JINGLE TIME

Have students turn to the Jingle Section in their books and recite the previously-taught jingles.

 GRAMMAR TIME

First-Year Option: Put the Practice Sentences from the box below on the board or on notebook paper. Use these sentences as you practice the concepts that have been taught. For the greatest benefit, students must participate orally with the teacher. **Second-Year Option:** Have students classify the Practice Sentences independently on notebook paper. Check students' sentences with the answers provided below. *(If you have the CDs for Practice Sentences, have students check their sentences with the CDs.)*

Chapter 10, Practice Sentences for Lesson 2
1. _____ Pine, oak, and dogwood trees are planted everywhere on our property.
2. _____ Were the poisonous mushrooms growing wildly along the bank of the river?

TEACHING SCRIPT FOR PRACTICING PATTERN 1 SENTENCES

Today, we will practice classifying Pattern 1 Sentences. We will classify the sentences together. Begin. *(You might have your students write the labels above the sentences at this time.)*

Question and Answer Flow for Sentence 1: Pine, oak, and dogwood trees are planted everywhere on our property.

1. What are planted everywhere on our property? trees - SN
2. What is being said about trees? trees are planted - V
3. Are - HV
4. Are planted where? everywhere - Adv
5. On - P
6. On what? property - OP
7. Whose property? our - PPA
8. What kind of trees? pine, oak, and dogwood - CAdj, CAdj, CAdj (compound adjective, compound adjective, compound adjective)
9. And - C
10. SN V P1 Check
11. (On our property) - Prepositional phrase
12. Period, statement, declarative sentence
13. Go back to the verb - divide the complete subject from the complete predicate.

Classified Sentence:

		CAdj	CAdj	C	CAdj	SN	HV	V		Adv		P	PPA	OP	
SN V		Pine,	oak,	and	dogwood	trees	/ are	planted		everywhere		(on	our	property).	D
P1															

CHAPTER 10 LESSON 2 CONTINUED

Question and Answer Flow for Sentence 2: Were the poisonous mushrooms growing wildly along the bank of the river?

1. What were growing wildly along the bank of the river? mushrooms - SN
2. What is being said about mushrooms? mushrooms were growing - V
3. Were - HV
4. Were growing how? wildly - Adv
5. Along - P
6. Along what? bank - OP
7. The - A
8. Of - P
9. Of what? river - OP
10. The - A
11. What kind of mushrooms? poisonous - Adj
12. The - A
13. SN V P1 Check
14. (Along the bank) - Prepositional phrase
15. (Of the river) - Prepositional phrase
16. Question mark, question, interrogative sentence
17. Go back to the verb - divide the complete subject from the complete predicate.
18. This sentence has predicate words in the complete subject. Underline the helping verb at the beginning of the sentence twice.

Classified Sentence:		HV	A	Adj	SN	V	Adv	P	A	OP	P	A	OP	
	SN V	Were	the	poisonous	mushrooms /	growing	wildly	(along	the	bank)	(of	the	river)?	Int
	P1													

TEACHING SCRIPT FOR INTRODUCING A PATTERN 1 PRACTICE SENTENCE

Put these words on the board: **Pattern 1 Sentence**

Get out a sheet of notebook paper. On the top line of your notebook paper, write the title *Pattern 1 Practice Sentence*. Look at the new words on the board: **Pattern 1 Sentence**. I will guide you again through the process as we learn to write a Pattern 1 sentence.

You have already learned how to write a Practice Sentence according to labels that have been provided for you. Today, you will learn how to write a Practice Sentence in which you select the parts of the sentence and the order they appear in your sentence. You will use only sentence parts of a Pattern 1 sentence.

Name the parts of a Pattern 1 sentence that YOU MUST USE. (*All Pattern 1 sentences must have a subject and a verb.*) Now, name the parts of a sentence that YOU CAN CHOOSE to add to your sentence. (*adjectives, adverbs, article adjectives, prepositional phrases, subject pronouns, possessive nouns, possessive pronouns, helping verbs, conjunctions, and interjections.*)

Let's write the labels for a Pattern 1 sentence on a sheet of notebook paper. First, write the *SN* and *V* labels that a Pattern 1 sentence must have, on your paper. Be sure to place them in the middle of your paper. (*Demonstrate by writing the SN and V labels on the board.*) Now, using what you know about writing Practice Sentences, we will decide what other parts we want to add to our Pattern 1 sentence. But first, we will look at a Reference box that will list all the parts that we can use. Turn to page 28 and look at Reference 32 (*Read and discuss the information in Reference 32 with your students. Reference 32 is reproduced for you on the next page.*)

CHAPTER 10 LESSON 2 CONTINUED

Reference 32: Sentence Parts That Can Be Used for a Pattern 1 Sentence

1. **Nouns**
   Use only subject nouns or object of the preposition nouns.
2. **Adverbs**
   Tell how, when, or where.
   Can be placed before or after verbs, at the beginning or end of a sentence, and in front of adjectives or other adverbs.
3. **Adjectives**
   Tell what kind, which one, or how many.
   Can be placed in front of nouns. Sometimes two or three adjectives can modify the same noun.
   Articles
   Adjectives that are used in front of nouns (a, an, the).

4. **Verbs** *(Can include helping verbs.)*
5. **Prepositional Phrases**
   Can be placed before or after nouns, after verbs, adverbs, or other prepositional phrases, and at the beginning or end of a sentence.
6. **Pronouns**
   (subjective, possessive, or objective)
7. **Conjunctions**
   Connecting words for compound parts: and, or, but.
8. **Interjections**
   Usually found at the beginning of a sentence. Can show strong or mild emotion.

Teacher's Note: You may want to make a poster of the information in the box above to show students that they are actually using the eight parts of speech from which to choose the different sentence parts that can be used for a Pattern 1 Sentence.

TEACHER INSTRUCTIONS

Use the information in the box above to help your students choose other parts to add to a Pattern 1 sentence. Help students select sentence labels and place them in the order in which they have decided. As students choose the sentence parts they want in their sentence, you should write the labels in the designated order on the board. Students should write the labels on their papers when they are ready to write a Pattern 1 Sentence. (*Students will have the same sentence labels in the same order this first time.*)

After your students have finished writing the <u>Teacher-guided</u> Pattern 1 Practice Sentence on their papers, each student should then write his or her own Pattern 1 sentence, choosing their own labels. Tell students they can use any sentence part listed in Reference 32 every time they write an independent Pattern 1 Sentence. Some students may add only adjectives, adverbs, and one or two prepositional phrases the first time. Other students may have the confidence to use a variety of sentence parts: pronouns, possessives, inverted order, adverb exceptions, etc.

TEACHING SCRIPT FOR THE IMPROVED SENTENCE

Under your Practice Sentence, write the title *Improved Sentence* on another line. To improve your Practice Sentence, you will make two synonym changes, one antonym change, and your choice of a complete word change or another synonym or antonym change. I will give you time to write your Improved Sentence. (*Always encourage students to use a thesaurus, synonym-antonym book, or a dictionary to help them develop an interesting and improved writing vocabulary.*) (*After students have finished, check and discuss students' Practice and Improved Sentences.*)

CHAPTER 10 LESSON 2 CONTINUED

SKILL TIME

TEACHING SCRIPT FOR INTRODUCING THE PUNCTUATION RULES

Turn to pages 29 and 30 in the Reference Section and look at References 33A and 33B in your student book. These are the rules for punctuation. The punctuation rules are organized into sections of similar rules. *(Read and discuss each section and the rules under each section.)* Your knowledge of punctuation rules will help you as you write and as you edit your writing. You will find that readers also appreciate writers who use punctuation rules well. Correct use of punctuation keeps writing clear and easy to understand. *(The punctuation rules are reproduced for you on the next two pages.)*

ACTIVITY / ASSIGNMENT TIME

Directions: Rewrite the following story. Use the symbol key below to help punctuate it.

honk john shouted sneeze beep honk did you see it hiccup honk did you see the shooting star hiccup honk it was a beautiful sight giggle beep honk john was dancing around and around because he was so excited groan

1. capitalization – honk
2. question mark – hiccup
3. exclamation point – giggle

4. comma – sneeze
5. period – groan
6. quotation marks – beep

Write a short story. Use the symbol key above to show how to punctuate your story. Give your story to several people and have them read the story and then punctuate it by following the symbols. Write another story and make up your own symbol key.

VOCABULARY TIME

Assign Chapter 10, Vocabulary Words #2 on page 8 in the Reference Section for students to define in their Vocabulary notebooks. Tell students they are to use a dictionary or thesaurus to look up the meanings of the vocabulary words. After they write each word and its meaning, students are to write a sentence using the vocabulary word.

Chapter 10, Vocabulary Words #2
(finish, commence, rude, impolite)

(End of lesson.)

CHAPTER 10 LESSON 2 CONTINUED

Reference 33A: Punctuation Rules

SECTION 1: END MARK PUNCTUATION

1. Use a (.) for the end punctuation of a sentence that makes a statement.
   (*Mom baked us a cake.*)
2. Use a (?) for the end punctuation of a sentence that asks a question.
   (*Are you going to town?*)
3. Use an (!) for the end punctuation of a sentence that expresses strong feeling.
   (*That bee stung me!*)
4. Use a (.) for the end punctuation of a sentence that gives a command or makes a request.
   (*Close the door.*)

SECTION 2: COMMAS TO SEPARATE TIME WORDS

5. Use a comma between the day of the week and the month. (*Friday, July 23*)
   Use a comma between the day and year. (*July 23, 2009*)
6. Use a comma to separate the year from the rest of the sentence when the year follows the month or the month and the day.
   (*We spent May, 2001, with Mom. We spent July 23, 2001, with Dad.*)

SECTION 3: COMMAS TO SEPARATE PLACE WORDS

7. Use a comma to separate the city from the state or country.
   (*I will go to Dallas, Texas. He is from Paris, France.*)
8. Use a comma to separate the state or country from the rest of the sentence when the name of the state or country follows the name of a city.
   (*We flew to Dallas, Texas, in June. We flew to Paris, France, in July.*)

SECTION 4: COMMAS TO MAKE MEANINGS CLEAR

9. Use a comma to separate words or phrases in a series.
   (*We had soup, crackers, and milk.*)
10. Use commas to separate introductory words such as *Yes, Well, Oh,* and *No* from the rest of a sentence.
    (*Oh, I didn't know that.*)
11. Use commas to set off most appositives. An appositive is a word, phrase, title, or degree used directly after another word or name to explain it or to rename it.
    (*Sue, the girl next door, likes to draw.*)
    One-word appositives can be written two different ways: *(1) My brother, Tim, is riding in the horse show. (2) My brother Tim is riding in the horse show. (Your assignments will require one-word appositives to be set off with commas.)*
12. Use commas to separate a noun of direct address (the name of a person directly spoken to) from the rest of the sentence.
    (*Mom, do I really have to go?*)

SECTION 5: PUNCTUATION IN GREETINGS AND CLOSINGS OF LETTERS

13. Use a comma (,) after the salutation (greeting) of a friendly letter. (*Dear Sam,*)
14. Use a comma (,) after the closing of any letter. (*Yours truly,*)
15. Use a colon (:) after the salutation (greeting) of a business letter. (*Dear Madam:*)

CHAPTER 10 LESSON 2 CONTINUED

Reference 33B: Punctuation Rules

SECTION 6: PERIODS

16. Use a period after most abbreviations or titles that are accepted in formal writing.
    (*Mr., Ms., Dr., Capt., St., Ave., St. Louis*) (*Note: These abbreviations cannot be used by themselves. They must always be used with a proper noun.*)

    In the abbreviations of many well-known organizations or words, periods are not required. (*USA, GM, TWA, GTE, AT&T, TV, AM, FM, GI, etc.*) Use only one period after an abbreviation at the end of a statement. Do not put an extra period for the end mark punctuation.

17. Use a period after initials.
    (*C. Smith, D.J. Brewton, Thomas A. Jones*)

18. Place a period after Roman numerals, Arabic numbers, and letters of the alphabet in an outline.
    (*II., IV., 5., 25., A., B.*)

SECTION 7: APOSTROPHES

19. Form a contraction by using an apostrophe in place of a letter or letters that have been left out.
    (*I'll, he's, isn't, wasn't, can't*)

20. Form the possessive of singular and plural nouns by using an apostrophe.
    (*boy's baseball, boys' baseball, children's baseball*)

21. Form the plurals of letters, symbols, numbers, and signs with the apostrophe plus *s* (*'s*). (*9's, B's, b's*)

SECTION 8: UNDERLINING

22. Use underlining or italics for titles of books, magazines, works of art, ships, newspapers, motion pictures, etc. (*A famous movie is <u>Gone With the Wind</u>. Our newspaper is the <u>Cabot Star Herald</u>.*) (*<u>Titanic</u>, <u>Charlotte's Web</u>, etc.*)

SECTION 9: QUOTATION MARKS

23. Use quotation marks to set off the titles of songs, short stories, short poems, articles, essays, short plays, and book chapters.
    (*Do you like to sing the song "America" in music class?*)

24. Quotation marks are used at the beginning and end of the person's words to separate what the person actually said from the rest of the sentence. Since the quotation tells what is being said, it will always have quotation marks around it.

25. The words that tell who is speaking are the explanatory words. Do not set explanatory words off with quotation marks. (*Fred said, "I'm here."*) (**Fred said** *are explanatory words and should not be set off with quotations.*)

26. A new paragraph is used to indicate a change of speaker.

27. When a speaker's speech is longer than one paragraph, quotation marks are used at the beginning of each paragraph and at the end of the last paragraph of that speaker's speech.

28. Use single quotation marks to enclose a quotation within a quotation.
    "My teddy bear says 'I love you' four different ways," said little Amy.

29. Use a period at the end of explanatory words that come at the end of a sentence.

30. Use a comma to separate a direct quotation from the explanatory words.

CHAPTER 10   LESSON 3

Objectives: Jingles, Grammar (Practice Sentences), Skills (capitalization and punctuation), Practice Exercise, Writing (journal), Study.

JINGLE TIME

Have students turn to the Jingle Section in their books and recite the previously-taught jingles.

GRAMMAR TIME

First-Year Option: Put the Practice Sentences from the box below on the board or on notebook paper. Use these sentences as you practice the concepts that have been taught. For the greatest benefit, students must participate orally with the teacher. **Second-Year Option:** Have students classify the Practice Sentences independently on notebook paper. Check students' sentences with the answers provided below. (*If you have the CDs for Practice Sentences, have students check their sentences with the CDs.*)

Chapter 10, Practice Sentences for Lesson 3
1. _____ Our wooden raft would not float on the water.
2. _____ Are you and your family staying for the picnic after church on Sunday?

TEACHING SCRIPT FOR PRACTICING PATTERN 1 SENTENCES

Today, we will practice classifying Pattern 1 Sentences. We will classify the sentences together. Begin. (*You might have your students write the labels above the sentences at this time.*)

Question and Answer Flow for Sentence 1: Our wooden raft would not float on the water.	
1. What would not float on the water? raft - SN	8. What kind of raft? wooden - Adj
2. What is being said about raft? raft would float - V	9. Whose raft? our - PPA
3. Would - HV	10. SN V P1 Check
4. Would float how? not - Adv	11. (On the water) - Prepositional phrase
5. On - P	12. Period, statement, declarative sentence
6. On what? water - OP	13. Go back to the verb - divide the complete subject
7. The - A	from the complete predicate.

Classified Sentence:

                    PPA   Adj   SN   HV   Adv V   P   A   OP

  SN V   Our wooden raft / would not float (on the water). **D**

  P1

CHAPTER 10 LESSON 3 CONTINUED

Question and Answer Flow for Sentence 2: Are you and your family staying for the picnic after church on Sunday?

1. Who are staying for the picnic after church on Sunday?
   you and family - CSP, CSN
2. What is being said about you and family?
   you and family are staying - V
3. Are - HV
4. For - P
5. For what? picnic - OP
6. The - A
7. After - P
8. After what? church - OP
9. On - P
10. On what? Sunday - OP

11. Whose family? your - PPA
12. And - C
13. SN V P1 Check
14. (For the picnic) - Prepositional phrase
15. (After church) - Prepositional phrase
16. (On Sunday) - Prepositional phrase
17. Question mark, question, interrogative sentence
18. Go back to the verb - divide the complete subject from the complete predicate.
19. This sentence has predicate words in the complete subject. Underline the helping verb at the beginning of the sentence twice.

Classified Sentence:

		HV	CSP	C	PPA	CSN	V	P	A	OP	P	OP	P	OP	
SN V		Are	you	and	your	family	/ staying	(for	the	picnic)	(after	church)	(on	Sunday)?	**Int**
P1															

SKILL TIME

TEACHING SCRIPT FOR CAPITALIZATION AND PUNCTUATION

You are ready to learn how to use the rules for capitalization and punctuation to edit sentences, paragraphs, and letters. It is important for you to know how to capitalize and punctuate any type of writing correctly. Expertise comes with years of practice and being able to apply all capitalization and punctuation rules automatically to edit your writing.

Teacher's Notes: You will find a copy of the capitalization rules at the end of Lesson 1 and the punctuation rules at the end of Lesson 2 in this chapter. Refer to them as needed.

Look at References 31, 33A, and 33B for the capitalization and punctuation rules on pages 27, 29, and 30 in the Reference Section of your book. You should know most of these rules by now, but I want you to know how the rules pages are set up with similar rules grouped in a given section. Let's read over the titles of all the sections on the rules pages. If you can find the right section, you'll be able to find the specific rule number.

TEACHER INSTRUCTIONS

Go over the different sections and one or two specific rules in each section of all three rules pages at this time. Reading over every capitalization and punctuation rule is not necessary. Students will get plenty of practice finding and applying these rules as they correct errors in the different exercises. They will learn the rules by using them over and over again while they are correcting the errors.

CHAPTER 10 LESSON 3 CONTINUED

You may have your students color-code the different sections. To make sure the color of their marker does not cover the rules or rule numbers, have students draw a box around each section instead of coloring each section.

Teacher's Notes: Make sure students understand the concept of proper adjectives during the discussion of the capitalization rules. Ask for examples of proper adjectives.

I'm going to show you how to use capitalization and punctuation rules to correct capitalization and punctuation errors. You will correct all capitalization errors first so you don't have to work with more than one page of rules at a time. For capitalization corrections, you will use only Reference 31, the capitalization rules page. You will correct all punctuation errors, using only Reference 33A and 33B, the punctuation rules pages. Using this method will prevent you from flipping back and forth from page to page for every correction.

Look at the *Capitalization and Punctuation Examples* on Reference 34 on page 31 in the Reference Section. Look at number 1. All capitalization errors have been corrected and bolded so we can clearly see them. Our job in this format is to supply only the correct rule numbers above the corrections that were made.

Look at the editing guide that is located under Sentence 1. The number beside CAPITALS in the editing guide tells how many total capitalization errors are in that sentence. There is a number 6 after the word CAPITALS. This means that there are 6 capitalization errors to correct. You are to write the rule number above each of the six corrections. Let's look at one bolded correction at a time and find the rule number listed on the rules page that matches the correction. (*Have students look up each capitalization rule number to see how it relates to each bolded correction.*)

Reference 34: Capitalization and Punctuation Examples

```
   1   6                    9   7                    14    14
1. No, I didn't see the pictures Mr. Jones took of his vacation in Paris, France.
   10   19                   16                          8       1
```

| Editing Guide for Sentence 1: | Capitals: 6 | Periods: 1 | Commas: 2 | Apostrophes: 1 | End Marks: 1 |

```
     Y    D                     R
2. yes, david, my brother's pen pal, is russian.
```

| Editing Guide for Sentence 2: | Capitals: 3 | Commas: 3 | Apostrophes: 1 | End Marks: 1 |

We will check the editing guide for the specific punctuation errors. If you see a number beside the word PERIODS, it is for the periods used after abbreviations and initials within the sentence. A period at the end of a sentence is listed beside the words END MARKS in the editing guide. (*Have students look up each punctuation rule number to see how it relates to each bolded correction.*)

Look at Sentence 2. For this sentence, we will make corrections only. We do not have to put the rule numbers. Look at how you are to correct capitalization mistakes. Do you see how a capital letter is put above each small letter that needs to be capitalized?

CHAPTER 10 LESSON 3 CONTINUED

Now, look at the punctuation examples. Do you see how you are to write each punctuation correction? Since punctuation is sometimes hard to see, you are to bold your punctuation answers by making them a little bigger and darker than normal. (*Lead students in a discussion of the corrections and why they were made.*)

 PRACTICE TIME

Have students turn to page 70 in the Practice Section of their book and find Chapter 10, Lesson 3, Practice. Go over the directions to make sure they understand what to do. Check and discuss the Practice after students have finished. (*Chapter 10, Lesson 3, Practice key is given below.*)

Chapter 10, Lesson 3, Practice: Use the Editing Guide below each sentence to know how many capitalization and punctuation errors to correct. For Sentence 1, write the capitalization and punctuation rule numbers for each correction in bold. For Sentence 2, write the capitalization and punctuation corrections. Use the capitalization and punctuation rule pages to help you.

(1 or 6)		11	11		8		

1. I'll be home on Friday, July 24 for Mother's birthday.
  19   5   20   1

Editing Guide for Sentence 1:	**Capitals: 4**	**Commas: 1**	**Apostrophes: 2**	**End Marks: 1**

  M   J   M   C   R   S   J
2. my sister, judy, will serve lunch for mother's friends at casey's restaurant on saturday, july 10.

Editing Guide for Sentence 2:	**Capitals: 7**	**Commas: 3**	**Apostrophes: 2**	**End Marks: 1**

Teacher's Note: Remind students to look at the Editing Guide several times for the total number of capitalization and punctuation mistakes.

 WRITING TIME

Have students make an entry in their journals.

 STUDY TIME

Have students study the vocabulary words in their vocabulary notebooks. Tell students that any vocabulary word in their notebooks could be on their test. Have students study any of the skills in the Practice Section that they need to review. Students should also study their homonym chart.

(End of lesson.)

CHAPTER 10   LESSON 4

Objectives: Jingles, Study, Test, Check, Activity, and Writing (journal).

JINGLE TIME

Have students turn to the Jingle Section in their books and recite the previously-taught jingles.

STUDY TIME

Have students study the vocabulary words in their vocabulary notebooks. Remind students that any vocabulary word in their notebooks could be on their test. Also, have students study any of the skills in the Practice Section that they need to review.

TEST TIME

Have students turn to page 106 in the Test Section of their book and find the Chapter 10 Test. Students should use the capitalization and punctuation rules in their Reference Section if needed. Go over the directions to make sure they understand what to do. (*Chapter 10 Test key is on the next page.*)

CHECK TIME

After students have finished, check and discuss their test papers. Make sure they understand why their answers are right or wrong. (*For total points, count each required answer as a point.*)

ACTIVITY / ASSIGNMENT TIME

Directions: Write a short story. Use the symbol key below or make up your own symbol key to show how to punctuate your story. Give your story to several people and have them read the story aloud and then punctuate it by following the symbols. Write another story and make up your own symbol key.

1. capitalization – honk
2. question mark – hiccup
3. exclamation point – giggle
4. comma – sneeze
5. period – groan
6. quotation marks – beep

(End of lesson.)

Chapter 10 Test
(Student Page 106)

Exercise 1: Classify each sentence.

<pre>
          SN   P OP   V   P A OP   P PPA Adj   OP
1. <u>SN V</u>   Droplets (of water) / formed (on the outside) (of her iced-tea glass). D
   P1
</pre>

<pre>
          I   PPA   SN   V   Adv   P PPA OP
2. <u>SN V</u>   Ouch! My suspenders / snapped tightly (against my back)! E
   P1
</pre>

<pre>
          SP HV Adv CV C CV   P   OP   P PPA Adj   OP
3. <u>SN V</u>   We / have not studied or learned (about fossils) (in our science class). D
   P1
</pre>

Exercise 2: Use Sentence 3 to underline the complete subject once and the complete predicate twice and to complete the table below.

List the Noun Used	List the Noun Job	Singular or Plural	Common or Proper	Simple Subject	Simple Predicate
1. fossils	2. OP	3. P	4. C	5. we	6. have studied/learned
7. class	8. OP	9. S	10. C		

Exercise 3: Name the eight parts of speech that you have studied. (*You may use abbreviations.*) **(The order may vary.)**

1. <u>noun</u> 2. <u>verb</u> 3. <u>adjective</u> 4. <u>adverb</u> 5. <u>preposition</u> 6. <u>pronoun</u> 7. <u>conjunction</u> 8. <u>interjection</u>

Exercise 4: Identify each pair of words as synonyms or antonyms by putting parentheses ( ) around *syn* or *ant*.

1. pail, bucket	**(syn)** ant	5. difficult, complex	**(syn)** ant	9. tales, stories	**(syn)** ant
2. petite, large	syn **(ant)**	6. fatigued, fresh	syn **(ant)**	10. pledge, promise	**(syn)** ant
3. accept, reject	syn **(ant)**	7. commence, finish	syn **(ant)**	11. impetuous, cautious	syn **(ant)**
4. rude, impolite	**(syn)** ant	8. rival, competitor	**(syn)** ant	12. common, unique	syn **(ant)**

Exercise 5: Underline the correct homonym in each sentence.

1. She loves the (sent, <u>scent</u>) of fresh roses.
2. He (<u>knew</u>, new) the solution immediately.
3. Do you (<u>know</u>, no) the most direct route?
4. We (<u>knew</u>, new) he was not well.
5. Yesterday, Billy (<u>sent</u>, scent) Travis home.
6. Will you (right, <u>write</u>) your grandmother?
7. There is (know, <u>no</u>) excuse for his tardiness.
8. I drove a (knew, <u>new</u>) car today.

Exercise 6: Use the Editing Guide below each sentence to know how many capitalization and punctuation errors to correct. For Sentence 1, write the capitalization and punctuation rule numbers for each correction in bold. For Sentence 2, make the capitalization and punctuation corrections. Use the capitalization and punctuation rule pages to help you.

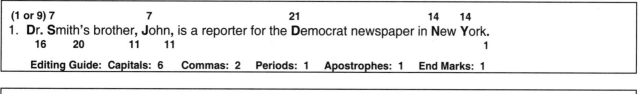

<pre>
   (1 or 9) 7   7   21   14   14
1. Dr. Smith's brother, John, is a reporter for the Democrat newspaper in New York.
   16   20   11   11   1
   Editing Guide: Capitals: 6   Commas: 2   Periods: 1   Apostrophes: 1   End Marks: 1
</pre>

<pre>
      M   I   Y   N   P   F   S   S
2. my brother and i went camping at yellowstone national park last friday, saturday, and sunday.

   Editing Guide: Capitals: 8   Commas: 2   End Marks: 1
</pre>

Exercise 7: In your journal, write a paragraph summarizing what you have learned this week.

CHAPTER 10 LESSON 4 CONTINUED

TEACHER INSTRUCTIONS

Use the Question and Answer Flows below for the sentences on the Chapter 10 Test.

Question and Answer Flow for Sentence 1: Droplets of water formed on the outside of her iced-tea glass.

1. What formed on the outside of her iced-tea glass? droplets - SN
2. What is being said about droplets? droplets formed - V
3. On - P
4. On what? outside - OP
5. The - A
6. Of - P
7. Of what? glass - OP
8. What kind of glass? iced-tea - Adj
9. Whose glass? her - PPA
10. Of - P
11. Of what? water - OP
12. SN V P1 Check
13. (Of water) - Prepositional phrase
14. (On the outside) - Prepositional phrase
15. (Of her iced-tea glass) - Prepositional phrase
16. Period, statement, declarative sentence
17. Go back to the verb - divide the complete subject from the complete predicate.

Classified Sentence:

```
            SN       P  OP    V    P  A   OP    P PPA  Adj   OP
  SN  V    Droplets (of water) / formed (on the outside) (of her iced-tea glass).  D
  ─────
   P1
```

Question and Answer Flow for Sentence 2: Ouch! My suspenders snapped tightly against my back!

1. What snapped tightly against my back? suspenders - SN
2. What is being said about suspenders? suspenders snapped - V
3. Snapped how? tightly - Adv
4. Against - P
5. Against what? back - OP
6. Whose back? my - PPA
7. Whose suspenders? my - PPA
8. Ouch - I
9. SN V P1 Check
10. (Against my back) - Prepositional phrase
11. Exclamation point, strong feeling, exclamatory sentence
12. Go back to the verb - divide the complete subject from the complete predicate.

Classified Sentence:

```
           I   PPA    SN          V    Adv   P   PPA OP
  SN  V   Ouch! My suspenders / snapped tightly (against my back)!  E
  ─────
   P1
```

Question and Answer Flow for Sentence 3: We have not studied or learned about fossils in our science class.

1. Who have not studied or learned about fossils in our science class? we - SP
2. What is being said about we? we have studied or learned - CV, CV
3. Have - HV
4. Have studied or learned how? not - Adv
5. Or - C
6. About - P
7. About what? fossils - OP
8. In - P
9. In what? class - OP 10. What kind of class? science - Adj
11. Whose class? our - PPA
12. SN V P1 Check
13. (About fossils) - Prepositional phrase
14. (In our science class) - Prepositional phrase
15. Period, statement, declarative sentence
16. Go back to the verb - divide the complete subject from the complete predicate.

Classified Sentence:

```
           SP  HV  Adv  CV   C   CV    P    OP     P PPA  Adj    OP
  SN  V   We / have not studied or learned (about fossils) (in our science class).  D
  ─────
   P1
```

CHAPTER 10   LESSON 5
Objectives: Writing (5-paragraph essay), Writing Assignment #11, and Bonus Option.

 WRITING TIME

Teacher's Notes:

1. Students will name or list three points they want to discuss about their topic.

2. As you work through the steps below, be sure to show students how an essay is divided into 5 paragraphs: the introduction, the first-point paragraph, the second-point paragraph, the third-point paragraph, and the conclusion.

3. Remind students that this is an expository essay, which means that its purpose is to inform or explain. The five-point format is another way of organizing an expository essay.

TEACHING SCRIPT FOR INTRODUCING HOW TO WRITE A 5-PARAGRAPH ESSAY

You have already learned how to write a three-paragraph essay. You also learned that an essay has three main parts: 1. Introduction 2. Body 3. Conclusion.

Today, you will learn how to write a five-paragraph essay. In a five-paragraph expository essay, there will be five paragraphs, no more and no fewer. The five-paragraph essay will also have the same three main parts: the introduction, body, and conclusion. The introduction forms the first paragraph, the body forms the second, third, and fourth paragraphs, and the conclusion forms the fifth paragraph of the essay. The title will again be the fourth component of a five-paragraph essay.

As you are learning to write a five-paragraph essay, it will help you to remember the outline for the three-paragraph essay that you have already learned. Look at the two outlines in Reference 35 on page 31 in your book.

Let's compare and discuss the differences between the three-paragraph essay and the five-paragraph essay. Notice that the introduction and conclusion are the same for both essays. Also, notice that the body of the five-paragraph essay has three paragraphs. Each point and its supporting sentences are a separate paragraph in the body of the five-paragraph essay.

CHAPTER 10 LESSON 5 CONTINUED

Reference 35: Three-Paragraph Essay and Five-Paragraph Essay	
Outline of a 3-Paragraph Essay	**Outline of a 5-Paragraph Essay**
I. Title	I. Title
II. Paragraph 1 – Introduction (3 sentences) 　A. Topic and general number sentence 　B. Extra information about the topic sentence 　C. Three-point sentence	II. Paragraph 1 - Introduction　　(3 sentences) 　A. Topic and general number sentence 　B. Extra information about the topic sentence 　C. Three-point sentence
III. Paragraph 2 – Body　　(6-9 sentences) 　A. **First-point** sentence 　B. One or two **supporting** sentences 　　for the first point 　C. **Second-point** sentence 　D. One or two **supporting** sentences 　　for the second point 　E. **Third-point** sentence 　F. One or two **supporting** sentences 　　for the third point	III. Paragraph 2 - First Point Body　　(3-4 sentences) 　A. **First-point** sentence 　B. Two or three **supporting** sentences for the first point IV. Paragraph 3 – Second Point Body　(3-4 sentences) 　A. **Second-point** sentence 　B. Two or three **supporting** sentences for the second 　　point V. Paragraph 4 – Third Point Body　(3-4 sentences) 　A. **Third-point** sentence 　B. Two or three **supporting** sentences for the third point
IV. Paragraph 3 – Conclusion (2 sentences) 　A. Concluding general statement 　B. Concluding summary sentence	VI. Paragraph 5 – Conclusion　　(2 sentences) 　A. Concluding general statement 　　(Restatement of the topic sentence) 　B. Concluding summary sentence 　　(Restatement of the 3-point sentence)

You will learn how to write each sentence and paragraph in the five-paragraph expository essay by following the steps in Reference 36 on pages 32 and 33 in your book. (*Read and discuss Reference 36 with your students. The reference box is located on the next page.*)

CHAPTER 10 LESSON 5 CONTINUED

Reference 36: Steps in Writing a Five-Paragraph Expository Essay

WRITING TOPIC: Playing a Musical Instrument

THREE MAIN POINTS

♦   Select the points to list about the topic.

1. **Opens the door to a new world of art**
2. **Teaches self-discipline**
3. **Creates a lifelong enjoyment of music**

WRITING THE INTRODUCTION AND TITLE

1. Sentence #1 - Topic Sentence
   Write the topic sentence by using the words in your topic and adding a general number word, such as
   several, many, some, or *numerous*, instead of the exact number of points you will discuss.
   (I have discovered that playing a musical instrument can provide many opportunities for people who love music.)

2. Sentence #2 - Extra Information about the topic sentence
   This sentence can clarify, explain, define, or just be an extra interesting comment about the topic
   sentence. If you need another sentence to complete your information, write an extra sentence here. If
   you write an extra sentence, your introductory paragraph will have four sentences in it instead of three.
   (Although many people focus solely on developing sports-related abilities, I think musical talents are just as important to develop.)

3. Sentence #3 - Three-point sentence
   This sentence will list the three points to be discussed in the order that you will present them in the body
   of your paper. You can list the points with or without the specific number in front.
   (Playing a musical instrument opens the door to a new world of art, teaches self-discipline, and creates a lifelong enjoyment of music.) or   **(The three reasons why I enjoy playing a musical instrument are that it opens the door to a new world of art, teaches self-discipline, and creates a lifelong enjoyment of music.)**

♦   The Title - Since there are many possibilities for titles, look at the topic and the three points listed about
   the topic. Use some of the words in the topic and write a phrase to tell what your paragraph is about.
   Your title can be short or long. Capitalize the first, last, and important words in your title.
   (The Benefits of Playing a Musical Instrument)

WRITING THE BODY

4. Sentence #4 - First Point - Write a sentence stating your first point.
   (One of the reasons I enjoy playing a musical instrument is that it opens the door to a new world of art.)

5. Sentences #5 - #7 - Supporting Sentences - Write two or three sentences that give more information
   about your first point. **(In learning to play different pieces of music on an instrument, one explores a wide range of artistic styles.) (In his or her career, a musician is able to explore numerous musical compositions.) (This exploration allows the musician to develop a taste for a variety of styles.)**

6. Sentence #8 - Second Point - Write a sentence stating your second point.
   (Another reason I enjoy playing a musical instrument is that it teaches self-discipline.)

7. Sentences #9 - #11 - Supporting Sentences - Write two or three sentences that give more information
   about your second point. **(Without a doubt, it requires devotion to the instrument.) (Many of the skills it takes to play well are acquired only through practice and patience.) (Often a musician must allow for extra hours of practice.)**

CHAPTER 10 LESSON 5 CONTINUED

Reference 36: Steps in Writing a Five-Paragraph Expository Essay (continued)

8. <u>Sentence #12 - Third Point</u> - Write a sentence stating your third point.
   (I also enjoy playing a musical instrument because it creates a lifelong enjoyment of music.)

9. <u>Sentences #13 - #15 - Supporting Sentences</u> - Write two or three sentences that give more information about your third point.
   (Acquiring these special skills creates many opportunities for one to perform for business or pleasure throughout the rest of his or her life.) (A musician can perform in an orchestra, ensemble, or just play solo.) (Whether his or her audience is a crowded auditorium or just Mom and Dad, the overwhelming feeling of achievement and enjoyment is astounding.)

WRITING THE CONCLUSION

10. <u>Sentence #16 - Concluding General Statement</u> - Read the topic sentence again and then rewrite it, using some of the same words to say the same thing in a different way.
    (Clearly, there are many advantages to playing a musical instrument.)

11. <u>Sentence #17 - Concluding Summary (final) Sentence</u> - Read the three-point sentence again and then rewrite it, using some of the same words to say the same thing in a different way.
    (For those who play a musical instrument, the skill can be very valuable in many ways.)

SAMPLE FIVE-PARAGRAPH ESSAY

The Benefits of Playing a Musical Instrument

I have discovered that playing a musical instrument can provide many opportunities for people who love music. Although many people focus solely on developing sports-related abilities, I think musical talents are just as important to develop. Playing a musical instrument opens the door to a new world of art, teaches self-discipline, and creates a lifelong enjoyment of music.

One of the reasons I enjoy playing a musical instrument is that it opens the door to a new world of art. In learning to play different pieces of music on an instrument, one explores a wide range of artistic styles. In his or her career, a musician is able to explore numerous musical compositions. This exploration allows the musician to develop a taste for a variety of styles.

Another reason I enjoy playing a musical instrument is that it teaches self-discipline. Without a doubt, it requires devotion to the instrument. Many of the skills it takes to play well are acquired only through practice and patience. Often a musician must allow for extra hours of practice.

I also enjoy playing a musical instrument because it creates a lifelong enjoyment of music. Acquiring these special skills creates many opportunities for one to perform for business or pleasure throughout the rest of his or her life. A musician can perform in an orchestra, ensemble, or just play solo. Whether his or her audience is a crowded auditorium or just Mom and Dad, the overwhelming feeling of achievement and enjoyment is astounding.

Clearly, there are many advantages to playing a musical instrument. For those who play a musical instrument, the skill can be very valuable in many ways.

CHAPTER 10 LESSON 5 CONTINUED

TEACHER INSTRUCTIONS FOR WRITING ASSIGNMENT

Give Writing Assignment #11 from the box below. For this writing assignment, students are to write a five-paragraph essay in first person. Remind students to follow the Writing Guidelines from Chapter 3 as they prepare their writings. Students are also encouraged to use the five-paragraph essay example and the essay outline in their Reference Section to do the writing assignment below.

Writing Assignment Box
Writing Assignment #11: Five-Paragraph Expository Essay (First Person) Remind students that the 5-paragraph essay still has three parts: 1. Introduction 2. Body 3. Conclusion. The body now has three paragraphs instead of one. **Writing topics: My Favorite Cartoons** or **Things That Make Me Happy** or **My Best Friends** or **Favorite Colors** **Bonus Option: To solve the puzzle for Psalms 119:11, Write the letter missing from each set of letters on notebook paper. (1. T   2. H) The two ** indicate the end of a word. There are 15 words.** Answer: (Thy word have I hid in mine heart, that I might not sin against thee.) King James Version

1. RSUV	7. BCEF**	13. EFGI	19. HJKL	25. OPQS	31. FGHJ**	37. MOPQ	43. XYZB	49. QRSU**
2. FGIJ	8. GIJK	14. GHJK	20. LMOP	26. SUVW**	32. KLNO	38. MNPQ	44. FHIJ	50. RSUV
3. VWXZ**	9. YZBC	15. ABCE**	21. BCDF**	27. RSUV	33. HJKL	39. SUVW**	45. YZBC	51. GIJK
4. UVXY	10. STUW	16. GHJK	22. GIJK	28. EFGI	34. EFHI	40. PQRT	46. GHJK	52. BCDF
5. LMNP	11. CDFG**	17. KLMO**	23. CDFG	29. XYZB	35. GIJK	41. FGHJ	47. MOPQ	53. DFGH
6. QSTU	12. HJKL**	18. LNOP	24. ZBCD	30. QRSU**	36. RSUV**	42. LMOP**	48. RTUV	

TEACHING SCRIPT FOR USING THE WRITING PROCESS FOR THIS WRITING ASSIGNMENT

As you begin this writing assignment, you will start through the writing process. First, you will think about your topic and gather any information you might need in order to do the writing. Second, you will write a rough draft. Remember, it is called a rough draft because it will be revised and edited. You do not have to worry about mistakes as you write your rough draft. After you write the first draft, you will make revisions, using the Revision Checklist in Reference 5. After you revise your writing, you will edit, using the Beginning Editing Checklist in Reference 5. Finally, after you are satisfied with your revising and editing, you will write a final paper, using the Final Paper Checklist in Reference 5. You will then give the finished writing assignment to me.

TEACHER INSTRUCTIONS FOR CHECKING WRITING ASSIGNMENT

Read, check, and discuss Writing Assignment #11 after students have finished their final paper. Use the editing checklist (*Reference 5 on teacher's page 12*) as you check and discuss students' papers. Make sure students are using the editing checklist correctly. In the beginning, you must also check students' papers carefully for <u>form</u> mistakes. This will ensure that students are learning the format correctly.

(End of lesson.)

CHAPTER 11   LESSON 1

Objectives: Jingles, Grammar (Practice Sentences, Oral Skill Builder Check), Skill (capitalization and punctuation of a friendly letter using rule numbers only), Practice Exercise, and Vocabulary #1.

 **JINGLE TIME**

Have students turn to the Jingle Section in their books and recite the previously-taught jingles.

 GRAMMAR TIME

First-Year Option: Put the Practice Sentences from the box below on the board or on notebook paper. Use these sentences as you practice the concepts that have been taught. For the greatest benefit, students must participate orally with the teacher. **Second-Year Option:** Have students classify the Practice Sentences independently on notebook paper. Check students' sentences with the answers provided below. *(If you have the CDs for Practice Sentences, have students check their sentences with the CDs.)*

Chapter 11, Practice Sentences for Lesson 1
1. _____ The hamburgers and hotdogs cooked quickly on Kelly's new grill.
2. _____ Eeek! That shrill sound grates on my nerves!

TEACHING SCRIPT FOR PRACTICING PATTERN 1 SENTENCES

We will practice classifying Pattern 1 Sentences. We will classify the sentences together. Begin. *(You might have your students write the labels above the sentences at this time.)*

Question and Answer Flow for Sentence 1: The hamburgers and hotdogs cooked quickly on Kelly's new grill.

1. What cooked quickly on Kelly's new grill?
   hamburgers and hotdogs - CSN, CSN
2. What is being said about hamburgers and hotdogs?
   hamburgers and hotdogs cooked - V
3. Cooked how? quickly - Adv
4. On - P
5. On what? grill - OP
6. What kind of grill? new - Adj

7. Whose grill? Kelly's - PNA
8. And - C
9. The - A
10. SN V P1 Check
11. (On Kelly's new grill) - Prepositional phrase
12. Period, statement, declarative sentence
13. Go back to the verb - divide the complete subject from the complete predicate.

Classified Sentence:

          A   CSN   C   CSN   V   Adv   P   PNA   Adj OP
  SN V   The hamburgers and hotdogs / cooked quickly (on Kelly's new grill). D
  P1

CHAPTER 11 LESSON 1 CONTINUED

Question and Answer Flow for Sentence 2: Eeek! That shrill sound grates on my nerves!

1. What grates on my nerves? sound - SN
2. What is being said about sound? sound grates - V
3. On - P
4. On what? nerves - OP
5. Whose nerves? my - PPA
6. What kind of sound? shrill - Adj
7. Which sound? that - Adj

8. Eeek - I
9. SN V P1 Check
10. (On my nerves) - Prepositional phrase
11. Exclamation point, strong feeling, exclamatory sentence
12. Go back to the verb - divide the complete subject from the complete predicate.

Classified Sentence:

	I	Adj	Adj	SN	V	P	PPA	OP

<u>SN V</u>   Eeek! That shrill sound / grates (on my nerves)! **E**
P1

Use Sentences 1-2 that you just classified with your students to do an Oral Skill Builder Check. Use the guidelines below.

Oral Skill Builder Check

1. **Noun check.**
   (Say the job and then say the noun. Circle each noun.)

2. **Identify the nouns as singular or plural.**
   (Write **S** or **P** above each noun.)

3. **Identify the nouns as common or proper.**
   (Follow established procedure for oral identification.)

4. **Do a vocabulary check.**
   (Follow established procedure for oral identification.)

5. **Identify the complete subject and the complete predicate.** (Underline the complete subject once and the complete predicate twice.)

6. **Identify the simple subject and simple predicate.**
   (Underline the simple subject once and the simple predicate twice. Bold, or highlight, the lines.)

7. **Recite the irregular verb chart.**
   (Located on student page 23 and teacher page 138.)

SKILL TIME

TEACHING SCRIPT FOR CAPITALIZATION AND PUNCTUATION OF A FRIENDLY LETTER, USING RULE NUMBERS ONLY

Today, you will learn how to apply the capitalization and punctuation rules to a friendly letter. A friendly letter is a letter written to talk to a friend or relative. The capitalization and punctuation rules apply to friendly letters in the same way they apply to any other type of writing. The only difference is that there are more address-related punctuation rules and a few new terms that you will learn as you punctuate letters. You do not have to learn the friendly-letter form at this time because it has already been set up for you.

The first friendly letter you will use in Practice Time has already been corrected. The corrections are identified in bold type. You need only to put the rule number above each correction in bold type that justifies each capitalization or mark of punctuation. I must also remind you to look at the editing guide to find the total number of errors you need to correct in each section. Remember that the end-mark total tells you how many sentences need end mark punctuation. For instance, if you have the number *seven* beside the words END MARKS in your editing guide, it means there are seven sentences in your letter. Also, make sure you pay attention to the greeting and closing of a friendly letter.

CHAPTER 11 LESSON 1 CONTINUED

 PRACTICE TIME

Have students turn to page 71 in the Practice Section of their books and find the skill under Chapter 11, Lesson 1, Practice. Go over the directions to make sure they understand what to do. Students must use the Reference Section in their books to find the capitalization and punctuation rule numbers to edit the friendly letter. They will write a rule number for each correction in bold type. Check and discuss the Practice after students have finished. (*Chapter 11, Lesson 1, Practice key is given below.*)

Chapter 11, Lesson 1, Practice: Write the capitalization and punctuation rule number for each correction in bold.

                                   15   **15**
                               3426 **T**aylor **C**ircle

                               14   **14**
                               Dallas, **T**exas 75224
                                       7

                             11
                             August 23, 20—
                                           5

2   **7**
Dear **B**illy,
        13

(1 or 6)   **1**   **23**   **23**
    I have great news! **M**y father bought extra tickets to the **D**allas **C**owboys football game this
                  3

11   **1**   **6**   **1**
Saturday. **H**e said **I** could ask you to go with us! **W**e have seats on the fifty-yard line.
   1   **3**   **1**
    My mom will call your parents about spending the weekend with me. **W**e'll have a great time!
                                  1 **19**   **3**

(1 or 6)
I hope to see you soon.
             1

                                         2
                                       Your pal,
                                          14

                                       7
                                       John

Editing Guide: Capitals: 20   Commas: 4   Apostrophes: 1   End Marks: 7

 VOCABULARY TIME

Assign Chapter 11, Vocabulary Words **#1** on page 8 in the Reference Section for students to define in their Vocabulary notebooks. After they write each word and its meaning, students are to write a sentence using the vocabulary word.

Chapter 11, Vocabulary Words #1
(fable, fiction, logical, silly)

(End of lesson.)

<table>
<tr><td colspan="2">CHAPTER 11 LESSON 2</td></tr>
</table>

Objectives: Jingles, Grammar (Practice Sentences), Independent Pattern 1 Practice Sentence, Skill (capitalization and punctuation of a friendly letter using corrections only), Practice Exercise, and Vocabulary #2.

JINGLE TIME

Have students turn to the Jingle Section in their books and recite the previously-taught jingles.

GRAMMAR TIME

First-Year Option: Put the Practice Sentences from the box below on the board or on notebook paper. Use these sentences as you practice the concepts that have been taught. For the greatest benefit, students must participate orally with the teacher. **Second-Year Option:** Have students classify the Practice Sentences independently on notebook paper. Check students' sentences with the answers provided below. (*If you have the CDs for Practice Sentences, have students check their sentences with the CDs.*)

Chapter 11, Practice Sentences for Lesson 2

1. _____ My friend's little brother could not sleep without his favorite blanket.
2. _____ The cast members and crew cheered after the first act of their play.

TEACHING SCRIPT FOR PRACTICING PATTERN 1 SENTENCES

We will practice classifying Pattern 1 Sentences. We will classify the sentences together. Begin. (*You might have your students write the labels above the sentences at this time.*)

Question and Answer Flow for Sentence 1: My friend's little brother could not sleep without his favorite blanket.

1. Who could not sleep without his favorite blanket?
   brother - SN
2. What is being said about brother? brother could sleep - V
3. Could - HV
4. Could sleep how? not - Adv
5. Without - P
6. Without what? blanket - OP
7. What kind of blanket? favorite - Adj
8. Whose blanket? his - PPA

9. Which brother? little - Adj
10. Whose brother? friend's - PNA
11. Whose friend? my - PPA
12. SN V P1 Check
13. (Without his favorite blanket) - Prepositional phrase
14. Period, statement, declarative sentence
15. Go back to the verb - divide the complete subject from the complete predicate.

Classified Sentence:

```
                        PPA PNA  Adj SN     HV  Adv  V      P  PPA  Adj    OP
              SN  V      My friend's little brother / could not sleep (without his favorite blanket).  D
              P1
```

CHAPTER 11 LESSON 2 CONTINUED

Question and Answer Flow for Sentence 2: The cast members and crew cheered after the first act of their play.

1. Who cheered after the first act of their play?
   members and crew - CSN, CSN
2. What is being said about members and crew?
   members and crew cheered - V
3. After - P
4. After what? act - OP
5. Which act? first - Adj
6. The - A
7. Of - P
8. Of what? play - OP

9. Whose play? their - PPA
10. And - C
11. What kind of members? cast - Adj
12. The - A
13. SN V P1 Check
14. (After the first act) - Prepositional phrase
15. (Of their play) - Prepositional phrase
16. Period, statement, declarative sentence
17. Go back to the verb - divide the complete subject
    from the complete predicate.

Classified Sentence:

		A	Adj	CSN	C	CSN	V	P	A	Adj	OP	P	PPA	OP

SN V / P1   The cast members and crew **/** cheered **(after the first act) (of their play). D**

TEACHER INSTRUCTIONS FOR A PATTERN 1 SENTENCE

Tell students that their sentence writing assignment today is to write a Pattern 1 sentence. They are to follow the same procedure used in the previous lessons. They should decide on their labels, arrange them in a selected order, write their sentences, and edit their sentences for improved word choices. (*Students do not have to write an Improved Sentence at this point unless you feel they need more one-on-one word choice writing practice.*) Make sure students check Reference 32 on page 28 in the Reference Section for the sentence parts that can be used in a Pattern 1 sentence. Check and discuss the Pattern 1 sentence after students have finished. (*Independent sentence assignments will be given in an assignment box like the one below.*)

Sentence Writing Assignment Box

Independent Pattern 1 Sentence
(In order to write a Pattern 1 sentence, students should decide on their labels, arrange them in a selected order, write their sentences, and edit their sentences for improved word choices.)

   SKILL TIME

TEACHING SCRIPT FOR CAPITALIZATION AND PUNCTUATION OF A FRIENDLY LETTER, USING CORRECTIONS ONLY

Your second friendly letter has not been punctuated. You are to write capitalization corrections above the capitalization mistakes and write the punctuation corrections where they belong in the letter. I must remind you again to look at the editing guide to find the total number of errors you need to correct in each section. Remember that the end mark total tells you how many sentences need end mark punctuation. You may also use your capitalization and punctuation rules as a reference if you need them.

CHAPTER 11 LESSON 2 CONTINUED

PRACTICE TIME

Have students turn to page 72 in the Practice Section of their book and find the skill under Chapter 11, Lesson 2, Practice. Go over the directions to make sure they understand what to do. Remind students to look at the editing guide to find the total number of errors they need to correct in each section. Students may also use their capitalization and punctuation rules as a reference if they need them. Check and discuss the Practice after students have finished. (*Chapter 11, Lesson 2, Practice key is given below.*)

Chapter 11, Lesson 2, Practice: Write the capitalization and punctuation corrections only.

                                                  B   T
176 buffalo trail
C   W
cody, wyoming 24431
F
february 19, 20—

D   C   P
dear cousin peggy,
    I   **G**   **J   A**
it doesn't seem possible that you and greg will be married twenty years in july. are you going
D   W   O   F   I   **M**
to disney world in orlando, florida? i know it will be a long trip by car. my family extends
                  D
congratulations. do let us know about your trip.

                                                A
affectionately yours,
                                                A
andy

Editing Guide: Capitals: 21   Commas: 5   Apostrophes: 1   End Marks: 5

VOCABULARY TIME

Assign Chapter 11, Vocabulary Words **#2** on page 8 in the Reference Section for students to define in their Vocabulary notebooks. Tell students they are to use a dictionary or thesaurus to look up the meanings of the vocabulary words. After they write each word and its meaning, students are to write a sentence using the vocabulary word.

Chapter 11, Vocabulary Words #2
(hesitate, pause, auction, buy)

(End of lesson.)

CHAPTER 11   LESSON 3

Objectives: Jingles, Grammar (Practice Sentences), Study, Test A, Check, and Writing (journal).

JINGLE TIME

Have students turn to the Jingle Section in their books and recite the previously-taught jingles.

GRAMMAR TIME

First-Year Option: Put the Practice Sentences from the box below on the board or on notebook paper. Use these sentences as you practice the concepts that have been taught. For the greatest benefit, students must participate orally with the teacher. **Second-Year Option:** Have students classify the Practice Sentences independently on notebook paper. Check students' sentences with the answers provided below. *(If you have the CDs for Practice Sentences, have students check their sentences with the CDs.)*

Chapter 11, Practice Sentences for Lesson 3
1. _____The football coach and his assistants shouted encouragingly to the players on the field.
2. _____ Were you hit in the face with a switch of the horse's tail?

TEACHING SCRIPT FOR PRACTICING PATTERN 1 SENTENCES

We will practice classifying Pattern 1 Sentences. We will classify the sentences together. Begin.

Question and Answer Flow for Sentence 1: The football coach and his assistants shouted encouragingly to the players on the field.

1. Who shouted encouragingly to the players on the field? coach and assistants - CSN, CSN
2. What is being said about coach and assistants? coach and assistants shouted - V
3. Shouted how? encouragingly - Adv
4. To - P
5. To whom? players - OP
6. The - A
7. On - P
8. On what? field - OP
9. The - A
10. Whose assistants? his - PPA
11. And - C
12. What kind of coach? football - Adj
13. The - A
14. SN V P1 Check
15. (To the players) - Prepositional phrase
16. (On the field) - Prepositional phrase
17. Period, statement, declarative sentence
18. Go back to the verb - divide the complete subject from the complete predicate.

Classified
Sentence:

		A	Adj	CSN	C	PPA	CSN		V		Adv		P	A	OP		P	A	OP	
SN V		The football coach and his assistants / shouted encouragingly (to the players) (on the field).																		**D**
P1																				

CHAPTER 11 LESSON 3 CONTINUED

Question and Answer Flow for Sentence 2: Were you hit in the face with a switch of the horse's tail?

1. Who were hit in the face with a switch of the horse's tail? you - SP
2. What is being said about you? you were hit - V
3. Were - HV
4. In - P
5. In what? face - OP
6. The - A
7. With - P
8. With what? switch - OP
9. A - A
10. Of - P
11. Of what? tail - OP
12. Whose tail? horse's - PNA

13. The - A
14. SN V P1 Check
15. (In the face) - Prepositional phrase
16. (With a switch) - Prepositional phrase
17. (Of the horse's tail) - Prepositional phrase
18. Question mark, question, interrogative sentence
19. Go back to the verb - divide the complete subject from the complete predicate.
20. This sentence has predicate words in the complete subject. Underline the helping verb at the beginning of the sentence twice.

Classified Sentence:

		HV	SP	V	P	A	OP	P	A	OP	P	A	PNA	OP	
SN V		Were	you /	hit	(in	the	face)	(with	a	switch)	(of	the	horse's	tail)?	Int
P1															

STUDY TIME

Have students study the vocabulary words in their vocabulary notebooks. Tell students that any vocabulary word in their notebooks could be on their test. Also, have students study any of the skills in the Practice Section that they need to review. Students should also study their homonym chart.

TEST TIME

Have students turn to page 107 in the Test Section of their book and find the Chapter 11 Test A. Students should use the Reference Section in their books to find the capitalization and punctuation rule numbers to edit the sentence and friendly letter. Go over the directions to make sure they understand what to do. (*Chapter 11 Test A key is on the next page.*)

CHECK TIME

After students have finished, check and discuss their test papers. Make sure they understand why their answers are right or wrong. (*For total points, count each required answer as a point.*)

(End of lesson.)

Chapter 11 Test A
(Student Page 107)

Exercise 1: <u>Sentence</u>: Write the capitalization and punctuation rule numbers for each correction in bold.

```
       1        9   10 10 7              22                    14      14
1.  His mother, Mrs. T. J. Smith, owned an Italian restaurant near Dallas, Texas.
        11    16 17 17   11                                    7    1
```

Editing Guide:	Capitals: 8	Commas: 3	Periods: 3	End Marks: 1

Exercise 2: <u>Friendly Letter</u>: Write the capitalization and punctuation corrections only.

```
                                                        C      D
                                                500 crimson drive
                                                C      I
                                                chicago, illinois 99542
                                                M
                                                may 18, 20—

     D    U   J
   dear uncle jim,
     T                                        M      M      D   T
     thank you so much for the flowers you sent mom for mother's day.  they were arranged
                              M                                         W
   perfectly in a beautiful vase.  mom was so surprised and happy to hear from you.  we look
                          E        S
   forward to seeing you when you return from europe.  see you soon.

                                                        Y
                                                your niece,
                                                T
                                                teresa
```

Editing Guide:	Capitals: 19	Commas: 4	Apostrophes: 1	End Marks: 5

Exercise 3: Name the eight parts of speech that you have studied. (*You may use abbreviations.*) **(The order may vary.)**

1. <u>**noun**</u>   2. <u>**verb**</u>   3. <u>**adjective**</u>   4. <u>**adverb**</u>   5. <u>**preposition**</u>   6. <u>**pronoun**</u>   7. <u>**conjunction**</u>   8. <u>**interjection**</u>

Exercise 4: Identify each pair of words as synonyms or antonyms by putting parentheses ( ) around *syn* or *ant*.

1. fiction, fable	**(syn)** ant	5. sharp, keen	**(syn)** ant	9. brawn, muscle	**(syn)** ant
2. uplift, depress	syn **(ant)**	6. complex, difficult	**(syn)** ant	10. creeping, rushing	syn **(ant)**
3. buy, auction	syn **(ant)**	7. silly, logical	syn **(ant)**	11. large, petite	syn **(ant)**
4. pause, hesitate	**(syn)** ant	8. feather, quill	**(syn)** ant	12. vivid, dingy	syn **(ant)**

Exercise 5: Underline the correct homonym in each sentence.

1. She writes on the prettiest (stationary, <u>stationery</u>).
2. Diplomats work hard to achieve (<u>peace</u>, piece).
3. The boy (<u>threw</u>, through) his shoes in the lake.
4. The train has been (<u>stationary</u>, stationery) for an hour.
5. I need a small (peace, <u>piece</u>) of chocolate.
6. He walked (threw, <u>through</u>) the hall alone.
7. What happened to (<u>your</u>, you're) hair?
8. I believe that (your, <u>you're</u>) a new student.

Exercise 6: In your journal, write a paragraph summarizing what you have learned this week.

CHAPTER 11   LESSON 4

Objectives: Test B, Check, Writing (journal), and Activity.

 TEST TIME

Have students turn to page 108 in the Test Section of their book and find the Chapter 11 Test B. Students should use the Reference Section in their books to find the capitalization and punctuation rule numbers to edit the sentence and friendly letter. Go over the directions to make sure they understand what to do. (*Chapter 11 Test B key is on the next page.*)

 CHECK TIME

After students have finished, check and discuss their test papers. Make sure they understand why their answers are right or wrong. (*For total points, count each required answer as a point.*)

 WRITING TIME

Have students make an entry in their journals.

 ACTIVITY / ASSIGNMENT TIME

Using Reference 34 on page 31 (*TM page 176*) as an example, write two original sentences with capitalization and punctuation errors. Make an editing guide for the sentences that tells how many mistakes are in each sentence. Bold the mistakes and write the rule numbers for the first sentence. Write the corrections only for the second sentence. (*Check and discuss the two sentences after students have finished.*)

(End of lesson.)

Chapter 11 Test B
(Student Page 108)

Exercise 1: Classify each sentence.

        A   SN   HV   V   Adv   P A Adj OP   P PPA OP

1. <u>SN V</u>   The goldfish / were swimming leisurely (around the fish tank) (in my room). **D**
   P1

      (You) SP   V   P   Adj   OP   P A Adj   OP

2. <u>SN V</u>   / Read (about current events) (in the daily newspaper). **Imp**
   P1

         PPA Adj Adj   SN   HV CV   C   CV   P OP Adv

3. <u>SN V</u>   Our new baby sister / is cooing and laughing (at us) now. **D**
   P1

Exercise 2: <u>Sentence</u>: Write the capitalization and punctuation corrections only.

     D   S   I   S   L   C   U

1.   david, sarah, and i helped build a house in salt lake city, utah, for a destitute family.

Editing Guide: Capitals: 7   Commas: 4   End Marks: 1

Exercise 3: <u>Friendly Letter</u>: Write the capitalization and punctuation rule numbers for each correction in bold.

                   15   15 15
                   12 **R**olling **H**ill **A**ve.
                              16
                   14   14   14
                   St. **P**aul, **M**innesota 72023
                     16   7
                   11
                   July 10, 20—
                         5

 2   7
Dear **M**ike,
      13

  (1 or 6)   (1 or 9) 7
  I won the state spelling bee last night. **M**s. **J**ames, my teacher, was so excited that she ran up on
                  1 16   11   11

                 (1 or6)   1
the stage to congratulate me. **I** received a trophy and a $100 gift certificate. **M**y mom told me that
               1   1

6   14   (1 or 6)   1
I'll now qualify for the national spelling bee in **W**ashington. **I** hope you can come. **W**rite soon.
                      1   1   1

                   2
                   Your cousin,
                       14

                   7
                   John

Editing Guide: Capitals: 20   · Commas: 6   Periods: 3   Apostrophes: 1   End Marks: 6

CHAPTER 11 LESSON 4 CONTINUED

TEACHER INSTRUCTIONS

Use the Question and Answer Flows below for the sentences on the Chapter 11 Test B.

Question and Answer Flow for Sentence 1: The goldfish were swimming leisurely around the fish tank in my room.

1. What were swimming leisurely around the fish tank in my room? goldfish - SN
2. What is being said about goldfish? goldfish were swimming - V
3. Were - HV
4. Were swimming how? leisurely - Adv
5. Around - P
6. Around what? tank - OP
7. What kind of tank? fish - Adj
8. The - A
9. In - P
10. In what? room - OP
11. Whose room? my - PPA
12. The - A
13. SN V P1 Check
14. (Around the fish tank) - Prepositional phrase
15. (In my room) - Prepositional phrase
16. Period, statement, declarative sentence
17. Go back to the verb - divide the complete subject from the complete predicate.

Classified Sentence:

```
              A    SN    HV     V       Adv       P   A  Adj  OP   P  PPA OP
      SN V   The goldfish / were swimming leisurely (around the fish tank) (in my room). D
      P1
```

Question and Answer Flow for Sentence 2: Read about current events in the daily newspaper.

1. Who read about current events in the daily newspaper? (You) - SP (Understood subject pronoun)
2. What is being said about you? you read - V
3. About - P
4. About what? events - OP
5. What kind of events? current - Adj
6. In - P
7. In what? newspaper - OP
8. What kind of newspaper? daily - Adj
9. The - A
10. SN V P1 Check
11. (About current events) - Prepositional phrase
12. (In the daily newspaper) - Prepositional phrase
13. Period, command, imperative sentence
14. Go back to the verb - divide the complete subject from the complete predicate.

Classified Sentence:

```
             (You) SP    V    P    Adj    OP    P  A  Adj    OP
      SN V         / Read (about current events) (in the daily newspaper). Imp
      P1
```

Question and Answer Flow for Sentence 3: Our new baby sister is cooing and laughing at us now.

1. Who is cooing and laughing at us now? sister - SN
2. What is being said about sister? sister is cooing and laughing - CV, CV
3. Is - HV
4. And - C
5. At - P
6. At whom? us - OP
7. Cooing and laughing when? now - Adv
8. Which sister? baby - Adj
9. What kind of sister? new - Adj
10. Whose sister? our - PPA
11. SN V P1 Check
12. (At us) - Prepositional phrase
13. Period, statement, declarative sentence
14. Go back to the verb - divide the complete subject from the complete predicate.

Classified Sentence:

```
             PPA Adj  Adj   SN  HV  CV    C   CV     P OP  Adv
      SN V   Our new baby sister / is cooing and laughing (at us) now. D
      P1
```

CHAPTER 11   LESSON 5
Objectives: Writing (persuasive essay) and Writing Assignment #12.

 WRITING TIME

TEACHING SCRIPT FOR A PERSUASIVE ESSAY

Persuasion means getting other people to see things your way. When you write a persuasive essay, your topic is something you want to "persuade" people to do or believe. A persuasive essay expresses an opinion and tries to convince the reader that this opinion is correct. Persuading someone to agree with you requires careful thinking and planning. As a writer, you must make the issue clear and present facts and reasons that give strong support to your opinion. You are encouraging your audience to take a certain action or to feel the same way you do.

In attempting to persuade anyone to your way of thinking, it is VERY important to consider just who the reader is that you are trying to persuade. Your reader is your audience. When you know who your reader is, you must use persuasive reasoning that will appeal to that reader. Know your reader well enough to use arguments that will appeal to him/her. You would not use the same kind of argument to persuade your five-year-old sister to tell you where she hid your skates that you would use to persuade your parents to allow you to have friends over for the night.

The three-point writing format is one of the best ways to present your persuasive argument because it gives you an organized way of stating your opinion and supporting it. The persuasive writing format is the same as your earlier expository writing format. They both use the three-point organization. The differences between persuasive and expository writing are your purpose for writing, the content of your paper, and the wording of your sentences.

You will find that the main difference is that the topic sentence is an opinion statement. In addition, all the points and supporting sentences are persuasive in nature and are intended to back up the opinion statement. Remember, persuasive writing states your opinion with supporting facts that try to convince your reader to think or act in a certain way, and expository writing attempts to give an explanation or information to your reader.

We will go through the steps for writing a persuasive essay by reading and discussing the guidelines for a three-paragraph persuasive essay in Reference 37 on page 34 in your book. You actually have two guidelines in your reference box. Let's go through the persuasive essay first so you will know all the parts. (*Read and discuss the parts of a persuasive essay below. Reference 37 is on page 200 in your TM.*)

Your first paragraph is an introductory paragraph and will have three sentences. Sentence #1 is the Topic Sentence. You will state your opinion in the topic sentence: **Everyone should wear a hat with his or her outfit.**

Sentence #2 is the Reason Sentence. You will give a general reason why you think the topic sentence is true: **Hats are the most exciting part of an outfit.**

Sentence #3 is the General Number Sentence. You will use a general number word and restate the main idea in the topic sentence: **There are numerous reasons why wearing a hat is beneficial.**

CHAPTER 11 LESSON 5 CONTINUED

The second paragraph is the body of the essay and will have 6 sentences. Sentence #4 is the <u>First-Point Persuasive Sentence</u>. You will give your first reason to support your opinion: **The first benefit of wearing a hat is protection from the sun.** Sentence #5 is the <u>First-Point Supporting Sentence</u>. You will give an example that supports and explains your first point: **Hats shield your head and face from harmful rays that can cause painful sunburns.**

Sentence #6 is the <u>Second-Point Persuasive Sentence</u>. You will give your second reason to support your opinion: **The second benefit for wearing a hat is that hats provide a simple form of self - expression.** Sentence #7 is the <u>Second-Point Supporting Sentence</u>. You will give an example that supports and explains your second point: **Different styles of hats show others a lot about you.**

Sentence #8 is the <u>Third-Point Persuasive Sentence</u>. You will give your third reason to support your opinion: **The third benefit of wearing a hat is that hats are not only fun, but also very versatile.** Sentence #9 is the <u>Third-Point Supporting Sentence</u>. You will give an example that supports and explains your third point: **You can find hats to match any outfit, style, or occasion.**

The third paragraph is the conclusion of the essay and will have two concluding sentences. The first concluding sentence is simply a restatement sentence that forcefully restates your original opinion in the topic sentence and usually starts with IN CONCLUSION. Sentence #10 is the <u>In Conclusion Sentence</u>: **In conclusion, every outfit should have a coordinating hat.**

The second concluding sentence is a summary sentence. This sentence summarizes one or more of the reasons stated. Sentence #11 is the <u>Final Summary Sentence</u>: **By providing protection and fun, hats become a necessity for every outfit.**

You have just learned how to write a three-paragraph persuasive essay. With that knowledge, I will now show you how to expand a three-paragraph persuasive essay into a five-paragraph persuasive essay. It will be structured much like the five-paragraph expository essay. Let's go over the steps.

1. The first paragraph has three sentences: the <u>Topic</u> sentence, the <u>Reason</u> sentence, and the <u>General</u> number sentence.
2. The second paragraph has the <u>First</u> point and two or three <u>Supporting</u> sentences for the first point.
3. The third paragraph has the <u>Second</u> point and two or three <u>Supporting</u> sentences for the second point.
4. The fourth paragraph has the <u>Third</u> point and two or three <u>Supporting</u> sentences for the third point.
5. The fifth paragraph has two sentences: the <u>In Conclusion</u> sentence and the <u>Final Summary</u> sentence.

Sometimes, you will only want to write a persuasive paragraph, not an essay. We will now go through the persuasive paragraph so you will know all the parts and will be familiar with the patterns for persuasive paragraphs and essays. Look at the persuasive paragraph guidelines in Reference 37. (*Read and discuss the guidelines for a persuasive paragraph and a persuasive essay in the reference box on the next page with your students. Make sure you use the sample essay to point out how each sentence is made.*)

CHAPTER 11 LESSON 5 CONTINUED

Reference 37: Persuasive Paragraph and Essay Guidelines	
Guidelines for a Persuasive Paragraph	**Guidelines for a 3-Paragraph Persuasive Essay**
Paragraph (10-13 sentences) A. **Topic** sentence (opinion statement) B. **General number** sentence C. **First-point** persuasive sentence D. 1 or 2 **supporting** sentences for the first point E. **Second-point** persuasive sentence F. 1 or 2 **supporting** sentences for the second point G. **Third-point** persuasive sentence H. 1 or 2 **supporting** sentences for the third point I. **In conclusion** sentence (Repeat topic idea) J. **Final summary** sentence (Summarize reasons)	I. Paragraph 1 – Introduction (3 sentences) 　　A. **Topic** sentence (opinion statement) 　　B. **Reason** sentence 　　C. **General number** sentence II. Paragraph 2 – Body (6-9 sentences) 　　A. **First-point** persuasive sentence 　　B. 1 or 2 **supporting** sentences for the first point 　　C. **Second-point** persuasive sentence 　　D. 1 or 2 **supporting** sentences for the second point 　　E. **Third-point** persuasive sentence 　　F. 1 or 2 **supporting** sentences for the third point III. Paragraph 3 – Conclusion (2 sentences) 　　A. **In conclusion** sentence (Repeat topic idea) 　　B. **Final summary** sentence (Summarize reasons)

Hats

Everyone should wear a hat with his or her outfit. Hats are the most exciting part of an outfit. There are numerous reasons why wearing a hat is beneficial.

The first benefit of wearing a hat is protection from the sun. Hats shield your head and face from harmful rays that can cause painful sunburns. The second benefit for wearing a hat is that hats provide a simple form of self-expression. Different styles of hats show others a lot about you. The third benefit of wearing a hat is that hats are not only fun, but also very versatile. You can find hats to match any outfit, style, or occasion.

In conclusion, every outfit should have a coordinating hat. By providing protection and fun, hats become a necessity for every outfit.

TEACHING SCRIPT FOR WRITING ASSIGNMENT

Now, you will write, revise, and edit a persuasive essay. As you edit, make sure you use all the checklists in Reference 5. Remember to read through the whole essay, starting with the title. After you are satisfied with your revising and editing, you will write a final paper, using the Final Paper Checklist in Reference 5. You will then give the finished writing assignment to me.

Writing Assignment Box

Writing Assignment #12: Three-Paragraph Persuasive Essay (First Person)
(Remind students that first person pronouns are *I, we, me, us, my, our, mine, and ours.*)

Writing topics: Why Reading Is Important or **Good Sportsmanship** or **Why We Need Prayer**

TEACHER INSTRUCTIONS FOR CHECKING WRITING ASSIGNMENT

Read, check, and discuss the final paper for Writing Assignment #12 after students have finished writing, revising, and editing their writing assignment. Use the checklists in Reference 5 as you check and discuss students' papers.

(End of lesson.)

CHAPTER 12   LESSON 1
Objectives: Jingles (Direct Object), Grammar (Introductory sentences, direct objects, transitive verbs, add direct objects to the Noun Check, Oral Skill Builder Check), Writing (journal), Vocabulary #1, and Activity.

 **JINGLE TIME**

Have students turn to the Jingle Section in their books and recite the previously-taught jingles. Then, lead students in reciting the new jingle (*The Direct Object*) below. Practice the new jingle several times until students can recite it smoothly. Emphasize reciting with a rhythm. Students and teacher should be together! (*Do not try to explain the jingle at this time. Just have fun reciting it.*)

Teacher's Notes: Again, do not spend a large amount of time practicing the new jingles. Students learn the jingles best by spending a small amount of time consistently, **every** day.

Jingle 16:   Direct Object Jingle
1. A direct object is a noun or pronoun.
2. A direct object completes the meaning of the sentence.
3. A direct object is located after the verb-transitive.
4. To find the direct object, ask WHAT or WHOM after your verb.

 GRAMMAR TIME

Put the introductory sentences from the box below on the board. Use these sentences as you go through each new concept covered in your teaching script. For the greatest benefit, students must participate orally with the teacher. (*You might put the introductory sentences on notebook paper if you are doing one-on-one instruction with your students.*)

Chapter 12, Introductory Sentences for Lesson 1
1. _____ The mailman delivered the package.
2. _____ The soldiers built the fort in a safe place.
3. _____ Did Joseph plant tomatoes in the tiny garden?

TEACHING SCRIPT FOR DIRECT OBJECTS AND TRANSITIVE VERBS

We have been studying Pattern 1, which has the (subject) noun and verb as its main parts (N V). Now, we will learn a new sentence pattern. This new sentence pattern is called Pattern 2, and it will have some new parts that you will learn today. Pattern 2 is different from Pattern 1 because its main parts are noun, verb, noun (N V N). The second noun is called a direct object. There are five things you need to know about a direct object. For this information, look at Reference 38 on page 35 in the Reference Section of your book and follow along as I read this information to you.

CHAPTER 12 LESSON 1 CONTINUED

I want you to notice that these five things are very similar to the Direct Object Jingle. You will read the example with me so you will know what to say when you classify Pattern 2 sentences. (*Read the information about direct objects to your students. Then, have students read and classify the sample sentence, with you.*)

Reference 38: Direct Object, Verb-transitive, and Pattern 2

1. A **direct object** is a noun or pronoun after the verb that completes the meaning of the sentence.

2. A **direct object** is labeled as **DO**.

3. To find the **direct object**, ask WHAT or WHOM after the verb.

4. A **direct object** must be verified to mean someone or something different from the subject noun.

5. A **verb-transitive** is an action verb with a direct object after it and is labeled V-t. (Whatever receives the action of a transitive verb is the direct object.)

Sample Sentence for the exact words to say to find the direct object and transitive verb.

1. Bob wrote a novel.
2. Who wrote a novel? Bob - SN
3. What is being said about Bob? Bob wrote - V
4. Bob wrote what? novel - verify the noun
5. Does novel mean the same thing as Bob? No.
6. Novel - DO (*Say: Novel - direct object.*)
7. Wrote - V-t (*Say: Wrote - verb-transitive.*)
8. A - A

9. SN V-t DO P2 Check
   (*Say: Subject Noun, Verb-transitive, Direct Object, Pattern 2, Check. This first check is to make sure the "t" is added to the verb.*)
10. Verb-transitive - check again.
    (*"Check again" means to check for prepositional phrases and then go through the rest of the Question and Answer Flow.*)
11. No prepositional phrases.
12. Period, statement, declarative sentence
13. Go back to the verb - divide the complete subject from the complete predicate.

Earlier you learned that nouns can have different jobs, or functions, in a sentence. You have studied two of these jobs already: A noun can be a subject, or a noun can be an object of a preposition. You must remember, however, that a noun used as a subject is a <u>core part of a sentence pattern</u> (like **SN V**). But a noun that is used as an object of a preposition is not part of the core pattern of a sentence. Nouns used as objects of prepositions can be used with every sentence pattern since they are not part of the core pattern.

You will now study how nouns function in different sentence patterns. The first pattern, **Pattern 1**, has a *Noun Verb* for the core sentence pattern and is written **N V**. However, notice that when you write Pattern 1 in Shurley English, you write **SN V** because you name the job of each core part as well, which is *Subject Noun / Verb*. You will also add the pattern number to each pattern to make it easier to identify. Therefore, the **first pattern** in Shurley English is *subject noun / verb / Pattern 1*, and it is written as **SN V P1**.

In the new sentence pattern, **Pattern 2**, there are two nouns in the core sentence pattern: **N V N**. The first noun is a subject noun and is still written as **SN**. The second noun will always come after the verb (*as its position in the pattern indicates*) and is required to complete the meaning of the sentence. This second noun is called a direct object and is written with the abbreviation **DO**. Any time there is a direct object in a sentence pattern, the verb is transitive and is written as **V-t** to indicate that it is an action verb used with a direct object noun. The **second pattern** in Shurley English is *subject noun / verb-transitive / direct object / Pattern 2,* and it is written as **SN V-t DO P2**.

CHAPTER 12 LESSON 1 CONTINUED

What is Pattern 2? (*SN V-t DO*) What are the core parts of a Pattern 2 sentence? (*SN V-t DO*) What parts of speech are used in a Pattern 2 sentence? (*N V N*) You will use what you have just learned as you classify Sentences 1-3 with me to find the direct object and verb-transitive. As we classify the sentences together, I will show you how to say the new part as we say the Question and Answer Flow. Begin.

Question and Answer Flow for Sentence 1: The mailman delivered the package.

1. Who delivered the package? mailman - SN
2. What is being said about mailman? mailman delivered - V
3. Mailman delivered what? package - verify the noun

Note: "Verify the noun" is a check to make sure the second noun does not mean the same thing as the subject noun. If it does not, then the second noun is a direct object.

4. Does package mean the same thing as mailman? No.
5. Package - DO (Direct Object)
6. Delivered - V-t (Verb-transitive)

Note: Always ask the WHAT or WHOM question immediately after finding the SN and V to get the DO. Mark the verb with a V until the DO has been identified. After you verify the noun is a direct object, mark your verb as transitive by adding the "t" to the main verb. Always get the core, SN V-t DO, before you classify the rest of the sentence.

7. The - A
8. The - A
9. SN V-t DO P2 Check

   (Subject noun, Verb-transitive, Direct object, Pattern 2 Check. Write *SN V-t DO P2* in the blank beside the sentence.)

10. Verb-transitive - Check again.

Note: Check for the "t" on the verb by saying, verb transitive. Check for prepositional phrases by saying, "check again."

11. No prepositional phrases.
12. Period, statement, declarative sentence
13. Go back to the verb - divide the complete subject from the complete predicate.

Classified Sentence:

```
             A    SN        V-t    A    DO
SN V-t    The mailman / delivered the package. D
DO P2
```

Teacher's Notes: A verb-transitive check has been added in Chapter 12 because students tend to forget to add the "t" to the verb, even after they say verb-transitive while classifying the direct object. If they leave the "t" off, it is wrong. This is the reason the verb-transitive check is so important for them to remember.

Question and Answer Flow for Sentence 2: The soldiers built the fort in a safe place.

1. Who built the fort in a safe place? soldiers - SN
2. What is being said about soldiers? soldiers built - V
3. Soldiers built what? fort - verify the noun
4. Does fort mean the same thing as soldiers? No.
5. Fort - DO
6. Built - V-t
7. The - A
8. In - P
9. In what? place - OP
10. What kind of place? safe - Adj
11. A - A
12. The - A
13. SN V-t DO P2 Check
14. Verb-transitive - Check again.
15. (In a safe place) - Prepositional phrase
16. Period, statement, declarative sentence
17. Go back to the verb - divide the complete subject from the complete predicate.

Classified Sentence:

```
             A    SN       V-t  A   DO   P  A  Adj  OP
SN V-t    The soldiers / built the fort (in a safe place). D
DO P2
```

CHAPTER 12 LESSON 1 CONTINUED

Question and Answer Flow for Sentence 3: Did Joseph plant tomatoes in the tiny garden?

1. Who did plant tomatoes in the tiny garden? Joseph - SN
2. What is being said about Joseph? Joseph did plant - V
3. Did - HV
4. Joseph did plant what? tomatoes - verify the noun
5. Do tomatoes mean the same thing as Joseph? No.
6. Tomatoes - DO
7. Plant - V-t
8. In - P
9. In what? garden - OP
10. What kind of garden? tiny - Adj

11. The - A
12. SN V-t DO P2 Check
13. Verb-transitive - Check again.
14. (In the tiny garden) - Prepositional phrase
15. Question mark, question, interrogative sentence
16. Go back to the verb - divide the complete subject from the complete predicate.
17. This sentence has predicate words in the complete subject. Underline the helping verb at the beginning of the sentence twice.

Classified Sentence:

                      HV   SN   V-t   DO   P A Adj OP

      SN V-t   <u>Did</u> Joseph / plant tomatoes (in the tiny garden)? **Int**

      DO P2

Teacher's Notes: Question and Answer Flow Notice.

For consistency, the Question and Answer Flow will verify the direct object by using the verb **Do** if the direct object is plural and **Does** if the direct object is singular.

> Example: Judy painted four pictures. Q & A: <u>Do pictures</u> mean the same thing as Judy?

On the other hand, you may prefer to use the singular form because you are actually saying, "Does the **word** *pictures* mean the same thing as Judy?" Therefore, if you choose to use the singular verb form, just make the necessary change whenever it occurs.

> Example: Judy painted four pictures. Q & A: <u>Does pictures</u> mean the same thing as Judy?

TEACHING SCRIPT FOR ADDING THE DIRECT OBJECTS TO THE NOUN CHECK

Name the noun jobs we have had before today. (*SN and OP*) Today, we have added another noun job. What is the new noun job that we have just added? (*direct object - DO*) So, if I want to find nouns in a sentence, where would I go? (*To the SN, OP, and DO jobs*) After I go to the subject noun, object of the preposition, and direct object jobs, what do I do next? (*As you do a Noun Check, look at each job to see if the word is a noun or a pronoun. If it is a pronoun, leave it alone and go to the next job. If it is a noun, circle it to indicate that it is a noun.*) (*Continue the Oral Sill Builder Check, using the guidelines below.*)

Oral Skill Builder Check

1. **Noun check.** (Say the job and then say the noun. Circle each noun.)	5. **Identify the complete subject and the complete predicate.** (Underline the complete subject once and the complete predicate twice.)
2. **Identify the nouns as singular or plural.** (Write **S** or **P** above each noun.)	
3. **Identify the nouns as common or proper.** (Follow established procedure for oral identification.)	6. **Identify the simple subject and simple predicate.** (Underline the simple subject once and the simple predicate twice. Bold, or highlight, the lines.)
4. **Do a vocabulary check.** (Follow established procedure for oral identification.)	7. **Recite the irregular verb chart.** (Located on student page 23 and teacher page 138.)

CHAPTER 12 LESSON 1 CONTINUED

 WRITING TIME

Have students make an entry in their journals.

 VOCABULARY TIME

Assign Chapter 12, Vocabulary Words **#1** on page 9 in the Section for students to define in their Vocabulary notebooks. Tell students they are to use a dictionary or thesaurus to look up the meanings of the vocabulary words. After they write each word and its meaning, students are to write a sentence using the vocabulary word.

Chapter 12, Vocabulary Words #1
(demand, suggest, endow, give)

 ACTIVITY / ASSIGNMENT TIME

Have students use the directions below to create a **personality poem** that uses parts of speech. Have students create a **personality poem** for themselves and one for each family member and for a friend or other relative. (*Write the directions and the example below on the board for your students.*)

Directions for each line of a personality poem:

1. Write your first name.
2. Write two adjectives that describe your personality.
3. Write four words that describe your appearance.
    (*adjective, noun, adjective, noun*).
4. Write five nouns naming things you enjoy.
5. Write any descriptive word you choose about yourself.

Example:

Amanda
Forgetful, happy
Blue eyes, big smile
Soccer, swimming, stamps, friends, jokes
Likeable

(End of lesson.)

CHAPTER 12   LESSON 2

Objectives: Jingles, Grammar (Practice Sentences, Oral Skill Builder Check, Independent Pattern 2 Practice Sentence), Vocabulary #2, and Activity.

JINGLE TIME

Have students turn to the Jingle Section in their books and recite the previously-taught jingles.

GRAMMAR TIME

First-Year Option: Put the Practice Sentences from the box below on the board or on notebook paper. Use these sentences as you practice the concepts that have been taught. For the greatest benefit, students must participate orally with the teacher. **Second-Year Option:** Have students classify the Practice Sentences independently on notebook paper. Check students' sentences with the answers provided below. (*If you have the CDs for Practice Sentences, have students check their sentences with the CDs.*)

Chapter 12, Practice Sentences for Lesson 2

1. _____ The designated batter sent the ball over the fence.
2. _____ Call your mother from the telephone in the hallway.
3. _____ The doctor sees many sick patients in his office daily.

TEACHING SCRIPT FOR PRACTICING PATTERN 2 SENTENCES

We will classify three different sentences to practice Pattern 2 sentences. We will classify the sentences together. Begin. (*You might have your students write the labels above the sentences at this time.*)

Question and Answer Flow for Sentence 1: The designated batter sent the ball over the fence.

1. Who sent the ball over the fence? batter - SN
2. What is being said about batter? batter sent - V
3. Batter sent what? ball - verify the noun
4. Does ball mean the same thing as batter? No.
5. Ball - DO
6. Sent - V-t
7. The - A
8. Over - P
9. Over what? fence - OP
10. The - A
11. What kind of batter? designated - Adj
12. The - A
13. SN V-t DO P2 Check
14. Verb-transitive - Check again.
15. (Over the fence) - Prepositional phrase
16. Period, statement, declarative sentence
17. Go back to the verb - divide the complete subject from the complete predicate.

Classified Sentence:

```
                           A     Adj    SN     V-t   A DO   P   A   OP
          SN  V-t    The designated batter / sent the ball (over the fence).  D
          DO  P2
```

CHAPTER 12 LESSON 2 CONTINUED

Question and Answer Flow for Sentence 2: Call your mother from the telephone in the hallway.

1. Who call your mother from the telephone in the hallway?
   You - SP (Understood subject pronoun)
2. What is being said about you? you call - V
3. You call whom? mother - verify the noun
4. Does mother mean the same thing as you? No.
5. Mother - DO
6. Call - V-t
7. Whose mother? your - PPA
8. From - P
9. From what? telephone - OP
10. The - A

11. In - P
12. In what? hallway - OP
13. The - A
14. SN V-t DO P2 Check
15. Verb-transitive - Check again.
16. (From the telephone) - Prepositional phrase
17. (In the hallway) - Prepositional phrase
18. Period, command, imperative sentence
19. Go back to the verb - divide the complete subject from the complete predicate.

Classified Sentence:

```
                    (You) SP   V-t  PPA   DO     P   A   OP        P   A   OP
                    SN V-t     / Call your mother (from the telephone) (in the hallway).  Imp
                    DO P2
```

Question and Answer Flow for Sentence 3: The doctor sees many sick patients in his office daily.

1. Who sees many sick patients in his office daily?
   doctor - SN
2. What is being said about doctor? doctor sees - V
3. Doctor sees whom? patients - verify the noun
4. Do patients mean the same thing as doctor? No.
5. Patients - DO
6. Sees - V-t
7. What kind of patients? sick - Adj
8. How many patients? many - Adj
9. In - P

10. In what? office - OP
11. Whose office? his - PPA
12. Sees when? daily - Adv
13. The - A
14. SN V-t DO P2 Check
15. Verb-transitive - Check again.
16. (In his office) - Prepositional phrase
17. Period, statement, declarative sentence
18. Go back to the verb - divide the complete subject from the complete predicate.

Classified Sentence:

```
                    A    SN    V-t  Adj  Adj   DO      P  PPA  OP    Adv
          SN V-t    The  doctor / sees many sick patients (in his office) daily.  D
          DO P2
```

TEACHER INSTRUCTIONS

Use Sentences 1-3 that you just classified with your students to do an Oral Skill Builder Check. Use the guidelines below.

Oral Skill Builder Check

1. **Noun check.**
   (Say the job and then say the noun. Circle each noun.)

2. **Identify the nouns as singular or plural.**
   (Write **S** or **P** above each noun.)

3. **Identify the nouns as common or proper.**
   (Follow established procedure for oral identification.)

4. **Do a vocabulary check.**
   (Follow established procedure for oral identification.)

5. **Identify the complete subject and the complete predicate.** (Underline the complete subject once and the complete predicate twice.)

6. **Identify the simple subject and simple predicate.**
   (Underline the simple subject once and the simple predicate twice. Bold, or highlight, the lines.)

7. **Recite the irregular verb chart.**
   (Located on student page 23 and teacher page 138.)

CHAPTER 12 LESSON 2 CONTINUED

TEACHING SCRIPT FOR INTRODUCING A PATTERN 2 PRACTICE SENTENCE

Put these words on the board: **Pattern 2 Practice Sentence**

Get out a sheet of notebook paper. On the top line of your notebook paper, write the title *Pattern 2 Practice Sentence*. Look at the new words on the board: **Pattern 2 Practice Sentence**. I will guide you again through the process as we learn to write a Pattern 2 sentence.

You have already learned how to write an independent Pattern 1 sentence according to labels you select. You will now learn how to write an independent Pattern 2 sentence the same way. First, you start out with the core labels for a Pattern 2 sentence. This means that you <u>must always have a subject, a verb-transitive, and a direct object before you add any extra parts</u>. (*SN V-t DO*)

Next, you build the rest of your Pattern 2 sentence from the regular sentence parts learned in Pattern 1. I will ask you a few questions to make sure you understand. What are the parts of a Pattern 2 sentence that YOU MUST USE? (*All Pattern 2 sentences must have a subject, a verb-transitive, and a direct object.*) I want you to name the extra sentence parts that you can use with your sentence. There are ten parts. (*adjectives, adverbs, articles, prepositional phrases, subject pronouns, possessive nouns, possessive pronouns, helping verbs, conjunctions, and interjections*) Remember, you will use the core parts of a Pattern 2 sentence and then add the extra parts that you want your sentence to have.

Let's write the labels for a Pattern 2 sentence on a sheet of notebook paper. First, on your paper, write the *SN V-t* and *DO* labels that a Pattern 2 sentence must have. Be sure to place them in the middle of your paper. (*Demonstrate by writing the SN V-t DO labels on the board.*) Using what you know about writing Practice Sentences, you decide which other parts you want to add to your Pattern 2 Practice Sentence. (*Have students finish writing a Pattern 2 sentence and turn it in to you. Students do not have to write an Improved Sentence at this point unless you feel they need the practice. If your students cannot handle this much independence so soon, give them the labels you want them to follow for a Pattern 2 sentence. (Example: A Adj SN V-t DO P A OP P OP) Check and discuss students' sentences after they have finished.*)

VOCABULARY TIME

Assign Chapter 12, Vocabulary Words **#2** on page 9 in the Reference Section for students to define in their Vocabulary notebooks. After they write each word and its meaning, students are to write a sentence using the vocabulary word.

Chapter 12, Vocabulary Words #2
(quick, agile, begins, originates)

ACTIVITY / ASSIGNMENT TIME

Have students write the three sentences that they classified at the beginning of the lesson on notebook paper. Have them tape-record the Question and Answer Flows for all three sentences. Students should write labels above the sentences as they classify them. They especially need the second practice if this is their first year in the program. (*After the students have finished, check the tape and sentence labels. Make sure students understand any mistakes they have made.*)

(End of lesson.)

CHAPTER 12 LESSON 3

Objectives: Jingles, Grammar (Practice Sentence), Skills (Editing Checklist), Practice Exercise, and Writing (journal).

JINGLE TIME

Have students turn to the Jingle Section in their books and recite the previously-taught jingles.

GRAMMAR TIME

First-Year Option: Put the Practice Sentences from the box below on the board or on notebook paper. Use these sentences as you practice the concepts that have been taught. For the greatest benefit, students must participate orally with the teacher. **Second-Year Option:** Have students classify the Practice Sentences independently on notebook paper. Check students' sentences with the answers provided below. *(If you have the CDs for Practice Sentences, have students check their sentences with the CDs.)*

Chapter 12, Practice Sentences for Lesson 3
1. _____ Did you find a penny on the ground?
2. _____ Taste Ann's famous punch recipe.
3. _____ My sister prepared her speech for the graduation ceremony.

TEACHING SCRIPT FOR PRACTICING PATTERN 2 SENTENCES

We will classify three different sentences to practice Pattern 2 sentences. We will classify the sentences together. Begin. *(You might have your students write the labels above the sentences at this time.)*

Question and Answer Flow for Sentence 1: Did you find a penny on the ground?

1. Who did find a penny on the ground? you -SP
2. What is being said about you? you did find - V
3. Did - HV
4. You did find what? penny - verify the noun
5. Does penny mean the same thing as you? No.
6. Penny - DO
7. Find - V-t
8. A - A
9. On - P
10. On what? ground - OP
11. The - A
12. SN V-t DO P2 Check
13. Verb-transitive - Check again.
14. (On the ground) - Prepositional phrase
15. Question mark, question, interrogative sentence
16. Go back to the verb - divide the complete subject from the complete predicate.
17. This sentence has predicate words in the complete subject. Underline the helping verb at the beginning of the sentence twice.

Classified Sentence:

```
                    HV  SP  V-t A DO   P A    OP
          SN V-t    Did you / find a penny (on the ground)? Int
          DO P2
```

CHAPTER 12 LESSON 3 CONTINUED

Question and Answer Flow for Sentence 2: Taste Ann's famous punch recipe.

1. Who taste Ann's famous punch recipe?
   (You) - SP (Understood subject pronoun)
2. What is being said about you? you taste - V
3. You taste what? recipe - verify the noun
4. Does recipe mean the same thing as you? No.
5. Recipe - DO
6. Taste - V-t
7. What kind of recipe? punch - Adj

8. What kind of recipe? famous - Adj
9. Whose recipe? Ann's - PNA
10. SN V-t DO P2 Check
11. Verb-transitive - Check again.
12. No prepositional phrases.
13. Period, command, imperative sentence
14. Go back to the verb - divide the complete
    subject from the complete predicate.

Classified Sentence:

	(You) SP	V-t	PNA	Adj	Adj	DO
SN V-t	/ Taste Ann's famous punch recipe. **Imp**					
DO P2						

Question and Answer Flow for Sentence 3: My sister prepared her speech for the graduation ceremony.

1. Who prepared her speech for the graduation
   ceremony? sister - SN
2. What is being said about sister? sister prepared - V
3. Sister prepared what? speech - verify the noun
4. Does speech mean the same thing as sister? No.
5. Speech - DO
6. Prepared - V-t
7. Whose speech? her - PPA
8. For - P
9. For what? ceremony - OP

10. What kind of ceremony? graduation - Adj
11. The - A
12. Whose sister? my - PPA
13. SN V-t DO P2 Check
14. Verb-transitive - Check again.
15. (For the graduation ceremony) - Prepositional phrase
16. Period, statement, declarative sentence
17. Go back to the verb - divide the complete subject
    from the complete predicate.

Classified Sentence:

	PPA	SN	V-t	PPA	DO	P	A	Adj	OP
SN V-t	My sister / prepared her speech (for the graduation ceremony) . **D**								
DO P2									

SKILL TIME

TEACHING SCRIPT FOR INTRODUCING A REGULAR EDITING CHECKLIST

The process of finding and correcting errors in writing is called editing. Remember, the writing that you edit is called a rough draft. Before we begin detailed editing, I want you to know that total editing is a slow, meticulous (careful) process. You do not get in a hurry when you edit. It is like being a detective. You have all the clues, but you must study the clues carefully in order to solve the editing mystery.

After a while, the editing process will become automatic, but you must remember that editing is never a fast process. As you mature in your writing ability, editing will become more and more important because, without it, you just cannot have a top-quality piece of writing. Editing is like icing on a cake: It puts the finishing touches on a paper.

CHAPTER 12 LESSON 3 CONTINUED

To make regular editing easier, you must have a system. If you have a system when you edit, you will get the maximum benefit of editing. The Shurley English editing system is simple: Use a checklist. All high-tech businesses use checklists to keep track of everything that's important and productive. They are simple but very effective when used correctly. Editing should become an automatic process that enables you to produce a top-quality writing product every time you write.

You have been using the Beginning Editing Checklist. That is a good checklist, but now you are ready to use the regular editing checklist. It is more detailed and establishes an editing routine that will be easy for you to follow. We will now go over the regular editing checklist, and then I will show you how to use it to edit a rough draft. Look at Reference 39 on page 36 in your Reference Section. *(The Editing Checklist below includes a few skills that students have not had. Add these skills as they are introduced during Skill Time.)*

Reference 39: Regular Editing Checklist

Read each sentence and go through the Sentence Checkpoints below.

_____ E1. Sentence sense check. (Check for words left out or words repeated.)

_____ E2. First word, capital letter check. End mark check. Any other capitalization check. Any other punctuation check.

_____ E3. Sentence structure and punctuation check.
(Check for correct construction and correct punctuation of a simple sentence, a simple sentence with compound parts, or a compound sentence.)

_____ E4. Spelling and homonym check.
(Check for misspelled words and incorrect homonym choices.)

_____ E5. Usage check.
(Check subject-verb agreement, a/an choice, pronoun/antecedent agreement, pronoun cases, degrees of adjectives, double negatives, verb tenses, and contractions.)

Read each paragraph and go through the Paragraph Checkpoints below.

_____ E6. Check to see that each paragraph is indented.

_____ E7. Check each paragraph for a topic sentence.

_____ E8. Check each sentence to make sure it supports the topic of the paragraph.

_____ E9. Check the content for interest and creativity. Do not begin all sentences with the same word, and use a variety of simple, compound, and complex sentences.

_____ E10. Check the type and format of the writing assigned.

Notice that each checkpoint on the editing guide has a capital *E* and a number beside it. The capital *E* refers to the editing checklist (*E* for editing). The number indicates which skill area is listed beside each checkpoint. So, *E1* means you are editing the first skill area. We will call *E1* checkpoint 1. What is being checked in checkpoint 1? (**E1:** *Sentence sense check. Check for words left out or words repeated.*) What is being checked in checkpoint 2? (**E2:** *First word, capital letter check. End mark check. Any other capitalization check. Any other punctuation check.*) What is being checked in checkpoint 3? (**E3:** *Sentence structure and punctuation check. Check for correct construction and correct punctuation of a simple sentence, a simple sentence with compound parts, a compound sentence, or a complex sentence.*)

CHAPTER 12 LESSON 3 CONTINUED

What is being checked in checkpoint 4? (**E4:** *Spelling and homonym check. Check for misspelled words and incorrect homonym choices.*) What is being checked in checkpoint 5? (**E5:** *Usage check. Check subject-verb agreement, a/an choice, pronoun/antecedent agreement, pronoun cases, degrees of adjectives, double negatives, verb tenses, and contractions.*)

These first five checkpoints will be used for each sentence as you do a sentence-by-sentence edit. The second five checkpoints are done as you check each paragraph. What are the five paragraph checkpoints? (**E6:** *Check to see that each paragraph is indented.* **E7:** *Check each paragraph for a topic sentence.* **E8:** *Check each sentence to make sure it supports the topic of the paragraph.* **E9:** *Check the content for interest and creativity. Do not begin all sentences with the same word, and use a variety of simple, compound, and complex sentences.* **E10:** *Check the type and format of the writing assigned.*)

Remember, editing is a slow, careful process that works best when you use your system. Your papers are not very long at this point, and it is crucial that you get in the habit of going through each sentence five times, one time for each sentence checkpoint. You'll know your paper pretty well by the time you finish, but that's the whole idea of editing. You should know your paper well enough to have corrected every mistake in it. This editing system may take you a little longer at the beginning, but it will save you from having to redo a poor editing job due to improper editing techniques.

I will guide you through an expository essay that has been edited so you can see the editing process. Look at the bottom of Reference 40 on page 37 in your book. *(Use the reference box below as you go through the teaching script that follows. Make sure you point out that all corrections are written on the line above each mistake.)* *(Do not go over the rough draft and final paper sections at this time. They will be discussed in later lessons.)*

Reference 40: Editing Example

Topic: **Reasons police officers use German shepherds**
Three main points: (**1. size   2. keen sense of smell   3. intelligence**)

Officers

German Shepherds for Police officers

→   U   S   G   (.) A
Police officers all over the united states use german shepherds for several reasons although German shepherds
  often   **a**
are oftan companion dogs, it is the police officer that has made the German shepherd an popular working dog. Three
 reasons   **their   their**   **their**   (.)
reason police officers use German shepherds are its size, its keen sense of smell, and its intelligence
                                                           their
   The first reason that police officers use German shepherds is there size. The strong, sleek body of the
 G   shepherd
german shepard is very intimidating to anyone who is a threat to police officers. The second reason that police
                        their   (,)   **many**   (,)
officers use German shepherds is there keen sense of smell. German shepherds like miny other dogs can use their
 noses   scents
nose's to follow cents left by criminals that humans would not be able to follow. The third reason that police officers
              their   **they're**
use German shepherds is its intelligence. Because German shepherds are a very smart breed of dog, their easily
              obey   (.)
trained to readily obeys the commands of their officer
                                              reasons   (')   (,)
   In conclusion, police officers use German shepherds for many reason. The German shepherds size keen sense of
  (,)   **make**   **police**   (.)
smell and intelligence makes them valuable working companions to the poliece officer

Total Mistakes: 34
Editing Guide: Sentence checkpoints: **E1, E2, E3, E4, E5**   Paragraph checkpoints: **E6, E7, E8, E9, E10**

CHAPTER 12 LESSON 3 CONTINUED

1. Check the title for capitalization and spelling mistakes. (***Capitalization check***-*correct* <u>officers</u> *with a capital O.* ***Spelling check*** *– no mistakes.*)

2. **Read the first sentence.** (Police officers all over the united states use german sheperds for several reasons)

3. Are there any mistakes for checkpoint 1? (*Read checkpoint 1 and check the sentence.*) (***Sentence sense check*** *– no mistakes.*)

4. Are there any mistakes for checkpoint 2? (*Read checkpoint 2 and check the sentence.*) (***First word, capital letter check*** *– no mistakes.* ***End mark check*** *– correct with a period.* ***Any other capitalization check*** *– correct* ***united states*** *with a capital U and S, correct* ***german*** *with a capital G.* ***Any other punctuation check*** *– no mistakes.*)

5. Are there any mistakes for checkpoint 3? (*Read checkpoint 3 and check the sentence.*) (***Sentence structure and sentence structure punctuation check*** *– no mistakes.*)

6. Are there any mistakes for checkpoint 4? (*Read checkpoint 4 and check the sentence.*) (***Spelling and homonym check*** *– no mistakes.*)

7. Are there any mistakes for checkpoint 5? You have to do an individual usage-by-usage check in checkpoint 5 because there are too many different skills to check as a group. (*Read checkpoint 5 and check the sentence.*) (*Subject-verb agreement check – no mistakes. A-An check – no mistakes. Pronoun/antecedent agreement check – no mistakes. Pronoun case check – no mistakes. Double negative check – no mistakes. Verb tense check – no mistakes. Contraction check – no mistakes.*)

Now, we start the checkpoints over again on the next sentence. You will make very few editing mistakes if you stick with this system until it becomes automatic. As soon as editing becomes automatic, you will go through the editing process with ease, so trust me on this. Begin.

1. **Read the second sentence.** (although German shepherds are oftan companion dogs, it is the police officer that has made the German shepherd an popular working dog.)

2. Are there any mistakes for checkpoint 1? (*Checkpoint 1: Sentence* ***sense check*** *– no mistakes.*)

3. Are there any mistakes for checkpoint 2? (*Checkpoint 2:* (***First word, capital letter check*** *– correct the first word with a capital* ***A.*** ***End mark check*** *– no mistakes.* ***Any other capitalization check*** *– no mistakes.* ***Any other punctuation check*** *– no mistakes.*)

4. Are there any mistakes for checkpoint 3? (*Checkpoint 3:* ***Sentence structure and sentence structure punctuation check*** *– no mistakes.*) (*They have not had a complex sentence yet, so just tell them the sentence is correct.*)

5. Are there any mistakes for checkpoint 4? (*Checkpoint 4:* ***Spelling and homonym check*** *– correct the spelling of* ***oftan*** *to* ***often.***)

6. Are there any mistakes for checkpoint 5? (*Checkpoint 5:* ***Subject-verb agreement check*** *– no mistakes.* ***A-An check*** *– change* ***an popular*** *to* ***a popular.*** ***Pronoun/antecedent agreement check*** *– no mistakes.* ***Pronoun case check*** *– no mistakes.* ***Double negative check*** *– no mistakes.* ***Verb tense check*** *– no mistakes.* ***Contraction check*** *– no mistakes.*)

1. **Read the third sentence.** (Three reason police officers use German shepherds are its size, its keen sense of smell, and its intelligence)

2. Are there any mistakes for checkpoint 1? (*Checkpoint 1:* ***Sentence sense check*** *– correct* <u>reason</u> *to* <u>reasons</u> *because there are three reasons.*)

3. Are there any mistakes for checkpoint 2? (*Checkpoint 2:* ***First word, capital letter check*** *– no mistakes.* ***End mark check*** *– correct with a* <u>period</u>*.* ***Any other capitalization check*** *– no mistakes.* ***Any other punctuation check*** *– no mistakes.*)

4. Are there any mistakes for checkpoint 3? (*Checkpoint 3:* ***Sentence structure and sentence structure punctuation check*** *– no mistakes.*)

CHAPTER 12 LESSON 3 CONTINUED

5. Are there any mistakes for checkpoint 4? (*Checkpoint 4:* **Spelling and homonym check** – *no mistakes.*)

6. Are there any mistakes for checkpoint 5? (*Checkpoint 5:* **Subject-verb agreement check** – *no mistakes.* **A-An check** – *no mistakes.* **Pronoun/antecedent agreement check** – *change each pronoun* <u>its</u> *to* <u>their</u> *to agree with the antecedent* <u>German shepherds</u>. *There will be three pronoun/antecedent corrections.* **Pronoun case check** – *no mistakes.* **Double negative check** – *no mistakes.* **Verb tense check** – *no mistakes.* **Contraction check** – *no mistakes.*)

Look at the first paragraph. Now we will do a paragraph check for the last five checkpoints.

1. Are there any mistakes for checkpoint 6? (*Read checkpoint 6 and check the first paragraph.*) (*Indent.*)
2. Are there any mistakes for checkpoint 7? (*Read checkpoint 7 and check the first paragraph.*) (*No corrections.*)
3. Are there any mistakes for checkpoint 8? (*Read checkpoint 8 and check the first paragraph.*) (*No corrections.*)
4. Are there any mistakes for checkpoint 9? (*Read checkpoint 9 and check the first paragraph.*) (*No corrections.*)
5. Are there any mistakes for checkpoint 10? (*Read checkpoint 10 and check the first paragraph.*) (*No corrections.*)

(*Work through the remaining sentences in the last two paragraphs.* **Make sure you take the time now to establish the editing routine that you want your students to follow.**)

PRACTICE TIME

Have students turn to page 72 in the Practice Section of their book and find the skill under Chapter 12, Lesson 3, Practice. Go over the directions to make sure they understand what to do. Check and discuss the Practice after students have finished. (*Chapter 12, Lesson 3, Practice key is given below.*)

Chapter 12, Lesson 3, Practice: Find each error and write the correction above it. Write the punctuation corrections where they belong.

(indent)   **are**   **(.) (T)**   **obvious**
Highlighters and markers is writing instruments that have many things in common the most obveous
are their   **a**   **page**
is there felt tip and similar size. Both writing instruments use an felt tip to mark on a paige. Both
         are   **a**   **instruments**
writing instruments is larger than an regular pen or pencil. Finally, both writing instuments can be
     write (,) highlight   **(.)**
used to wright highlite, or color

Total Mistakes: 16

WRITING TIME

Have students make an entry in their journals. After they have finished, have students study the vocabulary words in their vocabulary notebooks and any of the skills in the Practice Section that they need to review.

(End of lesson.)

CHAPTER 12   LESSON 4

Objectives: Jingles, Study, Test, Check, Writing (journal).

 JINGLE TIME

Have students turn to the Jingle Section in their books and recite the previously-taught jingles.

 STUDY TIME

Have students study the vocabulary words in their vocabulary notebooks. Remind students that any vocabulary word in their notebooks could be on their test. Also, have students study any of the skills in the Practice Section that they need to review.

 **TEST TIME**

Have students turn to page 109 in the Test Section of their book and find the Chapter 12 Test. Students are allowed to use the Reference Section to help them remember the new information and to check the capitalization and punctuation rules while they correct capitalization and punctuation errors in sentences. Go over the directions to make sure they understand what to do. (*Chapter 12 Test key is on the next page.*)

 CHECK TIME

After students have finished, check and discuss their test papers. Make sure they understand why their answers are right or wrong. (*For total points, count each required answer as a point.*)

(End of lesson.)

Chapter 12 Test
(Student Page 109)

Exercise 1: Classify each sentence.

```
        A    Adj     SN        V-t    A    Adj   Adj   DO    P   PPA  OP
1.  SN  V-t      A powerful hurricane / destroyed the beautiful white beaches (near our resort)!  E
    DO  P2

        A    SN     P    A    Adj   OP         V-t   PPA  DO   P    OP
2.  SN  V-t      The story (about the good Samaritan) / restored my faith (in mankind).  D
    DO  P2

             I      SP   HV   V-t    DO   P    Adj    Adj    OP
3.  SN  V-t      Good grief!  We / must seek shelter (from this blistering sun)!  E
    DO  P2
```

Exercise 2: Use Sentence 3 to underline the complete subject once and the complete predicate twice and to complete the table below.

List the Noun Used	List the Noun Job	Singular or Plural	Common or Proper	Simple Subject	Simple Predicate
1. shelter	2. DO	3. S	4. C	5. We	6. must seek
7. sun	8. OP	9. S	10. C		

Exercise 3: Identify each pair of words as synonyms or antonyms by putting parentheses ( ) around **syn** or **ant**.

1. endow, give	**(syn)** ant	5. finish, commence	syn **(ant)**	9. fiction, fable	**(syn)** ant
2. agile, quick	**(syn)** ant	6. demand, suggest	syn **(ant)**	10. rival, competitor	**(syn)** ant
3. hardy, robust	**(syn)** ant	7. originates, begins	**(syn)** ant	11. logical, silly	syn **(ant)**
4. rip, mend	syn **(ant)**	8. rude, impolite	**(syn)** ant	12. delight, displease	syn **(ant)**

Exercise 4: Underline the correct homonym in each sentence.

1. I will be gone for a (weak, <u>week</u>) or more.
2. Yesterday, she (lead, <u>led</u>) me to the kitchen.
3. He said he felt (<u>weak</u>, week) from the heat.
4. Did you (<u>hear</u>, here) the recess bell?
5. We have to use a number 2 (<u>lead</u>, led) pencil.
6. Put your coats over (hear, <u>here</u>), please.
7. Augusta is the (<u>capital</u>, capitol) of Maine.
8. Initials are written with (<u>capital</u>, capitol) letters.

Exercise 5: For Sentences 1 and 2: Write the capitalization and punctuation corrections only. For Sentence 3: Write the capitalization and punctuation rule numbers for each correction in bold.

```
    H        S                    B    M              K       S     C
1.  holly, did the swedish ambassador visit bangor, maine, on his way to the kennedy space center?
```

Editing Guide: Capitals: 7   Commas: 3   End Marks: 1

```
    T    M J      I            S              A        S   A
2.  today, mr. james and i visited a famous spanish mission called the alamo near san antonio.
```

Editing Guide: Capitals: 8   Commas: 1   Periods: 1   End Marks: 1

```
    1        9  10 10  7                     16     16      14        14
3.  Our captain, Mr. R. J. Nelson, showed us coral reefs in the Atlantic Ocean near Greenwich, England.
        11  16 17 17      11                                           7        1
```

Editing Guide: Capitals: 9   Commas: 3   Periods: 3   End Marks: 1

Exercise 6: In your journal, write a paragraph summarizing what you have learned this week.

CHAPTER 12 LESSON 4 CONTINUED

TEACHER INSTRUCTIONS

Use the Question and Answer Flows below for the sentences on the Chapter 12 Test.

Question and Answer Flow for Sentence 1: A powerful hurricane destroyed the beautiful white beaches near our resort!

1. What destroyed the beautiful white beaches near our resort? hurricane - SN
2. What is being said about hurricane? hurricane destroyed - V
3. Hurricane destroyed what? beaches - verify the noun
4. Do beaches mean the same thing as hurricane? No.
5. Beaches - DO
6. Destroyed - V-t
7. What kind of beaches? white - Adj
8. What kind of beaches? beautiful - Adj
9. The - A
10. Near - P
11. Near what? resort - OP
12. Whose resort? our - PPA
13. What kind of hurricane? powerful - Adj
14. A - A
15. SN V-t DO P2 Check
16. Verb-transitive - Check again.
17. (Near our resort) - Prepositional phrase
18. Exclamation point, strong feeling, exclamatory sentence
19. Go back to the verb - divide the complete subject from the complete predicate.

Classified Sentence:

```
              A   Adj    SN       V-t   A   Adj   Adj   DO    P  PPA  OP
   SN V-t    A powerful hurricane / destroyed the beautiful white beaches (near our resort)!  E
   DO P2
```

Question and Answer Flow for Sentence 2: The story about the good Samaritan restored my faith in mankind.

1. What restored my faith in mankind? story - SN
2. What is being said about story? story restored - V
3. Story restored what? faith - verify the noun
4. Does faith mean the same thing as story? No.
5. Faith - DO
6. Restored - V-t
7. Whose faith? my - PPA
8. In - P
9. In whom? mankind - OP
10. About - P
11. About whom? Samaritan – OP
12. What kind of Samaritan? good - Adj
13. The – A
14. The - A
15. SN V-t DO P2 Check
16. Verb-transitive - Check again.
17. (About the good Samaritan) - Prepositional phrase
18. (In mankind) - Prepositional phrase
19. Period, statement, declarative sentence
20. Go back to the verb - divide the complete subject from the complete predicate.

Classified Sentence:

```
            A   SN   P   A   Adj    OP        V-t    PPA  DO  P   OP
  SN V-t   The story (about the good Samaritan) / restored my faith (in mankind).  D
  DO P2
```

Question and Answer Flow for Sentence 3: Good grief! We must seek shelter from this blistering sun!

1. Who must seek shelter from this blistering sun? we - SP
2. What is being said about we? we must seek - V
3. Must - HV
4. We must seek what? shelter - verify the noun
5. Does shelter mean the same thing as we? No.
6. Shelter - DO
7. Seek - V-t
8. From - P
9. From what? sun - OP
10. What kind of sun? blistering - Adj
11. Which sun? this - Adj
12. Good grief - I
13. SN V-t DO P2 Check
14. Verb-transitive - Check again.
15. (From this blistering sun) - Prepositional phrase
16. Exclamation point, strong feeling, exclamatory sentence
17. Go back to the verb - divide the complete subject from the complete predicate.

Classified Sentence:

```
                   I      SP   HV  V-t   DO    P  Adj   Adj    OP
   SN V-t    Good grief! We / must seek shelter (from this blistering sun)!  E
   DO P2
```

(End of lesson.)

CHAPTER 12   LESSON 5

Objectives: Writing Assignments #13 and #14, Bonus Option.

 WRITING TIME

TEACHING SCRIPT FOR PRACTICING DIFFERENT KINDS OF WRITING

Today, you are assigned two different kinds of writing. You will write a five-paragraph persuasive essay and a three-paragraph expository essay. <u>You will revise and edit the five-paragraph persuasive essay.</u> (*Read the box below for more information about students' writing assignment.*) As you edit, make sure you use the checkpoints in the editing checklist provided in Reference 39. Remember to read through the whole essay, starting with the title, and then edit, sentence-by-sentence, using the five-sentence checkpoints for each sentence. Use the paragraph checkpoints to check each paragraph. Remember, your editing is now more detailed and more comprehensive, so take your time.

Writing Assignment Box #1

Writing Assignment #13: Five-Paragraph Persuasive Essay (First Person)
(Remember, first person pronouns are *I, we, me, us, my, our, mine,* and *ours.*)
Remind students that the 5-paragraph essay has three parts: 1. Introduction 2. Body 3. Conclusion. The body has three paragraphs instead of one. Have students use their regular editing checklist to edit this assignment.

Writing topics: Why Libraries Are Important or **Everyone Should Have Quiet Time** or **People Should Not Litter**

Your second writing assignment is to write a three-paragraph expository essay. (*Read the box below for more information about students' writing assignment.*) You do not have to edit this assignment with the editing checklist.

Writing Assignment Box #2

Writing Assignment #14: Three-Paragraph Expository Essay (First Person)
(Remember, first person pronouns are *I, we, me, us, my, our, mine,* and *ours.*)
Remind students that the 3-paragraph essay has three parts: 1. Introduction 2. Body 3. Conclusion. The body has one paragraph instead of three.

Writing topics: Big Events in My Life or **Favorite Video Games** or **My Favorite Bible Stories** or
                Reasons I Like the Circus/Zoo

<u>Bonus Option:</u> Do you memorize Bible verses? Do you know someone who does? Write the verses you know in your journal. From which book of the Bible have you memorized the most verses? Make a list of scripture you want to memorize in the future. Record the date in your Journal to see how long it takes you. Keep a record of different people who memorize Bible verses, and the verses they memorize.

TEACHER INSTRUCTIONS FOR WRITING ASSIGNMENTS

Read, check, and discuss Writing Assignment #13 after students have finished their final papers. Use the checklists as you check and discuss students' papers. Make sure students are using the regular editing checklist correctly. Read and discuss Writing Assignment #14 for fun and enrichment.

(End of lesson.)

Level 4 Homeschool Teacher's Manual

CHAPTER 13   LESSON 1

Objectives: Jingles, Grammar (Practice Sentences, Oral Skill Builder Check), Skills (identifying complete sentences and sentence fragments, correcting sentence fragments), Practice Exercise, Writing (journal) and Vocabulary #1.

JINGLE TIME

Have students turn to the Jingle Section in their books and recite the previously-taught jingles.

GRAMMAR TIME

First-Year Option: Put the Practice Sentences from the box below on the board or on notebook paper. Use these sentences as you practice the concepts that have been taught. For the greatest benefit, students must participate orally with the teacher. **Second-Year Option:** Have students classify the Practice Sentences independently on notebook paper. Check students' sentences with the answers provided below. (*If you have the CDs for Practice Sentences, have students check their sentences with the CDs.*)

Chapter 13, Practice Sentences for Lesson 1
1. _____ During the afternoon, my brother washed and waxed his truck.
2. _____ Can you play classical music on the old piano at Grandmother's house?

TEACHING SCRIPT FOR PRACTICING PATTERN 2 SENTENCES

We will practice classifying Pattern 2 sentences. We will classify the sentences together. Begin. (*You might have your students write the labels above the sentences at this time.*)

Question and Answer Flow for Sentence 1: During the afternoon, my brother washed and waxed his truck.

1. Who washed and waxed his truck? brother - SN
2. What is being said about brother?
   brother washed and waxed - CV, CV
3. Brother washed and waxed what? truck - verify the noun
4. Does tuck mean the same thing as brother? No.
5. Truck - DO
6. Washed and waxed - CV-t, CV-t
7. Whose truck? his - PPA
8. And - C
9. Whose brother? my - PPA
10. During - P
11. During what? afternoon - OP

12. The - A
13. SN V-t DO P2 Check
14. Verb-transitive - Check again.
15. (During the afternoon) - Prepositional phrase
16. Period, statement, declarative sentence
17. Go back to the verb - divide the complete subject from the complete predicate.
18. This sentence has predicate words in the complete subject. Underline the prepositional phrase at the beginning of the sentence twice.

Classified Sentence:

```
                        P    A    OP    PPA  SN    CV-t    C   CV-t  PPA  DO
          SN  V-t     (During the afternoon), my brother / washed and waxed his truck. D
          DO  P2
```

CHAPTER 13 LESSON 1 CONTINUED

Question and Answer Flow for Sentence 2: Can you play classical music on the old piano at Grandmother's house?

1. Who can play classical music on the old piano at Grandmother's house? you - SP
2. What is being said about you? you can play - V
3. Can - HV
4. You can play what? music - verify the noun
5. Does music mean the same thing as you? No.
6. Music - DO
7. Play - V-t
8. What kind of music? classical - Adj
9. On - P
10. On what? piano - OP
11. What kind of piano? old - Adj
12. The - A
13. At - P

14. At what? house - OP
15. Whose house? Grandmother's - PNA
16. SN V-t DO P2 Check
17. Verb-transitive - Check again.
18. (On the old piano) - Prepositional phrase
19. (At Grandmother's house) - Prepositional phrase
20. Question mark, question, interrogative sentence
21. Go back to the verb - divide the complete subject from the complete predicate.
22. This sentence has predicate words in the complete subject. Underline the helping verb at the beginning of the sentence twice.

Classified Sentence:

```
                            HV  SP   V-t   Adj    DO    P  A Adj  OP    P    PNA          OP
          SN  V-t      Can you / play classical music (on the old piano) (at Grandmother's house)? Int
          DO  P2
```

Use Sentences 1-2 that you just classified with your students to do an Oral Skill Builder Check. Use the guidelines below.

Oral Skill Builder Check

1. **Noun check.**
   (Say the job and then say the noun. Circle each noun.)
2. **Identify the nouns as singular or plural.**
   (Write **S** or **P** above each noun.)
3. **Identify the nouns as common or proper.**
   (Follow established procedure for oral identification.)
4. **Do a vocabulary check.**
   (Follow established procedure for oral identification.)

5. **Identify the complete subject and the complete predicate.** (Underline the complete subject once and the complete predicate twice.)
6. **Identify the simple subject and simple predicate.** (Underline the simple subject once and the simple predicate twice. Bold, or highlight, the lines.)
7. **Recite the irregular verb chart.** (Located on student page 23 and teacher page 138.)

SKILL TIME

TEACHING SCRIPT FOR IDENTIFYING COMPLETE SENTENCES AND SENTENCE FRAGMENTS

You should feel comfortable using a variety of sentences in your writing. A basic knowledge of different kinds of sentence structure is necessary for you to become a writer who is confident and effective. Today, we will learn to recognize and work with simple sentences and sentence fragments.

First, we are going to learn the difference between a complete sentence and a fragment. Most of the time you will have no trouble writing a complete sentence because you know the five rules that make a correct sentence. Let's repeat the Sentence Jingle again to make sure we are all focused on the same thing. (*Repeat the Sentence Jingle.*) When you are writing, sometimes you will put a thought down without checking the five parts. If your sentence **does not have a subject, a verb, and a complete thought**, you could have a sentence fragment. This lesson is to teach you how to recognize and prevent sentence fragments so all your sentences can be written correctly.

CHAPTER 13 LESSON 1 CONTINUED

Next, we will learn more about the simple sentence. A **simple sentence is one complete sentence**. It is also **one complete thought**. Adjectives, adverbs, and prepositional phrases add greater meaning, more life, and more color to simple sentences, but they are not necessary for a sentence to be a complete thought. A simple or complete sentence must have **a subject, a verb, and contain a complete thought**. The abbreviation for a simple sentence is the letter **S**. A sentence fragment does not express a complete thought because it always has one or more of the core parts missing. The abbreviation for a fragment is the letter **F**.

Find Reference 41 on page 37 in your book. Let's read the directions together. (*Read and discuss the directions*.) We will identify whether each sentence is a fragment or a simple sentence. After we decide what type of sentence it is, we will put the correct abbreviation in the blank at the left of each group of words. The abbreviations that you use are found in the directions. Remember, check each group of words for the main parts that make it a sentence: a subject, a verb, and a complete thought. (*Work through sentences 1–5, showing students how to identify each type of sentence and write the abbreviation in the blank*.)

Reference 41: Complete Sentences and Sentence Fragments

PART 1: Identifying Sentences and Fragments

Identifying simple sentences and fragments: Write **S** for a complete sentence and **F** for a sentence fragment on the line beside each group of words below.

S	1. The river flowed swiftly.
F	2. In their tracks.
S	3. Trumpets blared.
F	4. Crawling across the ceiling.
F	5. The enormous boulder.

PART 2: Sentence Fragments

Fragment Examples: (1) prepared to jump (2) all the happy children (3) because I snore too loudly (4) Washing the car.

Look at the title "Sentence Fragments" under Part 2 in the reference box. I am going to read several things about a fragment. As I read each one, you will read the fragment example that illustrates that point. I'll tell you when to read by saying "read." (*Teacher reads sentences 1-4 below. After each one, teacher says, "Read." Students will read the fragment from the box that illustrates the point just read by the teacher. You may want to do this part of the exercise again after your students realize what you are doing*.)

1. A fragment is a group of words that does not have a subject. Read fragment 1: (prepared to jump)
2. A fragment is a group of words that does not have a verb. Read fragment 2: (all the happy children)
3. A fragment is a group of words that does not complete a thought. Read fragment 3: (because I snore too loudly)
4. Sentence fragments should not be punctuated as complete sentences. Read fragment 4: (Washing the car.)

Remember, if a sentence is missing one of these three parts, a <u>subject</u>, a <u>verb</u>, or a <u>complete thought</u>, you probably have a sentence fragment.

TEACHING SCRIPT FOR CORRECTING SENTENCE FRAGMENTS

I want you to know how to add missing subject parts or missing predicate parts to make sentences complete. Look at the third part of Reference 41. It will help us learn how to correct fragments. Follow along as I go over it with you. These are all sentence fragments. We will make them complete sentences by adding the underlined part. (*Read the directions and work through the third part with your students. Part 3 is located on the next page*.)

CHAPTER 13 LESSON 1 CONTINUED

Reference 41: Complete Sentences and Sentence Fragments (continued)
PART 3: Correcting Sentence Fragments
Directions: Add the part that is underlined in parentheses to make each fragment into a complete sentence.
1. In the cave during the winter months. (subject part, predicate part, <u>both the subject and predicate</u>) (**The grizzly bear slept soundly** in the cave during the winter months.)
2. The chocolate milk. (subject part, <u>predicate part</u>, both the subject and predicate) (The chocolate milk **spilled on my dress**.)
3. Galloped excitedly by the creek during the storm. (<u>subject part</u>, predicate part, both the subject and predicate) (**The horses** galloped excitedly by the creek during the storm.)

 PRACTICE TIME

Have students turn to page 73 in the Practice Section of their book and find Chapter 13, Lesson 1, Practice (*1-2*). Go over the directions to make sure they understand what to do. Check and discuss the Practices after students have finished. (*Chapter 13, Lesson 1, Practice keys are given below*.)

Chapter 13, Lesson 1, Practice 1: On notebook paper, add the part that is underlined in the parentheses to make each fragment into a complete sentence. **(Sentences will vary.)**

1. Beside the pool after lunch   (subject part, predicate part, <u>both the subject and predicate</u>)
2. Cooked and cleaned after the party (<u>subject part</u>, predicate part, both the subject and predicate)
3. The funny little monkey at the zoo   (subject part, <u>predicate part</u>, both the subject and predicate)

Chapter 13, Lesson 1, Practice 2: Identify each kind of sentence by writing the abbreviation in the blank. **(S, F)**.

S	1.	The water churned rapidly.
F	2.	Above the sink in the bathroom and kitchen.
S	3.	The children ran happily to the playground.
F	4.	Signing his name to the document in the lawyer's office.
F	5.	The flat tire on the car in the middle of the road.

 WRITING TIME

Have students make an entry in their journals.

 VOCABULARY TIME

Assign Chapter 13, Vocabulary Words **#1** on page 9 in the Reference Section for students to define in their Vocabulary notebooks. Tell students they may use a dictionary or thesaurus. After they write each word and its meaning, students are to write a sentence using the vocabulary word.

Chapter 13, Vocabulary Words #1
(conceal, hide, fake, genuine)

(End of lesson.)

CHAPTER 13   LESSON 2
Objectives: Jingles, Grammar (Practice Sentences, Pattern 2 Practice Sentence), Skills (simple sentence with compound parts, run-on sentence), Practice Exercise, and Vocabulary #2.

JINGLE TIME

Have students turn to the Jingle Section in their books and recite the previously-taught jingles.

GRAMMAR TIME

First-Year Option: Put the Practice Sentences from the box below on the board or on notebook paper. Use these sentences as you practice the concepts that have been taught. For the greatest benefit, students must participate orally with the teacher. **Second-Year Option:** Have students classify the Practice Sentences independently on notebook paper. Check students' sentences with the answers provided below. *(If you have the CDs for Practice Sentences, have students check their sentences with the CDs.)*

Chapter 13, Practice Sentences for Lesson 2
1. _____ Yikes! The locusts have eaten the crops in the field to the ground!
2. _____ The brave young fireman rescued the dog from the blazing fire!

TEACHING SCRIPT FOR PRACTICING PATTERN 2 SENTENCES

We will practice classifying Pattern 2 sentences. We will classify the sentences together. Begin. *(You might have your students write the labels above the sentences at this time.)*

Question and Answer Flow for Sentence 1: Yikes! The locusts have eaten the crops in the field to the ground!	
1. What have eaten the crops in the field to the ground? locusts - SN	13. To what? ground - OP
2. What is being said about locusts? locusts have eaten - V	14. The - A
3. Have - HV	15. The - A
4. Locusts have eaten what? crops - verify the noun	16. Yikes - I
5. Do crops mean the same thing as locusts? No.	17. SN V-t DO P2 Check
6. Crops - DO	18. Verb-transitive - Check again.
7. Eaten - V-t	19. (In the field) - Prepositional phrase
8. The - A	20. (To the ground) - Prepositional phrase
9. In - P	21. Exclamation point, strong feeling, exclamatory sentence
10. In what? field - OP	22. Go back to the verb - divide the complete subject from the complete predicate.
11. The - A	
12. To - P	

Classified Sentence:

<pre>
                              I   A   SN   HV   V-t   A   DO   P A OP   P A   OP
              SN V-t   Yikes! The locusts / have eaten the crops (in the field) (to the ground)! E
              DO P2
</pre>

CHAPTER 13 LESSON 2 CONTINUED

Question and Answer Flow for Sentence 2: The brave young fireman rescued the dog from the blazing fire!

1. Who rescued the dog from the blazing fire? fireman - SN
2. What is being said about fireman? fireman rescued - V
3. Fireman rescued what? dog - verify the noun
4. Does dog mean the same thing as fireman? No.
5. Dog - DO
6. Rescued - V-t
7. The - A
8. From - P
9. From what? fire - OP
10. What kind of fire? blazing - Adj
11. The - A

12. What kind of fireman? young - Adj
13. What kind of fireman? brave - Adj
14. The - A
15. SN V-t DO P2 Check
16. Verb-transitive - Check again.
17. (From the blazing fire) - Prepositional phrase
18. Exclamation point, strong feeling, exclamatory sentence
19. Go back to the verb - divide the complete subject from the complete predicate.

	A	Adj	Adj	SN	V-t	A	DO	P	A	Adj	OP

Classified Sentence: <u>SN V-t</u> The brave young fireman **/** rescued the dog **(**from the blazing fire**)!** **E**
 DO P2

TEACHER INSTRUCTIONS FOR A PATTERN 2 SENTENCE

Tell students that their sentence writing assignment today is to write a Pattern 2 sentence. They are to follow the same procedure used in the previous lessons. They should decide on their labels, arrange them in a selected order, write their sentences, and edit their sentences for improved word choices. (*Students do not have to write an Improved Sentence at this point unless you feel they need more one-on-one word choice writing practice.*) Check and discuss the Pattern 2 sentence after students have finished.

 SKILL TIME

TEACHING SCRIPT FOR A SIMPLE SENTENCE WITH COMPOUND PARTS

In the previous lesson, we learned about the three main parts that make a complete sentence. What are the three main parts? (*subject, verb, complete sense*) We also learned that the abbreviation for a simple sentence is the letter **S** and the abbreviation for a fragment is the letter **F**.

Turn to Reference 42 on page 38 in your Reference Section. (*Reference 42 is located on the next page.*) Look at Example 1. This is an example of a simple sentence. Let's read the simple sentence together: **The red car rolled slowly down the hill.** (**S**) (*Do not read the (S) on the end.*) The (**S**) abbreviation in parentheses at the end is an identification symbol that indicates it is a simple sentence.

A simple sentence may have **compound parts, such as a compound subject or a compound verb**, even though it expresses only one complete thought. The abbreviation for a simple sentence with a compound subject is **SCS** (*simple sentence, compound subject*). The abbreviation for a simple sentence with a compound verb is **SCV** (*simple sentence, compound verb*).

Let's read Examples 2 and 3 together. Notice that the abbreviation at the end tells us what kind of sentence it is. (*Read the two sentences with your students.*) Example 2: **Stacy and Bonnie worked at the bank**. (**SCS**) Example 3: **Kim painted and decorated her bedroom**. (**SCV**)

CHAPTER 13 LESSON 2 CONTINUED

Reference 42: Simple Sentences, Compound Parts, and Fragments

Example 1: The red car rolled slowly down the hill. (**S**)
Example 2: <u>Stacy and Bonnie</u> worked at the bank. (**SCS**)
Example 3: Kim <u>painted and decorated</u> her bedroom. (**SCV**)

Part 1: Identify each kind of sentence by writing the abbreviation in the blank. (**S, SS, F, SCS, SCV**)

<u>SCV</u> 1. The students sang and danced in the play.
<u>SCS</u> 2. The horse and buggy arrived today.
<u>F</u> 3. After the trip to the zoo.
<u>S</u> 4. The ducks flew south for the winter.
<u>SS</u> 5. I turned on the air conditioner. It cooled the hot room.

Part 2: Put a slash to separate each run-on sentence below. Then, correct the run-on sentences by rewriting them as indicated by the labels in parentheses at the end of each sentence.

1. The young girl was crying / she was lost. (**SS**)
   The young girl was crying. She was lost.
2. The trophy is in the glass case / the medal is in the glass case. (**SCS**)
   The trophy and medal are in the glass case.
3. The toddler splashed in the water / she played in the water for hours. (**SCV**)
   The toddler splashed and played in the water for hours.

Look at Part 2. We will identify whether each sentence is a fragment, a simple sentence, a simple sentence with a compound subject, or a simple sentence with a compound verb. After we decide what type of sentence it is, we will discuss the correct abbreviation in the blank at the left of each sentence. The abbreviations are found at the end of the directions. (*Read the directions and work through sentences 1–5, showing students how to identify each type of sentence.*)

TEACHING SCRIPT FOR A RUN-ON SENTENCE

If two sentences are written together as one sentence without being punctuated correctly, it is called a run-on sentence. Go to Part 3 in your reference box and look at number 1: **The young girl was crying she was lost (SS)**. Is the first part of the sentence "The young girl was crying" a complete thought? *(yes)* Is the second part of the sentence "she was lost" a complete thought? *(yes)* The two complete thoughts are run together because they are written as one sentence.

There are several ways to correct a run-on sentence. First, we will put a slash between the two thoughts that are run together so we can see each sentence clearly. (*The young girl was crying / she was lost.*) Next, we will look at the abbreviation in parentheses at the end of number 1 to see how we are to correct this run-on sentence. Look at the end of number 1.

The (**SS**) in parentheses tells us to correct the run-on sentence by making it into two simple sentences. After we correct the run-on sentence, we will check the punctuation. (*The first word of each sentence must be capitalized, and each sentence must have end mark punctuation. Read the two simple sentences:* **The young girl was crying. She was lost.***)*

CHAPTER 13 LESSON 2 CONTINUED

We will now look at a second way to correct a run-on sentence. Look at number 2: **The trophy is in the glass case the medal is in the glass case.** **(SCS)** This is a run-on sentence that needs to be corrected. First, we will put a slash between the two thoughts that are run together so we can see each sentence clearly. (*The trophy is in the glass case / the medal is in the glass case.*)

Next, we will look at the abbreviation in parentheses at the end of number 2 to see how we are to correct the run-on sentence. Look at the end of number 2. The **(SCS)** in parentheses tells us to correct the run-on sentence by writing a simple sentence with a compound subject. When each sentence has a different subject, join the two subjects together with the conjunction *AND*. That will make a compound subject. If the subjects have additional subject words, include them as you write the compound subjects. (**The trophy and medal**)

Since both sentences have the same verb and complete predicate, the verb and complete predicate will stay the same except for one change. This change is a subject-verb agreement change. When *trophy* and *medal* were used as singular subjects, they each used the singular verb *is*. Now that *trophy* and *medal* have become a compound subject, the singular verb *is* <u>MUST</u> be changed to the plural verb *are* because a compound subject requires a plural verb form. This new sentence is called a simple sentence with a compound subject. (**The trophy and medal are in the glass case.**)

Now, we will look at a third way to correct a run-on sentence. Look at number 3: **The toddler splashed in the water she played in the water for hours.** **(SCV)** This is a run-on sentence that needs to be corrected. First, we will put a slash between the two thoughts that are run together so we can see each sentence clearly. (*The toddler splashed in the water / she played in the water for hours.*)

Next, we will look at the abbreviation in parentheses at the end of number 3 to see how we are to correct the run-on sentence. Look at the end of number 3. The **(SCV)** in parentheses tells us to correct the run-on sentence by writing a simple sentence with a compound verb. Since both sentences have the same subject (***toddler** and **she** are the same person*), the subject noun *toddler* is used.

Finally, we look at the verbs. Since each sentence has a different verb, the two verbs are joined together with the conjunction *AND*. Joining the verbs together with a conjunction makes a compound verb. If the verbs have additional predicate words, the predicate words are always included as the compound verbs are written. (**splashed and played in the water for hours**) This new sentence is called a simple sentence with a compound verb: **The toddler splashed and played in the water for hours.**

As you can see, there are several ways to correct a run-on sentence, but today, we concentrated on three ways to use the simple sentence to correct a run-on sentence.

CHAPTER 13 LESSON 2 CONTINUED

 PRACTICE TIME

Have students turn to page 73 in the Practice Section of their book and find Chapter 13, Lesson 2, Practice (*1-2*). Go over the directions to make sure they understand what to do. Check and discuss the Practices after students have finished. (*Chapter 13, Lesson 2, Practice keys are given below.*)

Chapter 13, Lesson 2, Practice 1: Put a slash to separate each run-on sentence below. Then, on notebook paper, correct the run-on sentences by rewriting them as indicated by the labels in parentheses at the end of each sentence.

1. Sam earned extra money **/** he spent it on baseball cards. **(SCV)**
   Sam earned extra money and spent it on baseball cards.
2. I am going to the library **/** Jason is going to the library. **(SCS)**
   Jason and I are going to the library.
3. My little puppy is very lovable **/** he likes to play with me. **(SS)**
   My little puppy is very lovable. He likes to play with me.

Chapter 13, Lesson 2, Practice 2: Identify each kind of sentence by writing the abbreviation in the blank.
(S, SS, F, SCS, SCV)

F	1.	Whenever the peaches are ripe.
SCV	2.	My mother cooked the meal and served the guests.
SCS	3.	Cauliflower and broccoli are healthy foods.
SS	4.	The tire went flat. Dad changed it.
S	5.	The invitation came in the mail.

 VOCABULARY TIME

Assign Chapter 13, Vocabulary Words **#2** on page 9 in the Reference Section for students to define in their Vocabulary notebooks. Tell students they are to use a dictionary or thesaurus to look up the meanings of the vocabulary words. After they write each word and its meaning, students are to write a sentence using the vocabulary word.

Chapter 13, Vocabulary Words #2
(adhere, stick, gallant, afraid)

(End of lesson.)

CHAPTER 13 LESSON 3
Objectives: Jingles, Grammar (Practice Sentences), Skills (compound sentence, comma splice, and run-on sentence), Practice Exercise.

JINGLE TIME

Have students turn to the Jingle Section in their books and recite the previously-taught jingles.

GRAMMAR TIME

First-Year Option: Put the Practice Sentences from the box below on the board or on notebook paper. Use these sentences as you practice the concepts that have been taught. For the greatest benefit, students must participate orally with the teacher. **Second-Year Option:** Have students classify the Practice Sentences independently on notebook paper. Check students' sentences with the answers provided below. *(If you have the CDs for Practice Sentences, have students check their sentences with the CDs.)*

Chapter 13, Practice Sentences for Lesson 3
1. _____ Finish your math assignment before bedtime.
2. _____ The president announced his executive decision on national television.

TEACHING SCRIPT FOR PRACTICING PATTERN 2 SENTENCES

We will practice classifying Pattern 2 sentences. We will classify the sentences together. Begin. (*You might have your students write the labels above the sentences at this time.*)

Question and Answer Flow for Sentence 1: Finish your math assignment before bedtime.
1. Who finish your math assignment before bedtime?   you - SP (Understood subject pronoun)   9. Before - P
2. What is being said about you? you finish - V   10. Before what? bedtime - OP
3. You finish what? assignment - verify the noun   11. SN V-t DO P2 Check
4. Does assignment mean the same thing as you? No.   12. Verb-transitive - Check again.
5. Assignment - DO   13. (Before bedtime) - Prepositional phrase
6. Finish - V-t   14. Period, command, imperative sentence
7. What kind of assignment? math - Adj   15. Go back to the verb - divide the complete
8. Whose assignment? your - PPA   subject from the complete predicate.

Classified Sentence:

```
          (You) SP    V-t   PPA Adj     DO       P    OP
          SN  V-t  / Finish your math assignment (before bedtime).  Imp
          DO  P2
```

CHAPTER 13 LESSON 3 CONTINUED

Question and Answer Flow for Sentence 2: The president announced his executive decision on national television.

1. Who announced his executive decision on national television? president - SN
2. What is being said about president? president announced - V
3. President announced what? decision - verify the noun
4. Does decision mean the same thing as president? No.
5. Decision - DO
6. Announced - V-t
7. What kind of decision? executive - Adj
8. Whose decision? his - PPA
9. On - P

10. On what? television - OP
11. What kind of television? national - Adj
12. The - A
13. SN V-t DO P2 Check
14. Verb-transitive - Check again.
15. (On national television) - Prepositional phrase
16. Period, statement, declarative sentence
17. Go back to the verb - divide the complete subject from the complete predicate.

Classified Sentence:

		A	SN	V-t	PPA	Adj	DO	P	Adj	OP
SN V-t		The president / announced his executive decision (on national television). **D**
DO P2

SKILL TIME

TEACHING SCRIPT FOR COMPOUND SENTENCES

Another kind of sentence you need to be able to recognize and write is the compound sentence. Look at the information about the compound sentence in Reference 43 on page 39 in your book. Pay special attention to the ways you can correctly join the parts of a compound sentence. (*Read the information about a compound sentence with your students. This information is reproduced for you.*) As you can see in Examples 1 and 2, the abbreviations at the end of the sentences give you the directions on how to correct the run-on sentences and fragments.

Reference 43: The Compound Sentence

1. Compound means two. A compound sentence is two complete sentences joined together correctly. The abbreviation for a compound sentence is **CD**.

2. One way to join two sentences and make a compound sentence is to use a comma and a conjunction. The formula for you to follow will always be given at the end of the sentence. The formula gives the abbreviation for the compound sentence and lists the conjunction to use (**CD, and**). Remember to place the comma BEFORE the conjunction.

   Example 1: We saw deer tracks in the **woods, and** we followed them. (CD, and)

3. Another way to join two sentences and make a compound sentence is to use a semicolon only. The formula to follow is given at the end of the sentence and lists the semicolon after the abbreviation of the compound sentence (**CD;**). (This method is usually used with short sentences that are closely related in thought.)

   Example 2: We saw deer tracks in the **woods; we** followed them. (CD;)

4. Compound sentences should be closely related in thought and importance.

   Correct: We saw deer tracks in the **woods, and** we followed them.
   Incorrect: We saw deer tracks in the **woods, and** my sister went shopping at the mall.

CHAPTER 13 LESSON 3 CONTINUED

TEACHING SCRIPT FOR COMMA SPLICE AND RUN-ON SENTENCE

Look at Reference 44 on page 39 on ways to correct compound sentence mistakes. (*Read the information below to the class.*)

Reference 44: Ways to Correct Compound Sentence Mistakes

When a compound sentence is not joined together correctly, you have a **comma splice or a run-on sentence.**
 	
 1. **A comma splice** is two sentences incorrectly connected with a comma and no conjunction. To correct a comma splice: Put a conjunction (*and, or, but*) after the comma.
 	
    <u>Incorrect</u>: I love **horses, I** ride every day.
    <u>Correct</u>:   I love **horses, and I** ride every day.
 	
 2. **A run-on sentence** is two or more sentences written together as one sentence, or two or more sentences written with a conjunction and no comma.
    <u>Incorrect</u>: I love **horses I** ride every day.
    <u>Incorrect</u>: I love **horses and I** ride every day.
 	
 3. Below are two ways to correct a run-on sentence:
 	
    1. Put a comma and a conjunction between the two complete thoughts.
    2. Put a semicolon between the two complete thoughts.
 	
    <u>Correct</u>: I love **horses, and I** ride every day.
    <u>Correct</u>: I love **horses; I** ride every day.

Now, we will review what you have just learned. First, compound sentences are correctly joined with conjunctions or semicolons. Second, conjunctions join words or sentences together to make compound subjects, compound verbs, or compound sentences. The three most common conjunctions are *and, or*, and *but*. Third, you must always use a comma with a conjunction when you join two sentences together to make a compound sentence.

The most important thing to remember is how to recognize the difference between a sentence with compound parts, such as compound subjects or compound verbs, and a compound sentence. The easiest way to do this is to find a subject and verb after the conjunction or semicolon. Remember, a compound sentence is two separate sentences joined together with a comma and a conjunction.

Look at the practice examples in Reference 45. We will work through the examples together. We will read the directions first to be sure we know what to do. (*Read the directions for Reference 45. Reference 45 is located on the next page.*)

CHAPTER 13 LESSON 3 CONTINUED

Reference 45: Using SCS, SCV, and CD Correctly

Put a slash to separate the two complete thoughts in each run-on sentence. Correct the run-on sentences or fragments as indicated by the labels in parentheses at the end of each sentence.

1. Samantha loves the state fair **/** she doesn't like the scary rides. (**CD**, but)
   Samantha loves the state fair, but she doesn't like the scary rides.

2. My dad owns a famous restaurant **/** the food is delicious! (**CD**;)
   My dad owns a famous restaurant; the food is delicious!

3. Beth sings in the church choir **/** Mary sings in the church choir. (**SCS**)
   Beth and Mary sing in the church choir. *(When the subject is compound, the verb is plural.)*

4. For extra money, David mows lawns **/** he cleans garages. (**SCV**)
   For extra money, David mows lawns and cleans garages.

Look at number 1. Is "Samantha loves the state fair" a complete sentence? (*Yes, except for an end mark.*) Is "she doesn't like the scary rides" a complete sentence? (*Yes - except for a capital letter and end mark.*) The directions tell us to put a slash between these two complete thoughts. (*Show students how the run-on sentence is divided with a slash.*)

Next, look at the end of number 1. The (**CD, but**) in parentheses tells us how to make these two sentences into a compound sentence. The (**CD**) stands for compound sentence, and the (**but**) tells which coordinate conjunction to use. Remember, we must also use a comma in front of the conjunction in order to punctuate the compound sentence correctly.

As you can see, the compound sentence has been written by using the information in parentheses (**CD, but**). (*Read the compound sentence:* **Samantha loves the state fair, but she doesn't like the scary rides**.) These two sentences are made into a compound sentence by using a comma and the coordinate conjunction *but* to join them.

TEACHER INSTRUCTIONS

Work through the rest of the Practice Sentences 2-4 in the same way. Make sure your students understand that the abbreviations in parentheses at the end of the sentences give directions on how to correct the run-on sentences and fragments.

Have students look at Reference 46. (*Reference 46 is located on the next page.*) Read the directions and work through Parts 1 and 2. Make sure students understand how each example was done because they will be tested in each format. (*In Part 2, point out that number 7 is a compound sentence because it has two sentences joined by a comma and conjunction. Number 8 is a simple sentence with a compound verb because it is only one sentence with a conjunction connecting two verbs. It does not have a second sentence and requires no commas.*)

CHAPTER 13 LESSON 3 CONTINUED

Reference 46: Identifying S, F, SCS, SCV, and CD

Part 1: Identify each kind of sentence by writing the abbreviation in the blank (**S, F, SCS, SCV, CD**)

  CD   1. Mr. Samson wanted to read the report, but he forgot his glasses.

  S   2. Dr. Robertson teaches first aid to the students at the high school.

  CD   3. We played tag at recess, but we did not play ball.

  SCS   4. Scott and Jerry rode the bus to the park.

  F   5. In the winter, the strong cold wind.

  SCV   6. My father climbed the tree and pulled my kite from the branches.

Part 2: On notebook paper, use the ways listed below to correct this run-on sentence: **I baked a cake I did not eat it.**

7. CD, but   **I baked a cake, but I did not eat it.**   8. SCV   **I baked a cake but did not eat it.**

PRACTICE TIME

Have students turn to page 74 in the Practice Section of their book and find Chapter 13, Lesson 3, Practice (*1-3*). Go over the directions to make sure they understand what to do. Check and discuss the Practices after students have finished. (*Chapter 13, Lesson 3 Practice keys are given below.*)

Chapter 13, Lesson 3, Practice 1: Put a slash to separate each run-on sentence below. Then, on notebook paper, correct the run-on sentences by rewriting them as indicated by the labels in parentheses at the end of each sentence.

1. The cattle broke through the fence **/** they grazed contentedly. (**SCV**)
   The cattle broke through the fence and grazed contentedly.
2. The cattle broke through the fence **/** they grazed contentedly. (**CD;**)
   The cattle broke through the fence; they grazed contentedly.
3. The cattle broke through the fence **/** they grazed contentedly. (**CD**, and)
   The cattle broke through the fence, and they grazed contentedly.
4. The cattle broke through the fence **/** the sheep broke through also. (**SCS**)
   The cattle and sheep broke through the fence.

Chapter 13, Lesson 3, Practice 2: Identify each kind of sentence by writing the abbreviation in the blank. (**S, F, SCS, SCV, CD**)

  SCV   1. The dog growled and barked at the mailman.

  CD   2. David fixed the fence, and Teresa planted the flowers.

  SCS   3. Her son and daughter were on the honor roll.

  F   4. Crashed during the terrible storm.

  CD   5. I like classical music; my sister likes rock and roll.

Chapter 13, Lesson 3, Practice 3: On a sheet of notebook paper, write two compound sentences, using these labels to guide you: ① (CD, but) ② (CD;) **(Sentences will vary.)**

(End of lesson.)

CHAPTER 13 LESSON 4

Objectives: Jingles, Study, Test, Check, Activity, and Writing (journal).

 JINGLE TIME

Have students turn to the Jingle Section in their books and recite the previously-taught jingles.

 STUDY TIME

Have students study the vocabulary words in their vocabulary notebooks. Remind students that any vocabulary word in their notebooks could be on their test. Also, have students study any of the skills in the Practice Section that they need to review.

 TEST TIME

Have students turn to page 110 in the Test Section of their book and find the Chapter 13 Test. Go over the directions to make sure they understand what to do. (*The chapter 13 Test key is on the next page.*)

 CHECK TIME

After students have finished, check and discuss their test papers. Make sure they understand why their answers are right or wrong. (*For total points, count each required answer as a point.*)

 ACTIVITY / ASSIGNMENT TIME

The **limerick** is a popular type of rhymed poem consisting of five lines. It was popularized in the United States by the poet Ogden Nash. The intent of the **limerick** is to evoke a smile or chuckle in the reader. Almost all **limericks** are humorous and are fun to write. The rules are simple. The first, second, and fifth lines contain three accents and rhyme with each other. The third and fourth lines contain two accents and rhyme with each other. Read and discuss the example below. Have students write their own limerick and then share it with others.

> There once was a gymnast named Curt
> Who vaulted without wearing a shirt.
> Then one day he crashed
> And two fingers got mashed;
> Poor guy, his ego was seriously hurt.

(End of lesson.)

Chapter 13 Test
(Student Page 110)

Exercise 1: Classify each sentence.

```
            A    Adj   SN   P    A    OP    V-t  PPA  DO   P    A   Adj   OP
```
1. <u>**SN V-t**</u>   The young man (down the street) / mowed my lawn (for a small fee). **D**
   <u>**DO P2**</u>

```
            CSN   C   CSN  V-t  DO    P   A     OP       P   PPA      OP
```
2. <u>**SN V-t**</u>   <u>Mom and Dad</u> / <u>ate lobster (at the restaurant) (on their anniversary)</u>. **D**
   <u>**DO P2**</u>

Exercise 2: Use Sentence 2 to underline the complete subject once and the complete predicate twice and to complete the table below.

List the Noun Used	List the Noun Job	Singular or Plural	Common or Proper	Simple Subject	Simple Predicate
1. **Mom**	2. **CSN**	3. **S**	4. **P**	5. **Mom/Dad**	6. **ate**
7. **Dad**	8. **CSN**	9. **S**	10. **P**		
11. **lobster**	12. **DO**	13. **S**	14. **C**		
15. **restaurant**	16. **OP**	17. **S**	18. **C**		
19. **anniversary**	20. **OP**	21. **S**	22. **C**		

Exercise 3: Identify each pair of words as synonyms or antonyms by putting parentheses ( ) around **syn** or **ant**.

1. conceal, hide	**(syn)** ant	5. quill, feather	**(syn)** ant	9. logical, silly	syn **(ant)**
2. auction, buy	syn **(ant)**	6. adhere, stick	**(syn)** ant	10. pursue, follow	**(syn)** ant
3. genuine, fake	syn **(ant)**	7. creeping, rushing	syn **(ant)**	11. gallant, afraid	syn **(ant)**
4. hesitate, pause	**(syn)** ant	8. quiver, shake	**(syn)** ant	12. proceed, cease	syn **(ant)**

Exercise 4: Put a slash to separate each run-on sentence below. Then, correct the run-on sentences by rewriting them on notebook paper as indicated by the labels in parentheses at the end of each sentence.

1. Dandelions are blooming / they cover the yard. (**CD;**)
   Dandelions are blooming; they cover the yard.
2. John whistled a tune / Debbie whistled a tune. (**SCS**)
   John and Debbie whistled a tune.
3. The boys put up a tent / they slept outside. (**SCV**)
   The boys put up a tent and slept outside.
4. The student wrote a poem / she read it to the class. (**CD**, and)
   The student wrote a poem, and she read it to the class.
5. Todd launched the boat / Ray helped him. (**SCS**)
   Todd and Ray launched the boat.
6. She coughed uncontrollably / she sneezed uncontrollably. (**SCV**)
   She coughed and sneezed uncontrollably.

Exercise 5: Identify each kind of sentence by writing the abbreviation in the blank. (**S, F, SCS, SCV, CD**)

<u>**SCS**</u>	1.	Monkeys and tigers are my favorite animals at the zoo.
<u>**CD**</u>	2.	The house shook, and the pictures fell off the wall.
<u>**F**</u>	3.	Walking along the beach during the summer.
<u>**SCV**</u>	4.	The plumber turned off the water and replaced the copper tubing.
<u>**CD**</u>	5.	The young student ran to class, but he was late.
<u>**S**</u>	6.	The detour through the country was very scenic.
<u>**CD**</u>	7.	She combs her hair, but she never brushes her teeth.

Exercise 6: On notebook paper, write one sentence for each of these labels: ① **S** ② **SCS** ③ **SCV** ④ **CD**. **(Answers will vary.)**

Exercise 7: In your journal, write a paragraph summarizing what you have learned this week.

CHAPTER 13 LESSON 4 CONTINUED

TEACHER INSTRUCTIONS

Use the Question and Answer Flows below for the sentences on the Chapter 13 Test.

Question and Answer Flow for Sentence 1: The young man down the street mowed my lawn for a small fee.

1. Who mowed my lawn for a small fee? man - SN
2. What is being said about man? man mowed - V
3. Man mowed what? lawn - verify the noun
4. Does lawn mean the same thing as man? No.
5. Lawn - DO
6. Mowed - V-t
7. Whose lawn? my - PPA
8. For - P
9. For what? fee - OP
10. What kind of fee? small - Adj
11. A - A
12. Down - P

13. Down what? street - OP
14. The - A
15. What kind of man? young - Adj
16. The - A
17. SN V-t DO P2 Check
18. Verb-transitive - Check again.
19. (Down the street) - Prepositional phrase
20. (For a small fee) - Prepositional phrase
21. Period, statement, declarative sentence
22. Go back to the verb - divide the complete subject from the complete predicate.

Classified Sentence:

```
                          A    Adj   SN    P    A    OP     V-t   PPA  DO   P   A  Adj  OP
              SN  V-t     The young man (down the street) / mowed my lawn (for a small fee).  D
              DO  P2
```

Question and Answer Flow for Sentence 2: Mom and Dad ate lobster at the restaurant on their anniversary.

1. Who ate lobster at the restaurant on their anniversary?
   Mom and Dad - CSN, CSN
2. What is being said about Mom and Dad?
   Mom and Dad ate - V
3. Mom and Dad ate what? lobster - verify the noun
4. Does lobster mean the same thing as Mom and Dad? No.
5. Lobster - DO
6. Ate - V-t
7. At - P
8. At what? restaurant - OP
9. The - A
10. On - P

11. On what? anniversary - OP
12. Whose anniversary? their - PPA
13. And - C
14. SN V-t DO P2 Check
15. Verb-transitive - Check again.
16. (At the restaurant) - Prepositional phrase
17. (On their anniversary) - Prepositional phrase
18. Period, statement, declarative sentence
19. Go back to the verb - divide the complete subject from the complete predicate.

Classified Sentence:

```
                          CSN  C  CSN  V-t  DO   P   A    OP      P  PPA    OP
              SN  V-t     Mom and Dad / ate lobster (at the restaurant) (on their anniversary).  D
              DO  P2
```

CHAPTER 13   LESSON 5

Objectives: Writing Assignments #15 and #16.

 WRITING TIME

TEACHING SCRIPT FOR PRACTICING DIFFERENT KINDS OF WRITING

Today, you are assigned two different kinds of writing. You will write a five-paragraph expository essay and a three-paragraph persuasive essay. <u>You will revise and edit the five-paragraph expository essay</u>. (*Read the box below for more information about students' writing assignment*.) As you edit, make sure you use the checkpoints in the editing checklist provided in Reference 39. Remember to read through the whole essay, starting with the title, and then edit, sentence-by-sentence, using the five sentence checkpoints for each sentence. Use the paragraph checkpoints to check each paragraph. After you are satisfied with your revising and editing, you will write a final paper, using the Final Paper Checklist in Reference 5.

Writing Assignment Box #1

Writing Assignment #15: Five-Paragraph Expository Essay (First Person)
(Remember, first person pronouns are *I, we, me, us, my, our, mine,* and *ours*.)

Remind students that the 5-paragraph essay has three parts: 1. Introduction 2. Body 3. Conclusion. The body has three paragraphs instead of one. Have students use their regular editing checklist to edit this assignment.

Writing topic: Things a Mother/Father Does or **People Who Influenced Me the Most** or
                          Ways to Have Fun at the Beach

Your second writing assignment is to write a three-paragraph persuasive essay. (*Read the box below for more information about the students' writing assignment*.) You do not have to edit this assignment with the editing checklist.

Writing Assignment Box #2

Writing Assignment #16: Three-Paragraph Persuasive Essay (First Person)
(Remember, first person pronouns are *I, we, me, us, my, our, mine,* and *ours*.)

Remind students that the 3-paragraph essay has three parts: 1. Introduction 2. Body 3. Conclusion. The body has one paragraph instead of three.

Writing topic: Why Every Country Needs a Flag or **Reasons Not to Smoke** or **A Good Attitude Is Important**

TEACHER INSTRUCTIONS FOR CHECKING WRITING ASSIGNMENT

Read, check, and discuss Writing Assignment #15 after students have finished their final papers. Use the checklists as you check and discuss students' papers. Make sure students are using the regular editing checklist correctly. Read and discuss Writing Assignment #16 for fun and enrichment.

(End of lesson.)

CHAPTER 14 LESSON 1

Objectives: Jingles, Grammar (Practice Sentences, Oral Skill Builder Check), Skills (personal pronouns and their antecedents, Oral Review), Practice Exercise, Writing (journal), and Vocabulary #1.

JINGLE TIME

Have students turn to the Jingle Section in their books and recite the previously-taught jingles.

GRAMMAR TIME

First-Year Option: Put the Practice Sentences from the box below on the board or on notebook paper. Use these sentences as you practice the concepts that have been taught. For the greatest benefit, students must participate orally with the teacher. **Second-Year Option:** Have students classify the Practice Sentences independently on notebook paper. Check students' sentences with the answers provided below. *(If you have the CDs for Practice Sentences, have students check their sentences with the CDs.)*

Chapter 14, Practice Sentences for Lesson 1
1. _____ The jungle receives heavy rainfall during the monsoon season.
2. _____ Jennifer's dog caught the Frisbee in the air with its teeth.

TEACHING SCRIPT FOR PRACTICING PATTERN 2 SENTENCES

We will practice classifying Pattern 2 sentences. We will classify the sentences together. Begin. *(You might have your students write the labels above the sentences at this time.)*

Question and Answer Flow for Sentence 1: The jungle receives heavy rainfall during the monsoon season.

1. What receives heavy rainfall during the monsoon season? jungle - SN
2. What is being said about jungle? jungle receives - V
3. Jungle receives what? rainfall - verify the noun
4. Does rainfall mean the same thing as jungle? No.
5. Rainfall - DO
6. Receives - V-t
7. What kind of rainfall? heavy - Adj
8. During - P
9. During what? season - OP
10. What kind of season? monsoon - Adj
11. The - A
12. The - A
13. SN V-t DO P2 Check
14. Verb-transitive - Check again.
15. (During the monsoon season) - Prepositional phrase
16. Period, statement, declarative sentence
17. Go back to the verb - divide the complete subject from the complete predicate.

Classified Sentence:

```
                       A   SN    V-t    Adj   DO   P   A   Adj    OP
        SN  V-t    The jungle / receives heavy rainfall (during the monsoon season).  D
        DO  P2
```

CHAPTER 14 LESSON 1 CONTINUED

Question and Answer Flow for Sentence 2: Jennifer's dog caught the Frisbee in the air with its teeth.

1. What caught the Frisbee in the air with its teeth?
   dog - SN
2. What is being said about dog? dog caught - V
3. Dog caught what? Frisbee - verify the noun
4. Does Frisbee mean the same thing as dog? No.
5. Frisbee - DO
6. Caught - V-t
7. The - A
8. In - P
9. In what? air - OP
10. The - A

11. With - P
12. With what? teeth - OP
13. Whose teeth? its - PPA
14. Whose dog? Jennifer's - PNA
15. SN V-t DO P2 Check
16. Verb-transitive - Check again.
17. (In the air) - Prepositional phrase
18. (With its teeth) - Prepositional phrase
19. Period, statement, declarative sentence
20. Go back to the verb - divide the complete subject
    from the complete predicate.

Classified Sentence:

	PNA	SN	V-t	A	DO	P	A	OP	P	PPA	OP

<u>SN V-t</u> Jennifer's dog **/** caught the Frisbee **(**in the air**) (**with its teeth**). D**
<u>DO P2</u>

Use Sentences 1-2 that you just classified with your students to do an Oral Skill Builder Check. Use the guidelines below.

Oral Skill Builder Check

1. **Noun check.**
   (Say the job and then say the noun. Circle each noun.)
2. **Identify the nouns as singular or plural.**
   (Write **S** or **P** above each noun.)
3. **Identify the nouns as common or proper.**
   (Follow established procedure for oral identification.)
4. **Do a vocabulary check.**
   (Follow established procedure for oral identification.)

5. **Identify the complete subject and the complete predicate.** (Underline the complete subject once and the complete predicate twice.)
6. **Identify the simple subject and simple predicate.**
   (Underline the simple subject once and the simple predicate twice. Bold, or highlight, the lines.)
7. **Recite the irregular verb chart.**
   (Located on student page 23 and teacher page 138.)

SKILL TIME

TEACHING SCRIPT FOR PERSONAL PRONOUNS AND THEIR ANTECEDENTS

You will now learn about personal pronouns and their antecedents. The more practice you have in working with pronouns and antecedents, the more likely you will use them correctly in your writing. The most common pronouns are known as personal pronouns. These are used to refer to yourself and to other people. You have learned most of the personal pronouns already through the Subject Pronoun Jingle, Possessive Pronoun Jingle, and Object Pronoun Jingle. (*I, she, his, him, them, themselves, etc.*)

Any time a personal pronoun is used in a sentence, it usually refers to a noun or another pronoun. The noun or pronoun to which a pronoun refers is called the **antecedent** of that pronoun. The antecedent can be in the same sentence as the pronoun, or it can be in a different sentence.

CHAPTER 14 LESSON 1 CONTINUED

Turn to page 41 and look at the two sample sentences in Reference 47. (*Read the two examples to your students: A. The little boy grinned playfully at his brother. B. The little boy gasped. He had just been stung.*) In the first example, the noun **boy** is the antecedent of the pronoun **his** because the pronoun **his** refers to the noun **boy**. In the second example, the noun **boy** is the antecedent of the pronoun **he** because the pronoun **he** refers to the noun *boy* in the first sentence. The second noun *wasp* is not an antecedent because there is not a pronoun that refers to the noun *wasp*.

Since antecedents determine the pronouns used, it is important for the pronoun to be as similar to the antecedent as possible in number and gender. The two guidelines for number and gender in Reference 47 will help you. (*Read and explain the rest of the information in Reference 47 with your students. Then, read and discuss the guided practice for antecedent agreement.*)

Reference 47: Personal Pronoun-Antecedent Agreement

antecedent	pronoun	antecedent	pronoun

A. The little **boy** grinned playfully at **his** brother. B. The little **boy** gasped. **He** had just been stung.

1. Decide if the antecedent is singular or plural, and then choose the pronoun that agrees in number.

   If the antecedent is singular, the pronoun must be singular. (man - he, him, his, etc.)
   If the antecedent is plural, the pronoun must be plural. (men - they, them, their, etc.)

2. Decide if the antecedent is male or female, and then choose the pronoun that agrees in gender.

   If the antecedent is masculine, the pronoun must be masculine gender. (boy-he)
   If the antecedent is feminine, the pronoun must be feminine gender. (girl-she)
   If the antecedent is neither masculine nor feminine, the pronoun must be the neuter gender. (book-it)
   (The plural pronouns *they* and *them* also show the neuter gender. The **toys** are damaged. **They** are broken.)

Guided Practice for Antecedent Agreement

Choose an answer from the pronoun choices in parentheses. Then, fill in the rest of the columns according to the titles. (**S** or **P** stands for singular or plural.)

Pronoun-Antecedent Agreement	Pronoun choice	S or P	Antecedent	S or P
1. The princess was proud of (<u>her</u>, their) crown.	her	S	princess	S
2. The doctor finally revealed (<u>his</u>, their) age.	his	S	doctor	S
3. The pheasants laid (its, <u>their</u>) eggs in the grass.	their	P	pheasants	P

Oral Review

To develop listening skills, give students a review of antecedent agreement orally. Repeat the nouns in bold and have students respond with the correct <u>possessive</u> pronoun that would refer to the noun.

patients - their	**shovel** - its	**piano** - its	**aunt** - her
feathers - their	**uncle** - his	**stamps** - their	**sister** - her
tornado - its	**manager** - his/her	**shoes** - their	**sand** - its
grandma - her	**salt** - its	**cousin** - his/her	**dad** - his
student - his/her	**Florida** - its	**halo** - its	**muscles** - their

CHAPTER 14 LESSON 1 CONTINUED

 PRACTICE TIME

Have students turn to pages 74 and 75 in the Practice Section of their book and find Chapter 14, Lesson 1, Practice (*1-2*). Go over the directions to make sure they understand what to do. Check and discuss the Practice after students have finished. (*Chapter 14, Lesson 1, Practice keys are given below.*)

Chapter 14, Lesson 1, Practice 1: Choose an answer from the pronoun choices in parentheses. Fill in the other columns according to the titles. (**S** or **P** stands for singular or plural.)

Pronoun-antecedent agreement	Pronoun Choice	S or P	Antecedent	S or P
1. The speaker unbuttoned (<u>his</u>, their) jacket.	his	S	speaker	S
2. Dad painted (<u>his</u>, their) truck yellow.	his	S	Dad	S
3. My aunt lost (<u>her</u>, their) pet chicken.	her	S	aunt	S
4. The protesters waved (his, <u>their</u>) flag.	their	P	protesters	P
5. The vinegar lost (<u>its</u>, their) flavor.	its	S	vinegar	S

Chapter 14, Lesson 1, Practice 2: Identify each kind of sentence by writing the abbreviation in the blank. (**S, F, SCS, SCV, CD**).

CD	1.	She wrote a novel, but it has not been published.
SCS	2.	Our aunt and uncle traveled to Europe with their friends.
F	3.	In the cafeteria for two hours.
S	4.	She washed the dishes for her mother.
SCV	5.	Larry's brother rested and ate under the shade tree.
CD	6.	The sun came out, but it was still raining.

 WRITING TIME

Have students make an entry in their journals.

 VOCABULARY TIME

Assign Chapter 14, Vocabulary Words **#1** on page 9 in the Reference Section for students to define in their Vocabulary notebooks. Tell students they are to use a dictionary or thesaurus to look up the meanings of the vocabulary words. After they write each word and its meaning, students are to write a sentence using the vocabulary word.

Chapter 14, Vocabulary Words #1
(emerge, disappear, shy, bashful)

(End of lesson.)

CHAPTER 14   LESSON 2
Objectives: Jingles, Grammar (Practice Sentences, Pattern 2 Practice Sentence), Practice Exercise, Vocabulary #2, and Activity.

JINGLE TIME

Have students turn to the Jingle Section in their books and recite the previously-taught jingles.

GRAMMAR TIME

First-Year Option: Put the Practice Sentences from the box below on the board or on notebook paper. Use these sentences as you practice the concepts that have been taught. For the greatest benefit, students must participate orally with the teacher. **Second-Year Option:** Have students classify the Practice Sentences independently on notebook paper. Check students' sentences with the answers provided below. (*If you have the CDs for Practice Sentences, have students check their sentences with the CDs.*)

Chapter 14, Practice Sentences for Lesson 2
1. _____ Did I leave my old straw hat at your house?
2. _____ The teacher showed a picture of the White House to our class.

TEACHING SCRIPT FOR PRACTICING PATTERN 2 SENTENCES

We will practice classifying Pattern 2 sentences. We will classify the sentences together. Begin. (*You might have your students write the labels above the sentences at this time.*)

Question and Answer Flow for Sentence 1: Did I leave my old straw hat at your house?
1. Who did leave my old straw hat at your house? I - SP
2. What is being said about I? I did leave - V
3. Did - HV
4. Did leave what? hat - verify the noun
5. Does hat mean the same thing as I? No.
6. Hat - DO
7. Leave - V-t
8. What kind of hat? straw - Adj
9. What kind of hat? old - Adj
10. Whose hat? my - PPA
11. At - P
12. At what? house - OP
13. Whose house? your - PPA
14. SN V-t DO P2 Check
15. Verb-transitive - Check again.
16. (At your house) - Prepositional phrase
17. Question mark, question, interrogative sentence
18. Go back to the verb - divide the complete subject from the complete predicate.
19. This sentence has predicate words in the complete subject. Underline the helping verb at the beginning of the sentence twice.

Classified Sentence:

HV SP V-t PPA Adj Adj DO P PPA OP

SN V-t   <u>Did</u> I / leave my old straw hat (at your house)? **Int**
DO P2

CHAPTER 14 LESSON 2 CONTINUED

Question and Answer Flow for Sentence 2: The teacher showed a picture of the White House to our class.

1. Who showed a picture of the White House to our class? teacher - SN
2. What is being said about teacher? teacher showed - V
3. Teacher showed what? picture - verify the noun
4. Does picture mean the same thing as teacher? No.
5. Picture - DO
6. Showed - V-t
7. A - A
8. Of - P
9. Of what? White House - OP
10. The - A
11. To - P
12. To whom? class - OP
13. Whose class? our - PPA
14. The - A
15. SN V-t DO P2 Check
16. Verb-transitive - Check again.
17. (Of the White House) - Prepositional phrase
18. (To our class) - Prepositional phrase
19. Period, statement, declarative sentence
20. Go back to the verb - divide the complete subject from the complete predicate.

Classified Sentence:

<pre>
                      A   SN   V-t A DO   P A   OP   P PPA OP
      SN V-t   The teacher / showed a picture (of the White House) (to our class). D
      DO P2
</pre>

TEACHER INSTRUCTIONS FOR A PATTERN 2 SENTENCE

Tell students that their sentence writing assignment today is to write a Pattern 2 sentence. They are to follow the same procedure used in the previous lessons. They should decide on their labels, arrange them in a selected order, write their sentence, and edit the sentence for improved word choices. (*Students do not have to write an Improved Sentence at this point unless you feel they need more one-on-one word choice writing practice.*) Check and discuss the Pattern 2 sentence after students have finished.

 PRACTICE TIME

Have students turn to pages 75 and 76 in the Practice Section of their book and find Chapter 14, Lesson 2, Practice (*1-3*). Go over the directions to make sure they understand what to do. Check and discuss the Practices after students have finished. (*Chapter 14, Lesson 2, Practice keys are given below and on the next page.*)

Chapter 14, Lesson 2, Practice 1: Choose an answer from the choices in parentheses. Fill in the other columns according to the titles. (**S or P** stands for singular or plural.)

Pronoun-antecedent agreement	Pronoun Choice	S or P	Antecedent	S or P
1. The student in the cafeteria lost (<u>his</u>, their) money.	his	S	student	S
2. The apartments had no numbers on (it, <u>them</u>).	them	P	apartments	P
3. The violinist played with (<u>his</u>, their) left hand.	his	S	violinist	S
4. The boys invested (his, <u>their</u>) money in bonds.	their	P	boys	P
5. The tulip lost (<u>its</u>, their) petals suddenly.	its	S	tulip	S
6. His sister lost (<u>her</u>, their) essay paper.	her	S	sister	S
7. The monkey made (<u>its</u>, their) bed with straw.	its	S	monkey	S
8. The turtles buried (its, <u>their</u>) eggs in sand.	their	P	turtles	P

Level 4 Homeschool Teacher's Manual

CHAPTER 14 LESSON 2 CONTINUED

Chapter 14, Lesson 2, Practice 2: Identify each kind of sentence by writing the abbreviation in the blank.
(S, F, SCS, SCV, CD)

F	1. Since the interstate is closed to traffic.
SCS	2. The judge and jury agreed on the verdict.
SCV	3. I smelled the fire and called for help.
CD	4. She ate her pancakes, but she was still hungry.
SCV	5. Seth entered and won the spelling contest.
CD	6. I walked my dog, and I carried our cat.
F	7. In the bedroom on top of the dresser.

Chapter 14, Lesson 2, Practice 3: On notebook paper, write two compound sentences, using these labels to guide you:
① (CD, but) ② (CD;) **(Sentences will vary.)**

 VOCABULARY TIME

Assign Chapter 14, Vocabulary Words **#2** on page 9 in the Reference Section for students to define in their Vocabulary notebooks. Tell students they are to use a dictionary or thesaurus to look up the meanings of the vocabulary words. After they write each word and its meaning, students are to write a sentence using the vocabulary word.

Chapter 14, Vocabulary Words #2
(treaty, agreement, flashy, plain)

 ACTIVITY / ASSIGNMENT TIME

Have students write a song that they like from memory. Have them sing the song or make up a new song that is funny or describes how they feel about something. Have students illustrate their songs. Have them share their songs and illustrations with other family members and friends.

(End of lesson.)

CHAPTER 14   LESSON 3

Objectives: Jingles, Grammar (Practice Sentences), and Practice Exercise.

JINGLE TIME

Have students turn to the Jingle Section in their books and recite the previously-taught jingles.

GRAMMAR TIME

First-Year Option: Put the Practice Sentences from the box below on the board or on notebook paper. Use these sentences as you practice the concepts that have been taught. For the greatest benefit, students must participate orally with the teacher. **Second-Year Option:** Have students classify the Practice Sentences independently on notebook paper. Check students' sentences with the answers provided below. (*If you have the CDs for Practice Sentences, have students check their sentences with the CDs.*)

Chapter 14, Practice Sentences for Lesson 3
1. _____ Yesterday, I borrowed a suit and tie from my brother for the formal dinner.
2. _____ The principal's secretary mailed the discipline notice to my parents.

TEACHING SCRIPT FOR PRACTICING PATTERN 2 SENTENCES

We will practice classifying Pattern 2 sentences. We will classify the sentences together. Begin. (*You might have your students write the labels above the sentences at this time.*)

Question and Answer Flow for Sentence 1: Yesterday, I borrowed a suit and tie from my brother for the formal dinner.

1. Who borrowed a suit and tie from my brother for the formal dinner? I - SP
2. What is being said about I? I borrowed - V
3. I borrowed what? suit and tie - verify the nouns
4. Do suit and tie mean the same thing as I? No.
5. Suit and tie - CDO, CDO
6. Borrowed - V-t
7. A - A
8. And - C
9. From - P
10. From whom? brother - OP
11. Whose brother? my - PPA
12. For - P
13. For what? dinner - OP
14. What kind of dinner? formal - Adj
15. The - A
16. Borrowed when? yesterday - Adv
17. SN V-t DO P2 Check
18. Verb-transitive - Check again.
19. (From my brother) - Prepositional phrase
20. (For the formal dinner) - Prepositional phrase
21. Period, statement, declarative sentence
22. Go back to the verb - divide the complete subject from the complete predicate.
23. This sentence has predicate words in the complete subject. Underline the adverb at the beginning of the sentence twice.

Classified Sentence:

               Adv   SP   V-t   A CDO C CDO P PPA OP   P A   Adj   OP

SN V-t   Yesterday, I / borrowed a suit and tie (from my brother) (for the formal dinner). **D**
DO P2

CHAPTER 14 LESSON 3 CONTINUED

Question and Answer Flow for Sentence 2: The principal's secretary mailed the discipline notice to my parents.

1. Who mailed the discipline notice to my parents? secretary - SN
2. What is being said about secretary? secretary mailed - V
3. Secretary mailed what? notice - verify the noun
4. Does notice mean the same thing as secretary? No.
5. Notice - DO
6. Mailed - V-t
7. What kind of notice? discipline - Adj
8. The - A
9. To - P
10. To whom? parents - OP
11. Whose parents? my - PPA
12. Whose secretary? principal's - PNA
13. The - A
14. SN V-t DO P2 Check
15. Verb-transitive - Check again.
16. (To my parents) - Prepositional phrase
17. Period, statement, declarative sentence
18. Go back to the verb - divide the complete subject from the complete predicate.

Classified Sentence:

```
                          A    PNA        SN      V-t  A   Adj    DO   P PPA OP
          SN  V-t    The principal's secretary / mailed the discipline notice (to my parents).  D
          DO  P2
```

 PRACTICE TIME

Have students turn to page 76 in the Practice Section of their book and find Chapter 14, Lesson 3, Practice (*1-2*). Go over the directions to make sure they understand what to do. Check and discuss the Practices after students have finished. (*Chapter 14, Lesson 3, Practice keys are given below.*)

Chapter 14, Lesson 3, Practice 1: Choose an answer from the choices in parentheses. Fill in the other columns according to the titles. (**S** or **P** stands for singular or plural.)

Pronoun-antecedent agreement

	Pronoun Choice	S or P	Antecedent	S or P
1. My nephew lives with (<u>his</u>, their) mother.	his	S	nephew	S
2. The envelopes have no names on (it, <u>them</u>).	them	P	envelopes	P
3. The prince wore (<u>his</u>, their) royal robes.	his	S	prince	S
4. The young boy washed (<u>his</u>, their) hands.	his	S	boy	S
5. The nation struggled for (<u>its</u>, their) independence.	its	S	nation	S
6. The tourists left (its, <u>their</u>) luggage in the taxi.	their	P	tourists	P
7. Sally wore (<u>her</u>, their) necklace to the prom.	her	S	Sally	S
8. The bluebirds hatch (its, <u>their</u>) eggs in a box.	their	P	bluebirds	P

Chapter 14, Lesson 3, Practice 2: Identify each kind of sentence by writing the abbreviation in the blank. (**S, F, SCS, SCV, CD**)

F	1. Where the brick wall used to stand.
SCS	2. The whales and sharks invaded the beach.
SCV	3. I answered the phone and listened to the recording.
CD	4. My dog growled, but I petted him anyway.
SCV	5. The talented singer laughed and sang with the audience.

(End of lesson.)

CHAPTER 14   LESSON 4

Objectives: Jingles, Study, Test, Check, Activity, and Writing (journal).

 JINGLE TIME

Have students turn to the Jingle Section in their books and recite the previously-taught jingles.

 STUDY TIME

Have students study the vocabulary words in their vocabulary notebooks. Remind students that any vocabulary word in their notebooks could be on their test. Also, have students study any of the skills in the Practice Section that they need to review.

 TEST TIME

Have students turn to page 111 in the Test Section of their book and find the Chapter 14 Test. Go over the directions to make sure they understand what to do. (*Chapter 14 Test key is on the next page.*)

 CHECK TIME

After students have finished, check and discuss their test papers. Make sure they understand why their answers are right or wrong. (*For total points, count each required answer as a point.*)

 ACTIVITY / ASSIGNMENT TIME

The **Parts-of-Speech Poem** is a directional poem in which one employs various parts of speech, following a prescribed formula. Teachers or students can design their own formulas to create different effects. Read and discuss the example below. Have students write their own **Parts-of-Speech Poem** using the directions below. Have them share their poems with others.

Line 1—One interjection	Oh yes!
Line 2—Two subject pronouns	He and I
Line 3—One verb phrase and one direct object	Have caught several turtles
Line 4—One prepositional phrase	On the muddy banks
Line 5—One prepositional phrase	Of the fishing lake
Line 6—One adverb	Before.

(End of lesson.)

Level 4 Homeschool Teacher's Manual

Chapter 14 Test
(Student Page 111)

Exercise 1: Classify each sentence.

```
           SP  CV-t  C  CV-t  A  DO   P  A  OP     P   PPA  Adj  OP
1. SN  V-t     I / traced  and  copied  a  picture (of a horse) (during my art class). D
   DO  P2

           PPA  SN    CV-t   C    CV-t   A    PNA      DO
2. SN  V-t     Our troops / invaded  and  occupied  the enemy's territory. D
   DO  P2
```

Exercise 2: Use Sentence 2 to underline the complete subject once and the complete predicate twice and to complete the table below.

List the Noun Used	List the Noun Job	Singular or Plural	Common or Proper	Simple Subject	Simple Predicate
1. **troops**	2. **SN**	3. **P**	4. **C**	5. **troops**	6. **invaded/occupied**
7. **territory**	8. **DO**	9. **S**	10. **C**		

Exercise 3: Identify each pair of words as synonyms or antonyms by putting parentheses ( ) around *syn* or *ant*.

1. quick, agile	**(syn)** ant	5. bashful, shy	**(syn)** ant	9. originates, begins	**(syn)** ant
2. flashy, plain	syn **(ant)**	6. endow, give	**(syn)** ant	10. treaty, agreement	**(syn)** ant
3. demand, suggest	syn **(ant)**	7. gallant, afraid	syn **(ant)**	11. complex, difficult	**(syn)** ant
4. mend, rip	syn **(ant)**	8. hardy, robust	**(syn)** ant	12. emerge, disappear	syn **(ant)**

Exercise 4: Choose an answer from the choices in parentheses. Fill in the other columns according to the titles. (**S** or **P** stands for singular or plural.)

Pronoun-antecedent agreement

1. The ships at sea have changed (its, <u>their</u>) course.
2. The small country won (<u>its</u>, their) independence.
3. The Sunday school teachers lost (his, <u>their</u>) lesson.
4. The doctor's wife misplaced (<u>her</u>, their) purse.
5. The wild pheasant lost (<u>its</u>, their) tail feathers.
6. The students in school brought (his, <u>their</u>) permission slip.

Pronoun Choice	S or P	Antecedent	S or P
their	P	ships	P
its	S	country	S
their	P	teachers	P
her	S	wife	S
its	S	pheasant	S
their	P	students	P

Exercise 5: Identify each kind of sentence by writing the abbreviation in the blank. (**S, F, SCS, SCV, CD**)

CD	1. Take your medicine, or you'll never get well.
S	2. I walked along the sandy beach.
SCS	3. The teachers and students cheered for our football team.
F	4. After lunch on Saturday.
CD	5. She never studies, but she makes good grades.
SCV	6. My sister cooked and cleaned our house today.
F	7. During the storm last night.

Exercise 6: On notebook paper, write one sentence for each of these labels: ① **S** ② **SCS** ③ **SCV** ④ **CD**. (**Answers will vary.**)

Exercise 7: In your journal, write a paragraph summarizing what you have learned this week.

CHAPTER 14 LESSON 4 CONTINUED

TEACHER INSTRUCTIONS

Use the Question and Answer Flows below for the sentences on the Chapter 14 Test.

Question and Answer Flow for Sentence 1: I traced and copied a picture of a horse during my art class.

1. Who traced and copied a picture of a horse during my art class? I - SP
2. What is being said about I? I traced and copied - CV, CV
3. I traced and copied what? picture - verify the noun
4. Does picture mean the same thing as I? No.
5. Picture - DO
6. Traced and copied - CV-t, CV-t
7. A - A
8. Of - P
9. Of what? horse - OP
10. A - A
11. During - P

12. During what? class - OP
13. What kind of class? art - Adj
14. Whose class? my - PPA
15. And - C
16. SN V-t DO P2 Check
17. Verb-transitive - Check again.
18. (Of a horse) - Prepositional phrase
19. (During my art class) - Prepositional phrase
20. Period, statement, declarative sentence
21. Go back to the verb - divide the complete subject from the complete predicate.

Classified Sentence:

<u>SN V-t</u>
DO P2

SP   CV-t   C   CV-t   A   DO   P   A   OP   P   PPA Adj OP
I / traced and copied a picture (of a horse) (during my art class). **D**

Question and Answer Flow for Sentence 2: Our troops invaded and occupied the enemy's territory.

1. Who invaded and occupied the enemy's territory?
   troops - SN
2. What is being said about troops?
   troops invaded and occupied - CV, CV
3. Troops invaded and occupied what?
   territory - verify the noun
4. Does territory mean the same thing as troops? No.
5. Territory - DO
6. Invaded and occupied - CV-t, CV-t
7. Whose territory? enemy's - PNA

8. The - A
9. And - C
10. Whose troops? our - PPA
11. SN V-t DO P2 Check
12. Verb-transitive - Check again.
13. No prepositional phrases.
14. Period, statement, declarative sentence
15. Go back to the verb - divide the complete subject from the complete predicate.

Classified Sentence:

<u>SN V-t</u>
DO P2

PPA SN   CV-t   C   CV-t   A   PNA   DO
Our troops / invaded and occupied the enemy's territory. **D**

CHAPTER 14   LESSON 5

Objectives: Writing Assignments #17 and #18.

 **WRITING TIME**

TEACHING SCRIPT FOR PRACTICING DIFFERENT KINDS OF WRITING

Today, you are assigned two different kinds of writing. You will write a five-paragraph persuasive essay and a three-paragraph expository essay. <u>You will revise and edit the five-paragraph persuasive essay.</u> (*Read the box below for more information about students' writing assignment.*) As you edit, make sure you use the checkpoints in the editing checklist provided in Reference 39. Remember to read through the whole essay, starting with the title, and then edit, sentence-by-sentence, using the five-sentence checkpoints for each sentence. Use the paragraph checkpoints to check each paragraph.

Writing Assignment Box #1

Writing Assignment #17: Five-Paragraph Persuasive Essay (First Person)
(Remember, first person pronouns are *I, we, me, us, my, our, mine,* and *ours.*)
Remind students that the 5-paragraph essay has three parts: 1. Introduction 2. Body 3. Conclusion. The body has three paragraphs instead of one. Have students use their regular editing checklist to edit this assignment.

Writing topics: Kids Need a Teen Center   or   **Why I Should/Should Not Go to College**   or
Memorizing Bible Verses

Your second writing assignment is to write a three-paragraph expository essay. (*Read the box below for more information about students' writing assignment.*) You do not have to edit this assignment with the editing checklist.

Writing Assignment Box #2

Writing Assignment #18: Three-Paragraph Expository Essay (First Person)
(Remember, first person pronouns are *I, we, me, us, my, our, mine,* and *ours.*)
Remind students that the 3-paragraph essay has three parts: 1. Introduction 2. Body 3. Conclusion. The body has one paragraph instead of three.

Writing topics: My Favorite Musical Instrument   or   **Things a Pet Needs**   or   **The Perfect Birthday Party**

TEACHER INSTRUCTIONS FOR CHECKING WRITING ASSIGNMENTS

Read, check, and discuss Writing Assignment #17 after students have finished their final papers. Use the checklists as you check and discuss students' papers. Make sure students are using the regular editing checklist correctly. Read and discuss Writing Assignment #18 for fun and enrichment.

(End of lesson.)

CHAPTER 15   LESSON 1

Objectives: Jingles, Grammar (Practice Sentences, Oral Skill Builder Check), Skill (possessive nouns), Practice Exercise, Writing (journal) and Vocabulary #1.

JINGLE TIME

Have students turn to the Jingle Section in their books and recite the previously-taught jingles.

GRAMMAR TIME

First-Year Option: Put the Practice Sentences from the box below on the board or on notebook paper. Use these sentences as you practice the concepts that have been taught. For the greatest benefit, students must participate orally with the teacher. **Second-Year Option:** Have students classify the Practice Sentences independently on notebook paper. Check students' sentences with the answers provided below. (*If you have the CDs for Practice Sentences, have students check their sentences with the CDs.*)

Chapter 15, Practice Sentences for Lesson 1

1. _____ The reputable carpenter built beautiful new homes and apartments in our neighborhood.
2. _____ Those menacing termites built tunnels in the walls of the house.

TEACHING SCRIPT FOR PRACTICING PATTERN 2 SENTENCES

We will practice classifying Pattern 2 sentences. We will classify the sentences together. Begin. (*You might have your child write the labels above the sentences at this time.*)

Question and Answer Flow for Sentence 1: The reputable carpenter built beautiful new homes and apartments in our neighborhood.

1. Who built beautiful new homes and apartments in our neighborhood? carpenter - SN
2. What is being said about carpenter? carpenter built - V
3. Carpenter built what? homes and apartments - verify the nouns
4. Do homes and apartments mean the same thing as carpenter? No.
5. Homes and apartments - CDO, CDO
6. Built - V-t
7. What kind of homes and apartments? new - Adj
8. What kind of homes and apartments? beautiful - Adj
9. And - C
10. In - P
11. In what? neighborhood - OP
12. Whose neighborhood? our - PPA
13. What kind of carpenter? reputable - Adj
14. The - A
15. SN V-t DO P2 Check
16. Verb-transitive - Check again.
17. (In our neighborhood) - Prepositional phrase
18. Period, statement, declarative sentence
19. Go back to the verb - divide the complete subject from the complete predicate.

Classified Sentence:

	A	Adj	SN	V-t	Adj	Adj	CDO	C	CDO	P	PPA	OP

SN V-t / DO P2   The reputable carpenter / built beautiful new homes and apartments (in our neighborhood). D

CHAPTER 15 LESSON 1 CONTINUED

Question and Answer Flow for Sentence 2: Those menacing termites built tunnels in the walls of the house.

1. What built tunnels in the walls of the house?
termites - SN
2. What is being said about termites? termites built - V
3. Termites built what? tunnels - verify the noun
4. Do tunnels mean the same thing as termites? No.
5. Tunnels - DO
6. Built - V-t
7. In - P
8. In what? walls - OP
9. The - A
10. Of - P
11. Of what? house - OP

12. The - A
13. What kind of termites? menacing - Adj
14. Which termites? those - Adj
15. SN V-t DO P2 Check
16. Verb-transitive - Check again.
17. (In the walls) - Prepositional phrase
18. (Of the house) - Prepositional phrase
19. Period, statement, declarative sentence
20. Go back to the verb - divide the complete subject from the complete predicate.

Classified Sentence:

Adj Adj SN V-t DO P A OP P A OP
SN V-t / Those menacing termites / built tunnels (in the walls) (of the house). D
DO P2

Use Sentences 1-2 that you just classified with your students to do an Oral Skill Builder Check. Use the guidelines below.

Oral Skill Builder Check

1. **Noun check.**
(Say the job and then say the noun. Circle each noun.)
2. **Identify the nouns as singular or plural.**
(Write **S** or **P** above each noun.)
3. **Identify the nouns as common or proper.**
(Follow established procedure for oral identification.)
4. **Do a vocabulary check.**
(Follow established procedure for oral identification.)

5. **Identify the complete subject and the complete predicate.** (Underline the complete subject once and the complete predicate twice.)
6. **Identify the simple subject and simple predicate.**
(Underline the simple subject once and the simple predicate twice. Bold, or highlight, the lines.)
7. **Recite the irregular verb chart.**
(Located on student page 23 and teacher page 138.)

SKILL TIME

TEACHING SCRIPT FOR MAKING NOUNS POSSESSIVE

Learning how to make nouns possessive is the next skill you will learn. This skill is really simple, but, again, students and adults alike have a lot of trouble with it when they write. The more practice you have in making nouns possessive, the more likely you will use possessive nouns correctly in your writing.

In order to form possessive nouns that show ownership, you must first decide if the noun is singular or plural before you add the apostrophe. After you know whether a noun is singular or plural, you can then use three rules to tell you how to make the noun possessive.

CHAPTER 15 LESSON 1 CONTINUED

Look at Reference 48 on page 41 in the Reference Section of your book and follow along as we go through the three rules and practice examples. (*The information and practice examples are reproduced for you below.*) Remember, we always read the directions first. Listen carefully because you have several things to do. (*Read the directions for Part A and Part B below.*)

Reference 48: Making Nouns Possessive						
1. For a singular noun - add (**'s**) **Rule 1: girl's**		2. For a plural noun that ends in **s** - add (**'**) **Rule 2: girls'**			3. For a plural noun that does not end in **s** - add (**'s**) **Rule 3: women's**	
Part A: Underline each noun to be made possessive and write singular or plural (S-P), the rule number, and the possessive form. Part B: Write each noun as singular possessive and then as plural possessive.						
Part A	**S-P**	**Rule**	**Possessive Form**	**Part B**	**Singular Poss**	**Plural Poss**
1. <u>magician</u> cape	S	1	magician's cape	5. knife	knife's	knives'
2. <u>nurses</u> patients	P	2	nurses' patients	6. broom	broom's	brooms'
3. <u>James</u> mailbox	S	1	James's mailbox	7. inventor	inventor's	inventors'
4. <u>children</u> voices	P	3	children's voices	8. man	man's	men's

TEACHING SCRIPT FOR MAKING NOUNS POSSESSIVE, PART A

For Part A, let's review the four things that the directions tell us to do. First, we decide which noun is to be made possessive and underline it. Second, we are going to identify the noun as singular or plural. Third, we are going to write the number of the rule to be followed from the rule box. Last, we are going to write the correct possessive form in the blank.

Look at number 1. The first thing we must do is underline the noun to be made possessive. An easy way to test for the correct noun to be made possessive is to do the "of" test. We would say "the cape **of** the magician, not the magician **of** the cape!" Now, we know the noun to make possessive. The word *magician* is underlined, as shown in the example.

Next, we must decide whether our underlined noun is singular or plural before we can make it possessive. Is *magician* singular or plural? (*singular*) The letter **S** is written in the blank under the column marked **S-P**.

Now, we will look at the rule box for making nouns possessive. Which rule do we use since *magician* is singular? (*Rule 1*) A number 1 is written in the blank under the column marked *Rule*. What does Rule 1 tell us to do? (*For a singular noun, add an apostrophe and s.*) The singular possessive noun *magician's* is written under the column marked *Possessive Form*. (*Work through the rest of Part A in the same way to make sure your students understand how to use the rule box for making nouns possessive.*)

TEACHING SCRIPT FOR MAKING NOUNS POSSESSIVE, PART B

Look at Part B. Every noun listed is singular. The directions tell us to do two things. First, we are going to write the singular possessive form of the noun. Second, we are going to change the singular noun to plural and then write the plural possessive form of the noun. <u>That means you may need to check a dictionary for the correct plural spelling of the noun. Dictionaries should always be available for looking up words.</u>

Look at number 5 under Part B. It says *knife*. Since we know that *knife* is singular, we go to Rule 1 so it will tell us how to make the word *knife* possessive. What does Rule 1 tell us to do? (*For a singular noun, add an apostrophe and s.*) The word *knife's* is written under the column marked *Singular Possessive*.

CHAPTER 15 LESSON 1 CONTINUED

We must change *knife* to its plural form before we can make it plural possessive. How do we make *knife* plural? (By changing the **f** to **v** and adding **es**: *knives*.) We still need to make the plural word *knives* possessive. Since the plural form of *knives* ends in an **s**, which rule do we need to follow? *(Rule 2)* What does Rule 2 say to add to *knives* to make it possessive? *(An apostrophe.)* The word *knives'* is written with an apostrophe in the *Plural Possessive* column. (*Work through the rest of Part B in the same way. After the singular possessive form has been demonstrated and discussed, make sure your students understand how the plural form of the noun is written before making it possessive with the apostrophe by following Rule 2 or Rule 3. Always encourage your students to use the dictionary to check plural spellings.*)

 PRACTICE TIME

Have students turn to page 77 in the Practice Section of their book and find Chapter 15, Lesson 1, Practice. Go over the directions to make sure they understand what to do. Guide students closely as they do the practice exercises for the first time. Check and discuss the Practice after students have finished. (*Chapter 15, Lesson 1, Practice key is given below.*)

Chapter 15, Lesson 1, Practice: Part A: Underline each noun to be made possessive and write singular or plural (**S-P**), the rule number, and the possessive form. Part B: Write each noun as singular possessive and then as plural possessive.

1. For a singular noun - add (**'s**)				2. For a plural noun that ends in **s** - add (**'**)	3. For a plural noun that does not end in **s** - add (**'s**)		
Rule 1: boy's				**Rule 2: boys'**	**Rule 3: men's**		
Part A	**S-P**	**Rule**	**Possessive Form**		**Part B**	**Singular Poss**	**Plural Poss**
1. <u>hedge</u> length	S	1	hedge's length		5. cousin	cousin's	cousins'
2. <u>donkeys</u> tails	P	2	donkeys' tails		6. postman	postman's	postmen's
3. <u>mirrors</u> lengths	P	2	mirrors' lengths		7. pirate	pirate's	pirates'
4. <u>women</u> efforts	P	3	women's efforts		8. buggy	buggy's	buggies'

 WRITING TIME

Have students make an entry in their journals.

 VOCABULARY TIME

Assign Chapter 15, Vocabulary Words **#1** on page 9 in the Reference Section for students to define in their Vocabulary notebooks. Tell students they are to use a dictionary or thesaurus to look up the meanings of the vocabulary words. After they write each word and its meaning, students are to write a sentence using the vocabulary word.

Chapter 15, Vocabulary Words #1
(delicious, tasty, approve, deplore)

(End of lesson.)

CHAPTER 15   LESSON 2
Objectives: Jingles, Grammar (Practice Sentences), Pattern 2 Practice Sentence, and Practice Exercise.

 JINGLE TIME

Have students turn to the Jingle Section in their books and recite the previously-taught jingles.

 GRAMMAR TIME

Put the Practice Sentences from the box below on the board. Use these sentences as you practice the concepts that have been taught. For the greatest benefit, students must participate orally with the teacher. (*You might put the Practice Sentences on notebook paper if you are doing one-on-one instruction with your child.*)

Chapter 15, Practice Sentences for Lesson 2
1. _____ Read the article about seatbelt safety on the front page of the newspaper.
2. _____ Jake and I finished our English assignment before the bell.

TEACHING SCRIPT FOR PRACTICING PATTERN 2 SENTENCES

We will practice classifying Pattern 2 sentences. We will classify the sentences together. Begin. (*You might have your child write the labels above the sentences at this time.*)

Question and Answer Flow for Sentence 1: Read the article about seatbelt safety on the front page of the newspaper.

1. Who read the article about seatbelt safety on the front page of the newspaper? you - SP
   (Understood subject pronoun)
2. What is being said about you? you read - V
3. You read what? article - verify the noun
4. Does article mean the same thing as you? No.
5. Article - DO
6. Read - V-t
7. The - A
8. About - P
9. About what? safety - OP
10. What kind of safety? seatbelt - Adj
11. On - P
12. On what? page - OP
13. Which page? front - Adj
14. The - A
15. Of - P
16. Of what? newspaper - OP
17. The - A
18. SN V-t DO P2 Check
19. Verb-transitive - Check again.
20. (About seatbelt safety) - Prepositional phrase
21. (On the front page) - Prepositional phrase
22. (Of the newspaper) - Prepositional phrase
23. Period, command, imperative sentence
24. Go back to the verb - divide the complete subject from the complete predicate.

Classified Sentence:

```
        (You) SP   V-t  A  DO    P    Adj  OP   P  A Adj  OP   P  A   OP
        SN  V-t  / Read the article (about seatbelt safety) (on the front page) (of the newspaper). Imp
        DO  P2
```

CHAPTER 15 LESSON 2 CONTINUED

Question and Answer Flow for Sentence 2: Jake and I finished our English assignment before the bell.	

1. Who finished our English assignment before the bell?
   Jake and I - CSN, CSP
2. What is being said about Jake and I?
   Jake and I finished - V
3. Jake and I finished what? assignment - verify the noun
4. Does assignment mean the same thing as Jake and I?
   No.
5. Assignment - DO
6. Finished - V-t
7. What kind of assignment? English - Adj
8. Whose assignment? our - PPA
9. Before - P

10. Before what? bell - OP
11. The - A
12. And - C
13. SN V-t DO P2 Check
14. Verb-transitive - Check again.
15. (Before the bell) - Prepositional phrase
16. Period, statement, declarative sentence
17. Go back to the verb - divide the complete subject
    from the complete predicate.

Classified Sentence:

		CSN	C	CSP	V-t	PPA	Adj	DO	P	A	OP
SN V-t		Jake	and	I /	finished	our	English	assignment	(before	the	bell). D
DO P2											

TEACHER INSTRUCTIONS FOR A PATTERN 2 PRACTICE SENTENCE

Tell students that their sentence writing assignment today is to write a Pattern 2 sentence. They are to follow the same procedure used in the previous lessons. They should decide on their labels, arrange them in a selected order, write their sentence, and edit the sentence for improved word choices. (*Students do not have to write an Improved Sentence at this point unless you feel they need more one-on-one word choice writing practice.*) Check and discuss the Pattern 2 sentence after students have finished.

 PRACTICE TIME

Students will continue their practice of making nouns possessive. Have students turn to page 77 in the Practice Section of their book and find Chapter 15, Lesson 2, Practice. Go over the directions to make sure they understand what to do. Check and discuss the Practice after students have finished. (*Chapter 15, Lesson 2, Practice key is given below.*)

Chapter 15, Lesson 2, Practice: Part A: Underline each noun to be made possessive and write singular or plural (**S-P**), the rule number, and the possessive form. Part B: Write each noun as singular possessive and then as plural possessive.

1. For a singular noun - add (**'s**)			2. For a plural noun that ends in **s** - add (**'**)		3. For a plural noun that does not end in **s** - add (**'s**)		
Rule 1: boy's			**Rule 2: boys'**		**Rule 3: men's**		
Part A	**S-P**	**Rule**	**Possessive Form**	**Part B**	**Singular Poss**	**Plural Poss**
1. <u>pigeons</u> roosts	P	2	**pigeons' roosts**	5. monkey	**monkey's**	**monkeys'**
2. <u>children</u> laughter	P	3	**children's laughter**	6. wife	**wife's**	**wives'**
3. <u>enemy</u> surrender	S	1	**enemy's surrender**	7. child	**child's**	**children's**
4. <u>class</u> decision	S	1	**class's decision**	8. axle	**axle's**	**axles'**

(End of lesson.)

CHAPTER 15   LESSON 3
Objectives: Jingles, Grammar (Practice Sentences), Practice Exercise, and Vocabulary #2.

 **JINGLE TIME**

Have students turn to the Jingle Section in their books and recite the previously-taught jingles.

 GRAMMAR TIME

First-Year Option: Put the Practice Sentences from the box below on the board or on notebook paper. Use these sentences as you practice the concepts that have been taught. For the greatest benefit, students must participate orally with the teacher. **Second-Year Option:** Have students classify the Practice Sentences independently on notebook paper. Check students' sentences with the answers provided below. *(If you have the CDs for Practice Sentences, have students check their sentences with the CDs.)*

Chapter 15, Practice Sentences for Lesson 3
1. _____ Dad and I had a small argument over the choice of television programs tonight.
2. _____ Frequently, Joey leaves his toys on the floor of his bedroom.

TEACHING SCRIPT FOR PRACTICING PATTERN 2 SENTENCES

We will practice classifying Pattern 2 sentences. We will classify the sentences together. Begin. *(You might have your students write the labels above the sentences at this time.)*

Question and Answer Flow for Sentence 1: Dad and I had a small argument over the choice of television programs tonight.

1. Who had a small argument over the choice of television programs tonight? Dad and I - CSN, CSP
2. What is being said about Dad and I? Dad and I had - V
3. Dad and I had what? argument - verify the noun
4. Does argument mean the same thing as Dad and I? No.
5. Argument - DO
6. Had - V-t
7. What kind of argument? small - Adj
8. A - A
9. Over - P
10. Over what? choice - OP
11. The - A
12. Of - P
13. Of what? programs - OP
14. What kind of programs? television - Adj
15. Had when? tonight - Adv
16. And - C
17. SN V-t DO P2 Check
18. Verb-transitive - Check again.
19. (Over the choice) - Prepositional phrase
20. (Of television programs) - Prepositional phrase
21. Period, statement, declarative sentence
22. Go back to the verb - divide the complete subject from the complete predicate.

Classified Sentence:		CSN	C	CSP	V-t	A	Adj	DO	P	A	OP	P	Adj	OP	Adv
SN V-t		Dad	and	I /	had	a	small	argument	(over	the	choice)	(of	television	programs)	tonight. **D**
DO P2															

CHAPTER 15 LESSON 3 CONTINUED

Question and Answer Flow for Sentence 2: Frequently, Joey leaves his toys on the floor of his bedroom.

1. Who leaves his toys on the floor of his bedroom? Joey - SN
2. What is being said about Joey? Joey leaves - V
3. Joey leaves what? toys - verify the noun
4. Do toys mean the same thing as Joey? No.
5. Toys - DO
6. Leaves - V-t
7. Whose toys? his - PPA
8. On - P
9. On what? floor - OP
10. The - A
11. Of - P
12. Of what? bedroom - OP
13. Whose bedroom? his - PPA
14. Leaves when? frequently - Adv
15. SN V-t DO P2 Check
16. Verb-transitive - Check again.
17. (On the floor) - Prepositional phrase
18. (Of his bedroom) - Prepositional phrase
19. Period, statement, declarative sentence
20. Go back to the verb - divide the complete subject from the complete predicate.
21. This sentence has predicate words in the complete subject. Underline the adverb at the beginning of this sentence twice.

Classified Sentence:

	Adv	SN	V-t	PPA DO	P A OP	P PPA OP
SN V-t	Frequently,	Joey /	leaves	his toys	(on the floor)	(of his bedroom). D
DO P2						

PRACTICE TIME

Students will continue their practice of making nouns possessive. Have students turn to page 78 in the Practice Section of their book and find Chapter 15, Lesson 3, Practice. Go over the directions to make sure they understand what to do. Check and discuss the Practice after students have finished. (*Chapter 15, Lesson 3, Practice key is given below.*)

Chapter 15, Lesson 3, Practice: Part A: Underline each noun to be made possessive and write singular or plural (**S-P**), the rule number, and the possessive form. Part B: Write each noun as singular possessive and then as plural possessive.

1. For a singular noun - add (**'s**)			2. For a plural noun that ends in **s** - add (**'**)		3. For a plural noun that does not end in **s** - add (**'s**)		
Rule 1: girl's			**Rule 2: girls'**		**Rule 3: women's**		
Part A	**S-P**	**Rule**	**Possessive Form**	**Part B**	**Singular Poss**	**Plural Poss**	
1. <u>bike</u> trail	S	1	bike's trail	5. baby	baby's	babies'	
2. <u>wolves</u> howls	P	2	wolves' howls	6. ally	ally's	allies'	
3. <u>women</u> scarves	P	3	women's scarves	7. alley	alley's	alleys'	
4. <u>pantries</u> shelves	P	2	pantries' shelves	8. scarf	scarf's	scarves'	

VOCABULARY TIME

Assign Chapter 15, Vocabulary Words **#2** on page 9 in the Reference Section for students to define in their Vocabulary notebooks. After they write each word and its meaning, students are to write a sentence using the vocabulary word. Have students study the vocabulary words when they have finished.

Chapter 15, Vocabulary Words #2
(hope, despair, influence, sway)

(End of lesson.)

CHAPTER 15   LESSON 4

Objectives: Jingles, Study, Test, Check, Activity, and Writing (journal).

JINGLE TIME

Have students turn to the Jingle Section in their books and recite the previously-taught jingles.

STUDY TIME

Have students study the vocabulary words in their vocabulary notebooks. Remind students that any vocabulary word in their notebooks could be on their test. Also, have students study any of the skills in the Practice Section that they need to review.

TEST TIME

Have students turn to page 112 in the Test Section of their book and find the Chapter 15 Test. Go over the directions to make sure they understand what to do. (*Chapter 15 Test key is on the next page.*)

CHECK TIME

After students have finished, check and discuss their test papers. Make sure they understand why their answers are right or wrong. (*For total points, count each required answer as a point.*)

ACTIVITY / ASSIGNMENT TIME

Read and discuss the new **Parts-of-Speech** formula and the example below. Have students write another **Parts-of-Speech Poem**, using the new formula below. Have them share their poems with others.

Line 1 - Write one noun (*the topic of your poem*).
Line 2 - Write two adjectives to describe the noun.
Line 3 - Write one verb and one prepositional phrase.
Line 4 - Write two adverbs describing the verb.
Line 5 - Write a sentence about the noun.

Fans,
Loud and excited,
Yell in the stands
Eagerly and noisily.
They are happy supporters.

(End of lesson.)

Chapter 15 Test
(Student Page 112)

Exercise 1: Classify each sentence.

       PPA   SN   V-t   A   DO   P PPA OP   P   A   Adj   OP

1. **SN V-t**   My grandmother / waters the flowers (in her yard) (during the summer months). **D**
  DO P2

           A   Adj   SN   HV Adv V-t A   DO   P   A   OP

2. **SN V-t**   The small child / would not eat the honeycomb (from the beehive). **D**
  DO P2

Exercise 2: Use Sentence 1 to underline the complete subject once and the complete predicate twice and to complete the table below.

List the Noun Used	List the Noun Job	Singular or Plural	Common or Proper	Simple Subject	Simple Predicate
1. **grandmother**	2. **SN**	3. **S**	4. **C**	5. **grandmother**	6. **waters**
7. **flowers**	8. **DO**	9. **P**	10. **C**		
11. **yard**	12. **OP**	13. **S**	14. **C**		
15. **months**	16. **OP**	17. **P**	18. **C**		

Exercise 3: Identify each pair of words as synonyms or antonyms by putting parentheses ( ) around **syn** or **ant**.

1. fable, fiction	**(syn)** ant	5. rude, impolite	**(syn)** ant	9. emerge, disappear	syn **(ant)**
2. hesitate, pause	**(syn)** ant	6. deplore, approve	syn **(ant)**	10. creeping, rushing	syn **(ant)**
3. hope, despair	syn **(ant)**	7. genuine, fake	syn **(ant)**	11. delicious, tasty	**(syn)** ant
4. conceal, hide	**(syn)** ant	8. sway, influence	**(syn)** ant	12. petite, large	syn **(ant)**

Exercise 4: Part A: Underline each noun to be made possessive and write singular or plural (**S-P**), the rule number, and the possessive form. Part B: Write each noun as singular possessive and then as plural possessive.

1. For a singular noun - add (**'s**)			2. For a plural noun that ends in **s** - add (**'**)		3. For a plural noun that does not end in **s** - add (**'s**)	
Rule 1: girl's			**Rule 2: girls'**		**Rule 3: women's**	
Part A	S-P	Rule	Possessive Form	Part B	Singular Poss	Plural Poss
1. tractor warranty	S	1	**tractor's warranty**	12. knife	**knife's**	**knives'**
2. actors roles	P	2	**actors' roles**	13. saddle	**saddle's**	**saddles'**
3. oxen yokes	P	3	**oxen's yokes**	14. penny	**penny's**	**pennies'**
4. lemon rind	S	1	**lemon's rind**	15. woman	**woman's**	**women's**
5. men wives	P	3	**men's wives**	16. monkey	**monkey's**	**monkeys'**
6. Jessie address	S	1	**Jessie's address**	17. captain	**captain's**	**captains'**
7. roses thorns	P	2	**roses' thorns**	18. child	**child's**	**children's**
8. patients rights	P	2	**patients' rights**	19. parrot	**parrot's**	**parrots'**
9. curtain design	S	1	**curtain's design**	20. party	**party's**	**parties'**
10. wives closets	P	2	**wives' closets**	21. wolf	**wolf's**	**wolves'**
11. children concerns	P	3	**children's concerns**	22. radio	**radio's**	**radios'**

Exercise 5: On notebook paper, write one sentence for each of these labels: ① **S** ② **SCS** ③ **SCV** ④ **CD**. **(Answers will vary.)**

Exercise 6: In your journal, write a paragraph summarizing what you have learned this week.

CHAPTER 15 LESSON 4 CONTINUED

TEACHER INSTRUCTIONS

Use the Question and Answer Flows below for the sentences on the Chapter 15 Test.

Question and Answer Flow for Sentence 1: My grandmother waters the flowers in her yard during the summer months.

1. Who waters the flowers in her yard during the summer months? grandmother - SN
2. What is being said about grandmother? grandmother waters - V
3. Grandmother waters what? flowers - verify the noun
4. Do flowers mean the same thing as grandmother? No.
5. Flowers - DO
6. Waters - V-t
7. The - A
8. In - P
9. In what? yard - OP
10. Whose yard? her - PPA
11. During - P
12. During what? months - OP
13. What kind of months? summer - Adj
14. The - A
15. Whose grandmother? my - PPA
16. SN V-t DO P2 Check
17. Verb-transitive - Check again.
18. (In her yard) - Prepositional phrase
19. (During the summer months) - Prepositional phrase
20. Period, statement, declarative sentence
21. Go back to the verb - divide the complete subject from the complete predicate.

Classified Sentence:

	PPA	SN		V-t	A	DO	P	PPA	OP	P	A	Adj	OP

SN V-t / DO P2   My grandmother / waters the flowers (in her yard) (during the summer months). D

Question and Answer Flow for Sentence 2: The small child would not eat the honeycomb from the beehive.

1. Who would not eat the honeycomb from the beehive? child - SN
2. What is being said about child? child would eat - V
3. Would - HV
4. Child would eat what? honeycomb - verify the noun
5. Does honeycomb mean the same thing as child? No.
6. Honeycomb - DO
7. Eat - V-t
8. The - A
9. From - P
10. From what? beehive - OP
11. The - A
12. Would eat how? not - Adv
13. What kind of child? small - Adj
14. The - A
15. SN V-t DO P2 Check
16. Verb-transitive - Check again.
17. (From the beehive) - Prepositional phrase
18. Period, statement, declarative sentence
19. Go back to the verb - divide the complete subject from the complete predicate.

Classified Sentence:

	A	Adj	SN	HV	Adv	V-t	A	DO	P	A	OP

SN V-t / DO P2   The small child / would not eat the honeycomb (from the beehive). D

CHAPTER 15   LESSON 5

Objectives: Writing Assignments #19 and #20.

 WRITING TIME

TEACHING SCRIPT FOR PRACTICING DIFFERENT KINDS OF WRITING

Today, you are assigned two different kinds of writing. You will write a five-paragraph expository essay and a three-paragraph persuasive essay. <u>You will revise and edit the five-paragraph expository essay</u>. (_Read the box below for more information about students' writing assignment._) As you edit, make sure you use the checkpoints in the editing checklist provided in Reference 39. Remember to read through the whole essay, starting with the title, and then edit, sentence-by-sentence, using the five-sentence checkpoints for each sentence. Use the paragraph checkpoints to check each paragraph. Remember, your editing is now more detailed and more comprehensive, so take your time.

Writing Assignment Box #1

Writing Assignment #19: Five-Paragraph Expository Essay (First Person)
(Remember, first person pronouns are _I, we, me, us, my, our, mine,_ and _ours._)
Remind students that the 5-paragraph essay has three parts: 1. Introduction 2. Body 3. Conclusion. The body has three paragraphs instead of one. Have students use their regular editing checklist to edit this assignment.

Writing topic: Ways to Make Friends   or   **Why I like to Use the Computer**   or   **Foods I Don't Like**

Your second writing assignment is to write a three-paragraph persuasive essay. (_Read the box below for more information about students' writing assignment._) You do not have to edit this assignment with the editing checklist.

Writing Assignment Box #2

Writing Assignment #20: Three-Paragraph Persuasive Essay (First Person)
(Remember, first person pronouns are _I, we, me, us, my, our, mine,_ and _ours._)
Remind students that the 3-paragraph essay has three parts: 1. Introduction 2. Body 3. Conclusion. The body has one paragraph instead of three.

Writing topic: Why I Should/Should Not Be Allowed to Decorate My Room or **Reasons for Sharing** or
Why I Should/Should Not Be Allowed to the Mall With My Friends

---

TEACHER INSTRUCTIONS FOR CHECKING WRITING ASSIGNMENTS

Read, check, and discuss Writing Assignment #19 after students have finished their final papers. Use the checklists as you check and discuss students' papers. Make sure students are using the regular editing checklist correctly. Read and discuss Writing Assignment #20 for fun and enrichment.

(End of lesson.)

CHAPTER 16   LESSON 1
Objectives: Jingle (Indirect Object), Grammar (Introductory Sentences, indirect objects, add the indirect object to the Noun Check, Oral Skill Builder Check), Practice Exercise, Writing (journal), and Vocabulary #1

JINGLE TIME

Have students turn to the Jingle Section in their books and recite the previously-taught jingles. Then, lead students in reciting the new jingle (*The Indirect Object*) below. Practice the new jingle several times until students can recite it smoothly. Emphasize reciting with a rhythm. Students and teacher should be together! (*Do not try to explain the jingle at this time. Just have fun reciting it.*)

Teacher's Notes: Again, do not spend a large amount of time practicing the new jingles. Students learn the jingles best by spending a small amount of time consistently, **every** day.

Jingle 17:   Indirect Object Jingle
1. An indirect object is a noun or pronoun.
2. An indirect object receives what the direct object names.
3. An indirect object is located between the verb-transitive and the direct object.
4. To find the indirect object, ask TO WHOM or FOR WHOM after the direct object.

GRAMMAR TIME

Put the introductory sentences from the box below on the board. Use these sentences as you go through each new concept covered in your teaching script. For the greatest benefit, students must participate orally with the teacher. (*You might put the introductory sentences on notebook paper if you are doing one-on-one instruction with your students.*)

Chapter 16, Introductory Sentences for Lesson 1
1. _____ Jeff gave Renee a beautiful diamond ring on their tenth anniversary.
2. _____ The salesman sold my mom a vacuum sweeper.
3. _____ Could you give me some help with this flat tire?

TEACHING SCRIPT FOR INDIRECT OBJECTS

Earlier, you learned that nouns can have different jobs, or functions, in a sentence. You have studied three of these jobs already: A noun can be a subject, an object of a preposition, or a direct object. You must remember, however, that a noun used as a subject or direct object is part of a core pattern: **SN V** or **SN V-t DO**. But a noun that is used as an object of a preposition is not part of a core sentence pattern.

Level 4 Homeschool Teacher's Manual

© SHURLEY INSTRUCTIONAL MATERIALS, INC.

CHAPTER 16 LESSON 1 CONTINUED

In the new sentence pattern, **Pattern 3**, there are three nouns in the core sentence pattern: **N V N N** The <u>first</u> noun is a subject noun and is still written as **SN**. The <u>third</u> noun is a direct object and is still written as **DO**. The verb is labeled **V-t** after identifying the direct object. The <u>second</u> noun is called an indirect object and is written with the abbreviation **IO**. The indirect object will *always* come between the verb and the direct object. This third pattern in Shurley English is *subject noun / verb-transitive / indirect object / direct object / Pattern 3,* and it is written as **SN V-t IO DO P3**.

There are five basic things you need to know about an indirect object. For this information, look at Reference 49 on page 42 in the Reference Section of your book and follow along as I read this information to you. I want you to notice that these five things are very similar to the Indirect Object Jingle. You will read the Question and Answer Flow for the Sample Sentence with me so you will know what to say when you classify Pattern 3 sentences. (*Read the information about indirect objects to your students. Then, have students read and classify the Sample Sentence orally with you.*)

Reference 49: Indirect Object and Pattern 3

1. An **indirect object** is a noun or pronoun.

2. An **indirect object** receives what the direct object names.

3. An **indirect object** is located between the verb-transitive and the direct object.

4. An **indirect object** is labeled as **IO**.

5. To find the **indirect object**, ask TO WHOM or FOR WHOM after the direct object.

Sample Sentence   for the exact words to say to find the indirect object.

1. Mother baked me a cake.
2. Who baked me a cake? Mother - SN
3. What is being said about Mother? Mother baked - V
4. Mother baked what? cake - verify the noun
5. Does cake mean the same thing as Mother? No.
6. Cake - DO
7. Baked - V-t
8. Mother baked cake for whom? me - IO
   (*Say: Me - indirect object.*)
9. A - A

10. SN V-t IO DO P3 Check
    (Say: Subject Noun, Verb-transitive, Indirect Object, Direct Object, Pattern 3, Check.) (This first check is to make sure the "t" is added to the verb.)

11. Verb-transitive - check again.
    ("Check again" means to check for prepositional phrases and then go through the rest of the Question and Answer Flow.)

12. No prepositional phrases.

13. Period, statement, declarative sentence.

14. Go back to the verb - divide the complete subject from the complete predicate.

I will now ask you some questions to make sure you understand what has been taught. What is Pattern 3? (*SN V-t IO DO*) What are the core parts of a Pattern 3 sentence? (*SN V-t IO DO*). What parts of speech are used in a Pattern 3 sentence use? (*N V N N*) You will use the information you have just learned as you classify this first set of sentences with me to find the indirect object. Begin.

CHAPTER 16 LESSON 1 CONTINUED

Question and Answer Flow for Sentence 1: Jeff gave Renee a beautiful diamond ring on their tenth anniversary.

1. Who gave Renee a beautiful diamond ring on their tenth anniversary? Jeff - SN
2. What is being said about Jeff? Jeff gave - V
3. Jeff gave what? ring - verify the noun
4. Does ring mean the same thing as Jeff? No.
5. Ring - DO
6. Gave - V-t

Note: Ask the indirect object question after the direct object has been identified.

7. Jeff gave ring to whom? Renee - IO (indirect object)

Note: Always get the core, SN V-t IO DO, before you classify the rest of the sentence.

8. What kind of ring? diamond - Adj
9. What kind of ring? beautiful - Adj
10. A - A
11. On - P
12. On what? anniversary - OP
13. Which anniversary? tenth - Adj
14. Whose anniversary? their - PPA
15. SN V-t IO DO P3 Check (Subject noun, verb-transitive, indirect object, direct object ,Pattern 3, Check)
16. Verb-transitive - Check again.
17. (On their tenth anniversary) - Prepositional phrase
18. Period, statement, declarative sentence
19. Go back to the verb - divide the complete subject from the complete predicate.

Classified Sentence:

SN V-t | IO A Adj Adj DO P PPA Adj OP

<u>SN V-t</u> / IO DO P3   Jeff / gave Renee a beautiful diamond ring (on their tenth anniversary). **D**

Question and Answer Flow for Sentence 2: The salesman sold my mom a vacuum sweeper.

1. Who sold my mom a vacuum sweeper? salesman - SN
2. What is being said about salesman? salesman sold - V
3. Salesman sold what? sweeper - verify the noun
4. Does sweeper mean the same thing as salesman? No.
5. Sweeper - DO
6. Sold - V-t
7. Salesman sold sweeper to whom? mom - IO
8. What kind of sweeper? vacuum - Adj
9. A - A
10. Whose mom? my - PPA
11. The - A
12. SN V-t IO DO P3 Check
13. Verb-transitive - Check again.
14. No prepositional phrases.
15. Period, statement, declarative sentence
16. Go back to the verb - divide the complete subject from the complete predicate.

Classified Sentence:

A SN V-t PPA IO A Adj DO

<u>SN V-t</u> / IO DO P3   The salesman / sold my mom a vacuum sweeper. **D**

Question and Answer Flow for Sentence 3: Could you give me some help with this flat tire?

1. Who could give me some help with this flat tire? you - SP
2. What is being said about you? you could give - V
3. Could - HV
4. You could give what? help - verify the noun
5. Does help mean the same thing as you? No.
6. Help - DO
7. Give - V-t
8. You could give help to whom? me - IO
9. What kind of help? some - Adj
10. With - P
11. With what? tire - OP
12. What kind of tire? flat - Adj
13. Which tire? this - Adj
14. SN V-t IO DO P3 Check
15. Verb-transitive - Check again.
16. (With this flat tire) - Prepositional phrase
17. Question mark, question, interrogative sentence
18. Go back to the verb - divide the complete subject from the complete predicate.
19. This sentence has predicate words in the complete subject. Underline the helping verb at the beginning of the sentence twice.

Classified Sentence:

HV SP V-t IO Adj DO P Adj Adj OP

<u>SN V-t</u> / IO DO P3   <u>Could</u> you / give me some help (with this flat tire)? **Int**

CHAPTER 16 LESSON 1 CONTINUED

Teacher's Notes: The verb-transitive check is continued for Pattern 3 because students might forget to add the "t" to the verb. If they leave the "t" off, it is wrong. This is the reason the verb-transitive check is so important for them to remember.

TEACHING SCRIPT FOR ADDING THE INDIRECT OBJECTS TO THE NOUN CHECK

Name the noun jobs we have had before today. (*SN, OP, and DO*) Today, we have added another noun job. What is the new noun job that we have just added? (*indirect object - IO*) So, if I want to find nouns in a sentence, where would I go? (*To the SN, OP, DO, or IO jobs*) After I go to the subject noun, object of the preposition, direct object, and indirect object jobs, what do I do next? (*Check each job to see if the word is a noun or a pronoun. If it is a pronoun, move to the next job. If it is a noun, circle it to indicate that it is a noun.*)

Oral Skill Builder Check	
1. Noun check. (Say the job and then say the noun. Circle each noun.)	**5. Identify the complete subject and the complete predicate.** (Underline the complete subject once and the complete predicate twice.)
2. Identify the nouns as singular or plural. (Write **S** or **P** above each noun.)	**6. Identify the simple subject and simple predicate.** (Underline the simple subject once and the simple predicate twice. Bold, or highlight, the lines.)
3. Identify the nouns as common or proper. (Follow established procedure for oral identification.)	
4. Do a vocabulary check. (Follow established procedure for oral identification.)	**7. Recite the irregular verb chart.** (Located on student page 23 and teacher page 138.)

 PRACTICE TIME

Students will continue their practice of making nouns possessive. Have students turn to pages 78 and 79 in the Practice Section of their book and find Chapter 16, Lesson 1, Practice (1-3). Go over the directions to make sure they understand what to do. Check and discuss the Practices after students have finished. (*Chapter 16, Lesson 1, Practice keys are given below and on the next page.*)

Chapter 16, Lesson 1, Practice 1: Part A: Underline each noun to be made possessive and write singular or plural (**S-P**), the rule number, and the possessive form. Part B: Write each noun as singular possessive and then as plural possessive.

1. For a singular noun - add (**'s**)			2. For a plural noun that ends in **s** - add (**'**)		3. For a plural noun that does not end in **s** - add (**'s**)		
Rule 1: girl's			**Rule 2: girls'**		**Rule 3: women's**		
Part A	**S-P**	**Rule**	**Possessive Form**	**Part B**	**Singular Poss**	**Plural Poss**	
1. <u>Ernie</u> idea	S	1	**Ernie's idea**	5. man	**man's**	**men's**	
2. <u>horse</u> mane	S	1	**horse's mane**	6. diary	**diary's**	**diaries'**	
3. <u>Helen</u> slipper	S	1	**Helen's slipper**	7. roof	**roof's**	**roofs'**	
4. <u>frogs</u> skin	P	2	**frogs' skin**	8. wolf	**wolf's**	**wolves'**	

CHAPTER 16 LESSON 1 CONTINUED

Chapter 16, Lesson 1, Practice 2: Choose an answer from the pronoun choices in parentheses. Fill in the other columns according to the titles. (**S** or **P** stands for singular or plural.)

Pronoun-antecedent agreement

1. The teacher asked the class to read to (<u>her</u>, them).
2. My parents painted (his, <u>their</u>) barn yesterday.
3. Connie admired her father and wrote about (her, <u>him</u>).
4. Mom hugged Joe and gave (<u>him</u>, her) encouragement.
5. The computers lost (its, <u>their</u>) connections.

Pronoun Choice	S or P	Antecedent	S or P
her	S	teacher	S
their	P	parents	P
him	S	father	S
him	S	Joe	S
their	P	computers	P

Chapter 16, Lesson 1, Practice 3: Identify each kind of sentence by writing the abbreviation in the blank. (**S, F, SCS, SCV, CD**).

<u>CD</u>   1. She wrote a novel, but it has not been published.

<u>SCS</u>   2. Our aunt and uncle traveled to Europe with their friends.

<u>F</u>   3. In the cafeteria for two hours.

<u>S</u>   4. She washed the dishes for her mother.

<u>SCV</u>   5. Larry's brother rested and ate under the shade tree.

<u>CD</u>   6. The sun came out, but it was still raining.

WRITING TIME

Have students make an entry in their journals.

VOCABULARY TIME

Assign Chapter 16, Vocabulary Words **#1** on page 9 in the Reference Section for students to define in their Vocabulary notebooks. Tell students they are to use a dictionary or thesaurus to look up the meanings of the vocabulary words. After they write each word and its meaning, students are to write a sentence using the vocabulary word.

Chapter 16, Vocabulary Words #1
(mock, mimic, drought, flood)

(End of lesson.)

CHAPTER 16 LESSON 2

Objectives: Jingles, Grammar (Practice Sentences, Oral Skill Builder Check), Independent Pattern 3 Practice Sentence, Vocabulary #2, and Practice Exercise.

JINGLE TIME

Have students turn to the Jingle Section in their books and recite the previously-taught jingles.

GRAMMAR TIME

First-Year Option: Put the Practice Sentences from the box below on the board or on notebook paper. Use these sentences as you practice the concepts that have been taught. For the greatest benefit, students must participate orally with the teacher. **Second-Year Option:** Have students classify the Practice Sentences independently on notebook paper. Check students' sentences with the answers provided below. (*If you have the CDs for Practice Sentences, have students check their sentences with the CDs.*)

Chapter 16, Practice Sentences for Lesson 2
1. _____ Did Ben give you a copy of the school newspaper?
2. _____ Sarah and Emily offered us punch and cookies at the reception.
3. _____ Give me the key to the front door.

TEACHING SCRIPT FOR PRACTICING PATTERN 3 SENTENCES

We will classify three different sentences to practice Pattern 3 sentences. We will classify the sentences together. Begin. (*You might have your students write the labels above the sentences at this time.*)

Question and Answer Flow for Sentence 1: Did Ben give you a copy of the school newspaper?

1. Who did give you a copy of the school newspaper? Ben - SN
2. What is being said about Ben? Ben did give - V
3. Did - HV
4. Ben did give what? copy - verify the noun
5. Does copy mean the same thing as Ben? No.
6. Copy - DO
7. Give - V-t
8. Ben did give copy to whom? you - IO
9. A - A
10. Of - P
11. Of what? newspaper - OP
12. What kind of newspaper? school - Adj
13. The - A
14. SN V-t IO DO P3 Check
15. Verb-transitive - Check again.
16. (Of the school newspaper) - Prepositional phrase
17. Question mark, question, interrogative sentence
18. Go back to the verb - divide the complete subject from the complete predicate.
19. This sentence has predicate words in the complete subject. Underline the helping verb at the beginning of the sentence twice.

Classified Sentence:

```
                        HV SN    V-t IO A DO   P A   Adj     OP
         SN  V-t       Did Ben / give you a copy (of the school newspaper)?  Int
         IO DO  P3
```

CHAPTER 16 LESSON 2 CONTINUED

Question and Answer Flow for Sentence 2: Sarah and Emily offered us punch and cookies at the reception.

1. Who offered us punch and cookies at the reception?
   Sarah and Emily - CSN, CSN
2. What is being said about Sarah and Emily?
   Sarah and Emily offered - V
3. Sarah and Emily offered what?
   punch and cookies - verify the nouns
4. Do punch and cookies mean the same thing as Sarah and Emily? No.
5. Punch and cookies - CDO, CDO
6. Offered - V-t
7. Sarah and Emily offered punch and cookies to whom?
   us - IO

8. And - C
9. At - P
10. At what? reception - OP
11. The - A
12. And - C
13. SN V-t IO DO P3 Check
14. Verb-transitive - Check again.
15. (At the reception) - Prepositional phrase
16. Period, statement, declarative sentence
17. Go back to the verb - divide the complete subject from the complete predicate.

Classified Sentence:

```
                              CSN  C  CSN   V-t  IO CDO  C  CDO   P  A    OP
         SN  V-t       Sarah and Emily / offered us punch and cookies (at the reception).  D
         IO DO P3
```

Question and Answer Flow for Sentence 3: Give me the key to the front door.

1. Who give me the key to the front door?
   you - SP (Understood subject pronoun)
2. What is being said about you? you give - V
3. You give what? key - verify the noun
4. Does key mean the same thing as you? No.
5. Key - DO
6. Give - V-t
7. You give key to whom? me - IO
8. The - A
9. To - P

10. To what? door - OP
11. What kind of door? front - Adj
12. The - A
13. SN V-t IO DO P3 Check
14. Verb-transitive - Check again.
15. (To the front door) - Prepositional phrase
16. Period, command, imperative sentence
17. Go back to the verb - divide the complete subject from the complete predicate.

Classified Sentence:

```
              (You) SP      V-t  IO  A  DO  P  A  Adj OP
              SN  V-t       / Give me the key (to the front door).  Imp
              IO DO P3
```

TEACHER INSTRUCTIONS

Use Sentences 1-3 that you just classified with your students to do an Oral Skill Builder Check.

Oral Skill Builder Check

1. **Noun check.**
   (Say the job and then say the noun. Circle each noun.)
2. **Identify the nouns as singular or plural.**
   (Write **S** or **P** above each noun.)
3. **Identify the nouns as common or proper.**
   (Follow established procedure for oral identification.)
4. **Do a vocabulary check.**
   (Follow established procedure for oral identification.)

5. **Identify the complete subject and the complete predicate.** (Underline the complete subject once and the complete predicate twice.)
6. **Identify the simple subject and simple predicate.**
   (Underline the simple subject once and the simple predicate twice. Bold, or highlight, the lines.)
7. **Recite the irregular verb chart.**
   (Located on student page 23 and teacher page 138.)

CHAPTER 16 LESSON 2 CONTINUED

TEACHING SCRIPT FOR INTRODUCING A PATTERN 3 PRACTICE SENTENCE

Get out a sheet of notebook paper. On the top line of your notebook paper, write the title *Pattern 3 Practice Sentence.* (*Put this title on the board:* **Pattern 3 Sentence**.) I will guide you through the process as we learn to write a Pattern 3 sentence.

You have already learned how to write independent Pattern 1 and Pattern 2 sentences according to labels you select. You will now learn how to write an independent Pattern 3 sentence the same way. First, you start out with the core labels for a Pattern 3 sentence. This means that you <u>must always have a subject, a verb-transitive, an indirect object, and a direct object before you add any extra parts</u>.

You build the rest of your Pattern 3 sentence from the regular sentence parts learned in Pattern 1. I will ask you a few questions to make sure you understand. What are the parts of a Pattern 3 sentence that YOU MUST USE? (*All Pattern 3 sentences must have a subject, a verb-transitive, an indirect object, and a direct object.*) I want you to name the extra sentence parts that you can use with your sentence. There are ten parts. (*adjectives, adverbs, articles, prepositional phrases, subject pronouns, possessive nouns, possessive pronouns, helping verbs, conjunctions, and interjections*) Remember, you will use the core parts of a Pattern 3 sentence and then add the extra parts that you want your sentence to have.

Let's write the labels for a Pattern 3 sentence on a sheet of notebook paper. First, write the *SN V-t IO* and *DO* labels that a Pattern 3 sentence must have on your paper. Be sure to place them in the middle of your paper. (*Demonstrate by writing the SN V-t IO DO labels on the board.*) Using what you know about writing Practice Sentences, you must decide what other parts you want to add to your Pattern 3 sentence. (*Have students finish writing a Pattern 3 sentence and turn it in to you. Students do not have to write an Improved Sentence at this point unless you feel they need the practice. If your students cannot handle this much independence so soon, give them the labels you want them to follow for a Pattern 3 sentence. Sample: (A Adj Adj SN V-t PPA IO A Adj Adj DO P PPA OP) Check and discuss students' sentences after they have finished.*)

 VOCABULARY TIME

Assign Chapter 16, Vocabulary Words **#2** on page 9 in the Reference Section for students to define in their Vocabulary notebooks. Tell students they are to use a dictionary or thesaurus to look up the meanings of the vocabulary words. After they write each word and its meaning, students are to write a sentence using the vocabulary word.

Chapter 16, Vocabulary Words #2
(nervous, uneasy, important, petty)

 PRACTICE TIME

Have students write the three sentences that they classify at the beginning of the lesson on a sheet of paper. Have them tape-record the Question and Answer Flows for all three sentences. Students should write labels above the sentences as they classify them. They especially need the second practice if this is their first year in the program. (*After the students have finished, check the tape and sentence labels. Make sure students understand any mistakes they have made.*)

(End of lesson.)

CHAPTER 16 LESSON 3

Objectives: Jingles, Grammar (Practice Sentences), and Practice Exercise.

JINGLE TIME

Have students turn to the Jingle Section in their books and recite the previously-taught jingles.

GRAMMAR TIME

First-Year Option: Put the Practice Sentences from the box below on the board or on notebook paper. Use these sentences as you practice the concepts that have been taught. For the greatest benefit, students must participate orally with the teacher. **Second-Year Option:** Have students classify the Practice Sentences independently on notebook paper. Check students' sentences with the answers provided below. (*If you have the CDs for Practice Sentences, have students check their sentences with the CDs.*)

Chapter 16, Practice Sentences for Lesson 3
1. _____ The tall city policeman gave my dad a warning for speeding.
2. _____ The sales woman at the mall handed my friends and me some perfume samples.
3. _____ Hooray! Mom fixed us our favorite dessert for dinner!

TEACHING SCRIPT FOR PRACTICING PATTERN 3 SENTENCES

We will classify three different sentences to practice Pattern 3 sentences. We will classify the sentences together. Begin. (*You might have your students write the labels above the sentences at this time.*)

Question and Answer Flow for Sentence 1: The tall city policeman gave my dad a warning for speeding.

1. Who gave my dad a warning for speeding? policeman - SN
2. What is being said about policeman? policeman gave - V
3. Policeman gave what? warning - verify the noun
4. Does warning mean the same thing as policeman? No.
5. Warning - DO
6. Gave - V-t
7. Policeman gave warning to whom? dad - IO
8. A - A
9. For - P
10. For what? speeding - OP
11. Whose dad? my - PPA
12. What kind of policeman? city - Adj
13. What kind of policeman? tall - Adj
14. The - A
15. SN V-t IO DO P3 Check
16. Verb-transitive - Check again.
17. (For speeding) - Prepositional phrase
18. Period, statement, declarative sentence
19. Go back to the verb - divide the complete subject from the complete predicate.

Classified Sentence:

```
                        A  Adj Adj   SN      V-t PPA IO A   DO    P    OP
     SN V-t     The  tall city policeman / gave my dad a warning (for speeding). D
     ‾‾‾‾‾‾
     IO DO P3
```

CHAPTER 16 LESSON 3 CONTINUED

Question and Answer Flow for Sentence 2: The sales woman at the mall handed my friends and me some perfume samples.

1. Who handed my friends and me some perfume samples? woman - SN
2. What is being said about woman? woman handed - V
3. Woman handed what? samples - verify the noun
4. Do samples mean the same thing as woman? No.
5. Samples - DO
6. Handed - V-t
7. Woman handed samples to whom? friends and me - CIO, CIO
8. What kind of samples? perfume - Adj
9. How many samples? some - Adj
10. And - C
11. Whose friends? my - PPA
12. At - P
13. At what? mall - OP
14. The - A
15. What kind of woman? sales - Adj
16. The - A
17. SN V-t IO DO P3 Check
18. Verb-transitive - Check again.
19. (At the mall) - Prepositional phrase
20. Period, statement, declarative sentence
21. Go back to the verb - divide the complete subject from the complete predicate.

Classified Sentence:			
	A Adj SN	P A OP	V-t PPA CIO C CIO Adj Adj DO
SN V-t IO DO P3	The sales woman (at the mall) / handed my friends and me some perfume samples. D

Question and Answer Flow for Sentence 3: Hooray! Mom fixed us our favorite dessert for dinner!

1. Who fixed us our favorite dessert for dinner? Mom - SN
2. What is being said about Mom? Mom fixed - V
3. Mom fixed what? dessert - verify the noun
4. Does dessert mean the same thing as Mom? No.
5. Dessert - DO
6. Fixed - V-t
7. Mom fixed dessert for whom? us - IO
8. What kind of dessert? favorite - Adj
9. Whose dessert? our - PPA
10. For - P
11. For what? dinner - OP
12. Hooray - I
13. SN V-t IO DO P3 Check
14. Verb-transitive - Check again.
15. (For dinner) - Prepositional phrase
16. Exclamation point, strong feeling, exclamatory sentence
17. Go back to the verb - divide the complete subject from the complete predicate.

Classified Sentence:	
	I SN V-t IO PPA Adj DO P OP
SN V-t IO DO P3	Hooray! Mom / fixed us our favorite dessert (for dinner)! E

 PRACTICE TIME

Have students turn to page 80 in the Practice Section of their book and find Chapter 16, Lesson 3, Practice. Go over the directions to make sure they understand what to do. Check and discuss the Practice after students have finished. (*Chapter 16, Lesson 3, Practice key is given below.*)

Chapter 16, Lesson 3, Practice: Part A: Underline each noun to be made possessive and write singular or plural **(S-P),** the rule number, and the possessive form. Part B: Write each noun as singular possessive and then as plural possessive.

1. For a singular noun - add (**'s**)			2. For a plural noun that ends in *s* - add (**'**)		3. For a plural noun that does not end in *s* - add (**'s**)		
Rule 1: girl's			**Rule 2: girls'**		**Rule 3: women's**		
Part A	**S-P**	**Rule**	**Possessive Form**	**Part B**	**Singular Poss**	**Plural Poss**	
1. <u>Sunday</u> sermon	S	1	**Sunday's sermon**	5. wife	**wife's**	**wives'**	
2. <u>wolves</u> howls	P	2	**wolves' howls**	6. glossary	**glossary's**	**glossaries'**	
3. <u>Bill</u> driveway	S	1	**Bill's driveway**	7. woman	**woman's**	**women's**	
4. <u>trucks</u> tires	P	2	**trucks' tires**	8. parent	**parent's**	**parents'**	

(End of lesson.)

CHAPTER 16   LESSON 4

Objectives: Jingles, Study, Test, Check, and Writing (journal).

 **JINGLE TIME**

Have students turn to the Jingle Section in their books and recite the previously-taught jingles.

 STUDY TIME

Have students study the vocabulary words in their vocabulary notebooks. Remind students that any vocabulary word in their notebooks could be on their test. Also, have students study any of the skills in the Practice Section that they need to review.

 TEST TIME

Have students turn to page 113 in the Test Section of their book and find the Chapter 16 Test. Go over the directions to make sure they understand what to do. (*Chapter 16 Test key is on the next page.*)

 CHECK TIME

After students have finished, check and discuss their test papers. Make sure they understand why their answers are right or wrong. (*For total points, count each required answer as a point.*)

(End of lesson.)

Level 4 Homeschool Teacher's Manual

Chapter 16 Test
(Student Page 113)

Exercise 1: Classify each sentence.

```
    (You) SP      V-t  IO  A  DO   P   PPA  Adj    Adj     OP
1.  SN  V-t       / Play us a song (on your new electric piano). Imp
    IO  DO  P3
```

```
              SP  V-t   IO   Adj  Adj  DO    P    A    Adj      OP      P   A   Adj   OP
2.  SN  V-t       I / bought you several new shoes (with the special discounts) (from the shoe store).  D
    IO  DO  P3
```

```
              HV   A    SN      V-t  PPA  IO   A   Adj    DO   P   A    OP
3.  SN  V-t       Did the curator / give your group an informative tour (of the museum)?  Int
    IO  DO  P3
```

Exercise 2: Use Sentence 3 to underline the complete subject once and the complete predicate twice and to complete the table below.

List the Noun Used	List the Noun Job	Singular or Plural	Common or Proper	Simple Subject	Simple Predicate
1. **curator**	2. **SN**	3. **S**	4. **C**	5. **curator**	6. **did give**
7. **group**	8. **IO**	9. **S**	10. **C**		
11. **tour**	12. **DO**	13. **S**	14. **C**		
15. **museum**	16. **OP**	17. **S**	18. **C**		

Exercise 3: Identify each pair of words as synonyms or antonyms by putting parentheses ( ) around *syn* or *ant*.

1. adhere, stick	**(syn)** ant	5. auction, buy	syn **(ant)**	9. delicious, tasty	**(syn)** ant
2. petty, important	syn **(ant)**	6. drought, flood	syn **(ant)**	10. finish, commence	syn **(ant)**
3. mock, mimic	**(syn)** ant	7. flashy, plain	syn **(ant)**	11. treaty, agreement	**(syn)** ant
4. bashful, shy	**(syn)** ant	8. nervous, uneasy	**(syn)** ant	12. impetuous, cautious	syn **(ant)**

Exercise 4: Underline the correct homonym in each sentence.

1. We (<u>knew</u>, new) better than to refuse.
2. (Their, <u>There</u>, They're) is the new student.
3. Your perfume has an odd (sent, <u>scent</u>).
4. I wonder if (their, there, <u>they're</u>) still going.
5. The store on the corner is (knew, <u>new</u>).
6. I like (<u>their</u>, there, they're) new swing.

Exercise 5: Identify each kind of sentence by writing the abbreviation in the blank. (**S, F, SCS, SCV, CD**)

  F   1. Beside the workbench in your dad's garage.
  SCS 2. The cat and dog played together.
  SCV 3. Kim researched and typed her essay.
  CD   4. I went to the beach, but I never got in the water.

Exercise 6: Part A: Underline each noun to be made possessive and write singular or plural (**S-P**), the rule number, and the possessive form. Part B: Write each noun as singular possessive and then as plural possessive.

Rule 1: boy's			Rule 2: boys'	Rule 3: men's		
Part A	**S-P**	**Rule**	**Possessive Form**	**Part B**	**Singular Poss**	**Plural Poss**
1. <u>Edgar</u> homer	**S**	**1**	**Edgar's homer**	5. wife	**wife's**	**wives'**
2. <u>officer</u> badge	**S**	**1**	**officer's badge**	6. fly	**fly's**	**flies'**
3. <u>Kent</u> suitcase	**S**	**1**	**Kent's suitcase**	7. dairy	**dairy's**	**dairies'**
4. <u>patients</u> rights	**P**	**2**	**patients' rights**	8. deer	**deer's**	**deer's**

Exercise 7: In your journal, write a paragraph summarizing what you have learned this week.

CHAPTER 16 LESSON 4 CONTINUED

TEACHER INSTRUCTIONS

Use the Question and Answer Flows below for the sentences on the Chapter 16 Test.

Question and Answer Flow for Sentence 1: Play us a song on your new electric piano.

1. Who play us a song on your new electric piano?
   (You) - SP (Understood subject pronoun)
2. What is being said about you? you play - V
3. You play what? song - verify the noun
4. Does song mean the same thing as you? No.
5. Song - DO
6. Play - V-t
7. You play song for whom? us - IO
8. A - A
9. On - P

10. On what? piano - OP
11. What kind of piano? electric - Adj
12. What kind of piano? new - Adj
13. Whose piano? your - PPA
14. SN V-t IO DO P3 Check
15. Verb-transitive - Check again.
16. (On your new electric piano) - Prepositional phrase
17. Period, command, imperative sentence
18. Go back to the verb - divide the complete subject
    from the complete predicate.

Classified Sentence:

	(You) SP		V-t	IO	A	DO	P	PPA	Adj	Adj	OP
SN V-t		/ Play us a song (on your new electric piano). **Imp**
IO DO P3	

Question and Answer Flow for Sentence 2: I bought you several new shoes with the special discounts from the shoe store.

1. Who bought you several new shoes with the special discounts from the shoe store? I - SP
2. What is being said about I? I bought - V
3. I bought what? shoes - verify the noun
4. Do shoes mean the same thing as I? No.
5. Shoes - DO
6. Bought - V-t
7. I bought shoes for whom? you - IO
8. What kind of shoes? new - Adj
9. How many shoes? several - Adj
10. With - P
11. With what? discounts - OP
12. What kind of discounts? special - Adj

13. The - A
14. From - P
15. From what? store - OP
16. What kind of store? shoe - Adj
17. The - A
18. SN V-t IO DO P3 Check
19. Verb-transitive - Check again.
20. (With the special discounts) - Prepositional phrase
21. (From the shoe store) - Prepositional phrase
22. Period, statement, declarative sentence
23. Go back to the verb - divide the complete subject
    from the complete predicate.

Classified Sentence:

	SP	V-t	IO	Adj	Adj	DO	P	A	Adj	OP	P	A	Adj	OP
SN V-t	I / bought you several new shoes (with the special discounts) (from the shoe store). **D**
IO DO P3

Question and Answer Flow for Sentence 3: Did the curator give your group an informative tour of the museum?

1. Who did give your group an informative tour of the museum? curator - SN
2. What is being said about curator? curator did give - V
3. Did - HV
4. Curator did give what? tour - verify the noun
5. Does tour mean the same thing as curator? No.
6. Tour - DO
7. Give - V-t
8. Curator did give tour to whom? group - IO
9. What kind of tour? informative - Adj
10. An - A
11. Of - P

12. Of what? museum - OP
13. The - A
14. Whose group? your - PPA
15. The - A
16. SN V-t IO DO P3 Check
17. Verb-transitive - Check again.
18. (Of the museum) - Prepositional phrase
19. Question mark, question, interrogative sentence
20. Go back to the verb - divide the complete subject
    from the complete predicate.
21. This sentence has predicate words in the
    complete subject. Underline the helping verb at
    the beginning of the sentence twice

Classified Sentence:

	HV	A	SN	V-t	PPA	IO	A	Adj	DO	P	A	OP
SN V-t	Did the curator / give your group an informative tour (of the museum)? **Int**
IO DO P3

CHAPTER 16   LESSON 5

Objectives: Writing Assignments #21 and #22, Bonus Option.

 WRITING TIME

TEACHING SCRIPT FOR PRACTICING DIFFERENT KINDS OF WRITING

Today, you are assigned two different kinds of writing. You will write a five-paragraph persuasive essay and a three-paragraph expository essay. <u>You will revise and edit the five-paragraph persuasive essay</u>. (*Read the box below for more information about students' writing assignment.*) As you edit, make sure you use the checkpoints in the editing checklist provided in Reference 39. Remember to read through the whole essay, starting with the title, and then edit, sentence-by-sentence, using the five-sentence checkpoints for each sentence. Use the paragraph checkpoints to check each paragraph.

Writing Assignment Box #1

Writing Assignment #21: Five-Paragraph Persuasive Essay (First or Third Person)
(Remember, first person pronouns are *I, we, me, us, my, our, mine,* and *ours.*)
Remind students that the 5-paragraph essay has three parts: 1. Introduction 2. Body 3. Conclusion. The body has three paragraphs instead of one. Have students use their regular editing checklist to edit this assignment.

Writing topics: Why I Should/Should Not Get an Allowance or **Why I Should Have My Own Computer** or
Snakes Make/Do Not Make Good Pets

Your second writing assignment is to write a three-paragraph expository essay. (*Read the box below for more information about students' writing assignment.*) You do not have to edit this assignment with the editing checklist.

Writing Assignment Box #2

Writing Assignment #22: Three-Paragraph Expository Essay (First or Third Person)
(Remember, first person pronouns are *I, we, me, us, my, our, mine,* and *ours.*)
Remind students that the 3-paragraph essay has three parts: 1. Introduction 2. Body 3. Conclusion. The body has one paragraph instead of three.

Writing topics: Things to Do During Severe Weather or **Insects I Hate** or **Favorite Famous Americans**

Bonus Option: How many books are in the Old Testament? (*39*) **Look up all the books of the Old Testament and list them in your Journal. Next, create a word search that contains all the books of the Old Testament. Be careful to spell all the names correctly. Give the word search to a family member to complete. Make a key so you can check the finished word search.**

TEACHER INSTRUCTIONS FOR CHECKING WRITING ASSIGNMENTS

Read, check, and discuss Writing Assignment #21 after students have finished their final papers. Use the checklists as you check and discuss students' papers. Make sure students are using the regular editing checklist correctly. Read and discuss Writing Assignment #22 for fun and enrichment.

(End of lesson.)

CHAPTER 17   LESSON 1

Objectives: Jingles, Grammar (Practice Sentences, Oral Skill Builder Check), Skills (beginning quotes, ending quotes), Practice Exercise, Writing (journal), and Vocabulary #1.

 JINGLE TIME

Have students turn to the Jingle Section in their books and recite the previously-taught jingles.

 GRAMMAR TIME

First-Year Option: Put the Practice Sentences from the box below on the board or on notebook paper. Use these sentences as you practice the concepts that have been taught. For the greatest benefit, students must participate orally with the teacher. **Second-Year Option:** Have students classify the Practice Sentences independently on notebook paper. Check students' sentences with the answers provided below. (*If you have the CDs for Practice Sentences, have students check their sentences with the CDs.*)

Chapter 17, Practice Sentences for Lesson 1
1. _____ Coach McGee ordered us new soccer uniforms for our championship game.
2. _____ Give me your address and telephone number for the church directory.

TEACHING SCRIPT FOR PRACTICING PATTERN 3 SENTENCES

We will practice Classifying Pattern 3 sentences. We will classify the sentences together. Begin. (*You might have your students write the labels above the sentences at this time.*)

Question and Answer Flow for Sentence 1: Coach McGee ordered us new soccer uniforms for our championship game.

1. Who ordered us new soccer uniforms for our championship game? Coach McGee - SN
2. What is being said about Coach McGee? Coach McGee ordered - V
3. Coach McGee ordered what? uniforms - verify the noun
4. Do uniforms mean the same thing as Coach McGee? No.
5. Uniforms - DO
6. Ordered - V-t
7. Coach McGee ordered uniforms for whom? us - IO
8. What kind of uniforms? soccer - Adj
9. What kind of uniforms? new - Adj
10. For - P
11. For what? game - OP
12. What kind of game? championship - Adj
13. Whose game? our - PPA
14. SN V-t IO DO P3 Check
15. Verb-transitive - Check again.
16. (For our championship game) - Prepositional phrase
17. Period, statement, declarative sentence
18. Go back to the verb - divide the complete subject from the complete predicate.

Classified Sentence:

		SN	V-t	IO Adj	Adj	DO	P	PPA	Adj	OP

SN V-t / Coach McGee / ordered us new soccer uniforms (for our championship game). **D**
IO DO P3

CHAPTER 17 LESSON 1 CONTINUED

Question and Answer Flow for Sentence 2: Give me your address and telephone number for the church directory.

1. Who give me your address and telephone number for the church directory? (You) - SP (Understood subject pronoun)
2. What is being said about you? you give - V
3. You give what? address and number - verify the nouns
4. Do address and number mean the same thing as you? No.
5. Address and number - CDO, CDO
6. Give - V-t
7. You give address and number to whom? me - IO
8. Whose address and number? your - PPA
9. And - C
10. What kind of number? telephone - Adj
11. For - P
12. For what? directory - OP
13. What kind of directory? church - Adj
14. The - A
15. SN V-t IO DO P3 Check
16. Verb-transitive - Check again.
17. (For the church directory) - Prepositional phrase
18. Period, command, imperative sentence
19. Go back to the verb - divide the complete subject from the complete predicate.

Classified Sentence:

(You) SP   V-t   IO   PPA   CDO   C   Adj   CDO   P   A   Adj   OP
SN V-t / Give me your address and telephone number (for the church directory). **Imp**
IO DO P3

Use Sentences 1-2 that you just classified with your students to do an Oral Skill Builder Check. Use the guidelines below.

Oral Skill Builder Check

1. **Noun check.**
   (Say the job and then say the noun. Circle each noun.)
2. **Identify the nouns as singular or plural.**
   (Write **S** or **P** above each noun.)
3. **Identify the nouns as common or proper.**
   (Follow established procedure for oral identification.)
4. **Do a vocabulary check.**
   (Follow established procedure for oral identification.)

5. **Identify the complete subject and the complete predicate.** (Underline the complete subject once and the complete predicate twice.)
6. **Identify the simple subject and simple predicate.**
   (Underline the simple subject once and the simple predicate twice. Bold, or highlight, the lines.)
7. **Recite the irregular verb chart.**
   (Located on student page 23 and teacher page 138.)

SKILL TIME

TEACHING SCRIPT FOR BEGINNING QUOTES

I am going to read you two short stories. They are the same story, but they are written two different ways. When I am finished, I want you to tell me if you enjoyed Story 1 or Story 2 the best.

Story 1

Laura and Audrey were bubbling with excitement. They were getting ready to stay all summer with their aunt in Colorado. Their flight would leave from the Dallas/Ft. Worth Airport at 2:00, and it was almost noon. Laura went through the checklist one more time to make sure that everything was packed. Audrey checked the flight times and memorized the gate numbers. Neither of the girls could relax. There was a lot of excitement in the air.

Story 2

> "I can hardly wait! A whole summer with Aunt Debbie!" exclaimed Audrey. She grabbed the tickets and sat down with them for one last look. Laura looked up from her checklist. "I'm excited too, but are you sure we have everything?" She looked back down and began making marks. "Hairbrush, make-up, toothbrush, toothpaste. Are you sure we packed the toothpaste?"
>
> "For the third time, yes! Even if we forgot it, don't you think Aunt Debbie would have toothpaste that we could use?" Audrey sighed and looked back at the tickets and began talking to herself. "The flight leaves at 2:00 from gate 12, or was it gate 21?"
>
> "I know I shouldn't worry so much, but I'm just so excited. We're going to have a wonderful summer!" Laura said as she sat down on the floor by the pile of suitcases.

Did you enjoy Story 1 or Story 2 the best? (*Discuss reasons your students give for their preferences.*) Quotations are used to make your writing come alive and to make your readers believe that they are right in the middle of the action. Quotations help build pictures for your readers as the story unfolds. In Story 2, the action was direct, vigorous, and strong. In Story 1, the action was indirect and a little weak, even though the meanings of the two stories were almost identical. You will use quotations more if you understand how to write them correctly. Quotations are fun to use, but, as all good writers know, to learn the basic rules requires a little effort.

Quotations are words spoken by someone, and quotation marks are used to set off the exact words that are spoken. The words set off by quotation marks are usually called a direct quotation. In your writing, you will often find it necessary to tell what someone has said, and you will need to know several rules of punctuation in order to write quotations.

We will start with how to punctuate beginning quotes. Look at Reference 50 on page 42 in the Reference Section of your book. We will go through each rule as we punctuate the guided sample sentence in the rule box for beginning quotes. (*It would be best to put the guided sentence on the board so students can follow each step as you write it. Read the step-by-step teaching script for beginning quotes on the next page.*)

Reference 50: Quotation Rules for Beginning Quotes

1. **Pattern:** "**C** -quote- **(,!?)** " explanatory words **(.)**
   (Quotation marks, capital letter, quote, end punctuation choice, quotation marks closed, explanatory words, period)
2. Underline **end explanatory words** and use a period at the end.
3. You should have a **beginning quote** – Use quotation marks at the beginning and end of what is said. Then, put a comma, question mark, or exclamation point (no period) after the quote but in front of the quotation marks.
4. **Capitalize** the beginning of the quote, any proper nouns, or the pronoun *I*.
5. **Punctuate** the rest of the sentence by checking for any apostrophes, periods, or commas that may be needed within the sentence.

Guided Practice
Sentence: the girls and i are writing invitations next monday with mrs kemp andy said

1. Pattern: "**C** -quote- **(,!?)** " explanatory words **(.)**
2. the girls and i are writing invitations next monday with mrs kemp **andy said(.)**
3. "the girls and i are writing invitations next monday with mrs kemp,**"** andy said.
4. "**The** girls and **I** are writing invitations next **Monday** with **Mrs Kemp**," Andy said.
5. "The girls and I are writing invitations next Monday with Mrs. Kemp," Andy said.
6. **Corrected Sentence:** "The girls and I are writing invitations next Monday with Mrs. Kemp," Andy said.

CHAPTER 17 LESSON 1 CONTINUED

You will never have trouble punctuating beginning quotations if you follow these simple quotation rules because they tell you exactly what to do to the whole sentence. Look at the sentence under the Guided Practice and read the sentence with me: (*the girls and i are writing invitations next monday with mrs kemp andy said*). We will break it up into sections, and then we will punctuate each section.

First, you always write a pattern to follow, so we will write the pattern for a beginning quote. That's number one under your rules. Let's read what the pattern says: **"C** *-quote- (,!?)* **"** *explanatory words* **(.).** I will translate the pattern for you: quotation marks, capital letter to begin a quote, the quote itself, a choice of end mark (,!?), quotation marks, explanatory words, and a period. You will understand it better as I explain each part to you.

Look at Rule 2. Rule 2 says to underline *end explanatory words* and use a period at the end. Explanatory words are the words that explain who is talking but are not part of the actual quote. Any time you have a beginning quote, your explanatory words will be at the end. What are the explanatory words at the end of this sentence? (*andy said*) (*Underline these explanatory words and put a period at the end.*)

Look at Rule 3. Rule 3 says, for beginning quotes, use quotation marks at the beginning and end of what is said. Which words need quotation marks at the beginning and end? (*"the girls and i are writing invitations next monday with mrs kemp "*) (*Put quotation marks around these words.*) Rule 3 also says to put a comma, question mark, or exclamation point (but no period) after the quote but in front of the quotation mark. Which punctuation mark would you use and why? (*Use a comma because the sentence is a statement, not a question or an exclamation.*) (*Put a comma after* **kemp** *but in front of the quotation marks.*)

Look at Rule 4. Rule 4 says to capitalize the beginning of the quote, any proper nouns, or the pronoun *I*. Which words would be capitalized in this sentence? (*The, I, Monday, Mrs, Kemp, Andy*) (*Capitalize these words.*)

Look at Rule 5. Rule 5 says to punctuate the rest of the sentence by checking for any apostrophes, periods, or commas that may be needed within the sentence. What punctuation is needed in this sentence? (*A period is needed after* **Mrs.** *because it is a person's title.*) (*Punctuate this abbreviation.*)

Now, we have a corrected sentence. Wasn't that easy? For a final check, I will go through the corrected sentence using the quotation pattern only. You will still have to remember to capitalize and punctuate the rest of the sentence, but this pattern will help you remember how to punctuate a beginning quote correctly. (*As you read each part of the quotation pattern, point out that part in the corrected sentence.*)
"C *-quote- (,!?)* **"** *explanatory words* **(.)**

TEACHING SCRIPT FOR ENDING QUOTES

Look at Reference 51 for end quotes on page 43. We will go through each rule as we punctuate the guided sample sentence in the rule box for end quotes. (*It would be best to put the guided sentence on the board so students can follow each step as you write it. Read the step-by-step teaching script for end quotes on the next page.*)

CHAPTER 17 LESSON 1 CONTINUED

Reference 51: Quotation Rules for End Quotes

1. **Pattern:** <u>C</u> - explanatory words(,) "**C** -quote- **(.!?)** "
   (Capital letter, explanatory words, comma, quotation marks, capital letter, quote, end punctuation choice, quotation marks closed)

2. Underline **beginning explanatory words** and use a comma after them.

3. You should have an **end quote** – Use quotation marks at the beginning and end of what is said. Then, put a period, question mark, or exclamation point (no comma) after the quote, but in front of the quotation marks.

4. **Capitalize** the first of the explanatory words at the beginning of a sentence, the beginning of the quote, and any proper nouns or the pronoun *I*.

5. **Punctuate** the rest of the sentence by checking for any apostrophes, periods, or commas that may be needed within the sentence.

Guided Practice

Sentence: andy said the girls and i are writing invitations next monday with mrs kemp

1. Pattern: <u>C</u> - explanatory words(,) "**C** -quote- **(.!?)** "

2. <u>**andy said**</u>**(,)** the girls and i are writing invitations next monday with mrs kemp

3. <u>andy said</u>, "the girls and i are writing invitations next monday with mrs kemp**.** "

4. <u>Andy said</u>, "The girls and **I** are writing invitations next **M**onday with **Mrs K**emp."

5. <u>Andy said</u>, "The girls and I are writing invitations next Monday with Mrs**.** Kemp."

6. **Corrected Sentence:** Andy said, "The girls and I are writing invitations next Monday with Mrs. Kemp."

You will never have trouble punctuating end quotations if you follow these simple rules because they tell you exactly what to do to the whole sentence. Look at the sentence under the Guided Practice and read the sentence with me: (*andy said the girls and i are writing invitations next Monday with mrs kemp*). We will break it up into sections, and then we will punctuate each section.

First, you always write a pattern to follow, so we will write the pattern for an end quote. That's number one under your rules. Let's read what the pattern says: *C -explanatory words(,) "C -quote- (.!?) "*. I will translate the pattern for you: capital letter to begin the explanatory words, the explanatory words, comma, quotation marks, capital letter to begin the quotation, a choice of end marks (.!?), and quotation marks.

Look at Rule 2. Rule 2 says to underline *beginning explanatory words* and use a comma after them. Remember, explanatory words are the words that explain who is talking but are not part of the actual quote. What are the explanatory words at the beginning of this sentence? (*andy said*) (*Underline these explanatory words and put a comma after* **said***.*)

Look at Rule 3. Rule 3 says, for end quotes, use quotation marks at the beginning and end of what is said. What words need quotation marks around them? (*"the girls and i are writing invitations next monday with mrs kemp"*) (*Put quotation marks around these words.*) Rule 3 also says to put a period, question mark, or exclamation point (but no comma) after the quote, but in front of the quotation marks. Which punctuation mark would you use and why? (*Use a period because the sentence is a statement, not a question or an exclamation.*) (*Put a period after* **kemp** *but in front of the quotation marks.*)

Look at Rule 4. Rule 4 says to capitalize the first of the explanatory words at the beginning of a sentence, the beginning of the quote, any proper nouns, or the pronoun *I*. Which words would be capitalized in this sentence? (*Andy, The, I, Monday, Mrs, Kemp*) (*Capitalize these words.*)

CHAPTER 17 LESSON 1 CONTINUED

Look at Rule 5. Rule 5 says to punctuate the rest of the sentence by checking for any apostrophes, periods, or commas that may be needed within the sentence. What punctuation is needed in this sentence? (*A period is needed after* **Mrs.** *because it is a person's title.*) (*Punctuate this abbreviation.*)

Now, we have a corrected sentence. For a final check, I will go through the corrected sentence using the quotation pattern only. You will still have to remember to capitalize and punctuate the rest of the sentence, but this pattern will help you remember how to punctuate end quotes correctly. (*As you read each part of the quotation pattern, point out that part in the corrected sentence.*)
<u>**C** -explanatory words</u>**(,) "C** -quote- **(.!?) "**

 PRACTICE TIME

Have students turn to page 80 in the Practice Section of their book and find Chapter 17, Lesson 1, Practice. Go over the directions to make sure they understand what to do. Guide students closely as they do the practice exercises for the first time. (*Students may use the Reference section in their books to help them remember the new information.*) Check and discuss the Practice after students have finished. (*Chapter 17, Lesson 1, Practice key is given below.*)

Chapter 17, Lesson 1, Practice: Use the Quotation Rules to help punctuate the quotations below. Underline the explanatory words.

    G   T   T
1. <u>governor thompson replied</u>, "this is our final offer."

    T   G   T
2. "this is our final offer," <u>governor thompson replied</u>.

    A   C   I   B
3. <u>after the christmas play i exclaimed</u>, "barbara, good job!"

    B   I   C
4. "barbara, good job!" <u>i exclaimed after the christmas play</u>.

 **WRITING TIME**

Have students make an entry in their journals.

 VOCABULARY TIME

Assign Chapter 17, Vocabulary Words **#1** on page 9 in the Reference Section for students to define in their Vocabulary notebooks. After they write each word and its meaning, students are to write a sentence using the vocabulary word.

Chapter 17, Vocabulary Words #1
(praise, commend, flimsy, sturdy)

(End of lesson.)

CHAPTER 17   LESSON 2

Objectives: Jingles, Grammar (Practice Sentences, Pattern 3 Practice Sentence), Practice Exercise, and Vocabulary #2.

 **JINGLE TIME**

Have students turn to the Jingle Section in their books and recite the previously-taught jingles.

 GRAMMAR TIME

First-Year Option: Put the Practice Sentences from the box below on the board or on notebook paper. Use these sentences as you practice the concepts that have been taught. For the greatest benefit, students must participate orally with the teacher. **Second-Year Option:** Have students classify the Practice Sentences independently on notebook paper. Check students' sentences with the answers provided below. (*If you have the CDs for Practice Sentences, have students check their sentences with the CDs.*)

Chapter 17, Practice Sentences for Lesson 2
1. _____ My father taught us Christian values by his example.
2. _____ Laura and John sent me some pictures of their five new puppies.

TEACHING SCRIPT FOR PRACTICING PATTERN 3 SENTENCES

We will practice classifying Pattern 3 sentences. We will classify the sentences together. Begin. (*You might have your students write the labels above the sentences at this time.*)

Question and Answer Flow for Sentence 1: My father taught us Christian values by his example.

1. Who taught us Christian values by his example? father - SN
2. What is being said about father? father taught - V
3. Father taught what? values - verify the noun
4. Do values mean the same thing as father? No.
5. Values - DO
6. Taught - V-t
7. Father taught values to whom? us - IO
8. What kind of values? Christian - Adj
9. By - P
10. By what? example - OP
11. Whose example? his - PPA
12. Whose father? my - PPA
13. SN V-t IO DO P3 Check
14. Verb-transitive - Check again.
15. (By his example) - Prepositional phrase
16. Period, statement, declarative sentence
17. Go back to the verb - divide the complete subject from the complete predicate.

Classified Sentence:

```
                              PPA SN    V-t  IO  Adj     DO    P  PPA  OP
                    SN V-t    My father / taught us Christian values (by his example).  D
                    IO DO P3
```

CHAPTER 17 LESSON 2 CONTINUED

Question and Answer Flow for Sentence 2: Laura and John sent me some pictures of their five new puppies.

1. Who sent me some pictures of their five new puppies?
   Laura and John - CSN, CSN
2. What is being said about Laura and John?
   Laura and John sent - V
3. Laura and John sent what? pictures- verify the noun
4. Do pictures mean the same thing as Laura and John? No.
5. Pictures - DO
6. Sent - V-t
7. Laura and John sent pictures to whom? me - IO
8. How many pictures? some - Adj
9. Of - P
10. Of what? puppies - OP
11. What kind of puppies? new - Adj
12. How many puppies? five - Adj
13. Whose puppies? their - PPA
14. And - C
15. SN V-t IO DO P3 Check
16. Verb-transitive - Check again.
17. (Of their five new puppies) - Prepositional phrase
18. Period, statement, declarative sentence
19. Go back to the verb - divide the complete subject from the complete predicate.

Classified Sentence:

	CSN	C	CSN	V-t	IO	Adj	DO	P	PPA	Adj	Adj	OP
SN V-t	Laura	and	John /	sent	me	some	pictures	(of	their	five	new	puppies). D
IO DO P3												

TEACHER INSTRUCTIONS FOR A PATTERN 3 PRACTICE SENTENCE

Tell students that their sentence writing assignment today is to write a Pattern 3 Practice Sentence. They are to follow the same procedure used in the previous lessons. They should decide on their labels, arrange them in a selected order, write their sentence, and edit the sentence for improved word choices. (*Students do not have to write an Improved Sentence at this point unless you feel they need more one-on-one word choice writing practice.*) Check and discuss the Pattern 3 Practices Sentence after students have finished.

 PRACTICE TIME

Students will continue punctuating direct quotations. Have students turn to pages 80 and 81 in the Practice Section of their book and find Chapter 17, Lesson 2, Practice (*1-3*). Go over the directions to make sure they understand what to do. Check and discuss the Practices after students have finished. (*Chapter 17, Lesson 2, Practice keys are given below and on the next page.*)

Chapter 17, Lesson 2, Practice 1: Use the Quotation Rules to help punctuate the quotations below. Underline the explanatory words.

    A **S**   **W**
1. <u>aunt sarah asked</u>, "will you close the door**?**"

    W   **A** **S**
2. "will you close the door**?**" <u>asked aunt sarah</u>.

    M   **T**
3. <u>mother said</u>, "take the trash out before you leave."

CHAPTER 17 LESSON 2 CONTINUED

Chapter 17, Lesson 2, Practice 2: Use the Quotation Rules to help punctuate the quotations below. Underline the explanatory words.

    W   R

1.   "watch out for that bee!" <u>roger yelled</u>.

    H   I   M

2.   "how can i call you if your phone is out of order?" <u>mandy asked</u>.

    S   I   O   S

3.   <u>sally said</u>, "i drove to oregon last september for a vacation."

    I   J   A   M

4.   "is your birthday in july or august?" <u>michael inquired</u>.

Chapter 17, Lesson 2, Practice 3: On notebook paper, write three sentences, demonstrating each of the two quotations: Beginning quote and end quote. **(Answers will vary.)**

VOCABULARY TIME

Assign Chapter 17, Vocabulary Words **#2** on page 9 in the Reference Section for students to define in their Vocabulary notebooks. Tell students they are to use a dictionary or thesaurus to look up the meanings of the vocabulary words. After they write each word and its meaning, students are to write a sentence using the vocabulary word.

Chapter 17, Vocabulary Words #2
(neutral, biased, young, youth)

(End of lesson.)

CHAPTER 17   LESSON 3

Objectives: Jingles, Grammar (Practice Sentences), Practice Exercise, and Study.

JINGLE TIME

Have students turn to the Jingle Section in their books and recite the previously-taught jingles.

GRAMMAR TIME

First-Year Option: Put the Practice Sentences from the box below on the board or on notebook paper. Use these sentences as you practice the concepts that have been taught. For the greatest benefit, students must participate orally with the teacher. **Second-Year Option:** Have students classify the Practice Sentences independently on notebook paper. Check students' sentences with the answers provided below. (*If you have the CDs for Practice Sentences, have students check their sentences with the CDs.*)

Chapter 17, Practice Sentences for Lesson 3

1. _____ Plants give us oxygen during the process of photosynthesis.
2. _____ Wow! The carnival rides gave me the thrill of my life!

TEACHING SCRIPT FOR PRACTICING PATTERN 3 SENTENCES

We will practice classifying Pattern 3 sentences. We will classify the sentences together. Begin. (*You might have your students write the labels above the sentences at this time.*)

Question and Answer Flow for Sentence 1: Plants give us oxygen during the process of photosynthesis.

1. What give us oxygen during the process of photosynthesis? plants - SN
2. What is being said about plants? plants give - V
3. Plants give what? oxygen - verify the noun
4. Does oxygen mean the same thing as plants? No.
5. Oxygen - DO
6. Give - V-t
7. Plants give oxygen to whom? us - IO
8. During - P
9. During what? process - OP
10. The - A
11. Of - P
12. Of what? photosynthesis - OP
13. SN V-t IO DO P3 Check
14. Verb-transitive - Check again.
15. (During the process) - Prepositional phrase
16. (Of photosynthesis) - Prepositional phrase
17. Period, statement, declarative sentence
18. Go back to the verb - divide the complete subject from the complete predicate.

Classified Sentence:

                                        SN   V-t IO   DO   P   A   OP   P   OP

        SN V-t   Plants **/** give us oxygen (during the process) (of photosynthesis). **D**

        IO DO P3

CHAPTER 17 LESSON 3 CONTINUED

Question and Answer Flow for Sentence 2: Wow! The carnival rides gave me the thrill of my life!

1. What gave me the thrill of my life? rides - SN
2. What is being said about rides? rides gave - V
3. Rides gave what? thrill - verify the noun
4. Does thrill mean the same thing as rides? No.
5. Thrill - DO
6. Gave - V-t
7. Rides gave thrill to whom? me - IO
8. The - A
9. Of - P
10. Of what? life - OP

11. Whose life? my - PPA
12. What kind of rides? carnival - Adj
13. The - A
14. Wow - I
15. SN V-t IO DO P3 Check
16. Verb-transitive - Check again.
17. (Of my life) - Prepositional phrase
18. Exclamation point, strong feeling, exclamatory sentence
19. Go back to the verb - divide the complete subject from the complete predicate.

Classified Sentence:

```
                              I    A   Adj   SN    V-t   IO  A  DO  P PPA OP
          SN  V-t       Wow!  The carnival rides / gave me the thrill (of my life)!  E
          ───────
          IO  DO  P3
```

PRACTICE TIME

Students will continue punctuating direct quotations. Have students turn to page 81 in the Practice Section of their book and find Chapter 17, Lesson 3, Practice(*1-2*). Go over the directions to make sure they understand what to do. Check and discuss the Practices after students have finished. (*Chapter 17, Lesson 3, Practice keys are given below.*)

Chapter 17, Lesson 3, Practice 1: Use the Quotation Rules to help punctuate the quotations below. Underline the explanatory words.

```
    I                                        Z    Z            M   S
```
1. "i will give you extra credit for your research paper on zig ziglar's life," said mrs. smith.

```
   M   S        I                                           Z    Z
```
2. mrs. smith said, "i will give you extra credit for your research paper on zig ziglar's life."

```
    W        W           D  C                              H
```
3. "will you visit washington, d. c., this summer with your family?" asked harry.

```
   H       W        W           D  C
```
4. harry asked, "will you visit washington, d. c., this summer with your family?"

Chapter 17, Lesson 3, Practice 2: On notebook paper, write two sentences, demonstrating each of these two quotations: Beginning quote and end quote. **(Answers will vary.)**

STUDY TIME

Have students study the vocabulary words in their vocabulary notebooks. Also, have students study any of the skills in the Practice Section that they need to review.

(End of lesson.)

CHAPTER 17   LESSON 4

Objectives: Jingles, Study, Test, Check, Activity, and Writing (journal).

 JINGLE TIME

Have students turn to the Jingle Section in their books and recite the previously-taught jingles.

 STUDY TIME

Have students study the vocabulary words in their vocabulary notebooks. Remind students that any vocabulary word in their notebooks could be on their test. Also, have students study any of the skills in the Practice Section that they need to review.

 TEST TIME

Have students turn to page 114 in the Test Section of their books and find the Chapter 17 Test. Go over the directions to make sure they understand what to do. (*Chapter 17 Test key is on the next page.*)

 CHECK TIME

After students have finished, check and discuss their test papers. Make sure they understand why their answers are right or wrong. (*For total points, count each required answer as a point.*)

 ACTIVITY / ASSIGNMENT TIME

Have students create their own **Parts-of-Speech Poem** formula. Then, have students design their own Parts-of-Speech poem, following the directions of their formula. Read and discuss their poems. Have them share their poems with other family members and friends.

(End of lesson.)

Chapter 17 Test
(Student Page 114)

Exercise 1: Classify each sentence.

```
     (You) SP    V-t  CIO  C   CIO  A  DO   P  A      Adj       OP      P  PPA  OP
1.  SN  V-t      / Give Clint and Craig a copy (of a United States map) (for their report).  Imp
    IO DO P3

                 PNA        SN       V-t   IO  A   DO    P  A  Adj  OP
2.  SN  V-t      Jennifer's parents / loaned her the money (for a new car).  D
    IO DO P3
```

Exercise 2: Use Sentence 2 to underline the complete subject once and the complete predicate twice and to complete the table below.

List the Noun Used	List the Noun Job	Singular or Plural	Common or Proper	Simple Subject	Simple Predicate
1. **parents**	2. **SN**	3. **P**	4. **C**	5. **parents**	6. **loaned**
7. **money**	8. **DO**	9. **S**	10. **C**		
11. **car**	12. **OP**	13. **S**	14. **C**		

Exercise 3: Identify each pair of words as synonyms or antonyms by putting parentheses ( ) around *syn* or *ant*.

1. praise, commend	**(syn)** ant	5. sway, influence	**(syn)** ant	9. adhere, stick	**(syn)** ant
2. deplore, approve	syn **(ant)**	6. hope, despair	syn **(ant)**	10. flimsy, sturdy	syn **(ant)**
3. gallant, afraid	syn **(ant)**	7. neutral, biased	syn **(ant)**	11. originates, begins	**(syn)** ant
4. youth, young	**(syn)** ant	8. give, endow	**(syn)** ant	12. suggest, demand	syn **(ant)**

Exercise 4: Use the Quotation Rules to help punctuate the quotations below. Underline the explanatory words.

```
        D                             I       B
1. . "did you get a part-time job after school?" i asked beth.


        B          I                    S     S    S
2.  beth answered, "i work three days a week at smith's shoe store."


        I                          I
3.  "is it hard to work and go to school?" i inquired.


        B               I          A        I
4.  beth stated proudly, "i get straight a's, and i like the extra money."
```

Exercise 5: On notebook paper, write one sentence for each of these labels: ① S ② SCS ③ SCV ④ CD.

Exercise 6: On notebook paper, write two sentences, demonstrating each of these two quotations: Beginning quote and end quote. **(Answers will vary.)**

Exercise 7: In your journal, write a paragraph summarizing what you have learned this week.

CHAPTER 17 LESSON 4 CONTINUED

TEACHER INSTRUCTIONS

Use the Question and Answer Flows below for the sentences on the Chapter 17 Tests.

Question and Answer Flow for Sentence 1: Give Clint and Craig a copy of a United States map for their report.

1. Who give Clint and Craig a copy of a United States map for their report? (You) - SP (Understood subject pronoun)
2. What is being said about you? you give - V
3. You give what? copy - verify the noun
4. Does copy mean the same thing as you? No.
5. Copy - DO
6. Give - V-t
7. You give copy to whom? Clint and Craig - CIO, CIO
8. A - A
9. Of - P
10. Of what? map - OP
11. What kind of map? United States - Adj
12. A - A
13. For - P
14. For what? report - OP
15. Whose report? their - PPA
16. And - C
17. SN V-t IO DO P3 Check
18. Verb-transitive - Check again.
19. (Of a United States map) - Prepositional phrase
20. (For their report) - Prepositional phrase
21. Period, command, imperative sentence
22. Go back to the verb - divide the complete subject from the complete predicate.

Classified	**(You) SP**		V-t	CIO	C	CIO	A	DO	P	A		Adj	OP	P	PPA	OP
Sentence:	SN V-t	/ Give	Clint	and	Craig	a	copy	(of	a	United States	map)	(for	their	report).	**Imp**
	IO DO P3														

Question and Answer Flow for Sentence 2: Jennifer's parents loaned her the money for a new car.

1. Who loaned her the money for a new car? parents - SN
2. What is being said about parents? parents loaned - V
3. Parents loaned what? money - verify the noun
4. Does money mean the same thing as parents? No.
5. Money - DO
6. Loaned - V-t
7. Parents loaned money to whom? her - IO
8. The - A
9. For - P
10. For what? car - OP
11. What kind of car? new - Adj
12. A - A
13. Whose parents? Jennifer's - PNA
14. SN V-t IO DO P3 Check
15. Verb-transitive - Check again.
16. (For a new car) - Prepositional phrase
17. Period, statement, declarative sentence
18. Go back to the verb - divide the complete subject from the complete predicate.

Classified Sentence:		**PNA**	SN	V-t	IO	A	DO	P	A	Adj	OP
	SN V-t	Jennifer's	parents	/ loaned	her	the	money	(for	a	new	car). **D**
	IO DO P3										

CHAPTER 17   LESSON 5

Objectives: Writing (narrative, writing with dialogue and without dialogue), and Writing Assignments #23 and #24.

 WRITING TIME

TEACHING SCRIPT FOR INTRODUCING NARRATIVE WRITING

Narrative writing is simply the telling of a story. When you compose stories, you are actually writing what professional writers call narratives, or short stories. Short stories have certain characteristics that make them different from other types of writing. You will study five characteristics known as Story Elements. These Story Elements are main idea, setting, characters, plot, and ending. Your narrative writing skills will be developed through the use of the Story Elements. Narrative writing will have a beginning, a middle, and an end.

You will now learn how to use the five Story Elements – main idea, setting, characters, plot, and ending – to make a Story Elements outline. This outline will help keep your writing focused and help you choose details and events that support the main idea of your story. Before you begin every story writing assignment, you will complete a Story Elements outline like the one in Reference 52 on page 44. (*Have students go to Reference 52 on student page 44. Read and discuss the story elements and sample story with them.*)

Reference 52: Story Elements Outline

1. **Main Idea (Tell the problem or situation that needs a solution.)**
   Dillon's mother was gone, and he was worried and scared.
2. **Setting (Tell when and where the story takes place, either clearly stated or implied.)**
   When - The story takes place in the evening. Where - The story takes place at Dillon's house.
3. **Character (Tell whom or what the story is about.)**
   The main characters are Dillon and his dog.
4. **Plot (Tell what the characters in the story do and what happens to them.)**
   The story is about a boy's frightening experience while his mom goes to the store.
5. **Ending (Use a strong ending that will bring the story to a close.)**
   The story ends with Dillon's relief that the scary creature was his dog.

Dillon's Scare

  Dillon sat quietly at the computer working on his history paper. His mom had gone to the store to get groceries for dinner that evening. It was getting late, and the sky began to darken outside. Dillon had stayed at home by himself many times, but his mom had been gone for a while now. He was getting worried.

  "She'll be home anytime," he said to himself as he left the computer to look out the window one more time. With no sign of his mom's car, he headed back to his chair. Before he could sit down, there was a sound coming from the other room.

  "Knock! Knock! Thump!" Dillon jumped and ran for the baseball bat he kept in the corner of his room. "Knock! Knock! Thump! Knock!" It sounded louder this time. Dillon slowly crept around the corner and into the other room. He glanced around the dark room and was about to leave when something in the far corner caught his attention. He flipped on the light switch.

  "Molly! You silly dog!" Molly got up from scratching her fleas. She let out one big "Woof!" as she headed toward Dillon with her big paws thumping on the floor.

CHAPTER 17 LESSON 5 CONTINUED

You will make a Story Elements outline when you get ready to write. I want to tell you about another special element that makes narrative writing especially interesting, and that is conversation. Remember, another word for conversation is **dialogue**. Writers use dialogue, or conversation, in their short stories because it helps move the plot along, and it helps the reader understand the characters better.

Dialogue "shows" instead of "tells" in narratives. It also "shows" what a character is like. It is much better than the writer's "telling" what a character is like. A character's personal quotations show the readers a great deal about the character.

Listen as I review the main punctuation rules to observe when working with dialogue.

1. Dialogue is always placed in quotation marks. This placement will separate dialogue from any explanatory words or other words that develop the plot of the story.
2. Periods, commas, question marks, and exclamation marks that punctuate dialogue always go INSIDE the quotation marks. You will follow the rules for punctuating quotations that you have already learned.
3. If more than one character is speaking, you must indent and create a new paragraph each time a different character speaks.

TEACHING SCRIPT FOR WRITING WITH DIALOGUE AND WITHOUT DIALOGUE

You will do two narrative writing assignments. The first narrative writing assignment will be a story without dialogue. The second narrative writing assignment will be the <u>same story</u> with dialogue. Both rough drafts will go through the revision and editing stages. (*Read the boxes below for more information about students' writing assignment.*) You will choose the point of view for each assignment.

Writing Assignment Box #1

Writing Assignment #23: A Narrative <u>without</u> dialogue (First or Third Person)
(Remember, first person pronouns are *I, we, me, us, my, our, mine,* and *ours.*)
Remind students to make a Story Elements outline.

Writing topics: Lost in the Mall/Jungle/Desert   or   My Crime-Fighting Machine   or
          Choose a story from the Bible or another favorite story and write it <u>without</u> dialogue.

Writing Assignment Box #2

Writing Assignment #24: A Narrative <u>with</u> dialogue (First or Third Person)
(Remember, first person pronouns are *I, we, me, us, my, our, mine,* and *ours.*)
Students will use the same Story Elements outline from Writing Assignment #24.

Writing topics: Lost in the Mall/Jungle/Desert   or   My Crime Fighting Machine   or
          Choose a story from the Bible or another favorite story and write it <u>with</u> dialogue.

TEACHER INSTRUCTIONS FOR CHECKING WRITING ASSIGNMENTS

Read, check, and discuss Writing Assignment #23 and #24 after students have finished their final papers. Use the checklists as you check and discuss students' papers. Make sure students are using the regular editing checklist and quotation rules correctly.

(End of lesson.)

CHAPTER 18   LESSON 1

Objectives: Jingles, Grammar (Practice Sentences, Oral Skill Builder Check), Skills (regular and irregular verbs), Practice Exercise, Vocabulary #1

JINGLE TIME

Have students turn to the Jingle Section in their books and recite the previously-taught jingles.

GRAMMAR TIME

First-Year Option: Put the Practice Sentences from the box below on the board or on notebook paper. Use these sentences as you practice the concepts that have been taught. For the greatest benefit, students must participate orally with the teacher. **Second-Year Option:** Have students classify the Practice Sentences independently on note paper. Check students' sentences with the answers provided below. (*If you have the CDs for Practice Sentences, have students check their sentences with the CDs.*)

Chapter 18, Practice Sentences for Lesson 1
1. _____ The church deacon passed us the offering plate during the worship service.
2. _____ Will you get Cameron a sharpened pencil from my desk drawer?

Question and Answer Flow for Sentence 1: The church deacon passed us the offering plate during the worship service.

1. Who passed us the offering plate during the worship service? deacon - SN
2. What is being said about deacon? deacon passed - V
3. Deacon passed what? plate - verify the noun
4. Does plate mean the same thing as deacon? No.
5. Plate - DO
6. Passed - V-t
7. Deacon passed plate to whom? us - IO
8. What kind of plate? offering - Adj
9. The - A
10. During - P
11. During what? service - OP
12. What kind of service? worship - Adj
13. The - A
14. What kind of deacon? church - Adj
15. The - A
16. SN V-t IO DO P3 Check
17. Verb-transitive - Check again.
18. (During the worship service) - Prepositional phrase
19. Period, statement, declarative sentence
20. Go back to the verb - divide the complete subject from the complete predicate.

Classified Sentence:

```
                        A   Adj   SN      V-t  IO A  Adj   DO    P   A   Adj    OP
             SN  V-t    The church deacon / passed us the offering plate (during the worship service).  D
             IO  DO  P3
```

CHAPTER 18 LESSON 1 CONTINUED

Question and Answer Flow for Sentence 2: Will you get Cameron a sharpened pencil from my desk drawer?

1. Who will get Cameron a sharpened pencil from my desk drawer? you - SP
2. What is being said about you? you will get - V
3. Will - HV
4. You will get what? pencil - verify the noun
5. Does pencil mean the same thing as you? No.
6. Pencil - DO
7. Get - V-t
8. You will get pencil for whom? Cameron - IO
9. What kind of pencil? sharpened - Adj
10. A - A
11. From - P
12. From what? drawer - OP
13. What kind of drawer? desk - Adj
14. Whose drawer? my - PPA
15. SN V-t IO DO P3 Check
16. Verb-transitive - Check again.
17. (From my desk drawer) - Prepositional phrase
18. Question mark, question, interrogative sentence
19. Go back to the verb - divide the complete subject from the complete predicate.
20. This sentence has predicate words in the complete subject. Underline the helping verb at the beginning of the sentence twice.

Classified Sentence:

```
                            HV  SP  V-t   IO    A   Adj       DO      P  PPA Adj   OP
            SN  V-t        Will you / get Cameron a sharpened pencil (from my desk drawer)? Int
            IO DO P3
```

Use Sentences 1-2 that your students classified to do an Oral Skill Builder Check.

Oral Skill Builder Check

1. **Noun check.**
   (Say the job and then say the noun. Circle each noun.)

2. **Identify the nouns as singular or plural.**
   (Write **S** or **P** above each noun.)

3. **Identify the nouns as common or proper.**
   (Follow established procedure for oral identification.)

4. **Do a vocabulary check.**
   (Follow established procedure for oral identification.)

5. **Identify the complete subject and the complete predicate.** (Underline the complete subject once and the complete predicate twice.)

6. **Identify the simple subject and simple predicate.** (Underline the simple subject once and the simple predicate twice. Bold, or highlight, the lines.)

7. **Recite the irregular verb chart.** (Located on student page 23 and teacher page 138.)

SKILL TIME

TEACHING SCRIPT FOR IDENTIFYING REGULAR AND IRREGULAR VERBS

You are going to learn three interesting things about verbs that will help you make correct verb choices when you speak and write. You will learn how to identify regular and irregular verbs, how to identify the simple verb tenses, and how to identify the tenses of helping verbs. Turn to page 45 and look at Reference 53. Follow along as I go over this important information with you. (*Read the information to your students and work through the guided examples provided for each concept. This information and the guided examples are reproduced for you on the next page.*)

CHAPTER 18 LESSON 1 CONTINUED

Reference 53: Regular and Irregular Verbs

Most verbs are **regular verbs**. This means that they form the past tense merely by adding **-ed**, **-d**, or **-t** to the main verb: *pace, paced*. This simple procedure makes regular verbs easy to identify. Some verbs, however, do not form their past tense this way. For that reason, they are called **irregular verbs**. Most irregular verbs form the past tense by having a **vowel spelling change** in the word. For example: *dr<u>i</u>ve, dr<u>o</u>ve, dr<u>i</u>ven* or *r<u>i</u>ng, r<u>a</u>ng, r<u>u</u>ng.*

To decide if a verb is regular or irregular, remember these two things:

1. Look only at the main verb. If the main verb is made past tense with an *-ed, -d, or -t* ending, it is a regular verb. (*pace, paced, paced*)
2. Look only at the main verb. If the main verb is made past tense with a vowel spelling change, it is an irregular verb. (*ring, rang, rung*)

A partial listing of the most common irregular verbs is on the irregular verb chart located in Reference 27 on page 23 in the student book. (*Page 138 in the Teacher's Manual.*) Refer to this chart whenever necessary.

Identify each verb as regular or irregular and put **R** or **I** in the blank. Then, write the past tense form.

ride	I	rode	sign	R	signed	eat	I	ate
try	R	tried	drive	I	drove	build	R	built

 PRACTICE TIME

Have students turn to page 82 in the Practice Section of their book and find Chapter 18, Lesson 1, Practice. Go over the directions to make sure they understand what to do. Check and discuss the Practice after students have finished. (*Chapter 18, Lesson 1, Practice key is given below.*)

Chapter 18, Lesson 1, Practice: Identify each verb as regular or irregular by writing **R** or **I** in the first blank and the past tense form in the second blank. Also, underline each verb or verb phrase in sentences 5-9.

Verb		R or I	Past Tense	Underline the Verb	R or I	Past Tense
1.	sting	I	stung	5. Gloria <u>sits</u> on the front row.	I	sat
2.	worry	R	worried	6. Donnie <u>gnawed</u> on the apple.	R	gnawed
3.	carve	R	carved	7. Marcie <u>is singing</u> in the choir.	I	sang
4.	wear	I	wore	8. Sam <u>drives</u> a new car.	I	drove
				9. Clay <u>loves</u> model airplanes.	R	loved

 VOCABULARY TIME

Assign Chapter 18, Vocabulary Words **#1** on page 9 in the Reference Section for students to define in their Vocabulary notebooks. After they write each word and its meaning, students are to write a sentence using the vocabulary word.

Chapter 18, Vocabulary Words #1
(escalate, decrease, danger, peril)

(End of lesson.)

CHAPTER 18 LESSON 2

Objectives: Jingles, Grammar (Practice Sentences, Pattern 3 Practice Sentence), Skills (simple verb tenses, tenses of helping verbs), Practice Exercise, Writing (journal), and Vocabulary #2.

JINGLE TIME

Have students turn to the Jingle Section in their books and recite the previously-taught jingles.

GRAMMAR TIME

First-Year Option: Put the Practice Sentences from the box below on the board or notebook paper. Use these sentences as you practice the concepts that have been taught. For the greatest benefit, students must participate orally with the teacher. **Second-Year Option:** Have students classify the Practice Sentences independently on notebook paper. Check students' sentences with the answers provided below. (*If you have the CDs for Practice Sentences, have students check their sentences with the CDs.*)

Chapter 18, Practice Sentences for Lesson 2
1. _____ Stupendous! My parents bought me a new bicycle for my birthday present!
2. _____ Will our tour guide give us a stern lecture about untreated water?

Question and Answer Flow for Sentence 1: Stupendous! My parents bought me a new bicycle for my birthday present!

1. Who bought me a new bicycle for my birthday present? parents - SN
2. What is being said about parents? parents bought - V
3. Parents bought what? bicycle - verify the noun
4. Does bicycle mean the same thing as parents? No.
5. Bicycle - DO
6. Bought - V-t
7. Parents bought bicycle for whom? me - IO
8. What kind of bicycle? new - Adj
9. A - A
10. For - P
11. For what? present - OP
12. What kind of present? birthday - Adj
13. Whose present? my - PPA
14. Whose parents? my - PPA
15. Stupendous - I
16. SN V-t IO DO P3 Check
17. Verb-transitive - Check again.
18. (For my birthday present) - Prepositional phrase
19. Exclamation point, strong feeling, exclamatory sentence
20. Go back to the verb - divide the complete subject from the complete predicate.

Classified Sentence:

```
                        I      PPA SN     V-t   IO A Adj  DO   P PPA Adj   OP
         SN V-t     Stupendous! My parents / bought me a new bicycle (for my birthday present)! E
         IO DO P3
```

CHAPTER 18 LESSON 2 CONTINUED

Question and Answer Flow for Sentence 2: Will our tour guide give us a stern lecture about untreated water?

1. Who will give us a stern lecture about untreated water? guide - SN
2. What is being said about guide? guide will give - V
3. Will - HV
4. Guide will give what? lecture - verify the noun
5. Does lecture mean the same thing as guide? No.
6. Lecture - DO
7. Give - V-t
8. Guide will give lecture to whom? us - IO
9. What kind of lecture? stern - Adj
10. A - A
11. About - P
12. About what? water - OP
13. What kind of water? untreated - Adj
14. What kind of guide? tour - Adj
15. Whose guide? our - PPA
16. SN V-t IO DO P3 Check
17. Verb-transitive - Check again.
18. (About untreated water) - Prepositional phrase
19. Question mark, question, interrogative sentence
20. Go back to the verb - divide the complete subject from the complete predicate.
21. This sentence has predicate words in the complete subject. Underline the helping verb at the beginning of the sentence twice.

Classified Sentence:

	HV	PPA	Adj	SN		V-t	IO	A	Adj	DO	P		Adj	OP	
SN V-t	<u>Will</u>	our	tour	guide	/	give	us	a	stern	lecture	(about		untreated	water)?	Int
IO DO P3															

TEACHER INSTRUCTIONS FOR A PATTERN 3 PRACTICE SENTENCE

Tell students that their sentence writing assignment today is to write a Pattern 3 Practice Sentence. They are to follow the same procedure used in the previous lessons. They should decide on their labels, arrange them in a selected order, write their sentences, and edit their sentences for improved word choices. (*Students do not have to write an Improved Sentence at this point unless you feel they need more one-on-one word choice writing practice.*) Check and discuss the Pattern 3 Practice Sentence after students have finished.

SKILL TIME

TEACHING SCRIPT FOR IDENTIFYING SIMPLE VERB TENSES AND THE TENSES OF HELPING VERBS

You are going to learn more about verbs to help you better understand how verbs function. Look at References 54 and 55 on pages 45 and 46 while I go over this important information with you. (*Read the information to your students and work through the guided examples provided. This information is reproduced for you on the next two pages.*)

CHAPTER 18 LESSON 2 CONTINUED

Reference 54: Simple Verb Tenses

When you are writing paragraphs, you must use verbs that are in the same tense. Tense means time. The tense of a verb shows the time of the action. There are three basic tenses that show when an action takes place. They are **present tense, past tense,** and **future tense**. These tenses are known as the simple tenses.

1. The **simple present tense** shows that something is happening now, in the present. The present tense form usually ends in *s, es,* or in a *plain ending*.
   (Regular present tense form: *climb, climbs*) (Irregular present tense form: *ride, rides*)
   (**Examples:** Jerry climbs a tall ladder. Carla rides wild horses.)

2. The **simple past tense** shows that something has happened sometime in the past. The regular past tense form usually ends in *-ed, -d, -t*. Most irregular past tense forms should be memorized.
   (Regular past tense form: *climbed*) (Irregular past tense form: *rode*)
   (**Examples:** Jerry climbed a tall ladder. Carla rode wild horses.)

3. The **future tense** shows that something will happen sometime in the future. The future tense form always has the helping verb *will* or *shall* before the main verb.
   (Regular future tense form: *will climb*) (Irregular future tense form: *will ride*)
   (**Examples:** Jerry will climb a tall ladder. Carla will ride wild horses.)

Simple Present Tense	Simple Past Tense	Simple Future Tense
What to look for: **one verb** With s, es, or plain ending.	What to look for: **one verb** With -ed, -d, -t, or irr spelling change.	What to look for: **will** or **shall** With a main verb.
1. He goes on a hike. 2. He does his homework.	1. He went on a hike. 2. He did his homework.	1. He will go on a hike. 2. He will do his homework.

CHAPTER 18 LESSON 2 CONTINUED

Reference 55: Tenses of Helping Verbs

1. If there is only a main verb in a sentence, the tense is determined by the main verb and will be either present tense or past tense.
2. If there is a helping verb with a main verb, the tense of both verbs will be determined by the helping verb, not the main verb.

<u>Since the helping verb determines a verb's tense</u>, it is important to learn the tenses of the 14 helping verbs you will be using. You should memorize the list below so you will never have trouble with tenses.

Present tense helping verbs: **am, is, are, has, have, does, do**
Past tense helping verbs: **was, were, had, did, been**
Future tense helping verbs: **will, shall**

If you use a present tense helping verb, it is considered present tense even though the main verb has an -*ed* ending and it doesn't sound like present tense. (*I have walked - present tense.*) In later grades, you will learn that certain helping verbs help form other tenses called the perfect tenses.

Example 1: Underline each verb or verb phrase. Identify the verb tense by writing a number **1** for present tense, a number **2** for past tense, or a number **3** for future tense. Write the past tense form and **R** or **I** for Regular or Irregular

Verb Tense		Main Verb Past Tense Form	R or I
1	1. The bluebird <u>has built</u> a nest.	built	R
2	2. She <u>had written</u> her name in pencil.	wrote	I
3	3. The boys <u>will close</u> the gate.	closed	R

Example 2: List the present tense and past tense helping verbs below.

Present tense:	1. **am**	2. **is**	3. **are**	4. **has**	5. **have**	6. **does**	7. **do**
Past tense:	8. **was**	9. **were**	10. **had**	11. **did**	12. **been**		

CHAPTER 18 LESSON 2 CONTINUED

 PRACTICE TIME

Have students turn to page 82 in the Practice Section of their book and find Chapter 18, Lesson 2, Practice. Go over the directions to make sure they understand what to do. Check and discuss the Practice after students have finished. (*Chapter 18, Lesson 2, Practice key is given below.*)

Chapter 18, Lesson 2, Practice: Underline each verb or verb phrase. Identify the verb tense by writing a number **1** for present tense, a number **2** for past tense, or a number **3** for future tense. Write the past tense form and **R** or **I** for Regular or Irregular.

Verb Tense				Main Verb Past Tense Form	R or I
2	1.	The paint <u>had begun</u> to peel.		began	I
1	2.	Julie <u>is painting</u> her nails.		painted	R
1	3.	I <u>am washing</u> the car now.		washed	R
3	4.	Tonight, we <u>will stay</u> at a motel.		stayed	R
1	5.	She <u>has built</u> a sand castle.		built	R
3	6.	Sheila <u>will do</u> the swan dive.		did	I
2	7.	Rhonda <u>had written</u> the poems.		wrote	I
2	8.	He <u>carved</u> his name in stone.		carved	R
1	9.	We <u>have driven</u> all night.		drove	I

 WRITING TIME

Have students make an entry in their journals.

 VOCABULARY TIME

Assign Chapter 18, Vocabulary Words **#2** on page 9 in the Reference Section for students to define in their Vocabulary notebooks. Tell students they are to use a dictionary or thesaurus to look up the meanings of the vocabulary words. After they write each word and its meaning, students are to write a sentence using the vocabulary word.

Chapter 18, Vocabulary Words #2
(bicker, agree, error, wrong)

(End of lesson.)

CHAPTER 18   LESSON 3

Objectives: Jingles, Grammar (Practice Sentences), Skill (changing verbs to different tenses in a paragraph), Practice Exercise.

JINGLE TIME

Have students turn to the Jingle Section in their books and recite the previously-taught jingles.

GRAMMAR TIME

First-Year Option: Put the Practice Sentences from the box below on the board or notebook paper. Use these sentences as you practice the concepts that have been taught. For the greatest benefit, students must participate orally with the teacher. **Second-Year Option:** Have students classify the Practice Sentences independently on notebook paper. Check students' sentences with the answers provided below. *(If you have the CDs for Practice Sentences, have students check their sentences with the CDs.)*

Chapter 18, Practice Sentences for Lesson 3
1. _____ Give her the Governor's report on education reform.
2. _____ Yesterday, Terry's brother bought him a microwave for his apartment.

Question and Answer Flow for Sentence 1: Give her the Governor's report on education reform.

1. Who give her the Governor's report on education reform?
   you - SP (Understood subject pronoun)
2. What is being said about you? you give - V
3. You give what? report - verify the noun
4. Does report mean the same thing as you? No.
5. Report - DO
6. Give - V-t
7. You give report to whom? her - IO
8. Whose report? Governor's - PNA
9. The - A

10. On - P
11. On what? reform - OP
12. What kind of reform? education - Adj
13. SN V-t IO DO P3 Check
14. Verb-transitive - Check again.
15. (On education reform) - Prepositional phrase
16. Period, command, imperative sentence
17. Go back to the verb - divide the complete
    subject from the complete predicate.

Classified Sentence:

```
                  (You) SP     V-t IO  A     PNA      DO  P   Adj     OP
                  SN  V-t      / Give her the Governor's report (on education reform).  Imp
                  IO DO  P3
```

CHAPTER 18 LESSON 3 CONTINUED

Question and Answer Flow for Sentence 2: Yesterday, Terry's brother bought him a microwave for his apartment.

1. Who bought him a microwave for his apartment? brother - SN
2. What is being said about brother? brother bought - V
3. Brother bought what? microwave - verify the noun
4. Does microwave mean the same thing as brother? No.
5. Microwave - DO
6. Bought - V-t
7. Brother bought microwave for whom? him - IO
8. A - A
9. For - P
10. For what? apartment - OP
11. Whose apartment? his - PPA
12. Whose brother? Terry's - PNA

13. Bought when? yesterday - Adv
14. SN V-t IO DO P3 Check
15. Verb-transitive - Check again.
16. (For his apartment) - Prepositional phrase
17. Period, statement, declarative sentence
18. Go back to the verb - divide the complete subject from the complete predicate.
19. This sentence has predicate words in the complete subject. Underline the adverb at the beginning of the sentence twice.

Classified Sentence:

| | Adv | PNA | SN | V-t | IO | A | DO | P | PPA | OP |

<u>SN V-t</u> <u>Yesterday</u>, Terry's brother **/** bought him a microwave (for his apartment). **D**
<u>IO DO P3</u>

SKILL TIME

TEACHING SCRIPT FOR CHANGING VERBS TO DIFFERENT TENSES IN A PARAGRAPH

It is very important to study verb tenses because you will use what you learn in your writing. Remember, verb tenses in sentences are used to tell the reader the time period an event takes place. In writing, one of the most common mistakes students make is mixing present tense and past tense verbs. Mixing verb tenses can make your writing awkward and confusing to your reader. Look at this example. (_Put the example on the board._) Example: **The performer <u>smiles</u> and <u>waved</u> to the audience as he <u>walks</u> around the stage.**

In this sentence, _waved_ is past tense, and _smiles_ and _walks_ are present tense. The shift from present to past and back to present leaves your reader wondering about the time these actions take place. To make your writing clear and effective, choose a verb tense, or time, for your writing and stick to it.

We will now work with verb tenses in a paragraph format. We will do several things to help you understand how the different tenses are used. First, we will identify the tense used in a sample paragraph as either present tense or past tense. Next, we will change from one tense to another tense in a paragraph. Then, we will work with mixed tenses. This means that a paragraph has a mixture of present and past tense verbs. Since past tense and present tense are usually not used together in the same paragraph, we will change all the mixed verbs to the tense indicated.

As I read the sample paragraph to you, listen very carefully to the verbs. After I have finished, I will ask you the tense of the paragraph. (_Read the sample paragraph in Reference 56 on the next page to your students. Do not allow them to look at the paragraph in their books, yet._) What is the tense of the paragraph? (_present tense_) We will now change the paragraph to past tense. To do this, we must change each verb to past tense, one at a time. After we have finished, I will read both paragraphs again so you can train your ear to hear the difference between present tense and past tense. (_Have students go to the first guided example in Reference 56 on page 47 and follow along as you show them how to change each present tense verb to a past tense verb._)

CHAPTER 18 LESSON 3 CONTINUED

Reference 56: Changing Tenses in Paragraphs

Guided Example 1: Change the underlined present tense verbs in Paragraph 1 to past tense verbs in Paragraph 2.

Paragraph 1: Present Tense

Lindsay **fills** her jar with lightening bugs every June. She **chases** them down hillsides and **grabs** them with her fingers. Once she **captures** them, she **drops** them into her see-through container, one at a time. She **prizes** them like jewels and **lets** them flash all night on the stand beside her bed.

Paragraph 2: Past Tense

Lindsay **filled** her jar with lightening bugs every June. She **chased** them down hillsides and **grabbed** them with her fingers. Once she **captured** them, she **dropped** them into her see-through container, one at a time. She **prized** them like jewels and **let** them flash all night on the stand beside her bed.

Guided Example 2: Change the underlined mixed tense verbs in Paragraph 1 to present tense verbs in Paragraph 2.

Paragraph 3: Mixed Tenses

My brother **went** fishing several times during the summer. He **throws** his line in the water and **caught** a fish almost every time. He **cleans** them and **grilled** them over an open fire. He usually **seasoned** them with Cajun spices. He **sat** under a shade tree in the evening breeze and **ate** them. Then, he **drifts** off to sleep.

Paragraph 4: Present Tense

My brother **goes** fishing several times during the summer. He **throws** his line in the water and **catches** a fish almost every time. He **cleans** them and **grills** them over an open fire. He usually **seasons** them with Cajun spices. He **sits** under a shade tree in the evening breeze and **eats** them. Then, he **drifts** off to sleep.

 PRACTICE TIME

Students will continue their practice of verb tenses. Have students turn to pages 82, 83, and 84 in the Practice Section of their books and find Chapter 18, Lesson 3, Practice (*1-4*). Go over the directions to make sure they understand what to do. Check and discuss the Practices after students have finished. (*Chapter 18, Lesson 3, Practice keys are given below and on the next page.*)

Chapter 18, Lesson 3, Practice 1: Underline each verb or verb phrase. Identify the verb tense by writing a number **1** for present tense, a number **2** for past tense, or a number **3** for future tense. Write the past tense form and **R** or **I** for Regular or Irregular.

Verb Tense			Main Verb Past Tense Form	R or I
2	1.	The Coast Guard <u>had</u> <u>rescued</u> a ship.	rescued	R
3	2.	<u>Will</u> you <u>adjust</u> the margins?	adjusted	R
3	3.	He <u>will</u> <u>be</u> <u>writing</u> a novel.	wrote	I
1	4.	I <u>am</u> <u>defending</u> myself in court.	defended	R

CHAPTER 18 LESSON 3 CONTINUED

Chapter 18, Lesson 3, Practice 2: Change the underlined present tense verbs in Paragraph 1 to past tense verbs in Paragraph 2.

Paragraph 1: Present Tense

My grandfather **raises** cattle. He **owns** a large farm in eastern Texas, and I **visit** him at least twice a year. I **help** him do chores around the farm. We **load** bags of grain onto the trailer and **ride** into the field to feed the cattle. We **tear** open the bags and **pour** the feed into a large feed trough for the cattle. Then, we **spray** their backs with fly repellant. When we **finish**, we **return** to the house for afternoon snacks and a tall glass of my grandmother's homemade lemonade. I **love** my grandfather and his farm!

Paragraph 2: Past Tense

My grandfather **raised** cattle. He **owned** a large farm in eastern Texas, and I **visited** him at least twice a year. I **helped** him do chores around the farm. We **loaded** bags of grain onto the trailer and **rode** into the field to feed the cattle. We **tore** open the bags and **poured** the feed into a large feed trough for the cattle. Then, we **sprayed** their backs with fly repellant. When we **finished**, we **returned** to the house for afternoon snacks and a tall glass of my grandmother's homemade lemonade. I **loved** my grandfather and his farm!

Chapter 18, Lesson 3, Practice 3: Write the seven present tense helping verbs, the five past tense helping verbs, and the two future tense helping verbs. **(The order of answers may vary.)** (Present: **am, is, are, has, have, do, does**; Past: **was, were, had, did, been**; Future: **will, shall**)

Chapter 18, Lesson 3, Practice 4: Change the underlined mixed tense verbs in Paragraph 1 to present tense verbs in Paragraph 2.

Paragraph 1: Mixed Tenses

Cathy **watched** as the horses **prance** across the arena. The horses **held** their heads with such great elegance, and the riders **modeled** perfect riding posture. They **file** into a straight line and **wove** in and out of the obstacles. The lead rider **carries** a flag that he **left** on the final obstacle. As the horses **exited** the arena, the crowd **cheers** loudly. Cathy **closed** her eyes and **imagines** being the star of such a magnificent performance.

Paragraph 2: Present Tense

Cathy **watches** as the horses **prance** across the arena. The horses **hold** their heads with such great elegance, and the riders **model** perfect riding posture. They **file** into a straight line and **weave** in and out of the obstacles. The lead rider **carries** a flag that he **leaves** on the final obstacle. As the horses **exit** the arena, the crowd **cheers** loudly. Cathy **closes** her eyes and **imagines** being the star of such a magnificent performance.

(End of lesson.)

CHAPTER 18   LESSON 4

Objectives: Jingles, Study, Test A and B, Check, Writing (journal).

 JINGLE TIME

Have students turn to the Jingle Section in their books and recite the previously-taught jingles.

 STUDY TIME

Have students study the vocabulary words in their vocabulary notebooks. Remind students that any vocabulary word in their notebooks could be on their test. Also, have students study any of the skills in the Practice Section that they need to review.

 TEST TIME

Have students turn to pages 115 and 116 in the Test Section of their books and find the Chapter 18 Tests A and B. Go over the directions to make sure they understand what to do. (*Chapter 18 A and B keys are on the next two pages.*)

 CHECK TIME

After students have finished, check and discuss their test papers. Make sure they understand why their answers are right or wrong. (*For total points, count each required answer as a point.*)

(End of lesson.)

Chapter 18A Test
(Student Page 115)

Exercise 1: Classify each sentence.

         I   PPA Adj   SN   V-t IO A DO   P   PPA   OP   P   OP

1. **SN V-t**   Wow! My best friend / sent me a present (from her hometown) (in Uruguay)! **E**
   IO DO P3

          HV   SP   V-t   PPA   IO   A DO   P   PPA   OP   P PPA Adj OP

2. **SN V-t**   Did you / make your grandparents a card (for their anniversary) (in your art class)? **Int**
   IO DO P3

Exercise 2: Use Sentence 2 to underline the complete subject once and the complete predicate twice and to complete the table below.

List the Noun Used	List the Noun Job	Singular or Plural	Common or Proper	Simple Subject	Simple Predicate
1. grandparents	2. IO	3. P	4. C	5. you	6. did make
7. card	8. DO	9. S	10. C		
11. anniversary	12. OP	13. S	14. C		
15. class	16. OP	17. S	18. C		

Exercise 3: Identify each pair of words as synonyms or antonyms by putting parentheses ( ) around **syn** or **ant**.

1. mock, mimic	**(syn)** ant	5. peril, danger	**(syn)** ant	9. error, wrong	**(syn)** ant
2. bicker, agree	syn **(ant)**	6. flimsy, sturdy	syn **(ant)**	10. escalate, decrease	syn **(ant)**
3. genuine, fake	syn **(ant)**	7. petty, important	syn **(ant)**	11. hardy, robust	**(syn)** ant
4. agile, quick	**(syn)** ant	8. youth, young	**(syn)** ant	12. conceal, hide	**(syn)** ant

Exercise 4: Underline each verb or verb phrase. Identify the verb tense by writing a number **1** for present tense, a number **2** for past tense, or a number **3** for future tense. Write the past tense form and **R** or **I** for Regular or Irregular.

Verb Tense			Main Verb Past Tense Form	R or I
1	1.	She is moving to an apartment.	moved	R
3	2.	The caller will leave a message.	left	I
2	3.	Was she washing the windows?	washed	R
1	4.	The cattle are wading in the creek.	waded	R
2	5.	The coach had instructed his players.	instructed	R
3	6.	Kim will eat the strawberries.	ate	I
2	7.	I pretended not to see.	pretended	R
1	8.	They have built bonfires before.	built	R
1	9.	Stuart is leaving for home.	left	I
2	10.	He was running very fast.	ran	I

Exercise 5: Identify each kind of sentence by writing the abbreviation in the blank. (**S, F, SCS, SCV, CD**)

    CD   1. She collected seashells, and her brother sold them.
   SCV   2. We stopped for a hamburger and were on our way.
   SCS   3. The cowboy and his dogs herded the cattle.
     F   4. Besides the cost of shipping.
    CD   5. The actor missed his cue, and we all laughed.

Chapter 18B Test
(Student Page 116)

Exercise 6: Change the underlined present tense verbs in Paragraph 1 to past tense verbs in Paragraph 2.

Paragraph 1: Present Tense

    I **crawl** into bed and **reach** for my favorite book. I **snuggle** under my covers and **open** my book. Reading **is** an adventure for me. The story **comes** alive as I **read**. My heart **pounds** as the mystery **builds**. I **sniff** and **wipe** my eyes at the sad or romantic scenes. Reading **is** better than a movie! Finally, my eyes no longer **stay** open. I **sigh** and **close** my book. Reluctantly, I **turn** off the light and **continue** my reading adventures in my dreams!

Paragraph 2: Past Tense

    I **crawled** into bed and **reached** for my favorite book. I **snuggled** under my covers and **opened** my book. Reading **was** an adventure for me. The story **came** alive as I **read**. My heart **pounded** as the mystery **built**. I **sniffed** and **wiped** my eyes at the sad or romantic scenes. Reading **was** better than a movie! Finally, my eyes no longer **stayed** open. I **sighed** and **closed** my book. Reluctantly, I **turned** off the light and **continued** my reading adventures in my dreams!

Exercise 7: Change the underlined mixed tense verbs in Paragraph 1 to present tense verbs in Paragraph 2.

Paragraph 1: Mixed Tense

    I **open** my jewelry box and **gasped**. My grandmother's gold necklace **is** not there! I **was** frantic! I **move** everything off my desk and anxiously **searched** for my grandmother's heirloom. I **looked** under my bed and in my closet. Finally, I **sat** on the bed, and tears of frustration **fill** my eyes. Suddenly, my daughter **walked** into my room with my grandmother's gold necklace around her neck. She **hugged** me and **thanks** me for the loan of the necklace. She **was wearing** it to the antique banquet!

Paragraph 2: Present Tense

    I **open** my jewelry box and **gasp**. My grandmother's gold necklace **is** not there! I **am** frantic! I **move** everything off my desk and anxiously **search** for my grandmother's heirloom. I **look** under my bed and in my closet. Finally, I **sit** on the bed, and tears of frustration **fill** my eyes. Suddenly, my daughter **walks** into my room with my grandmother's gold necklace around her neck. She **hugs** me and **thanks** me for the loan of the necklace. She **is wearing** it to the antique banquet!

Exercise 8: On notebook paper, write one sentence for each of these labels: ① **(S)** ② **(SCS)** ③ **(SCV)** ④ **(CD)** **(Sentences will vary.)**

Exercise 9: On notebook paper, write three sentences, demonstrating each of the three kinds of quotations: Beginning quote and end quote. **(Sentences will vary.)**

Exercise 10: On notebook paper, write the seven present tense helping verbs, the five past tense helping verbs, and the two future tense helping verbs. **(The order of answers may vary.)** (Present: **am, is, are, has, have, do, does;** Past: **was, were, had, did, been;** Future: **will, shall**)

Exercise 11: In your journal, write a paragraph summarizing what you have learned this week.

CHAPTER 18 LESSON 4 CONTINUED

TEACHER INSTRUCTIONS

Use the Question and Answer Flows below for the sentences on the Chapter 18 Tests.

Question and Answer Flow for Sentence 1: Wow! My best friend sent me a present from her hometown in Uruguay!

1. Who sent me a present from her hometown in Uruguay? friend - SN
2. What is being said about friend? friend sent - V
3. Friend sent what? present - verify the noun
4. Does present mean the same thing as friend? No.
5. Present - DO
6. Sent - V-t
7. Friend sent present to whom? me - IO
8. A - A
9. From - P
10. From what? hometown - OP
11. Whose hometown? her - PPA
12. In - P
13. In what? Uruguay - OP
14. What kind of friend? best - Adj
15. Whose friend? my - PPA
16. Wow - I
17. SN V-t IO DO P3 Check
18. Verb-transitive - Check again.
19. (From her hometown) - Prepositional phrase
20. (In Uruguay) - Prepositional phrase
21. Exclamation point, strong feeling, exclamatory sentence
22. Go back to the verb - divide the complete subject from the complete predicate.

Classified Sentence:

```
                              I    PPA Adj  SN    V-t  IO A  DO    P  PPA   OP      P   OP
          SN  V-t    Wow!  My best friend / sent me a present (from her hometown) (in Uruguay)!  E
          IO DO P3
```

Question and Answer Flow for Sentence 2: Did you make your grandparents a card for their anniversary in your art class?

1. Who did make your grandparents a card for their anniversary in your art class? you - SP
2. What is being said about you? you did make - V
3. Did - HV
4. You did make what? card - verify the noun
5. Does card mean the same thing as you? No.
6. Card - DO
7. Make - V-t
8. You did make card for whom? grandparents - IO
9. A - A
10. For - P
11. For what? anniversary - OP
12. Whose anniversary? their - PPA
13. In - P
14. In what? class - OP
15. What kind of class? art - Adj
16. Whose class? your - PPA
17. Whose grandparents? your - PPA
18. SN V-t IO DO P3 Check
19. Verb-transitive - Check again.
20. (For their anniversary) - Prepositional phrase
21. (In your art class) - Prepositional phrase
22. Question mark, question, interrogative sentence
23. Go back to the verb - divide the complete subject from the complete predicate.
24. This sentence has predicate words in the complete subject. Underline the helping verb at the beginning of the sentence twice.

Classified Sentence:

```
                      HV  SP   V-t  PPA     IO     A DO  P  PPA   OP       P  PPA Adj OP
          SN  V-t    Did you / make your grandparents a card (for their anniversary) (in your art class)?  Int
          IO DO P3
```

(End of lesson.)

CHAPTER 18   LESSON 5
Objectives: Writing Assignments #25 and #26, Bonus Option.

 WRITING TIME

TEACHING SCRIPT FOR NARRATIVE WRITING ASSIGNMENTS

You will do two narrative writing assignments. The first narrative writing assignment will be a story without dialogue. The second narrative writing assignment will be a <u>different story</u> with dialogue. You will make a Story Elements outline for both stories. Both rough drafts will go through the revision and editing process. (*Read the boxes below for more information about the students' writing assignment*.) You will choose the point of view for each assignment.

Writing Assignment Box #1

Writing Assignment #25: Narrative Essay <u>Without</u> Dialogue (First or Third Person)

Remind students to make a Story Elements Outline.

Writing topics: The Best Way to Spend a Day or **The Only Time My Opinion Counts** or **The Mighty Mississippi**

Writing Assignment Box #2

Writing Assignment #26: Narrative Essay <u>With</u> Dialogue (First or Third Person)

Remind students to make a Story Elements Outline.

Writing topics: My Act in a Talent Show or **Surviving a Flood/Tornado/ Hurricane** or **A Secret Message**

<u>**Bonus Option:**</u> **How many books are in the New Testament?** (27) **Look up all the books of the New Testament and list them in your Journal. Next, create a word search that contains all the books of the New Testament. Be careful to spell all the names correctly. Give the word search to a family member to complete. Make a key so you can check the finished word search.**

TEACHER INSTRUCTIONS FOR CHECKING WRITING ASSIGNMENTS #25 AND #26

Read, check, and discuss Writing Assignments #25 and #26 after students have finished their final papers. Use the editing checklist as you check and discuss students' papers. Make sure students are using the editing checklist correctly.

(End of lesson.)

Level 4 Homeschool Teacher's Manual

<table>
<tr><td colspan="2">CHAPTER 19   LESSON 1</td></tr>
<tr><td colspan="2">Objectives: Jingles, Grammar (Introductory Sentences, mixed patterns, Oral Skill Builder Check), Practice Exercise, Vocabulary #1, and Activity.</td></tr>
</table>

JINGLE TIME

Have students turn to the Jingle Section in their books and recite the previously-taught jingles.

GRAMMAR TIME

Put the introductory sentences from the box below on the board. Use these sentences as you go through each new concept covered in your teaching script. (*You might put the introductory sentences on notebook paper if you are doing one-on-one instruction with your students.*)

Chapter 19, Introductory Sentences for Lesson 1

1. _____ The efficient manager gave the new employees a tour of the facilities.
2. _____ The landscape artist created a peaceful garden with a variety of native plants.
3. _____ Erosion of the earth's soil occurs naturally with water and wind.

TEACHING SCRIPT FOR INTRODUCING MIXED PATTERNS

You have studied each sentence pattern separately. Today, we will mix up the patterns in a set of sentences. You must decide if a sentence is a Pattern 1, Pattern 2, or Pattern 3 and write the correct pattern in the blank after you classify the sentence. We will classify the three sentences to practice identifying the different sentence patterns. Begin. (*You might have your students write the labels above the sentences at this time.*)

Question and Answer Flow for Sentence 1: The efficient manager gave the new employees a tour of the facilities.

1. Who gave the new employees a tour of the facilities? manager - SN
2. What is being said about manager? manager gave - V
3. Manager gave what? tour - verify the noun
4. Does tour mean the same thing as manager? No.
5. Tour - DO
6. Gave - V-t
7. Manager gave tour to whom? employees - IO
8. A - A
9. Of - P
10. Of what? facilities - OP
11. The - A

12. What kind of employees? new - Adj
13. The - A
14. What kind of manager? efficient - Adj
15. The - A
16. SN V-t IO DO P3 Check
17. Verb-transitive - Check again.
18. (Of the facilities) - Prepositional phrase
19. Period, statement, declarative sentence
20. Go back to the verb - divide the complete subject from the complete predicate.

Classified Sentence:

<pre>
                          A   Adj   SN   V-t A   Adj   IO   A DO P A   OP
          SN V-t   The efficient manager / gave the new employees a tour (of the facilities). D
          IO DO P3
</pre>

CHAPTER 19 LESSON 1 CONTINUED

Question and Answer Flow for Sentence 2: The landscape artist created a peaceful garden with a variety of native plants.

1. Who created a peaceful garden with a variety of native plants? artist - SN
2. What is being said about artist? artist created - V
3. Artist created what? garden - verify the noun
4. Does garden mean the same thing as artist? No.
5. Garden - DO
6. Created - V-t
7. What kind of garden? peaceful - Adj
8. A - A
9. With - P
10. With what? variety - OP
11. A - A

12. Of - P
13. Of what? plants - OP
14. What kind of plants? native - Adj
15. What kind of artist? landscape - Adj
16. The - A
17. SN V-t DO P2 Check
18. Verb-transitive - Check again.
19. (With a variety) - Prepositional phrase
20. (Of native plants) - Prepositional phrase
21. Period, statement, declarative sentence
22. Go back to the verb - divide the complete subject from the complete predicate.

Classified Sentence:		A	Adj	SN	V-t	A	Adj	DO	P	A	OP	P	Adj	OP

SN V-t / DO P2   The landscape artist / created a peaceful garden (with a variety) (of native plants). **D**

Question and Answer Flow for Sentence 3: Erosion of the earth's soil occurs naturally with water and wind.

1. What occurs naturally with water and wind? erosion - SN
2. What is being said about erosion? erosion occurs - V
3. Occurs how? naturally - Adv
4. With - P
5. With what? water and wind - COP, COP
6. And - C
7. Of - P
8. Of what? soil - OP

9. Whose soil? earth's - PNA
10. The - A
11. SN V P1 Check
12. (Of the earth's soil) - Prepositional phrase
13. (With water and wind) - Prepositional phrase
14. Period, statement, declarative sentence
15. Go back to the verb - divide the complete subject from the complete predicate.

Classified Sentence:		SN	P	A	PNA	OP	V	Adv	P	COP	C	COP

SN V / P1   Erosion (of the earth's soil) / occurs naturally (with water and wind). **D**

Use Sentences 1-3 that you just classified with your students to do an Oral Skill Builder Check.

Oral Skill Builder Check

1. **Noun check.**
   (Say the job and then say the noun. Circle each noun.)
2. **Identify the nouns as singular or plural.**
   (Write **S** or **P** above each noun.)
3. **Identify the nouns as common or proper.**
   (Follow established procedure for oral identification.)
4. **Do a vocabulary check.**
   (Follow established procedure for oral identification.)

5. **Identify the complete subject and the complete predicate.** (Underline the complete subject once and the complete predicate twice.)
6. **Identify the simple subject and simple predicate.** (Underline the simple subject once and the simple predicate twice. Bold, or highlight, the lines.)
7. **Recite the irregular verb chart.** (Located on student page 23 and teacher page 138.)

CHAPTER 19 LESSON 1 CONTINUED

PRACTICE TIME

Have students write the three sentences that they classified at the beginning of the lesson on a sheet of paper. Have them tape-record the Question and Answer Flows for all three sentences. Students should write labels above the sentences as they classify them. They especially need the second practice if this is their first year in the program. (*After the students have finished, check the tape and sentence labels. Make sure students understand any mistakes they have made.*)

VOCABULARY TIME

Assign Chapter 19, Vocabulary Words **#1** on page 9 in the Reference Section for students to define in their Vocabulary notebooks. Tell students they are to use a dictionary or thesaurus to look up the meanings of the vocabulary words. After they write each word and its meaning, students are to write a sentence using the vocabulary word.

Chapter 19, Vocabulary Words #1
(remain, stay, dim, bright)

ACTIVITY / ASSIGNMENT TIME

Have students make a booklet and title it, "Little Known Facts About Interesting People." They should interview one person a week for several weeks and organize their facts into a pleasing format. They may want to add photographs, artwork, etc. (*This can also be done on the computer.*) Students may use the suggestions below as they compile information for their folders. Suggested people to interview: parents, grandparents, friends, mayor, police chief, nurses, doctors, preachers, aunts, uncles, cousins, brothers, sisters, etc. (*Students might like to give the people they interviewed a copy of their report.*)

Full name, Date/place of birth, City of residence, Occupation, If retired, date of retirement, Spouse, How I met my spouse, Date/place of marriage, Names of children, Number of grandchildren/great grandchildren.

My favorite color is…, My favorite month is…, My favorite school subject was…, My favorite real food is…., My favorite junk food is…, My favorite dessert is…, My favorite restaurant is…, My favorite room in the house is…, My favorite author/book is…, My favorite kind of music/song is…, My favorite movie is…, My favorite TV show is…, My teenage idol was…, My hobbies are…, My pet peeve is…, The greatest invention during my lifetime is…, If I could live in another time period, I'd choose…, If I could go anywhere in the world, I'd go to…, If I won a million dollars, I'd…, If I've learned one thing in life, it's…, I wish I was better at…, I like people who…, When I'm nervous, I…, When I was a kid, I wanted to be…, My favorite childhood memory is…, My best vacation was…, The person who influenced me the most was…, My proudest accomplishments are…, My words of wisdom for others are…

(End of lesson.)

CHAPTER 19   LESSON 2

Objectives: Jingles, Grammar (Practice Sentences, mixed patterns, Practice Sentence), Skill (double negatives), Practice Exercise and Vocabulary #2.

 JINGLE TIME

Have students turn to the Jingle Section in their books and recite the previously-taught jingles.

 GRAMMAR TIME

First-Year Option: Put the Practice Sentences from the box below on the board or notebook paper. Use these sentences as you practice the concepts that have been taught. For the greatest benefit, students must participate orally with the teacher. **Second-Year Option:** Have students classify the Practice Sentences independently on notebook paper. Check students' sentences with the answers provided below. *(If you have the CDs for Practice Sentences, have students check their sentences with the CDs.)*

Chapter 19, Practice Sentences for Lesson 2
1. _____ Our family explored the main islands of Hawaii during our summer vacation.
2. _____ The lady at the ticket counter gave us a coupon for some popcorn at the concession stand.
3. _____ Did Mom stop by the newspaper office for a short chat with the editor?

TEACHING SCRIPT FOR PRACTICING MIXED PATTERNS

We will practice classifying Mixed Patterns. We will classify the sentences together. Begin. *(You might have your students write the labels above the sentences at this time.)*

Question and Answer Flow for Sentence 1: Our family explored the main islands of Hawaii during our summer vacation.

1. Who explored the main islands of Hawaii during our summer vacation? family - SN
2. What is being said about family? family explored - V
3. Family explored what? islands - verify the noun
4. Do islands mean the same thing as family? No.
5. Islands - DO
6. Explored - V-t
7. Which islands? main - Adj
8. The - A
9. Of - P
10. Of what? Hawaii - OP
11. During - P
12. During what? vacation - OP
13. What kind of vacation? summer - Adj
14. Whose vacation? our - PPA
15. Whose family? our - PPA
16. SN V-t DO P2 Check
17. Verb-transitive - Check again.
18. (Of Hawaii) - Prepositional phrase
19. (During our summer vacation) - Prepositional phrase
20. Period, statement, declarative sentence
21. Go back to the verb - divide the complete subject from the complete predicate.

Classified Sentence:

	PPA	SN		V-t	A	Adj	DO		P	OP		P	PPA	Adj	OP	
SN V-t	Our	family	/	explored	the	main	islands	(of	Hawaii)		(during	our	summer	vacation).	D
DO P2																

Level 4 Homeschool Teacher's Manual

CHAPTER 19 LESSON 2 CONTINUED

Question and Answer Flow for Sentence 2: The lady at the ticket counter gave us a coupon for some popcorn at the concession stand.

1. Who gave us a coupon for some popcorn at the concession stand? lady - SN
2. What is being said about lady? lady gave - V
3. Lady gave what? coupon - verify the noun
4. Does coupon mean the same thing as lady? No.
5. Coupon - DO
6. Gave - V-t
7. Lady gave coupon to whom? us - IO
8. A - A
9. For - P
10. For what? popcorn - OP
11. How much popcorn? some - Adj
12. At - P
13. At what? stand - OP
14. What kind of stand? concession - Adj
15. The - A
16. At - P
17. At what? counter - OP
18. What kind of counter? ticket - Adj
19. The - A
20. The - A
21. SN V-t IO DO P3 Check
22. Verb-transitive - Check again.
23. (At the ticket counter) - Prepositional phrase
24. (For some popcorn) - Prepositional phrase
25. (At the concession stand) - Prepositional phrase
26. Period, statement, declarative sentence
27. Go back to the verb - divide the complete subject from the complete predicate.

Classified Sentence:	SN V-t	A SN P A Adj OP V-t IO A DO P Adj OP P A Adj
		The lady (at the ticket counter) / gave us a coupon (for some popcorn) (at the concession
	IO DO P3	OP
		stand). **D**

Question and Answer Flow for Sentence 3: Did Mom stop by the newspaper office for a short chat with the editor?

1. Who did stop by the newspaper office for a short chat with the editor? Mom - SN
2. What is being said about Mom? Mom did stop - V
3. Did - HV
4. By - P
5. By what? office - OP
6. What kind of office? newspaper - Adj
7. The - A
8. For - P
9. For what? chat - OP
10. What kind of chat? short - Adj
11. A - A
12. With - P
13. With whom? editor - OP
14. The - A
15. SN V P1 Check
16. (By the newspaper office) - Prepositional phrase
17. (For a short chat) - Prepositional phrase
18. (With the editor) - Prepositional phrase
19. Question mark, question, interrogative sentence
20. Go back to the verb - divide the complete subject from the complete predicate.
21. This sentence has predicate words in the complete subject. Underline the helping verb at the beginning of the sentence twice.

Classified Sentence:	SN V	HV SN V P A Adj OP P A Adj OP P A OP
	P1	Did Mom / stop (by the newspaper office) (for a short chat) (with the editor)? **Int**

TEACHER INSTRUCTIONS FOR A PRACTICE SENTENCE

Tell students that their sentence writing assignment today is to write a sentence pattern of their choice. They may choose any Pattern, 1-3, for a Practice Sentence. They are to follow the same procedure used in the previous lessons. They should decide on their labels, arrange them in a selected order, write their sentence, and edit the sentence for improved word choices. (*Students do not have to write an Improved Sentence at this point unless you feel they need more one-on-one word choice writing practice.*) Check and discuss the sentence pattern chosen after students have finished.

CHAPTER 19 LESSON 2 CONTINUED

SKILL TIME

TEACHING SCRIPT FOR DOUBLE NEGATIVES

Today, we are going to learn how to correct double negative mistakes in writing. The first thing we need to know is what it means to have a double negative mistake. Double means TWO, and negative means NOT. We have a **double negative** mistake when we use two negative words that both mean NOT in the same sentence. Most negative words begin with the letter *n*. Other negative words do not begin with the letter *n* but are negative in meaning. There are also some prefixes that give words a negative meaning.

Look at Reference 57 on page 48 in your book. First, we will go over the most commonly-used negative words and prefixes. Then, we'll learn three ways to correct double negative mistakes, and, finally, we'll see different ways to change negative words to positive words. (*Read and discuss the information in Reference 57 below with your students.*)

Reference 57: Double Negatives						
Negative Words That Begin With *N*					**Other Negative Words**	**Negative Prefixes**
neither	no	no one	not (n't)	nowhere	barely, hardly, scarcely	dis, non, un
never	nobody	none	nothing			

Three Ways to Correct a Double Negative

Rule 1. **Change** the second negative to a positive:
    Wrong: The crowd **couldn't** see **nothing**.
    Right: The crowd **couldn't** see **anything**.

Rule 2. **Take out** the negative part of a contraction:
    Wrong: The crowd **couldn't** see **nothing**.
    Right: The crowd **could** see **nothing**.

Rule 3. **Remove** the first negative word (possibility of a verb change):
    Wrong: The crowd **couldn't** see **nothing**.
    Right: The crowd **saw nothing**.

Changing Negative Words to Positive Words

1. Change *no* or *none* to *any*.
2. Change *nobody* to *anybody*.
3. Change *no one* to *anyone*.
4. Change *nothing* to *anything*.
5. Change *nowhere* to *anywhere*.
6. Change *never* to *ever*.
7. Change *neither* to *either*.
8. Remove the *n't* from a contraction.

Examples: Underline the negative words in each sentence. Rewrite each sentence and correct the double-negative mistake as indicated by the rule number in parentheses at the end of the sentence.

  1. She <u>doesn't</u> have <u>no</u> money for lunch. (Rule 3) **She has no money for lunch.**
  2. The seniors <u>can't</u> <u>hardly</u> wait for graduation. (Rule 2) **The seniors can hardly wait for graduation.**
  3. He <u>hasn't</u> done <u>nothing</u> for his report. (Rule 1) **He hasn't done anything for his report.**

Go through the guided examples with your students. Make sure students know how to make the double-negative correction according to the rule provided at the end of each sentence. (*Remember, the reference answers are keyed to give students guided examples.*)

CHAPTER 19 LESSON 2 CONTINUED

PRACTICE TIME

Have students turn to pages 84 and 85 in the Practice Section of their book and find Chapter 19, Lesson 2, Practice (*1-2*). Go over the directions to make sure they understand what to do. Check and discuss the Practices after students have finished. (*Chapter 19, Lesson 2, Practice keys are given below.*)

Chapter 19, Lesson 2, Practice 1: Underline the negative words in each sentence. Rewrite each sentence on notebook paper and correct the double negative mistake as indicated by the rule number in parentheses at the end of the sentence.

Rule 1	Rule 2	Rule 3
Change the second negative to a positive.	Take out the negative part of a contraction.	Remove the first negative word (verb change).

1. There <u>wasn't</u> <u>no</u> sauce left. (Rule 1)
   There wasn't any sauce left.
2. Julia <u>doesn't</u> have <u>no</u> sister. (Rule 3)
   Julia has no sister.
3. We <u>don't</u> see <u>nothing</u> in the box. (Rule 1)
   We don't see anything in the box.
4. Sally <u>couldn't</u> find <u>no</u> paint. (Rule 1)
   Sally couldn't find any paint.

5. John <u>hadn't</u> <u>never</u> climbed that hill. (Rule 2)
   John had never climbed that hill.
6. They <u>didn't</u> hear <u>nothing</u> about the test. (Rule 2)
   They did hear nothing about the test.
7. <u>Don't</u> <u>never</u> miss your bus. (Rule 1)
   Don't ever miss your bus.
8. The jury <u>didn't</u> have <u>no</u> questions. (Rule 3)
   The jury had no questions.

Chapter 19, Lesson 2, Practice 2: Underline each verb or verb phrase. Identify the verb tense by writing a number **1** for present tense, a number **2** for past tense, or a number **3** for future tense. Write the past tense form and **R** or **I** for Regular or Irregular.

Verb Tense		Main Verb Past Tense Form	R or I
1	1. The boys <u>are</u> <u>building</u> a fort.	built	R
2	2. <u>Did</u> you <u>swim</u> in the pool?	swam	I
1	3. The toddler <u>has</u> <u>grown</u> three inches.	grew	I
1	4. I <u>am</u> <u>cooking</u> the meal.	cooked	R
3	5. I <u>will</u> <u>be</u> <u>riding</u> home with you.	rode	I
1	6. Two monkeys <u>swing</u> on the tree vine.	swung	I
1	7. We <u>have</u> <u>skipped</u> a report.	skipped	R
3	8. The lesson <u>will</u> <u>begin</u> at four o'clock.	began	I

VOCABULARY TIME

Assign Chapter 19, Vocabulary Words **#2** on page 9 in the Reference Section for students to define in their Vocabulary notebooks. After they write each word and its meaning, students are to write a sentence using the vocabulary word.

Chapter 19, Vocabulary Words #2
(connect, separate, puzzle, mystery)

(End of lesson.)

CHAPTER 19   LESSON 3

Objectives: Jingles, Grammar (Practice Sentences, mixed patterns), Skill (contractions), Practice Exercise, Writing (journal).

JINGLE TIME

Have students turn to the Jingle Section in their books and recite the previously-taught jingles.

GRAMMAR TIME

First-Year Option: Put the Practice Sentences from the box below on the board or notebook paper. Use these sentences as you practice the concepts that have been taught. For the greatest benefit, students must participate orally with the teacher. **Second-Year Option:** Have students classify the Practice Sentences independently on notebook paper. Check students' sentences with the answers provided below. (*If you have the CDs for Practice Sentences, have students check their sentences with the CDs.*)

Chapter 19, Practice Sentences for Lesson 3
1. _____ Penguins can swim at a very high rate of speed underwater.
2. _____ The restaurant offered us a choice of chocolate, lemon, or coconut pie.
3. _____ The native plants in our yard attract several kinds of birds, insects, and animals.

TEACHING SCRIPT FOR PRACTICING MIXED PATTERNS

We will practice classifying Mixed Patterns. We will classify the sentences together. Begin. (*You might have your students write the labels above the sentences at this time.*)

Question and Answer Flow for Sentence 1: Penguins can swim at a very high rate of speed underwater.

1. What can swim at a very high rate of speed underwater?
   penguins - SN
2. What is being said about penguins?
   penguins can swim - V
3. Can - HV
4. At - P
5. At what? rate - OP
6. What kind of rate? high - Adj
7. How high? very - Adv

8. A - A
9. Of - P
10. Of what? speed - OP
11. Can swim where? underwater - Adv
12. SN V P1 Check
13. (At a very high rate) - Prepositional phrase
14. (Of speed) - Prepositional phrase
15. Period, statement, declarative sentence
16. Go back to the verb - divide the complete subject from the complete predicate.

Classified Sentence:

		SN	HV	V	P	A	Adv	Adj	OP	P	OP		Adv
SN V		Penguins /	can	swim	(at	a	very	high	rate)	(of	speed)	underwater.	**D**
P1													

Level 4 Homeschool Teacher's Manual

CHAPTER 19 LESSON 3 CONTINUED

Question and Answer Flow for Sentence 2: The restaurant offered us a choice of chocolate, lemon, or coconut pie.

1. What offered us a choice of chocolate, lemon, or coconut pie? restaurant - SN
2. What is being said about restaurant? restaurant offered - V
3. Restaurant offered what? choice - verify the noun
4. Does choice mean the same thing as restaurant? No.
5. Choice - DO
6. Offered - V-t
7. Restaurant offered choice to whom? us - IO
8. A - A
9. Of - P
10. Of what? pie - OP
11. What kind of pie? chocolate, lemon, or coconut - CAdj, CAdj, CAdj
12. Or - C
13. The - A
14. SN V-t IO DO P3 Check
15. Verb-transitive - Check again.
16. (Of chocolate, lemon, or coconut pie) - Prepositional phrase
17. Period, statement, declarative sentence
18. Go back to the verb - divide the complete subject from the complete predicate.

Classified Sentence:

<pre>
              A   SN   V-t   IO A DO   P   CAdj   CAdj C CAdj OP
SN V-t   The restaurant / offered us a choice (of chocolate, lemon, or coconut pie). D
IO DO P3
</pre>

Question and Answer Flow for Sentence 3: The native plants in our yard attract several kinds of birds, insects, and animals.

1. What attract several kinds of birds, insects, and animals? plants - SN
2. What is being said about plants? plants attract - V
3. Plants attract what? kinds - verify the noun
4. Do kinds mean the same thing as plants? No.
5. Kinds - DO
6. Attract - V-t
7. How many kinds? several - Adj
8. Of - P
9. Of what? birds, insects, and animals - COP, COP, COP
10. And - C
11. In - P
12. In what? yard - OP
13. Whose yard? our - PPA
14. What kind of plants? native - Adj
15. The - A
16. SN V-t DO P2 Check
17. Verb-transitive - Check again.
18. (In our yard) - Prepositional phrase
19. (Of birds, insects, and animals) - Prepositional phrase
20. Period, statement, declarative sentence
21. Go back to the verb - divide the complete subject from the complete predicate.

Classified Sentence:

<pre>
              A   Adj SN   P PPA OP   V-t   Adj   DO   P COP COP   C   COP
SN V-t   The native plants (in our yard) / attract several kinds (of birds, insects, and animals). D
DO P2
</pre>

SKILL TIME

TEACHING SCRIPT FOR INTRODUCING CONTRACTIONS

A contraction is two words shortened into one word, and the new word always has an apostrophe. The apostrophe takes the place of the letters that have been left out. When we worked with homonyms, you learned how important it was to choose the correct word. You had to constantly be aware of the spelling of certain words and their meanings. This will still be important as you work with contractions. You must know how to spell contractions correctly and which contraction is correct. And, of course, some contractions can be confused with possessive pronouns, so you must always be aware of the right choices.

CHAPTER 19 LESSON 3 CONTINUED

Look at Reference 58 on page 49. I want you to repeat with me the words from which the contraction is made and then repeat the contraction. (*Go over all the contractions in this manner. This will help your students see them, say them, and hear them correctly. Develop a singsong chant that has enough rhythm to sound good and to be fun at the same time. The contraction chart is reproduced for you on the next page.*)

 PRACTICE TIME

Have students turn to pages 85 and 86 in the Practice Section of their book and find the skill under Chapter 19, Lesson 3, Practice (*1-3*). Go over the directions to make sure they understand what to do. Check and discuss the Practices after students have finished. (*Use the contraction chart on the next page to help students check the Lesson 3, Practice below. Chapter 19, Lesson 3, Practice keys are given below.*)

Chapter 19, Lesson 3, Practice 1: Copy the following words and contractions on notebook paper. Write the correct contraction beside each word; then, write the correct word beside each contraction. **Key: (Words: can't, let's, don't, wasn't, they're, aren't, hadn't, isn't, she's, who's, you're, didn't, it's, we're, weren't, doesn't, hasn't, I'm, I've, I'd, won't, I'll, wouldn't, I'd.)** (**Contractions: he is, that is, you have, they have, he had or he would, she had or she would, he will, we will, we had or we would, they had or they would, should not, could not.**)

Words: cannot, let us, do not, was not, they are, are not, had not, is not, she is, who is, you are, did not, it is, we are, were not, does not, has not, I am, I have, I had, will not, I will, would not, I would.
Contractions: he's, that's, you've, they've, he'd, she'd, he'll, we'll, we'd, they'd, shouldn't, couldn't.

Chapter 19, Lesson 3, Practice 2: Underline the negative words in each sentence. Rewrite each sentence on notebook paper and correct the double-negative mistake as indicated by the rule number in parentheses at the end of the sentence.

Rule 1	Rule 2	Rule 3
Change the second negative to a positive.	Take out the negative part of a contraction.	Remove the first negative word (verb change).

1. She <u>couldn't</u> find <u>nothing</u> in her desk. (Rule 2)
   She could find nothing in her desk.
2. Doug <u>hadn't</u> <u>never</u> played basketball. (Rule 2)
   Doug had never played basketball.
3. They <u>don't</u> know <u>nothing</u> about it. (Rule 1)
   They don't know anything about it.
4. He <u>doesn't</u> have <u>no</u> pets. (Rule 3)
   He has no pets.
5. There <u>wasn't</u> <u>no</u> time left. (Rule 1)
   There wasn't any time left.
6. I <u>didn't</u> find <u>no</u> key. (Rule 3)
   I found no key.

Chapter 19, Lesson 3, Practice 3: Underline each verb or verb phrase. Identify the verb tense by writing a number **1** for present tense, a number **2** for past tense, or a number **3** for future tense. Write the past tense form and **R** or **I** for Regular or Irregular.

Verb Tense			Main Verb Past Tense Form	R or I
1	1.	The pictures <u>are</u> <u>falling</u> off the walls.	fell	I
2	2.	The volunteers <u>worked</u> diligently.	worked	R
1	3.	She <u>has</u> <u>called</u> three times.	called	R
1	4.	The church <u>is</u> <u>changing</u> locations.	changed	R
3	5.	The water <u>will</u> <u>feel</u> too cold.	felt	I

 WRITING TIME

Have students make an entry in their journals.

CHAPTER 19 LESSON 3 CONTINUED

Reference 58: Contraction Chart					Pronoun	Contraction
AM		**HAS**			**its**	**it's**
I am	– I'm	has not	– hasn't		(owns)	(it is)
		he has	– he's		*its coat*	*it's cute*
IS		she has	– she's			
is not	– isn't					
he is	– he's	**HAVE**			**your**	**you're**
she is	– she's	have not	– haven't		(owns)	(you are)
it is	– it's	I have	– I've		*your car*	*you're right*
who is	– who's	you have	– you've			
that is	– that's	we have	– we've			
what is	– what's	they have	– they've			
there is	– there's				**their**	**they're**
		HAD			(owns)	(they are)
ARE		had not	– hadn't		*their house*	*they're gone*
are not	– aren't	I had	– I'd			
you are	– you're	he had	– he'd			
we are	– we're	she had	– she'd		**whose**	**who's**
they are	– they're	you had	– you'd		(owns)	(who is)
		we had	– we'd		*whose cat*	*who's going*
WAS, WERE		they had	– they'd			
was not	– wasn't					
were not	– weren't	**WILL, SHALL**				
		will not	– won't			
DO, DOES, DID		I will	– I'll			
do not	– don't	he will	– he'll			
does not	– doesn't	she will	– she'll			
did not	– didn't	you will	– you'll			
		we will	– we'll			
CAN		they will	– they'll			
cannot	– can't					
		WOULD				
LET		would not	– wouldn't			
let us	– let's	I would	– I'd			
		he would	– he'd			
		she would	– she'd			
		you would	– you'd			
		we would	– we'd			
		they would	– they'd			
		SHOULD, COULD				
		should not	– shouldn't			
		could not	– couldn't			

(End of lesson.)

CHAPTER 19   LESSON 4
Objectives: Jingles, Study, Test, Check and Writing (journal).

JINGLE TIME

Have students turn to the Jingle Section in their books and recite the previously-taught jingles.

STUDY TIME

Have students study the vocabulary words in their vocabulary notebooks. Remind students that any vocabulary word in their notebooks could be on their test. Also, have students study any of the skills in the Practice Section that they need to review.

TEST TIME

Have students turn to page 117 in the Test Section of their book and find the Chapter 19 Test. Go over the directions to make sure they understand what to do. (*Chapter 19 Test key is on the next page.*)

CHECK TIME

After students have finished, check and discuss their test papers. Make sure they understand why their answers are right or wrong. (*For total points, count each required answer as a point.*)

(End of lesson.)

Chapter 19 Test
(Student Page 117)

Exercise 1: Classify each sentence.

```
    (You) SP    V    P   OP  P   A     OP      P   OP
1. SN  V          / Go (with us) (to the museum) (on Friday).  Imp
   P1
```

```
                 PPA   SN    V-t  Adj  Adj  DO   P  A    OP      P PPA    OP
2. SN  V-t       Our mother / gave daily piano lessons (to the children) (in our neighborhood).  D
   DO  P2
```

```
                 PPA Adj  PNA   Adj  SN   V-t  IO   Adj    DO    P PPA OP
3. SN  V-t       My little sister's new shoes / gave her terrible blisters (on her feet).  D
   IO DO  P3
```

Exercise 2: Identify each pair of words as synonyms or antonyms by putting parentheses ( ) around *syn* or *ant*.

1. remain, stay	**(syn)** ant	5. hope, despair	syn **(ant)**	9. sway, influence	**(syn)** ant
2. drought, flood	syn **(ant)**	6. biased, neutral	syn **(ant)**	10. dim, bright	syn **(ant)**
3. praise, commend	**(syn)** ant	7. connect, separate	syn **(ant)**	11. uneasy, nervous	**(syn)** ant
4. shy, bashful	**(syn)** ant	8. puzzle, mystery	**(syn)** ant	12. emerge, disappear	syn **(ant)**

Exercise 3: Change the underlined mixed tense verbs in Paragraph 1 to past tense verbs in Paragraph 2.

Paragraph 1: Mixed Tenses

The weather **was** hot, and the builders **are** tired. The thermometer **read** well above one hundred degrees. The sweat from the builders' foreheads **dripped** down their cheeks and **streaks** their dusty faces. Their water jugs **are** almost empty, and it <u>is</u> only mid-afternoon. The tired workers **send** a young crew member to refill the coolers. Before he **returned**, the neighborhood children **offer** the men several pitchers of ice-cold lemonade. The thirsty builders **smile** blissfully as they **guzzled** down the sweet treat.

Paragraph 2: Past Tense

The weather **was** hot, and the builders **were** tired. The thermometer **read** well above one hundred degrees. The sweat from the builders' foreheads **dripped** down their cheeks and **streaked** their dusty faces. Their water jugs **were** almost empty, and it **was** only mid-afternoon. The tired workers **sent** a young crew member to refill the coolers. Before he **returned**, the neighborhood children **offered** the men several pitchers of ice-cold lemonade. The thirsty builders **smiled** blissfully as they **guzzled** down the sweet treat.

Exercise 4: Copy the following words on notebook paper. Write the correct contraction beside each word.
(Key: you've, there's, isn't, they'll, won't, it's, he'll, let's, we'd, I'll, you'll, wasn't, don't, they've, I'm, doesn't, haven't.)
Words: you have, there is, is not, they will, will not, it is, he will, let us, we would, I will, you will, was not, do not, they have, I am, does not, have not.

Exercise 5: Copy the following contractions on notebook paper. Write the correct word beside each contraction. **(Key: they are, he is or he has, you are, has not, you had or you would, we have, does not, had not, cannot, I had, do not.)**
Contractions: they're, he's, you're, hasn't, you'd, we've, doesn't, hadn't, can't, I'd, don't.

Exercise 6: Write the seven present tense helping verbs, the five past tense helping verbs, and the two future tense helping verbs on notebook paper. **(The order of answers may vary).** (Present: **am, is, are, has, have, do, does**; Past: **was, were, had, did, been**; Future: **will, shall**)

Exercise 7: In your journal, write a paragraph summarizing what you have learned this week.

CHAPTER 19 LESSON 4 CONTINUED

TEACHER INSTRUCTIONS

Use the Question and Answer Flows below for the sentences on the Chapter 19 Tests.

Question and Answer Flow for Sentence 1: Go with us to the museum on Friday.

1. Who go with us to the museum on Friday?
   you - SP (understood subject pronoun)
2. What is being said about you? you go - V
3. With - P
4. With whom? us - OP
5. To - P
6. To what? museum - OP
7. The - A
8. On - P

9. On what? Friday - OP
10. SN V P1 Check
11. (With us) - Prepositional phrase
12. (To the museum) - Prepositional phrase
13. (On Friday) - Prepositional phrase
14. Period, command, imperative sentence
15. Go back to the verb - divide the complete subject from the complete predicate.

Classified Sentence:

	(You) SP	V	P	OP	P	A	OP	P	OP
SN V	/ Go	(with us)	(to the museum)	(on Friday). **Imp**
P1			

Question and Answer Flow for Sentence 2: Our mother gave daily piano lessons to the children in our neighborhood.

1. Who gave daily piano lessons to the children in our neighborhood? mother - SN
2. What is being said about mother? mother gave - V
3. Mother gave what? lessons - verify the noun
4. Do lessons mean the same thing as mother? No.
5. Lessons - DO
6. Gave - V-t
7. What kind of lessons? piano - Adj
8. What kind of lessons? daily - Adj
9. To - P
10. To whom? children - OP
11. The - A

12. In - P
13. In what? neighborhood - OP
14. Whose neighborhood? our - PPA
15. Whose mother? our - PPA
16. SN V-t DO P2 Check
17. Verb-transitive - Check again.
18. (To the children) - Prepositional phrase
19. (In our neighborhood) - Prepositional phrase
20. Period, statement, declarative sentence
21. Go back to the verb - divide the complete subject from the complete predicate.

Classified Sentence:

	PPA SN	V-t	Adj	Adj	DO	P	A	OP	P	PPA	OP
SN V-t	Our mother / gave daily piano lessons (to the children) (in our neighborhood). **D**
DO P2		

Question and Answer Flow for Sentence 3: My little sister's new shoes gave her terrible blisters on her feet.

1. What gave her terrible blisters on her feet? shoes - SN
2. What is being said about shoes? shoes gave - V
3. Shoes gave what? blisters - verify the noun
4. Do blisters mean the same thing as shoes? No.
5. Blisters - DO
6. Gave - V-t
7. Gave blisters to whom? her - IO
8. What kind of blisters? terrible - Adj
9. On - P
10. On what? feet - OP

11. Whose feet? her - PPA
12. What kind of shoes? new - Adj
13. Whose shoes? sister's - PNA
14. Which sister? little - Adj
15. Whose sister? my - PPA
16. SN V-t IO DO P3 Check
17. Verb-transitive - Check again.
18. (On her feet) - Prepositional phrase
19. Period, statement, declarative sentence
20. Go back to the verb - divide the complete subject from the complete predicate.

Classified Sentence:

	PPA Adj	PNA	Adj	SN	V-t	IO	Adj	DO	P	PPA	OP
SN V-t	My little sister's new shoes / gave her terrible blisters (on her feet). **D**
IO DO P3		

CHAPTER 19 LESSON 5

Objectives: Writing Assignments #27 and #28.

 **WRITING TIME**

TEACHING SCRIPT FOR WRITING ASSIGNMENTS

You will do two writing assignments. The first writing assignment will be a narrative essay with or without dialogue. It's your choice. The second writing assignment will be a five-paragraph expository essay. You should make a Story Elements outline for the narrative writing. Both rough drafts will go through the revision and editing stages. As you revise and edit, make sure you use the checkpoints in the Regular Editing Checklist provided in Reference 39. (*Read the boxes below for more information about students' writing assignment.*)

Writing Assignment Box

Writing Assignment #27: Three-Paragraph Narrative Essay <u>With/Without</u> Dialogue (First or Third Person)

Remind students to make a Story Elements outline for their story.

**Writing topic choices: The Unexpected Roller Coaster Ride   or   The Day My Pet Could Talk or
                         The Day No One Could Talk**

Writing Assignment Box

Writing Assignment #28: Five-Paragraph Expository Essay (First Person)

Writing topic choices: My Favorite Eating Places   or   Our Family Traditions   or   My Favorite Things to Wear

---

TEACHER INSTRUCTIONS FOR CHECKING WRITING ASSIGNMENTS

Read, check, and discuss Writing Assignments #27 and #28 after students have finished their final papers. Use the editing checklist as you check and discuss students' papers.

(End of lesson.)

CHAPTER 20   LESSON 1
Objectives: Jingles, Grammar (Practice Sentences, Oral Skill Builder Check), Linking Verbs, Practice Exercise, Writing (journal), and Vocabulary #1.

JINGLE TIME

Have students turn to the Jingle Section in their books and recite the previously-taught jingles.

GRAMMAR TIME

First-Year Option: Put the Practice Sentences from the box below on the board or notebook paper. Use these sentences as you practice the concepts that have been taught. For the greatest benefit, students must participate orally with the teacher. **Second-Year Option:** Have students classify the Practice Sentences independently on notebook paper. Check students' sentences with the answers provided below. *(If you have the CDs for Practice Sentences, have students check their sentences with the CDs.)*

Chapter 20, Practice Sentences for Lesson 1
1. _____ The young boy played in the driveway for hours on his new bicycle.
2. _____ He gave the talented students voice lessons after school.

Question and Answer Flow for Sentence 1: The young boy played in the driveway for hours on his new bicycle.

1. Who played in the driveway for hours on his new bicycle? boy - SN
2. What is being said about boy? boy played - V
3. In - P
4. In what? driveway - OP
5. The - A
6. For - P
7. For what? hours - OP
8. On - P
9. On what? bicycle - OP
10. What kind of bicycle? new - Adj
11. Whose bicycle? his - PPA
12. Which boy? young - Adj
13. The - A
14. SN V P1 Check
15. (In the driveway) - Prepositional phrase
16. (For hours) - Prepositional phrase
17. (On his new bicycle) - Prepositional phrase
18. Period, statement, declarative sentence
19. Go back to the verb - divide the complete subject from the complete predicate.

Classified Sentence:

		A	Adj	SN	V	P	A	OP		P	OP		P	PPA	Adj	OP	
SN V		The young boy / played (in the driveway) (for hours) (on his new bicycle).															D
P1																	

CHAPTER 20 LESSON 1 CONTINUED

Question and Answer Flow for Sentence 2: He gave the talented students voice lessons after school.

1. Who gave the talented students voice lessons after school? he - SP
2. What is being said about he? he gave - V
3. He gave what? lessons - verify the noun
4. Do lessons mean the same thing as he? No.
5. Lessons - DO
6. Gave - V-t
7. He gave lessons to whom? students - IO
8. What kind of lessons? voice - Adj
9. After - P

10. After what? school - OP
11. What kind of students? talented - Adj
12. The - A
13. SN V-t IO DO P3 Check
14. Verb-transitive - Check again.
15. (After school) - Prepositional phrase
16. Period, statement, declarative sentence
17. Go back to the verb - divide the complete subject from the complete predicate.

Classified Sentence:

		SP	V-t	A	Adj	IO	Adj	DO	P	OP

SN V-t   He / gave the talented students voice lessons (after school). D
IO DO P3

Use Sentences 1-2 that you just classified with your students to do an Oral Skill Builder Check. Use the guidelines below.

Oral Skill Builder Check

1. **Noun check.**
   (Say the job and then say the noun. Circle each noun.)
2. **Identify the nouns as singular or plural.**
   (Write **S** or **P** above each noun.)
3. **Identify the nouns as common or proper.**
   (Follow established procedure for oral identification.)
4. **Do a vocabulary check.**
   (Follow established procedure for oral identification.)

5. **Identify the complete subject and the complete predicate.** (Underline the complete subject once and the complete predicate twice.)
6. **Identify the simple subject and simple predicate.** (Underline the simple subject once and the simple predicate twice. Bold, or highlight, the lines.)
7. **Recite the irregular verb chart.**
   (Located on student page 23 and teacher page 138.)

TEACHING SCRIPT FOR LINKING VERBS

The verbs that you have studied in Patterns 1-3 are action verbs because they show what the subjects do. Today, you will study a new kind of verb called a linking verb. This verb does not show action. The linking verb does exactly what its name says it does: it links, or connects, a word in the predicate to the subject of the sentence. Turn to Reference 59 on page 50 in the Reference Section of your book. Follow along as I read how to identify linking verbs. (*Reference 59 is located on the next page.*)

CHAPTER 20 LESSON 1 CONTINUED

Reference 59: Linking Verbs

An action verb shows action. It tells what the subject does. A linking verb does not show action. It does not tell what the subject does. A linking verb is called a state of being verb because it tells **what the subject is or is like**. To decide if a verb is linking or action, remember these two things**:**

1. A linking verb may have a noun in the predicate that means the same thing as the subject:

A linking verb connects a noun in the predicate that means the same thing as the subject to the subject of the sentence. This noun is called a predicate noun and is identified with the abbreviation **PrN**.

(Mrs. Reid is the aunt.)   (They are the players.)   (Kim is the friend.)   (Son is the actor.)

SN LV	PrN	SP LV	PrN	SN LV	PrN	SN LV	PrN

Mrs. Reid **is** my (aunt).   They **are** soccer (players).   Kim **is** my best (friend).   My son **is** a talented (actor).

2. A linking verb may also have an adjective in the predicate that tells what kind of subject:

A linking verb connects an adjective in the predicate that describes the subject of the sentence. This adjective is called a predicate adjective and is identified with the abbreviation **PA**.

(What kind of coach? happy) (What kind of Joe? hungry) (What kind of grass? green) (What kind of they? doubtful)

SN LV PA	SN LV PA	SN LV PA	SP LV PA

The coach **is** (happy).   Joe **was** (hungry).   The grass **is** (green).   They **were** very (doubtful).

These are the <u>most common</u> linking verbs: *am, is, are, was, were, be, been, seem, become.*

These <u>sensory verbs</u> can be linking or action: *taste, sound, smell, feel, look.*

A good rule to follow:
If a sentence has a predicate noun (**PrN**) or a predicate adjective (**PA**), it has a linking verb.
If a sentence <u>does not have</u> a predicate noun (**PrN**) or a predicate adjective (**PA**), it probably has an action verb.

Example: Underline each subject and fill in each column according to the title.

	List each Verb	Write PrN, PA, or None	Write L or A
1. The clouds are dark.	are	PA	L
2. The choir sings well.	sings	None	A
3. Tony is my first cousin.	is	PrN	L
4. The squirrel is climbing the tree.	is climbing	None	A

 PRACTICE TIME

Have students turn to page 86 in the Practice Section of their book and find the instructions under Chapter 20, Lesson 1, Practice (*1-2*). Go over the directions to make sure they understand what to do. If students need a review, have them study the information in the Reference Section of their books. Check and discuss the Practices after students have finished. (*Chapter 20, Lesson 1, Practice keys are on the next page*.)

Level 4 Homeschool Teacher's Manual

CHAPTER 20 LESSON 1 CONTINUED

Chapter 20, Lesson 1, Practice 1: Underline each subject and fill in each column according to the title.

	List each Verb	Write PrN, PA, or None	Write L or A
1. Those <u>pickles</u> are sour.	are	PA	L
2. Our new <u>home</u> is beautiful.	is	PA	L
3. <u>They</u> rushed to the store.	rushed	None	A
4. <u>Panthers</u> are fierce creatures.	are	PrN	L
5. <u>She</u> is our new principal.	is	PrN	L
6. All the <u>glasses</u> are dirty.	are	PA	L
7. That <u>movie</u> was very popular.	was	PA	L
8. <u>Sally</u> rode in the parade.	rode	None	A
9. <u>They</u> visited our school.	visited	None	A
10. <u>Travis</u> is a new student.	is	PrN	L
11. My <u>brother</u> is riding his horse.	is riding	None	A
12. <u>Hudson</u> is a small country town.	is	PrN	L
13. The <u>landscape</u> was beautiful.	was	PA	L
14. <u>Adam</u> is the oldest child.	is	PrN	L

Chapter 20, Lesson 1, Practice 2: Copy the following **words** and **contractions** on notebook paper. Write the correct contraction beside each word; then, write the correct word beside each contraction. **Key: (<u>Words</u>: he's, haven't, we've, he'd, you'd, he'll, they'll, we'd, they'd, shouldn't, couldn't, didn't, he's, what's, he'd, she's, hasn't, I'm, you've, she'd, won't, I'll.) (<u>Contractions</u>: I am, it is, who is, are not, you are, they are, was not, were not, does not, did not, cannot, has not, will not.)**

<u>Words:</u> he has, have not, we have, he had, you had, he will, they will, we would, they would, should not, could not, did not, he is, what is, he would, she has, has not, I am, you have, she had, will not, I will.

<u>Contractions:</u> I'm, it's, who's, aren't, you're, they're, wasn't, weren't, doesn't, didn't, can't, hasn't, won't.

WRITING TIME

Have students make an entry in their journals.

VOCABULARY TIME

Assign Chapter 20, Vocabulary Words **#1** on page 9 in the Reference Section for students to define in their Vocabulary notebooks. After they write each word and its meaning, students are to write a sentence using the vocabulary word.

Chapter 20, Vocabulary Words #1
(dwell, live, subordinate, leader)

(End of lesson.)

CHAPTER 20   LESSON 2

Objectives: Jingles, Grammar (Practice Sentences, Practice Sentence), Skills (form the plurals of nouns with different endings), Practice Exercise, Writing (journal), and Vocabulary #2.

JINGLE TIME

Have students turn to the Jingle Section in their books and recite the previously-taught jingles.

GRAMMAR TIME

First-Year Option: Put the Practice Sentences from the box below on the board or notebook paper. Use these sentences as you practice the concepts that have been taught. For the greatest benefit, students must participate orally with the teacher. **Second-Year Option:** Have students classify the Practice Sentences independently on notebook paper. Check students' sentences with the answers provided below. (*If you have the CDs for Practice Sentences, have students check their sentences with the CDs.*)

Chapter 20, Practice Sentences for Lesson 2
1. _____ The drummers beat a steady rhythm on their drums.
2. _____ The tiny tadpole swam quickly away from the large fish.

Question and Answer Flow for Sentence 1: The drummers beat a steady rhythm on their drums.

1. Who beat a steady rhythm on their drums? drummers - SN
2. What is being said about drummers? drummers beat - V
3. Drummers beat what? rhythm - verify the noun
4. Does rhythm mean the same thing as drummers? No.
5. Rhythm - DO
6. Beat - V-t
7. What kind of rhythm? steady - Adj
8. A - A
9. On - P
10. On what? drums - OP
11. Whose drums? their - PPA
12. The - A
13. SN V-t DO P2 Check
14. Verb-transitive - Check again.
15. (On their drums) - Prepositional phrase
16. Period, statement, declarative sentence
17. Go back to the verb - divide the complete subject from the complete predicate.

Classified Sentence:

```
              A    SN       V-t A Adj  DO    P PPA OP
   SN V-t    The drummers / beat a steady rhythm (on their drums).  D
   DO P2
```

CHAPTER 20 LESSON 2 CONTINUED

Question and Answer Flow for Sentence 2: The tiny tadpole swam quickly away from the large fish.

1. What swam quickly away from the large fish?
   tadpole - SN
2. What is being said about tadpole? tadpole swam - V
3. Swam how? quickly - Adv
4. Swam where? away - Adv
5. From - P
6. From what? fish - OP
7. What kind of fish? large - Adj

8. The - A
9. What kind of tadpole? tiny - Adj
10. The - A
11. SN V P1 Check
12. (From the large fish) - Prepositional phrase
13. Period, statement, declarative sentence
14. Go back to the verb - divide the complete subject from the complete predicate.

				A Adj SN	V	Adv	Adv	P	A Adj OP

Classified Sentence:

SN V   The tiny tadpole / swam quickly away (from the large fish). **D**
P1

TEACHER INSTRUCTIONS FOR A PRACTICE SENTENCE

Tell students that their sentence writing assignment today is to write a sentence pattern of their choice. They may choose any Pattern, 1-3, for a Practice Sentence. They are to follow the same procedure used in the previous lessons. They should decide on their labels, arrange them in a selected order, write their sentences, and edit their sentences for improved word choices. (_Students do not have to write an Improved Sentence at this point unless you feel they need more one-on-one word choice writing practice._) Check and discuss the sentence pattern chosen after students have finished.

SKILL TIME

TEACHING SCRIPT FOR HOW TO FORM THE PLURALS OF NOUNS WITH DIFFERENT ENDINGS

Today, we will learn how to form the plurals of nouns with different endings. Look at Reference 60 on page 51. This is a box of rules that will make it a little easier to form the plurals of nouns with different endings. Let's read the rules and discuss how each one is used. (_Read and discuss the rules in the reference box below._)

Reference 60: Rules for the Plurals of Nouns with Different Endings	
1. "ch, sh, z, s, ss, x" – add "es."	6. "f" or "ff," add "s."
2. a vowel plus "y," add an "s."	7. a vowel plus "o," add "s."
3. a consonant plus "y," change "y" to "i" and add "es."	8. a consonant plus "o," add "es."
4. "f" or "fe," change the "f" or "fe" to "v" and add "es."	9. stays the same for S and P.
5. irregular nouns – change spellings completely.	10. regular nouns – add "s".

Use the rules above to write the correct plural form of these nouns:

	Rule	Plural Form			Rule	Plural Form
1. donkey	2	donkeys	3.	proof	6	proofs
2. elf	4	elves	4.	fish	9 or 1	fish or fishes

CHAPTER 20 LESSON 2 CONTINUED

After reading the rules, we know 3 things:

1. Which rule you choose will usually depend on the last two letters of a word.
2. You will have to decide whether some letters are vowels or consonants before you can choose a rule.
3. There are some plurals that you will just have to memorize if you don't want to look them up in a dictionary.

I am going to help you form the plurals of a few words so you will see how the rules work. Look at the word **donkey** on your sheet. What are the two letters at the end of **donkey**? *(ey)* Is the 'e' a consonant or vowel? *(vowel)* What is the number of the rule that tells you what to do when you have a vowel plus 'y'? *(Rule 2)*

We will put the number 2 in the small blank beside **donkey**. Now, we will read Rule 2 to find out how to make **donkey** plural. What does Rule 2 tell you to do to make **donkey** plural? *(add an s)* How do you spell the plural of **donkey**? *(d-o-n-k-e-y-s)* Write the correct plural spelling in the blank beside **donkey**.

Look at the next two words on your sheet. They are **elf** and **proof**. What is the letter at the end of each of these words? *(f)* What two rules deal with the letter 'f'? *(Rules 4 and 6)* By reading these two rules, can you tell how to make **elf** and **proof** plural? *(no)*

The only time you know for sure you can use Rule 4 is when you have a word that ends in "fe" *(like knife – knives)*. The only time you know for sure you can use Rule 6 is when you have a word that ends in "ff" *(like cuff - cuffs)*. Words that end only in "f" *(like elf and proof)* must be looked up in the dictionary if you do not already know how to form their plurals. The correct spelling for words like **elf** and **proof** that do not follow a definite rule will have to be memorized.

TEACHER INSTRUCTIONS: At this point, either look up **elf** and **proof** in the dictionary or ask your students to spell these plurals correctly. Write them on the board for the students to see. Encourage the students to use the dictionary when they are not sure of the spellings. This is a valuable skill that will carry into adult life. (*You could even allow them to use a dictionary on their test; it will help them remember the words they do not know.*)

Have your students write the rule numbers and correct plural spellings for ELF and PROOF on their papers. Show students how to find the rules that will help them spell the plural words correctly.

 PRACTICE TIME

Have students turn to page 87 in the Practice Section of their book and find Chapter 20, Lesson 2, Practice (*1-4*). Go over the directions to make sure they understand what to do. Check and discuss the Practices after students have finished. (Chapter 20, Lesson 2, Practice keys are given below and on the next page.)

Chapter 20, Lesson 2, Practice 1: Write the rule number from Reference 60 and the correct plural form of the nouns below.

		Rule	Plural Form			Rule	Plural Form
1.	pulley	2	**pulleys**	6.	tax	1	**taxes**
2.	wife	4	**wives**	7.	studio	7	**studios**
3.	reef	6	**reefs**	8.	potato	8	**potatoes**
4.	moose	9	**moose**	9.	trip	10	**trips**
5.	woman	5	**women**	10.	fly	3	**flies**

CHAPTER 20 LESSON 2 CONTINUED

Chapter 20, Lesson 2, Practice 2: Underline each subject and fill in each column according to the title.

	List each Verb	Write PrN, PA, or None	Write L or A
1. <u>Today</u> is Friday.	is	PrN	L
2. Our <u>luggage</u> was blue.	was	PA	L
3. The <u>doctors</u> went to Russia.	went	None	A
4. Next <u>month</u> is December.	is	PrN	L
5. Our <u>campus</u> is efficient.	is	PA	L
6. <u>Anna</u> is very polite.	is	PA	L
7. <u>Samson</u> was an excellent athlete.	was	PrN	L
8. <u>We</u> bought her paintings.	bought	None	A
9. <u>He</u> went to Missouri.	went	None	A
10. Those <u>snakes</u> are poisonous.	are	PA	L

Chapter 20, Lesson 2, Practice 3: Copy the following **words** and **contractions** on notebook paper. Write the correct contraction beside each word; then, write the correct word beside each contraction. **Key: (<u>Words</u>: that's, there's, they've, we'd, they're, aren't, hadn't, isn't, she's, who's, you're.) (<u>Contractions</u>: is not, she is, what is, we are, do not, let us, he is, she is, have not, I have, we have, you had or you would, we had or we would, I will, I had or I would.)**

<u>Words:</u> that is, there is, they have, we had, they are, are not, had not, is not, she is, who is, you are.

<u>Contractions:</u> isn't, she's, what's, we're, don't, let's, he's, she's, haven't, I've, we've, you'd, we'd, I'll, I'd.

Chapter 20, Lesson 2, Practice 4: On notebook paper, write a beginning quote and an end quote. Underline the explanatory words. (**Answers will vary.**)

WRITING TIME

Have students make an entry in their journals.

VOCABULARY TIME

Assign Chapter 20, Vocabulary Words **#2** on page 9 in the Reference Section for students to define in their Vocabulary notebooks. Tell students they are to use a dictionary or thesaurus to look up the meanings of the vocabulary words. After they write each word and its meaning, students are to write a sentence using the vocabulary word.

Chapter 20, Vocabulary Words #2
(mistake, blunder, allow, forbid)

(End of lesson.)

CHAPTER 20   LESSON 3
Objectives: Jingles, Grammar (Practice Sentences), Skills (similes and metaphors), and Practice Exercise.

 JINGLE TIME

Have students turn to the Jingle Section in their books and recite the previously-taught jingles.

 GRAMMAR TIME

First-Year Option: Put the Practice Sentences from the box below on the board or on notebook paper. Use these sentences as you practice the concepts that have been taught. For the greatest benefit, students must participate orally with the teacher. **Second-Year Option:** Have students classify the Practice Sentences independently on notebook paper. Check students' sentences with the answers provided below. (*If you have the CDs for Practice Sentences, have students check their sentences with the CDs.*)

Chapter 20, Practice Sentences for Lesson 3
1. _____ The veteran teacher gave the rude students a stern lecture on good manners.
2. _____ Wow! He ate the whole pie!

Question and Answer Flow for Sentence 1: The veteran teacher gave the rude students a stern lecture on good manners.

1. Who gave the rude students a stern lecture on good manners? teacher - SN
2. What is being said about teacher? teacher gave - V
3. Teacher gave what? lecture - verify the noun
4. Does lecture mean the same thing as teacher? No.
5. Lecture - DO
6. Gave - V-t
7. Teacher gave lecture to whom? students - IO
8. What kind of lecture? stern - Adj
9. A - A
10. On - P
11. On what? manners - OP

12. What kind of manners? good - Adj
13. What kind of students? rude - Adj
14. The - A
15. What kind of teacher? veteran - Adj
16. The - A
17. SN V-t IO DO P3 Check
18. Verb-transitive - Check again.
19. (On good manners) - Prepositional phrase
20. Period, statement, declarative sentence
21. Go back to the verb - divide the complete subject from the complete predicate.

Classified Sentence:

	A	Adj	SN		V-t	A	Adj	IO		A	Adj	DO	P	Adj	OP
SN V-t	The	veteran	teacher	/	gave	the	rude	students		a	stern	lecture	(on	good	manners). D
IO DO P3															

CHAPTER 20 LESSON 3 CONTINUED

Question and Answer Flow for Sentence 2: Wow! He ate the whole pie!

1. Who ate the whole pie? he - SP
2. What is being said about he? he ate - V
3. He ate what? pie - verify the noun
4. Does pie mean the same thing as he? No.
5. Pie - DO
6. Ate - V-t
7. Which pie? whole - Adj
8. The - A

9. Wow - I
10. SN V-t DO P2 Check
11. No prepositional phrases.
12. Exclamation point, strong feeling, exclamatory sentence
13. Go back to the verb - divide the complete subject from the complete predicate.

Classified Sentence:

```
                          I    SP  V-t A   Adj  DO
      SN  V-t       Wow!  He / ate the whole pie!  E
      DO  P2
```

SKILL TIME

TEACHING SCRIPT FOR SIMILES AND METAPHORS

Discuss the following information about similes and metaphors. When a writer uses words to draw a picture of two things that he is comparing, it is called a figure of speech. Two figures of speech that writers use most often are **simile** and **metaphor**.

A simile: draws a picture by comparing one noun to another noun in the sentence using "like" or "as."

        Examples: My brother is as slow as a turtle.   Her pillow was as soft as a cloud.
                    Her eyes fluttered like a butterfly.   The crowd flocked towards the stage like angry geese.

A metaphor: draws a picture by showing how two very different things can be alike. It will use linking verbs (*am, is, are, was, were*) to connect the noun in the predicate to the subject.

        Examples: The scream was a knife that pierced the night's silence. Her presence was the sunshine that filled the room.

Assignment: Have students write ten sentences using similes (*like* or *as*) and 5 sentences using metaphors (*linking verb* and *predicate noun*). Discuss the similes and metaphors in the students' sentences. Act out some of the sentences if possible. **Option:** Write and share a short story using similes and metaphors.

PRACTICE TIME

Have students turn to pages 88 and 89 in the Practice Section of their books and find Chapter 20, Lesson 3, Practice (*1-5*). Go over the directions to make sure they understand what to do. If students need a review, have them study the information and examples in the Reference Section of their books. Check and discuss the Practices after students have finished. (*Chapter 20, Lesson 3, Practice keys are given on the next page.*)

CHAPTER 20 LESSON 3 CONTINUED

Chapter 20, Lesson 3, Practice 1: Underline each subject and fill in each column according to the title.

	List each Verb	Write PrN, PA, or None	Write L or A
1. <u>Spanish</u> is a beautiful language.	is	PrN	L
2. <u>She</u> washed her hands in the sink.	washed	None	A
3. The <u>letters</u> are slanted.	are	PA	L
4. The <u>mouse</u> ate the crumb.	ate	None	A
5. Those two <u>boys</u> are brothers.	are	PrN	L
6. My <u>muscles</u> are sore.	are	PA	L

Chapter 20, Lesson 3, Practice 2: Write the rule number from Reference 60 and the correct plural form of the nouns below.

		Rule	Plural Form			Rule	Plural Form
1.	monkey	2	monkeys	6.	fox	1	foxes
2.	wharf	4 or 6	wharves or wharfs	7.	stereo	7	stereos
3.	spoof	6	spoofs	8.	potato	8	potatoes
4.	fish	1 or 9	fish or fishes	9.	author	10	authors
5.	man	5	men	10.	bully	3	bullies

Chapter 20, Lesson 3, Practice 3: Underline the negative words in each sentence. Rewrite each sentence on notebook paper and correct the double negative mistake as indicated by the rule number in parentheses at the end of the sentence.

Rule 1	Rule 2	Rule 3
Change the second negative to a positive.	Take out the negative part of a contraction.	Remove the first negative word (verb change).

1. She <u>didn't</u> want <u>nothing</u> to eat. (Rule 1)
   She didn't want anything to eat.
2. We <u>hadn't</u> <u>never</u> been to New York. (Rule 2)
   We had never been to New York.
3. She <u>doesn't</u> want <u>no</u> scholarships. (Rule 1)
   She doesn't want any scholarships.
4. The boys <u>didn't</u> catch <u>no</u> fish. (Rule 3)
   The boys caught no fish.

Chapter 20, Lesson 3, Practice 4: Underline each verb or verb phrase. Identify the verb tense by writing a number **1** for present tense, a number **2** for past tense, or a number **3** for future tense. Write the past tense form and **R** or **I** for Regular or Irregular.

Verb Tense		Main Verb Past Tense Form	R or I
2	1. <u>Did</u> you <u>win</u> the lottery?	won	I
3	2. They <u>will</u> <u>rebuild</u> the church.	rebuilt	R
2	3. In class, he <u>was</u> <u>eating</u> an apple.	ate	I
1	4. I <u>want</u> a different truck.	wanted	R

Chapter 20, Lesson 3, Practice 5: Copy the following **words** and **contractions** on notebook paper. Write the correct contraction beside each word; then, write the correct word beside each contraction. **Key: (Words: can't, let's, don't, wasn't, they're, aren't, hadn't, isn't, she'll, who's, you're.) (Contractions: you had or you would, would not, we are, cannot, he had or he would, should not, they are, who is, there is, she is, he is, I had or I would.)**

<u>Words:</u> cannot, let us, do not, was not, they are, are not, had not, is not, she will, who is, you are.
<u>Contractions:</u> you'd, wouldn't, we're, can't, he'd, shouldn't, they're, who's, there's, she's, he's, I'd.

(End of lesson.)

CHAPTER 20   LESSON 4

Objectives: Jingles, Study, Test, Check, Activity, Writing (journal).

JINGLE TIME

Have students turn to the Jingle Section in their books and recite the previously-taught jingles.

STUDY TIME

Have students study the vocabulary words in their vocabulary notebooks. Remind students that any vocabulary word in their notebooks could be on their test. Also, have students study any of the skills in the Practice Section that they need to review.

TEST TIME

Have students turn to page 118 in the Test Section of their books and find the Chapter 20 Test. Go over the directions to make sure they understand what to do. (*Chapter 20 Test key is on the next page.*)

CHECK TIME

After students have finished, check and discuss their test papers. Make sure they understand why their answers are right or wrong. (*For total points, count each required answer as a point.*)

ACTIVITY / ASSIGNMENT TIME

Read and discuss the example below of a color poem containing similes with your students. Have them follow the directions given to write their own color poem. (*Write the poem and directions on the board.*)

1. Choose a color for a title.
2. Write similes using *like* or *as*. Write one line for each of the five senses below:

	Green
sight	Looks like dancing summer leaves
smell	Smells like a freshly-cut lawn
taste	Tastes as sour as a lime
hearing	Sounds like a grasshopper's song
touch	And feels as scaly as a lizard.

(End of lesson.)

Chapter 20 Test
(Student Page 118)

Exercise 1: Classify each sentence.

```
        PNA      SN        V-t   IO A Adj  DO   P    A    OP
1.  SN  V-t    Julie's grandmother / gave her a tender hug (before the ceremony).  D
    IO DO  P3
```

```
        PPA CSN  C CSP CV  Adv   C   CV    Adv     P    A    Adj  OP
2.  SN  V      My brother and I / yelled wildly and raced frantically (after the departing bus)!  E
    P1
```

Exercise 2: Identify each pair of words as synonyms or antonyms by putting parentheses ( ) around **syn** or **ant**.

1. bicker, agree	syn **(ant)**	4. escalate, decrease	syn **(ant)**	7. peril, danger	**(syn)** ant
2. dwell, live	**(syn)** ant	5. allow, forbid	syn **(ant)**	8. wrong, error	**(syn)** ant
3. flashy, plain	syn **(ant)**	6. blunder, mistake	**(syn)** ant	9. subordinate, leader	syn **(ant)**

Exercise 3: Underline each subject and fill in each column according to the title.

	List each Verb	Write PrN, PA, or None	Write L or A
1. A wedding <u>gown</u> is expensive.	is	PA	L
2. <u>Giants</u> have big feet.	have	None	A
3. <u>Rhode Island</u> is the smallest state.	is	PrN	L
4. <u>Florida</u> is a peninsula.	is	PrN	L
5. <u>Beets</u> are very healthy.	are	PA	L
6. The <u>chef</u> prepared a fine dessert.	prepared	None	A

Exercise 4: Write the rule number from Reference 60 and the correct plural form of the nouns below.

		Rule	Plural Form			Rule	Plural Form
1.	donkey	2	**donkeys**	6.	church	1	**churches**
2.	doily	3	**doilies**	7.	ox	5	**oxen**
3.	louse	5	**lice**	8.	fish	9 or 1	**fish or fishes**
4.	patio	7	**patios**	9.	half	4	**halves**
5.	wife	4	**wives**	10.	bluff	6	**bluffs**

Exercise 5: Underline the negative words in each sentence. Rewrite each sentence on notebook paper and correct the double negative mistake as indicated by the rule number in parentheses at the end of the sentence.

Rule 1	Rule 2	Rule 3
Change the second negative to a positive.	Take out the negative part of a contraction.	Remove the first negative word (verb change).

1. The pen <u>doesn't</u> have <u>no</u> ink. (Rule 3)
   The pen has no ink.
2. My goldfish <u>wouldn't</u> eat <u>no</u> food. (Rule 2)
   My goldfish would eat no food.
3. Paul <u>didn't</u> want <u>no</u> bread. (Rule 1)
   Paul didn't want any bread.
4. The driver <u>didn't</u> <u>never</u> change lanes. (Rule 3)
   The driver never changed lanes.
5. This recipe <u>doesn't</u> call for <u>no</u> sugar. (Rule 1)
   This recipe doesn't call for any sugar.
6. I <u>wouldn't</u> <u>never</u> repeat that. (Rule 2)
   I would never repeat that.

Exercise 6: Copy the following words on notebook paper. Write the correct contraction beside each word.
Key: can't, let's, don't, wasn't, they're, aren't, hadn't, isn't, she's, who's, you're, didn't, it's.
Words: cannot, let us, do not, was not, they are, are not, had not, is not, she is, who is, you are, did not, it is.

Exercise 7: In your journal, write a paragraph summarizing what you have learned this week.

CHAPTER 20 LESSON 4 CONTINUED

TEACHER INSTRUCTIONS

Use the Question and Answer Flows below for the sentences on the Chapter 20 Tests.

Question and Answer Flow for Sentence 1: Julie's grandmother gave her a tender hug before the ceremony.

1. Who gave her a tender hug before the ceremony? grandmother - SN
2. What is being said about grandmother? grandmother gave - V
3. Grandmother gave what? hug - verify the noun
4. Does hug mean the same thing as grandmother? No.
5. Hug - DO
6. Gave - V-t
7. Grandmother gave hug to whom? her - IO
8. What kind of hug? tender - Adj
9. A - A
10. Before - P
11. Before what? ceremony - OP
12. The - A
13. Whose grandmother? Julie's - PNA
14. SN V-t IO DO P3 Check
15. Verb-transitive - Check again.
16. (Before the ceremony) - Prepositional phrase
17. Period, statement, declarative sentence
18. Go back to the verb - divide the complete subject from the complete predicate.

Classified Sentence:

	PNA	SN	V-t	IO	A	Adj	DO	P	A	OP

SN V-t / IO DO P3   Julie's grandmother / gave her a tender hug (before the ceremony). D

Question and Answer Flow for Sentence 2: My brother and I yelled wildly and raced frantically after the departing bus!

1. Who yelled wildly and raced frantically after the departing bus? brother and I - CSN, CSP
2. What is being said about brother and I? brother and I yelled and raced - CV, CV
3. Raced how? frantically - Adv
4. After - P
5. After what? bus - OP
6. Which bus? departing - Adj.
7. The - A
8. And - C
9. Yelled how? wildly - Adv
10. And - C
11. Whose brother? my - PPA
12. SN V P1 Check
13. (After the departing bus) - Prepositional phrase
14. Exclamation point, strong feeling, exclamatory sentence
15. Go back to the verb - divide the complete subject from the complete predicate.

Classified Sentence:

	PPA	CSN	C	CSP	CV	Adv	C	CV	Adv	P	A	Adj	OP

SN V / P1   My brother and I / yelled wildly and raced frantically (after the departing bus)! E

(End of lesson.)

CHAPTER 20 LESSON 5

Objectives: Writing (descriptive) and Writing Assignments #29 and #30.

 **WRITING TIME**

TEACHING SCRIPT FOR INTRODUCING DESCRIPTIVE WRITING

An artist paints a picture on canvas with paint. A descriptive writer paints a picture on paper with words. Both the artist and writer must select what they will include in their picture. Descriptive writing **shows** the reader what is being described. It does not just **tell** him about it.

Even though you can use description in expository, narrative, and persuasive writing, sometimes you are asked to write only a descriptive piece of writing. Then, you must know that a **descriptive paragraph** gives a detailed picture of a person, place, thing, or idea.

A descriptive paragraph will usually start with an overall impression of what you are describing. That will be your topic sentence. Then, you will add supporting sentences that give details about the topic. To make a description clear and vivid, these detail sentences should include as much information as possible about how the topic looks, sounds, feels, or tastes. The sensory details that you include will depend on what you are describing. Since all the senses are not significant in all situations, the following guidelines about descriptive writing will give you the types of details that you should consider when you are describing certain topics.

Look at Reference 61 on page 51 in your Reference Section. Follow along as I read the guidelines for descriptive writing. This reference will give you ideas and help guide you as you write descriptive paragraphs. (*Read and discuss Reference 61 below with your students. You might even want to make a descriptive - guidelines poster for the wall so students can have a visual guide as they write descriptive paragraphs.*)

Reference 61: Guidelines for Descriptive Writing

1. **When describing people,** it is helpful to notice these types of details: appearance, walk, voice, manner, gestures, personality traits, any special incident related to the person being described, and any striking details that make that person stand out in your mind.

2. **When describing places or things,** it is helpful to notice these types of details: the physical features of a place or thing (color, texture, smell, shape, size, age), any unusual features, any special incident related to the place or thing being described, and whether or not the place or thing is special to you.

3. **When describing nature,** it is helpful to notice these types of details: the special features of the season, the sights, smells, sounds, colors, animals, insects, birds, and any special incident related to the scene being described.

4. **When describing an incident or an event,** it is helpful to notice these types of details: the order in which the event takes place, any specific facts that will keep the story moving from a beginning to an ending, the answers to any of the *who, what, when, where, why*, and *how* questions that the reader needs to know, and especially the details that will create a clear picture, such as how things look, sound, smell, feel, etc.

CHAPTER 20 LESSON 5 CONTINUED

Look at Reference 62 on page 52. Follow along as I go over the steps in writing a descriptive paragraph. *(Read the samples below as students follow along in the reference box.)*

♦ Writing Topic: **A Weekend at the Cabin**
♦ <u>The Title</u> - Since there are many possibilities for titles, decide if you want to leave the topic as your title or if you want to write a different phrase to tell what your paragraph is about.
(A Weekend at the Cabin)

1. Sentence #1 - Write a topic sentence that introduces what is being described.
   (Almost every weekend, my family and I pack our bags and drive to the lake for a weekend stay in our cabin.)

2. Sentences #2 - #8 -Write sentences that give a description of your topic. *(Use the descriptive writing guidelines in Reference 61 to help you.)*

   (When we arrive, we spend the rest of the evening sitting by a small campfire near the edge of the lake. Dad unpacks his guitar and strums a few relaxing tunes. Mom dozes off in the hammock while Daniel and I comb the shoreline for unique treasures. We return to the cabin before dusk with a few old bobbers, a rusty can, and an empty glass bottle. We tromp up the front porch stairs and head inside to tell of our adventure. A little later, the family gathers in the front room to watch a movie. Daniel and I try to stay awake, but we soon fall fast asleep.)

3. Sentence #9 -Write a concluding (final) sentence that summarizes your paragraph or relates it back to the topic sentence. Read the topic sentence again and then restate it by using some of the same words to say the same thing in a different way.
   (Even though our trips to the cabin can be very tiresome, it is my favorite place to go on the weekend.)

Reference 62: Descriptive Paragraph Guidelines

A. Sentence 1 is the topic sentence that introduces **what is being described**.
B. For sentences 2-8, use **the descriptive details** in Reference 61.
C. Sentence 9 is a concluding sentence that **restates, or relates back to, the topic sentence**.

A Weekend at the Cabin

Almost every weekend, my family and I pack our bags and drive to the lake for a weekend stay in our cabin. When we arrive, we spend the rest of the evening sitting by a small campfire near the edge of the lake. Dad unpacks his guitar and strums a few relaxing tunes. Mom dozes off in the hammock while Daniel and I comb the shoreline for unique treasures. We return to the cabin before dusk with a few old bobbers, a rusty can, and an empty glass bottle. We tromp up the front porch stairs and head inside to tell of our adventure. A little later, the family gathers in the front room to watch a movie. Daniel and I try to stay awake, but we soon fall fast asleep. Even though our trips to the cabin can be very tiresome, it is my favorite place to go on the weekend.

CHAPTER 20 LESSON 5 CONTINUED

Teacher's Notes: The descriptive writing guideline is a suggested guide to help students as they learn to write descriptive paragraphs. However, some students will be able to organize their ideas and stick to the topic without following the guideline exactly. The number of sentences may also vary.

TEACHING SCRIPT FOR WRITING ASSIGNMENTS

You will write two descriptive paragraphs. You should use the descriptive paragraph guidelines to help you notice and describe different types of details. <u>You will revise and edit both writing assignments.</u> (*Read the box below for more information about students' writing assignment.*) As you edit, make sure you use the checkpoints in the editing checklist provided in Reference 39. Remember to read through the whole paragraph, starting with the title, and then edit, sentence-by-sentence, using the five-sentence checkpoints for each sentence. Use the paragraph checkpoints to check each paragraph.

Writing Assignment Box #1

Writing Assignment #29: Descriptive Paragraph (First Person)

Writing topic choices: Grandmother's House or My Unusual Pet or A Special Gift or Sights and Sounds of the woods at night/baseball game/basketball game/football game

---

Writing Assignment Box #2

Writing Assignment #30: Descriptive Paragraph (First or Third Person)

Writing topic choices: Favorite Biblical Character or An Unforgettable Vacation or Winter Wonderland or Choose your own topic.

TEACHER INSTRUCTIONS FOR CHECKING WRITING ASSIGNMENTS

Read, check, and discuss Writing Assignments #29 and #30 after students have finished their final papers. Use the editing checklist as you check and discuss students' papers. Make sure students are using the editing checklist correctly.

(End of lesson.)

CHAPTER 21   LESSON 1

Objectives: Jingles, Grammar (Practice Sentences), Skills (parts of a friendly letter, parts of an envelope), Practice Exercise, Writing (journal), and Vocabulary #1.

JINGLE TIME

Have students turn to the Jingle Section in their books and recite the previously-taught jingles.

GRAMMAR TIME

First-Year Option: Put the Practice Sentences from the box below on the board or on notebook paper. Use these sentences as you practice the concepts that have been taught. For the greatest benefit, students must participate orally with the teacher. **Second-Year Option:** Have students classify the Practice Sentences independently on notebook paper. Check students' sentences with the answers provided below. (*If you have the CDs for Practice Sentences, have students check their sentences with the CDs.*)

Chapter 21, Practice Sentences for Lesson 1

1. _____ My older brother had a bag of licorice for my sister and me.
2. _____ The excited crowd gave the American players a standing ovation for their excellent performance!

TEACHING SCRIPT FOR PRACTICING MIXED PATTERNS

We will practice classifying Mixed Patterns. We will classify the sentences together. Begin. (*You might have your students write the labels above the sentences at this time.*)

Question and Answer Flow for Sentence 1: My older brother had a bag of licorice for my sister and me.

1. Who had a bag of licorice for my sister and me? brother - SN	12. And - C
2. What is being said about brother? brother had - V	13. Whose sister? my - PPA
3. Brother had what? bag - verify the noun	14. Which brother? older - Adj
4. Does bag mean the same thing as brother? No.	15. Whose brother? my - PPA
5. Bag - DO	16. SN V-t DO P2 Check
6. Had - V-t	17. Verb-transitive - Check again.
7. A - A	18. (Of licorice) - Prepositional phrase
8. Of - P	19. (For my sister and me) - Prepositional phrase
9. Of what? licorice - OP	20. Period, statement, declarative sentence
10. For - P	21. Go back to the verb - divide the complete subject
11. For whom? sister and me - COP, COP	from the complete predicate.

Classified   PPA Adj   SN   V-t A DO   P   OP   P PPA COP C COP
Sentence: SN V-t   My older brother **/** had a bag (of licorice) (for my sister and me). **D**
                  DO P2

CHAPTER 21 LESSON 1 CONTINUED

Question and Answer Flow for Sentence 2: The excited crowd gave the American players a standing ovation for their excellent performance!

1. Who gave the American players a standing ovation for their excellent performance? crowd - SN
2. What is being said about crowd? crowd gave - V
3. Crowd gave what? ovation - verify the noun
4. Does ovation mean the same thing as crowd? No.
5. Ovation - DO
6. Gave - V-t
7. Crowd gave ovation to whom? players - IO
8. What kind of ovation? Standing - Adj
9. A - A
10. For - P
11. For what? performance - OP
12. What kind of performance? excellent - Adj
13. Whose performance? their - PPA
14. Which players? American - Adj
15. The - A
16. What kind of crowd? excited - Adj
17. The - A
18. SN V-t IO DO P3 Check
19. Verb-transitive - Check again.
20. (For their excellent performance) - Prepositional phrase
21. Exclamation point, strong feeling, exclamatory sentence
22. Go back to the verb - divide the complete subject from the complete predicate.

Classified Sentence:	A Adj SN V-t A Adj IO A Adj DO P PPA Adj
	The excited crowd / gave the American players a standing ovation (for their excellent
SN V-t	OP
IO DO P3	performance)! E

SKILL TIME

TEACHING SCRIPT FOR THE PARTS OF A FRIENDLY LETTER

Close your eyes. Picture a good friend or favorite relative that you really like but don't get to see very often. Open your eyes. The memory of that favorite person in your life brought a smile to your face, didn't it? Remember, keeping in touch with favorite people brings smiles to their faces, too, and writing a letter is a great way to stay in touch with people you care about and who care about you.

A letter written to or received from friends or relatives is called a **friendly letter**. Listen carefully to some tips that will make your friendly letter interesting and enjoyable to read. (*Read and discuss the tips below. Option: You might choose to dictate the writing tips to your students to enhance their listening skills.*)

Tips for Writing Friendly Letters

Tip #1: Write as if you were talking to the person face-to-face. Share information about yourself and mutual friends. Tell stories, conversations, or jokes. Share photographs, articles, drawings, poems, etc. Avoid saying something about someone else that you'll be sorry for later.

Tip #2: If you are writing a return letter, be sure to answer any questions that were asked. Repeat the question so that your reader will know what you are writing about. (You asked about . . .)

Tip #3: End your letter in a positive way so that your reader will want to write a return letter.

CHAPTER 21 LESSON 1 CONTINUED

Now that you know what things to write about, you must learn to put your friendly letter in the correct friendly-letter format. The friendly letter has five parts: the heading; the friendly greeting, which is also called the salutation; the body; the closing; and the signature.

Each of the parts of a friendly letter has a specific place where it should be written in order for your letter to have correct friendly-letter form. Look at the five parts of a friendly letter and the friendly letter example in Reference 63 on page 52 in your book. We will now go over each of the five parts, what information is contained in each part, and where each part is placed in a friendly-letter form. (*Go over the letter parts and the letter example reproduced below with your students.*)

Reference 63: The Five Parts of a Friendly Letter

1. Heading
1. Box or street address of writer
2. City, state, zip code of writer
3. Date letter was written
4. Placement: upper right-hand corner

2. Friendly Greeting or Salutation
1. Begins with *Dear*
2. Names person receiving the letter
3. Has comma after person's name
4. Placement: at left margin, two lines below heading

3. Body
1. Tells reason the letter was written
2. Can have one or more paragraphs
3. Has indented paragraphs
4. Is placed one line below the greeting
5. Skips one line between each paragraph

4. Closing
1. Closes letter with a personal phrase - (Your friend, With love,)
2. Capitalizes only first word
3. Is followed by a comma
4. Is placed two lines below the body
5. Begins just to the right of the middle of the letter

5. Signature
1. Tells who wrote the letter
2. Is usually signed in cursive
3. Uses first name only unless there is a question as to which friend or relative you are
4. Is placed beneath the closing

Friendly Letter Example

1. Heading

5481 Victory Blvd.
Stocktown, WV 50009
June 8, 20___

2. Friendly Greeting, (or Salutation)

Dear Tim,

3. Body (Indent Paragraphs)

    As you know, your Uncle James and I will be going to Europe next month. We need someone to watch the house and take care of our dog. We thought you would be the perfect person for the job since you are on summer vacation. If you don't already have plans, we'd love for you to house-sit for us!

4. Closing,

Sincerely yours,

5. Signature

Aunt Tracey

CHAPTER 21 LESSON 1 CONTINUED

TEACHING SCRIPT FOR THE PARTS OF AN ENVELOPE

In order to address the envelope of your friendly letter correctly, you must know the parts that go on the envelope and where to write them. Look at Reference 64 on page 53 and follow along as I read the information about the parts of an envelope. Notice what information is contained in the two parts, and where each part is placed on the envelope. (*Go over the information below with your students.*)

Reference 64: Friendly Envelope Parts	
Envelope Parts	**Friendly Envelope Example**
The return address: 1. Name of the person writing the letter 2. Box or street address of the writer 3. City, state, zip code of the writer **The mailing address:** 1. Name of the person receiving the letter 2. Street address of the person receiving the letter 3. City, state, zip code of the person receiving the letter	**Return Address** Stamp Tracey Graves 5481 Victory Blvd. Stocktown, WV 50009 **Mailing Address** Tim Smith 123 Mockingbird Lane Jacksonville, FL 70006

PRACTICE TIME

Have students turn to page 89 in the Practice Section of their book and find Chapter 21, Lesson 1, Practice. Go over the directions to make sure they understand what to do. Check and discuss the Practice after students have finished. (*Chapter 21, Lesson 1, Practice instructions are given below.*)

Chapter 21, Lesson 1, Practice: Use butcher paper, large pieces of construction paper, or poster board to make a colorful wall poster identifying the five parts of a friendly letter and the parts of an envelope. Write the title and an example for each of the five parts. Illustrate your work. Then, give an oral presentation about the friendly letter and the envelope when you have finished. (*This project may take several days.*)

WRITING TIME

Have students make an entry in their journals.

VOCABULARY TIME

Assign Chapter 21, Vocabulary Words **#1** on page 9 in the Reference Section for students to define in their Vocabulary notebooks. After they write each word and its meaning, students are to write a sentence using the vocabulary word.

Chapter 21, Vocabulary Words #1
(terror, fear, compete, cooperate)

(End of lesson.)

     Level 4 Homeschool Teacher's Manual

CHAPTER 21   LESSON 2

Objectives: Jingles, Grammar (Practice Sentences , Practice Sentence), Practice Exercise, and Writing (journal)

JINGLE TIME

Have students turn to the Jingle Section in their books and recite the previously-taught jingles.

GRAMMAR TIME

First-Year Option: Put the Practice Sentences from the box below on the board or notebook paper. Use these sentences as you practice the concepts that have been taught. For the greatest benefit, students must participate orally with the teacher. **Second-Year Option:** Have students classify the Practice Sentences independently on notebook paper. Check students' sentences with the answers provided below. *(If you have the CDs for Practice Sentences, have students check their sentences with the CDs.)*

Chapter 21, Practice Sentences for Lesson 2
1. _____ Pass me another slice of Nancy's homemade apple pie.
2. _____ The tired and weary miners struck gold during the gold rush in California.

TEACHING SCRIPT FOR PRACTICING MIXED PATTERNS

We will practice classifying Mixed Patterns. We will classify the sentences together. Begin. (*You might have your students write the labels above the sentences at this time.*)

Question and Answer Flow for Sentence 1: Pass me another slice of Nancy's homemade apple pie.

1. Who pass me another slice of Nancy's homemade apple pie? you - SP (Understood subject pronoun)
2. What is being said about you? you pass - V
3. You pass what? slice - verify the noun
4. Does slice mean the same thing as you? No.
5. Slice - DO
6. Pass - V-t
7. You pass slice to whom? me - IO
8. Which slice? another - Adj
9. Of - P
10. Of what? pie - OP
11. What kind of pie? apple - Adj
12. What kind of pie? homemade - Adj
13. Whose pie? Nancy's - PNA
14. SN V-t IO DO P3 Check
15. Verb-transitive - Check again.
16. (Of Nancy's homemade apple pie) - Prepositional phrase
17. Period, command, imperative sentence
18. Go back to the verb - divide the complete subject from the complete predicate.

Classified Sentence:

             (You) SP   **V-t IO Adj DO P PNA Adj Adj OP**

             SN V-t   **/ Pass me another slice (of Nancy's homemade apple pie). Imp**

             IO DO P3

CHAPTER 21 LESSON 2 CONTINUED

Question and Answer Flow for Sentence 2: The tired and weary miners struck gold during the gold rush in California.

1. Who struck gold during the gold rush in California? miners - SN
2. What is being said about miners? miners struck - V
3. Miners struck what? gold - verify the noun
4. Does gold mean the same thing as miners? No.
5. Gold - DO
6. Struck - V-t
7. During - P
8. During what? rush - OP
9. What kind of rush? gold - Adj
10. The - A
11. In - P
12. In what? California - OP
13. What kind of miners? tired and weary - CAdj, CAdj
14. And - C
15. The - A
16. SN V-t DO P2 Check
17. (During the gold rush) - Prepositional phrase
18. (In California) - Prepositional phrase
19. Period, statement, declarative sentence
20. Go back to the verb - divide the complete subject from the complete predicate.

Classified Sentence:

                   A CAdj C CAdj SN   V-t   DO   P   A Adj OP   P   OP

<u>SN V-t</u>   The tired and weary miners / struck gold (during the gold rush) (in California). **D**

DO P2

TEACHER INSTRUCTIONS FOR A PRACTICE SENTENCE

Tell students that their sentence writing assignment today is to write a sentence in the pattern of their choice. They may choose any Pattern, 1-3, for a Practice Sentence. They are to follow the same procedure used in the previous lessons. They should decide on their labels, arrange them in a selected order, write their sentences, and edit their sentences for improved word choices. (*Students do not have to write an Improved Sentence at this point unless you feel they need more one-on-one word choice writing practice.*) Check and discuss the sentence pattern chosen after students have finished.

 PRACTICE TIME

Students will continue letter writing activities. Have students turn to page 89 in the Practice Section of their book and find Chapter 21, Lesson 2, Practice. Go over the directions to make sure they understand what to do. Check and discuss the Practice after students have finished. (*Chapter 21, Lesson 2, Practice instructions are given below.*)

Chapter 21, Lesson 2, Practice: Write a friendly letter to a special friend or relative. Before you start, review the references and tips for writing friendly letters. After your letter has been edited, fold the letter and put it in an envelope. Address the envelope properly and mail it. Don't forget the stamp. (E-mail does not take the place of this assignment.)

 WRITING TIME

Have students make an entry in their journals.

(End of lesson.)

CHAPTER 21 LESSON 3

Objectives: Jingles, Grammar (Practice Sentences), Practice Exercise, and Vocabulary #2.

JINGLE TIME

Have students turn to the Jingle Section in their books and recite the previously-taught jingles.

GRAMMAR TIME

First-Year Option: Put the Practice Sentences from the box below on the board or on notebook paper. Use these sentences as you practice the concepts that have been taught. For the greatest benefit, students must participate orally with the teacher. **Second-Year Option:** Have students classify the Practice Sentences independently on notebook paper. Check students' sentences with the answers provided below. *(If you have the CDs for Practice Sentences, have students check their sentences with the CDs.)*

Chapter 21, Practice Sentences for Lesson 3
1. _____ Did your mother talk to the minister about the new church?
2. _____ After the storm, my mother will take you to the store.

TEACHING SCRIPT FOR PRACTICING MIXED PATTERNS

We will practice classifying Mixed Patterns. We will classify the sentences together. Begin. *(You might have your students write the labels above the sentences at this time.)*

Question and Answer Flow for Sentence 1: Did your mother talk to the minister about the new church?	
1. Who did talk to the minister about the new church? mother - SN	11. Whose mother? your - PPA
2. What is being said about mother? mother did talk - V	12. SN V P1 Check
3. Did - HV	13. (To the minister) - Prepositional phrase
4. To - P	14. (About the new church) - Prepositional phrase
5. To whom? minister - OP	15. Question mark, question, interrogative sentence
6. The - A	16. Go back to the verb - divide the complete subject from the complete predicate.
7. About - P	17. This sentence has predicate words in the complete subject. Underline the helping verb at the beginning of the sentence twice.
8. About what? church - OP	
9. What kind of church? new - Adj	
10. The - A	

Classified Sentence:

	HV	PPA	SN	V	P	A	OP	P	A	Adj	OP	
SN V	Did	your	mother /	talk	(to	the	minister)	(about	the	new	church)?	**Int**
P1												

CHAPTER 21 LESSON 3 CONTINUED

Question and Answer Flow for Sentence 2: After the storm, my mother will take you to the store.

1. Who will take you to the store? mother - SN
2. What is being said about mother? mother will take - V
3. Will - HV
4. Mother will take whom? you - verify the pronoun
5. Does you mean the same thing as mother? No.
6. You - DO
7. Take - V-t
8. To - P
9. To what? store - OP
10. The - A
11. Whose mother? my - PPA
12. After - P

13. After what? storm - OP
14. The - A
15. SN V-t DO P2 Check
16. Verb-transitive - Check again.
17. (After the storm) - Prepositional phrase
18. (To the store) - Prepositional phrase
19. Period, statement, declarative sentence
20. Go back to the verb - divide the complete subject from the complete predicate.
21. This sentence has predicate words in the complete subject. Underline the prepositional phrase at the beginning of the sentence twice.

Classified Sentence:

                              P   A   OP   PPA SN   HV V-t DO P A   OP
SN V-t   (After the storm), my mother / will take you (to the store). D
DO P2

PRACTICE TIME

Have students turn to page 89 in the Practice Section of their books and find Chapter 21, Lesson 3, Practice (*1-2*). Go over the directions to make sure they understand what to do. Check and discuss the Practices after students have finished. (*Chapter 21, Lesson 3, Practice instructions are given below.*)

Chapter 21, Lesson 3, Practice 1: On notebook paper, identify the parts of a friendly letter and envelope by writing the titles and an example for each title. Use References 63-64 to help you. (**Use References 63-64 to check the parts of a friendly letter and envelope.**)

Chapter 21, Lesson 3, Practice 2: Write a friendly letter to a neighbor, nursing home resident, or relative. This person must be someone different from the person chosen in the previous lesson. Before you start, review the references and tips for writing friendly letters. After your letter has been edited, fold the letter and put it in an envelope. Address the envelope properly and mail it. Don't forget the stamp.

VOCABULARY TIME

Assign Chapter 21, Vocabulary Words **#2** on page 9 in the Reference Section for students to define in their Vocabulary notebooks. They should write each word, its meaning, and a sentence using the word.

Chapter 21, Vocabulary Words #2
(safe, secure, clutter, order)

(End of lesson.)

CHAPTER 21   LESSON 4

Objectives: Jingles, Study, Test, Check, Activity, and Writing (journal).

JINGLE TIME

Have students turn to the Jingle Section in their books and recite the previously-taught jingles.

STUDY TIME

Have students study the vocabulary words in their vocabulary notebooks. Remind students that any vocabulary word in their notebooks could be on their test. Also, have students study any of the skills in the Practice Section that they need to review.

TEST TIME

Have students turn to page 119 in the Test Section of their books and find the Chapter 21 Test. Go over the directions to make sure they understand what to do. (*Chapter 21 Test key is on the next page.*)

CHECK TIME

After students have finished, check and discuss their test papers. Make sure they understand why their answers are right or wrong. (*For total points, count each required answer as a point.*)

ACTIVITY / ASSIGNMENT TIME

Get some potting soil, 8 different packages of flower seeds, and 8 plastic cups. Tell students they will plant an English flower garden. Then, have students follow the directions below.

1. Name your flower garden by printing the eight parts of speech on the 8 cups with a black magic marker.
2. Draw or cut out and paste a picture of each flower you will plant in the 8 cups. (Each cup should have different flower seeds, if possible.)
3. Put potting soil in the 8 cups and plant 2-3 flower seeds into the soil of the appropriate cup.
4. Place the cups in the window and water daily with an eyedropper.
5. Watch the seeds grow. Record the progress of your flower garden in a journal.
6. As the seeds become flowers, research the flowers in the different cups.
7. Find as much information as possible about the flowers and write a report.
8. Draw, label, and color all the basic parts of a flower on a poster board.
9. Present your report to family members and friends.
10. Use the flowers in the cups and the illustrations on the poster board to help you demonstrate your presentation.

(End of lesson.)

Chapter 21 Test
(Student Page 119)

Exercise 1: Classify each sentence.

          A   Adj   SN   V-t IO A Adj   DO P PPA   OP   Adv

1. <u>**SN V-t**</u>   The green apples / gave me a terrible pain (in my stomach) yesterday. **D**
   IO DO P3

                PPA   CSN C CSP V-t   Adj   DO   P A   OP   P   PPA   OP

2. <u>**SN V-t**</u>   My brother and I / picked wild berries (in the woods) (behind our house). **D**
   DO P2

Exercise 2: Identify each pair of words as synonyms or antonyms by putting parentheses ( ) around *syn* or *ant*.

1. oppose, agree	syn **(ant)**	4. degrade, praise	syn **(ant)**	7. endow, give	**(syn)** ant
2. neutral, biased	syn **(ant)**	5. safe, secure	**(syn)** ant	8. shame, dishonor	**(syn)** ant
3. terror, fear	**(syn)** ant	6. clutter, order	syn **(ant)**	9. compete, cooperate	syn **(ant)**

Exercise 3: Choose an answer from the choices in parentheses. Then, fill in the rest of the columns according to the titles. (**S** or **P** stands for singular or plural.)

Pronoun-antecedent agreement

1. I think the farmer has lost (<u>his</u>, their) cows.
2. The entrance with (<u>its</u>, their) flashing lights was beautiful.
3. Both turtles have lost (its, <u>their</u>) shells.
4. Her sandals needed (its, <u>their</u>) straps tightened.
5. The wind lost (<u>its</u>, their) intensity after the storm.
6. The bubbles made (its, <u>their</u>) way to the clouds.
7. My tooth has (<u>its</u>, their) root exposed.

Pronoun Choice	S or P	Antecedent	S or P
his	S	farmer	S
its	S	entrance	S
their	P	turtles	P
their	P	sandals	P
its	S	wind	S
their	P	bubbles	P
its	S	tooth	S

Exercise 4: Write the rule number from Reference 60 and the correct plural form of the nouns below.

		Rule	Plural Form				Rule	Plural Form
1.	key	2	**keys**		6.	box	1	**boxes**
2.	holly	3	**hollies**		7.	child	5	**children**
3.	mouse	5	**mice**		8.	deer	9	**deer**
4.	radio	7	**radios**		9.	knife	4	**knives**
5.	leaf	4	**leaves**		10.	cliff	6	**cliffs**

Exercise 5: Write the seven present tense helping verbs, the five past tense helping verbs, and the two future tense helping verbs. (Present: **am, is, are, has, have, do, does;** Past: **was, were, had, did, been;** Future: **will, shall.**) (**The order of answers may vary.**)

Exercise 6: Copy the following words on notebook paper. Write the correct contraction beside each word.
Key: can't, let's, don't, wasn't, they're, aren't, hadn't, isn't, she's, who's, you're, didn't, it's, we're, weren't, doesn't, hasn't, I'm, I've, I'd, won't, I'll, wouldn't, shouldn't, couldn't, they'd.
Words: cannot, let us, do not, was not, they are, are not, had not, is not, she is, who is, you are, did not, it is, we are, were not, does not, has not, I am, I have, I had or I would, will not, I will, would not, should not, could not, they would.

Exercise 7: On notebook paper, identify the parts of a friendly letter and envelope by writing the titles and an example for each title. Use References 63 and 64 to help you. (**Use References 63-64 to check the friendly letter and envelope parts**.)

Exercise 8: In your journal, write a paragraph summarizing what you have learned this week.

CHAPTER 21 LESSON 4 CONTINUED

TEACHER INSTRUCTIONS

Use the Question and Answer Flows below for the sentences on the Chapter 21 Test.

Question and Answer Flow for Sentence 1: The green apples gave me a terrible pain in my stomach yesterday.

1. What gave me a terrible pain in my stomach yesterday?
   apples - SN
2. What is being said about apples? apples gave - V
3. Apples gave what? pain - verify the noun
4. Does pain mean the same thing as apples? No.
5. Pain - DO
6. Gave - V-t
7. Apples gave pain to whom? me - IO
8. What kind of pain? terrible - Adj
9. A - A
10. In - P
11. In what? stomach - OP
12. Whose stomach? my - PPA
13. Gave when? yesterday - Adv
14. What kind of apples? green - Adj
15. The - A
16. SN V-t IO DO P3 Check
17. Verb-transitive - Check again.
18. (In my stomach) - Prepositional phrase
19. Period, statement, declarative sentence
20. Go back to the verb - divide the complete subject from the complete predicate.

Classified Sentence:

SN V-t / IO DO P3

A   Adj   SN   V-t IO A Adj   DO P PPA OP   Adv
The green apples / gave me a terrible pain (in my stomach) yesterday. D

Question and Answer Flow for Sentence 2: My brother and I picked wild berries in the woods behind our house.

1. Who picked wild berries in the woods behind our house?
   brother and I - CSN, CSP
2. What is being said about brother and I?
   brother and I picked - V
3. Brother and I picked what? berries - verify the noun
4. Do berries mean the same thing as brother and I? No.
5. Berries - DO
6. Picked - V-t
7. What kind of berries? wild - Adj
8. In - P
9. In what? woods - OP
10. The - A
11. Behind - P
12. Behind what? house - OP
13. Whose house? our - PPA
14. And - C
15. Whose brother? my - PPA
16. SN V-t DO P2 Check
17. Verb-transitive - Check again.
18. (In the woods) - Prepositional phrase
19. (Behind our house) - Prepositional phrase
20. Period, statement, declarative sentence
21. Go back to the verb - divide the complete subject from the complete predicate.

Classified Sentence:

SN V-t / DO P2

PPA CSN   C CSP V-t Adj DO   P A OP   P PPA OP
My brother and I / picked wild berries (in the woods) (behind our house). D

CHAPTER 21   LESSON 5

Objectives: Writing Assignments #31 and #32, Bonus Option.

 **WRITING TIME**

TEACHING SCRIPT FOR WRITING ASSIGNMENTS

Today, you are assigned two different kinds of writing. You will write a descriptive paragraph and a friendly letter. <u>You will revise and edit both writing assignments</u>. (_Read the box below for more information about students' writing assignment._) As you edit, make sure you use the checkpoints in the editing checklist provided in Reference 39. Remember to read through the whole paragraph, starting with the title, and then edit, sentence-by-sentence, using the five-sentence checkpoints for each sentence. Use the paragraph checkpoints to check the paragraph.

Writing Assignment Box #1

Writing Assignment #31: Descriptive Paragraph (First or Third Person)
(Remember, first person pronouns are _I, we, me, us, my, our, mine,_ and _ours._)

Remind students to use the descriptive guidelines to help them notice and describe different types of details. Have students use their regular editing checklist to edit this assignment.

Writing topics: My Pet's Behavior When He/She Is Happy   or   **Your Favorite Flower/Tree**   or   **The Family Car**
            or   **Describe something that belongs to someone you love**

Your second writing assignment is to write a friendly letter. (_Read the box below for more information about students' writing assignment._)

Writing Assignment Box #2

Writing Assignment #32: Write a friendly letter to a person of your choice. Before you start, review the tips for writing friendly letters and any references about friendly letters. After your letter has been edited, fold the letter and put it in an envelope. Address the envelope properly and mail it. Don't forget the stamp.

Bonus Option: Write John 3:16 in your Journal from memory. Then, write an essay that explains what this verse in the Bible means to you. If you do not have this verse memorized, record in your Journal how long it takes to memorize it.

TEACHER INSTRUCTIONS FOR CHECKING WRITING ASSIGNMENTS

Read, check, and discuss Writing Assignment #31 after students have finished their final papers. Use the checklists as you check and discuss students' papers. Make sure students are using the regular editing checklist correctly. Read and discuss Writing Assignment #32 for fun and enrichment.

(End of lesson.)

CHAPTER 22   LESSON 1

Objectives: Jingles, Grammar (Practice Sentences, Oral Skill Builder Check), Skills (parts of a business letter, parts of a business envelope), Practice Exercise, Writing (journal), and Vocabulary #1.

JINGLE TIME

Have students turn to the Jingle Section in their books and recite the previously-taught jingles.

GRAMMAR TIME

First-Year Option: Put the Practice Sentences from the box below on the board or on notebook paper. Use these sentences as you practice the concepts that have been taught. For the greatest benefit, students must participate orally with the teacher. **Second-Year Option:** Have students classify the Practice Sentences independently on notebook paper. Check students' sentences with the answers provided below. (*If you have the CDs for Practice Sentences, have students check their sentences with the CDs.*)

Chapter 22, Practice Sentences for Lesson 1
1. _____ The polar bear swam playfully through the ice-cold water.
2. _____ We cooked dinner for the entire church staff on Monday.

TEACHING SCRIPT FOR PRACTICING MIXED PATTERNS

We will practice classifying Mixed Patterns. We will classify the sentences together. Begin. (*You might have your students write the labels above the sentences at this time.*)

Question and Answer Flow for Sentence 1: The polar bear swam playfully through the ice-cold water.

1. What swam playfully through the ice-cold water? bear - SN
2. What is being said about bear? bear swam - V
3. Bear swam how? playfully - Adv
4. Through - P
5. Through what? water - OP
6. What kind of water? ice-cold - Adj
7. The - A

8. What kind of bear? polar - Adj
9. The - A
10. SN V P1 Check
11. (Through the ice-cold water) - Prepositional phrase
12. Period, statement, declarative sentence
13. Go back to the verb - divide the complete subject from the complete predicate.

Classified Sentence:

```
                        A   Adj  SN    V     Adv     P    A   Adj    OP
        SN  V          The polar bear / swam playfully (through the ice-cold water).  D
        P1
```

CHAPTER 22 LESSON 1 CONTINUED

Question and Answer Flow for Sentence 2: We cooked dinner for the entire church staff on Monday.

1. Who cooked dinner for the entire church staff on Monday? we - SP
2. What is being said about we? we cooked - V
3. We cooked what? dinner - verify the noun
4. Does dinner mean the same thing as we? No.
5. Dinner - DO
6. Cooked - V-t
7. For - P
8. For whom? staff - OP
9. What kind of staff? church - Adj
10. Which staff? entire - Adj
11. The - A
12. On - P
13. On what? Monday - OP
14. SN V-t DO P2 Check
15. Verb-transitive - Check again.
16. (For the entire church staff) - Prepositional phrase
17. (On Monday) - Prepositional phrase
18. Period, statement, declarative sentence
19. Go back to the verb - divide the complete subject from the complete predicate.

Classified Sentence:

```
                              SP    V-t    DO    P  A  Adj  Adj  OP   P   OP
               SN  V-t        We / cooked dinner (for the entire church staff) (on Monday).  D
               DO  P2
```

Use Sentences 1-2 that you just classified with your students to do an Oral Skill Builder Check. Use the guidelines below.

Oral Skill Builder Check

1. **Noun check.**
   (Say the job and then say the noun. Circle each noun.)
2. **Identify the nouns as singular or plural.**
   (Write **S** or **P** above each noun.)
3. **Identify the nouns as common or proper.**
   (Follow established procedure for oral identification.)
4. **Do a vocabulary check.**
   (Follow established procedure for oral identification.)

5. **Identify the complete subject and the complete predicate.** (Underline the complete subject once and the complete predicate twice.)
6. **Identify the simple subject and simple predicate.**
   (Underline the simple subject once and the simple predicate twice. Bold, or highlight, the lines.)
7. **Recite the irregular verb chart.**
   (Located on student page 23 and teacher page 138.)

SKILL TIME

TEACHING SCRIPT FOR THE PARTS OF A BUSINESS LETTER

Sharing information with a friend or relative is not the only reason to write a letter. Sometimes, you may need to write a letter to someone you do not know about something that is not personal in nature. This kind of letter is called a **business letter**. Even if you are not in business, there are several reasons why you may need to write a business letter. We will discuss four reasons for writing business letters, and then we will study the four types of business letters and the type of information that should be included in each one. Look at Reference 65 on page 54 and follow along as I read the information about business letters. (*Reference 65 is reproduced for you on the next page.*)

CHAPTER 22 LESSON 1 CONTINUED

Reference 65: Four Types of Business Letters	
Four common reasons to write business letters and information about the four types: 1. If you need to send for information - letter of inquiry. 2. If you want to order a product - letter of request or order. 3. If you want to express an opinion - letter to an editor or official. 4. If you want to complain about a product - letter of complaint.	
Letter of Inquiry	**Letter of Request or Order**
1. Ask for information or answers to your questions. 2. Keep the letter short and to the point. 3. Word the letter so that there can be no question as to what it is you need to know.	1. Carefully and clearly describe the product. 2. Keep the letter short and to the point. 3. Include information on how and where the product should be shipped. 4. Include information on how you will pay for the product.
Letter to an Editor or Official	**Letter of Complaint About a Product**
1. Clearly explain the problem or situation. 2. Offer your opinion of the cause and possible solutions. 3. Support your opinions with facts and examples. 4. Suggest ways to change or improve the situation.	1. Carefully and clearly describe the product. 2. Describe the problem and what may have caused it. (Don't spend too much time explaining how unhappy you are.) 3. Explain any action you have already taken to solve the problem. 4. End your letter with the action you would like the company to take to solve the problem.

The form of a business letter is like the friendly letter except that a business letter uses language that is more formal. A business letter also has an inside address above the greeting that tells who is receiving the letter. The inside address saves companies or business people time because they do not have to read the entire letter in order to know which person in the company receives the letter.

TEACHING SCRIPT FOR THE SIX PARTS OF A BUSINESS LETTER

Now that you know the different reasons to write business letters, you must learn to put your business letter into correct business-letter form. The business letter has six parts: the heading; the inside address; the formal greeting, which is also called the salutation; the body; the closing; and the signature. I will briefly tell you some extra information about the new things that you will find in a business letter.

First, how you write the inside address will depend on what you know about the business or company that will receive the letter. If you know the name of a person in the company who can help you, you will use that name as part of the inside address. If you do not know the name of a person in the company who can help you, you will just use the name of the company.

Second, greetings in business letters are formal. This means that you use the title and last name of the person who is receiving the letter, followed by a colon. If you do not know the name of the person receiving the letter, you should use **sir** or **madam**.

CHAPTER 22 LESSON 1 CONTINUED

Third, when writing the signature of a business letter, you should always sign your first and last name. Each of the parts of a business letter has a specific place it should be written in order for your letter to have correct business letter form. Look at the business letter example in Reference 66 on page 54 in your book. We will now go over each of the six parts, what information is contained in each part, and where each part is placed in the business letter. (*Go over the example reproduced below with your students.*)

Reference 66: Business Letter Example

1. HEADING

47 Benton Road
Boise, Idaho 40007
March 30, 20__

2. INSIDE ADDRESS

Mr. Stanley Wolfe
Tucson Tickets and Travel
2737 Baxter Drive
Tucson, Arizona 20001

3. FORMAL GREETING, (OR SALUTATION)

Dear Mr. Wolfe:

4. BODY (INDENT PARAGRAPHS)

  Our company is planning a semi-annual conference in June. We would like some information about the lodging and attractions that would be available to us. Any information you could send us would be much appreciated.

5. FORMAL CLOSING,

Sincerely yours,

6. SIGNATURE

Ken Jarvis

TEACHING SCRIPT FOR THE PARTS OF A BUSINESS ENVELOPE

In order to address the envelope of your business letter correctly, you must know the parts that go on the envelope and where to write them. The parts of a business envelope are similar to the parts of an envelope for a friendly letter. There are two differences in the mailing address for the business envelope that you should remember.

(1) You must put the name of the person within the company to whom you are writing and his/her title (if you know it) on the first line of the mailing address. If you do not know the name of a particular person in the company who would handle your request or problem, you can just choose a department within the company (such as SALES, SHIPPING, ACCOUNTING, etc.). Then, you can write the name of the department on the first line of your mailing address, or you can leave the first line blank.

(2) You must put the name of the company on the second line of the mailing address.

Look at Reference 67 on page 55 for an example of the parts of a business envelope. (*Go over the information and example reproduced on the next page with your students.*)

Seahorse

CHAPTER 22 LESSON 1 CONTINUED

Reference 67: Business Envelope Parts	
Envelope Parts	**Business Envelope Example**
The return address: 1. Name of the person writing the letter 2. Box or street address of the writer 3. City, state, zip code of the writer **The mailing address:** 1. Name of the person receiving the letter 2. Name of the company receiving the letter 3. Street address of the person receiving the letter 4. City, state, zip code of the person receiving the letter	Return Address Stamp Ken Jarvis 47 Benton Road Boise, Idaho 40007 Mailing Address Mr. Stanley Wolfe Tucson Tickets and Travel 2737 Baxter Drive Tucson, Arizona 20001

PRACTICE TIME

Have students turn to page 90 in the Practice Section of their book and find Chapter 22, Lesson 1, Practice. Go over the directions to make sure they understand what to do. Check and discuss the Practice after students have finished. (*Chapter 22, Lesson 1, Practice instructions are given below.*)

Chapter 22, Lesson 1, Practice: Use butcher paper, large pieces of construction paper, or poster board to make a colorful wall poster identifying the six parts of a business letter and the parts of a business envelope. Write the title and an example for each of the six parts of the business letter and envelope. Illustrate your work. Then, give an oral presentation about the business letter and the envelope when you have finished. (*This project may take several days.*)

WRITING TIME

Have students make an entry in their journals.

VOCABULARY TIME

Assign Chapter 22, Vocabulary Words **#1** on page 9 in the Reference Section for students to define in their Vocabulary notebooks. Tell students they are to use a dictionary or thesaurus to look up the meanings of the vocabulary words. After they write each word and its meaning, students are to write a sentence using the vocabulary word.

Chapter 22, Vocabulary Words #1
(stern, hard, harshness, sweetness)

(End of lesson.)

CHAPTER 22 LESSON 2

Objectives: Jingles, Grammar (Practice Sentences, Practice Sentence), and Practice Exercise.

JINGLE TIME

Have students turn to the Jingle Section in their books and recite the previously-taught jingles.

GRAMMAR TIME

First-Year Option: Put the Practice Sentences from the box below on the board or on notebook paper. Use these sentences as you practice the concepts that have been taught. For the greatest benefit, students must participate orally with the teacher. **Second-Year Option:** Have students classify the Practice Sentences independently on notebook paper. Check students' sentences with the answers provided below. (*If you have the CDs for Practice Sentences, have students check their sentences with the CDs.*)

Chapter 22, Practice Sentences for Lesson 2
1. _____ Hey! The man in the black coat grabbed the poor lady's purse!
2. _____ The children were waiting patiently for the ice-cream truck on the hot summer day.

TEACHING SCRIPT FOR PRACTICING MIXED PATTERNS

We will practice classifying Mixed Patterns. We will classify the sentences together. Begin. (*You might have your students write the labels above the sentences at this time.*)

Question and Answer Flow for Sentence 1: Hey! The man in the black coat grabbed the poor lady's purse!

1. Who grabbed the poor lady's purse? man - SN
2. What is being said about man? man grabbed - V
3. Man grabbed what? purse - verify the noun
4. Does purse mean the same thing as man? No.
5. Purse - DO
6. Grabbed - V-t
7. Whose purse? lady's - PNA
8. What kind of lady? poor - Adj
9. The - A
10. In - P
11. In what? coat - OP

12. What kind of coat? black - Adj
13. The - A
14. The - A
15. Hey - I
16. SN V-t DO P2 Check
17. Verb-transitive - Check again.
18. (In the black coat) - Prepositional phrase
19. Exclamation point, strong feeling, exclamatory sentence
20. Go back to the verb - divide the complete subject from the complete predicate.

Classified Sentence:

	I	A	SN	P	A	Adj	OP	V-t	A	Adj	PNA	DO	

<u>SN V-t</u>   Hey! The man (in the black coat) **/** grabbed the poor lady's purse! **E**
DO P2

CHAPTER 22 LESSON 2 CONTINUED

Question and Answer Flow for Sentence 2: The children were waiting patiently for the ice-cream truck on the hot summer day.

1. Who were waiting patiently for the ice-cream truck on the hot summer day? children - SN
2. What is being said about children? children were waiting - V
3. Were - HV
4. Children were waiting how? patiently - Adv
5. For - P
6. For what? truck - OP
7. What kind of truck? ice-cream - Adj
8. The - A
9. On - P

10. On what? day - OP
11. What kind of day? summer - Adj
12. What kind of day? hot - Adj
13. The - A
14. The - A
15. SN V P1 Check
16. (For the ice-cream truck) - Prepositional phrase
17. (On the hot summer day) - Prepositional phrase
18. Period, statement, declarative sentence
19. Go back to the verb - divide the complete subject from the complete predicate.

		A	SN	HV	V	Adv	P	A	Adj	OP	P	A	Adj	Adj	OP
Classified															
Sentence:	SN V	The children / were waiting patiently (for the ice-cream truck) (on the hot summer day). D
	P1	

TEACHER INSTRUCTIONS FOR A PRACTICE SENTENCE

Tell students that their sentence writing assignment today is to write a sentence pattern of their choice. They may choose any Pattern, 1-3, for a Practice Sentence. They are to follow the same procedure used in the previous lessons. They should decide on their labels, arrange them in a selected order, write their sentences, and edit their sentences for improved word choices. (*Students do not have to write an Improved Sentence at this point unless you feel they need more one-on-one word choice writing practice.*) Check and discuss the sentence pattern chosen after students have finished.

 PRACTICE TIME

Have students turn to page 90 in the Practice Section of their book and find Chapter 22, Lesson 2, Practice (*1-2*). Go over the directions to make sure they understand what to do. Check and discuss the Practices after students have finished. (*Chapter 22, Lesson 2, Practice instructions are given below.*)

Chapter 22, Lesson 2, Practice 1: Write a friendly letter to a special friend or relative. Before you start, review the references and tips for writing friendly letters. After your letter has been edited, fold the letter and put it in an envelope. Address the envelope properly and mail it. Don't forget the stamp.

Chapter 22, Lesson 2, Practice 2: Write a business letter. You may invent the company and the situation for which you are writing. Before you begin, review the reasons for writing business letters and the four types of business letters (*Reference 65 on page 54*). After your letter has been edited, fold the letter and put it in an envelope. Address the envelope properly.

(End of lesson.)

CHAPTER 22   LESSON 3
Objectives: Jingles, Grammar (Practice Sentences), Practice Exercise, and Vocabulary #2.

JINGLE TIME

Have students turn to the Jingle Section in their books and recite the previously-taught jingles.

GRAMMAR TIME

First-Year Option: Put the Practice Sentences from the box below on the board or on notebook paper. Use these sentences as you practice the concepts that have been taught. For the greatest benefit, students must participate orally with the teacher. **Second-Year Option:** Have students classify the Practice Sentences independently on notebook paper. Check students' sentences with the answers provided below. *(If you have the CDs for Practice Sentences, have students check their sentences with the CDs.)*

Chapter 22, Practice Sentences for Lesson 3
1. _____ The wrinkled shirt gave the man a sloppy appearance.
2. _____ The sea captain spotted a beacon of light from the lighthouse on the seashore.

TEACHING SCRIPT FOR PRACTICING MIXED PATTERNS

We will practice classifying Mixed Patterns. We will classify the sentences together. Begin. *(You might have your students write the labels above the sentences at this time.)*

Question and Answer Flow for Sentence 1: The wrinkled shirt gave the man a sloppy appearance.

1. What gave the man a sloppy appearance? shirt - SN
2. What is being said about shirt? shirt gave - V
3. Shirt gave what? appearance - verify the noun
4. Does appearance mean the same thing as shirt? No.
5. Appearance - DO
6. Gave - V-t
7. Shirt gave appearance to whom? man - IO
8. What kind of appearance? sloppy - Adj
9. A - A

10. The - A
11. What kind of shirt? wrinkled - Adj
12. The - A
13. SN V-t IO DO P3 Check
14. Verb-transitive - Check again.
15. No prepositional phrases.
16. Period, statement, declarative sentence
17. Go back to the verb - divide the complete subject from the complete predicate.

Classified Sentence:

<pre>
                          A   Adj   SN   V-t A IO A   Adj   DO
          SN V-t   The wrinkled shirt / gave the man a sloppy appearance. D
          IO DO P3
</pre>

Question and Answer Flow for Sentence 2: The sea captain spotted a beacon of light from the lighthouse on the seashore.

1. Who spotted a beacon of light from the lighthouse on the seashore? captain - SN
2. What is being said about captain? captain spotted - V
3. Captain spotted what? beacon - verify the noun
4. Does beacon mean the same thing as captain? No.
5. Beacon - DO
6. Spotted - V-t
7. A - A
8. Of - P
9. Of what? light - OP
10. From - P
11. From what? lighthouse - OP
12. The - A
13. On - P
14. On what? seashore - OP
15. The - A
16. What kind of captain? sea - Adj
17. The - A
18. SN V-t DO P2 Check
19. Verb-transitive - Check again.
20. (Of light) - Prepositional phrase
21. (From the lighthouse) - Prepositional phrase
22. (On the seashore) - Prepositional phrase
23. Period, statement, declarative sentence
24. Go back to the verb - divide the complete subject from the complete predicate.

Classified Sentence:

```
                    A  Adj   SN        V-t  A  DO    P  OP    P   A    OP        P   A    OP
   SN V-t          The sea captain / spotted a beacon (of light) (from the lighthouse) (on the seashore).  D
   DO  P2
```

PRACTICE TIME

Have students turn to page 90 in the Practice Section of their books and find the instructions under Chapter 22, Lesson 3, Practice (*1-2*). Go over the directions to make sure they understand what to do. Check and discuss the Practices after students have finished. (*Chapter 22, Lesson 3, Practice instructions are given below.*)

Chapter 22, Lesson 3, Practice 1: On notebook paper, identify the parts of a business letter and envelope by writing the titles and an example for each title. Use References 66 and 67 to help you. (*Use References 66 and 67 to check the parts of a business letter and envelope.*)

Chapter 22, Lesson 3, Practice 2: Write a business letter. You may invent another company and the situation for which you are writing. Before you begin, review the reasons for writing business letters and the four types of business letters (Reference 65). This business must be different from the business chosen in the previous lesson. After your letter has been edited, fold the letter and put it in an envelope. Address the envelope properly.

VOCABULARY TIME

Assign Chapter 22, Vocabulary Words **#2** on page 9 in the Reference Section for students to define in their Vocabulary notebooks. They should write each word, its meaning, and a sentence using the word.

Chapter 22, Vocabulary Words #2
(innocent, guilty, remember, retain)

(End of lesson.)

CHAPTER 22   LESSON 4
Objectives: Jingles, Study, Test, Check, Activity, and Writing (journal).

JINGLE TIME

Have students turn to the Jingle Section in their books and recite the previously-taught jingles.

STUDY TIME

Have students study the vocabulary words in their vocabulary notebooks. Remind students that any vocabulary word in their notebooks could be on their test. Also, have students study any of the skills in the Practice Section that they need to review.

TEST TIME

Have students turn to page 120 in the Test Section of their books and find the Chapter 22 Test. Go over the directions to make sure they understand what to do. (*Chapter 22 Test key is on the next page.*)

CHECK TIME

After students have finished, check and discuss their test papers. Make sure they understand why their answers are right or wrong. (*For total points, count each required answer as a point.*)

ACTIVITY / ASSIGNMENT TIME

Have students choose a state that they would like to visit. Have students write several letters requesting information about the state. (*Have them research the different places to send the letters.*) Next, have the students research encyclopedias, newspapers, magazines, and even the Internet about the places they would like to visit in their chosen state. They will continue different aspects of this project for several weeks. Students will continue learning about the state they have chosen as they are given new things to do in future lessons.

(End of lesson.)

Chapter 22 Test
(Student Page 120)

Exercise 1: Classify each sentence.

              A   Adj   SN   V   P   A   Adj   OP   P   A   OP   Adv

1. <u>**SN V**</u>   The red schooner / raced (through the choppy water) (on the lake) today. **D**
     P1

           CSN   C   CSN   V-t   PPA   Adj   Adj   DO   P   A   Adj   OP

2. <u>**SN V-t**</u>   Roger and Tina / sell their handmade woven baskets (at the fall festival). **D**
     DO P2

Exercise 2: Identify each pair of words as synonyms or antonyms by putting parentheses ( ) around ***syn*** or ***ant***.

1. innocent, guilty	syn **(ant)**	4. compete, cooperate	syn **(ant)**	7. safe, secure	**(syn)** ant
2. connect, separate	syn **(ant)**	5. retain, remember	**(syn)** ant	8. terror, fear	**(syn)** ant
3. stern, hard	**(syn)** ant	6. clutter, order	syn **(ant)**	9. harshness, sweetness	syn **(ant)**

Exercise 3: Use the Quotation Rules to help punctuate the quotations below. Underline the explanatory words.

       N   B   M   K

1.   "**nancy,** do you want to go to blackwood mall tomorrow**?**" <u>asked katherine</u>**.**

      K   A   A   L

2.   <u>kevin shouted loudly to amy and amber</u>**,** "**look** out for that power line**!**"

      I   S   K

3.   "**i** would like to see susan's new dress shop today**,**" <u>kimberly said to her mother</u>**.**

    T   I   M D

4.   <u>the new employee stated boldly</u> **,** "**i** would like to work the evening shift if possible**, mr. davis.**"

    T   J

5.   "**that** bull is going to trample the cowboy**!**" <u>gasped julie to her brother</u>**.**

Exercise 4: On notebook paper, identify the parts of a business letter and envelope by writing the titles and an example for each title. Use References 66 and 67 to help you. (***Use References 66 and 67 to check the assignment.***)

Exercise 5: On notebook paper, identify the parts of a friendly letter and envelope by writing the titles and an example for each title. Use References 63 and 64 to help you. (***Use Reference 63 and 64 to check the assignment.***)

Exercise 6: On notebook paper, write one sentence for each of these labels: ① **(S)** ② **(SCS)** ③ **(SCV)** ④ **(CD)**. **(Sentences will vary.)**

Exercise 7: On notebook paper, write the seven present tense helping verbs, the five past tense helping verbs, and the two future tense helping verbs. **(The order of answers may vary.)** (Present: am, is, are, has, have, do, does; Past: was, were, had, did, been; Future: will, shall)

Exercise 8: In your journal, write a paragraph summarizing what you have learned this week.

CHAPTER 22 LESSON 4 CONTINUED

TEACHER INSTRUCTIONS

Use the Question and Answer Flows below for the sentences on the Chapter 22 Test.

Question and Answer Flow for Sentence 1: The red schooner raced through the choppy water on the lake today.

1. What raced through the choppy water on the lake today? schooner - SN
2. What is being said about schooner? schooner raced - V
3. Through - P
4. Through what? water - OP
5. What kind of water? choppy - Adj
6. The - A
7. On - P
8. On what? lake - OP
9. The - A
10. Raced when? today - Adv
11. What kind of schooner? red - Adj
12. The - A
13. SN V P1 Check
14. (Through the choppy water) - Prepositional phrase
15. (On the lake) - Prepositional phrase
16. Period, statement, declarative sentence
17. Go back to the verb - divide the complete subject from the complete predicate.

Classified Sentence:

```
                      A  Adj  SN      V      P   A   Adj  OP   P  A  OP  Adv
      SN  V          The red schooner / raced (through the choppy water) (on the lake) today.  D
      P1
```

Question and Answer Flow for Sentence 2: Roger and Tina sell their handmade woven baskets at the fall festival.

1. Who sell their handmade woven baskets at the fall festival? Roger and Tina - CSN, CSN
2. What is being said about Roger and Tina? Roger and Tina sell - V
3. Roger and Tina sell what? baskets - verify the noun
4. Do baskets mean the same thing as Roger and Tina? No.
5. Baskets - DO
6. Sell - V-t
7. What kind of baskets? woven - Adj
8. What kind of baskets? handmade - Adj
9. Whose baskets? their - PPA
10. At - P
11. At what? festival - OP
12. What kind of festival? fall - Adj
13. The - A
14. And - C
15. SN V-t DO P2 Check
16. Verb-transitive - Check again.
17. (At the fall festival) - Prepositional phrase
18. Period, statement, declarative sentence
19. Go back to the verb - divide the complete subject from the complete predicate.

Classified Sentence:

```
                       CSN  C CSN  V-t PPA    Adj      Adj    DO    P  A Adj  OP
      SN  V-t         Roger and Tina / sell their handmade woven baskets (at the fall festival).  D
      DO  P2
```

CHAPTER 22   LESSON 5

Objectives: Writing Assignments #33 and #34.

 WRITING TIME

TEACHING SCRIPT FOR WRITING ASSIGNMENTS

Today, you are assigned two different kinds of writing. You will write a descriptive paragraph and a business letter. <u>You will revise and edit both writing assignments.</u> (*Read the box below for more information about the students' writing assignment.*) As you edit, make sure you use the checkpoints in the editing checklist provided in Reference 39. Remember to read through the whole paragraph, starting with the title, and then edit, sentence-by-sentence, using the five-sentence checkpoints for each sentence. Use the paragraph checkpoints to check the paragraph.

Writing Assignment Box #1

Writing Assignment #33: Descriptive Paragraph (First or Third Person)

Writing topic choices: The Most Interesting Bible Character or A Treasured Pet or An Unforgettable Dream or Choose your own topic.

Your second writing assignment is to write a business letter. (*Read the box below for more information about students' writing assignment.*)

Writing Assignment Box #2

Writing Assignment #34: Write a business letter. You may invent a company and a situation for which you are writing. Before you begin, review the reasons for writing business letters and the four types of business letters (Reference 65 on page 54). This business must be different from the businesses chosen in the previous lessons. After your letter has been edited, fold the letter and put it in an envelope. Address the envelope properly.

TEACHER INSTRUCTIONS FOR CHECKING WRITING ASSINGMENTS

Read, check, and discuss Writing Assignments #33 and #34 after students have finished their final papers. Use the editing checklist as you check and discuss students' papers. Make sure students are using the editing checklist correctly.

(End of lesson.)

CHAPTER 23   LESSON 1
Objectives: Jingles, Grammar (Practice Sentences), Skill (thank-you notes), and Practice Exercise.

JINGLE TIME

Have students turn to the Jingle Section in their books and recite the previously-taught jingles.

GRAMMAR TIME

First-Year Option: Put the Practice Sentences from the box below on the board or on notebook paper. Use these sentences as you practice the concepts that have been taught. For the greatest benefit, students must participate orally with the teacher. **Second-Year Option:** Have students classify the Practice Sentences independently on notebook paper. Check students' sentences with the answers provided below. (*If you have the CDs for Practice Sentences, have students check their sentences with the CDs.*)

Chapter 23, Practice Sentences for Lesson 1
1. _____ Did you see spotted giraffes, pink flamingos, and striped zebras at the zoo?
2. _____ The honeybee takes pollen and nectar from blossoms of flowers.

TEACHING SCRIPT FOR PRACTICING MIXED PATTERNS

We will practice classifying Mixed Patterns. We will classify the sentences together. Begin. (*You might have your students write the labels above the sentences at this time.*)

Question and Answer Flow for Sentence 1: Did you see spotted giraffes, pink flamingos, and striped zebras at the zoo?

1. Who did see spotted giraffes, pink flamingos, and striped zebras at the zoo? you - SP
2. What is being said about you? you did see - V
3. Did - HV
4. You did see what?
   giraffes, flamingos, and zebras - verify the nouns
5. Do giraffes, flamingos, and zebras mean the same thing as you? No.
6. Giraffes, flamingos, and zebras - CDO, CDO, CDO
7. See - V-t
8. What kind of giraffes? spotted - Adj
9. What kind of flamingos? pink - Adj
10. And - C
11. What kind of zebras? striped - Adj
12. At - P
13. At what? zoo - OP
14. The - A
15. SN V-t DO P2 Check
16. Verb-transitive - Check again.
17. (At the zoo) - Prepositional phrase
18. Question mark, question, interrogative sentence
19. Go back to the verb - divide the complete subject from the complete predicate.
20. This sentence has predicate words in the complete subject. Underline the helping verb at the beginning of the sentence twice.

Classified Sentence:

```
                        HV SP   V-t   Adj   CDO   Adj   CDO    C  Adj    CDO   P A  OP
              SN V-t    Did you / see spotted giraffes, pink flamingos, and striped zebras (at the zoo)? Int
              DO P2
```

CHAPTER 23 LESSON 1 CONTINUED

Question and Answer Flow for Sentence 2: The honeybee takes pollen and nectar from blossoms of flowers.

1. What takes pollen and nectar from blossoms of flowers?
   honeybee - SN
2. What is being said about honeybee? honeybee takes - V
3. Honeybee takes what? pollen and nectar - verify the nouns
4. Do pollen and nectar mean the same thing as honeybee? No.
5. Pollen and nectar - CDO, CDO
6. Takes - V-t
7. And - C
8. From - P
9. From what? blossoms - OP

10. Of - P
11. Of what? flowers - OP
12. The - A
13. SN V-t DO P2 Check
14. Verb-transitive - Check again.
15. (From blossoms) - Prepositional phrase
16. (Of flowers) - Prepositional phrase
17. Period, statement, declarative sentence
18. Go back to the verb - divide the complete subject from the complete predicate.

Classified Sentence:

```
              A      SN      V-t  CDO  C  CDO   P    OP    P   OP
    SN  V-t   The honeybee / takes pollen and nectar (from blossoms) (of flowers).  D
    DO  P2
```

SKILL TIME

TEACHING SCRIPT FOR THANK-YOU NOTES

Close your eyes. Relax and clear your mind of clutter. Now, think of a person who has done something nice for you or has given you a gift. Sometimes, a person even gives a gift of time, so a gift does not always mean a "physical" gift. After you have thought of someone, open your eyes. That person deserves a thank-you note from you after such a nice gesture. Therefore, it is time we learn about thank-you notes.

You usually write thank-you notes to thank someone for a gift or for doing something nice. In either case, a thank-you note should include at least three statements.

1. **You should tell the person <u>what</u> you are thanking him/her for.**
2. **You should tell the person <u>how the gift was used</u> or <u>how it helped</u>.**
3. **You should tell the person <u>how much you appreciated the gift or action</u>.**

A thank-you note should follow the same form as a friendly letter: heading, greeting, body, closing, and signature. Look at Reference 68 on page 55 and follow along as I read the information about thank-you notes. (*Go over the information and examples reproduced on the next page with your students.*)

CHAPTER 23 LESSON 1 CONTINUED

Reference 68: Thank-You Notes		
For a Gift		**For an Action**
What - Thank you for... (tell color, kind, and item)	**What** -	Thank you for... (tell action)
Use - Tell how the gift is used.	**Helped** -	Tell how the action helped.
Thanks - I appreciate your remembering me with this special gift.	**Thanks** -	I appreciate your thinking of me at this time.

Example 1: Gift

202 Shady Lane
Gopher, Missouri 21161
January 12, 20__

Dear Lorene,

    The red scarf you sent me for Christmas is absolutely beautiful. I will always think of you as I wear it this winter. I appreciate this special gift that you made especially for me.

Much love,
Aunt Ellen

Example 2: Action

420 Elmwood Place
Harpoon, Louisiana 47705
June 26, 20__

Dear Steven,

    Thank you so much for helping with the landscaping project in front of City Hall. The area is far more eye-catching today than it was a week ago. You are a good worker and a dependable friend.

Special thanks,
Cody

PRACTICE TIME

Have students turn to page 90 in the Practice Section of their book and find Chapter 23, Lesson 1, Practice. Go over the directions to make sure they understand what to do. Check and discuss the Practice after students have finished. (*Chapter 23, Lesson 1, Practice instructions are given below.*)

Chapter 23, Lesson 1, Practice: Write your own thank-you note. First, think of a person who has done something nice for you or has given you a gift (even the gift of time). Next, write that person a thank-you note, using the information in the Reference Section as a guide. (*Check and discuss students' thank-you notes after they are finished.*)

VOCABULARY TIME

Students will no longer have assigned Vocabulary Words. As they find new or interesting words, have students add them to their list in their Vocabulary notebook.

(End of lesson.)

CHAPTER 23   LESSON 2
Objectives: Jingles, Grammar (Practice Sentences, Practice Sentence), Skill (invitations), Practice Exercise, and Writing (journal).

JINGLE TIME

Have students turn to the Jingle Section in their books and recite the previously-taught jingles.

GRAMMAR TIME

First-Year Option: Put the Practice Sentences from the box below on the board or on notebook paper. Use these sentences as you practice the concepts that have been taught. For the greatest benefit, students must participate orally with the teacher. **Second-Year Option:** Have students classify the Practice Sentences independently on notebook paper. Check students' sentences with the answers provided below. *(If you have the CDs for Practice Sentences, have students check their sentences with the CDs.)*

Chapter 23, Practice Sentences for Lesson 2
1. _____ The librarian gave us a tour of the new city library.
2. _____ Awesome! Steve and Mary rode to the prom in a white limousine!

TEACHING SCRIPT FOR PRACTICING MIXED PATTERNS

We will practice classifying Mixed Patterns. We will classify the sentences together. Begin. *(You might have your students write the labels above the sentences at this time.)*

Question and Answer Flow for Sentence 1: The librarian gave us a tour of the new city library.	
1. Who gave us a tour of the new city library? librarian - SN	12. What kind of library? new - Adj
2. What is being said about librarian? librarian gave - V	13. The - A
3. Librarian gave what? tour - verify the noun	14. The - A
4. Does tour mean the same thing as librarian? No.	15. SN V-t IO DO P3 Check
5. Tour - DO	16. Verb-transitive - Check again.
6. Gave - V-t	17. (Of the new city library) - Prepositional phrase
7. Librarian gave tour to whom? us - IO	18. Period, statement, declarative sentence
8. A - A	19. Go back to the verb - divide the complete subject
9. Of - P	from the complete predicate.
10. Of what? library - OP	
11. What kind of library? city - Adj	

Classified Sentence:

```
                          A    SN      V-t IO A DO  P A  Adj Adj OP
             SN  V-t      The librarian / gave us a tour (of the new city library).  D
             ─────────
             IO DO P3
```

CHAPTER 23 LESSON 2 CONTINUED

Question and Answer Flow for Sentence 2: Awesome! Steve and Mary rode to the prom in a white limousine!	
1. Who rode to the prom in a white limousine? Steve and Mary - CSN, CSN	9. A - A
2. What is being said about Steve and Mary? Steve and Mary rode - V	10. And - C
	11. Awesome - I
3. To - P	12. SN V P1 Check
4. To what? prom - OP	13. (To the prom) - Prepositional phrase
5. The - A	14. (In a white limousine) - Prepositional phrase
6. In - P	15. Exclamation point, strong feeling, exclamatory sentence
7. In what? limousine - OP	16. Go back to the verb - divide the complete subject
8. What kind of limousine? white - Adj	from the complete predicate.

Classified Sentence:

                             I   CSN   C   CSN   V   P A OP   P A Adj   OP

SN V _____   Awesome! Steve and Mary / rode (to the prom) (in a white limousine)! E

P1

TEACHER INSTRUCTIONS FOR A PRACTICE SENTENCE

Tell students that their sentence writing assignment today is to write a sentence in the pattern of their choice. They may choose any Pattern, 1-3, for a Practice Sentence. They are to follow the same procedure used in the previous lessons. They should decide on their labels, arrange them in a selected order, write their sentence, and edit the sentence for improved word choices. (*Students do not have to write an Improved Sentence at this point unless you feel they need more one-on-one word choice writing practice.*) Check and discuss the sentence pattern chosen after students have finished.

SKILL TIME

TEACHING SCRIPT FOR INVITATIONS

With all the commercial cards today, the art of personal, unique, and individual invitations is almost obsolete. And whether you ever have an occasion to write personal invitations or not, as an astute student of English, it is your responsibility to learn how, especially since it is so easy. Today, each of you will plan a special event or occasion and make an invitation to send out. It is time we learn about writing invitations. It is always best to make an outline for an invitation. Your invitation outline should include the following information in any logical order.

1. **What - Tell what the event or special occasion is.**
2. **Who - Tell whom the event is for.**
3. **Where - Tell where the event will take place.**
4. **When - Tell the date and time of the event.**
5. **Whipped-cream statement: A polite statement written to make the person feel welcome.**

An invitation will sometimes have an RSVP. This is a French expression that means "please respond," and a reply is needed. If a phone number is included, reply by phone. Otherwise, a written reply is expected. An invitation should follow the same form as a friendly letter: **heading, greeting, body, closing, and signature**. Now, we will go over the five outline parts of an invitation again and see how they are used in a sample invitation.

CHAPTER 23 LESSON 2 CONTINUED

Look at Reference 69 on page 56 and follow along as I read the information about invitations. (*Go over the information and examples reproduced below with your students.*)

Reference 69: Invitations		
1.	What	– a special celebration luncheon
2.	Who	– for all the members of the Community Helpers Organization
3.	Where	– Community Center on Lighthouse Drive in Sherwood
4.	When	– on March 28, at 11:30
5.	Whipped Cream	– We hope you can come!

752 Firefly Road
Wichita, Kansas 70006
February 4, 20__

Dear Judy Morris,
    You are cordially invited to <u>a special celebration luncheon</u> <u>for all the members of the Community Helpers Organization</u>. We will be honoring dedicated members who have actively changed the face of our community. The luncheon will be held on <u>March 28</u>, at the <u>Community Center on Lighthouse Drive in Sherwood</u>. We will begin serving lunch <u>at 11:30</u>. <u>We hope you can come!</u>

Sincerely,

Tina Woods

Student Note: Notice that the five parts of an invitation are underlined in the example; however, you would not underline them in an actual invitation.

 PRACTICE TIME

Students will continue letter writing activities. Have students turn to page 90 in the Practice Section of their book and find Chapter 23, Lesson 2, Practice. Go over the directions to make sure they understand what to do. If students need a review, have them study the information and examples in the Reference Section of their books. Check and discuss the Practice after students have finished. (*Chapter 23, Lesson 2, Practice instructions are given below.*)

Chapter 23, Lesson 2, Practice: Make your own invitation card. First, think of a special event or occasion and who will be invited. Next, make an invitation to send out, using the information in the Reference Section as a guide. Illustrate your card appropriately. (*Check and discuss students' invitation cards after they are finished.*)

 WRITING TIME

Have students make an entry in their journals.

(End of lesson.)

CHAPTER 23   LESSON 3

Objectives: Skill (introduce parts of a book), Practice Exercise

SKILL TIME

TEACHING SCRIPT FOR INTRODUCING PARTS OF A BOOK

Do you know the parts of a book? Let's see how many we can name. (_Call on students to name the parts they know. See the parts below._) Actually, the parts of a book can be divided into the front part and back part. We will learn the front parts of a book, and then we will learn the back parts. Anytime you use a nonfiction book to help you with an assignment, it is necessary to understand how to use that book efficiently.

Knowing the parts of a book will help you make full use of the special features that are sometimes found in nonfiction books. I will now give you a brief description of each of the features that could appear in a book. We will start with the front parts of a book. Look at Reference 70 on page 56 in the Reference Section of your book. (_Read and discuss the parts of a book below with your students._)

Reference 70: Parts of a Book

AT THE FRONT:

1. **Title Page.** This page has the full title of the book, the author's name, the illustrator's name, the name of the publishing company, and the city where the book was published.

2. **Copyright Page.** This page is right after the title page and tells the year in which the book was published and who owns the copyright. If the book has an ISBN number (International Standard Book Number), it is listed here.

3. **Preface** (also called **introduction**). If a book has this page, it will come before the table of contents and will usually tell you briefly why the book was written and what it is about.

4. **Table of Contents.** This section lists the major divisions of the book by units or chapters and tells their page numbers.

5. **Body.** This is the main section, or text, of the book.

AT THE BACK:

6. **Appendix.** This section includes extra informative material such as maps, charts, tables, diagrams, letters, etc. It is always wise to find out what is in the appendix, since it may contain supplementary material that you could otherwise find only by going to the library.

7. **Glossary.** This section is like a dictionary and gives the meanings of some of the important words in the book.

8. **Bibliography.** This section includes a list of books used by the author. It could serve as a guide for further reading on a topic.

9. **Index.** This will probably be your most useful section. The purpose of the index is to help you quickly locate information about the topics in the book. It has an alphabetical list of specific topics and tells on which page that information can be found. It is similar to the table of contents, but it is much more detailed.

CHAPTER 23 LESSON 3 CONTINUED

 PRACTICE TIME

Have students turn to page 91 in the Practice Section of their book and find the instructions under Chapter 23, Lesson 3, Practice (*1-5*). Go over the directions to make sure they understand what to do. If students need a review, have them study the information and examples in the Reference Section of their books. Check and discuss the Practices after students have finished. (*Chapter 23, Lesson 3, Practice keys are below*.)

Chapter 23, Lesson 3, Practice 1: Match each part of a book listed below with the type of information it may give you. Write the appropriate letter in the blank. You may use each letter only once.

| A. Title page | B. Copyright page | C. Index | D. Bibliography | E. Appendix | F. Glossary |

1. __D__ A list of books used by the author as references

2. __B__ ISBN number

3. __C__ Used to locate topics quickly

Chapter 23, Lesson 3, Practice 2: Match each part of a book listed below with the type of information it may give you. Write the appropriate letter in the blank. You may use each letter only once.

| A. Title page | C. Copyright page | E. Bibliography | G. Body |
| B. Table of contents | D. Index | F. Preface | |

1. __D__ Exact page numbers for a particular topic

2. __G__ Text of the book

3. __F__ Reason the book was written

4. __E__ Books listed for finding more information

Chapter 23, Lesson 3, Practice 3: On notebook paper, write the five parts found at the front of a book. **(Title Page, Copyright Page, Preface, Table of Contents, Body) (The order of answers may vary.)**

Chapter 23, Lesson 3, Practice 4: On notebook paper, write the four parts found at the back of a book. **(Appendix, Glossary, Bibliography, Index) (The order of answers may vary.)**

Chapter 23, Lesson 3, Practice 5: Write the nine parts of a book on a poster and write a description beside each part. Illustrate and color the nine parts. **(Title Page, Copyright Page, Preface, Table of Contents, Body, Appendix, Glossary, Bibliography, Index)** (*Check and discuss students' definitions and illustrations after they have finished. Note: Students may use their reference pages to help them.*)

(End of lesson.)

CHAPTER 23   LESSON 4

Objectives: Jingles, Study, Test, Check, Activity (continued), and Writing (journal).

JINGLE TIME

Have students turn to the Jingle Section in their books and recite the previously-taught jingles.

STUDY TIME

Have students study the vocabulary words in their vocabulary notebooks. Remind students that any vocabulary word in their notebooks could be on their test. Also, have students study any of the skills in the Practice Section that they need to review.

TEST TIME

Have students turn to page 121 in the Test Section of their books and find the Chapter 23 Test. Go over the directions to make sure they understand what to do. (*Chapter 23 Test key is on the next page.*)

CHECK TIME

After students have finished, check and discuss the test. Make sure they understand why their test questions and answers are right or wrong. (*For total points, count each required answer as a point.*)

ACTIVITY / ASSIGNMENT TIME

In the last activity, students wrote letters for information about the state that they would like to visit. They also researched reference materials and the Internet for more information about the places that they would like to visit in their chosen state.

For the last portion of this project, have students write about the things that make their chosen state important to the rest of the world. They should include interesting facts about their state (weather, population, main industries, natural resources, etc.) and tell what impressed them the most. Finally, they should compare their own state to their chosen state. What are the differences and likeness? After they write their state report, have them illustrate it. Have students put the report and illustrations in a booklet, write a title on the front cover of the booklet, and illustrate the cover. After they have finished, have them give their reports to other family members and friends to read.

(End of lesson.)

Chapter 23 Test
(Student Page 121)

Exercise 1: Classify each sentence.

```
          A    Adj   Adj       SN     V-t  A   DO    P   OP    P   OP
1. SN V-t     The lovely bluebonnet flowers / cover the prairies (in parts) (of Texas). D
   DO P2

              SN   CV   C    CV     P   PPA  OP     P   A   OP    P   A   OP
2. SN V       Ellen / talked and laughed (with her sister) (for an hour) (on the phone). D
   P1
```

Exercise 2: Match each part of a book listed below with the type of information it may give you. Write the appropriate letter in the blank. You may use each letter only once.

A. Title page	B. Copyright page	C. Index	D. Bibliography	E. Appendix	F. Glossary

1. __D__ A list of books used by the author as references   4. __B__ ISBN number

2. __F__ Meanings of important words in the book   5. __C__ Used to locate topics quickly

3. __A__ Publisher's name and city where the book was published   6. __E__ Extra maps in a book

Exercise 3: Match each part of a book listed below with the type of information it may give you. Write the appropriate letter in the blank. You may use each letter only once.

A. Title page	C. Copyright page	E. Bibliography	G. Body
B. Table of contents	D. Index	F. Preface	

1. __D__ Exact page numbers for a particular topic   4. __G__ Text of the book

2. __A__ Author's name, title of book, and illustrator's name   5. __F__ Reason the book was written

3. __E__ Books listed for finding more information   6. __B__ Titles of units and chapters

7. __C__ Copyright date

Exercise 4: On notebook paper, write the five parts found at the front of a book. **(Title Page, Copyright Page, Preface, Table of Contents, Body) (The order of answers may vary.)**

Exercise 5: On notebook paper, write the four parts found at the back of a book. **(Appendix, Glossary, Bibliography, Index) (The order of answers may vary.)**

Exercise 6: Write a thank-you note. First, think of a person who has done something nice for you or has given you a gift (even the gift of time). Next, write that person a thank-you note, using the information in the Reference Section as a guide. **(Answers will vary.)**

Exercise 7: Make an invitation card. First, think of a special event or occasion and who will be invited. Next, make an invitation to send out, using the information in the Reference Section as a guide. Illustrate your card appropriately. **(Answers will vary.)**

Exercise 8: In your journal, write a paragraph summarizing what you have learned this week.

CHAPTER 23 LESSON 4 CONTINUED

TEACHER INSTRUCTIONS

Use the Question and Answer Flows below for the sentences on the Chapter 23 Test.

Question and Answer Flow for Sentence 1: The lovely bluebonnet flowers cover the prairies in parts of Texas.

1. What cover the prairies in parts of Texas? flowers - SN
2. What is being said about flowers? flowers cover - V
3. Flowers cover what? prairies - verify the noun
4. Do prairies mean the same as flowers? No.
5. Prairies - DO
6. Cover - V-t
7. The - A
8. In - P
9. In what? parts - OP
10. Of - P
11. Of what? Texas - OP
12. What kind of flowers? bluebonnet - Adj
13. What kind of flowers? lovely - Adj
14. The - A
15. SN V-t DO P2 Check
16. Verb-transitive - Check again.
17. (In parts) - Prepositional phrase
18. (Of Texas) - Prepositional phrase
19. Period, statement, declarative sentence
20. Go back to the verb - divide the complete subject from the complete predicate.

Classified Sentence:

```
                    A   Adj    Adj    SN    V-t  A    DO     P  OP  P  OP
SN  V-t    The lovely bluebonnet flowers / cover the prairies (in parts) (of Texas).  D
DO  P2
```

Question and Answer Flow for Sentence 2: Ellen talked and laughed with her sister for an hour on the phone.

1. Who talked and laughed with her sister for an hour on the phone? Ellen - SN
2. What is being said about Ellen? Ellen talked and laughed - CV, CV
3. With - P
4. With whom? sister - OP
5. Whose sister? her - PPA
6. For - P
7. For what? hour - OP
8. An - A
9. On - P
10. On what? phone - OP
11. The - A
12. And - C
13. SN V P1 Check
14. (With her sister) - Prepositional phrase
15. (For an hour) - Prepositional phrase
16. (On the phone) - Prepositional phrase
17. Period, statement, declarative sentence
18. Go back to the verb - divide the complete subject from the complete predicate.

Classified Sentence:

```
                 SN    CV   C    CV    P  PPA  OP    P  A  OP   P  A  OP
SN  V     Ellen / talked and laughed (with her sister) (for an hour) (on the phone).  D
P1
```

(End of lesson.)

CHAPTER 23 LESSON 5

Objectives: Writing Assignments #35 and #36, Bonus Option.

 **WRITING TIME**

TEACHING SCRIPT FOR WRITING ASSIGNMENTS

Today, you are assigned two different kinds of writing. You will write a business letter for the first writing assignment. For the second writing assignment, you will have a choice of topics. This assignment will require a title that will accurately reflect the content of your paragraph or essay. You will revise and edit both writing assignments. (*Read the box below for more information about students' writing assignment.*) As you edit, make sure you use the checkpoints in the editing checklist provided in Reference 39.

Writing Assignment Box #1

Writing Assignment #35: Write a business letter. You may invent a company and a situation for which you are writing. Before you begin, review the reasons for writing business letters and the four types of business letters (Reference 65 on page 54). This business must be different from the businesses chosen in the previous lessons. After your letter has been edited, fold the letter and put it in an envelope. Address the envelope properly.

Writing Assignment Box #2

Writing Assignment #36: Your choice (First or Third Person)

Writing choices: (1) **Expository** (2) **Persuasive** (3) **Narrative** (4) **Descriptive**

Bonus Option: Think about several scriptures in the Bible that would make good topics for a sermon. Write a sermon in your Journal, using the scripture you have chosen. Deliver your sermon to family members and friends. As time goes by, you could write other sermons. Keep your sermons and refer to them when you are an adult. You could also show them to your children.

TEACHER INSTRUCTIONS FOR CHECKING WRITING ASSIGNMENTS

Read, check, and discuss Writing Assignments #35 and #36 after students have finished their final papers. Use the editing checklist as you check and discuss students' papers. Make sure students are using the editing checklist correctly.

(End of lesson.)

CHAPTER 24   LESSON 1

Objectives: Skill (main parts of the library), Practice Exercise, and Activity.

SKILL TIME

TEACHING SCRIPT FOR INTRODUCING MAIN PARTS OF THE LIBRARY

A library is a good place to find information. In order to make the library an easy and fun experience, you will need to know about some of the major sections in the library and the most common materials found in the library. As we study the different sections, we can put the information on different colored construction paper. Look at Reference 71 on page 57 as we study the main parts of the library.

Teacher's Notes: Make cards from large sheets of different colored construction paper. Write these titles on them: *Fiction Section, Nonfiction Section, Reference Section, Dictionary, Encyclopedia, Atlas, Almanac, The Readers' Guide to Periodical Literature*, and the *Card Catalog*. Under each title, write the information provided below. You and your students might also illustrate and laminate the cards.

Reference 71: Main Parts of the Library

Fiction Section
Fiction books contain stories about people, places, or things that are not true. Fiction books are arranged on the shelves in alphabetical order according to the authors' last names. Since fiction stories are made-up, they cannot be used when you research your report topic.

Non-Fiction Section
Non-Fiction books contain information and stories that are true.

Reference Section
The Reference Section is designed to help you find information on many topics. The Reference Section contains many different kinds of reference books and materials. Some of the ones that you need to know about will now be discussed.

- **Dictionary** (Reference Book)
  The dictionary gives the definition, spelling, pronunciation, and correct usage of words and tells briefly about famous people and places.

- **Encyclopedia** (Reference Book)
  The encyclopedia gives concise, accurate information about persons, places, and events of world-wide interest.

- **Atlas** (Reference Book)
  The atlas is primarily a book of maps, but it often contains facts about oceans, lakes, mountains, areas, population, products, and climates of every part of the world.

2

CHAPTER 24 LESSON 1 CONTINUED

Reference 71: Main Parts of the Library (continued)

- **Almanac** (Reference Book)
  The World Almanac and *Information Please Almanac* are published once a year and contain brief, up-to-date information on a variety of topics.

- ***The Readers' Guide to Periodical Literature*** (Reference Book)
  The Readers' Guide to Periodical Literature is an index for magazines. It is a monthly booklet that lists the titles of articles, stories, and poems published in all leading magazines. These titles are listed under topics that are arranged alphabetically. The monthly issues of *The Readers' Guide to Periodical Literature* are bound together in a single volume once a year and filed in the library. By using the *Readers' Guide*, a person researching a topic can know which back issues of magazines might be helpful.

- **Card Catalog** (Reference File)
  The card catalog is a file of cards, arranged alphabetically, and usually placed in the drawers of a cabinet called the card catalog. It is an index to the library. Some libraries now have computer terminals that show the same information as the card catalog, but the information is stored in a computer. Often, the computer listing will also tell whether or not the book is currently on loan from the library.

In a card catalog, the cards inside the drawers are arranged in alphabetical order. The labels on the drawers tell which cards are in each drawer. The cards inside the card catalog contain information about every book and nearly all the other materials located in the library. (*A sample card catalog is provided below for you to demonstrate what the card catalog looks like.*)

Sample Card Catalog

A-Az	Fed-Gus	L-Mz	S-Sz	W-Wz
=	=	=	=	=
B-Cam	Gut-Iz	N-Pz	T-Tz	X-Yz
=	=	=	=	=
Can-Fec	J-Kz	Q-Rz	U-Vz	Z-Zz
=	=	=	=	=

A book is listed in the library in three ways – by author, by title, and by subject. The card catalog has three kinds of cards: the **author card**, the **title card**, and the **subject card**. All three kinds of cards are arranged alphabetically by the words on the top line.

Look at Reference 72 on page 58 in your Reference Section. This gives you an example of the three cards as we talk about them. All three kinds of cards – the author card, the title card, and the subject card – give the name of the book, the name of the author, and the call number of the book. They also give the place and date of publication, the publisher, the number of pages in the book, and other important information.

Reference 72: Card Catalog Cards

Author Card	Title Card	Subject Card

586.3
Author-Pacton, James R.
Title   Science for Kids and Parents
    Ill. by Charles Finley
    Children's Press, Chicago
    (c1990) 116p.
	586.3
	Title Science for Kids and Parents
	Author-Pacton, James R.
	    Ill. by Charles Finley
	    Children's Press, Chicago
	    (c1990) 116p.
		586.3
		Topic Science Projects
		Author-Pacton, James R.
		Title Science for Kids and Parents
		    Ill. by Charles Finley
		    Children's Press, Chicago
		    (c1990) 116p.

CHAPTER 24 LESSON 1 CONTINUED

Author cards have the name of the author of the book on the top line, and author cards are filed alphabetically by the author's last name. **Title cards** have the title of the book on the top line, and title cards are filed alphabetically by the first word of the title (except *A, An,* or *The*). **Subject cards** will have the subject of the book on the top line, and subject cards are filed alphabetically by the first word of the subject (except *A, An,* or *The*).

We are going to discuss how to find nonfiction books in the card catalog and on the library shelves. To find out if your library has a certain nonfiction book, look in the card catalog for the title card of that book. If you don't know the title, but do know the author, look for the author card. If you don't know the title or the author, look under the subject of the book. Also, look under the subject if you are interested in finding several books about your topic.

After you find the card for the book you want in the card catalog, you must know how to find the book on the library shelves. Nonfiction books are arranged on the shelves in **numerical order**, which is number order, according to a **call number**. A call number is the number located on the spine of nonfiction books.

The *Dewey Decimal System* is a way of identifying books by numbers, and a **call number** is part of that system. Since the Dewey Decimal System is a number system for locating nonfiction books, all nonfiction books are given a call number, which will identify where they are located on the shelf. Be sure to write the call number down on paper before you look for the book on the shelves.

When you go to the library shelf, look at the call numbers printed on the spines of the books until you find the same number on the book that you copied from the catalog card. All three catalog cards for a book will have the same call number in the top left corner of the cards. It is important to note that individual biographies and autobiographies are arranged on a separate shelf by the last name of the person about whom they are written.

We are going to discuss how to find fiction books in the card catalog and on the library shelves. To find out if your library has a certain fiction book, look in the card catalog for the title card of that book. If you don't know the title, but do know the author, look for the author card. If you don't know the title or the author, look under the subject of the book. Also, look under the subject if you are interested in finding several books about your topic. Sometimes, fiction books are not classified by subject like other books. You must then look for the title or author of the book.

After you find the card for the book you want in the card catalog, you must know how to find the book on the library shelves. Fiction books are arranged on the shelves in **alphabetical order** according to the **authors' last names**; therefore, a fiction book is located not by title but by the author's last name.

If you look on the spine of a fiction book, you will see only a letter(s). This is the first letter in the author's last name, and all three catalog cards will have the first letter of the author's last name in the top left corner of each card. Be sure to write the author's last name and the book title down on paper before you look for the book on the shelves.

When you go to the library shelf, look at the letter(s) printed on the spines of the books until you find the same letter(s) on the book that you copied from the catalog card. If two authors have the same last name, their books are arranged in alphabetical order according to the authors' first names. If there are two or more books by the same author, they are arranged in alphabetical order by titles. (*You might want to take your students to the library for a demonstration of what they have just learned.*)

CHAPTER 24 LESSON 1 CONTINUED

PRACTICE TIME

Have students turn to page 92 in the Practice Section of their book and find Chapter 24, Lesson 1, Practice (1-4). Go over the directions to make sure they understand what to do. Check and discuss the Practices after students have finished. (*Chapter 24, Lesson 1, Practice keys are given below.*)

Chapter 24, Lesson 1, Practice 1: Underline the correct answers for numbers 1-3. Write the correct answers for numbers 4-5.

1. Biographies and autobiographies are arranged on the shelves in (**numerical order, <u>alphabetical order</u>**).

2. The main reference book that is primarily a book of maps is the
(**encyclopedia, dictionary, <u>atlas</u>, almanac**).

3. The main reference book that is published once a year with a variety of up-to-date information is the
(**encyclopedia, dictionary, atlas, <u>almanac</u>**).

4. What would you find by going to *The Readers' Guide to Periodical Literature*? (**magazine articles**)

5. What are the names of the three types of cards located in the card catalog? (**author card, title card, subject card**)

Chapter 24, Lesson 1, Practice 2: Write True or False after each statement.
1. The title of the book is always the first line on each of the catalog cards. **False**
2. The *Readers' Guide to Periodical Literature* is an index to magazines. **True**
3. Biographies are arranged on the shelves according to the author's last name. **False**
4. The books in the nonfiction section are arranged numerically by a call number. **True**
5. Fiction and nonfiction books have numbers on their spines to locate them on a shelf. **False**

Chapter 24, Lesson 1, Practice 3: Select eight of your favorite fiction books and alphabetize them on notebook paper by the authors' last names.

Chapter 24, Lesson 1, Practice 4: Draw and label the three catalog cards for this book on notebook paper: 822.14 *One Writer's Secret* by Andrea Paige, Thompson Press, Dallas, 1994, 264 p. (*About Emily Dickinson*)

1. Author Card

822.14
Author   **Paige, Andrea**
Title   **<u>One Writer's Secret</u>**
        Thompson Press, Dallas
        (c 1994) 264p.

2. Title Card

822.14
Title   **<u>One Writer's Secret</u>**
Author   **Paige, Andrea**
        Thompson Press, Dallas
        (c 1994) 264p.

3. Subject Card

822.14
Topic   **Emily Dickinson**
Author **Paige, Andrea**
Title   **<u>One Writer's Secret</u>**
        Thompson Press, Dallas
        (c 1994) 264p.

ACTIVITY / ASSIGNMENT TIME

Take students on a field trip to visit their local library. Have them take pencils and notebooks to take notes and draw a diagram of the library. After they return home, have students design a library and put it on poster board. They are to label and illustrate as many areas in the library as possible. Finally, have students write a report about their study of the library. They will finish their library project during the next lesson.

(End of lesson.)

CHAPTER 24   LESSON 2

Objectives: Skills (alphabetizing, guide words), Practice Exercise, and Activity.

SKILL TIME

TEACHING SCRIPT FOR INTRODUCING ALPHABETIZING

Sometimes studying involves looking words up in a dictionary. You may need to see if you have spelled a word correctly, or you may want to check a word's meaning. A dictionary gives you the correct spelling, pronunciation, meanings, and usage of words. Today, we are going to learn about alphabetizing because words are arranged in alphabetical order in a dictionary. The best way to learn alphabetizing is to alphabetize words for practice. Look at Reference 73 on page 58 in your Reference section.

There is a simple way to put words in alphabetical order. When the first letter of the words to be alphabetized is different, you only have to look at the first letter to put words in alphabetical order. Let's read the directions for the example. (*Read the directions.*) Look at the two words under the title "Music Words." In the words *guitar* and *drums*, the first letters, *g* and *d*, are different. Since *d* comes before *g* in the alphabet, *drums* comes before *guitar*. A number *1* has been written in the blank in front of *drums* and a number *2* has been written in the blank in front of *guitar* as demonstrated in the example.

Reference 73: Alphabetical Order									
Example: Put each group of words in alphabetical order. Use numbers to show the order in each column.									
Music Words		**"B" Words**		**Math Words**		**Science Words**		**"T" Words**	
2	1. guitar	2	3. barn	2	5. subtract	2	7. nucleus	1	9. tent
1	2. drums	1	4. bacon	1	6. multiply	1	8. neutron	2	10. test

When the first letters of words to be alphabetized are the same, you will have to look at the second or third letters to put them in alphabetical order. Now, look at the two words *barn* and *bacon* under "B Words." In the words *barn* and *bacon*, the first two letters are the same. Go to the third letter in each word. Since *c* comes before *r* in the alphabet, *bacon* comes before *barn*. A number *1* has been written in the blank in front of *bacon* and a number *2* has been written in the blank in front of *barn* as demonstrated in the example. (*Call on students to demonstrate this process orally, with the rest of the sample words.*)

TEACHING SCRIPT FOR INTRODUCING GUIDE WORDS

When you are looking a word up in the dictionary, you look first under the first letter of the word. After you have found that letter in the dictionary, you can use special words, called **guide words**, which are found at the top of the dictionary pages, to keep you from having to look at every word on every page until you find your word. When you are looking a word up in the dictionary, you need to know how to use guide words.

CHAPTER 24 LESSON 2 CONTINUED

Guide words are the two words listed at the top of each dictionary page. Guide words tell the first and last words on the page. When you are looking up a word in the dictionary, you can save yourself time by using the guide words to help you see if the word you want to look up is on a particular page. To do this, see if your word comes between the guide words in an alphabetical order check. If it does, then your word is found on that page.

Look at Reference 74 on page 58 in the Reference Section of your book. Let's do the example to learn how to use guide words. Look at number 1. If you want to find the word *decoy* in the dictionary, there is a process you go through. Usually, this process is automatic. Now, you will decide if the word *decoy* is located on page 294 or on page 295.

1. First, you look at the guide words *decoration* and *deduct* at the top of page 294.
2. Next, you decide if *decoy* is on page 294 by putting *decoration*, *deduct* and *decoy* in alphabetical order. (*Write the example on the board:* __1__ decoration __2__ decoy __3__ deduct)
3. Now, you know that *decoy* is found on page 294 because it comes between the two guide words listed on that page. The page number *294* is written in the blank beside *decoy*.

Reference 74: Guide Words

Example: Below are the tops of two dictionary pages. Write the page number on which each word listed would appear.

decoration	Page	**deduct**
(first word)	294	(last word)

deductible	Page	**defense**
(first word)	295	(last word)

Page

__294__ 1. decoy

__295__ 2. deep

Next, you will decide if the word *deep* is located on page 294 or on page 295. You started the process all over again.

1. First, you look at the guide words, *decoration* and *deduct*, at the top of page 294
2. Next, you decide if *deep* is on page 294 by putting *decoration*, *deduct* and *deep* in alphabetical order. (*Write the example on the board:* __1__ decoration __2__ deduct __3__ deep.)
3. Now, you know that *deep* is not found on page 294 because it does not come between the two guide words listed on that page. *deep* comes **after** *deduct*. So, you go to the next page and check the guide words to see if *deep* comes between them. Now, you start the process all over again, using the guide words on page 295.

1. First, you look at the guide words, *deductible* and *defense*, at the top of page 295.
2. Next, you decide if *deep* is on page 295 by putting *deductible*, *defense* and *deep* in alphabetical order. (*Write the example on the board:* __1__ deductible __2__ deep __3__ defense.)
3. Now, you know that *deep* is found on page 295 because it comes between the two guide words listed on that page. The page number *295* is written in the blank beside *deep*.

CHAPTER 24 LESSON 2 CONTINUED

 PRACTICE TIME

Have students turn to page 93 in the Practice Section of their book and find Chapter 24, Lesson 2, Practice (*1-2*). Go over the directions to make sure they understand what to do. If students need a review, have them study the information and examples in the Reference Section of their books. Check and discuss the Practices after students have finished. (*Chapter 24, Lesson 2, Practice keys are given below.*)

Chapter 24, Lesson 2, Practice 1: Put each group of words in alphabetical order. Write numbers in the blanks to show the order in each column.

	Car Words		Medical Words		"Q" Words		People Words		"V" Words
3	1. hood	**2**	7. cast	**1**	13. quaint	**3**	19. friends	**1**	25. valley
5	2. vents	**3**	8. compress	**6**	14. quote	**1**	20. actors	**3**	26. vibrant
4	3. horn	**1**	9. arteries	**2**	15. quart	**4**	21. heirs	**6**	27. voice
2	4. engine	**5**	10. scapula	**3**	16. quartz	**6**	22. students	**2**	28. vent
1	5. brakes	**6**	11. vaccine	**5**	17. quest	**2**	23. citizens	**4**	29. victory
6	6. wipers	**4**	12. coronary	**4**	18. queen	**5**	24. sisters	**5**	30. violet

Chapter 24, Lesson 2, Practice 2: Below are the tops of two dictionary pages. Write the page number on which each word listed would appear.

patriarch (first word)	Page 363	**pavilion** (last word)		**pedestrian** (first word)	Page 364	**penurious** (last word)

Page
364 1. pedigree

363 2. pattern

Page
364 3. pelican

364 4. penicillin

Page
363 5. pauper

364 6. pelts

Page
364 7. pennant

363 8. patrol

 ACTIVITY / ASSIGNMENT TIME

Have students finish their library illustrations and report. Students will read and discuss their library project and library reports with family members or friends.

CHAPTER 24   LESSON 3

Objectives: Skills (dictionary, entry words), and Practice Exercise

SKILL TIME

TEACHING SCRIPT FOR INTRODUCING THE DICTIONARY AND ENTRY WORDS

Today, we will learn about the dictionary and dictionary entry words. A dictionary gives many kinds of information. Look at Reference 75 on page 59. Follow along as I read the information about the dictionary and the parts of a dictionary entry word to you. (*Read and discuss Reference 75 below.*)

Reference 75: The Dictionary

1. The words listed in a dictionary are called entry words and are in bold face type.
2. The entry words are listed in alphabetical order (ABC order).
3. The dictionary tells how to spell the word and how to pronounce the word.
4. The dictionary tells what the word means and gives an example to explain the meaning.
5. The dictionary tells how to use the word and gives the part of speech for the word.

Entry Words

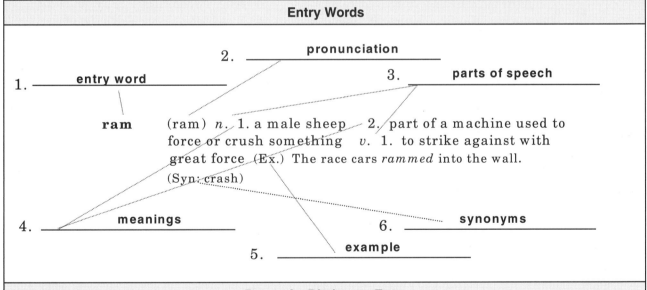

Parts of a Dictionary Entry

1. The entry word – gives correct spelling and divides the word into syllables.
2. Pronunciation – tells how to pronounce a word. It is usually put in parentheses.
3. Part of speech – uses small *n.* for noun, small *v.* for verb, *adj.* for adjective, etc.
4. Meanings – are numbered definitions listed according to the part of speech.
5. Example – a sentence using the entry word to illustrate a meaning. Shown as (Ex.)
6. Synonyms – words that have similar meanings to the entry word. Shown as (Syn:)

CHAPTER 24 LESSON 3 CONTINUED

PRACTICE TIME

Have students turn to pages 93 and 94 in the Practice Section of their book and find Chapter 24, Lesson 3, Practice (*1-3*). Go over the directions to make sure they understand what to do. Check and discuss the Practices after students have finished. (*Chapter 24, Lesson 3, Practice keys are given below.*)

Chapter 24, Lesson 3, Practice 1: Match the definitions of the parts of a dictionary entry below. Write the correct letter of the word beside each definition.

E	1. small *n.* for noun, small *v.* for verb, *adj.* for adjective, etc.	A.	pronunciation
F	2. sentences using the entry word to illustrate a meaning	B.	meanings
D	3. words that have similar meanings to the entry word	C.	entry word
A	4. shows how to pronounce a word, usually put in parentheses	D.	synonyms
C	5. correct spelling and divides the word into syllables	E.	parts of speech
B	6. numbered definitions listed according to the part of speech	F.	examples

Chapter 24, Lesson 3, Practice 2: Label each part of the dictionary entry below. Use the definitions in the matching exercise to help you.

2. **pronunciation**

1. **entry word**

3. **parts of speech**

up•set   (up set') *v.* 1. to interfere. 2. to knock over.
(Syn: spill) 3. to defeat unexpectedly. *adj.* 1. worried, anxious.
2. sick. (Ex.) Jane had an upset stomach after eating pizza.

6. **synonyms**

4. **meanings**

5. **example**

Chapter 24, Lesson 3, Practice 3: Write the meaning and the part of speech for each underlined word on the lines below.

		Word Meaning	Part of Speech
1.	By accident, I <u>upset</u> the vase of flowers.	to knock over	V
2.	We were <u>upset</u> by the phone call.	worried	Adj
3.	Our team <u>upset</u> the champions.	to defeat unexpectedly	V
4.	Her <u>upset</u> stomach was the result of too many sweets.	sick	Adj

(End of lesson.)

Level 4 Homeschool Teacher's Manual

CHAPTER 24   LESSON 4

Objectives: Study, Test A, Test B, Check, Activity, and Writing (journal).

JINGLE TIME

Have students turn to the Jingle Section in their books and recite the previously-taught jingles.

STUDY TIME

Have students study any of the skills in the Practice Section that they need to review.

TEST TIME

Have students turn to pages 122 and 123 in the Test Section of their books and find the Chapter 24 tests A and B. Go over the directions to make sure they understand what to do. (*Chapter 24 A and B keys are on the next two pages.*)

CHECK TIME

After students have finished, check and discuss the test. Make sure they understand why their test questions and answers are right or wrong. (*For total points, count each required answer as a point.*)

ACTIVITY / ASSIGNMENT TIME

Have students look up information about the library or their favorite hobby on the Internet. Have them take notes and give you a short oral report on their chosen topic.

(End of lesson.)

Chapter 24 Test A
(Student Page 122)

Exercise 1: Classify each sentence.

            SN   V-t   A   DO   P A   OP

1. **SN V-t**   Jason / stacked the wood (by the porch). **D**
   DO P2

            A   SN   V-t A IO A   DO   P A   OP

2. **SN V-t**   An eyewitness / gave the police a description (of the criminal). **D**
   IO DO P3

Exercise 2: Put each group of words in alphabetical order. Use numbers to show the order in each column.

Animal Words	Month Words	"B" Words	Car Words	"L" Words
_3_ 1. hamster	_3_ 5. July	_1_ 9. blunder	_3_ 13. muffler	_1_ 17. laughter
_1_ 2. baboon	_2_ 6. August	_4_ 10. bull	_1_ 14. bumper	_4_ 18. llama
_4_ 3. skunk	_1_ 7. April	_2_ 11. brazen	_4_ 15. tailpipe	_3_ 19. livery
_2_ 4. guinea	_4_ 8. October	_3_ 12. buffalo	_2_ 16. generator	_2_ 20. licorice

Exercise 3: Below are the tops of two dictionary pages. Write the page number on which each word listed would appear.

floor	Page	**fluid**
(first word)	178	(last word)

focus	Page	**footstool**
(first word)	179	(last word)

Page		**Page**		**Page**		**Page**	
_178_	1. flour	_179_	3. foliage	_179_	5. folklore	_179_	7. folksy
_179_	2. food	_178_	4. flourish	_179_	6. football	_178_	8. flop

Exercise 4: Match the definitions of the parts of a dictionary entry below. Write the correct letter of the word beside each definition.

_E_	1. small *n.* for noun, small *v.* for verb, *adj.* for adjective, etc.	A. pronunciation
_F_	2. sentences using the entry word to illustrate a meaning	B. meanings
_D_	3. words that have similar meanings to the entry word	C. entry word
_A_	4. shows how to pronounce a word, usually put in parentheses	D. synonyms
_C_	5. correct spelling and divides the word into syllables	E. parts of speech
_B_	6. numbered definitions listed according to the part of speech	F. examples

Chapter 24 Test B
(Student Page 123)

Exercise 5: Underline the correct answer for numbers 1-5. Write the correct answers for numbers 6-7.

1. Nonfiction books are arranged on the shelves in (**<u>numerical order</u>, alphabetical order**).
2. Fiction books are arranged on the shelves in (**numerical order, <u>alphabetical order</u>**).
3. The main reference book that is primarily a book of maps is the (**encyclopedia, dictionary, <u>atlas</u>, almanac**).
4. The main reference book that gives the definition, spelling, and pronunciation of words is the (**encyclopedia, <u>dictionary</u>, atlas, almanac**).
5. The main reference book that is published once a year with a variety of up-to-date information is the (**encyclopedia, dictionary, atlas, <u>almanac</u>**).
6. What would you find by going to *The Readers' Guide to Periodical Literature*? (**magazine articles**)
7. What are the names of the three types of cards located in the card catalog? (**author card, title card, subject card**)

Exercise 6: Put the fiction books below in the correct order to go on the shelves. Write numbers 1-4 in the blanks to show the correct order. *(Alphabetize fiction books by authors' last names.)*

1. *Ulysses* by James Joyce   <u>4</u>
2. *The Old Man and the Sea* by Ernest Hemingway   <u>2</u>
3. *Now in November* by Josephine Johnson   <u>3</u>
4. *The Scarlet Letter* by Nathaniel Hawthorne   <u>1</u>

Exercise 7: Write True or False after each statement.

1. Fiction and nonfiction books have numbers on their spines to locate them on a shelf. **False**
2. The title of the book is always the first line on each of the catalog cards. **False**
3. The books in the fiction section are arranged alphabetically by the author's last name. **True**
4. The *Readers' Guide to Periodical Literature* is an index to magazines. **True**
5. Biographies are arranged on the shelves according to the author's last name. **False**
6. The books in the nonfiction section are arranged numerically by a call number. **True**

Exercise 8: Draw and label the three types of catalog cards for this book on notebook paper: 833.6 *Writers on Writing* by Charles Tyndall, Fulton Press, Houston, 1997, 265p. *(Use the catalog card examples in Reference 72.)*

Exercise 9: In your journal, write a paragraph summarizing what you have learned this week.

CHAPTER 24 LESSON 4 CONTINUED

TEACHER INSTRUCTIONS

Use the Question and Answer Flows below for the sentences on the Chapter 24 Test A.

Question and Answer Flow for Sentence 1: Jason stacked the wood by the porch.

1. Who stacked the wood by the porch? Jason - SN
2. What is being said about Jason? Jason stacked - V
3. Jason stacked what? wood - verify the noun
4. Does wood mean the same thing as Jason? No.
5. Wood - DO
6. Stacked - V-t
7. The - A
8. By - P
9. By what? porch - OP
10. The - A
11. SN V-t DO P2 Check
12. Verb-transitive - Check again.
13. (By the porch) - Prepositional phrase
14. Period, statement, declarative sentence
15. Go back to the verb - divide the complete subject from the complete predicate.

Classified Sentence:

| | SN | V-t | A | DO | P | A | OP |

SN V-t   Jason / stacked the wood (by the porch). **D**
DO P2

Question and Answer Flow for Sentence 2: An eyewitness gave the police a description of the criminal.

1. Who gave the police a description of the criminal? eyewitness - SN
2. What is being said about eyewitness? eyewitness gave - V
3. Eyewitness gave what? description - verify the noun
4. Does description mean the same thing as eyewitness? No.
5. Description - DO
6. Gave - V-t
7. Eyewitness gave description to whom? police - IO
8. A - A
9. Of - P
10. Of whom? criminal - OP
11. The - A
12. The - A
13. An - A
14. SN V-t IO DO P3 Check
15. Verb-transitive - Check again.
16. (Of the criminal) - Prepositional phrase
17. Period, statement, declarative sentence
18. Go back to the verb - divide the complete subject from the complete predicate.

Classified Sentence:

| A | SN | | V-t | A | IO | A | DO | P | A | OP |

SN V-t   An eyewitness / gave the police a description (of the criminal). **D**
IO DO P3

Use the three catalog cards below to check the answers for Exercise 8 on the Chapter 24 Test B.

Key for Exercise 8: Draw and label the three catalog cards for this book on notebook paper: 833.6 *Writers on Writing* by Charles Tyndall, Fulton Press, Houston, 1997, 265 p.

1. Author Card
833.6
Author   **Tyndall, Charles**
Title   <u>**Writers on Writing**</u>
Fulton Press, Houston
(c 1997) 265p.

2. Title Card
833.6
Title   <u>**Writers on Writing**</u>
Author   **Tnydall, Charles**
Fulton Press, Houston
(c 1997) 265p.

3. Subject Card
833.6
Topic   **Writers Thoughts**
Author   **Tyndall, Charles**
Title   <u>**Writers on Writing**</u>
Fulton Press, Houston
(c 1997) 265p.

CHAPTER 24   LESSON 5

Objectives: Writing Assignments #37 and #38.

 **WRITING TIME**

TEACHING SCRIPT FOR WRITING ASSIGNMENTS

Today, you are assigned two different kinds of writing. You will write a five-paragraph persuasive essay and a descriptive paragraph. <u>You will revise and edit the five-paragraph persuasive essay.</u> (*Read the box below for more information about students' writing assignment.*) As you edit, make sure you use the checkpoints in the editing checklist. Remember to read through the whole essay, starting with the title, and then edit, sentence-by-sentence, using the five-sentence checkpoints for each sentence. Use the paragraph checkpoints to check each paragraph.

Writing Assignment Box #1

Writing Assignment #37: Five-Paragraph Persuasive Essay (First or Third Person)
(Remember, first person pronouns are *I, we, me, us, my, our, mine,* and *ours.*)
Remind students that the 5-paragraph essay has three parts: 1. Introduction 2. Body 3. Conclusion. The body has three paragraphs instead of one. Have students use their regular editing checklist to edit this assignment.

Writing topics: Why a Firm Handshake Is Important   or   **Why I Think ____ Is an Admirable Person**   or
                    Reasons I Should Go to Concerts

Your second writing assignment is to write a descriptive paragraph. (*Read the box below for more information about students' writing assignment.*) You do not have to edit this assignment with the editing checklist.

Writing Assignment Box #2

Writing Assignment #38: Descriptive paragraph (First or Third Person)

Writing topic choices: Sunday Dinner at My House   or   **My Best Friend**   or   **My Favorite Sandwich**

TEACHER INSTRUCTIONS FOR CHECKING WRITING ASSIGNMENTS

Read, check, and discuss Writing Assignment #37 after students have finished their final papers. Use the checklists as you check and discuss students' papers. Make sure students are using the regular editing checklist correctly. Read and discuss Writing Assignment #38 for fun and enrichment.

(End of lesson.)

| **CHAPTER 25   LESSON 1** |
| Objectives: Skills (outlining), and Practice Exercise. |

SKILL TIME

TEACHING SCRIPT FOR INTRODUCING THE OUTLINE

In order to develop good report writing techniques, you must learn how to make and use an outline effectively. Making an outline will give you a visual map of your report. Today, you will learn the vocabulary of outlines and how outlines are organized. There are two reasons to use an outline when you plan to write. First, outlining helps to put ideas and information in the correct order for writing. Second, outlining helps you remember information more easily.

There are two kinds of outlines: the **topic outline** and the **sentence outline**. In a *topic* outline, information is written in single words or phrases. In a *sentence* outline, information is written in complete sentences. Outlines have very rigid rules about how they are organized and formatted. Even though the topic outline and the sentence outline are formatted the same, you cannot combine the two styles by using a mixture of phrases and complete sentences.

Outlines have a vocabulary and set of rules that are unique to outlining. All outlines follow the same basic plan. Since the *topic* outline is the easiest and most commonly-used outline, you will learn about outline format by studying the topic outline. Look at Reference 76 on page 59 as we study the information about outlines. (*References 76 and 77 are reproduced below and on the next page. Read and discuss the information with your students.*)

Reference 76: Outlines	
Outline Guide	**Sample Outline**
Title	Fishing Trips
I. Introduction	I. Introduction

II. Main Topic (First main point)
   A. Subtopic (Supports first main point)
      1. Details (Supports subtopic)
      2. Details (Supports subtopic)
   B. Subtopic (Supports first main point)
   C. Subtopic (Supports first main point)
	II. Preparation
	   A. Gathering bait
	      1. Digging worms
	      2. Making dough balls
	   B. Checking the poles
	   C. Stocking the tackle box

III. Main Topic (Second main point)
   A. Subtopic (Supports second main point)
   B. Subtopic (Supports second main point)
	III. Departure
	   A. Fuel the car
	   B. Eat on the way

IV. Main Topic (Third main point)
   A. Subtopic (Supports third main point)
   B. Subtopic (Supports third main point)
	IV. Arrival
	   A. Baiting the hooks
	   B. Stringing the fish

V. Conclusion	V. Conclusion

CHAPTER 25 LESSON 1 CONTINUED

Reference 77: Outline Information

First, an outline has a TITLE.
(*Direct students' attention to the title at the top of the Outline Guide in Reference 76.*)

- At first, your outline title should be the same or similar to your narrowed topic. This will help you stay focused on the main idea of your report. If you decide to change the title for your final paper, you must remember to change your outline title.

- Capitalizing rules for titles are the same for outlines as for final papers: Capitalize the first word, the last word, and all the important words in between them. Conjunctions, articles, and prepositions with fewer than five letters are not usually capitalized unless they are the first or last word. Titles for reports are not underlined or placed in quotation marks unless the title is a quotation.

Second, an outline has Roman numerals denoting MAIN TOPICS.
(*Explain Roman numerals if necessary—I, II, III, IV—and direct students' attention to the main topics beside each Roman numeral.*)

- There must always be two or more Roman numerals. There can never be just one. For each Roman numeral, there is a paragraph. (Three Roman numerals - three paragraphs.)

- The information following a Roman numeral is called the main topic and gives the main idea, or main point, of each paragraph. It will be used to form the topic sentence of the paragraph.

- Every first word in a main topic is always capitalized.

- The periods after the Roman numerals must be lined up under each other.

Third, an outline has capital letters denoting SUBTOPICS.
(*Direct students' attention to the subtopics beside each capital letter.*)

- There must always be two or more capital letters. If you only have one, do not put it on the outline. Each capital letter is indented under the first word of the main topic.

- The information beside a capital letter is called the subtopic and gives details that support the main topic, or main point, of the paragraph.

- Every first word in a subtopic is always capitalized.

- The periods after the capital letters must be lined up under each other.

Fourth, an outline sometimes has Arabic numerals denoting DETAILS.
(*Explain Arabic numerals if necessary—1, 2, 3—and direct students' attention to the details beside each Arabic numeral.*)

- There must always be two or more Arabic numerals. If you only have one, do not put it on the outline. Each Arabic numeral is indented under the first word of the subtopic.

- The information beside an Arabic numeral is called a detail and tells specific information about the subtopic of the paragraph.

- Every first word in a detail is always capitalized.

- The periods after the Arabic numerals must be lined up under each other.

CHAPTER 25 LESSON 1 CONTINUED

Now, I will summarize the basic rules you have just learned. See if you can find these rules in your reference box as I summarize the *rules for outlining*. (1) Put periods after Roman numerals, capital letters, Arabic numerals, and any word that would require a period in a sentence. (2) Capitalize the first word of each line and any word that would be capitalized in a sentence. (3) You cannot have a Roman numeral I. without a Roman numeral II., an A. without a B., or a 1. without a 2.

Remember, you can always utilize the information in this Reference box if you forget how to organize your outline.

TEACHER INSTRUCTIONS

Compare the <u>Outline Guide</u> with the <u>Sample Outline</u> in Reference 76 with your students. Show students how the titles (topics, subtopics, and details) in the Outline Guide explain how to organize the Sample Outline.

 PRACTICE TIME

Have students turn to page 94 in the Practice Section of their book and find Chapter 25, Lesson 1, Practice. Go over the directions to make sure they understand what to do. If students need a review, have them study the information and examples in the Reference Section of their books. Check and discuss the Practice after students have finished. (*Chapter 25, Lesson 1, Practice instructions are given below.*)

Chapter 25, Lesson 1, Practice: Give an oral report on the main points of an outline that are given below. Make an outline as a visual aid to help in your presentation. (You may use Reference 77 as your guide.)

(1) Put periods after Roman numerals, capital letters, Arabic numerals, and any word that would require a period in a sentence.

(2) Capitalize the first word of each entry and any word that would be capitalized in a sentence.

(3) You cannot have a Roman numeral I. without a Roman numeral II., an A. without a B., or a 1. without a 2.

(End of lesson.)

CHAPTER 25   LESSON 2

Objectives: Practice Exercise, and Writing (journal).

 PRACTICE TIME

Have students turn to page 95 in the Practice Section of their book and find Chapter 25, Lesson 2, Practice. Go over the directions to make sure they understand what to do. If students need a review, have them study the information and examples in the Reference Section of their books. Check and discuss the Practice after students have finished. (*Chapter 25, Lesson 2, Practice key is given below.*)

Chapter 25, Lesson 2, Practice: Copy the notes below into a two-point outline.

Notes	Outline
two types of summer jobs	**Two Types of Summer Jobs**
inside jobs	**I. Inside jobs**
grocery sackers	**A. Grocery sackers**
ticket takers	**B. Ticket takers**
outdoor jobs	**II. Outside jobs**
landscaper	**A. Landscaper**
lifeguard	**B. Lifeguard**

 WRITING TIME

Have students make an entry in their journals.

(End of lesson.)

CHAPTER 25   LESSON 3
Objectives: Practice Exercise, and Study.

 PRACTICE TIME

Have students turn to page 95 in the Practice Section of their book and find Chapter 25, Lesson 3, Practice. Go over the directions to make sure they understand what to do. If students need a review, have them study the information and examples in the Reference Section of their books. Check and discuss the Practice after students have finished. (*Chapter 25, Lesson 3, Practice key is given below.*)

Chapter 25, Lesson 3, Practice: Copy the notes below into a two-point outline.

Notes	Outline
two types of camping-out	**Two Types of Camping-Out**
in the woods	I. In the Woods
using a tent	A. Using a tent
using a camper	B. Using a camper
at a motel	II. At a Motel
with air conditioning	A. With air conditioning
with room service	B. With room service

 STUDY TIME

Have students study any of the skills in the Reference Section or the Practice Section that they need to review.

(End of lesson.)

CHAPTER 25   LESSON 4

Objectives: Jingles, Study, Test, Check, and Writing (journal).

JINGLE TIME

Have students turn to the Jingle Section in their books and recite the previously-taught jingles.

STUDY TIME

Have students study any of the skills in the Reference Section or the Practice Section that they need to review.

TEST TIME

Have students turn to page 124 in the Test Section of their books and find the Chapter 25 Test. Go over the directions to make sure they understand what to do. (*Chapter 25 Test key is on the next page.*)

CHECK TIME

After students have finished, check and discuss the test. Make sure they understand why their test questions and answers are right or wrong. (*For total points, count each required answer as a point.*)

(End of lesson.)

Chapter 25 Test
(Student Page 124)

Exercise 1: Classify each sentence.

	A	CSN	C	CSN	P	A	Adj	OP	V	P	A	Adj	OP

1. **SN V**   The girls and boys (on the debate team) / competed (for the first-place trophy). **D**
   P1

           A   SN   CV-t   C   CV-t A   Adj   DO   P A   OP

2. **SN V-t**   The cowboys / chase and lasso the runaway calves (at the ranch). **D**
   DO P2

          PPA   SN   V-t   IO A   DO   P   Adj   COP   C   COP

3. **SN V-t**   My parents / gave me a lecture (about bicycle helmets and safety). **D**
   IO DO P3

Exercise 2: Copy the notes below into a two-point outline.

Notes	Outline
preparing for exams	**Preparing for Exams**
studying alone	**I. Studying alone**
reviewing class notes	**A. Reviewing class notes**
skimming headlines	**B. Skimming headlines**
studying with others	**II. Studying with others**
rap sessions	**A. Rap sessions**
oral quizzes	**B. Oral quizzes**

Exercise 3: On notebook paper, write all the jingles that you can recall from memory. There is a total of 17. *(Check students' jingles from the Jingle Section in their books.)*

Exercise 4: In your journal, write a paragraph summarizing what you have learned this week.

CHAPTER 25 LESSON 4 CONTINUED

TEACHER INSTRUCTIONS

Use the Question and Answer Flows below for the sentences on the Chapter 25 Test.

Question and Answer Flow for Sentence 1: The girls and boys on the debate team competed for the first-place trophy.

1. Who competed for the first-place trophy?
   girls and boys - CSN, CSN
2. What is being said about girls and boys?
   girls and boys competed - V
3. For - P
4. For what? trophy - OP
5. What kind of trophy? first-place - Adj
6. The - A
7. On - P
8. On what? team - OP
9. What kind of team? debate - Adj
10. The - A
11. And - C
12. The - A
13. SN V P1 Check
14. (On the debate team) - Prepositional phrase
15. (For the first-place trophy) - Prepositional phrase
16. Period, statement, declarative sentence
17. Go back to the verb - divide the complete subject from the complete predicate.

Classified Sentence:

```
                    A   CSN C  CSN  P  A   Adj   OP       V      P  A   Adj    OP
        SN  V       The girls and boys (on the debate team) / competed (for the first-place trophy).  D
        ____
        P1
```

Question and Answer Flow for Sentence 2: The cowboys chase and lasso the runaway calves at the ranch.

1. Who chase and lasso the runaway calves at the ranch?
   cowboys - SN
2. What is being said about cowboys? cowboys chase and lasso - CV, CV
3. Cowboys chase and lasso what? calves - verify the noun
4. Do calves mean the same thing as cowboys? No.
5. Calves - DO
6. Chase and lasso - CV-t, CV-t
7. What kind of calves? runaway - Adj
8. The - A
9. At - P
10. At what? ranch - OP
11. The - A
12. And - C
13. The - A
14. SN V-t DO P2 Check
15. Verb-transitive - Check again.
16. (At the ranch) - Prepositional phrase
17. Period, statement, declarative sentence
18. Go back to the verb - divide the complete subject from the complete predicate.

Classified Sentence:

```
                    A    SN      CV-t  C  CV-t  A   Adj     DO    P  A   OP
        SN  V-t     The cowboys / chase and lasso the runaway calves (at the ranch).  D
        _____
        DO  P2
```

Question and Answer Flow for Sentence 3: My parents gave me a lecture about bicycle helmets and safety.

1. Who gave me a lecture about bicycle helmets and safety? parents - SN
2. What is being said about parents? parents gave - V
3. Parents gave what? lecture - verify the noun
4. Does lecture mean the same thing as parents? No.
5. Lecture - DO
6. Gave - V-t
7. Parents gave lecture to whom? me - IO
8. A - A
9. About - P
10. About what? helmets and safety - COP, COP
11. And - C
12. What kind of helmets and safety? bicycle - Adj
13. Whose parents? my - PPA
14. SN V-t IO DO P3 Check
15. Verb-transitive - Check again
16. (About bicycle helmets and safety) - Prepositional phrase
17. Period, statement, declarative sentence
18. Go back to the verb - divide the complete subject from the complete predicate.

Classified Sentence:

```
                    PPA SN      V-t  IO A  DO     P   Adj    COP  C  COP
        SN  V-t     My parents / gave me a lecture (about bicycle helmets and safety).  D
        _____
        IO  DO  P3
```

CHAPTER 25   LESSON 5

Objectives: Writing Assignments #39 and #40, Bonus Option.

 **WRITING TIME**

TEACHING SCRIPT FOR WRITING ASSIGNMENTS

Today, you will be given two writing assignments. With each, you will have a choice of assignments. Once you have drafted your writings, you will then revise and edit both assignments. The second assignment will require a title that will accurately reflect the content of your paragraph or essay.

Writing Assignment Box #1

Writing Assignment #39: Your choice

Writing choices: (1) **Friendly Letter**   (2) **Business Letter**   (3) **Thank You Note**

Rather than choose the same type of writing you used in your last assignment, select a different one for this second writing assignment. You may write a paragraph or an essay.

Writing Assignment Box #2

Writing Assignment #40: Your choice (First or Third Person)

Writing choices: (1) **Expository**   (2) **Persuasive**   (3) **Narrative**   (4) **Descriptive**

Bonus Option: Make Bible Memory Markers. Begin by selecting a book of the Bible. Cut a piece of colored construction paper into a strip. Make the strip as wide and as long as you want your bookmarker to be. At the top of the strip, write the name of the book of the Bible you have chosen. Underneath the name, write Old Testament or New Testament. Illustrate your Memory Marker.

Now, make a Memory Marker for each book in the Bible. (This activity may take several days.) When you are finished creating all 66 Memory Markers, store the strips in a handy box. As you study different books of the Bible, use the appropriate marker. You may have several markers in your Bible at any given time. On the back of each marker, record the chapter and verses that you have memorized. Don't forget to put the date.

TEACHER INSTRUCTIONS FOR CHECKING WRITING ASSIGNMENTS

Read, check, and discuss Writing Assignments #39 and #40 after students have finished their final papers. Use the editing checklist as you check and discuss students' papers. Make sure students are using the editing checklist correctly.

(End of lesson.)

CHAPTER 26   LESSON 1

Objectives: Writing (A Remarkable Person "Me Booklet").

 WRITING TIME

TEACHING SCRIPT

Every year you grow and change. Today, we will start a booklet that will record some of those changes. Look at Reference 78A on page 61 as we go over the directions in the reference box. (*Have students follow along as you read and discuss the information in the reference box below.*)

Reference 78A: A Remarkable Person – Me

This activity produces a booklet about you. The instructions on how to make this booklet are given below. You will also be given directions on how to add artwork for each topic. Remember, this is a unique opportunity to express who you are at this stage of your life. This booklet would also make a wonderful gift to your parents, or you may save it and read it at different times as you grow older. You will certainly enjoy remembering what you were like as a fourth grader.

1. Have two sheets of construction paper. Use one sheet for the title page of your booklet and one sheet for the back cover.

2. Make a title page and illustrate it (or put a picture of yourself on it).

3. Make a separate page for each topic. Make each page special by doing some artwork for each topic. (*Example: Draw a big football and put "Goals for My Life" inside the football, and write your paragraph inside the football. You might want to add goal posts at the top and bottom of the page. Draw weights for "My Strengths," etc. Use creativity to match each topic with different kinds of artwork.*)

4. Do neat work.

5. Put the back cover on and staple your booklet on the left-hand side when you are finished. You can be proud of this booklet. No one else has one quite like it. It is an original, just like you!

(Title Page)	(Page 1)
A Booklet About A Remarkable Person **ME!** Written by (put your name here) Illustrated by (put your name here)	**Things I Like to Do** ...with a friend. ...with my family. ...by myself. ...that cost money. ...that are different. ...that are special.

(End of lesson.)

CHAPTER 26   LESSON 2

Objectives: Writing (A Remarkable Person "Me Booklet" continued).

 **WRITING TIME**

TEACHING SCRIPT

Today we will continue working on our "me booklets". Look at Reference 78B on page 62 as we go over the information in the reference box.

Reference 78B: A Remarkable Person – Me	
(Page 2) Goals for My Life	(Page 3) Goals for the Rest of This School Year
(Page 4) My Strengths	(Page 5) My Weaknesses
(Page 6) My Special Feelings I am happy when... I am angry when... I hope that... I finally... I love... I admire... I want to be like... I get excited when... I need... I feel safe when... I am thankful for... I am afraid of... I feel sorry for... I am proud of... I am really good at...	(Page 7) My Family Other Special People

(End of lesson.)

CHAPTER 26   LESSON 3

Objectives: Writing (autobiographies).

WRITING TIME

TEACHING SCRIPT

An autobiography is an account of a writer's life. Look at Reference 79 on page 63 in your book. You will now write your autobiography. You will use this outline to guide you. *(Read and discuss Reference 79 with your students before they begin writing their autobiography.)*

Reference 79: My Autobiography

Title: My Autobiography   Introductory sentence: My name is ____ _____ , and I am ___ years old.

I. Family
   A. Birth
   B. Parents
   C. Brothers and sisters
   D. Grandparents

II. Family life
   A. Chores and responsibilities
   B. How we celebrate special holidays
   C. Family vacations
   D. Special things about my family

III. School days
   A. Friends
   B. Teachers
   C. Best/worst subjects
   D. Special things about school

IV. Special interests
   A. Hobbies
   B. My achievements
   C. My likes and dislikes
   D. Other

(End of lesson.)

CHAPTER 26   LESSON 4

Objectives: Writing ("Me Booklets" and autobiographies concluded).

CHECK TIME

TEACHER INSTRUCTIONS

Read, discuss, and enjoy students' "Me Booklets" and autobiographies.

(End of lesson.)

TEACHER INDEX

Due to the tremendous amount of review of concepts provided, this index lists only the page numbers on which the topic is introduced.

TEACHER INDEX

Due to the tremendous amount of review of concepts provided, this index lists only the page numbers on which the topic is introduced.

Level 4
Jingles & Introductory Sentences

Shurley Instructional Materials, Inc.
366 SIM Drive
Cabot, AR 72023